T0299297

STRATEGIC ALLIANCE MANAGEMENT

Strategic Alliance Management presents an academically grounded alliance development framework, detailing eight stages of alliance development with consideration for specific management challenges. For each stage, readers are presented with theoretical insights, evidence-based managerial guidelines and a business case illustration. Other chapters consider alliance attributes, alliance competences, and alliance challenges, and cover topics such as innovation, co-branding, coopetition, business ecosystems, alliance professionals, alliance capabilities, societal alliances and a tension-based alliance mindset.

This fully revised third edition leverages the book's strengths in marrying theory with practical insight. All the chapters have been updated to reflect the current academic literature, whilst new international case studies are incorporated throughout. Two new chapters feature in this edition, considering the importance of the mindset required to successfully navigate alliance arrangements, and emerging alliance practices, exploring how new technologies, sustainability and the external environment have disrupted alliance management. In-chapter text boxes discussing emerging themes provide opportunity for discussion and analysis.

The textbook remains highly valuable core and recommended reading for postgraduate students of Strategic Management and Corporate Strategy, MBA and Executive MBA, as well as reflective practitioners in the field. Online resources include chapter-by-chapter lecture slides, two long case studies and short interviews with alliance executives.

Brian Tjemkes holds a PhD from Radboud University Nijmegen and is currently employed as Professor of Strategic Management at the Vrije Universiteit Amsterdam. He is Head of the Strategy section, Director of the International Business Administration programme and Director of the VU Knowledge Hub for Ecosystems. His research interests centre on strategic alliances, business ecosystems and strategic leadership. His work has been disseminated through various academic and professional conferences and publications in, among others, *Journal of Management Studies, Human Relations, International Journal of Management Reviews, Journal of International Management* and *Journal of Cross-Cultural Psychology*. He is co-author of the books *Strategic Alliance Management* and *Transformative Strategizing*. He is devoted to sharing his insights with practice via executive education, workshops, presentations and professional publications. Orcid: 000-0001-9071-5947

Pepijn Vos works at the Netherlands Organization for Applied Scientific Research (TNO) as Researcher and Consultant in the field of managing strategic alliances, public–private partnerships and innovation. He holds a Bachelor in Food Technology Management from the University of Applied Science HAS in Den Bosch and an MSc in Business Administration at the Radboud University in Nijmegen. In 2008, he joined TNO in the Netherlands as a researcher and consultant in the field of open innovation, co-creation, alliance management and cross sector collaboration. His main interests are in the fields of managing strategic alliances, (inter-organizational) collaboration and innovation. He works on projects in different fields such as open innovation, organized crime, energy transition, safety and security. He is co-author of *Strategic Alliance Management* and *Samen werken—Samen winnen* (a Dutch book on public–private partnerships).

Koen Burgers is an all-round alliance professional. He has experience as Management Consultant at Kirkman Company. Next, Koen was Director of Strategy and Business Transformation at Damen Shipyards. Currently, Koen is CEO of SolarDuck, a company active in offshore floating solar which he co-founded. Koen is an alliance professional and applies state of the art academic insights and alliance experience in his management activities. He is co-author of *Strategic Alliance Management*.

STRATEGIC ALLIANCE MANAGEMENT

Third edition

Brian Tjemkes, Pepijn Vos and Koen Burgers

Routledge
Taylor & Francis Group

LONDON AND NEW YORK

Designed cover image: mycola

First published 2023
by Routledge
4 Park Square, Milton Park, Abingdon, Oxon OX14 4RN

and by Routledge
605 Third Avenue, New York, NY 10158

Routledge is an imprint of the Taylor & Francis Group, an informa business

© 2023 Brian Tjemkes, Pepijn Vos and Koen Burgers

The right of Brian Tjemkes, Pepijn Vos and Koen Burgers to be identified as authors
of this work has been asserted in accordance with sections 77 and 78 of the Copyright,
Designs and Patents Act 1988.

All rights reserved. No part of this book may be reprinted or reproduced or utilised in
any form or by any electronic, mechanical, or other means, now known or hereafter
invented, including photocopying and recording, or in any information storage or
retrieval system, without permission in writing from the publishers.

Trademark notice: Product or corporate names may be trademarks or registered
trademarks, and are used only for identification and explanation without intent to
infringe.

British Library Cataloguing-in-Publication Data
A catalogue record for this book is available from the British Library

ISBN: 978-1-032-11928-1 (hbk)
ISBN: 978-1-032-11925-0 (pbk)
ISBN: 978-1-003-22218-7 (ebk)

DOI: 10.4324/9781003222187

Typeset in Bembo
by Apex CoVantage, LLC

Access the Support Material: www.routledge.com/9781032119281

CONTENTS

List of Figures   x
List of Tables   xi
List of Boxes   xiii
Preface   xiv

1 Strategic alliance management   **1**
The meaning of an alliance   2
Alliance activity   3
Alliance failure   6
An academically grounded alliance development framework   7
Alliance challenges   11

2 Alliance strategy formulation   **13**
Three prototypical governance modes   13
Governance mode rationales   15
Alliance strategy formulation: decision-making steps   25
Summary   28
Case: Google–HubSpot   28

3 Alliance partner selection   **30**
Types of partner fit   30
Alliance partner selection: decision-making steps   35
Summary   39
Case: SolarDuck   39

4 Alliance negotiation   **43**

Negotiation behaviour   43

Valuation   48

Alliance negotiation: decision-making steps   48

Summary   53

Case: Renault–Nissan   54

5 Alliance design   **57**

Governance form   57

Alliance contracts   64

Management control   67

Structural configuration   69

Alliance design: decision-making steps   71

Summary   75

Case: Organovo   75

6 Alliance launch   **78**

Alliance launch objectives and challenges   78

Alliance launch attributes   81

Alliance launch: decision-making steps   85

Summary   89

Case: Capgemini–Eneco   89

7 Alliance management   **92**

Alliance management approaches   92

Alliance design and management   101

Alliance management: decision-making steps   103

Summary   106

Case: TNO–Hoogendoorn   107

8 Alliance evaluation   **109**

Issues with alliance performance and metrics   109

Performance metric approaches   112

Alliance evaluation: decision-making steps   117

Summary   120

Case: DBS Singapore   121

9 Alliance termination   **124**

Alliance termination types, trajectories and motives   124

Planning alliance termination   129

Alliance termination: decision-making steps   131

Summary   134

Case: Nokia–Microsoft   135

10 Supplier alliances   **139**
 The supplier alliance challenge   139
 Managing supplier alliances   142
 Supplier alliances: decision-making steps   146
 Summary   151
 Case: NAM–GLT Plus   151

11 Learning alliances   **156**
 The learning alliance challenge   156
 Managing learning alliances   159
 Learning alliances: decision-making steps   164
 Summary   170
 Case: Holst Centre   170

12 Co-branding alliances   **173**
 The co-branding alliance challenge   173
 Managing co-branding alliances   175
 Co-branding alliances: decision-making steps   181
 Summary   185
 Case: Heineken–James Bond   186

13 International alliances   **189**
 The international alliance challenge   189
 The nature of national culture   191
 Managing international alliances   196
 International alliances: decision-making steps   198
 Summary   203
 Case: Damen Shipyards   204

14 Asymmetrical alliances   **208**
 The asymmetrical alliance challenge   208
 Managing asymmetrical alliances   211
 Asymmetrical alliances: decision-making steps   215
 Summary   219
 Case: Disney–Pixar   219

15 Cross-sector alliances   **222**
 The cross-sector alliance challenge   222
 Managing cross-sector alliances   226
 Cross-sector alliances: decision-making steps   228
 Summary   232
 Case: Marks & Spencer–Oxfam   232

16   Coopetition alliances 236

The coopetition alliance challenge 236

Managing coopetition alliances 240

Coopetition alliances: decision-making steps 244

Summary 250

Case: Reckitt Benckiser 250

17   Multi-partner alliances 253

The multi-partner alliance challenge 253

Managing multi-partner alliances 255

Multi-partner alliances: decision-making steps 259

Summary 263

Case: Skyteam 264

18   Alliance portfolios 267

The meaning of an alliance portfolio 267

Alliance portfolio governance 269

Alliance portfolio: decision-making steps 277

Summary 281

Case: General Electric 281

19   Alliance networks 284

The meaning of an alliance network 284

Alliance network governance 286

Alliance network: decision-making steps 293

Summary 297

Case: IBM 297

20   Business ecosystems 300

The business ecosystem challenge 300

Business ecosystem attributes 303

Managing business ecosystems 309

Business ecosystems: decision-making steps 312

Summary 316

Case: Apple vs Amazon 317

21   Alliance professionals 320

Alliance professionals: a unique job 320

Hierarchical positions and alliance roles 324

Alliance manager: attributes and competences 327

Alliance professionals: decision-making steps 330

Summary 332

Case: Ivan Vogels 333

22	**Alliance teams**	**336**
	The alliance team challenge	336
	Alliance team types	337
	Managing alliance teams	340
	Alliance teams: decision-making steps	346
	Summary	349
	Case: Dutch Optics Centre	349
23	**Alliance capabilities**	**352**
	The meaning of alliance capabilities	352
	Building and deploying alliance capabilities	358
	Alliance capabilities: decision-making steps	360
	Summary	362
	Case: Philips	363
24	**Alliance mindset**	**365**
	The meaning of alliance mindset	365
	Alliance tensions	367
	Summary	373
	Case: Microsoft	374
25	**Alliance system**	**376**
	A co-evolutionary view	376
	Drivers of alliance co-evolution	379
	Summary	386
	Case: Oral care appliances	386
26	**Contemporary alliances**	**389**
	Technological innovation	389
	Societal responsibility	392
	Theoretical implications for strategic alliance management	394
	Summary	396
	Case: Torvald Klaveness	397
27	**Strategic alliance management: science and art**	**400**
	The science of strategic alliance management	401
	The art of strategic alliance management	402
	The future of strategic alliance management	404
	Appendix	410
	References	415
	Index	449

FIGURES

1.1	Alliance development stages	8
1.2	Structure of the book	11
2.1	Decision-making steps: alliance strategy formulation	25
3.1	Decision-making steps: alliance partner selection	36
4.1	Decision-making steps: alliance negotiation	49
5.1	Alliance mirror design	70
5.2	Decision-making steps: alliance design	71
6.1	Decision-making steps: alliance launch	86
7.1	Decision-making steps: alliance management	104
8.1	Decision-making steps: alliance evaluation	118
9.1	Decision-making steps: alliance termination	131
10.1	Alliance development framework: supplier alliances	147
11.1	Alliance development framework: learning alliances	165
12.1	Alliance development framework: co-branding alliances	182
13.1	Alliance development framework: international alliances	199
14.1	Alliance development framework: asymmetrical alliances	215
15.1	Alliance development framework: cross-sector alliances	229
16.1	Alliance development framework: coopetition alliances	245
17.1	Alliance development framework: multi-partner alliances	260
18.1	Generic alliance portfolio configurations	274
18.2	Alliance development framework: alliance portfolios	278
19.1	Alliance network configurations	289
19.2	Alliance development framework: alliance networks	293
20.1	Alliance development framework: business ecosystems	313
21.1	Decision-making steps: alliance professionals	330
22.1	Alliance multi-team system	345
22.2	Decision-making steps: alliance teams	347
23.1	Decision-making steps: alliance capabilities	360
25.1	Alliance system	383
27.1	Strategic alliance management: science and art	401

TABLES

1.1	Examples of alliances	3
1.2	Advantages and disadvantages of alliances	5
2.1	Prototypical governance modes: make, buy and ally	14
2.2	Theoretical perspectives: alliance formation	24
3.1	Partner fit types	32
4.1	Negotiation strategies and tactics	45
5.1	Non-equity and equity-based arrangements	61
5.2	Contractual clauses	65
6.1	Alliance launch misconceptions	80
6.2	Alliance launch attributes	82
7.1	Four alliance management approaches	93
8.1	Issues with performance metric	110
8.2	Six performance metrics approaches	113
9.1	Theoretical perspectives and alliance termination	128
10.1	Two views on buyer–supplier exchanges	140
10.2	Examples of supplier alliances	141
10.3	Managing supplier alliances	143
11.1	Examples of learning alliances	157
11.2	Managing learning alliances	159
12.1	Examples of co-branding alliances	174
12.2	Managing co-branding alliances	177
13.1	Examples of international alliances	190
13.2	Hofstede's five cultural dimensions	192
14.1	Examples of asymmetrical alliances	209
14.2	Managing asymmetrical alliances	212
15.1	Examples of cross-sector alliances	223
15.2	Cross-sector alliance partners	224
16.1	Examples of coopetition alliances	237
16.2	Managing coopetition alliances	241
17.1	Examples of multi-partner alliances	254

17.2	Managing multi-partner alliances	256
18.1	Examples of alliance portfolios	268
18.2	Alliance portfolio governance	271
19.1	Examples of alliance networks	285
19.2	Alliance network governance	287
20.1	Examples of business ecosystems	301
20.2	What is a business ecosystem, and not?	304
20.3	Ecosystem types	308
20.4	Business ecosystem management	310
21.1	Alliance professionals job advertisements (excerpts)	321
21.2	Examples of alliance professionals' roles	324
22.1	Examples of alliance team types	338
22.2	Alliance team management	341
23.1	Alliance capability instruments	355
23.2	Alliance tools	357
23.3	Alliance capability competence levels	359
24.1	Two examples of tensions in alliances	367
24.2	Four key tensions in alliances	369
25.1	Driving and inhibiting forces of alliance adaptation	377
25.2	Four co-evolutionary trajectories	378
26.1	Examples of contemporary alliance arrangements	390
26.2	Contemporary alliances: description and implications	395
A.1	Managerial checklist	410

BOXES

1.1	Alliance segmentation	9
2.1	Some other governance mode explanations	16
5.1	Joint ventures: a separate stream of research	59
5.2	Alliance mirror design	70
6.1	Alliance relaunch	88
7.1	Types of trust	94
7.2	Organizational justice	96
8.1	Development and implementation metrics	112
8.2	Balanced performance metrics in the Dutch shipbuilding industry	117
9.1	The Skoltech project	126
10.1	Global supply chains	146
11.1	Open innovation	158
12.1	Alternative forms of co-branding	176
13.1	High and low context cultures	195
13.2	Market entry governance modes	200
14.1	Small firms and alliances	210
16.1	Competition law	246
18.1	Toyota's suppliers' portfolio	270
21.1	ASAP Certification	329
22.1	Multi-dimensional conceptualization of alliance teams	339
22.2	Alliance team leadership	343
23.1	Designing an alliance office	361
24.1	Alliance mindset: theoretical perspectives	370
25.1	Nexia's co-evolution	380
26.1	Multi-sided platforms	391
27.1	Suggestions for empirical alliance research	408

PREFACE

Since the first (2012) and second edition (2017) of *Strategic Alliance Management*, the world has changed dramatically. Spurred by technological advancements (e.g. cloud computing, artificial intelligence, blockchain technology), firms increasingly operate at a global scale. By contrast, globalization intertwines with an increasing awareness that a firm's responsibility extends beyond profit-maximization—firms also have a responsibility to assume ownership of ecological and societal challenges. The common denominator across these developments however is that strategic alliances are and will remain cornerstones for the (competitive) strategy of many firms and (non-profit) organizations, enabling them to achieve objectives that otherwise would be difficult to realize. To successfully navigate the unknowns of today's world, organizations resort to traditional alliance management practices, but new alliance constellations (e.g. purpose-based ecosystems and multi-lateral societal alliances), and thus practices, have emerged. The alliance landscape is continuously changing and evolving, making strategic alliance management as relevant today as it was 50 years ago.

Like its predecessors, this third edition attempts to synthesize academic insights (traditional and contemporary) with managerial experience via a 'guided tour' of various aspects of strategic alliance management. Building on an academically grounded alliance development framework, the book elaborates on unique decision-making situations tied to alliance development stages. In light of a burgeoning and expanding field, the book should be considered as a foundational work offering deep insights in the fundamentals of strategic alliance management, but not detailing on each new (anecdotic) insight and discovery. Nonetheless, in recognition of the fact that distinct alliance objectives, alliance partners and alliance constellations constitute unique management challenges, the book also elaborates on these specific conditions. Furthermore, the ability to create successful alliances, which reflects learning about alliance management and leveraging alliance knowledge inside the company, is an alliance competence. To provide understanding about such competences, the book looks in detail at alliance professionals, alliance teams and alliance capabilities, which all contribute to successful strategic alliance management. Furthermore, we detail on the alliance mindset, suggesting that successful alliance practices originate alliance managers' ability to reconcile tensions. Taking a broader perspective, we also detail on the alliance system and contemporary alliance constellations. The conclusion builds on these insights and offers new avenues for future strategic alliance management research. The intended result is a more comprehensive book than has previously been available, which acknowledges that decision making constitutes a critical success condition.

With regard to this third edition, several amendments to the first and second editions have been made. First, the second edition contains two new chapters: Chapter 24 discussing an alliance manager's mindset (i.e. tension-based) and Chapter 26 detailing on emerging alliance constellations (e.g. technological and societal alliances). Second, we reorganized the structure of the book to present a more coherent story. After the introduction, Chapters 2–9 systematically introduce the alliance development framework, Chapters 10–12 detail on alliance objectives, Chapter 13–16 detail on alliance partners, Chapters 17–20 detail on alliance constellations, Chapters 21–23 detail on alliance competences and Chapters 24–26 detail on alliance challenges before we conclude the book. Third, in addition to new chapters, the academic literature has been updated where applicable, and some chapters have been rewritten to capture new insights (e.g. Chapter 20 Business ecosystems). Fourth, we have added new examples to illustrate a chapter's content, and relatively older cases have been replaced by more recent ones.

This third edition is (again) written with an even-handed appreciation for theory and practice. Readers possessing management knowledge, combined with the book's logic, concept and implications, will be able to absorb the information. Readers are assumed to have a basic understanding of strategic management and organizations, obtained either through study or experience. Therefore, students participating in advanced courses in graduate and MBA programmes in business schools will find this book useful, as will professionals seeking a deeper understanding of the subject.

In preparing this book (editions 1–3), the authors have received considerable assistance from colleagues who provided detailed feedback on our treatment of the academic literature, alliance experts who reviewed our decision-making steps, students who raised questions, and executives who provided us with relevant examples. We specifically acknowledge the companies and alliance managers that have provided insights, examples and feedback on the case material (editions 1–3). Thanks are due to Pallas Agterberg (Alliander); Ingrid Kylstad and Morten Skedsmo (Torvald Klaveness); Steven Twait (AstraZeneca); Hans de Roos (KLM); Frits Zegeling (Grolsch); Rose Verdurmen (TNT); Jaap Lombaers (Holst Centre); Michiel Jansen, Tako Keja and Alfred Vrieling (NAM); Berry Vetjens, Nathalie van Schie and Erik Ham (TNO); Ron van Vianen and Peter van Duijn (Hoogendoorn); Ivan Vogels (SAP); Enri Leufkens (CapGemini); Michael Kaschke (Reckitt Benckiser); Anoop Nathwani (Consortio Consulting); Henk Raven (Habraken Rutten Advocaten); Justin Philippens (The3); and Bruce Dönszelmann (KLM). We also thank Peter Simoons and members of the alliance roundtable for their input to the second and third edition.

We also appreciate the support of staff of the Vrije Universiteit Amsterdam, Nyenrode University and TNO, who offered us critical reflections on earlier drafts of the book. We also acknowledge Elisabeth Caswell and James Morrison, whose text editing has been invaluable, as well as Sophia Levine, Rupert Spurrier, Terry Clague, Alexander Krause, Izzy Fitzharris and Manon Lute, who provided editorial assistance in the preparation of the final manuscript. Although we received much-appreciated support in writing the book, any errors remain the responsibility of the authors. Enjoy reading.

Brian Tjemkes, Amsterdam
Pepijn Vos, The Hague
Koen Burgers, Nijmegen

1

STRATEGIC ALLIANCE MANAGEMENT

In the early industrial age, firms created value by transforming raw materials into finished products. The economy was based primarily on tangible resources—inventory, land, factories, equipment—and a firm could formulate and execute its business strategy by operating autonomously and interacting with its environment through market transactions. But times have changed. In the current age, businesses must create and deploy intangible resources, including employee skills, information technologies and corporate culture, to encourage innovation, promote sustainability and improve their competitive strength. Value does not reside in any individual intangible resource, however. Rather, it arises from the entire set of resources and the strategy that links them. Valuable resources cannot be considered separately from the organizations in which they are embedded. In turn, to develop and maintain competitive advantages, many firms turn increasingly to alliances; instead of just acquiring resources, they enjoy the benefits of combining their own resources with the assets of others.

Alliances thus have become cornerstones of the competitive strategy of many firms, enabling them to achieve objectives that otherwise would be difficult to realize.[1] For example, alliances provide firms with an opportunity to increase their innovative capacity, improve their market response, effectuate corporate social responsibility, achieve efficiency and share investment risks with partner firms. Yet this increased focus on and use of alliances by firms is paralleled by empirical research that indicates moderate to high alliance failure rates. Extant academic and professional literature indicates that to reap the benefits from alliances, firms must overcome internal and external adversities by efficiently and effectively managing their alliances. Even as alliance literature offers a vast amount of theoretical and practical insights though, it lacks any systematic framework for decision making. Such a framework would be of great benefit to (novice) alliance professionals by enabling them to manage their alliances systematically and aim towards success.

Accordingly, the objective of this book is to connect existing theoretical and practical insights and thereby present a much needed, coherent and academically grounded development framework of strategic alliance management. The framework focuses on unique decision-making situations tied to the management of alliances as they progress from formation

DOI: 10.4324/9781003222187-1

to termination. Our unique alliance development framework is also grounded in theoretical perspectives (i.e. know-what), supported by practice-oriented decision-making guidelines (i.e. know-how) and illustrated by real-life alliance cases. It also incorporates both generic and specific decision-making situations tied to unique alliance contexts. Before we proceed to introduce our Alliance Development Framework though, we establish a foundation for this book in this opening chapter. To this end, we first outline our book's scope and provide a clear definition of an alliance. In the following two sections, we elaborate on why firms increasingly use alliances as instruments to develop and sustain a competitive advantage, as well as the causes for alliance failure. In the final section, after explaining the need for a book on strategic alliance management, we present the structure of the book.

The meaning of an alliance

An alliance is a voluntary, long-term, contractual relationship between two or more autonomous and independent organizations (i.e. firms), designed to achieve mutual and individual objectives by sharing and/or creating resources (Ariño *et al.* 2001, p. 110; Gulati 1995b). This definition encompasses inter-organizational relationships, such as joint ventures, purchase partnerships, research and development partnerships, co-makerships, co-creation efforts, multi-partner alliances, public–private partnerships and consortia, but it excludes arrangements such as simple market transactions, mergers and acquisitions. In Table 1.1, we list examples of alliances consistent with our definition.

Four important implications derive from this definition. First, an alliance is an instrument that firms use to achieve their objectives, ultimately to develop and sustain their competitive advantage (Ireland *et al.* 2002). Therefore, alliance management constitutes a strategic activity within firms. Second, the definition indicates that an alliance consists of two or more firms which remain independent organizational entities but connect voluntarily through an alliance contract. Although alliances thus offer firms flexibility in achieving their objectives, they also represent relatively unstable organizational arrangements because there is an absence of hierarchical governance (Litwak and Hylton 1962). Third, as critical resources get exchanged, firms engaged in alliances grow increasingly dependent on each other to realize their joint and individual objectives. This situation implies that firms must manage their alliances proactively to resolve any tension between cooperative forces focused on value creation and competitive forces oriented towards value appropriation (Dyer *et al.* 2008). Fourth, our definition implies that alliances are transitional entities because firms can dissolve them at any convenient time. The threat of premature termination requires systematic management attention to resolve any emerging adversities.

Compared with other organizational entities, such as stand-alone organizations, alliances thus represent unique arrangements with specific management challenges (Albers *et al.* 2016). For example, interdependent parties in alliances must develop joint business propositions, share control and management, accept overlapping roles and responsibilities, engage in adaptation through mutual cooperation, install internal and proactive monitoring mechanisms and develop long-term incentive systems. However, parallel to cooperation, competition between the partners exists because partners simultaneously compete with one another to attain individual objectives, occasionally at the expense of their counterparts. In other words, if alliances are relatively unstable and complex entities, the question emerges: why do firms engage in alliance activity?

TABLE 1.1 Examples of alliances

Company	Description
DSM	DSM establishes a number of partnerships for its Pharma and Bulk Chemicals activities in order to streamline and simplify its core portfolio in Nutrition and Performance Materials. In 2011, DSM established a 50/50 joint venture with Sinochem to develop, produce and sell pharmaceutical ingredients and finished dosages. In 2015, DSM formed ChemicaInvest, a new joint venture (35% equity) with CVC Capital Partners. ChemicaInvest is a global leader in the production and supply of caprolactam and the leading European supplier of acrylonitrile and composite resins. In 2022, DSM and the World Food Programme (WFP) agreed to extend their partnership and scale up rice fortification worldwide. The partnership will seek to improve the availability and accessibility of nutritious foods in order to reach vulnerable people.
IBM	IBM forges a number of global partnerships to achieve economies of scale and scope, enhance its innovative capability and support its global footprint and market leadership. In 2014, IBM and Twitter forged a global partnership, integrating Twitter data with IBM analytics services, to enrich cloud services for clients, to deliver a set of enterprise applications to help improve business decisions across industries and professions and to enrich consulting services for clients across business. In 2015, IBM and Box announced a global partnership that would combine the best-in-class technologies of both companies to create simple and secure IT (cloud-based) solutions. In 2016, IBM and Teva expanded their existing global e-Health alliance with a focus on the discovery of new treatment options and improving chronic disease management. Both projects will run on the IBM Watson Health Cloud.
Walmart	Walmart has revolutionized the way retail companies manage relationships and partnerships within the supply chain. Walmart shares its vast trove of real-time sales data with the firms that stock its shelves and even goes so far as to create large teams to work with partners to streamline costs. In addition, Walmart forges partnerships to effectuate a positive change with regards to risks and social issues in consumer goods supply chains. Walmart is a founding member of the Alliance for Bangladesh Worker Safety, a group of brands and retailers seeking to drive safer working conditions for the men and women in the ready-made garment industry. In 2014, Walmart joined the Fair Food programme through a partnership with the Coalition of Immokalee Workers (CIW) and Florida tomato suppliers. The Global Social Compliance Programme (GSCP) is a business-driven programme created to promote the continuous improvement of working and environment conditions in global supply chains. Walmart is one of five leading companies that helped to create GSCP. In 2021, Walmart and Netflix partnered up to bring products celebrating some of the streaming service's most popular kids' shows to store shelves across the country in a partnership they're calling the Netflix Hub.

Sources: DSM (2016, 2022); IBM (2016); Walmart (2016, 2021).

Alliance activity

Alliances are critical weapons in firms' competitive arsenals, and in recent decades, alliance activity has increased substantially (Duysters *et al.* 2012; Gomes *et al.* 2016; Bamford *et al.* 2022). According to Kang and Sakai (2001), the number of alliances in 1999 was six times higher than a decade before. Duysters *et al.* (1999) report a similar exponential increase in strategic technology alliances during the period 1970–1996, and Anand and Khanna (2000) count, during 1990–1993, more than 9,000 alliances just in the US manufacturing sector. On the basis of their research, Dyer *et al.* (2001) conclude that in 2001, the top 500 global businesses averaged 60 major alliances each. De Man (2005) reports the number of alliances by high-tech companies during the period 1998–2002: IBM (168), Cisco (56), Eli Lilly (40) and Philips–EU (61). Furthermore, the impact of alliances appears to be growing steadily. As Harbison and Pekar (1998) find, the percentage of the annual revenue of the 1,000 largest US companies earned from alliances grew from less than 2 per cent in 1980 to 19 per cent by 1996 and was expected to reach 35 per cent by 2002. With respect to predictions for the future, survey research indicates that managers consider alliances primary vehicles for growth (Schifrin 2001). Banks, for example, are becoming more open to the idea of partnering with startups to push their growth strategy forward. Between 2013 and 2014, a 200 per cent jump in the value of US fintech (partnership) deals was observed (Accenture 2016). Results from the Global CEO Survey indicate that 49 per cent of the participating CEOs will forge an alliance/joint venture agreement in 2016, compared to 51 per cent in 2015, and 44 per cent in 2014 (PWC 2016). Analysis of the 96 largest companies in the world, across eight industries, shows that new partnership formations are surging worldwide, up 173 per cent in 2021 compared to 2020 (Bamford *et al.* 2022*)*. Moreover, in a post-pandemic world, alliances and ecosystems (in addition to mergers and acquisitions) are considered critical instruments to grow, create competitive advantage and be disruptive (Macmillan *et al.* 2022). These illustrations imply that firms cannot create value on a stand-alone basis; the way business is conducted today is based on partnerships (for more alliance examples see Turiera and Cros 2013).

The rationales for engaging in alliances shift with economic and industry developments (Doz and Hamel 1998). During the 1970s for example, firms focused on product performance (i.e. efficiency and quality) and engaged in alliances to obtain access to technology and new domestic and international markets, as well as to realize market stability. During the 1980s, the focus shifted to obtaining flexible market positions as continuing globalization, increasing competition and more demanding customers required firms to become flexible. Their alliances provided flexibility, deployed to build industry stature, consolidate industry positions and gain economies of scale and scope. Then during the 1990s and 2000s, firms switched their attention to learning and capability development for innovation; they began using alliances to ensure a constant stream of prospects for advancing technology and to proactively maximize value, optimize their total cost for product or customer segments and gain an ability to respond to changing internal and external conditions. More recent upsurges in alliance activity appear triggered by a focus on corporate social responsibility: alliances help firms comply with institutional and market demands for societal and ecological responsibility. Also, new alliance-based organizational arrangements (e.g. ecosystem, meta-organizations) have emerged in response to technological advances. Regardless of the rationale, though, the strategic value of alliances is apparent, especially in a contemporary context of rapidly growing and changing markets, global competition, network organizations and dynamic, complex, expensive technologies.

Today alliances represent strategic instruments that offer various advantages (see Table 1.2). Firms enter alliances to access valuable and complementary resources they do not already possess (Das and Teng 2000b), including capital, technology and specialized knowledge. To expand product volume and achieve economies of scale, firms also establish partnerships. Furthermore, they might engage in alliances to reduce operational and strategic risks, accelerate internal growth or increase speed to market. Alliances also can function as learning vehicles, providing a means to obtain, exchange and harvest knowledge (Lubatkin *et al.* 2001). They can even shift external dependencies to the firm's advantage by blocking competitors or inducing group-to-group competition (Gimeno 2004). If an alliance offers legitimacy and reputation effects (Stuart 2000), it can reinforce the firm's corporate social responsibility policies and lobbying activities (London *et al.* 2006; Yin and Jamali 2021). Finally, alliances offer a way to assess potential acquisition partners (Hagedoorn and Sadowski 1999), in that shared experiences reduce the costs related to integration. Thus, alliances provide more flexibility than hierarchies or markets and are subject to less regulation than mergers and acquisitions.

TABLE 1.2 Advantages and disadvantages of alliances

Advantages	*Disadvantages*
• Access to resources: firms form alliances to gain access to capital, specialized skills, market and technological knowledge, or production facilities, which can help them focus on core competences. • Economies of scale: high fixed costs require firms to collaborate to expand production volume. • Risk and cost sharing: alliances enable firms to share the risk and cost of particular investments. • Access to a (foreign) market: partnering with another firm is often the only way to obtain access to a (foreign) market. • Learning and innovation: alliances offer firms an opportunity to learn from their partners; for example, lean manufacturing, product development, management know-how or technology capabilities. • Speed to market: firms with complementary skills collaborate to increase speed to market and capture first-mover advantages. • Reputation: firms form alliances to increase their reputation and legitimization. Lobbying activities and collective pressure prompt governments to adopt policies that favour specific industries. • Neutralizing or blocking competitors: firms can gain competencies and market power to neutralize or block the moves of a competitor (e.g. entry barriers). • Assessing acquisition partner: alliances offer a way to know a potential acquisition candidate better and decrease information asymmetry. • Flexibility: alliances provide more flexibility than hierarchies and markets and are subject to less regulation than mergers and acquisitions.	• Loss of proprietary information: proprietary information can be lost to a partner who is a competitor or eventually will become one. • Management complexities: because alliances require the combined effort of multiple firms, they entail coordination complexities, often resulting in conflicts, frustrations and costly delays. • Financial and organizational risks: the opportunistic behaviour of partners can undermine the value creation logic of an alliance. Inter-organizational routines also may make it difficult for a firm to act independently. • Risk of becoming dependent: a power imbalance arises if one partner becomes overly dependent on the other. This situation increases the risk of opportunism, exploitation and (hostile) acquisitions. • Loss of decision autonomy: joint planning and decision making may result in a loss of decision-making autonomy and control. • Loss of flexibility: establishing an alliance with one partner may prevent partnerships with other potential firms. • Antitrust implications: the benefits of alliances disappear if they are challenged on antitrust grounds. Some countries have strict regulations that prohibit certain business relationships. • Learning barriers: although alliances provide access to knowledge, learning barriers may make it difficult to integrate and exploit new knowledge. • Long-term viability: despite predetermined objectives and end dates, internal and external contingencies often cause premature termination.

Source: Adapted from Barringer and Harrison (2000).

However, alliance activity creates several disadvantages. For example, firms may lose proprietary information to a competitor, which weakens their competitive advantage (Kale *et al.* 2000); the managerial complexities due to reciprocal and interdependent relationships may create substantial coordination costs that jeopardize joint value creation (Gulati and Singh 1998); their voluntarily collaboration increases the risk of opportunistic conduct, which undermines value appropriation efforts (Wathne and Heide 2000); firms can become locked into a relationship, reducing their bargaining power; and the loss of decision autonomy could inhibit the firm's ability to steer the alliance towards its own objectives (Glaister *et al.* 2003), just as the loss of organizational flexibility may restrain its ability to pursue alternative, potentially more valuable arrangements. Furthermore, laws and regulations often inhibit an alliance's potential (Oxley 1999), and inter-firm learning may be difficult due to learning barriers that limit a firm's absorptive capacity (Hamel 1991). Finally, unforeseen internal and external contingencies constitute a threat to long-term stability (Das and Teng 2000a).

Alliance failure

Paradoxically, even as firms increase their focus on and use of alliances, their failure rates seem to keep climbing (Hoang and Rothaermel 2005; Pekar and Allio 1994). Researchers report failure rates as high as 70 per cent (Harrigan 1988), though in other settings, Franko (1971) and Killing (1983) find 24 and 30 per cent premature alliance dissolutions, respectively. Porter (1987) considers 33 randomly chosen US firms, a sample that produced a dissolution rate of 50.3 per cent during 1950–1986. Kok and Wildeman (1997) and Dacin *et al.* (1997) calculate approximately 60 per cent failure rates for alliances, whereas Park and Ungson (1997) find a dissolution rate of 43 per cent during 1979–1995 among a US–Japanese sample. De Man (2005) reports an average failure rate of 52 per cent for a sample of 140 European and US firms. Based on a repetitive study among alliance professionals (i.e. 2002, 2007, 2009, 2011), Duysters (2012) and colleagues conclude that the alliance failure rates remain stable at approximately 50 per cent. These reports in combination confirm that even if firms consider alliances attractive methods to achieve their objectives, they are subject to widespread failure and premature dissolution.

A plethora of factors contribute to or inhibit the achievement of superior performance (Hoffmann and Schlosser 2001; Nemeth and Nippa 2013; Robson *et al.* 2002; Ryan-Charleton *et al.* 2022). For example, the success or failure of alliances might be attributed to environmental contingencies (Koza and Lewin 1998), the cultural distance between partners (Barkema *et al.* 1996), broad or narrow alliance scopes (Khanna 1998), the alliance contract (Hagedoorn and Hesen 2007), the governance form adopted (Sampson 2004a), emerging alliance instability (Das and Teng 2000a), management control (Yan and Gray 1994), the quality of the working relationship (Ariño *et al.* 2001) or learning processes (Lane *et al.* 2001). We postulate that whereas premature dissolution results from mismanagement and ad hoc decision making, alliance success stems from the adoption of a systematic approach to alliance management.

Specifically, we address three key reasons that encompass this plethora of potential deal breakers. First, failure stems from a lack of understanding of the potential pitfalls and hazards that pertain to the different alliance development stages. Alliances typically develop through a sequence of stages, and during each, partner firms direct their attention to specific design and management decisions. For example, during the alliance strategy formulation stage, decisions should focus on developing a business proposition and selecting an appropriate governance mode (i.e. make, buy or ally). But during the alliance management stage, decisions instead must focus on the day-to-day operations. Second, failure can be attributed to an unawareness of the unique challenges imposed on them by different alliance objectives, diverging partner firm characteristics and unique alliance contexts. For example, whereas learning alliances require firms to focus on knowledge sharing and protection mechanisms, co-branding alliances necessitate that they direct their attention towards reputation management. Third, alliance failure is more likely when firms neglect the institutionalization of their alliance know-how and know-what—which we refer to as alliance capabilities. For example, firms that possess strong alliance capabilities, implying that they have invested in an alliance function, databases and checklists, tend to outperform firms without these capabilities. Moreover, firms employing alliance professionals who possess an 'alliance mindset' are more likely to experience success.

To reap the benefits from alliances, firms must deal systematically with these three issues, which will enable them to achieve, efficiently and effectively, a good design and management approach to their alliance relationships. Observing the high failure rates in practice, it seems, however, that firms are not sufficiently prepared. Therefore, we need an academically grounded framework that offers a coherent understanding of the unique nature of strategic alliance management.

An academically grounded alliance development framework

Before and during alliance development, managers confront varied, unique decision-making situations. Each situation requires that firms conceptualize it in terms of problem, solutions and implementation. That is, firms must tackle any situation by defining the problem, developing a set of solutions, selecting one solution, and then implementing it efficiently and effectively. To this end, they need to be aware of decision-making rationales, that is, the underlying principles, guidelines and theories that may inform their decision. Academic research is rife with theories that attempt to explain these decision-making rationales; we draw on theories from alliance literature to discuss the decision-making content, the alternatives, and the theoretical rationales for these various alternatives. In addition, decision makers in firms must understand the necessary steps for arriving at an appropriate solution, which we refer to as decision-making steps. Management literature is informative in this context. By combining these varied concepts and research streams, we propose an academically grounded framework for strategic alliance management that consists of three main parts: (1) alliance development stages, (2) alliance attributes and (3) alliance competences.

Alliance development stages

The foundation details the development stages through which alliances progress. Building on prior alliance development literature (D'Aunno and Zuckerman 1987; Das and Teng 2002; Dyer *et al.* 2001; Kanter 1994), we distinguish eight stages: (1) alliance strategy formulation, (2) alliance partner selection, (3) alliance negotiation, (4) alliance design, (5) alliance launch,

(6) alliance management, (7) alliance evaluation and (8) alliance termination (see Figure 1.1). Each development stage depicts a specific decision-making situation that requires unique know-what and know-how (see Box 1.1 for other segmentation approaches). An alliance transforms and proceeds to the next stage only after it has achieved the objectives of the preceding stage. Thus, each development stage is characterized by specific issues and requires specific decision-making rationales and steps.

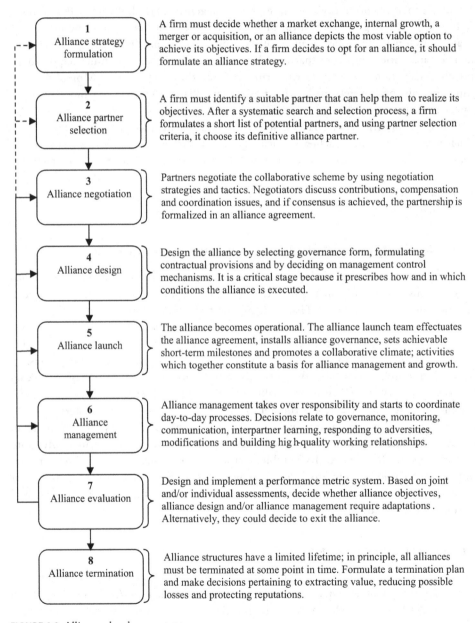

1 Alliance strategy formulation
A firm must decide whether a market exchange, internal growth, a merger or acquisition, or an alliance depicts the most viable option to achieve its objectives. If a firm decides to opt for an alliance, it should formulate an alliance strategy.

2 Alliance partner selection
A firm must identify a suitable partner that can help them to realize its objectives. After a systematic search and selection process, a firm formulates a short list of potential partners, and using partner selection criteria, it choose its definitive alliance partner.

3 Alliance negotiation
Partners negotiate the collaborative scheme by using negotiation strategies and tactics. Negotiators discuss contributions, compensation and coordination issues, and if consensus is achieved, the partnership is formalized in an alliance agreement.

4 Alliance design
Design the alliance by selecting governance form, formulating contractual provisions and by deciding on management control mechanisms. It is a critical stage because it prescribes how and in which conditions the alliance is executed.

5 Alliance launch
The alliance becomes operational. The alliance launch team effectuates the alliance agreement, installs alliance governance, sets achievable short-term milestones and promotes a collaborative climate; activities which together constitute a basis for alliance management and growth.

6 Alliance management
Alliance management takes over responsibility and starts to coordinate day-to-day processes. Decisions relate to governance, monitoring, communication, interpartner learning, responding to adversities, modifications and building high-quality working relationships.

7 Alliance evaluation
Design and implement a performance metric system. Based on joint and/or individual assessments, decide whether alliance objectives, alliance design and/or alliance management require adaptations. Alternatively, they could decide to exit the alliance.

8 Alliance termination
Alliance structures have a limited lifetime; in principle, all alliances must be terminated at some point in time. Formulate a termination plan and make decisions pertaining to extracting value, reducing possible losses and protecting reputations.

FIGURE 1.1 Alliance development stages

BOX 1.1 ALLIANCE SEGMENTATION

Alliance segmentation entails an approach to distinguish between different types of alliance relationships. Segmentation is academically relevant to clarify the object of the study and organize theory and empirical evidence systematically. In this book, for example, we use various alliance segmentation approaches, including alliance development (e.g. design versus management), alliance objectives (e.g. learning versus co-branding), partner characteristics (e.g. cross-sector versus competition) and governance forms (e.g. equity versus non-equity). Whereas the academic segmentations outlined in this book are critical to alliance professionals as it helps them to organize and focus their attention, in practice, other segmentations do exist. For example, alliance leadership may organize a set of alliance relationships based on the extent to which a partner holds promise for the future and the extent to which this partner is strategically important to the firm. Consequently, four alliance types are distinguished. First, a corporate alliance is strategically important and holds a key to future success. These relationships require extant managerial attention as often multiple ties exist with a (rival) partner, including supplier, learning and customer relationships. In addition to exploiting existing and joint resource combinations, innovation is often part of the long-term agenda. Second, a business alliance entails a single-tie relationship, exhibiting low strategic importance and low potential for future synergies. Such a relationship extends beyond a mere transactional exchange, and alliance management is relatively straightforward with a focus on monitoring relationship progress and attaining objectives. Third, relationship alliances hold great promise for the future, as for example joint research and development efforts may lead to marketable innovations. However, the present strategic value is low, thus alliance management should primarily focus attention on unlocking the relationship's potential. Fourth, strategic alliances are of critical importance to the firm as, for example, a partner may provide access to a unique distribution channel or supply a critical component. Even if future synergies are unlikely, relationship continuation is imperative. Depending on the nature and objectives of the firm, other pragmatic segmentation approaches, for example, based on the extent of integration, the extent of learning or the extent of equity, may be more suited and managerially effective.

Alliances are, however, purposeful entities that can learn and adapt to changing circumstances, indicating that alliance development also entails a repetitive sequence of goal formulation, implementation and modification based on lessons learned or changed intentions among the partner firms (Ariño and de la Torre 1998). The alliance development framework incorporates a cyclical approach, such that the eight stages remain interlinked through learning and adaptation. All decisions made in one stage have effects on subsequent stages, and alliance development can follow an iterative development path, such that stages may be revisited if needed. Alliance failure often results when organizations skip one or more stages and/or managers fail to complete their decision-making tasks for each development stage. Management thus plays a critical role (i.e. decision making) in successful alliances, as organizations must be actively managed and guided through various stages to increase chances for success.

Chapters 2 to 9 present the foundation of our alliance development framework and detail, for each development stage, the content and steps associated with decision-making situations. Before engaging in an alliance, a firm must conduct a strategic analysis to determine the appropriate governance mode (Chapter 2). A firm then conducts a partner analysis to select an appropriate partner (Chapter 3). Building on these two pre-design stages, the firm starts alliance negotiations (Chapter 4), with the result that the outcomes of the negotiations are formalized in an alliance design (Chapter 5), which provides the foundation for alliance launch (Chapter 6) and alliance management (Chapter 7). As the alliance develops, performance assessments are required to monitor the relationship's progress (Chapter 8), and the firm must manage the alliance dissolution too (Chapter 9).

Alliance attributes

Because each alliance is surrounded by unique circumstances, we augment our framework by elaborating on unique decision-making situations originating in unique alliance attributes. Distinct alliance objectives, alliances with different types of partners and specific alliance constellations are likely to require idiosyncratic know-what and know-how, so we must offer more detail in our framework. We first focus on alliance objectives and their management challenges, as distinct alliance objectives impose constraints on decision making within each alliance development stage. We give detail on supplier alliances (Chapter 10), learning alliances (Chapter 11) and co-branding alliances (Chapter 12). In addition, the impact of partner characteristics on decision making is discussed, as diverging philosophies, orientations and backgrounds between partners constitute a potential barrier to effective decision making. We detail international alliances (Chapter 13), asymmetrical alliances (Chapter 14), cross-sector alliances (Chapter 15) and coopetition alliances (Chapter 16). Alliance arrangements also come in constellations composed of more than two alliance partners. Unique alliance constellations bring about unique decision-making challenges. Specific attention is given to multi-partner alliances (Chapter 17), alliance portfolios (Chapter 18), alliance networks (Chapter 19) and business ecosystems (Chapter 20). Other alliance objectives, partner characteristics and alliance constellations may affect strategic alliance management as well, but we suggest that taken together, these chapters present a coherent overview covering a wide-range of topics. All chapters are replete with illustrative case descriptions.

Alliance competence

The ability to create successful alliances, which reflects learning about alliance management and then leveraging alliance knowledge within the company, constitutes an alliance capability. To build alliance capabilities, organizations must not only learn and manage alliances but also exploit their own alliance competences appropriately. Firms that capitalize on their prior experience with alliances likely develop and deploy their alliance capabilities and, therefore, tend to outperform firms without alliance experience or capabilities. Another critical element of a firm's alliance competence pertains to the selection, training and management of people involved in alliance relationships; thus we detail the role and competences of alliance professionals (Chapter 21) and explicate how partner representatives may work together in alliance teams (Chapter 22) before we define alliance capabilities, detail why they are important, and describe decision making in terms of building and deploying alliance capabilities (Chapter 23).

Alliance challenges

Whereas Chapters 2–23 offer instrumental knowledge about strategic alliance management, we acknowledge that high-performing alliances require more than pre-set solutions. A manager's experience, expertise and creativity contribute to developing an alliance mindset. An alliance mindset refers to the cognitive frame alliance managers use to identify and deal with tensions with alliance arrangements, including cooperative versus competitive, structure versus process, deliberate versus emergent and corporate versus societal tensions. We provide an

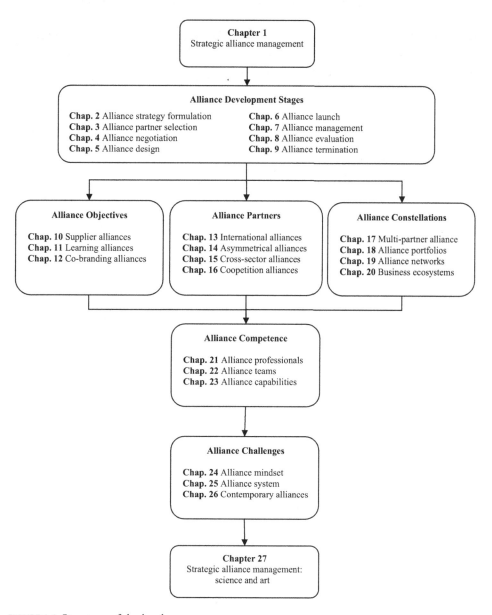

FIGURE 1.2 Structure of the book

understanding of how managers can identify and resolve these alliance tensions (Chapter 24). In addition, understanding the interplay between partner firm, alliance and external environment poses a challenge which needs to be understood to successfully steer alliances towards success. We detail on a co-evolutionary approach, which at the core approaches alliance management from a system perspective (Chapter 25). Undeniably, alliances constitute the cornerstone of firms' competitive strategy. Not surprisingly, new forms of alliance arrangements are created and effectuated. Accounting for technological, ecological and sociological developments, we detail on new alliance forms, among which include Industry 4.0 alliances, blockchain alliances, environmental collaborations and societal alliances (Chapter 26).

In Chapter 27, we postulate that, in addition to being a Science, strategic alliance management constitutes an Art. We conclude the book with themes likely to become salient to the future of strategic alliance management. Taken together, this book takes readers on a guided tour of strategic alliance management, as we depict in Figure 1.2.

Note

1 The main focus of the book is on business, hence we use the label 'firm' or 'organization' if a broader context is implied. The insights offered in this book, however, also apply to other organization forms, including non-profit and non-governmental organizations.

2

ALLIANCE STRATEGY FORMULATION

During the alliance strategy formulation stage, a firm decides which governance mode is appropriate for realizing its objectives, that is, how it will organize the procurement of its desired resources. We distinguish three prototypical types: 'make', such that firms gather resources internally through inter-unit exchanges or through mergers and acquisitions; 'buy', which means firms procure resources through discrete market transactions organized by simple contracts; and 'ally', which refers to alliance arrangements organized through complex contracts with external parties to procure resources. This chapter is divided as follows. To inform their decisions about alliance strategy formulation, managers must understand the difference between alternative governance modes (first section) and comprehend the rationales underpinning each of them (second section). When a firm adopts the ally governance mode, it also must formulate an alliance strategy to detail the requirements that the alliance should meet. We therefore wind up this chapter with three sections describing a set of decision-making steps, a summary for alliance strategy formulation and a case illustration.

Three prototypical governance modes

In the context of governance modes, a firm's boundary pertains to its demarcation from its external environment, though these boundaries are constantly subject to change as firms rearrange their portfolios of activities to achieve their objectives. Such restructuring occurs through three types of prototypical governance modes that define exchanges and that we compare in Table 2.1: make, buy and ally[1] (Gulati and Nickerson 2008).

The 'make' governance mode indicates that firms seek to realize their objectives through internal procurement (Gulati and Nickerson 2008). For example, in inter-unit exchanges, firms autonomously invest in and develop their existing resources and capabilities to market their products and services. Prior to their internal procurement though, some firms internalize previously external resources by engaging in mergers and acquisitions. In such a transaction, two firms agree to integrate their operations because they possess resources that, when combined, create synergies. Through internal procurement, organizations obtain property rights and thus a competitive advantage because they can develop products and services out of sight of competitors. In this case, they also might attain control over their margins and

DOI: 10.4324/9781003222187-2

TABLE 2.1 Prototypical governance modes: make, buy and ally

	Make		Buy	Ally
	Internal growth	*Merger and acquisition*	*Market*	*Alliance*
Form	Internal growth	Merger and acquisition	Market	Alliance
Description	Activities and resources developed internally	Activities and resources internalized through a transaction in which two firms agree to merge	Activities and resources procured through a market transaction	Access to activities and resources obtained through collaboration with external firm(s)
Coordination	Hierarchy	Hierarchy	Price	Relational (supplemented with hierarchical and price)
Characteristics	• No or limited interdependencies with external organizations • Full control over resources	• Relatively few interdependencies with external organizations after integration • Full control over resources	• Low interdependencies with external organizations • Full control over resources	• High interdependencies with external organizations • Partial control over all resources
Advantages	• Proprietary rights and ownership • Protecting and building competences • Adaptation to internal and external demands	• Quick access to similar markets • Authority over activity • Tax benefits • Small impact on industry capacity • Building competences	• Quick access to commodities • Efficient information processing • High-powered incentives	• Quick access to complementary resources • Speed and flexibility • Shared investments and risks
Downside	• Slow and costly development • Uncertainty • Limited growth and expansion	• Required finances • Complex negotiation and integration challenges • Bureaucracy • Loss of flexibility and high risk • High failure costs	• High transaction costs due to market failure • High uncertainty • Inseparability of resources • Information asymmetries • Subject to market power	• Shared returns • Lack of control • Questionable long-term viability • Difficult to integrate learning • Need for performance monitoring

Sources: Gulati and Nickerson (2008); Powell (1990); Williamson (1991).

markets. However, the 'make' decision imposes hazards on the firm in that it might increase the level of bureaucracy because the firm has full control over an activity (Williamson 1991). It also reduces flexibility; building or integrating new resources requires substantial investments, which may be difficult to recoup if the firm fails.

The 'buy' governance mode instead implies that firms procure resources through discrete market transactions, organized in the form of a simple contract. Market transactions are well suited to exchanging commodities because 'supply and demand' governs the exchange. The exchange is organized by price (Powell 1990), so the level of organizational and financial integration between the transacting firms is low. Because markets process information efficiently, buyers gain good access to different types of relevant information, including prices, alternative suppliers and quality. However, market transactions also involve potential hazards. The main disadvantage of the 'buy' governance mode therefore pertains to the opposing objectives of the transacting organizations: the buying firm aims to lower costs, whereas the selling organization hopes to increase revenues. The conflict may induce opportunistic behaviour and increase transaction costs. Furthermore, markets may fail in response to the uncertainty surrounding the supply of resources, information asymmetries between buyers and suppliers may result in higher prices and suppliers may use their market power to increase their margins.

Finally, the third governance mode, 'ally', suggests that firms establish alliances with external parties to obtain access to desired resources. Alliances provide a viable alternative when internal and external conditions lead the firm to desire some degree of control over the resources but not to internalize them. For example, when markets fail, firms may use an alliance to obtain access to external resources. Alliances offer several advantages: an alliance governance mode enables a firm to access complementary resources without obtaining proprietary rights. It provides the firm with speed and flexibility in obtaining access and exploiting desired resources. Furthermore, through collaborations, firms can share investments, which may reduce risk. However, sharing resources may also impose the risk of creating increased competition. Furthermore, it may be difficult to integrate learning into the firm, and the long-term viability of an alliance is questionable. When partners have reaped the benefits from the relationship, they are then likely to terminate it.

The three governance modes offer alternative strategic options for building and sustaining a competitive advantage. However, it is also important to note the plethora of intermediate governance forms on the make–buy continuum (Powell 1990). For example, alliances constitute a hybrid governance mode between hierarchy and market exchanges, whereas joint ventures (i.e. where two firms establish a new organizational entity) tend to verge on hierarchical governance. In contrast, licence agreements are more closely associated with market exchange. Despite these varied intermediate forms, the logic for choosing a governance mode can rely mainly on the three prototypical types.

Governance mode rationales

Numerous theoretical perspectives permeate alliance literature, providing rationales for cooperative strategies and governance mode decisions (Salvato *et al.* 2017). Contingent on a theory's assumptions and related key constructs, each theory provides alternative explanations. For reasons of parsimony (see Box 2.1 for other perspectives), we focus here on seven theoretical perspectives that tend to dominate alliance literature: (1) transaction cost economics, (2) resource-based view, (3) resource dependence perspective, (4) strategic management theory, (5) social network theory, (6) organizational learning perspective and (7) institutional theory.

BOX 2.1 SOME OTHER GOVERNANCE MODE EXPLANATIONS

Extending beyond more established theoretical perspectives, such as transaction cost economics, resource-based view and institutional theory, other theoretical perspectives have been introduced to the alliance field. Real options represent a firm's investment in assets, which allow the firm to respond to future events in a contingent fashion. Initial work by Kogut (1991)—advocating that the establishment of a joint venture (JV) depicts a real option decision—laid the foundation of a series of studies drawing on real options theory (see Reuer and Tong 2005). These studies investigated topics such as the initiation of equity arrangements as option purchases, valuations of JV terminations, risk implications of JV investments and conditions under which real options are used in JVs. More recent, one ramification of real options theory extends to alliance management and details on the extent to which (real) options can be identified and exploited (Berard and Perez 2014). Real options theory thus explicates how alliance decisions could be viewed as a way to attain risk reduction in the present by having a right but not the obligation to undertake future investments and to capitalize on emerging opportunities. Agency theory is concerned with the governance mechanisms that organize the relationship between principals (e.g. shareholders) and agents (e.g. board), as these parties inherently have conflicting interests and access to different sets of information. According to agency theory, a tension exists between principals having a need to impose control and agents acting within their own interest, a tension which can be resolved, for example, by contracts. Within an alliance setting, agency theory is used to explain joint venture investment decisions, and empirical evidence suggests that the presence of agency hazards affects firms' decisions to opt for equity-based arrangements (Reuer and Ragozzino 2005). It also stipulates that effective alliance decision making and relationships result from imposing monitoring and incentive systems that align alliance managers' interests (i.e. agents) with owners' interests (i.e. principals).

Sources: Berard and Perez (2014); Kogut (1991); Reuer and Ragozzino (2005); Reuer and Tong (2005); Wang (2015).

Transaction cost economics (TCE)

TCE offers a coherent framework for exploring choices of governance modes (Williamson 1975, 1991). It stresses efficiency and cost minimization rationales for cooperation and advances insights by recognizing the role of partners' motives, the nature of the investments and the specific character of the transactions. It states that transaction costs should be minimized when a governance mode matches the transaction exchange conditions. These costs of running the economic system include both ex-ante and ex-post costs (Williamson 1985). The ex-ante costs relate mainly to drafting, negotiating and safeguarding a contractual agreement, whereas the ex-post costs entail the time and resources invested in repairing misalignments and bonding. In this sense, transaction costs differ from production costs, which are generated from the primary functions of the organization, that is, producing goods and services.

Two assumptions and three exchange conditions constitute the core of TCE logic. The first assumption involves opportunism, or behaviour that is self-interested and deceptive. The logic thus holds that managers are inclined to break, whether implicitly and explicitly, the rules that govern a transaction. A second assumption refers to bounded rationality. That is, despite the firm's efforts to deal with complexity and unpredictability, managers have only limited ability to plan for the future and predict various contingencies that may arise. The potential for opportunistic behaviour and the constraints of bounded rationality pose severe problems for governing transactions because they drive transaction costs higher and require firms to protect themselves against exploitation. Accordingly, TCE predicts that distinct transactions with variations in frequency, asset specificity and uncertainty demand alternative governance modes to be organized efficiently. Frequency refers to the number of exchanges that constitute the transaction. Asset specificity occurs when investments specifically support an exchange relationship, such that if the relationship were to be terminated, the value of these assets would be largely lost. Finally, uncertainty implies that the consequences of a situation are unpredictable.

If market transactions dominate, exchanges are likely to be straightforward and non-repetitive and require few transaction-specific investments. In such conditions, the market itself, backed by contract law, can provide effective safeguards. However, if transactions produce uncertain outcomes, recur frequently and require substantial investments (i.e. asset specificity), they can be organized more efficiently through hierarchical governance. The transaction costs for market exchanges are greater than those of long-term relational exchanges, so increased transaction costs should prompt a shift from external to internal governance. A vulnerable firm that lacks information its exchange partners already have may benefit similarly from internalizing transactions or activities. However, if a transaction involves mixed asset specificity and recurs, an alliance, a form of hybrid governance, is likely to be the appropriate governance mode. Such hybrid governance modes demand mutual dependence, mutual commitments to resource contributions and accepted compensation mechanisms. Although alliances thus offer advantages, including the avoidance of uncertainty caused by market failure, their uneasy control position implies an inherent instability.

Critics of TCE also refer to limitations of the TCE to explain governance mode decisions (see e.g. David and Han 2004; de Wulf and Odekerken-Schroder 2001; Ghoshal and Moran 1996; Weitz and Jap 1995). First, studies that draw on different conceptualizations of asset specificity and uncertainty produce some mixed results. Masten *et al.* (1991) find that vertical integration in the shipbuilding industry became more likely in the presence of relationship-specific human capital, but Joskow's (1985) research suggests that physical and site specificity increase the length of contracts among coal suppliers. Moreover, TCE fails to recognize the potential value of transaction-specific investments (Madhok and Tallman 1998), even if the value creation potential of an alliance outweighs the costs associated with coordination and protection. In contrast with TCE-based predictions, Russo (1992) indicates that uncertainty relates negatively to backward integration, even as Poppo and Zenger (2002) argue that when uncertainty interacts with asset specificity and relational norms, the likelihood of relational exchanges increases. Clearly more empirical testing is called for. Second, TCE may place too much emphasis on opportunistic behaviour (Ghoshal and Moran 1996), neglecting the role of relational governance (Heide and John 1992) and emphasizing hierarchical control as a protection against opportunism, even if trust reduces transaction costs and makes alliances more suitable governance modes. Third, only limited evidence really shows that governance modes aligned with exchange conditions outperform misaligned governance modes (David and Han 2004), such as when Sampson (2004a) reveals that governance modes designed to match the predictions of TCE experience improved innovation performance compared with misaligned governance modes.

Resource-based view (RBV)

A firm can maximize its value by pooling and exploiting its valuable resources. According to the RBV, firms attempt to find an optimal resource boundary that ensures the value of their resources is realized best, compared with other resource combinations (Barney 1991). A competitive advantage results when the firm can implement a value-creating strategy (Hitt et al. 2000) that is not being implemented simultaneously by its (potential) competitors. Specifically, a competitive advantage requires the firm to possess valuable, scarce, not imitable and non-substitutable resources. Such characteristics also imply that the resources are difficult to move across firm boundaries, such that they constitute barriers to external procurement. Thus market exchanges are not pivotal in the RBV; resources subject to such transactions tend instead to be available, mobile and imitable, and their acquisition does not increase the firm's competitive advantage. If all desirable resources were available for acquisition through market exchange at fair prices, it would be unwise for firms to get involved in alliances, which usually entail high governance costs and some sacrifice of organizational control. Therefore, the RBV seems particularly appropriate for examining alliances or mergers and acquisitions; firms engage in boundary-spanning activities to access and obtain resources that they do not own but need in order to strengthen their competitive position.

In turn the RBV defines both merger and acquisitions and alliances as strategies for gaining access to other firms' resources, for the purpose of bringing them together and attaining otherwise unavailable value (Das and Teng 2000b). When a firm does not possess the entire bundle of resources and capabilities it needs, markets cannot bundle the required resources or alternatives to attaining those resources are too costly, then it engages in mergers and acquisitions, or alliances. Mergers and acquisitions and alliances work towards the same overall objective, namely, obtaining resources, but the RBV suggests that two conditions particularly favour alliances. First, an alliance constitutes a more viable alternative when not all the resources owned by the target are valuable to the firm. Second, disposing of redundant or less valuable resources induces a cost because such resources may be tied to the desired resources. Alliances enable the focal firm to obtain only its desired resources, while bypassing undesired ones.

Furthermore, unlike mergers and acquisitions, alliances enable firms to protect their own valuable resources. For example, if a firm wants to exploit certain resources but lacks the competences to do so, alliances help them retain those resources and capitalize on their value, only temporarily giving up control. The firm retains its access to its valuable resources and can exploit them for future internal development. Alliances thus form when the realized value of resources contributed to the alliance is greater than their value when realized through internal uses or relinquishment. This scenario is especially likely for resources characterized by imperfect mobility—resources which are inimitable and non-substitutable.

Of course, with respect to governance mode decisions, there are also criticisms of the RBV. First, even though prior RBV research offers a plethora of resources (e.g. reputation, culture, brands, organizational routines) that might contribute to a firm's competitive advantage, systematic empirical testing of their impact on governance decisions is relatively scarce (see for exceptions Gu and Lu 2014; Villalonga and McGahan 2005). Second, the RBV primarily focuses on the possession of resources, not the costs of resource deployment, even though using resources, whether autonomously or collaboratively, imposes coordination and value appropriation costs. Although a complete RBV theory related to governance decisions is thus lacking (Das and Teng 2000b), we note that it contributes valuable insights to value creation within alliances. For a coherent RBV, further substantial conceptual and empirical research is required.

Resource dependence perspective (RDP)

The RDP is rooted in an open system framework: firms are embedded sets of relationships, which render them dependent on their external environment (Pfeffer and Salancik 1978). According to Aldrich and Pfeffer (1976), firms cannot generate all the resources or functions they need to maintain themselves, so they must enter into transactions and relations with external actors that can supply those required resources. A firm's ability to control external resources determines its survival and provides power over external parties. Power originates through resource scarcity, which reflects three sources. First, the importance of an external resource—or the extent to which the firm needs the resource to survive—reduces a firm's relative power. In particular, intangible resources such as patents, trademarks, market or technological know-how and human competences tend to be pivotal, whereas tangible resources, such as commodities, can be effectively obtained through market exchanges. Second, a firm's discretion over the resource allocation and use (e.g. ownership rights, access) increases its relative power. Third, the extent to which desired resources can be substituted by alternative resources increases the firm's relative power. With this focus on desired resources, the RDP contributes insights into why firms engage in mergers and acquisitions and alliances.

At the heart of the RDP rests the notion that two firms prefer to avoid becoming dependent on each other's resources (Blankenburg Holm *et al.* 1999). To reduce uncertainty and increase its relative power, a firm may seek to become autonomous by managing its external relationships with a two-fold strategy to acquire control over (1) critical resources to decrease dependence on other firms and (2) resources that increase the dependence of other firms on it. Mergers and acquisitions and alliances can help execute this dual strategy. When firms ally to obtain access to critical resources, their long-term relationship probably enables them to exercise some degree of external control, though mergers and acquisitions should be preferable when the firm needs more control over its partner (Finkelstein 1997). Alliances provide a firm with more flexibility and options to scale investments up or down; mergers and acquisitions offer more control over joint resources (Yin and Shanley 2008). With flexible arrangements, firms can take advantage of changed circumstances, but they lose the capability to exploit opportunities. Commitment and control over resources offer other benefits, but again at a cost: the potential loss of investment and foregone opportunities. Thus, though resource scarcity may encourage competition between firms, it also may stimulate cooperation, producing mergers and acquisitions that aim to increase command over external resources or alliances based on mutual support rather than domination.

We also note two main limitations of the RDP. First, despite the intuitive understanding it offers of rationales for distinct governance modes, strong empirical evidence about the distinct conditions that favour specific governance modes remains lacking (Fink *et al.* 2006). For example, internalizing resources through mergers and acquisitions could increase independence, but it may also impose high costs because acquiring capabilities tends to be expensive, and integrating capabilities takes time and effort. Similarly, obtaining resources through market exchange increases a firm's dependence on its external environment, yet the costs are relatively low. Second, the RDP tends to neglect the importance of prior relationships, even though social connectedness may affect alliance formation decisions (Gulati 1995b). An account that focuses only on interdependence cannot explain how firms learn about new alliances and overcome the threats of partnerships. The RDP implicitly assumes that all information is freely available and equally accessible and thus that firms have equal opportunities to ally. Despite these critiques, the RDP provides a clear indication that a firm's survival depends on its ability to command external resources. A firm is effective when it resolves the trade-off between flexibility (i.e. market exchange and alliance) and commitment (i.e. internalization), while also satisfying the demands of partners in its environment on which it relies most, and which contribute most to its existence.

Strategic management theory (SMT)

To maximize their competitive strength, firms may adopt distinct governance modes, though their underlying motives tend to converge. Therefore, the SMT imagines the governance mode decision as a trade-off among distinct strategic motives, even if the strategic motives identified by SMT literature tend to be similar across modes. For example, Walter and Barney (1990) provide a list of strategic drivers for mergers and acquisitions, and Glaister and Buckley (1996) issue a similar list of strategic (and learning) motives that drive alliance formation. For parsimony, we focus on key strategic motives for alliances.

In this setting, the SMT cites the need for prospective partners to achieve synergies across their business strategies, such that an alliance can contribute to the realization of their strategic objectives. Reasons to establish partnerships are vast: short-term efficiency, resource access, market position, geographical expansion, risk reduction, competitive blockades, economies of scale, speed to market, minimized transaction costs, shared investments and so on. To organize these reasons, Barringer and Harrison (2000) divide the strategic motives to form alliances into four internally focused categories:

1   Increase market power. By erecting entry barriers or forming clusters with other firms, alliances enable firms to adopt monopoly-like behaviour and increase their market power.
2   Increase political power. Individual firms team up to influence governing bodies more effectively, whether nationally or internationally.
3   Increase efficiency. Being able to tap into others' resources and share the load can result in significant reductions of costs and economies of scale. Such partnerships often focus on production, though they also might include marketing or even pre-competitive research.
4   Differentiation. Partnerships within and across sectors in pursuit of new customers and innovation enable firms to differentiate offers from those of competitors.

Faulkner (1995) also recognizes external strategic motives. For example, globalization and regionalization increase international turbulence and uncertainty, such that firms confront the need for vast (financial) resources to deal with technological changes and shorter product life cycles.

Burgeoning literature on strategic management thus offers many relevant insights, including analyses of the reasons for establishing alliances, alliance objectives and areas of potential conflict. Despite this focus on strategic motives, few studies provide clear-cut insights into governance mode decisions. Whereas the breadth of SMT constitutes one of its greatest strengths, it also represents its greatest weakness: motivations arising from nearly all other perspectives can be incorporated into the SMT, and its underlying logic could be applied to any governance mode. For example, realizing economics of scale implies forward/backward integration through mergers and acquisitions and alliances, as also explained by TCE. Increasing political power reflects an institutional stream of thought, and obtaining and accessing resources relates to the RBV. Thus though the SMT provides theoretical and managerial insights in the strategic rationales that underlie alliance formation, its primary contribution is its pragmatism.

Social network theory (SNT)

The social context that surrounds prior alliances influences alliance formation decisions (Gulati 1995b). Thus SNT views firms not as stand-alone entities but rather according to their location within the network of inter-organizational relationships that determine their success and survival. Although SNT has not developed sufficiently to inform governance mode decisions, it asserts that a firm's social network facilitates new alliances by providing valuable information about the location of critical resources and the partner's reliability. Repeated collaborations might provide information that helps firms learn about new opportunities and enhance their trust in current and potential partners, though indirect relationships through common partners also function as important referral mechanisms. Recognizing the ambiguities and uncertainty associated with alliances, access to valuable information thus might lower search costs and alleviate risks of opportunism, which can make firms more likely to enter alliances.

In the social network, potential partners become aware of one another's existence, as well as their needs, capabilities and alliance requirements. Social networks also provide information about partners' reliability. For example, a partner that behaves opportunistically imposes greater risk on any firm that enters into an alliance with it, but a rich social network contains clues about past behaviours, so the firm can incorporate the partner's network reputation into its alliance formation decision. Although SNT thus offers a novel view on alliance formation, we find again that the empirical evidence is virtually absent, in this case with regard to how distinct social network resources prompt distinct governance mode decisions. For example, are firms with central positions in an inter-firm network, which gives them access to high-quality information (i.e. superior network resources), more inclined to establish hierarchical governance modes, compared with firms with more peripheral network positions? Yet SNT offers a relevant explanation for the emergence of alliances: social networks (of prior alliances) function as conduits for valuable information and thus play an important role in shaping future alliance formation.

Organizational learning perspective (OLP)

Firms might enter into partnerships primarily to learn new skills or acquire tacit knowledge (Hamel 1991). According to the OLP, firms form alliances because the superior knowledge they can gain will enhance their competitive position. Firms that place a high priority on the acquisition of intangible knowledge (e.g. technological know-how) are likely to consider alliances important instruments because in alliances, learning occurs on both macro and micro levels (Knight 2002). At the macro level, alliances provide a means for firms to share and acquire knowledge, which may improve their competitiveness and profitability. At the micro level of analysis, interpersonal links offer members of the firms an opportunity to share and learn skills from one another. That is, alliances might add value to firms by providing (1) the possibility for firm innovation and enhancement and (2) employees with the chance to exchange professional practices that can show them how to perform their tasks better.

In terms of governance mode preferences though, OLP insights are less conclusive. In general, hierarchical governance modes appear more appropriate for learning rather than market exchanges because learning requires long-term and frequent interactions. However, alliances constitute a particularly effective means for knowledge exchange, particularly if that knowledge cannot be obtained easily in the market (Mowery *et al.* 1996) or internally developed. An alliance is preferable if the desired knowledge is tacit and difficult to evaluate; internal learning may prevent novel insights. Thus a firm that wants to learn a particular skill stands a better chance of doing so if it forms an alliance with an expert firm and can absorb external knowledge (Deeds and Hill 1996). Yet OLP neglects the costs and risks of learning through alliances. In particular, knowledge transfers demand substantial investments in training, education, relationship building and organizational adaptations (Lane and Lubatkin 1998). The risks pertain primarily to the unwanted transfer of proprietary knowledge because firms in a learning alliance may compete for valuable knowledge (Hamel 1991). Thus, the gains from learning alliances must be balanced against the pains of the dilution of firm-specific resources, the deterioration of integrative capabilities and the high demands on management attention.

Institutional theory (IT)

With an open system perspective, IT states that firms are strongly influenced by their external environments (Scott 2003). Influenced by economic factors, such as industry regulations, rival behaviour and socially constructed norms and beliefs, firms organize their boundary-spanning activities to mimic other firms. That is, firms pursue activities that increase their legitimacy and cause them to appear in agreement with the prevailing rules, requirements and norms in their business environments (Dimaggio and Powell 1983), as these rules establish bases for production, exchange and distribution. With this logic, IT can answer how and why firms adopt distinct governance modes, such as alliances, for example. In particular, this school of thought states that alliances aim for legitimacy and social approval rather than effectiveness or efficiency. Legitimacy in the alliance process helps ensure that the initiative receives a certain level of acceptance; without it, the initiative is unlikely to persist. Such legitimacy can be enhanced by governance mode decisions because partnering with well-known, reputed partners improves the focal firm's reputation or congruence with prevailing norms. Common alliance practices thus emerge as collaborating becomes a more widely accepted and desirable phenomenon, and firms copy rivals in their use of this strategy (Teng 2005).

When social behaviour becomes accepted, it turns into an institution, and institutions give industry members a clearly laid route to success and lead to a bandwagon effect (Venkatraman *et al.* 1994). Pangarkar and Klein (1998) suggest that bandwagon pressures, which they capture as the proportion of firms in a peer group that undertake alliances and their average number of alliances, influence both the probability and number of alliances a firm undertakes. Such bandwagon pressures also imply a lack of clarity in the firm's cost–benefit calculations. Confronted with bandwagon pressure, firms are likely to adopt the alliance behaviours modelled by their peers indiscriminately to ensure legitimacy, without considering the actual outcomes of their alliance partnerships. Alternatively, this pressure might induce firms to hire managers with similar industry backgrounds and experiences, who are familiar with industry practices.

Beyond bandwagon pressures, firms may engage in status-driven imitations of their peers, especially the alliance behaviour performed by large and prestigious firms. Partnering with an organization that promotes socially desirable objectives may enhance a firm's reputation more widely; high-profile charitable organizations thus can benefit from such a legitimacy strategy. This view of strategic alliances implies a process of mimetic isomorphism: firms follow established rules and norms and copy, consciously or not, the strategies of their successful peers. The resulting legitimacy and reputation can open doors to other relationships that help the firm gain access to additional critical resources.

The IT thus offers a narrow, behaviourally oriented explanation of alliance formation (Barringer and Harrison 2000). It cannot determine why particular governance modes exist or why firms engage in boundary-spanning activities that deviate from the status quo. Furthermore, if every firm adopts similar governance modes, there is little opportunity for sustainable competitive advantage. In the biotechnology field for example, alliance-based competition has become prevalent, such that firms may experience difficulty in differentiating themselves through alliances. However, IT advances literature with its assertion that firms form alliances to respond to bandwagon pressure and obtain social approval and legitimacy, rather than to realize economic outcomes.

Overview

This concise overview of theoretical perspectives on governance mode decisions reveals the varied and numerous insights that have been produced, ranging from economic to behavioural motives (see Table 2.2). Among the economic explanations, TCE focuses on cost minimization, whereas the RBV emphasizes value creation. At the other end of the spectrum, IT offers a behavioural explanation: firms' behaviour is guided by their legitimacy motives. The OLP also adopts a behavioural explanation but also suggests economic undertones with its proposal that inter-firm learning enables firms to reduce costs and improve profitability. The RDP, SMT and SNT fall in the middle of this spectrum. The RDP originates in organizational theory but adopts economic explanations to explain why firms engage in alliances, namely, to gain control over scarce resources. In contrast, the SMT is primarily economically based, but recent studies have incorporated behavioural motives, such as inter-firm learning. Finally, the SNT emphasizes behavioural explanations but also incorporates economic arguments to explain the influence of network resources on alliance formation.

Academics and managers can certainly benefit from considering each theoretical perspective, but by blending them, they also might obtain a more useful understanding of governance mode decisions. For example, if we combine TCE with OLP explanations, we might predict that inter-firm learning will reduce transaction costs (Nooteboom 2004). A blend of OLP with SNT, as exemplified by Powell et al. (1996), indicates that industries with widely dispersed sources of expertise require learning in networks rather than in individual firms. Augmenting TCE with the RBV suggests that cost minimization and value maximization together drive

TABLE 2.2 Theoretical perspectives: alliance formation

	Transaction cost economics	Resource-based view	Resource dependence perspective	Strategic management theory	Social network theory	Organizational learning perspective	Institutional theory
Description	Firms organize their boundary-spanning activities to minimize transaction costs.	Firms organize their boundary-spanning activities to maximize value creation.	Firms engage in resource exchanges with external parties to reduce uncertainty and obtain control.	Firms forge alliances to achieve synergies between business strategies.	Inter-firm networks constitute conduits of information, shaping alliance decisions.	Firms engage in inter-firm learning to improve their (core) competences.	Firms organize their boundary-spanning activities to conform with prevailing norms imposed by their environment.
Alliance formation logic	Alliances reduce uncertainty caused by market failure and reduce costs associated with hierarchy.	Alliances create value when procurement of resources is difficult through market or internal development.	Alliances enable firms to minimize dependence on external parties or maximize control over scarce resources.	Alliances enable firms to build and sustain a competitive advantage.	Firms use network resources, such as reputation and referral, to inform alliance formation.	Alliances function as learning vehicles to access, obtain and exploit (intangible) knowledge.	Firms form alliances to obtain legitimization by mimicking competitors' alliance behaviour.
Limitations	Neglects social context and value creation motives.	Neglects costs and investments of resource deployment.	Neglects social context in which exchanges are embedded.	Encompasses a variety of strategic motives tied to other perspectives.	Neglects other prototypical types of governance modes.	Neglects costs and investments required to enable inter-firm learning.	Neglects alternative motives, including economic and strategic.

governance mode decisions (Zajac and Olsen 1993). The SNT may be especially open to combinations with other perspectives, such as TCE and RDP, because then it can illustrate how firms create and manage alliances as strategic responses to competitive uncertainties. The IT school of thought also accords with Gulati's (1995b) findings that alliances form within partner firms' social networks; for example, the strength of a firm's reputation and closeness in the network of past alliances are strong predictors of alliance formation, and the likelihood of alliance formation also relates positively to the complementarity of the partners' capabilities, status similarity and social capital arising from direct and indirect collaborative experiences. Finally, SMT provides a more holistic perspective and potentially could incorporate elements from the other perspectives. Building on this observation, we outline some managerial implications in the next section.

Alliance strategy formulation: decision-making steps

During alliance strategy formulation, firms must decide which governance mode fits their objectives and situation. However, governance mode decisions are complex because firms confront a plethora of reasons, occasionally opposing, that provide support for a specific governance mode. To organize decision making, we suggest that alliance strategy formulation overall comprises five sequential decision-making steps (see Figure 2.1). If, after careful analysis, a firm prefers an 'ally' governance mode, it must then explicate its alliance strategy and prepare for partner selection.

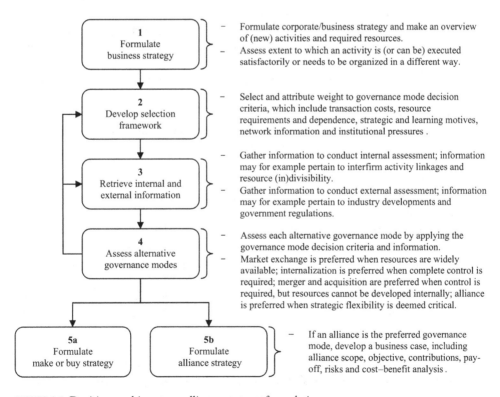

FIGURE 2.1 Decision-making steps: alliance strategy formulation

Step 1: formulate business strategy

A firm first must decide on its strategy, derived from its mission and its vision. The strategy describes how the firm aims to achieve its long-term objectives. To realize those objectives, the firm chooses some primary activities, new and/or existing ones, and identifies resources needed to execute these activities. In turn, a firm must determine the extent to which it is able to execute these activities satisfactorily. Such an overview should grant insights into the objective(s), required tasks and feasibility to perform the activity. Once a firm has a complete overview, it may enter the next step.

Step 2: develop a governance mode selection framework

To evaluate and decide on an appropriate governance mode for a specific activity, selected from the overview, it should be clear which decision criteria apply and how they affect the governance mode decision. In particular, decision criteria might be organized according to the theoretical perspectives presented in this chapter. Thus the analysis might include the following:

1   Transaction-based motives, such as the frequency of the activity, uncertainty surrounding the activity and degree of asset specificity; an alliance is preferred when a transaction is recurring, surrounded by moderate uncertainty and requires mixed alliance-specific investments.
2   Resource-based motives, including the nature of existing and desired resources, divisibility of resources and their availability; an alliance is preferred when an external party possesses valuable and scarce resources (i.e. blocking market exchange), but the desired resources are part of a larger and indivisible resource endowment (i.e. blocking a merger).
3   Dependence-based motives, such as the degree to which existing and desired resources are critical to the activity and freely available; an alliance is preferred when a firm seeks flexible control over external resources.
4   Strategic motives, such as market power, market entry, blocking competitors and international expansion: an alliance is preferred when it enables a firm to realize strategic objectives.
5   Network criteria or information about a potential partner's credibility and reliability and referrals; an alliance (partner) is preferred when a firm receives supportive information via its alliance network.
6   Organizational learning criteria, including the extent to which fast access to knowledge is required, the extent to which knowledge must be recombined and the extent of speed required in generating new knowledge; an alliance is preferred when speed, flexibility and knowledge recombination are imperative.
7   Institutional-based motives, incorporating criteria such as legitimacy, reputation and status; an alliance is preferred when external pressure imposes partnering as common practice.

To complement the selection framework, firms should assign each criterion a relative weight. For example, a firm might decide that obtaining legitimacy outweighs economic benefits, commanding external control over scarce resources outweighs prior established reputations or acquiring valuable market know-how outweighs improving market position. The choice of governance mode should rely on a cost–benefit analysis of the trade-offs among distinct decision criteria.

Step 3: retrieve internal and external information

To apply their selection framework, firms should conduct internal and external assessments to obtain the necessary information. The internal analysis involves gathering detailed information within the firm about the nature of the activity, the required resources, inter-firm activity linkages, organizational culture, and systems and procedures. An external analysis should feature information about, for example, industry developments and regulations, competitor strategies and actions, and governmental policies. Building on such information, the firm can evaluate and decide on the governance mode that is most appropriate for any selected activity.

Step 4: assess alternative governance modes

Against the backdrop of the selection framework, supportive guidelines and gathered information about the internal and external contexts, firms must recognize that each governance mode entails its own unique advantages and disadvantages (see Table 2.1) as they decide on the most appropriate governance mode for any specific activity. In short, a market exchange is preferable when the required resources are relatively easily available but do not necessarily enhance a firm's competitive advantage. Internal procurement or mergers and acquisitions are ideal if unified ownership and control rights permit more thorough exploitation of combined organizational resources, even if such exploitations demand higher investments (e.g. physical, human, intangible resources) and increased governance costs. Alliances, which cannot exploit joint assets as intensively as mergers and acquisitions but which offer more flexibility, are preferable if continuing cooperation is beneficial and centralized control could harm value creation. A firm might conclude this step with the following questions:

- Does the chosen governance mode generate strategic value or competitive power?
- Does it impose a risk of losing competitive strength to rivals?
- Does the mode disrupt an activity's interrelatedness with other firm's activities?

If the answers to these critical questions are unsatisfactory, a firm may need to reconsider its decision and re-engage in Steps 2 and 3. However, if a firm, on the basis of extensive analysis, decides that an 'ally' governance mode is its best option, the next step is to explicate its alliance strategy.

Step 5: formulate alliance strategy

The final step formalizes the alliance strategy. The firm should decide which external source(s) of resources it wants to deploy in support of the selected activity to attain its objectives. An alliance strategy summarizes these decisions, often formalized in the form of a business case that describes the scope of activities taken into account, the objective of the alliance, the nature of the partnership and a cost–benefit analysis. A clear business case is critical to approach and select potential partners and serves as input for alliance negotiation and design.

Summary

In this chapter, we have provided overviews of the dominant theoretical perspectives that attempt to explain governance mode decisions. Transaction costs, resource synergies, dependence, informational advantages, strategic motives, inter-firm learning and institutional pressures all impact the choice between 'make', 'buy' and 'ally'. We argue that in order to arrive at a governance mode decision, executives should consider all motives. To this end, we suggest a five-step procedure for firms to help them to make governance mode decisions and achieve a well-formulated alliance strategy. Much of the logic described herein, however, also applies to alliance-oriented governance form decisions (e.g. alliance structure). That is, the governance mode decision of a firm, which itself might be influenced by transaction costs, resource alignment and institutional pressures, for example, influences the firm's structural preference in terms of non-equity versus equity-based governance forms. We go into detail on structural preferences in Chapter 5, but a combined analysis of governance mode (e.g. make, buy, ally) and governance form (e.g. equity, non-equity) may be beneficial.

CASE: GOOGLE–HUBSPOT[2]

Larry Page and Sergey Brin were both students at Stanford University studying computer sciences. During their stay at Stanford, in 1996, they developed an algorithm able to search the internet effectively. This algorithm was known as 'BackRub'. On 4 September 1998, Google was officially founded as a company, and the search engine proved very successful. In 2000, Google began selling advertisements which were based on search keywords. The company eventually moved to Mountain View in 2003 and was taken public in 2004. The company experienced a fast growth and soon became one of the largest media companies in the world. The company launched a number of new features in a relatively short time span. In 2002, Google News was introduced; in 2004, Gmail; followed by Google Maps in 2005. In 2006, it bought YouTube, and Google Chrome was introduced in 2008.

With its growing success, its competition became more fierce also. Microsoft offered Bing as a search engine and offered a competing webmail service under the name of Hotmail. Also Microsoft offered Windows Live Local as an alternative for Google Maps. Google had already introduced Chrome as a web browser, but it also began competing with Microsoft's operating system, Windows, by introducing the Linux-based operating system Chrome OS. Google was hit hard by the financial crisis in 2007 and 2008. Revenues from selling advertisements declined sharply. To improve its efficacy in selling ads, Google agreed to buy DoubleClick in 2007. This marked the start of cookie-based tracking. Google grew further, and in 2014, the company had more than 70 offices in 41 countries.

In growing the company, utilizing the competencies of others has been crucial. Getting access to competencies can be achieved either through acquisitions, such as YouTube, or partnerships. Google had been very active in forging partnerships. For instance, Google teamed up with NASA in 2005 to explore large-scale data management and distributed computing. Part of this collaboration was the building of a Google Research and Development centre at the Ames Research Centre of NASA. Another partnership is the one with GeoEye in which it launched a satellite which provided Google with high-resolution imagery for Google Earth. Another way of getting access to resources is investing in startups and scale-ups. On 31 March 2009, Google established a $100 million fund. This commitment was raised to $300 million annually. Since 2015, Google Ventures has been renamed GV. One of the companies in which Google Ventures has invested is HubSpot.

HubSpot was established at the Massachusetts Institute of Technology (MIT) by Brian Halligan and Dharmesh Shah in 2006. It develops and markets software products for inbound marketing, sales and customer services. In the years 2007 to 2010, it witnessed step growth in revenues and raised a total of €33.5 million in three equity rounds. Then, in March 2011, it raised another $32 million from, amongst others, Google Ventures. The changing way people shop, learn and buy requires new way of marketing and sales. The software of HubSpot helps business to transform accordingly. An important element in this change is the move away from outbound marketing (cold calls, email blasts and direct mail) to inbound marketing (Google, blogs, social media, mobile). Google shares the 'belief that search engines, social media and mobile devices have fundamentally changed how businesses should market themselves'. The investment allowed HubSpot to further penetrate the market of small- and medium-sized enterprises. Since the investment, HubSpot integrated many Google features, such as Google Calendar, Gmail, AdWords, Docs and Drive. In 2018, HubSpot announced the expanding of the partnership between the two companies through the adoption of Google Cloud to expand its international cloud infrastructure. This allowed HubSpot to invest more in its current Google Cloud integrations. Next, customers would benefit from increased data security. The combination of Google analytical capabilities with HubSpot of turning data into actions is the sweet spot of the collaboration. Given this integration and close collaboration between the two, there has been some debate as to Google buying HubSpot and further integrating the two platforms. Up till date, Google did not buy the platform, and the two are thus still collaborating as strategic partners.

Questions

1   What are (strategic) motives for Google to prefer collaborative agreements over mergers and/or internal growth?
2   What problems may Google and HubSpot experience as the alliance progresses? How can they overcome these problems?
3   To what extent is the alliance agreement between Google and HubSpot typical for the ICT industry? Explain whether the alliance is likely to change industry structure and competitors' strategic behaviour.

Notes

1   Williamson (1985) calls the three governance modes hierarchy, market and hybrid.
2   Crunchbase (2022); Google (2022); Hubspot (2022a, 2022b).

3
ALLIANCE PARTNER SELECTION

The alliance partner selection stage involves the choice of a partner or group of partners with which a firm seeks to realize its objectives. Questions that need to be addressed during this stage include which potential partners exist, which partner is most suitable and what are potential strengths and weaknesses of each potential partner? Answering these questions requires an understanding of the notion of partner fit—that is, of the comparative inter-firm differences related to certain attributes or dimensions that continually shape the pattern of interaction between partners. If partners are highly compatible, such as in their culture or networks, they may be more likely to realize their objectives. Partner misfit instead tends to jeopardize the relationship; therefore, pre-existing knowledge about the degree and content of misfit provides valuable information for improving the design and management of any alliance. To inform their alliance partner selection, managers must understand the differences among various types of fit and comprehend the rationales that underpin partner selection (described in the first section). The following two sections provide a systematic framework containing a set of decision-making steps for alliance partner selection, along with a summary. The final section concludes with a case illustration.

Types of partner fit

In alliance literature, partner fit relies on two related concepts, each with a specific logic. The first type pertains to resource complementarity between partners as a means to enhance the alliance's collaborative effectiveness; Parkhe (1991) calls it Type I diversity. In contrast, a second type of partner fit refers to the extent to which inter-firm characteristics, including strategic, cultural, organizational and operational features, are compatible, which we refer to as partner fit compatibility and which is akin to Type II diversity. Incompatibility negatively affects alliance functioning and, without proper intervention, can result in the premature dissolution of the relationship. Both types of partner fit can explain how (mis)fit affects partners' ability to work jointly and effectively, but their underlying logic varies: complementarity functions as a rationale for alliance formation; incompatibility impedes alliance development.

DOI: 10.4324/9781003222187-3

Partner fit: resource complementarity

Resource complementarity refers to the extent to which the joint use of distinct sets of resources yields a higher total return than the sum of returns earned if each set of resources were used independently (Chi 1994; Dyer and Singh 1998). In this definition, alliances give an option to a firm that lacks the entire bundle of resources and capabilities it needs to sustain a competitive edge in a particular domain of activity or the capability to develop them competitively (Mowery *et al.* 1998). Resource complementarity is thus an important partner selection criterion; a firm should prefer a potential partner that creates higher relative fit between resource foundations and resource provisions. Lambe *et al.* (2002) indicate that resource complementarity enables parties to develop an idiosyncratic resource foundation which fosters joint value creation. According to Hitt *et al.* (2000), emerging market firms concentrate more on financial assets, technical capabilities, intangible assets and willingness to share expertise than do developed market firms. Developed market firms instead want to leverage their resources, such as local market knowledge and access, through partner selection. Thus, to increase an alliance's value creation potential, firms seek the specific partners with which they can align their particular resources.

But resource complementarity as a guiding principle constitutes a mixed blessing because not all contributed resources can be used effectively in an alliance (Das and Teng 2000b). Consider four types of resource alignment configurations; the first pair centres on resource synergies, but the second pair focuses on resource under-performance in alliances:

1 Complementary resource alignment occurs when firms contribute dissimilar resources because their complementarity enables them to create synergy and capitalize on non-redundant distinctive competences.
2 Supplementary resource alignment occurs when firms supply similar resources to an alliance, such as to obtain economies of scale, increase their market power, or supply financial resources, essential to the formation of an alliance.
3 Surplus resource alignment suggests that firms contribute dissimilar resources that are not utilized fully. For example, a firm could contribute more manufacturing capacity than needed. Such slack resources may be redundant, though the surplus also might provide protection against future contingencies.
4 Wasteful resource alignment occurs when similar resources under-perform. For example, managerial know-how cannot be integrated in another firm, such that it simply becomes an additional cost of the alliance.

In addition, though resource complementarity might reduce the risk of opportunistic behaviour and goal conflicts, because the long-term value creation is likely to outweigh the short-term rewards, it increases risks for misappropriation and unwanted knowledge spillovers. Partnering firms that contribute complementary resources confront a tempting opportunity to gather up the valuable new resources provided by their counterparts. As noted by Cohen and Levinthal (1990), overlap in knowledge resources actually improves partners' ability to absorb knowledge, and their in-depth understanding of the potential value and deployment of resources allows them to interact more and share knowledge more easily and effectively. Resource complementarity thus may stimulate inter-firm learning—which increases the likelihood of involuntary transfers of critical resources. The initial resource-based motives for value creation therefore could undermine a firm's competitive position over time. Thus, firms must consider the extent to which a partner's anticipated resource contributions will be sufficient motive to forge an alliance.

Partner fit: compatibility

Compatibility refers to the degree to which partner firms share similar characteristics (Douma *et al.* 2000; Liu *et al.* 2015). This sort of partner fit reinforces collective strength and positively influences alliance effectiveness because it facilitates alliance processes. For example, the propensity for opportunistic behaviour declines when the parties in an alliance have well-matched firm characteristics because compatibility increases the quality of the relationship (Saxton 1997). Furthermore, compatibility determines the extent to which organizations can get along and realize anticipated synergies to achieve alliance success, such that alliances are more successful when partners have similar management styles, cultures, asset sizes and venture experience levels (Harrigan 1988; Lavie *et al.* 2012). However, misfit jeopardizes alliance functioning by impeding inter-firm collaboration. Emphasizing compatibility during partner selection enables firms to select appropriate partners or develop and implement corrective measures if misfit occurs. We consider five types of fit: (1) strategic, (2) organizational, (3) operational, (4) cultural and (5) human (see Table 3.1).

TABLE 3.1 Partner fit types

	Description	*Implications*
Resource complementarity	Resource alignment yields a higher return than the sum of returns if each set of resources were used independently.	• Resource complementarity provides a motive for alliance formation. • Threat of resource leakage and cost of non-performing resources.
Strategic fit	Compatibility in partners' strategic view and orientation.	• Good fit signals long-term commitment. • Misfit creates strategic conflicts that undermine joint business proposition.
Organizational fit	Compatibility in partners' organizational structure and routines.	• Good fit reduces uncertainty about intentions, interests and competences. • Misfit undermines collective sense making and increases risk of decision-making conflicts.
Operational fit	Compatibility in partners' operational systems.	• Good fit enables partners to integrate alliance activities. • Misfit impedes the execution of day-to-day alliance operations.
Cultural fit	Compatibility in partners' organizational culture.	• Good fit stimulates joint sense making. • Misfit undermines the quality of the working relationship at different levels in the alliance.
Human fit	Compatibility in partners' employee backgrounds and experiences.	• Good fit stimulates trust building and inter-partner learning. • Misfit fosters interpersonal conflicts and impedes communication and information exchange.

Sources: Douma *et al.* (2000); Hennart and Zeng (2005); Sarkar *et al.* (2001).

Strategic fit

Drawing on strategic management theory, alliance research has emphasized the concept of strategic fit among partners (Douma *et al.* 2000). Highly compatible business and alliance goals, appropriate competitive positions, compatible strategic missions and visions, mutual dependence on one another's resources, similar views about present and future developments and a shared understanding of the business rationale constitute indicators of strategic fit. Appreciation by the market (i.e. financial analysts) is an important driver of such strategic fit. Thus good strategic fit is a prerequisite for any alliance because it implies that individual interests are carefully weighed against the potential benefits and hazards of the alliance. Partners have perceived the added value for their individual businesses and recognize the important role they play in terms of alliance success. Selecting a partner with good strategic fit increases the long-term value creation potential of alliances by signalling that partners have converging long-term interests and are not likely to engage in behaviour that poses a competitive threat.

A strategic misfit is a threat, however. In the long term, partners with poor fit may be less committed and allocate resources to alternative, more valuable arrangements. Signals for strategic misfit include partners acting competitively in the areas on which the alliance focuses, varying perceptions of the importance of the alliance, divergent industry visions, the pursuit of potentially conflicting alliance objectives and market rejection of the alliance. If limited strategic fit is present, firms must carefully consider whether it can be strengthened; otherwise, they should not collaborate. Corrective measures might attempt to encourage top management dialogue about the strategic vision, reduce or expand the alliance scope, realign alliance strategies, emphasize added value and communicate carefully with stakeholders about the importance of the alliance. That is, if firms pursue an alliance with poor strategic fit, they face greater demands on their alliance design and management.

Organizational fit

The degree to which partners' organizations are compatible reflects their organizational characteristics, such as management styles, operating procedures, information systems, decision-making level (e.g. centralized versus decentralized), management style (participatory versus authoritarian) and reliance on formal planning and control systems (Parkhe 1991). Thus Douma *et al.* (2000) call organizational fit a critical factor for alliance success, one that reduces uncertainty about the partner's intentions, interests or competences. Partners with similar organizational attributes, such as customers, manufacturing capabilities and other organizational processes, are more likely to enjoy synergies (Saxton 1997). However, alliance partners almost always differ in some organization characteristics, so the goal is to arrive at a profound understanding of these differences and initiate corrective measures.

Poor organizational fit jeopardizes alliance development and could limit partners' ability to engage in collective sense making, joint decision making or inter-firm learning. If a firm with a centralized, mechanistic structure collaborates with a firm with an organic, decentralized structure, the resulting misfit impedes their constructive collaboration (Parkhe 1991). Similarly, when established firms collaborate with entrepreneurial firms, their decision-making structures do not naturally align, which often leads to conflict, misunderstanding and frustration. If partners exhibit different management styles and institutionalized different internal task routines, they are less likely to attain relational trust, which in turn impedes alliance performance (Lavie *et al.* 2012). To overcome these potential hazards, alliance partners should anticipate organizational misfit during the alliance design and management stages and emphasize the need for flexibility and adaptation. Manageability increases with relatively simple alliance designs, characterized by limited alliance scope, few alliance partners, contracts with contingency clauses and clear task divisions. In addition, proactive alliance management, achieved by building relational capital and emphasizing constructive partner interactions, can overcome the risks associated with organizational misfit. If well managed then, organization misfit might even help partners align their organizational differences.

Operational fit

Operational fit, or firms' procedural capabilities, can be captured by effective management, operational aspects of the business model, operational standards, working procedures and operational systems (Sarkar *et al.* 2001). Good operational fit indicates that alliance partners can collaborate effectively at the operational level, which gives alliances a better chance of success because the links between the partners' operations are transparent. For example, when two manufacturers seek to collaborate, the extent to which they can jointly create value largely depends on their ability to integrate operational facilities. With good operational fit, the partners can work together efficiently, reduce the costs required for coordination, resolve emerging operational issues quickly and discover potential areas for improvements. Thus, good strategic and organizational fit is a prerequisite for long-term commitment; operational fit is critical for determining the extent to which alliance partners can realize the potential benefits.

Poor operational fit creates the risk that processes will stall or produce inadequate output, thus jeopardizing value creation. When the operational processes do not match, or assumptions about the capabilities and capacities of either partner go unchecked, the seeds are planted for future operational problems. They can also lead to poor communication among operational staff, which impedes quick conflict resolution. Poor operational fit creates ambiguity about each partner's roles and skills, which impedes decision-making. Furthermore, it undermines alliance leadership and performance management, both of which are required to monitor and manage the alliance's progress. However, to overcome the risks resulting from poor operational fit, potential alliance partners simply need to incorporate partner differences in their alliance design and management. Joint training and education, personnel transfer across partners and codevelopment of operational systems could prevent the emergence of any of these concerns.

Cultural fit

Partners' cultures, including their ideologies, values and practices, should not come into too much conflict (Park and Ungson 1997). Organization culture, interwoven into the very fabric of the partners, is manifest in the distribution of power and control, commitment to the alliance, openness of the organization, innovation intentions and willingness to collaborate. Cultural fit suggests that partners have sufficient awareness and flexibility to work constructively and learn from their cultural differences to achieve strength. Cultural fit acts as a lubricant in the relationship.

A cultural misfit instead gums up the works. It can cause conflicts in corporate boardrooms, frictions at the operational level and mistrust between the partners. Social incompatibility may lead to partners' inability to develop harmonious relationships (Sarkar *et al.* 2001). If alliance employees resist an understanding of their partner's culture, the complete failure of the alliance is likely. To deal with their different cultures, partners can adopt several approaches. In non-equity based alliances, for example, partners may decide to allow the cultures to coexist, whereas for joint ventures, partners might engage in a process of cultural assimilation, combining the positive elements of both cultures to develop a new culture. In any case, the partners must initiate activities that stimulate cultural awareness, such as joint sessions, cultural training or employee transfers. If well managed, a cultural misfit may even improve alliance performance and lead to spin-offs and positive cultural changes in the partnering organizations.

Human fit

Finally, human fit refers to the degree to which individuals or teams of individuals who will work together in the alliance have converging backgrounds, experiences and personalities (Douma *et al.* 2000). Because the behaviours of employees influence profitability, customer satisfaction and other important outcomes directly, managing human fit is utterly critical. Trust building and learning between employees can ensure the development of strong relationships and high-quality learning interfaces. Common backgrounds, experiences and personalities support employees' mutual understanding, ease interactions and streamline employee behaviour. In addition, human fit encourages collaboration in alliance teams, which often determines alliance success.

But poor human fit likely inhibits alliance progress; misunderstandings and conflicts among alliance employees undermine alliance progress. High-quality interpersonal interactions are prerequisites for the transfer of tacit know-how about markets, management and technologies. To mitigate the impact of poor human fit, alliance partners should undertake human resource management activities, including formal policies and everyday practices focused on training and monitoring. Partners might reward employees by offering alliance team-based incentives tied to overall performance. In addition, motivating and retaining key employees is an important task for alliance management to help employees adjust to new alliance environments and then interact and work effectively with employees from their new alliance partner.

Overall partner fit thus drives the partner selection stage. Complementary resources stimulate joint coordination, which increases profitability and competitive advantages. Parties should participate in learning processes to exploit these synergies, explore complementary resource strengths, and thus achieve greater alliance performance. Compatibility enables parties to cooperate efficiently and effectively; resource complementarity gives parties incentives to sacrifice their short-term individual goals to achieve long-term value creation. Partner fit in terms of compatibility also facilitates learning by creating the perception that benefits for the partner are in the best interests of the focal firm. Finally, it reduces misappropriation concerns, mitigates the risk of conflicts, contributes to the development of trust and commitment and enables inter-partner learning. However, when confronted with an undesired misfit, firms must decide whether to continue collaborating or take appropriate measures in the design and management phase to deal with the potential hazards.

Alliance partner selection: decision-making steps

During the alliance partner selection stage, firms identify the partner that fits best with their organization and objectives. The focus is on achieving collective alignment across the partners' resources, strategies, organizations, operations, cultures and people. To evaluate the degree of

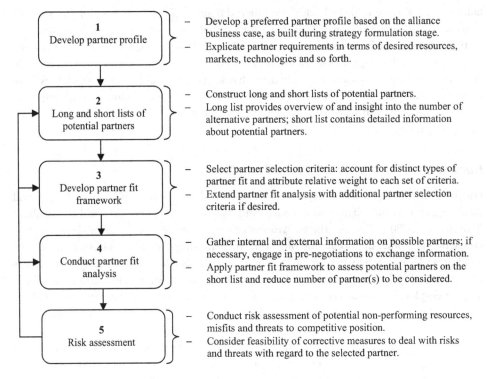

FIGURE 3.1 Decision-making steps: alliance partner selection

fit, and thus the feasibility of the alliance, two questions are key: how can fit be measured, and what degree of fit is required for a successful alliance? A systematic analysis of partner fit provides clear insights into the chances for success, along with a better understanding of the nature and magnitude of corrective measures needed to mitigate negative effects. Firms must recognize though that managing partner fit effectively may require considerable investments, which implies the greater importance of careful partner selection. To this end, we suggest that alliance partner selection should involve a (repetitive) sequence of five decision-making steps (see Figure 3.1).

Step 1: develop partner profile

A partner profile describes the ideal alliance partner, according to the firm's own requirements and intentions. It thus constitutes an important preparatory activity. The firm's intentions might be explicated partially in its business case, which is the end product of the alliance strategy formulation stage. To this end product, the firm should add generic partner fit criteria. Firms can map the important resources and competences of potential partners and how they would contribute to the alliance. Furthermore, they should explicate requirements, in terms of desired markets, products, services and technologies. They can also explicate details such as the ideal size, organization structure, reputation and image of a preferred partner. In terms of operational fit, firms should note required technologies and operational systems; cultural and human fit criteria should include optimal organizational culture and desired competences and skills. In addition, they might incorporate financial and legal criteria into partner profiles or mention a potential partner's preferred reputation in managing alliances. Developing a complete partner profile enables firms to recognize good potential partners when they appear.

Step 2: create long and short lists of potential partners

A long list of potential partners summarizes all possible partners, which is important for two reasons. First, the long list enables the firm to make informed decisions about which potential partners are appropriate. Second, it reveals the multiple alternatives available, which signals a strong bargaining position. Potential partners can be identified through different sources—intermediaries, the internet, trade associations, business networks, conferences, line of industries or (patent) databases, to name just a few. Information about foreign alliances is available from foreign investment agencies, government embassies and consulates. And a firm can seek referrals through its existing alliance partners. Even more detailed company information might be found in websites, print articles, work documents, blogs and annual reports or gathered from the insights of people in personal networks. Whereas the long list provides an overview, a short list enables firms to conduct in-depth analyses of potential partners. Scrutinizing all potential partners demands substantial resources and time. Against the backdrop of the partner selection criteria in Step 1, the firms can compare information about these potential partners to reduce their long list to the short list. This transfer demands that firms do the following:

- Collect as much pertinent, publicly available information on potential partners as possible.
- Assess the degree to which potential partners meet the partner profile.
- Decide which potential partners are most suitable for the short list because they can supply the desired resources and exhibit good compatibility with the firm.

Step 3: build partner fit framework

With this step, a firm develops a detailed partner fit framework to prepare for assessments of potential partners on the short list. To this end, it first explicates indicators for each type of partner fit and then prioritizes those types by indicating their relative importance. The partner fit framework thus comprises partner dimensions, indicators and the relative weight of each dimension:

- Resource complementarity indicators include the extent to which resources are complementary, and anticipated resource contributions will enhance the performance of the alliance.
- Strategic fit indicators include alignment between partners' mission and vision, business strategy, industry threats and opportunities, technological developments, mutual dependence, strategic importance, balanced power and a win–win situation.
- Organizational fit entails compatibility in firm size, authority structure, decision-making approaches, planning and control systems, accounting systems, information systems, management style and incentive systems.
- Operational fit includes operational standards and procedures, systems, allocation of tasks, coordination and performance measurement.

- Cultural fit indicators include alignment in ideologies, values, beliefs and attitudes, as well as ethical matters and management styles. Other potential indicators might involve experience with the partner, respect and balance, ease of doing business, communication style and commitment. When considering allying abroad, issues such as the political or economic climate and national culture also should be taken into consideration.
- Human fit entails the 'click' in personal styles and attitudes, openness, flexibility, employment policies, reward systems, training and education.

Step 4: execute partner fit analysis

Now that the partner selection criteria and the relative weight of each has been determined, the firm must reanalyze existing information and collect any additional information that might be needed. To identify the fit between the firm and its presumed partner(s), relevant, often detailed, information must be acquired about each aspect in the fit analysis framework. This information pertains not only to a potential partner but also to the focal firm. For each potential partner on the short list, relevant information can be acquired through internet searches, annual reports and third parties. Alliance databases are also useful tools for gathering information. But the firm still needs to consider the information about itself that indicates which individuals, teams, departments or business units will be most involved to ensure that they are ready to enter an alliance. The systematic reporting of the partner fit analysis thus provides a foundation for decision making. Such reports can include a textual partner fit report, accompanied by figures and tables.

Collecting some types of information (e.g. human, operational fit) can be cumbersome. Thus firms might agree to organize a preliminary meeting with a potential partner in order to involve it in the partner analysis. The meeting should be clearly exploratory, but the firm also might ask the partner firm to sign a non-disclosure agreement. Such a meeting enables the firm and the potential partner to get to know each other and retrieve pertinent information. For example, they might obtain insights about both partners' strengths, personal chemistry, need to protect intellectual property and potential hazards. With the information from the fit analyses and the evaluation meetings, the firm can begin to consider seriously alliances with one or more partners.

Step 5: conduct risk assessment

The last step in the partner selection analysis requires the firm to conduct a risk assessment of the selected (potential) partner(s). It is unlikely that a firm possesses great fit with the preferred partner on every indicator. Rather, the evaluation helps the firm identify and discuss potential risks and hazards. Risks associated with resource complementarity primarily pertain to idle resources and the threat of resource leakage. Non- or under-performing resources hamper joint value creation, but the unwanted transfer of resources can undermine the firm's own competitive advantage. Organizational alignment risks involve incompatible organization designs (e.g. structure, decision making, management style), which may require a firm to reorganize. The operational risks refer to the costs associated with securing alignment, such as setting up new departments or units to support the alliance. Integrating control and operating systems demand additional coordination efforts. Cultural and human risks derive from incompatibilities in partners' day-to-day functioning. To develop a steady, collaborative culture, with trusting teams and committed individuals, firms should offer training and education, as well as recognize the importance of incentives. The results of this analysis can be presented in a risk-and-yield analysis, featuring an overview of partner fit criteria, the degree of fit, the associated risk and corrective measures.

Following these five steps for partner selection does not mean a clear-cut recipe for instant alliance success. Rather, by using the partner selection framework, alliance managers can better design and manage their alliances and explicate and focus their conversations with potential partners. A partner selection analysis means doing the necessary homework; occasionally, firms will need to retrace their steps. If the results of the risk assessment stage are unsatisfying and a potential partner emerges as inappropriate, the firm should reconsider Steps 2–4. At the end of the day though, the key to any alliance remains in the hand of the managers who are responsible for the next alliance development stage, for which this analysis should set the agenda: the alliance negotiation.

Summary

We have provided an overview of the drivers of alliance partner selection. Whereas partner fit in terms of resource complementarity emphasizes a value creation logic, partner fit related to compatibility functions as a lubricant for inter-firm collaboration. When confronted with an undesired misfit, firms must decide whether to continue collaborating or take appropriate measures in the design and management phase to deal with the potential hazards. We have also presented a five-step procedure for firms to use in their partner selection decisions. Its application results in the selection of a partner with which to enter into alliance negotiations. Moreover, a firm may have achieved partner fit, but as the alliance is executed, unseen contingencies, both internal and external, continuously issue challenges to the maintenance of partner fit. Without deliberate managerial action, even an alliance with an ideal partner fit can in the end produce disappointing results. To guide managerial action, firms might reapply the partner analysis framework as the alliance progresses.

CASE: SOLARDUCK[1]

Carbon dioxide levels in the atmosphere have been rising increasingly over the past decades and have reached levels which have not been seen for the past 800,000 years. Although sometimes heavily debated in society, a general consensus exists about the connection between greenhouse gas concentrations in the atmosphere and global average temperatures. Based on the studies of Dr Charles Keeling, in the late fifties and sixties of the last century, the first indication were given for 'anthropogenic' (human caused) contributions to global warming. In 1972, the Club of Rome published a ground-breaking report titled 'The Limits to Growth'. In this report, the exhaustion of natural resources was highlighted as a factor which would ultimately lead to a decline in economic growth, availability of food and could even result in societal collapse. However, the report contained a message of hope. Human kind is able to live on the earth indefinitely if limits are imposed allowing for a restoration of the equilibrium between economic activity and earth's ability to sustain those. Even though the publication of this report increased environmental awareness, carbon emissions have increased further. In 2015, a turning point was reached. The Paris Agreement is a legally binding international treaty on climate change which was adopted by 196 countries. Its objective is to limit global warming to well below 2 degrees Celsius, compared to the pre-industrial age. At its core, the Paris Agreement provides a framework for financial, technical and capacity building; stimulating international collaboration; accelerating technology development; and increasing international solidarity. The agreement also changed the way in which human kind generates the energy it demands.

An important aspect in restoring the balance between economic development and earth's resources is changing the way in which energy is generated. Since the Industrial Revolution, fossils fuels have become the most dominant source for energy. In 2019, coal, oil and gas still accounted for almost 80 per cent of the global primary energy consumption. However, the energy mix is fast decarbonizing. According to the International Energy Agency (IEA), fossil fuels will peak this decade, while non-fossil energy sources have become dominant in the supply of energy. Renewables sources of energy are gaining in importance fast. The rapid advancement of technologies allows increased yield and lowered costs. For instance, wind turbines have been in existence for more than a century; however, the upscaling of the technology over the past decades has resulted in reduced pricing and a sharp increase in its deployment. In the rapid changing energy market, old technologies are becoming obsolete, new technologies are being developed and new companies are entering the arena.

One example of a new company is SolarDuck, established in 2019 in the Netherlands. As a spin-off of Damen Shipyards, the biggest shipbuilder in the Netherlands and a prominent member of the Dutch offshore industry, SolarDuck was founded on the conviction that wind energy alone will not suffice. Large parts of the world population are living in wind-scarce but sun-rich regions. Solar energy is the most competitive form of renewable energy in these parts of the world. However, land constraints are becoming increasingly apparent. One solution is to let solar float on inland waters like lakes. However, many islands and energy dense locations around the world have no sizeable inland waters at their disposal. But, many of these locations are located in coastal regions. The ability to deploy solar energy offshore will open up a new horizon for solar energy. As such, SolarDuck primarily focuses on more benign locations such as sun-rich regions in South East Asia, the Mediterranean and the Caribbean.

Since the start of the company in 2019, it has seen a rapid development. By the end of 2020, it had filed its first patents, which included the triangular-shaped platforms, which is unique for SolarDuck. As triangles have three axes of rotational freedom, it can far better cope with waves than a square-shaped platform and thus is one of the cornerstones of the SolarDuck design. Beginning in 2021, it launched its first floating powerplant. Damen Shipyards constructed this first plant. For practical reasons related to permitting and accessibility, the system was not located offshore but in the river Waal, the biggest river of the Netherlands. To show its ability to withstand extreme conditions, the powerplant was towed 50 kilometres upstream to its testing site near the city of Tiel. In August 2021, Solar-Duck received an Approval in Principle of the certification agency Bureau Veritas, which was a world's first for offshore floating solar technology. Both in developing the technology and in commercialization, the ability to leverage the expertise of others is vital for the growth of SolarDuck.

Partnering constitutes the cornerstone for further developing the business. From an operational perspective, SolarDuck requires specific competencies and the ability to allow for worldwide scaling. These factors play a dominant role in assessing partner fit. SolarDuck aims to be a technology integrator: subcontractors produce the semi-finished products, and final assembly and commissioning takes place close to the project site, which can be anywhere in the world. This requires a range of supply-chain partners. Based on dependencies, specific arrangements are made, ranging to extensive partnership structures for highly specialized components. In other words, being a small and relatively young company with pre-bankable technology, its global reach can only be realized through forging alliances. The alliance approach ranges from relatively simple intermediation agreements with well-networked local representatives to multi-purpose strategic partnerships.

The Dutch offshore industry has been taking advantage of the offshore wind developments that have taken place on the North Sea. The Netherlands aims to have 11.5Gw installed capacity by 2030. The execution of these ambitions relies on a close cooperation between states and private parties that are able to develop and deploy the required technology. In September 2021, SolarDuck signed a partnership with the Dutch developer Pondera for development projects located in the Netherlands and South East Asia. Since the start of the company in 2007, Pondera has played a critical role in reducing greenhouse gas emissions as, with their (global) projects, they support the transition to a renewable energy system. Offering consultancy services to a variety of clients, Pondera's offerings range from government policy research to supporting renewable energy project development at all stages of the project lifecycle. In the partnership, SolarDuck contributes the technology, whereas Pondera brings in its project development and project financing expertise. In 2022, SolarDuck and RWE forged a partnership. Established in 1898, the Rheinisch-Westfälisches-Elekrizitätswerk (RWE) had a vision to provide low-cost energy by establishing large-scale powerplants and high-performance grids, which included factories and households. In 2009, RWE became a major player in the Dutch energy market after the takeover of Dutch-based Essent B.V. After several restructurings, RWE became one of the world's largest renewable energy producers. In 2021, RWE announced its investment and growth strategy 'Growing Green', in which it will invest 50 billion Euro until 2030 in the energy transition. As part of that strategy, RWE actively scouts new technologies that can support the energy transitions and supports (smaller sized) companies in developing those technologies to be relevant in utility scale energy generation. Responding to the Dutch offshore wind tender 'Hollandse Kust West' (HKW), both parties engaged in negotiation to include SolarDuck technology in the bid for HKW. As a result of these negotiations, RWE committed to invest in the deployment of SolarDuck's full-scale offshore pilot in the North Sea. Next, SolarDuck was selected as the exclusive provider for offshore floating solar PV technology with integrated storage in RWE's bid for offshore wind park Hollandse Kust West in the Netherlands. Furthermore, RWE and SolarDuck agreed to explore and develop offshore floating solar parks in identified key markets in Europe. On November 10, 2022, the Dutch authorities awarded the construction of Hollandse Kust West to RWE, and as a consequence, SolarDuck will be constructing the largest offshore solar plant up till date.

Pondera's and RWE's commitment to support the energy transition represents a valuable asset for SolarDuck to further accelerate the development of the market and the deployment of its technology. In assessing these partners, Solar Duck did not only review capabilities and contributions but also the entrepreneurial spirit of the firms. Since offshore floating solar is a new market, SolarDuck seeks partners that are willing to further develop this market and take some risk. Next, good personal connections with the people that are responsible for the alliance is essential in generating value to all partners. Through these alliances, SolarDuck can further develop its offshore floating solar technology towards bankable, commercial technology and speed up the roll-out of this new technology globally.

Questions

1 Regarding resource complementarity, explain how SolarDuck's resource endowments interrelate with Pondera's and RWE's contributions to the partnership.
2 Regarding compatibility, which types of partner (mis)fit may SolarDuck experience in its partnerships with Pondera and RWE? What measures should SolarDuck consider to reinforce fit and mitigate the effects of misfit?
3 The execution of the alliance was characterized by intense and constructive collaboration among the partners. Describe how the degree of partner (mis)fit may have affected the partners' post-formation behaviours.

Note

1 Climate (2022); Clubofrome (2022); Pondera (2022); Ritchie and Roser (2022); RWE (2021, 2022); SolarDuck (2022); UNFCCC (2022).

4

ALLIANCE NEGOTIATION

Alliance negotiation constitutes yet another critical stage in the alliance development framework. Many alliance initiatives are terminated before they can be executed; if they are executed, the negotiation processes and outcomes establish the foundation for the future progress of the alliance. This stage entails establishing the actual complementarities in the collaboration and defining carefully the nature and amount of resources that will be available to the partnership, the ownership, the anticipated outcomes and the contractual provisions. Because alliance partners are interdependent, reaching an agreement demands some negotiation, usually through a dialogue among representatives of partner firms, with the goal of reaching outcomes that fulfil the various interests of the partners in a way that is acceptable to everyone. Thus the key questions to be addressed during this stage refer to which negotiation outcomes will enable the alliance partners to obtain the greatest possible level of synergy, and what negotiation outcomes would provide the best deal for the partner firms. To inform their alliance negotiations, negotiators thus need a good understanding of the differences among various negotiation strategies and tactics (described in the first section), as well as how to value their resource contributions responsibly (shown in the second section). The following two sections provide a systematic framework with a set of decision-making steps for alliance negotiation and a summary. The final section concludes with a case illustration.

Negotiation behaviour

Firms establish alliances to maximize synergies by aligning potentially complementary resources. The partner firms remain independent though, so to be successful in an alliance negotiation, they must recognize their conflicting aims (Das and Kumar 2010). First, they need an outcome that maximizes the potential value of the alliance. Second, they need to protect their individual firms' interest and negotiate an outcome that maximizes value for the firm specifically. Negotiating an alliance thus entails seeking a relationship between partners that enables them to achieve business success together, without either partner needing to accept a loss of finances, identity or independence (Child and Faulkner 1998). Alliance partners should conclude their negotiations with the feeling that they have achieved a workable deal that benefits them individually as well. To resolve this conundrum, negotiation behaviour

DOI: 10.4324/9781003222187-4

encompasses all activities exploited by negotiators during a negotiation process, with the aim of coming to terms with the negotiating partner. To this end, negotiators formulate and deploy different strategies and tactics, switching among them as alliance negotiations progress (Thompson 1990).

Negotiation strategies

A negotiation strategy reflects a party's disposition towards reconciling and integrating the interests of the partners. Prior research has remarked that negotiation strategies typically have been categorized as either integrative or distributive (Kersten 2001). Integrative negotiations address (and attempt to accommodate) the underlying interests of both parties, which is useful for generating joint gain, particularly in positive-sum negotiations. In such a negotiation situation, the amount of benefits to be divided is variable (i.e. unknown), and partners may profit without sacrifice if they can increase the overall pie. Moreover, partner interests likely converge because their value realization depends on their long-term commitment. Integrative negotiation enables partners to solve problems, develop win–win solutions, achieve value creation and create synergies beyond what would have been possible alone (Pruitt and Lewis 1975). When parties adopt a problem-solving orientation, they likely identify similarities in their interests and pursue common objectives (Ariño and Reuer 2004). Transparency, and the speed and reliability with which partners learn about each other's actions, also result in proposals and counter-proposals, discussions about the solutions and efforts to uncover mutual interests (Olekalns *et al.* 1996). To overcome potentially incompatible interests, negotiators seek settlements that are better for all parties involved. Integrative negotiation thus requires flexibility among parties and willingness to think creatively in order to discover efficient negotiation outcomes.

In contrast, distributive negotiation seeks to create individual gain by persuading the other party to make concessions. The focus is on securing individual interests, appropriating value through the alliance and sharing the pie (Jap 2001), which might be appropriate if the amount of resources is fixed (i.e. a zero-sum game). Partner interests are often diametrically opposed, so they focus on the realization of immediate outcomes, even at the expense of their partner. This type of negotiation is characterized by minimal information exchanges, greater commitment to individual interests and increased hostility (Lax and Sebenius 1986). Yet it also means the exchange of information is crucial because parties work to maximize the amount of information they receive while also minimizing the amount of information they grant (Wolfe and McGinn 2005). The parties' sole aim is to direct efforts towards negotiation outcomes that enable them to appropriate future benefits.

Building on these two dimensions, various typologies of negotiation strategies (for an overview, see Das and Kumar 2010) adopt different foci, including conflict cultures (Gelfand *et al.* 2006), negotiation models (Lewicki *et al.* 1992) and negotiation strategies (Pruitt 1983). By comparing these distinct typologies, we note five negotiation strategies that appear appropriate as categories for classifying negotiation behaviour (Child and Faulkner 1998). First, collaborating suggests concern for individual and partner's interests, with a focus on problem solving. Second, competing indicates that the primary concern with individual interests leads to an attempt to force the partner to back down. Third, avoiding means that partners do not pursue either party's interests and refuse to consider the issue. Fourth, accommodating suggests that a partner's interests are the primary concern, so the focal firm backs down. Fifth and finally, a compromising strategy indicates moderate concerns for a partner's interests, such that they agree to split the difference (see Table 4.1).

TABLE 4.1 Negotiation strategies and tactics

	Description	*Tactics*	*Implications*
Collaborating	Primary concern for individual and partner's interests; focus on problem solving.	Primary focus on soft tactics to build high-quality working relationship; hard tactics only employed to defend interests.	Strengthening of pre-existing relationships; preventing conflict escalation.
Competing	Primary concern for individual interests; focus on imposing outcomes on counterpart.	Focus on hard tactics to exploit power advantage and obtain compliance.	Jeopardizing long-term relationships; conflicts that are costly to resolve.
Avoiding	Limited concern for individual and partner's interests; focus on neglecting negotiation.	Limited use of tactics.	Integrative solution is not achieved, likelihood of premature dissolution.
Accommodating	Primary concern for partner's interests; focus on compliance with counterpart's demands.	Primary focus on hard and rational tactics to deal pre-emptively with counterpart's demand.	Short-term success, but risk of exploitation remains because an integrative outcome is not achieved.
Compromising	Moderate concern for individual and partner's interests; focus on quick consensus solutions.	Primary focus on rational tactics to obtain compliance.	Short-term success, but fundamental issues persist as the alliance progresses.

Sources: Das and Kumar (2010); Lax and Sebenius (1986); Rao and Schmidt (1998).

In a comparison of these negotiation approaches, collaborating seems fruitful for alliance negotiations (Das and Kumar 2010) because it maximizes the negotiation outcome through a strong focus by both parties on each other's and their own outcomes. To develop win–win alliances, partners need to negotiate generously and ensure that their partner receives a good deal, which might mean sub-optimal immediate outcomes as they lay the groundwork for long-term success. Negotiators may be more sensitive to the absence of agreement than to failure to attain an ideal agreement. With flexibility, firms are willing to back down from their initial interests and consider alternative negotiation solutions. Although collaborating cannot guarantee a successful negotiation even if employed by all partners, it is likely to result in outcomes associated with trust-building. If partners invest in relational capital during their initial alliance negotiations, they should enjoy collaborative decision making as the alliance progresses. Moreover, collaborative negotiations are often supplemented by informal, collective sense-making processes that contribute to enhance partner interactions as the alliance progresses.

Negotiation tactics

Negotiation tactics refer to the means used to execute the negotiation strategy. Parties can use a variety of negotiation instruments to achieve this objective (Lax and Sebenius 1986). For example, through communication and persuasion, a negotiator may coerce another party to accept a compensation structure that conflicts with its interests. A firm might present information in such a manner that it looks like a win–win situation, even if it benefits that focal firm primarily. Some negotiators derive power from their possession of specialized knowledge or unique information. Identifying with a charismatic person, which often relies on the negotiator's skill in building good personal relationships, also may exert influence, as can advocacy of normative conformity (i.e. claiming that a position is correct, legitimate or principled). To organize these distinct types of tactics, a three-category classification is identified: hard, soft and rational (Kipnis and Schmidt 1985; Rao and Schmidt 1998).

Hard tactics generally result when negotiators develop a subjective assessment that the counterpart will comply with their demands. This assessment causes them to develop a focus on maximizing their own value and pursuing whatever joint positive value is available. As a leading principle, they aim to fulfil self-interest by creating fear in the opposing party, using threats, demands and sanctions. Because counterparts face high costs if they fail to comply, they usually accommodate the hard negotiators' demands. This scenario also implies reduced dependency, in that the negotiator will describe the multiple alternatives available to realize its objectives, while increasing the partner's dependence and switching costs, such as by setting firm deadlines, demanding concessions, acting forcefully or threatening to terminate negotiations. Such hard influence tactics seek to weaken the other party's position, increase the credibility of the negotiator's own position and impose negotiation outcomes. In the case of conflicts, contracts supported by legal systems serve to resolve the situation. With a focus on differences, these power-based negotiations are characterized by a strong motivation to pursue individual interests at the expense of the partner.

Soft tactics instead emphasize friendliness and assume counterparts have an option of noncompliance with little cost. Thus the aim is to strive for fairness by building a high-quality relationship marked by interpersonal liking, a sense of obligation and reciprocity. Compliance through soft tactics arises because of the bilateral focus and concern for partners' interests. For example, negotiators may emphasize interdependence and actively communicate the limited number of alternatives. Another indicator of soft tactics is a willingness to make alliance-specific investments, which signals commitment and a voluntary exposure to potential exploitation (i.e. a hold-up situation). These influence tactics thus emphasize openness, informality and long-time horizons. If conflicts emerge, their resolution proceeds through active consensus seeking and joint problem solving, with a focus on what partners have in common rather than their differences. Soft tactics indicate a strong motivation to seek solutions and identify a binding common objective, as well as a willingness to recognize both sides' interests as valid.

Rational tactics rely on logic, data and information to obtain compliance. They feature unemotional arguments, but compliance is not taken for granted. The aim is to persuade a counterpart through objective information; the logically presented facts and information cause any request to appear detailed and well prepared. The negotiator also comes off as a competent and reasonable counterpart. Gaining compliance then requires a bilateral focus and concern for partners' interests. For example, negotiators might emphasize facts and figures related to joint business development, industry dynamics and other sources of relevant information.

Negotiation dynamics

To resolve the tension between common and individual interests—and despite our distinction between them—alliance negotiations tend to feature both integrative and distributive negotiation approaches. For example, to find solutions, parties might prefer joint gain but also seek a solution that maximizes their own gain, if they can convince the partner to accept it. Switching between approaches is difficult, however; it involves role reversal by the negotiators, which may be misinterpreted. Alliance negotiations often involve a mixture of trust-building and bargaining power games, which can reinforce a perception of mixed signals about long-term commitment. In addition, adopting an integrative strategy poses a risk because the party becomes vulnerable to opportunism in the negotiation. Being open about one's own interests and preferences to achieve joint gains might provoke a partner to adopt a distributive orientation and exploit this openness to strengthen its own position. Yet proactively adopting a distributive orientation can be perceived as hostile, which may fuel a negative escalation in the negotiation. That is, a distributive strategy may minimize vulnerability to exploitation, but it leaves significant potential joint gain on the table.

Negotiators tend to have learned about distributive strategies and hard tactics, but in alliance negotiations specifically, such tactics produce sub-optimal results. Alliances require more integrative negotiation strategies and soft tactics. A key success factor in any negotiation is recognizing the importance of the relationship, so negotiators might consider the following approaches (Das and Kumar 2010; Pruitt and Lewis 1975):

- Develop super-ordinate goals. Negotiators should focus on developing super-ordinate goals rather than pursuing individual targets. With such a focus, negotiators can resolve conflicts and seek negotiation outcomes in both partners' interests.
- Consider interests. Positions are the demands the negotiator makes; interests are the underlying demands. By concentrating on interests, negotiators can identify shared and incompatible interests, isolate the latter as potential deal breakers and continue the negotiation.
- Separate people from the problem. Personal involvement often translates into emotions, perceptions and beliefs that deteriorate judgemental capabilities. By excluding such involvement, negotiators can focus on the problem instead of personalities.
- Make multiple proposals. With more than one option, the negotiator can identify what the other party values and develop creative trade-offs.
- Engage in creative thinking. The act of creation needs to be separate from judgements of alternatives.
- Focus on fair. When confronted with incompatible interests, the parties need to understand and agree on fairness criteria.
- Work towards clarity. Negotiators should define the scope, objectives, priorities, important tasks, milestones and performance measures for their negotiation.

Alliance negotiation skills can be learned. In general, enhanced negotiation and contracting skills are often manifested in an increased level of contractual detail. For example, Reuer and Ariño (2007) find that prior relationships (i.e. learning) lead to less detailed coordination provisions but do not have an effect on enforcement provisions. Ryall and Sampson (2009) show that firms with prior deals tend to write more detailed contracts regarding partners' rights and obligations, and with more extensive penalty clauses. Ariño et al. (2014) show that the length of prior relationships has a U-shaped association with negotiating time, such that the length of a prior relationship will lower the negotiation time at first, but then it increases the negotiation time. In addition, their results indicate that the length of prior relationships moderates the effect of procedures for termination on negotiation time but not the effect of financial consequences of termination. Taken together, these findings suggest that alliance negotiators learn from prior (negotiation) experiences with partners: they tend to tailor contractual stipulations and details to the specific alliance context and adapt negotiation strategies to new emerging circumstances (e.g. trust as substitute for contractual detail) as the alliance advances.

Valuation

Valuing partners' resource contributions is both important and difficult (Child and Faulkner 1998). Alliance negotiations tend to be lengthy and confidential, and market mechanisms (i.e. price) are rarely appropriate for valuing resources. The future value of resource contributions is also uncertain because value creation depends on the partners' commitment to make the alliance work. Decisions with respect to the alliance design may also affect this valuation. For example, the boundaries of an alliance are clearly demarcated in a joint venture, but non-equity alliances tend to have diffuse boundaries. And yet, an alliance negotiation absolutely necessitates resource valuation because value assessments directly affect negotiation behaviour (Contractor and Ra 2000). In this inexact process, partners' attitudes, and the way they get managed and evolve over time, play a key role. Furthermore, valuations of contributions largely depend on the measurability of those contributions. Tangible resources such as fixed assets offer high measurability, so negotiators likely have a clear assessment of their value, perhaps based on (market) costs, uniqueness, replacement value or net present value calculated on the basis of an expected income stream and discount rate. Working capital might be valued at face value, unless there are reasons to discount it, such as when a joint venture will incorporate bad debts. Intangible resources are difficult to measure due to their tacit nature, and their valuation is more likely to result in conflicts and disagreements between partners.

To provide some insights on valuation, Contractor (2001) distinguishes three types of intangible resources: intellectual property rights, intellectual assets and human and organizational capital. Intellectual property rights (IPR) are formally registered assets, such as patents and brand names, which makes them relatively easy to transfer among alliance partners. To value IPR, negotiators likely use a market-based benchmark. For example, it is possible to assign a value to a brand name by employing a market mechanism: firms are often willing to pay large sums to obtain the rights to such brands. Intellectual assets comprise both IPR and codified but unregistered corporate knowledge, such as drawings, software, databases, manuals and trade secrets—in written form, but deliberately not registered with government authorities. Measuring such resources becomes more difficult, as does their transferability, although it is difficult to attribute a value to such resources except perhaps through royalties and commissions for sales. Human and organizational capital refers to uncodified know-how or expertise that resides in employees' skills, routines and organizational culture. These resources are the most difficult to measure and often inseparable from the firm. For example, expertise is generally ignored in valuation exercises, even though it might constitute a key motive for forging an alliance. Technological capabilities are similarly difficult to value due to their intangible nature, though royalties, licence agreements and discount calculations could provide some insights. Thus whereas tangible assets are often valued at their cost, the valuation of intangible assets tends to be ignored or assigned a value on the basis of equity principles (Child and Faulkner 1998).

Alliance negotiation: decision-making steps

Negotiations in alliances must achieve win–win outcomes because the partners ultimately seek a long-term relationship. To increase the likelihood of smooth collaboration, it is important that partners consider alliance negotiations a positive-sum game, in which integrative

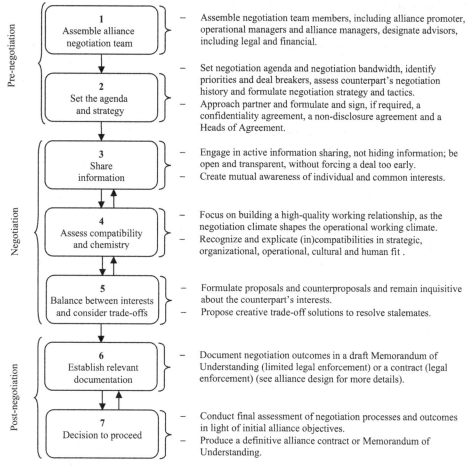

Pre-negotiation

1
Assemble alliance
negotiation team

– Assemble negotiation team members, including alliance promoter, operational managers and alliance managers, designate advisors, including legal and financial.

2
Set the agenda
and strategy

– Set negotiation agenda and negotiation bandwidth, identify priorities and deal breakers, assess counterpart's negotiation history and formulate negotiation strategy and tactics.
– Approach partner and formulate and sign, if required, a confidentiality agreement, a non-disclosure agreement and a Heads of Agreement.

Negotiation

3
Share
information

– Engage in active information sharing, not hiding information; be open and transparent, without forcing a deal too early.
– Create mutual awareness of individual and common interests.

4
Assess compatibility
and chemistry

– Focus on building a high-quality working relationship, as the negotiation climate shapes the operational working climate.
– Recognize and explicate (in)compatibilities in strategic, organizational, operational, cultural and human fit .

5
Balance between interests
and consider trade-offs

– Formulate proposals and counterproposals and remain inquisitive about the counterpart's interests.
– Propose creative trade-off solutions to resolve stalemates.

Post-negotiation

6
Establish relevant
documentation

– Document negotiation outcomes in a draft Memorandum of Understanding (limited legal enforcement) or a contract (legal enforcement) (see alliance design for more details).

7
Decision to proceed

– Conduct final assessment of negotiation processes and outcomes in light of initial alliance objectives.
– Produce a definitive alliance contract or Memorandum of Understanding.

FIGURE 4.1 Decision-making steps: alliance negotiation

negotiations supported by soft tactics lead to better outcomes for all partners. Their efforts should focus on learning their partner's concerns, considering benefits and costs, becoming aware of their partner's negotiation strengths (i.e. bargaining power) and accommodating each other in valuing resource contributions. To guide successful alliance negotiations, we distinguish three negotiation stages—pre-negotiation, negotiation and post-negotiation—each with multiple steps, as we detail next (see Figure 4.1).

Pre-negotiation

During the pre-negotiation stage, a firm prepares for the alliance negotiation by assembling an alliance team and formulating a negotiation strategy. In addition, each party should gather all possible information about the partner in terms of its current position, including its financial status, key capabilities, vulnerabilities, personnel, technologies and key markets. The firm might simultaneously undertake a similar analysis of its own organization to find any potential (in)compatibilities. A combination of these activities helps the firm to calculate its negotiation bandwidth before entering the actual negotiation stage.

Step 1: assemble alliance negotiation team

Assembling an effective alliance negotiation team can prevent the escalation of tension during negotiations, which might occur when a single negotiator becomes too emotionally involved and loses a sense of objective judgement. All involved partners should establish their own teams, set to take part cooperatively at the negotiating table. In addition, the negotiation teams should have access to all information gathered in preceding alliance development stages (i.e. strategy formulation and partner selection). The team generally consists of an alliance promoter (or champion), senior-level managers, operational managers and alliance managers. The alliance promoter works to gain trust, support and legitimacy within the organization while also establishing the vision for the alliance, informing important actors and procuring sufficient resources within the organization. The senior managers need to take part in discussions related to financial and strategic objectives; they also can encourage firm-wide commitment to the alliance. Involving operational managers, such as division heads, financial managers and technical or marketing managers—that is, the people who will execute the alliance—gives a sense of operational fit and helps build support for decisions and trust. Finally, alliance managers, who are responsible for alliance execution and day-to-day operations, should receive support from both alliance partners and thus must be involved in the negotiations. Legal and tax professionals might help formalize partnerships, but because the main objective of the negotiation stage is to create a business framework, they rarely join the negotiation team, functioning instead as advisors, especially when the negotiation and alliance design stages are concurrent.

Step 2: set the agenda and strategy

In the next step, but still in advance of the actual negotiation, the team attempts to set the agenda. Coming to a negotiation table without sufficient preparation can hinder both the process and its outcomes. After identifying negotiation issues, the team should establish its negotiation bandwidth to determine the worst possible condition it would accept in relation to each specific issue. The step-by-step process therefore encompasses the following:

1   Establish a list of negotiation points, including the alliance strategy and objectives, the resources provided by the different parties, protections and how to deal with changes.
2   Develop a common view of deal breakers and how to deal with them.
3   Gather information about the negotiation history of the potential partner, perhaps from network contacts, including the experience and background of its counterpart's negotiation team. When the alliance includes a foreign partner, a critical judgement relates to the level of knowledge of the foreign business culture.
4   Use this information to determine a negotiation strategy and tactics for each negotiation issue. For example, negotiating about the value of intangible resources favours an integrative strategy, whereas negotiating financial compensation benefits from a distributive strategy.

A firm may also approach its counterpart and decide together to formulate and sign a confidentiality agreement (i.e. non-disclosure agreement) to regulate the information exchanged during the negotiation and protect them from unwanted interference by external stakeholders. For example, a joint venture announcement tends to influence stockholder value, so the confidentiality agreement might prevent the parties from discussing the negotiations with stockholders or the market. In addition, the basic principles of the alliance agreement might be formalized in a letter of intent or Heads of Agreement. Such a document enables the parties to concentrate on establishing the fundamental principles of the venture, provides a basis for public announcements, helps keep negotiations moving forward and provides a draft for the definitive alliance agreement. Even when these emerge, they are rarely legally binding. During this pre-negotiation stage, parties may request due diligence, perhaps to assess financial matters and technology. The results of this exercise help negotiators assess the value of inputs, outputs and organizational requirements.

Negotiation

During the negotiation stage, negotiation teams meet in person and jointly develop an alliance roadmap by exchanging relevant information, assessing their computability and chemistry, balancing their interests and considering alternatives. We analytically distinguish these activities, but they are often simultaneous. The primary risk in this stage is that negotiators might place too much emphasis on their firm's rather than shared interests, creating tense alliance negotiations. Thus all parties should monitor actively the level of anxiety and manage it if necessary.

Step 3: share information

Alliance negotiation means information sharing, and the objective is two-fold: to strengthen relations between the potential partners and their negotiators, and to obtain a shared understanding of super-ordinate goals. Negotiators should expect to abide by the following rules:

- Be open and honest because hiding relevant information could harm the negotiation process in a later stage.
- Do not force a deal by mentioning legal threats because early meetings have softer objectives, such as getting to know each other and gaining an understanding of the other's vision of the alliance and culture.
- Balance information sharing and gathering; avoid being an open book while the other party sits silent and absorbs information.
- Share only the information that is relevant for the alliance. Remain aware of not only what is discussed but also the matters that are not discussed.

Step 4: assess compatibility and chemistry

Good collaborations often feature partners that understand each other and the way their counterpart works. Assessing compatibility and chemistry is therefore crucial as negotiations progress. Investing in a stronger relationship pays off when more difficult negotiation issues arise, so negotiators should consider several issues. First, with regard to partner fit, they should understand the areas in which the partner firms are compatible or incompatible. For example, incompatibility might create conflict to the detriment of integrative solutions. Second, they should assess the support offered by extant senior-level and operational managers of both sides. A lack of commitment may jeopardize alliance negotiations. Third, negotiators should assess the degree to which the values and way of doing business are compatible across partners. Incompatible values may be ignored during negotiations, but they are likely to emerge and create conflicts once the alliance is executed. Collective awareness about these issues enables negotiators to develop solutions before they even arise, which contributes to a relationship based on mutual trust.

Step 5: balance between interests and consider trade-offs

Balancing interests is a sensitive matter during alliance negotiations, which inherently involve conflicting objectives and even personal interests. Therefore, one tactic is to have one negotiation team make the first set of proposals, which prompts inquiry rather than immediate counter-proposals. The negotiation teams should be oriented towards creating win–win situations through integrative negotiations. With this orientation they also should avoid an emphasis on power or control over the negotiation, which tends to induce distributive negotiation strategies. Instead negotiators can focus on the potential for mutually beneficial agreements and try to use problem-solving strategies that support both individual organizations' goals. For example, in a careful assessment of the partner's resource contribution, the negotiator should take into account human capital, in the form of professional, expertise, reputation and network capital. Yet this analysis also must consider the potential losses that result from investing in an alliance. Creativity also is required to determine compensation because different alliance payments provide different incentives. For example, a lump sum fee paid at the start of the agreement might reduce long-term commitment; royalties, indexed as a percentage of alliance sales, might increase it. Dividends as returns on equity positions also function as mutual hostages. Commitment to an alliance reflects the partners' motivation to collaborate, which itself depends on the potential value of the alliances and their anticipated benefits. The goal is to build trust with the potential partner, create momentum, develop consensus and signal commitment, through both verbal and non-verbal communication.

Post-negotiation

In the last phase, the negotiation outcomes are transcribed into a legal contract that codifies each party's rights, duties and responsibilities and specifies the goals, policies and strategies underlying the anticipated cooperation. Thus a common understanding must exist regarding how the results are measured and managed. Governance structures, such as performance management, should have been discussed and accepted in the alliance economics stage so they can be included in the documentation. Even after such documentation though, the parties must conduct a final check: does the negotiation agreement fit the original alliance objectives, and have the negotiators established a constructive working climate?

Step 6: establish relevant documentation

The results of the negotiation are documented in a preliminary alliance contract (legally binding) or Memorandum of Understanding (limited legal enforcement), which contains an outline of the negotiated points and, if required, issues that need further negotiation. Other documented elements may include the objective and purpose of the alliance, partners' resource contributions, a draft of a potential alliance design, division of tasks and responsibilities, decision-making and conflict resolutions procedures, rules and procedures in case the alliance is terminated due to unforeseen events and possible future projects for the alliance (see Chapter 5 for more details).

Step 7: decision to proceed

The last task means completing the alliance negotiation and deciding to initiate the next stage, alliance launch (see Chapter 6). Therefore, to assess whether the objectives of the negotiation have been achieved and whether to draw up the definitive alliance contract, the negotiation teams must confirm the following:

- The mission statement is clearly articulated and understood by both parties.
- There is a clarity about the alliance design, including governance form, contractual provisions and management control.
- There is a clear understanding of the operational, technological, legal, marketing and decision-making procedures.
- Consensus about (resource) inputs has been reached, with balanced trade-offs between partners.
- Both parties intend to continue the alliance until objectives are achieved; however, there exists a common perception of how to deal with conflict.
- There is a clear understanding of important issues, including the protection of intellectual property or ownership rights resulting from the alliance.
- There is sufficient insight into the effect of the alliance on organizational processes (managerial, decision making, operational etc.).
- The understanding includes the impact on certain organizational departments and units, with support gained from those affected by any potential reorganization or disruption.

Summary

In this chapter, we have provided an overview of critical issues in alliance negotiation. Resolving the inherent tension between collaboration and competition requires that negotiators understand the implications of distinct negotiation approaches and their underlying dynamics. With such understanding, negotiators can assess the implications of their behaviour, including conflict, which is generally germane to alliance negotiations. The appropriate use of negotiation strategies and tactics provides an effective mechanism for pre-emptively managing conflicts about coordination, compensation and contributions. In addition, alliance negotiations often constitute a first encounter between partners and, thus, a first opportunity to develop relational norms and capital. Distributive negotiations accompanied by hard tactics may let the firm realize its negotiation objectives, but only at the expense of the counterpart and to the jeopardy of the alliance's execution. In contrast, integrative negotiations leading to win–win outcomes can reinforce initial trust and commitment. High-quality partner interactions are prerequisites for developing productive alliances and constitute an important part of alliance management. Building on the insights presented, we distinguished three negotiation stages analytically and suggested that negotiations proceed in this order (the stages are, of course, interrelated).

Moreover, we distinguish analytically and sequentially between alliance negotiation and alliance design: in practice, these development stages are often concurrent. For example, negotiations could last from weeks to years—and it would not be advisable for the partners to wait to document contractual provisions determined six months previously because they want to conclude the entire negotiation stage first.

CASE: RENAULT–NISSAN[1]

Renault, the French automotive company, was founded in 1899 and now holds a leading position in the European and Latin American car markets. Throughout its history, Renault has introduced ground-breaking cars, such as the Espace and Megane Scenic. In the late 1990s, despite being in a financially sound position, Renault recognized that it needed to make changes in order to remain competitive. At this time the automobile industry exhibited a pattern of rapid consolidation, and Renault was very dependent on its home market and nearby European markets. The merger between Daimler and Chrysler in 1998 led Renault to recognize the need to economize on costs and increase its presence in the global automotive market.

Nissan Motors has produced cars since 1933 (its predecessors having done so since 1914) and has become one of the leading car manufacturers in the world. As the second-largest Japanese car manufacturer, after Toyota, Nissan has been able to establish a strong market presence in the Japanese and Asian markets, the United States and Europe. Starting in 1991, however, Nissan was confronted with several challenges. It experienced substantial losses due to decreasing sales in key markets, it was unable to develop successful new models, it had difficulty standardizing its products and it had a huge debt position of US$20 billion.

To deal with their own adversities and changing industry and market conditions (such as over-capacity), Renault and Nissan decided to establish an alliance in 1999. Renault's senior management realized that an attempt to acquire Nissan would be opposed by key stakeholders and the Japanese public, so it proposed an alliance between the firms, to which Nissan responded positively. Although both companies were experiencing difficulties and analysts were sceptical about the alliance, the resource and market complementarity between the two firms was high. Renault had strong marketing and design capabilities, while Nissan was renowned for its engineering capabilities. Furthermore, the two companies were geographically complementary to each other: Renault mainly served the European and Latin American markets, while Nissan served the Japanese, Asian and North American markets. Renault sought a partner that would provide it with the opportunity to expand from a regional player into a global player, whereas Nissan was looking for a partner with a strong financial position.

Both companies realized that the cultural distance and experience in working together would present potential obstacles to forging a win–win partnership. Consequently, they decided to adopt a non-conventional negotiation approach. Instead of the traditional static analytical 'due diligence' approach, the partners recognized that the key to success was a climate of mutual trust and proof of both companies' ability to actually work together. Prior to the negotiations, the companies' senior management held numerous discussions about interests and objectives. The teams were kept small, which enabled them to become acquainted and to develop a high-quality relationship. After these initial meetings, both companies selected engineers and managers to form a team that would explore concrete opportunities of collaboration and possible synergies. As a way of supporting the integrative nature of the negotiations, no formal goals were imposed on the team, and team members were encouraged to let go of any cultural stereotypes. The teams examined collaborative opportunities in a range of areas, such as purchasing, engines and gearboxes, car platforms, production and international markets. Based on team reports, the senior management from both firms concluded that sufficient synergies could be realized, so they decided to proceed with making a deal.

The companies signed a Memorandum of Understanding, through which they expressed a commitment to evaluate further possible synergies and start formal negotiations. During this period, Renault signalled its commitment by refraining to impose an equity exchange on Nissan. At that time, Nissan did not have the financial resources to fund the acquisition of Renault shares, and Renault agreed to postpone the matter. Further analysis of the companies' operations was being made by 21 intercompany teams. Information was shared in an open atmosphere that was unusual for the car industry.

Renault executives began to further refine the concept of the alliance. Building on past experiences and reviewing other alliances, such as the Ford–Mazda partnership, emphasis was placed on financial and cultural dimensions. Renault executives took Japanese language classes, which eased communication. The companies focused on two major issues. First, during the formal negotiations, the companies had to take account of multiple stakeholders. For example, Renault was partly state-owned and had strong unions to deal with. Nissan was part of the Fuyo Keiretsu, in which its most powerful stakeholders (Fuji Bank, Industrial Bank of Japan, and Dai-Ichi Metal Insurance) were organized. Second, prior to the formal negotiation, Nissan set four pre-conditions that Renault had to meet: (1) retention of the Nissan name, (2) protection of jobs, (3) support for the restructuring of the Nissan organization and (4) selection of the CEO from the Nissan organization. Renault was able to meet these pre-conditions, which allowed both firms to take the next step.

The actual negotiations benefitted from prior investments in relationship building. Both companies gained an understanding about each other's backgrounds, believed in the alliance and were fully aware of potential areas for collaboration. Instead of securing private interests and resorting to distributive tactics, both companies expressed a willingness to accommodate the other's interests. However, a serious issue emerged when Nissan asked Renault to invest US$6 billion to ease financial pressure on the Japanese company. Renault could not accommodate this request, which forced Nissan to explore other alternatives, including partnerships with DaimlerChrysler and Ford. Recognizing the importance of the Nissan alliance, Renault arranged additional financial resources and approached Nissan to restart negotiations. Because the Nissan attempt to partner with DaimlerChrysler had failed, Nissan complied with Renault's request. Although Renault was not able to provide conclusive financial details, it had now obtained a bargaining power advantage. However, it did not exercise this advantage in the interests of safeguarding the important relationship between the firms. When negotiations were completed, Renault agreed to invest US$5.4 billion in exchange for 36.8 per cent of the Nissan Motor shares, 15.2 per cent of the Nissan Diesel shares and ownership of Nissan's financial subsidiaries in Europe.

The alliance quickly proved successful. For example, Renault Mexico was established in 2000 with Nissan's support, and Renault was able to re-enter the Australian market in 2001. In 2000, Nissan established a presence in Brazil with Renault's help. In 2001, both partners set up a joint purchasing organization: Renault Argentina started importing Nissans for the Argentinean market, and Renault entered the Indonesian market through the local Nissan dealer network. In 2002, Nissan was able to buy a 13.5 per cent stake in Renault, which it increased later that year to 15 per cent, thereby honouring its earlier agreements. Since then, the alliance has grown and proved successful. In terms of synergies, the alliance reported savings of more than US$1.5 billion. The alliance now actively promotes sharing best practices. The 'Nissan Production Way' has been the foundation for the 'Système de Production Renault', which is now the standard used by all Renault factories.

The collaboration expanded successfully over the years. In 2010, the alliance announced a broad strategic cooperation with Daimler with the aim of developing small cars and sharing technology. In 2014, the alliance announced that production and development will be fully integrated, anticipating a cost saving of US$4.3 billion. In 2016, Mitsubishi entered the alliance as an equal partner after Nissan acquired a controlling stake in Mitsubishi. In September 2017, the name of the alliance was officially changed to Renault–Nissan–Mitsubishi. The alliance became the largest car manufacturer in the world. With regard to product development, the alliance committed US$4 billion into the development of electric vehicles, aiming to become the leader in zero-emission transportation. Although sales have been slower than anticipated, the alliance has delivered six electric car models as of 2016. Although the alliance has been performing well, there has been a conflict over control since 2014. Despite the fact that Nissan is far larger than Renault, Renault has a far larger voting stake in Nissan. Moreover, Renault is well represented in the Board of Nissan. Next, in 2014, the French Government passed the 'Florange Law' to strengthen French shareholder control over French companies. Being the largest shareholder in Renault, this meant that the French state could increase its voting power in Nissan. This tension was manged by a pledge by Renault that it would never oppose the Nissan Board at a company shareholder meeting. The arrest of Carlos Ghosn, then the CEO of both Nissan and Renault, led to tensions, as the French wanted a merger between Renault and Nissan and to name the next Chairmen of Nissan. Nissan did not agree with these demands.

Despite these conflicts, all three partners regard the alliance as vital for long-term viability. However, the structure of the alliance was changed in 2019 through the signing of a Memorandum of Understanding by which an Alliance Operating Board was established which operates under supervision of a Chairman and the three CEOs as equal members (Renault–Nissan–Mitsubishi Alliance). In January 2022, the alliance announced a common roadmap for the alliance, named Alliance 2030, in which it will further increase the use of common platforms while deploying a 'smart differentiation strategy'. The partners will invest a total of US$26 billion in five years' time to support electrification leading to 35 new EV models by 2030.

Questions

1 Renault and Nissan adopted a non-conventional negotiation approach. How does this approach differ from a traditional approach, and to what extent has it contributed to the success of the alliance?

2 How did the diverging organizational, cultural and institutional backgrounds of Renault and Nissan affect the negotiation trajectory in terms of negotiation approach, processes and outcomes?

3 Considering the Renault–Nissan alliance, how do governments influence alliance negotiations, and what tactics can partners use to deal with this influence?

Note

1 Globenewswire (2022a); Horrel (2016); Lewis (2004); Renault (2010); Renault–Nissan–Mitsubishi Alliance (2022); Weis (2011); corporate website: www.nissan-global.com/EN/index.html (accessed 2 August 2011).

5
ALLIANCE DESIGN

The problem of how alliance partners can exercise sufficient control over the direction of their alliance is well recognized. In the alliance design stage, partner firms confront the challenge of designing an alliance structure that provides them with sufficient control to realize their objectives. Insufficient control limits a partner's ability not only to protect but also to use the resources it provides efficiently. Alliance partners thus are motivated to create an alliance design that fulfils the following objectives: to increase the likelihood of attaining individual and collective objectives, to create safeguards to reduce the impact of potential exchange hazards and to increase their ability to respond to unforeseen circumstances. The guiding questions for this stage thus refer to the most suitable governance form, the required contractual provisions and the supplementary management controls to be installed. To this end, managers must understand the primary function of governance forms (shown in the first section), alliance contracts (second section) and management control (third section). In addition, the following two sections discuss how these design elements interrelate, and they provide a systematic, five-step framework to assist alliance managers in their alliance design decisions. The chapter concludes with a summary and a case illustration.

Governance form

A governance form consists of the configuration of an alliance's structural building blocks, which aim to organize the partners' coordination and contractual enforcement legally (Williamson 1985). With minimum cost, an appropriate governance form can ensure the control that parties need before they will come to believe that engaging in the alliance will be of benefit to them (Dyer 1997). Accordingly, a governance form should align parties' interests by creating an incentive structure that stimulates the creation of long-term gains through cooperation, while reducing short-term gains from competition. In addition to its coordinative function, an appropriate governance form also reduces the likelihood of exchange hazards and, in turn, contributes positively to the likelihood of superior alliance performance. The primary purpose is to protect alliance partners against two types of exchange hazards: (1) opportunistic behaviour and (2) misappropriation of benefits.

DOI: 10.4324/9781003222187-5

Williamson (1975) defines opportunistic behaviour as self-interested behaviour with guile, which may include making hollow promises or window-dressing efforts, unresponsiveness, unreasonable demands, misrepresentations of abilities, a reluctance to fulfil a commitment, withholding and incomplete disclosure of information, expropriation of know-how and/ or exploitation of partner-specific assets (Williamson 1985). Various forms of opportunistic behaviour emerge in alliance contexts, including the hold-up problem (Klein *et al.* 1978), shirking (Wathne and Heide 2000) and free riding (Hennart and Zeng 2005):

- Hold-up problems arise when one party exploits the other party's dependence on the alliance, often due to the presence of assets and investments with value specific to the relationship, which thus creates incentives for opportunism. If a party is tied to the alliance through specialized investments, it cannot dissolve the alliance without incurring substantial costs associated with the loss of non-recoverable investments.
- Shirking refers to situations in which one party avoids its obligations and contracted duties to increase its own short-term rewards (e.g. immediate cost saving), even though doing so imposes costs on the alliance and jeopardizes long-term value creation.
- Free riding arises when one party fails to fulfil its obligations to supply the required inputs to its partner. For example, if parties contractually agree to exploit resources, but it is difficult to determine if the agreed amount or quality of resources has been provided, a party that fails to provide its share reaps additional benefits from its free riding.

After an alliance has formed, parties may have concerns about the misappropriation of their benefits too (Gulati and Singh 1998). Appropriation concerns originate from the presence of behavioural uncertainty, combined with the difficulties of specifying intellectual property rights, as well as the challenges of contractual monitoring and enforcement (Oxley 1997). Uncertainties associated with future performance and problems in observing partners' contributions aggravate the potential that a party might not receive its anticipated share of benefits. The presence of a knowledge component in an alliance raises additional appropriation concerns because knowledge is difficult to bind, monitor and codify. A partner firm may acquire valuable knowledge that is not part of the initial alliance agreement and use it for purposes outside the alliance (Khanna 1998). As the alliance develops, the likelihood of such misappropriation may increase as a result of various internal and external dynamics (Yan and Zeng 1999), which could give rise to goal conflicts. Goal conflicts constitute a threat to alliance continuity in that incompatible or misaligned goals reduce the incentives for parties to cooperate and contribute to the achievement of the other party's objectives.

In order to determine the extent to which they need to safeguard against exchange hazards, firms need to assess the level of governance required. A first decision relates to the type of governance form, which differs when alliance partners take actual ownership of the alliance structure (e.g. joint venture) versus when they rely on non-equity-based arrangements.

Non-equity and equity-based governance forms

A non-equity arrangement implies that the alliance agreement is organized through an alliance contract, without any transfer of equity between the partners (Pisano 1989). This type of arrangement is relatively easily established because it relies solely on a relatively simple contractual agreement. The rules of the game are well specified, and a failure by either party to deliver on the contracted commitments can be resolved through litigation. Non-equity arrangements often involve a series of small tasks or projects, even if over a long period, but one party usually dominates, such that relationship power and information are asymmetrical. Non-equity arrangements mimic market transactions and exclude relational elements, so the contractual terms of exchange are binding and specific, and efficiencies of the market exchange enable them to maximize their profits (Ganesan 1993). Examples of such partnerships include production or marketing alliances, which offer the key advantage of speed in forging the relationship. Because of the low degree of integration and reciprocal relationships, partners can dissolve these relationships with minimal costs. However, non-equity arrangements offer only limited protection against exchange hazards and demand increasingly explicit and close controls over alliance activities and partner behaviour.

In contrast, in an equity-based arrangement, the partners transfer equity or establish a new organizational entity, called a joint venture (see Box 5.1), in which they both participate with

BOX 5.1 JOINT VENTURES: A SEPARATE STREAM OF RESEARCH

A joint venture (JV) is a newly established organization created by two or more parties, generally characterized by shared ownership, shared returns and risks and shared governance; They resemble hierarchy-based organizations. Setting up a separate legal entity is expensive and often time-consuming, and as a consequence, flexibility is reduced. Yet JVs offer profit-and-loss transparency, long-term incentives and a minimal threat to the partner firms' images in case of a reputational stumble. Due to these unique properties within the broader alliance field, a separate stream of research emerged, addressing a variety of topics inherently tied to this equity-based alliance arrangement. Here we suggest that generic alliance insights, however, also apply to joint ventures, although specific topics warrant attention when a JV is the preferred governance form. For example, specific attention needs to be given to the number of partners included, the valuation of initial contributions and the ownership split among the parents. To avoid adversities, clarity about the geographic, product, technology and value-chain scope is required. The legal form needs to support the JV's objectives and should be aligned with the incentive system. Governance and control pertains to generic alliance coordination mechanisms, but specific attention needs to be given to board composition, management structure and staffing. As part of the alliance contract, exit and evolution provisions need to be stipulated to curb exit-adversities and organize a smooth withdrawal/divestment. As partners work together in a new organization, cultural, organizational and operational alignment is prerequisite, as well as setting-up parent–JV interfaces. Exploring these themes more in-depth, initial research focused primarily on the motives and design of joint ventures and explored for example the antecedents and consequences of equity stakes (Yan and Luo 2001). The ownership structure (e.g. minority, 50/50, majority stake) is for example shown to impact the parent firm incentive schemes (e.g. dividend and profit sharing), the parent's strategies (e.g. market scope) and governance and control of a JV (e.g. board composition). More recently, studies explored JV processes and dynamics, including topics such as how minority owners in a joint venture can proactively deal with conflicts and prevent premature JV termination (Westman and Thorgren 2016) and how parent companies, JV organization and JV environment co-evolve (van der Meer-Kooistra and Kamminga 2015). A subset of studies focuses on international joint ventures (IJVs). Viewed as vehicles for market entry and learning, IJVs pose specific management challenges due to cross-cultural differences (Reuer *et al.* 2014). For example, countries may have specific rules and regulations with regard to JV formation and legal forms, organizations may have different practices, tensions may exist between foreign and local control and people may have different values and norms. Taken together, (I)JVs represent a unique alliance arrangement with an idiosyncratic set of management tasks. It is beyond the scope of this book to go into detail on all intricacies, however, extant literature on (I)JVs is available.

Sources: Kogut (1988); Reuer *et al.* (2014); van der Meer-Kooistra and Kamminga (2015); Westman and Thorgren (2016); Yan and Luo (2001).

equity (Hennart 1988). The exchange of equity thus provides an additional protection against exchange hazards because partners become dependent on each other to achieve their objectives. Equity-based arrangements usually reflect a long-term commitment and a sense of mutual cooperation, shared risks and benefits. They are characterized by high levels of interdependence, financial and organizational integration, and often extensive contracts. The main advantage of such equity-based alliances is the partial ownership and the direct control that follows from it. Ownership also assures greater transparency in terms of shared costs, potential revenue and risks. Direct control reduces the risk of opportunistic partner behaviour because of the higher likelihood of detection. However, equity-based alliances also require increased integration, which may cause problems in fields such as finance, human resources or information technology.

Furthermore, if equity is exchanged, firms must determine whether to opt for a minority, an equal or a majority share. If a firm has less than 50 per cent of the equity, it has less control over the alliance, acquires fewer profits and usually needs to expend more effort in lobbying activities to influence the process and results. However, the risks involved are relatively lower, the impact on the organization is smaller and the demands on management resources decline. In contrast, when the firm has more than a 50 per cent equity share, it takes more responsibility for the alliance process and invests more in the partnership; it also obtains more control over alliance processes, can push its own interests to the front and reaps a relatively larger share of the created value. Finally, in an equal share arrangement, the partners share costs and risks equally, and their interest and commitment are equally important. However, this form demands complex control, agreement from all participants and a loss of speed.

A specific type of equity-based alliance is the joint venture (see Box 5.1): partner firms establish and become owners of a new independent entity. They resemble hierarchy-based organizations, such that joint ventures are subject to different problems than market exchange-type alliances, including the need to design coordination and misappropriation tactics. Setting up a separate legal entity is expensive and often time-consuming; the new entity must then build its own image and reputation. Finally, flexibility is minimal because the strong organizational and financial relationships between the partners impede either's effort to exit, possibly including high exit fees. Despite these disadvantages, joint ventures offer profit-and-loss transparency, shared and direct control through partial ownership, long-term incentives and a minimal threat to the partner firms' images in case of a reputational stumble.

Both non-equity and equity arrangements can enable firms to realize their objectives, but they do so in different ways, which influence firms' governance decisions (see Table 5.1).

TABLE 5.1 Non-equity and equity-based arrangements

	Non-equity arrangement	Equity arrangement with recurrent entity			Equity arrangement with new entity
		Minority share	Equal share	Majority share	
Description	Agreement based on formalized alliance contract.*	Firm has less than 50% equity share.	Firms both have 50% equity share.	Firm has more than 50% equity share.	Founding of new organizational entity; joint venture.
Advantages	Limited integration, keep own identity, focus on activities, flexibility, easy exit.	Less risk, less organizational change and impact, less need for alliance management.	Sharing cost and risks equally, equal commitment and interests.	More control, push own interests, fewer debates.	Transparent cost and profit sharing, risk sharing, ownership provides control and monitoring, long-term incentives, fewer reputational effects.
Disadvantages	Lack of control, requires alliance management skills, risk of opportunism, good preparation and negotiation needed, less learning and synergetic benefits.	Less profit, less control, more lobbying, risk of opportunism.	Complex control, agreement needed at all decision points, loss of speed.	Large responsibility, high investments.	Difficulties with integration, transfer of staff, required set-up time, costs and legal implications to exit or amend joint venture.

Note: * Franchise and (cross-)licence agreements tend to be more transactional-oriented than non-equity-based alliances and are, therefore, not incorporated in this table.
Sources: Dwyer *et al.* (1987); Hennart (1988); Pisano (1989).

Non-equity arrangements enable firms to realize their objectives without resorting to full integration, such that they resemble market transactions and focus on short-term outcomes. In contrast, the degree of integration in equity-based arrangements is relatively higher, which creates stronger incentives for long-term commitments, akin to a hierarchical arrangement. Without additional measures (e.g. contractual, control mechanisms), a non-equity arrangement offers limited safeguards against exploitation and opportunistic conduct, whereas an equity arrangement provides substantial protection—though the costs associated with forging and monitoring such an equity arrangement may outweigh its benefits. Thus, both governance forms offer unique advantages, and both entail limitations. The choice of a governance form depends on the risks and level of influence a firm prefers over its alliance activities.

Governance form selection

Alliance literature draws on several theoretical perspectives to provide rationales for governance form decisions. These perspectives are similar to those in Chapter 2; for parsimony, we do not repeat an in-depth discussion of these theories here but rather cite key implications for governance form decisions.

Transaction cost economics (TCE) notes that transaction costs are minimized when a governance form matches the exchange conditions (Williamson 1975, 1991). In general, when a transaction involves mixed asset specificity and is recurrent, an alliance is appropriate. Different governance form preferences thus represent responses to appropriation concerns: firms resort to equity arrangements to reduce transaction costs when there is a risk of opportunism but not to mandate hierarchical internalization. Equity participation is a feasible countermeasure to opportunism and appropriation concerns because opportunism by the equity partner invokes penalties in the form of the reduced value of its equity stake. In addition, asset specificity provides an important indicator of structural preference. As firms make more specialized investments, they tend to prefer equity-based arrangements, which offer protection against the exploitation of a hold-up situation. Furthermore, when creation, transfer and exploitation of knowledge are part of the alliance, an equity arrangement is preferable because this type of joint ownership aligns partner interests and provides superior monitoring (Gulati and Singh 1998). Empirical studies generally provide support for these predictions (Osborn and Baughn 1990; Oxley 1997; Pisano 1989).

The resource-based view (RBV) emphasizes value maximization through pooling and employing valuable resources (Zajac and Olsen 1993). The resources exchanged are intimately connected with alliance performance and can determine the preferred type of alliances and chosen governance structure. The focus thus shifts from safeguarding against exchange hazards to improving knowledge flows between partner firms. In distinguishing between proprietary and knowledge-based resources (Das and Teng 2000b), a firm prefers a governance form that enables it to procure external resources without losing control over its own resources. Property-based resources are protected by property rights laws; non-equity arrangements often provide enough security for collaboration. If the exchange entails knowledge-based resources, they are less identifiable and more difficult to manage, so direct control through an equity alliance is preferable over non-equity agreements. Mellewigt and Das (2010) examine structural preferences in the German telecommunications industry and find that the exchange of knowledge-based resources tends to lead to equity agreements that safeguard against opportunism and knowledge leakage. Finally, if resource contributions become heterogeneous, the risk of unwanted resource transfers increases, a threat that can be countered by equity arrangements (Sampson 2004a).

The resource dependence perspective (RDP), concerned with a firm's external arrangements, suggests that partner firms contribute critical resources to ensure their survival (Pfeffer and Salancik 1978). When resources are not readily or sufficiently available through market exchange, firms engage in boundary-spanning activities and forge relationships with other parties in order to obtain them and reduce external uncertainty. Non-equity-based arrangements provide more flexibility and the options to scale up or scale down an investment; equity-based arrangements offer more control over joint resources. Flexible arrangements mean that the firm can take advantage of changed circumstances, though at the cost of the extent of its capability to exploit opportunities. The more interdependent the firms are, perhaps due to their interdependencies in purchases and sales, the more likely they are to prefer an equity arrangement (Pfeffer and Nowak 1976). As the importance of the alliance increases (i.e. fewer alternatives become available), firms tend to prefer equity arrangements in order to gain more control (Blodgett 1991a).

Social network theory (SNT) states that the social context emerging from prior alliances influences governance decisions (Gulati 1995b). Repeated collaborations with the same partners provide information that helps firms learn about new opportunities and enhances their trust in current and potential partners. Indirect relationships through common partners function as important referral mechanisms. Successive alliances reduce behavioural uncertainty and the need for more sophisticated governance forms. Trust and the development of inter-organizational routines also increase the predictability of partner firms' behaviour, which reduces the need for equity-based protection. That is, prior ties between partners reduce contracting costs and require less complex contracts; moreover, if the prior collaborations were preceded by extensive negotiations, those prior agreements can usually be embodied in new contracts at little cost. Gulati (1995a) reaffirms these claims: his study suggests that repeated alliances are less likely than other alliances to be organized using equity.

An organizational learning perspective (OLP) states that firms enter into partnerships to learn new skills or acquire tacit knowledge (Kogut 1988). The primary motive for forming alliances is that superior knowledge enhances their competitive position. In terms of governance forms, OLP suggests that equity-based arrangements are more appropriate as learning vehicles than are non-equity arrangements. If alliances involve knowledge, it can be difficult to circumscribe, monitor and codify this resource rather than giving rise to free riding or misappropriation. Such concerns are compounded because knowledge is so difficult to value without complete information. A firm that wants to learn a particular skill thus stands a better chance of realizing this objective if it forms an equity-based arrangement, which is better equipped to handle the knowledge management processes required for knowledge creation, transfer and exploitation (Inkpen 2000). In addition, reciprocal relationships typical of equity arrangements offer better protection against knowledge spillovers.

Institutional theory (IT) argues that alliances aim for legitimacy and social approval rather than effectiveness or efficiency. Common alliance practices emerge when collaborating becomes an accepted phenomenon, and firms copy their rivals in their use of this strategy (Venkatraman *et al.* 1994). In addition, entering strategic alliances increases legitimacy because partnering with well-known and reputed partners improves the focal firm's reputation and congruence with prevailing norms in the institutional environment (Lin *et al.* 2009). The choice of non-equity or equity-based arrangements thus may be shaped by institutional pressures.

This concise overview of theoretical perspectives on governance form decisions summarizes the many unique insights into motives that range from economic to behavioural. Yet choosing a governance form remains relatively straightforward. A simple non-equity-based arrangement may suffice if the resources and information to be transferred are precise and highly explicit. As the alliance becomes more complex and the likelihood of exchange hazards increases, equity-based arrangements tend to be more appropriate. However, governance form is not the only decision to make when structuring an alliance. Alliance managers have considerable flexibility in designating duties and responsibilities through alliance contracts and management control mechanisms.

Alliance contracts

An alliance contract provides a legally binding, institutional framework that codifies each party's rights, duties and responsibilities and specifies the goals, policies and strategies that underlie the anticipated cooperation (Luo 2002; Mayer and Argyres 2004). These promises or obligations to perform particular actions in the future explain the contribution of an alliance contract to alliance development and outcomes. That is, an alliance contract safeguards investments and property against misappropriation by a partner and codifies the penalties a firm can impose on a counterpart if the latter violates the alliance agreement. An alliance contract also provides a clear overview of the tasks and responsibilities of each party, such that it also functions as a coordination mechanism. In order to cope with additional internal and external challenges that may emerge unexpectedly as the partnership unfolds, alliance contracts can enable adaptation. This so-called contingency adaptability refers to the specification of principles or guidelines that describe how to handle changing situations. Finally, an alliance contract signals commitment as a tangible expression of trust and loyalty between partners.

The degree to which contractual terms actually appear in an alliance contract (see Table 5.2) is often referred to as contractual completeness (Luo 2002), and it directly affects alliance development and outcomes (Hagedoorn and Hesen 2007). Contractor and Reuer (2014) present a continuum of alliance contracts, which comprises simple performance contracts on the one hand to complete equity-based joint venture contracts with side agreements on the other. Simple performance contracts entail, for example, the exchange of intellectual property rights, but other contractual terms could be left wide open, such that firms have to interpret the content as relevant to the situation or renegotiate terms as necessary. At the other end, in a complete and complex joint venture, multiple contract terms could be detailed closely, leaving no room for interpretation. The more complex the contract is, the greater the specification of promises, obligations and processes for dispute resolution. For example, complex contracts could specify procedures for monitoring, penalties for non-compliance, inputs to be provided and outcomes to be delivered. As exchange hazards rise, so must contractual safeguards to reduce the threat of costs and performance losses.

Contractor and Reuer (2014) suggest that contract completeness depends on deal-specific, relational and environmental factors. Deal-specific factors, among which include size of financial and personal commitment, tacit knowledge, asset specificity, interdependence and risk of opportunism, induce more complex contracts. For example, if partners agree to make alliance-specific investments, complete contracts are needed to protect against opportunism. That is, such investments need long-term alliances to provide benefits, so the potential for threats of termination and unfavourable conditions imposed by non-investing counterparts usually demand contractual safeguarding. The perceived risk of opportunistic behaviour is also likely to determine contract completeness because the partners seek to reduce behavioural uncertainty. Performance measurement ambiguity and alliance uncertainty also necessitate

TABLE 5.2 Contractual clauses

- The spirit of the venture or social contract should be embodied in the alliance contract. The parties might agree to the same terms on paper but have different expectations about how the agreement will work in practice.
- Technically, a business plan is not a legal document, and it is not expected that disagreements result in legal claims. It is important however to document common and individual alliance objectives.
- Scope and exclusivity refer to the delineation of alliance activities in terms of product, country, technology and period.
- The governance form should be specified in the alliance contract: non-equity or equity. It is important to specify ownership (if applicable). The partners may decide to equally share ownership in a joint venture. Alternatively, partners may take a majority or minority equity stake.
- Contributions should be specified: what each partner supplies to the alliance in terms of assets, business, services, technology and people.
- Funding should be specified: is initial capital provided in cash or non-cash assets, what are future legal obligations and does the alliance require outside financing?
- Compensation mechanisms depict the rewards parties can expect, such as profits, royalties, dividends or intellectual property. A hybrid compensation structure is preferred because it provides short- and long-term incentives.
- The alliance's management structure is usually formalized in an alliance contract. Issues include the right to appoint directors and delegates in the management team, authority given to managers from partners and reserved matters.
- Roles, tasks and authority specify who has the right to make decisions in which areas, and the decision-making procedures, such as majority voting, consensus, consent, blocking votes, lead partner ruling, based on proportion of investment and a 'one person, one vote' principle.
- Protection, such as of intellectual property rights (i.e. patents and licences), enables firms to prevent partners from using certain organizational resources in a competitive manner.

- With non-compete and exclusivity clauses, partners can limit their cooperation (or the results of their cooperation) to certain products, markets, technologies or geographical areas.
- Adaptation and contingency clauses provide guidelines and solutions about how partners should act when confronted with unanticipated circumstances. They may be incorporated in the contract as independent terms or as related clauses in specific areas.
- Exit provisions detail the consequences and obligations of parties when one or both partners want to exit the alliance. They detail implications tied to unilateral termination, such as the right to sell to a third party, put/call options in a joint venture, preemption rights and obligations. Exit provisions also may detail exit triggers, such as insolvency, change of control and contract breaches. In joint ventures, different resolutions to buy-outs can be incorporated, including right of first refusal, right of first offer, drag along or a shoot-out procedure.
- Conflict resolution provisions provide guidelines. The most effective conflict resolution strategy is joint problem solving, but procedures may also entail third-party arbitration and votes.
- An alliance's communication structure is often specified because high-quality communication is critical to effective functioning. It might list different fixed contact points across different levels, boundary-spanning agents, frequency of meetings and the ICT infrastructure.
- Location of operation is often specified. Activities may take place at different locations; to reduce the risk of hazards, partners need to specify the working procedures.
- Other contractual clauses may pertain to setting the accounting principles to be adopted by the alliance (e.g. international joint venture); the governing law if partners operate in different countries; timing issues related to third-party consent (e.g. antitrust, shareholder approval); major contracts with existing customers and suppliers; employees and taxes.

contractual protections because in these conditions, partners have incentives to limit their contributions. In contrast, relational aspects, such as relational quality, prior experiences and past ties, may reduce the need for more complete contracts. This is because mutual trust may substitute for formal governance (see Chapter 6 for more detail on the relationship between formal and relational governance). Environmental factors, such as the intensity of competition, the level of technological and market uncertainty, political risks, appropriability regimes and legal enforceability, industry norms and reputation, also affect contract completeness. For example, when compared to emerging countries with less-developed legal systems, legal systems in developed countries function to enforce intellectual property rights, thus reducing the need for complete contracts. However, because crafting complete contracts is costly, partners do so only when the risk of contractual breaches is high. Whereas contract completeness deters behaviours that could jeopardize the performance of an alliance, it increases contracting costs and potentially damages initial trust building. Contract completeness may thus enhance alliance performance (Poppo and Zenger 2002), but this effect really is conditional on the degree of cooperation between partners, such that when contracts are more complete, cooperation contributes more to performance (Luo 2002). Moreover, if enforcement is difficult, as in highly volatile environments, the costs of complete contracts may not outweigh their benefits.

Contract standardization implies instead the application of similar contracts or terms across a range of contractual transactions (Vlaar 2006). On a continuum, a tailored contract would represent one end, whereas the standardized contract would be the other. A tailored contract is designed especially for the alliance and tends to be fairly complex; a standard contract is intended to apply to multiple contractual relationships, so its terms are not designed for any specific collaboration (Ariño and Reuer 2004). Standardized contracts can be quickly and efficiently implemented; tailored contracts can be designed according to the specific situation, although doing so demands significantly higher costs. The applicability of standardized contracts also depends on the variation in alliance schemes. Low variation supports opportunities for using standardized documents; high variation makes tailored contracts seem more appropriate. Poppo and Zenger (2002) thus find that firms using customized contracts can improve their alliance performance, but only if a high level of relational governance exists.

Another important distinction separates pre-specified and open-ended alliances (Reuer and Ariño 2007). When an alliance's time horizon is pre-specified, alliance managers tend to be more concerned about ownership of proprietary knowledge, disclosure of confidential information or the means for ending the alliance. The risk of opportunistic behaviours is higher in alliances with a pre-specified duration because the counterparts have few possibilities to reciprocate for opportunistic behaviour. Yet the costs of predicting future economic conditions for open-ended alliances and crafting appropriate contractual provisions are significant, forcing alliance managers to rely more on incomplete contracts. In open-ended alliances of long anticipated duration, the thought of future benefits safeguards against opportunism because the 'shadow of the future' shifts dispositions towards win–win instead of win–lose perspectives (Heide and Miner 1992).

A well-designed alliance contract is thus consistent with the alliance objectives and the partners' interests, whatever those may be. Even if alliance partners have a clear understanding, however, designing an alliance contract that anticipates all possible unforeseen circumstances is simply not feasible. Alliances tend to be even more common in uncertain environments because they offer firms flexibility. Alliance managers therefore need to balance the costs of negotiating, monitoring and enforcing alliance contracts against the threat of potential exchange hazards. They are likely to be left with the use of incomplete contracts, with their adaptation problems and room for opportunistic conduct. In this case, the governance form and alliance contract may need to be supplemented with additional management control mechanisms.

Management control

Management control in alliances refers to control mechanisms that alliance partners might use but are not likely to formalize in an alliance contract. Their primary purpose is to encourage coordination and ensure the partners achieve their predetermined objectives (Dekker 2004). Control mechanisms organize the coordination of interdependent tasks; firms might put command and authority systems in place to force their partner to comply with the tasks required to achieve alliance objectives or allocate resources even if the partner is unwilling to do so. Management control also enables a firm to acquire influence over alliance development and outcomes by installing incentive systems, standard operating procedures and conflict resolution procedures, which provide incentives to collaborate. Reducing appropriation concerns and fulfilling coordination requirements are thus critical rationales for management control. Management control may also be embodied in alliance contracts, but it extends beyond governance form; for example, control is not a strict consequence of ownership (e.g. joint venture) but rather results from a variety of control mechanisms.

Control modes

We begin by differentiating three control modes (Dekker 2004): output, behavioural and social. Output and behavioural control are based on formal control mechanisms, often but not necessarily incorporated into an alliance contract (Chen *et al.* 2009; Patzelt and Shepherd 2008). The former specify the objectives to be realized by the alliance and its partners, and then monitor the realization of such targets. For example, outcome controls might set alliance objectives, create incentive and reward systems and outline monitoring procedures, which together clarify mutual expectations and increase goal congruence. Behavioural control refers to how the partners should act and monitors whether their actual behaviours comply with these predetermined behaviours. Reports, meetings, planning, operating rules and routines, standard procedures and conflict resolution procedures are typical examples. Social control mechanisms are not formalized in an alliance contract but rather reflect relational norms that guide partner firms' behaviours and result from socialization processes (MacNeil 1978). Social control thus influences alliance activities through partner interactions that facilitate shared values and common understanding. It requires significant communication through organizational mechanisms such as rituals, ceremonies, teams, task forces and other socialization methods. The choice of output, behavioural or social modes of management control depends on three factors:

1 If the resources contributed to the alliance relate closely to the partner firms' core competences, the risk of misuse creates a serious threat. Firms can reduce this threat with output and behavioural controls; for example, alliance contract clauses might specify restrictions on the use of resources and establish monitoring procedures that increase detection of misuse and thus help alliance partners legally protect their contributions.

2   Alliance activities often range from achieving economies of scale to developing new concepts; the nature of these activities affects management control decisions. In alliances with clear task specialization, focused management control is desirable, preferably accompanied by dedicated output and behavioural controls.

3   When measurability of outputs is ambiguous, social control enables firms to protect themselves against misappropriation because relational norms and capital encourage partners to act in the interest of their counterparts. If uncertainty and ambiguity surround resource contributions and outcomes are difficult to measure, social control again is most appropriate because it reduces the risk of exchange hazards.

Control dimensions

Geringer and Hebert (1989) also identify three dimensions of management control: the mechanisms alliance partners use to exercise control, the degree of control realized by the partners and the focus of the control. The mechanisms that partners use to exercise control can vary, including power, authority or a wide range of bureaucratic, cultural and informal mechanisms. For example, Schaan (1983) suggests two main categories of control mechanisms: positive and negative. Positive control refers to mechanisms that firms employ to promote constructive behaviours, often exercised through informal mechanisms such as staffing, participation in the planning process and reporting relationships. Negative control, which relies principally on formal agreements, helps firms stop or prevent alliance partners from implementing destructive activities or decisions. In addition, Caniëls and Gelderman (2010) suggest that firms may employ administrative controls to influence decision making, enforced through contractual provisions that stipulate how to handle conflicts, the specific penalties for opportunistic behaviour and which behaviours are allowed. Bargaining power may also function as a control mechanism: a dependent partner has a strong incentive to continue the relationship, to avoid the various costs of termination, and it also avoids opportunistic behaviour for fear of retaliation by the dominant partner. Anderson and colleagues (2015) present three frameworks for management control. The first framework focuses on how control can be achieved through shared beliefs, diagnosis and interactions (i.e. behavioural); a second framework emphasizes the object of control, including personnel, actions and results (i.e. economic); whereas a third framework focuses on accounting and governance tools of control (i.e. transaction efficiency), such as decision rights, rewards, sanctions and performance. Empirical results suggest that alliances that have value-creation as the root use combinations of transaction, economic and behavioural control. All these types of control grant alliance partners influence over alliance activities, while also protecting them from opportunistic behaviours.

Next, the degree of control refers to partners' decision-making authority (Killing 1983). One partner may obtain a dominant decision-making role, perhaps through dominance in board representation, the right to veto decisions, representation in alliance management, departmentalization of activities, planning and budgeting mechanisms or performance evaluations (Makhija and Ganesh 1997). When a firm has dominant control, it can manage the alliance more easily and, for example, direct resource allocations better (Child 2002). However, partners may also share management control and play active and equal roles in making decisions. Shared control provides partners with signals of long-term commitment, eases information exchange and enables them to deal flexibly with unforeseen circumstances, which should improve alliance outcomes (Beamish 1993). In a joint venture setting, perhaps neither partner is involved in decision making because an independent joint venture manager enjoys decision-making autonomy. Glaister *et al.* (2003) propose that joint venture autonomy enhances alliance performance, but once performance deteriorates, parents become involved in decision making and operations. Yet the overall empirical evidence on the required degree of decision-making authority is inconclusive: firms need to consider the alliance's circumstances carefully and make an informed decision about the degree of control they desire. Moreover, control designs in alliances may evolve over time, for example, from shared to autonomous types (Zhang and Li 2001).

The focus dimension of management control suggests that partner firms may seek to obtain control over specific alliance activities rather than control overall. Focusing management control in areas where its resources get utilized improves the firm's ability to detect misuse and free riding. Prior alliance studies thus distinguish strategic and operational control (Yan and Gray 2001); having a majority equity share tends to result in strategic control, whereas providing non-capital resources leads to operational control (Child and Yan 1999). In addition, Yan and Gray (2001) find that operational control positively influences the realization of the partner's objectives, but strategic control has no impact. Whereas ownership and overall control might provide general insights in alliance progress, focused control appears to enable firms to monitor critical alliance activities more closely.

In summary, governance form constitutes the foundation of an alliance design, but non-equity and equity arrangements also can be augmented with alliance contracts and management control mechanisms. Alliance contracts depict formalized agreements between alliance partners and detail partners' promises and obligations. However, not all design decisions can or should be formalized, in which case additional management control mechanisms, such as social and focused control, may be used to develop a coherent alliance design.

Structural configuration

Despite even their best efforts to deal with complexity and unpredictability, managers remain limited in their ability to plan for the future and predict the various contingencies that may arise, which creates the need for contracting and formalization. However, limited information may also result in misaligned governance forms or incomplete contracts because it is too costly for managers to negotiate and write claims that fully describe each party's responsibilities and rights for all contingencies that could reasonably occur during the alliance. When new circumstances arise, a contract must specify, in its adaptation clauses, how to deal with them; otherwise, the parties will need to engage in costly renegotiations or terminate the alliance prematurely. Accordingly, alliance partners need a balance across governance form, alliance contract and management control to minimize the costs of negotiating, contracting and monitoring, while still providing sufficient coordination and protection against exchange hazards (Das and Rahman 2001).

We suggest that firms can design an optimal structural configuration (see Box 5.2) with a constellation of mutually supportive structural safeguards, including governance form, contractual provisions and management control mechanisms. Equity arrangements outperform non-equity arrangements with respect to reducing the likelihood of exchange hazards, but decisions about contractual design and management control also affect the likelihood of exchange hazards. Alliance partners may agree about hybrid compensation structures, share decision-making rights or commit themselves to non-recoverable investments, which in combination create reciprocal relationships akin to hierarchical control, though without resorting to equity-based arrangements. Furthermore, they may install management control mechanisms, such as shared decision making, monitoring and mimicking hierarchical elements. This type of quasi-hierarchical control reduces parties' vulnerability to exchange hazards and enables them to protect individual interests, potentially rendering an equity governance form redundant.

BOX 5.2 ALLIANCE MIRROR DESIGN

A widely adopted alliance design is the mirror structure design, also known as the multiple points of contact model, which aligns governance form, alliance contract and management control. In a mirror structure, the partner firms mirror each other, such that at each organizational level, representatives are appointed to participate in the alliance management. The resultant structure covers strategic, tactical and operational levels of the organizations. The strategic direction of the alliance is managed by executives from all participating organizations, who form an executive board (with cross-board positions) or oversight committee. Their primary role is to provide the strategic direction for the alliance and guard its fit with the strategic targets of their organization. Involvement in the day-to-day practices of the alliance is generally low. In addition, an alliance steering committee is installed and, depending on the size and scope of the alliance, it might consist of a strategic and an operational management team. The strategic management team focuses on translating the strategic direction provided by the executive board into plans and priorities. Often members of the management team conduct periodic meetings to discuss the operational direction of the alliance and resolve issues. If the management team cannot resolve issues or conflicts, the matter goes to the executive board, which makes the final decision. On a day-to-day basis, the alliance is managed by representatives from the participating organizations who are directly involved with its activities. Sometimes specific groups work on specific assignments or projects. The operational management team then acts as a steering committee for working groups. One key advantage of the mirror structure is that alliance partners can use it for both equity- and non-equity-based arrangements.

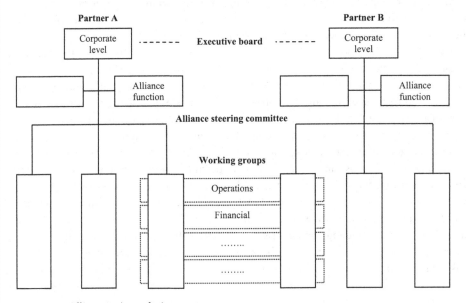

FIGURE 5.1 Alliance mirror design

Source: De Man (2013).

Child (2002) reaffirms this view by revealing various successful structural configurations within the context of international joint ventures. Joint ventures with a majority foreign equity share that receive heavy support from the foreign parent and give local managers an active role outperform similar joint ventures with minimal local manager contribution. Joint ventures with equal equity stakes tend to perform well when they also feature shared management and aligned goals; joint ventures with a minority equity share experience higher performance when the foreign partner has operational control. In summary, designing alliances requires managers to resolve a series of trade-offs rather than seeking a single, ultimate alliance design.

Alliance design: decision-making steps

In the preceding chapter, we focused on alliance negotiations and processes resulting in alliance outcomes. In the alliance design stage, firms formalize these outcomes. Consistent with win–win negotiations, a definitive formalized alliance design enables partners to realize common objectives, while also protecting individual interests. The focus is on designing an alliance structure with a governance form, contractual provisions and management control that aligns partners' objectives and offers a constructive foundation for executing the alliance. But what should be formalized in an alliance design, how and for what reasons? To resolve these questions, we propose a (repetitive) sequence of five decision-making steps (see Figure 5.2).

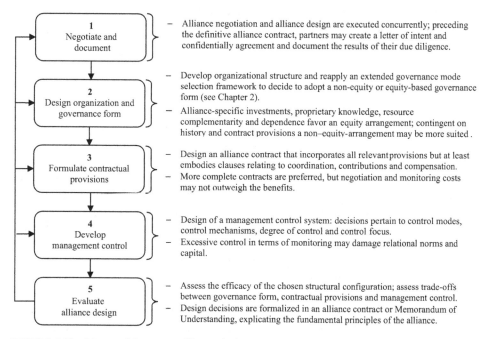

FIGURE 5.2 Decision-making steps: alliance design

Step 1: negotiate and document

Alliance negotiation and alliance design are often executed concurrently. As the negotiation progresses, negotiators draft documents that provide initial input, prior to the definitive alliance agreement. Building on the pre-negotiation outcomes, the first document is a confidentiality agreement that details the rules of engagement and regulates the information exchange between partners. The next document to be drafted in the alliance design stage is the Heads of Agreement. This brief document establishes the (commercial) fundamentals of the alliance. It is not a legal document but rather a road map that nurtures communication between negotiation parties. The negotiators should discuss the terms of this document, including at least the following issues:

- Spirit of the alliance, including shared values and visions.
- Fundamentals of the alliance, including alliance objectives, scope, location of operation and exclusivity of negotiations.
- Anticipated contributions and the partners' provision of resources in terms of tangible (e.g. financial) and intangible (e.g. know-how) assets.
- Anticipated compensation, including reward mechanisms described in terms of royalties, fees, lump-sum payments and dividends, as well as ownership and rights over technologies developed by the alliance, their use (e.g. licensing) and future developments.
- Coordination and tentative ideas about governance form, contractual provisions and management control mechanisms, including the management and communication structure.
- Public announcements that detail who will release a press release announcing the alliance to inform external stakeholders and when this will be done; stock exchange regulations that must be adhered to.
- Other agreements, including product development, pricing, cost sharing of marketing campaigns, marketing rights of products and technologies in case the partnership ends, and legal, tax and financial matters.

Step 2: design organization and governance form

Before opting for a governance form, it is critical that the alliance partners design the organizational structure (Albers *et al.* 2016). Specifically, they first have to decide upon the hierarchical arrangement required to organize alliance activities. For example, the relationships between an executive board, a steering committee and working groups needs to be determined, as well as decision-making authority. Second, the partners must decide which teams are required to execute alliance tasks and how they interact. For example, if the objective is to commoditize a new innovative product, activities between R&D, engineering and marketing staff need to be organized and aligned. Third, as part of the alliance organization, partners must establish and formalize linkages to their organizations. Appointing gatekeepers and boundary-spanning agents is imperative. Once, the organization has been set (i.e. a blueprint has been made), the partner may decide upon the governance form.

An appropriate alliance governance form provides control and conditions—that is, a context for executing the alliance successfully. The guidelines for the proper governance form are not straightforward. Negotiators must find the delicate balance across negotiation, contracting and monitoring costs to protect their interests and anticipated benefits. Furthermore, governance form decisions should be aligned with decisions about contractual provisions and management control mechanisms. To discuss some of these considerations, we simplify matters by taking a one-sided perspective, such that we note non-equity arrangements are preferred when a firm does the following:

- Expects to make limited alliance-specific investments; otherwise, an equity-based arrangement is more appropriate because it offers better protection against exploitation.
- Expects to supply primarily property-based rather than knowledge-based resources; otherwise, an equity-based arrangement offers better protection against knowledge leaks.
- Considers the alliance of moderate strategic importance; otherwise, an equity-based arrangement better protects against the unwanted transfer of critical resources.
- Expects that the degree of required learning is low; otherwise, an equity-based arrangement is beneficial by functioning as a learning vehicle.
- Possesses a history of collaboration with this partner; otherwise, an equity-based arrangement is more appropriate because trust and inter-organizational routines have not yet been developed.

In addition to the choice between non-equity and equity-based arrangements, various types of equity-based arrangements might be chosen. For example, a joint venture is preferable if the firm seeks to divest resources but wants to continue exploiting their value. Protection of the market and the firm's reputation may prompt firms to adopt a joint venture form or separate out risky investments. The choice of minority versus majority equity-based arrangements depends on the importance of the relationship to the firm and its desire to possess ownership and exercise influence.

Step 3: formulate contractual provisions

A governance form alone is not sufficient to govern an alliance. Alliance partners can augment their selected governance form with contractual provisions, whose choice and content can alter the initial governance form decision. That is, using negotiation about the content of the specific contractual provisions, a firm can acquire strategic and organizational control and decision-making authority, in which case the equity-based governance form may become obsolete. Resource contributions vulnerable to exploitation also could be protected with nonexclusive protection provisions. A reward system with ex-ante and residual sharing would provide long-term incentives to partners to remain committed; however, an absence of adequate contractual protection may suggest that equity governance is more appropriate to safeguard the firm's interests. The more complete an alliance contract is, the less need for equity-based governance forms, as reinforced by a mutual history of collaboration. However, at the least, the contractual provisions should include the following:

- A business plan specifying the alliance's common and individual objectives.
- The governance form, whether non-equity or equity-based.
- The alliance's management structure in terms of board representations, decision-making rights, veto decisions and the alliance steering committee.
- Partners' resource contributions, including both property-based and knowledge-based resources.

- Clauses specifying compensation mechanisms, such as royalties, dividends and lump sum payments.
- Non-compete and exclusivity clauses that specify target markets and the use of technologies.
- Protection clauses, including intellectual property rights, patents and licences.
- Conflict resolution techniques, such as arbitration and mediation.
- Exit clauses, including triggers of termination and termination trajectories.
- Regulations for accounting principles and timing issues, contracts with existing customers and suppliers, employees and taxes.

Step 4: develop management control

Alliance partners might also supplement an alliance design with management control mechanisms that are not formalized in an alliance contract. It is important to recall the spirit of collaboration when deciding on management control mechanisms. Control systems should not be based on who has more or less control, but rather on the right persons or organization to control a specific area based on their abilities or experience, the possession of appropriate tools to exercise control and control of the moment. Ill-designed management control systems may suggest the appearance of control, but in reality, they provide inaccurate information and tend to jeopardize the quality of the working relationship. Management control might include the following:

- Modes of management control: contingent on the alliance objectives and initial design decisions, partner firms may use a combination of outcome, behavioural and social controls to monitor partners' behaviour and alliance progress.
- Mechanisms of management control: partners may use combinations of positive and negative controls and employ administrative or power-based control.
- Degree of management control: partners need to consider in which areas they require dominant control or whether shared management is more likely to foster alliance performance.
- Focus of management control: partners may install focused control in critical areas that appear vulnerable to misappropriation.

Depending on the management control system, firms should make an organizational chart that depicts the different roles, functions and reporting directions for each firm. In addition, they can specify meeting frequency and communication and reporting systems. If applicable, alliance partners may also opt to explicate a code of conduct: how do the partners expect their employees to behave? Such codes are becoming increasingly popular in cross-sector alliances between profit and non-profit organizations (see Chapter 15).

Step 5: evaluate alliance design

Building on these preceding decisions, alliance partners should evaluate the definitive alliance design: does the alliance design provide sufficient incentives and enforcement for long-term commitment, while protecting the partners' individual interests? If so, these decisions should be clearly documented in the alliance contract (or Memorandum of Understanding), which guides its execution. As part of the evaluation, alliance partners should pay sufficient attention to the alliance implementation plan. Launching an alliance without a carefully prepared plan is like starting a business without a business plan.

Summary

We have provided an overview of three structural building blocks of alliance design: governance form, alliance contract and management control. Each block of alliance design functions to align partners' interests, enable coordination and reduce the risk of exchange hazards. Rather than considering them as discrete one-off decisions, we present them as interrelated. Governance form decisions affect the content of contractual provisions, and vice versa. Deficiencies in an alliance contract may be overcome through management control mechanisms. Alliance negotiators should account for these relationships when negotiating the alliance design. To this end, we have provided a five-step procedure for firms that may assist them in alliance design decisions and prepare the partners to execute the alliance. However, alliance design alone is insufficient to secure coordination and protection against exchange hazards. Alliance management and in particular relational governance also offers a critical coordination mechanism. Before detailing on alliance management, however, in the next chapter we first elaborate on the alliance launch stage.

CASE: ORGANOVO[1]

Organovo was founded in 2007 with the intention of commercializing organ printing technology developed by the University of Missouri—Columbia. In 2009, Organovo opened its laboratory in San Diego and focused primarily on printing blood vessels. In 2012, Organovo went public and started a partnership with Autodesk research to develop 3D bioprinting software. In the following year, Organovo became involved in cancer research and received a stock listing at the New York Stock Exchange. In 2014, Organovo released the exVive3D Human Liver Tissue. The printed tissues remained stable and functional for more than 40 days and were made available for preclinical in vitro testing to provide predictive liver tissue—specific toxicity marker assessment. Following these technological advances, Organovo forged multiple partnerships.

In 2015, L'Oréal's Technology Incubator announced a partnership with Organovo to develop 3D bioprinted human skin tissue. L'Oréal S.A. is a French cosmetics company with its headquarters in Clichy, France. Although L'Oréal started with hair colouring products, after the Second World War, the company soon ventured into other fields of the beauty industry. Currently L'Oréal offers more than 500 brands and several thousands of individual products in all sectors of the beauty business. L'Oréal aims to be an innovative frontrunner in the business. Therefore, the company has developed a technology incubator that enables it to develop technologies and uncover disruptive innovations across industries that have the potential to transform the beauty business. One focus area concerns products with skin applications. The availability of human skin is critical for L'Oréal to develop its products. L'Oréal also offers skin to implant on the human body to replace damaged or diseased skin tissue. The production of human skin is a costly and time-consuming activity. L'Oréal tries to avoid animal testing and therefore farms human tissue using its research laboratory in Lyon. L'Oréal produces approximately 100,000 skin samples annually, which translates to roughly 5 m^2 of skin per year. This is a complex procedure that requires donations from plastic surgery patients in France. To increase skin production and accelerate skin production through increased automation, L'Oréal turned to Organovo and initiated a research partnership. Specifically, the partnership aims to develop 3D printed human tissues, which can be used for product evaluation and other areas of advanced research. Organovo will introduce its proprietary NovoGen Bioprinting Platform. This 3D printing platform has been developed by Organovo and its partner Invetech to print human tissue. The initial application of this platform was printing blood vessels and nerve conduit, but Organovo has expressed that potentially any tissue or organ can be built. Together with L'Oréal's expertise in skin engineering, the two partners aim to develop a commercially viable solution. The partnership design consists of three consecutive phases. During the solution development stage, the partners deploy a stage gate design. At each stage gate, the partners have the ability to end the collaboration. During this phase, a technological and viable solution is developed. According to Organovo, the printing of human skin will be roughly similar to that of printing liver samples. Although the actual printing is not very different from ordinary 3D printing, the nourishment of the cells requires in-depth scientific knowledge. The technology developed will be thoroughly tested in the following phase. Given the objective, L'Oréal seeks the ability to speed up the production of human skin. This requires Organovo to further industrialize the technology to become economically viable. This is the focus of the second stage of the partnership. For both these phases, L'Oréal will provide up-front funding. The third and final phase of the partnership consists of the development of a viable business model. In this phase, L'Oréal and Organovo will create a commercial supply agreement that will include customary licensing and royalty terms. The agreement will provide L'Oréal with exclusive rights to the skin tissue that the two companies develop. These rights will remain intact for the purposes of development, testing, manufacturing, evaluation and sale of non-prescription skincare products and nutraceutical supplements. Organovo will retain the rights to these tissue models for efficacy testing of prescription drugs, toxicity tests and the development and testing of therapeutic or surgically transplanted tissues. For Organovo, this partnership is the first application of the technology that the company created in the beauty industry. Through the technology, Organovo can automate the creation of skin tissue while mimicking the form and function of native tissues in the body.

After its founding, Organovo pushed an innovation agenda seeking to become a leader in the 3D bioprinter space. As a result, it generated a broad set of patents that provide foundational claims in the bioprinting space. In order to broaden the impact of the technology and serve the needs of researchers and users of bioprinting, Organovo seeks to make these patents available for licensing. In 2022, Organovo and BICO forged a licensing agreement on Bioprinting Patents. BICO (formerly CELLINK) was founded in 2016. As the leading bioconvergence company in the world, BICO aims to reduce organ shortage and speed up drug development by providing accessible life science solutions that combine biology and technology, fundamentally shifting the global healthcare industry. The agreement provides BICO's division CELLINK with possibilities to access Organovo's bioprinting technologies, which will further empower the company to continue to advance and expand its product portfolio. Before coming to this agreement however, Organovo and BICO were engaged in several legal disputes regarding (alleged) patent infringements. Under the new agreement, all civil actions regarding potential infringement and intellectual property rights concerning validity of Organovo's patents are dismissed and/or terminated. The partners also have released each other from all previous claims, demands, liabilities and costs in favour of the beneficial and sustainable solution created through this patent licence agreement. Instead of spending resources on legal disputes, the new agreement will strengthen BICO's offering by obtaining access to new technologies, and BICO will have the freedom to operate globally with the strongest and most extensive bioprinting portfolio on the market. In the words of Organovo Executive Chairman Keith Murphy:

> Organovo celebrates the success of CELLINK's bioprinting product lines in opening up the horizons of 3D bioprinting to customers. We are proud to be a part of enabling CELLINK and BICO to grow these products and we look forward with excitement to their next generation of bioprinters.

The agreement will enable BICO to effectuate an innovative and ground-breaking commercial agenda, speed up development for their customers (e.g. new instruments) and enhance its market position and share, resulting in improved profitability in the long run.

———————————————————

Questions

1   Why would L'Oréal and Organovo opt for a non-equity governance form, and which supportive contractual clauses could be used to steer the alliance towards its objectives?
2   What control and coordination mechanisms are used (or should have been used) to enforce relationship governance and deter opportunistic behaviour?
3   Comparing the Organovo–L'Oreal and Organovo–BICO partnerships, what alliance design differences exist, and why?

Note

1   Bico (2022); King (2015); Organovo (2015, 2022).

6

ALLIANCE LAUNCH

Bringing an alliance alive depends on a smooth transition from the alliance formation stage—including partner selection, negotiation and design—to the alliance management stage. Academics and practitioners consider alliance launch critical to the long-term success of an alliance. In practice, however, managers tend to underestimate the difficulties and adversities surrounding the execution of an alliance arrangement. Alliance launches are often executed with the idea of 'we don't have time for it', 'let's focus on the key objective' and 'we will address issues when we encounter them'. The desire to get to work is understandable, but a failure to systematically prepare and organize an alliance launch—both internally and across the alliance—will most likely result in operating inefficiencies, poor decision-making, escalating conflicts and ultimately the destruction of the alliance. Too many deals have been thrown over the fence from those who are responsible for alliance negotiation and design to those responsible for managing the relationship. Alliance partners commonly think that an alliance is up and running as soon as a kick-off meeting has taken place. However, a lot more work needs to be done before an alliance can be steered towards its objectives. People need to be brought up to speed, teams need to be established, operational plans need to be implemented, resources need to be secured and partners need to invest in relational understanding and collaborative routines. The first section of this chapter explores in detail the challenges associated with alliance launch. The second section elaborates on drivers that contribute to a successful startup of an alliance arrangement. The third section presents a framework to guide managerial decision-making. The chapter concludes with two sections that present a summary and a case illustration.

Alliance launch objectives and challenges

In contrast to partner selection, negotiation, design, management and evaluation, few firms consider alliance launch management to be a distinct stage. This is unfortunate because there is strong evidence that systematically organizing alliance execution is essential to long-term value creation (Bamford *et al.* 2004). The alliance launch stage depicts the bridge between alliance formation, with its focus on deal-making, and alliance management, with a focus on extracting the collaborative value. Therefore, the main responsibility of managers during the

DOI: 10.4324/9781003222187-6

alliance launch is to organize the transition from 'drawing board' to 'day-to-day' operations. Specifically, launch managers need to simultaneously attain (at least) three objectives during this stage: secure strategic alignment, erect a new organization and build collaborative and meaningful relations (Bamford *et al.* 2004; Visioni *et al.* 2010).

Launch objectives

A first critical objective during the alliance launch is to secure alignment between the alliance strategy and partners' (strategic) interests, ambitions and plans (Bamford *et al.* 2004). Although the deal has been made and the contract has been signed, asymmetries in strategic interests may become manifest during alliance execution, or interests may change. Many conflicts of interest surface only when the partners dig deep into operation details and start to run the alliance. In order to build a solid foundation, launch managers need to reconcile these adverse asymmetries and communicate the strategic intent to all involved in the relationship. Furthermore, to incentivize partners and generate smooth collaborative processes, it is critical to secure alignment between alliance strategy and partners, communication, administration and decision-making systems. Misalignment between alliance strategy, individual interests and reporting systems could lead to serious delays in the attainment of short- and long-term milestones. Without strategic alignment, the future of the alliance will be jeopardized even before the relationship is effectuated.

A second critical objective for launch managers is the building of a new organization (Bamford *et al.* 2004). Although alliance partners formally agreed on paper how the new organization should look, it is the launch manager's responsibility to create an operational governance system that promotes shared decision making, provides protection and does not stifle entrepreneurship. Governance adversities during the startup can quickly escalate and pave the way for a premature termination of the deal. The new organization should fit with the alliance business plan and create an environment in which the personnel of each partner are able to contribute to a high-performing alliance. Launch managers should become familiar with their partner's preferences and design and implement structures that facilitate high-quality decision making. They should appoint strong and motivational leaders who are able to build and lead effective teams. As such, during the startup, the people involved can make timely and quick decisions and create and participate in open and transparent dialogues, while providing partner organizations with sufficient control. Overall, launch managers who build effective and efficient alliance organizations obtain commitment from staff across partners and hierarchies because they carefully leverage and manage interdependencies (such as capital, materials, people and intellectual property) between alliance partners.

A third objective for launch managers pertains to building productive relations between and across staff. Alliance success depends on relationship issues such as trust, chemistry, smooth communications, clarity about roles and responsibilities and dealing with cultural differences between partners. Relationship aspects are especially crucial in the early stages of an alliance, which are fraught with uncertainty, ambiguity and the legacy of alliance negotiation. Cultural differences between partners could create tensions, mis-communication and conflict that disturb the development of the alliance. Therefore, cultural differences should be managed actively to secure commitment from the key staff in order to create compelling value proposition for employees involved in the alliance. Working together quickly to solve alliance problems and accomplish results that could not have achieved before will help build trust. Moreover, personnel working in the alliance should learn about each other and each other's organization. This can be achieved by stimulating and facilitating constructive communication and by reducing or preventing miscommunication. Creating collaborative behaviour and routines enhances collective sense-making—the latter is critical to alliance success.

Launch impediments

The alliance launch stage comes with unique objectives, and if firms do not pay sufficient attention, failure to achieve them can ruin the relationship and cause alliance failure (Bamford *et al.* 2004). Although managerial perceptions and biases may impede alliance execution (see Table 6.1), the failure to attain alliance launch objectives is primarily caused by underestimating the salience of two alliance launch impediments.

The first impediment pertains to the difficulties surrounding the organization of hand-offs. Within an alliance launch context, a hand-off represents the transfer of tangible and intangible knowledge between people involved during alliance formation and people responsible for alliance management. For example, a hand-off takes place between the negotiation and design team who, 'on paper', assigned tasks and responsibilities to engineers and the alliance

TABLE 6.1 Alliance launch misconceptions

Misconception	Assumption	Worst practice
We don't have time for it.	Alliance leadership assumes that speed is critical to alliance success, as deal-making has already taken too much time.	Fast startup of an alliance can be extremely risky for partners. This approach is characterized by imposing pressure on working staff to work on and achieve long-term objectives without considering the need to develop collaborative routines, build relational quality, and enhance decision-making.
We are able to 'self-organize'.	Alliance leadership assumes that those working on the alliance are skilled, have subject matter expertise and experience such that they can and will take the actions needed to (over time) coalesce into a collaborative value-creating arrangement.	Relying on the ability to 'self-organize' may undermine an alliance's value potential. This approach is often facilitated by a joint kick-off meeting without further planning and support. Structures develop organically, unique challenges are not addressed and alliance leadership ends up revisiting decisions to ensure alignment and develop the necessary protocols.
We have a collective understanding.	Alliance leadership assumes that all key personnel have a complete and shared understanding of the context for and intent of the alliance. This assumption often includes a belief that the contract is a description of the alliance.	Building an alliance on an alleged collective understanding and sense-making will create conflicts and misperceptions and can derail an alliance. This approach is often characterized by influential stakeholders who lack sensitivity for external collaboration and operational processes. Alliance success hinges on the efficiency and quality of day-to-day interactions as much as (often more than) it does on interactions between alliance managers and formal governance meetings.

managers who supervise these engineers on the day-to-day execution of their tasks. Analogous to a relay race, a good hand-off involves transferring the correct baton at the right time with the right intent. If a hand-off is not smooth and technically precise, it can cause disorganization, mistrust, reinforce 'us-versus-them' perceptions and delay the execution of critical collaborative processes. In contrast, a well-organized hand-off will accelerate alliance growth. In addition to providing insight in the alliance contract, the people involved in deal-making should offer information about the context in which the contract was formulated, the intentions and spirit of partners, an overview of people who were involved and the issues that were discussed. Such knowledge is critical because it provides the management team with an opportunity to develop the alliance further where the deal-making team left off, rather than start with a blank slate. Thus, a good hand-off requires the right constellation of staff and sufficient connections between them to allow for intensive communication. Strong hand-offs across organizational boundaries and hierarchical levels improve the speed, energy and spirit in the alliance, and organizing these hand-offs effectively is a challenge for alliance launch managers.

The second impediment that can obfuscate an alliance launch is the inevitability of staff changes as the alliance becomes operational. New staff are assigned to the alliance (such as scientists, engineers, marketers) while initial deal-makers (such as negotiators, lawyers and CEOs) withdraw—or at least take a more distal position—from the relationship (Kelly et al. 2002). The new people will often have not worked with each other before, will not know each other and will not have participated in the process of forming the alliance, and will therefore have limited background information about the ideas, the expectations and decisions made in the process. They bring different assumptions, attitudes and expectations about the alliance, as well as private fears about their role. This may cause resistance, communication issues, a break-down of sense-making, or, in a worst-case scenario, new people with disparate interest may raise unwarranted challenges to the goal, scope and intentions of the partners to collaborate. Perhaps more importantly, staff who partake in alliance formation, who may have educated new people, will most likely have been assigned different tasks or returned to their regular jobs. Thus, a systematic launch involves an extended set of individuals who partake during the early and later stages of alliance development and will interact in some way during the alliance launch. The challenge is to remove communication barriers, lingering suspicions about partner motives and latent opposition in the partner companies. Preparing new staff to work within the alliance context is a critical challenge that must be addressed in order to avoid a delay in the development of the alliance.

Alliance launch attributes

A systematic process and insight in the drivers for alliance execution is necessary in order to effectively deal with the challenges inherently tied to launching an alliance. By following an organized process for launching new alliances, partners can build the types of working relationships, detailed strategies and operating plans that enable them to capitalize on value-creating opportunities. Regardless of whether alliance launch managers occupy permanent and distinct positions within an organization, will remain involved as alliance managers, or have been acting as deal-maker during alliance formation (Bamford et al. 2003), a successful alliance launch depends on the interplay between a set of five attributes (see Table 6.2).

TABLE 6.2 Alliance launch attributes

Attribute	Description	Key Elements	If not, then . . .
Assemble launch team	The launch team is responsible for articulating and implementing the alliance launch strategy.	Generate favourable short-term process and outcomes during transition period. Launch team starts planning when partners explicate intention to collaborate. Balanced team with leader who has earned respect and has interest in the success of the alliance.	Launch managers who operate solitarily tend to make biased decisions due to emotional involvement. Imbalanced teams with over- and under-representation tend to invoke favouritism.
Articulate launch strategy	The launch strategy entails a detailed and interrelated set of plans, activities and short-term milestones that combine to create a foundation for long-term value creation.	Develop a 100-day roadmap to be used as an implementation framework and checklist. Formulate operational plans, unconstrained by one partner's ideas, practices and structures. Plan and design implementation activities, including kick-off and follow-up meetings.	Activity misalignment during alliance execution creates loss of value. Not knowing who should be involved for what reason generates coordination and relational conflicts.
Create launch speed	Proactive planning and immediate execution following contract signing is essential for the rapid development of collaborative processes and outcomes.	Launch planning begins during negotiation and design development stages. Fast and clear decisions are key for promoting stability and creating energy in the alliance. Small steps at the start create confidence, build trust and allow partners to learn.	Fear and indecision will be an obstacle to rapid decision-making and proactiveness. Procrastination in launching invokes performance and relational risks.
Organize communication	Active and timely communication to internal and external stakeholders creates commitment and involvement.	Communication from alliance leadership must be significant, constant and consistent. Clarity about the motive, scope and intent should be conveyed to management and operational staff. Proactive issue spotting through dialogue eases operational and functional collaboration.	Collective sense-making processes tend to break-down and inhibit progress. Support from internal and external stakeholders will diminish.
Align measurement	Create short-term target and milestones for all functional areas, consistent with the long-term alliance strategy.	Provide a clear definition of short-term milestones, tailored to the alliance context. Establish a performance monitoring system to track alliance launch progress. Acknowledge that performance metrics change as the alliance progresses towards maturity.	Without appropriate launch metrics, alliance leadership makes erroneous decisions. Escalation of conflicts and withdrawal of commitment become realistic threats.

Sources: Bamford et al. (2004); Kelly et al. (2002); Segil (1998).

Assemble the alliance launch team

The (joint) alliance launch team is composed of staff who are employed by the partners involved in the alliance. The team is typically established during alliance negotiation and design, but internal preparations may extend before partner selection (that is, intent to collaborate). It is preferable to establish a team because appointing a single alliance launch manager may be ineffective. Personal preferences, favouritism and emotional attachments of a launch manager may bias decision making and thus render an alliance unstable from the start. Team members typically dedicate themselves full-time to the launch process, as alliance execution involves the management of demanding, uncertain and sometimes conflicting processes. In order to resolve conflicts and serve partners' interests, team member representation is preferably balanced between the partners. The team leader, who is ultimately responsible for the alliance launch, will preferably be an ambitious, confident and fully dedicated senior executive who disavows all biases stemming from the leader's own organization. The team's main responsibility is to formulate and implement the launch strategy, while considering the interests of all stakeholders. To this end, among other activities, the team will develop operational plans, set milestones, contact champions in the partner organizations and obtain their support, identify potential hand-off adversities and resolve partner misfits before they can undermine value creation processes. The team sets the right tone for the alliance and manages the technical/operational and relationship aspects during the transition period. In addition to being business savvy and possessing corporate and business know-how, team members tend to have excellent interpersonal skills. Team members should be chosen based on their ability to work in cooperative and uncertain environments.

Articulate the alliance launch strategy

The alliance launch strategy entails the formulation and implementation of an alliance execution plan. It provides an answer to the question: what do partners need to do to effectuate the alliance contract and get operations going? The launch team is responsible for developing this 'grand' execution plan, which generally consists of a detailed 100-day road map. For example, day 1 may refer to sending out a press release and day 100 may refer to the formal withdrawal of the launch team. Operationalization of intent and plans—the translation of the alliance contract and partners' ambitions into an execution plan—is critical because successful launches depend on the quality and detail of operational planning. Such plans—with clear functional goals, activities, results and milestones, for example—secure commitment from key staff and create compelling value propositions for employees to become involved in the alliance. An effective alliance launch strategy also identifies and explicates (new) opportunities for value creation as the rapid achievement of intentional and emergent milestones instils confidence among the partners that long-term alliance objectives are also attainable. In writing these plans, decisions should follow a neutral, objective decision-making process so that the solutions employed reflect the interests of all parties. It is also critical to set attainable short-term milestones as the attainment of these will create trust, stimulate interaction and learning, and reinforce the spirit of the alliance. As part of the launch strategy, planning its implementation is critical. As part of the execution plan, it makes sense to identify which employees (and other stakeholders) from which partners require preparation and need to be involved during the launch. The launch team is also responsible for orchestrating key launch activities (such as workshops and meetings) and translating and deepening the strategy (as formulated in the contract) along a series of operational dimensions. In order to maintain neutrality and promote an alliance of equals, it is important to act with an open mind and not be constrained by partner organization ideas, practices, structures and systems. Launch decisions should follow from neutral, objective decision-making processes to, for example, ensure incentives to secure talent and critical resources from each partner and to create an aligned and working governance structure. To accomplish these tasks, it is critical that the launch team begins to prepare on time, is involved in contractual negotiations, obtains commitment and legitimacy, and sets milestones essential for alliance growth.

Create speed in launching the alliance

Anecdotal evidence suggests that alliances stumble during the first 100–180 days, losing critical time and momentum while failing to build an effective collaboration infrastructure (Bamford *et al.* 2003). Therefore, a successful alliance launch implies careful preparation and swift execution. Alliance launch planning precedes the formalization of the contractual agreement; once partners sign the contract, alliance execution is imminent. Starting on time, with solid preparation, is essential for rapidly installing a collaborative process. Formulating and executing launch plans prevents fear and indecisiveness from becoming an obstacle to alliance progress. Timely decisions are the key to promoting stability and creating belief in and commitment to the alliance. Working together quickly to solve problems and accomplish results that could not have been achieved before helps to build trust. In order to maintain the speed, energy and spirit in the alliance, a smooth hand-off between formation and management is crucial. If the timing and the speed is not in sync between the people involved, it will immediately jeopardize progress. To maintain speed, the launch team must identify and manage the hand-off situation. Despite the importance of speed, beginning with small 'baby steps' is a prerequisite for creating confidence in one another's intentions, capabilities and contributions. Ultimately, the early completion of a launch project can mitigate relational and performance risks and enable the early realization of alliance benefits.

Organize communication efforts

Communication is critical during the alliance launch. Alliance leadership must be significant, constant and consistent in the content, frequency and timing of communication. With regard to content, employees and external stakeholders are informed, for example, about alliance motives, scope and governance, and insights into why their organization participates. As alliance execution progresses, launch managers should provide information frequently, for example, during launch meetings, workshops and bilateral encounters. Over-communication depicts a driver of successful organizational alignment and integration. Launch managers should also offer updates about performance progress and milestone achievement as such information is critical to maintain continuity commitment. High-quality communication promotes openness and trust and allows partners to quickly resolve adversities that emerge once an alliance becomes operational. Openly discussing issues also redirects partners' attention to blind spots; thus, communication reduces unexpected surprises and helps to build confidence.

Align launch measures with strategy

Building a set of aligned measures implies that the performance system in place fits with the development stage of the alliance (Segil 1998). During alliance formation, metrics should inform management about why the alliance is valuable; during the management stage, metrics should inform about the extent to which the alliance is attaining its objectives (see also Box 8.1). During the launch stage, metrics focus on the extent to which alliance execution progresses according to partners' expectations. Target and milestones must capture all functional areas of the scope and focus particularly on the measurement of short-term alliance outcomes and processes. Doing so requires clear definitions and articulation of tailored milestones, which are aligned with the alliance strategy. It also demands an effective tracking system to monitor progress and identify areas for improvement. During this stage, metrics primarily capture aspects of relationship quality (such as harmony, trust and commitment), decision-making (quality, effectiveness and speed), governance (learning, flexibility and adaptability) and initial alliance objectives (such as spending on research and development, and operating efficiency). The launch team is responsible for creating and implementing the launch metrics and for communicating the results of performance assessments to relevant staff. Based on systematic analysis, the launch team leader should present a consistent set of priorities, in collaboration with functional and operational managers, to accelerate alliance execution.

Alliance launch: decision-making steps

The main objective during the alliance launch stage is to accomplish an effective and efficient transition from alliance formation to alliance management. To increase the likelihood of an alliance attaining its long-term objectives, it is important that partners allocate sufficient time and energy to transition processes and decision-making. Although the formal launch phase of an alliance begins after the contract is signed, those who will drive the alliance launch need to be engaged long before the ink is dry. This is because once the alliance becomes operational, multiple hand-offs between and across hierarchical levels need to be organized simultaneously, under dynamic conditions, as staff changes occur. In order to build a value-creating partnership, management should focus on assembling a launch team, on strongly supporting the execution of the alliance and on joint learning. To guide a successful alliance launch, we have distinguished five steps that should inform decision making during alliance launch (see Figure 6.1).

Step 1: prepare alliance launch

During the launch preparation stage, partner firms individually prepare to launch the alliance by assembling the alliance launch team and formulating a tentative launch strategy. To this end, they gather all possible information about resource needs/gaps, essentials with regard to internal communication, staffing possibilities and adversities that could potentially inhibit collaborative processes during alliance execution, including partner misfits, tensions developed during negotiations and blind spots in the governance structure. This internal preparation helps launch managers to immediately initiate launch activities once the deal-makers conclude their business, formalize an agreement and send a press release to external stakeholders (such as journalists and investors). No later than this point, launch managers representing their organizations should come together and combine their insights, discuss pitfalls and start developing plans to organize a smooth transition from formation to management.

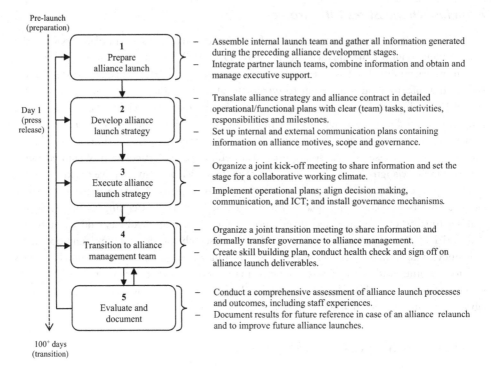

FIGURE 6.1 Decision-making steps: alliance launch

Assembling a joint alliance launch team makes it possible to identify and (preemptively) resolve conflicts that emerge once the alliance becomes operational. The alliance launch team should have full access to all information gathered in preceding alliance development stages (for example, strategy, partner selection, negotiation and design) and to information pertinent to the future of the alliance. For example, members of the launch team may participate in exploratory conversations and even sit in on the negotiations. During these preliminary stages, they play an advisory role rather than participating in deal-making. Nevertheless, they may observe the proceedings and get to know key individuals. By the time the contract is signed, the launch managers are ready and eager to take charge. The team generally consists of experienced alliance managers who have strong connections in their organizations. Their corporate know-how and know-what enables them to speed up decision making, assess the impact of decisions on the functional areas and, in case of conflicts, identify and contact staff who can resolve problems. They also coordinate efforts with senior level support and input. Implementing the right leadership structure to support a launch is an essential component of ensuring alliance launch success.

Step 2: develop alliance launch strategy

The launch team is responsible for developing the launch strategy, which entails several interrelated plans and activities. The team must develop a 100-day road map and provide an account of tasks, activities, results and milestones that need to be executed and achieved during the first phase of alliance execution. This road map contains detailed operational plans, an overview of launch metrics, solutions to overcome partner differences and an overview of alliance launch activities. Specifically, an implementation plan should include the following topics:

- Time span for achieving alliance objectives and performance metrics system.
- Personnel plans to allocate the roles to key persons involved in the alliance; training and education of personnel and personnel rotation programmes.
- Resource plans to secure timely resource provisions after the alliance starts (e.g. funding, patents, software systems).
- Marketing plan to secure the integration of sales and service systems and joint distribution.
- Operational plans to support operational linkages between the firms and enable the integration of business processes.
- Communication plan to identify requirements for effective formal and informal communication during all stages of the alliance, including briefings with operational managers and reporting to executive managers.
- Contingency plan that specifies responses when dealing with unforeseen circumstances, such as product launches and market failure.

The launch team should also organize training and provide tools to assist staff in conducting their tasks. For example, it is most helpful to participate in joint training so that partners share common vocabulary, skills and even concrete job aids to enable collaboration. Joint training also provides an opportunity for partners to get to know one another and build effective relationships. This familiarity forms the basis for more constructive interactions and represents an insurance policy against interpersonal and functional breakdowns. Furthermore, planning often lacks involvement from the teams and individuals who will lead implementation, which can breed misunderstanding and erode support. Good planning involves key staff early, and successful alliances are based on a well-coordinated hand-off from design to management through launch.

Step 3: execute alliance launch strategy

Well-designed alliance launch strategies must lead to action. In an alliance, this implies coordinated and collaborative action. As the first step in execution, the launch team should organize a kick-off meeting that involves the alliance core team. During this meeting, mutual expectations, ambitions, governance issues and other relevant topics are discussed. In other kick-off meetings that also involve non-core staff, an overview of the structure and status should be offered, governance committees and functional/operational teams installed and put to work, work streams identified and accountabilities given. Next, the alliance metrics must be implemented in order to monitor progression towards attaining the alliance objectives. This requires setting up management systems, which might also imply the implementation of supporting ICT infrastructure that enables the alliance management team to effectively govern the alliance.

Step 4: transition to alliance management team

After 100 days (or another agreed-upon period), alliance management is formally transferred from the launch team to the managers responsible for the day-to-day management. Although some launch team members may continue their work, other members are likely to be assigned to new alliances and/or tasks. In order to signal to internal stakeholders that the alliance is entering into a new stage, a post kick-off meeting needs to be organized. During this meeting, information is shared about the status of the alliance and next steps that will be taken. The launch team creates a skill-building plan, conducts a final health check and approves alliance launch deliverables. The transition to the alliance management team requires a specific and carefully designed strategy. This requires the entire launch team to transfer their collective responsibilities at a specified moment in time when the alliance management team will assume responsibility for managing the alliance. This 'big bang' transfer of responsibilities ensures clarity about who is in control of the alliance relationship.

However, this approach involves some risks. A first risk is that the new team is not fully introduced in the alliance dynamics. This could jeopardize the collaboration within the team and the functioning of the alliance as a whole. Next, a new team presents new team challenges. A new 'social structure' needs to be built, which may require time. An alternative to a big bang approach is a phased approach in which positions are changed gradually over time. This enables the new people to become accustomed to their new roles. However, it also poses a risk of ambiguous responsibilities and tensions between old and new team members who are either hesitant to let go or anxious to take control. In short, the transition from the launch team to the management team requires consideration and a careful execution.

Step 5: evaluate and document

Learning from the alliance launch is critical because experiences may prevent future alliances from premature termination. To this end, the launch team needs to conduct a comprehensive assessment of alliance launch processes and outcomes, with a specific focus on staff experiences. The results of alliance health-checks and other performance reports also depict critical input for a systematic review of the alliance launch process. The results should be documented for future reference and be used as input for other alliance relationships. However, the documents should also be available to alliance management taking over management tasks (see Step 4) as it will enhance their understanding of prior decisions. In case of an alliance relaunch (see Box 6.1), these documents may also be of critical importance as they should contain detailed information on successes but also on tensions, adversities and conflicts.

BOX 6.1 ALLIANCE RELAUNCH

No matter how well an alliance is launched, changes in circumstances may warrant a relaunch of the alliance relationship. For example, changes in partners' strategies and organization, unforeseen competitor moves, new technologies and break-down in alliance performance and commitment may damage an alliance beyond normal repair. In these circumstances, it is often easier to opt for a (radical) alliance relaunch than to seek performance improvement through incremental change. However, the need for a relaunch is sometimes less obvious. Although the alliance is strategically critical to the partners, alliance outcomes and processes are slowly deteriorating. In order to identify clues, partners need a systematic and comprehensive performance system to identify adversities indicative of an alliance relaunch. Metrics may focus on signs, such as slow and dead-locked decision making, a substantial number of communication errors, escalating operational conflicts, employee attrition, high absentee rates during critical meetings and implicit and/or explicit violations of agreements. Ideally, during the initial launch of an alliance, some time would be spent discussing and defining triggers that would indicate the need for a relaunch and can be jointly monitored (whether as part of the alliance scorecard or independently).

Sources: Eaves *et al.* (2003); Visioni *et al.* (2010).

Summary

In this chapter, we have pointed out why the startup phase is a crucial phase for the success of the alliance. We have detailed the alliance launch objectives, challenges, barriers and drivers and provided an overview of the managerial guidelines that enable firms to launch an alliance effectively and efficiently. However, we have not suggested that a 'one-size-fits-all' solution to alliance launch exists. Launch managers need to formulate trade-offs and creatively tailor the launch strategy and derived plans to the idiosyncrasies of the alliance. For example, when comparing non-equity with joint venture arrangements, specific launch activities may deserve more weight. Within a non-equity arrangement, information systems and cultural differences may need to be aligned, whereas in a newly established joint venture, new systems and cultures may need to be created. As joint ventures tend to be more complex with regard to finance, organization and legislation, the alliance launch teams responsible for their execution would benefit from specialist members. Also, the formal transition of management to alliance managers responsible for the day-to-day operations may involve more hand-offs (functional and hierarchical, for example) than a non-equity arrangement. Other conditions that may affect alliance launch activities include alliance objectives, partners' backgrounds and experience, and environmental dynamics.

CASE: CAPGEMINI–ENECO[1]

Capgemini is one of the world's foremost providers of consulting, technology and outsourcing services. With 180,000 staff working in more than 40 countries, together with its clients, Capgemini creates and delivers business, technology and digital solutions that fit their needs, enabling them to achieve innovation and competitiveness. To enable future growth and development, Capgemini developed the Utility to Energy Services (U2ES) transformation proposition. With U2ES, Capgemini aims to improve customer satisfaction and build new customer and strategic relationships, enabling operational excellence and creating new business models and new revenue streams. Fuelled by the U2ES transformation programme, in 2015, Capgemini signed an alliance partner agreement with Eneco Group (Eneco, Stedin, Joulz, Ecofys), the leading Dutch sustainable energy group dedicated to helping its clients to save, use, exchange or sell energy. The joint objective is to engage and collaborate in business innovation and digital transformation, and accelerate innovation and new value creation for both partners. The agreement builds upon Capgemini's worldwide sector knowledge and best practices in digital utilities transformation and Eneco's leadership in energy services and new business models.

The agreement will also drive industry-wide innovation for utility organizations, as Eneco and Capgemini plan to make a number of newly developed energy services available to other industry players through Capgemini's U2ES transformation programme, which is helping utility companies transform into energy services companies. Driven by its mission of sustainable energy for everyone, Eneco's success will depend on its ability to innovate and transform its current IT landscape and capabilities in order to reduce total cost of ownership and create a launch platform for its future services. In the words of Joeri Kamp, CIO of Eneco Group, 'Our customers are changing the way they use energy in their homes and for their businesses dramatically. Decentralized and renewable energy have become the standard. Our focus is on facilitating this transformation with agile products and services'. Thus, the collaboration enables partners to innovate by integrating IT solutions with knowledge of sustainable energy and utilizing energy infrastructures. Specifically, the alliance helps to improve and transform Eneco's IT landscape, as well as to create joint technology exploration, joint intellectual property (IP) and business development. Preliminary and early focus areas will include home energy management, electric vehicle charging, local energy generation and digital customer services.

During their discussions and while shaping the alliance, the partners recognized that making this alliance successful would require that they work together; therefore, they entered the launch phase and determined what they needed to do to position themselves for success. To organize the alliance launch, innovation directors and two to three other executives from both partners combined to set the scene and create internal commitment on a larger scale. It was considered vital to focus on an open and transparent relationship with time to establish personal connections. A two-day workshop was chosen as the launch event, with a focus on sharing opportunities and best practices, but also to make sure people would have time at the bar to build an eagerness to join forces. In other words, the launch team defined the enablers of success.

In April 2015, this two-day workshop was held. Top-level executives and key specialists from both partners came together to share and discuss ambitions, market views, challenges and solutions, as well as spend time together to establish a cultural and personal click. Bringing tangible experience and solutions to the table opened eyes on both sides and quickly established credibility and eagerness to team up. This resulted in an extensive list of areas for potential cooperation and joint value generation. For example, during this meeting the launch team facilitated conversations aimed at clarifying ambiguous goals and drilling down into a meaningful level of specificity beneath such high-level objectives as 'meet end-customer needs' and 'create value'. They then helped both sides work together to develop detailed operation plans to achieve their goals. Following this kick-off meeting, within a matter of weeks the partners had a jointly agreed-upon operational plan that clearly defined focus areas for the next 12 months.

With regard to governance, the partners decided that, to guarantee alliance progress, a '90-day partnership heart beat' would be the preferred rhythm. Thus, immediately following the kick-off meeting, a series of quarterly steering committee meetings were organized. During these initial meetings, an informal atmosphere was maintained to share how ongoing initiatives could be accelerated and how a 'skin in the game' attitude and approach could be established and supported. A small investment pool was created to allow initiatives to take quick steps forward. Also, the first Dutch core team meeting was organized within a year after signing. The core team is responsible for providing guidance and control on a frequent and operational basis.

Several joint activities were organized in order to celebrate short-term success. For example, in June 2015, Capgemini and Eneco gave a joint presentation at the Capgemini Global Analyst Day held in Paris. Also, senior executives from both partners went on trips to the United States, visiting other utilities and potential partners and visiting Capgemini's Applied Innovation Exchange (AIE) in San Francisco. The AIE is a dedicated space to enable joint innovation between Capgemini and its clients and partners, and between clients and other companies. The AIE's aim is to enable participants to attain a competitive advantage in today's fast-pace innovation market landscape by compressing the cycle time from the discovery to deployment of innovation. The AIE in San Francisco provided a strong link to the US start-up community and accelerated initiatives to bring start-up solutions to Eneco.

To systemically organize activities during the first year, the partners decided to use Capgemini's project approach to generate and execute the project initiatives part of the agreement. That is, a four-gate-based approach to secure project evaluation and prioritization was employed. The four gates pertain to project idea generation (Gate 0), project proposal (Gate 1), project confirmed (Gate 2) and project execution (Gate 3). During the alliance launch, the partners together decided on the portfolio of project initiatives to be developed, based on business need and potential value. For each initiative, they completed a review that contained information about the initiative's impact on customer experience, ambition, status, progress and which partner takes the lead. This approach enables the partners, from the start, to have a comprehensive and jointly agreed project portfolio with sufficient operational detail to guide day-to-day work.

Taken together, as a result of a systematic alliance launch, the first year of the Capgemini–Eneco alliance enabled the partners to celebrate successes and build a solid foundation. They obtained a deeper understanding of one another's organization (culturally and operationally) and installed a governance structure tailored to the new relationship with a clear project organization. Capgemini and Eneco were able to collaborate effectively and efficiently, even in the face of unexpected disagreements and conflicts. The Capgemini–Eneco relationship has become stronger over time, generating extant collaborative and innovation opportunities within the realm of energy.

Questions

1 To what extent do you think that Capgemini's alliance launch approach contributed to alliance success? What more could they have done?
2 To monitor launch progress, what metrics would you suggest, and how would the application of these metrics inform decision-making?

Note

1 Interview with senior executive of Capgemini.

7

ALLIANCE MANAGEMENT

The alliance management stage confronts alliance partners with the next challenge: monitor and coordinate alliance activities, and if required impose changes, to the purpose of creating value-creating conditions and mitigating the potential threat of exchange hazards. Alliance managers must oversee whether the partners deploy their resource contributions, adhere to coordination mechanisms, act on expressed commitments and execute and complete the tasks assigned to them. The decisions made during the preceding alliance development stages, particularly alliance launch, may ease the task of alliance management, but as the relationship progresses, the focus should be on day-to-day coordination related to partners' ability to align their contributions and efforts to ensure efficiency and effectiveness. This stage also introduces partners to new uncertainties and ambiguities, emerging from both internal and external contingencies. An alliance manager's task is to respond to these contingencies and steer the relationship towards its objectives. To inform their alliance management, managers need to recognize how to deploy a range of soft approaches (shown in the first section). The following two sections provide detail on the relationship between alliance design and alliance management, and a systematic framework and decision-making steps for alliance management. The chapter concludes with a summary and a case illustration.

Alliance management approaches

Alliance management encompasses both organizational and inter-organizational routines, systems and procedures that make an alliance work (or not). Its objective is to optimize conditions to enable communication, conflict resolution, decision making and evaluation, which in turn foster alliance performance (Ireland *et al.* 2002). Yet an alliance's value creation potential is continuously at risk. Environmental conditions such as industry dynamics, regulations and laws could pose a threat or provide an opportunity—for example, the industrial and political environment may render an alliance agreement obsolete, or competitors may introduce new technologies that force alliance partners to reconsider their alliance contract. Changes within the partners' firms also create dynamics that demand active alliance management. Internal reorganizations, corporate strategy shifts or transitions in the board of directors may hinder alliance progress. Furthermore, causes endogenous to the alliance can prompt managerial action: the alliance's performance might fall below initial expectations, the partners may

DOI: 10.4324/9781003222187-7

TABLE 7.1 Four alliance management approaches

	Relational governance	Conflict management	Response strategies	Inter-partner learning
Description	Social institutions that govern and guide alliance partners to behave in a mutually beneficial manner.	Conflicts are inherently tied to alliances and tend to hinder alliance collaboration and outcomes.	Adversities require managers to react with relationship-preserving or destroying response strategies.	A regular and repeatable pattern of routines, supporting knowledge and information transfer.
Logic	Relational norms and relational capital function as self-enforcing governance mechanisms.	The impact of dysfunctional conflicts needs to be mitigated; functional conflicts should be exploited.	Understanding the range of responses and their causes enables alliance partners to predict response strategies.	Learning about partners reduces costs and increases ease of adaptation in the alliance.
Implications	Protects alliance partners against misappropriation and opportunism and functions as a lubricant for cooperation and adaptation.	Active conflict management enables alliance partners to improve the quality of alliance processes.	Improved resource allocation as firm can anticipate partner's responses to adversity.	Increases likelihood of alliance success, specifically in terms of learning objectives.
Downside	Requires investments; an optimal alliance governance form does not exist.	Requires substantial investments; misuse may exacerbate tensions.	Requires further validation; governance and outcome implications are unclear.	Potential threat of knowledge leakage; learning requires substantial investments.

update their expectations or the governance form may become inefficient. We previously explicated how alliance design can safeguard against unforeseen circumstances, but here we discuss four alliance management approaches that suggest unique perspectives on how to deal with the soft side of alliance management: (1) relational governance, (2) conflict management, (3) response strategies and (4) inter-partner learning (see Table 7.1).

Relational governance theory (RGT)

Relational governance theory (RGT) offers a valuable complement to classical contracting (MacNeil 1978) by emphasizing the importance of social and relational processes as building blocks of efficient and effective alliances. Classical contract law relied primarily on the legal framework as a mechanism to plan exchanges, (re)negotiate contracts and resolve contractual conflicts; RGT considers legal mechanisms costly in terms of resources and time. Alternatively, relational governance thus governs and guides parties such that they behave in a mutually bene-ficial manner because of their common understanding of relational norms and relational capital.

Relational norms rest on the premise that for alliance contracts to function, a set of com-mon unwritten social rules must exist to describe the unwritten social rules that guide partner firms' behaviours in particular situations and enhance cooperation and outcomes. Relational norms generally pertain to notions of flexibility, solidarity and information exchange (Heide and John 1992). Flexibility implies that partners expect to make adjustments in their ongoing relationship in order to fit changing circumstances; it facilitates adaptation to unforeseen contingencies. Solidarity norms pertain to partners' anticipation of efforts to preserve the relationship; they signal commitment to continuing the relationship. Information exchange norms mean that parties will provide certain information that might help their partner, such that it facilitates problem solving and adaptation. In alliances with high levels of relational norms, partners can respond effectively to environmental contingencies, extend the time horizon for evaluating the outcomes of their relationships and refrain from relationship-damaging behaviours (Palmatier *et al.* 2007). Relational norms promote collaboration, which operates as a safeguard that allows the parties to work on the relationship and respond to problematic situations without continuously referring to a contract. Thus normative behaviours operate as self-enforcing governance mechanisms, such that managers respond to good social relationships by acting to support the relationship. When relational norms are absent, however, managers are likely to respond to poor social relationships with uncooperative behaviours. In the resulting destructive interaction pattern, partners may engage in repeated efforts to exploit their counterpart's vulnerability by behaving opportunistically in order to extract additional rewards.

Relational capital is a response to the inadequacies of contracts that enables alliance partners to deal with their bounded rationality and opportunism (White *et al.* 2007). It refers to the extent to which parties feel comfortable, rely on trust in their dealings with one another and commit to the relationship (Ariño *et al.* 2001). Trust reflects the willingness of a party to be vulnerable to the actions of another party (see Box 7.1), with the expectation that the other party will perform a particular action important to the party that employs trust, irrespective of its ability to monitor or control that other party. Trust-based relational capital contributes to a freer, greater exchange of information and know-how because decision makers do not worry about protecting themselves from opportunistic behaviour. In turn, commitment refers to an expectation that behaviours will be directed towards relationship maintenance, with a high value placed on the joint relationship. Greater commitment enables both parties to achieve individual and joint goals without raising the spectre of opportunism. Because more committed partners exert effort and balance short-term problems with long-term goal achievement, higher levels of commitment should be associated with partnership success. If they have a

BOX 7.1 TYPES OF TRUST

The alliance literature identifies different types of trust:

- Trust refers to a structural component, that is when an alliance design invokes trust. For example, alliance-specific investments create a mutual hostage situation.
- Trust refers to a behavioural component, that is when partners' conduct invoke trust. For example, confidence that individual partners have in their mutual reliability and integrity.
- Knowledge-based trust emerges through partner interactions as they learn about each other and develop trust around norms of equity.
- Deterrence-based trust entails utilitarian considerations that lead a firm to believe that a partner will not engage in opportunistic behaviour because of the costly sanctions that are likely to arise.

- Good-will trust refers to the belief that a partner intends to allocate its resources and capabilities rather than engage in opportunistic conduct.
- Competence trust pertains to the belief that a partner does possess enough resources and capabilities to meet the agreements of the alliance contract.
- Calculative trust entails the belief that the possible gains realized through the alliance outweigh the possible costs.

Sources: Boersma *et al.* (2003); Das and Teng (2001); Gulati (1995a); Madhok (1995).

good relationship, the parties might discuss and resolve their potential tensions, such that relational capital attenuates concerns about goal conflicts, opportunism and misappropriation. As a critical catalyst of alliance progress, it encourages economically efficient alliances, even in conditions of uncertainty, ambiguity or incomplete information (Palmatier *et al.* 2007).

Relational governance (i.e. relational norms and capital) thus emerges in alliances that include socialization between the partners, which itself results in shared beliefs and values, and influences partners' behaviour so as to increase commitment to the alliance (Das and Teng 2001). However, relational capital focuses on expectations of partner behaviour, whereas relational norms are mechanisms to influence behaviour. Frequent and successful partner interactions might drive the development of close personal relationships that contribute to relational capital building, but these interactions also reinforce the development of relational norms. These different concepts still tend to have similar implications for alliance management, however, such that in an alliance characterized by relational governance, alliance partners are more willing to accommodate one another's needs and overcome adversity. Accordingly, they can implement necessary adjustments to the alliance and rebalance the alliance system, such that parties are confident that any changes are in their interests. Furthermore, relational governance pushes parties to focus on mutually beneficial strategies, rather than exploitation and misappropriation, by shifting their focus from self-centred behaviours towards behaviours that foster unity through common responsibilities. Tensions that arise in the course of the relationship thus will be treated as joint concerns; counterparts maintain agreements, perform competently and behave honourably, even without explicit promises or performance guarantees (Boersma *et al.* 2003). The task for alliance management is to reinforce the priority of investing in the development of relational norms and capital.

Yet relational governance also suffers several disadvantages. A good relationship eliminates costly contracts and coordination mechanisms by reducing the need to monitor partners' behaviour (Dyer 1997). But building a high-quality relationship also demands time and resources, without any guarantee that the counterpart will cooperate (Ariño *et al.* 2001). Moreover, trust in one's counterpart may precisely induce adverse behaviours, such as betrayal and setting (too) high expectations, as the counterpart may expect to be forgiven (Ekici 2013). Furthermore, despite widespread recognition of the importance of relational governance, prior research has not prescribed the optimal types of governance for dealing with specific exchange characteristics. Research that examines relationships between relational governance and other alliance variables (e.g. contracts, alliance-specific investments) has tended to produce fragmented findings (Palmatier *et al.* 2007). With the conceptual framework provided in extant relational governance literature, however, we provide insights into the dimensions and dynamics that underlie alliances, as well as the belief structures and activities necessary for successful alliance relationships (see Box 7.2 for a more recent view).

BOX 7.2 ORGANIZATIONAL JUSTICE

Recent alliance research has drawn on equity and organizational justice theory to explain alliance behaviour. Organizational justice theory states that (in)equity, (in)justice or (un) fairness affect the behaviour of alliance partners. Inequity exists when the perceived inputs and/or outcomes for one firm are inconsistent with the perceived inputs and/or outcomes of the partner firm. Perceived inequities lead exchange partners to feel as though they are being under- or over-rewarded, then affect their behaviours in subsequent periods by encouraging parties to change their inputs, which likely results in suspicion and mistrust by the exchange partner. Equitable outcomes instead create confidence that the parties will not take advantage of each other but rather are concerned about the other's welfare. For example, Scheer *et al.* (2003) find that Dutch automobile dealers react adversely to positive and negative inequities in their relationships with automobile suppliers, and Luo (2005) shows that alliance profitability increases when parties share their perceptions of procedural justice, especially compared with situations marked by asymmetrical perceptions. Despite recent advances, more research is needed to achieve coherent explanations for alliance behaviour. Poppo and Zhou (2014) demonstrate that procedural fairness partially mediates the effect of contractual complexity, whereas distributive fairness partially mediates the effect of contractual recurrence in fostering exchange performance. Luo and colleagues (2015) show that the effect of strong form opportunism on alliance performance is attenuated by distributive justice, whereas the effect of weak form opportunism is suppressed by procedural justice and interactional justice. This suggests that while distributive justice acts to preserve the formal structure of the exchange, procedural justice and interactional justice support the informal mechanisms of cooperative interaction. Taken together, the organizational justice theory holds great promise to explain alliance behaviours, as alliance studies suggest that alliance governance and management must go beyond their coordinating and safeguarding functions to establish a fair frame of reference.

Sources: Greenberg (1987); Luo (2005); Luo *et al.* (2015); Poppo and Zhou (2014); Scheer *et al.* (2003).

Conflict management

Conflicts in alliances pertain to a perceived divergence of interests, or the belief that partners' current aspirations cannot be achieved simultaneously (White *et al.* 2007). Conflict is generally imagined as destructive because it creates negative reactions that can intensify partner tensions (Peng and Shenkar 2002). Moreover, conflicts induce heightened competitive processes, create misperceptions of alliance progress and stimulate a sense of the inequitable distribution of alliance outcomes. They also can give rise to distrust and anxiety, reduce the level of cooperation and efficient integration of activities and hamper alliance performance (Ding 1997). When conflict leads to overt aggression or passive resistance, it harms alliance performance in another way. Thus dysfunctional conflicts have negative effects in terms of strategic alliance collaboration, and partners who perceive them tend to consider themselves obstructed from achieving their objectives.

Dysfunctional conflicts arise for various reasons. Ring and Van de Ven (1994) argue that coordination and efficiency concerns due to opportunism and injustice are responsible for inter-partner conflict, but Khanna (1998) cites incompatibilities between private and common benefits. Das and Teng (2002) also suggest that conflicts result from misfit across organizational routines, technologies, decision-making styles and preferences; emerging private interests and opportunistic behaviour; or fierce competitions outside the alliance. White et al. (2007) instead attribute conflicts to cultural differences between partners engaged in international alliances. Thus, the initial alliance conditions and internal and external contingencies induce conflicts and require a response from alliance managers.

To deal with conflict, researchers propose various conflict resolution strategies—some of which are akin to negotiation strategies. Bradford et al. (2004) thus distinguish among collaboration (explore integrative solutions), accommodation (accept counterpart's perspective) and confrontation (advocacy of one perspective), whereas White and colleagues (2007) distinguish a harmony strategy, which stresses cooperative behaviour, from a confrontation strategy, with a focus on competitive behaviour, and from a regulatory strategy, stressing rule-based behaviour. Lin and Germain (1998) present problem solving (seeking mutually satisfying solutions), compromising (seeking middle ground), forcing (imposing solution) and legalistic (resorting to contract) strategies. However, conflict resolution tends to be conditional on the type of strategy used and its match with the type of conflict at issue. Lin and Germain (1998) thus reveal that a problem-solving strategy improves joint venture performance, but a legalistic strategy has a negative influence. According to Bradford et al. (2004), a collaborative conflict reduction strategy thus reduces the negative effect of conflicts for relational and task conflicts, but an accommodation strategy only reduces relational conflicts, the confrontation conflict strategy only reduces task conflicts and any misalignment exacerbates the impact of conflicts.

In all these classifications, however, the apparently destructive nature of conflicts is primary, even if other studies suggest that conflicts may not be very detrimental to alliances. Functional conflicts create a positive effect and a constructive contribution to the collaboration (Morgan and Hunt 1994) because such conflicts stimulate interactions among alliance partners. Knowledge sharing and creation results from functional conflict in trusting conditions because trust improves the quality of dialogue and discussions in the alliance (Panteli and Sockalingam 2005). Refusing to discuss conflicts means inhibiting creativity and innovation. Any conflicts resolved amicably can be regarded as functional because they ultimately prevent stagnation, stimulate interest and curiosity, and provide a means to resolve the conflicts, which then increases productivity. Functional conflicts also might initiate a critical review of past actions, more frequent and effective communications between alliance partners, a more equitable distribution of system resources and standardization of the conflict resolution modes available.

Active management of conflicts thus forces alliance members to disagree and debate the merits of their alternative solutions, which can mitigate the negative effects of conflicts and exploit their beneficial aspects. However, if conflicts cannot be resolved, tensions escalate and the dissolution of the partnership becomes inevitable. Despite the importance of dealing actively with conflicts, we also need to consider the hazards associated with conflict management. It demands substantial investments, during both the formation and management stages. Designing conflict resolution mechanisms ex ante and applying them ex post is particularly costly. The misuse of conflict resolution techniques may also have detrimental consequences for alliance continuity. If managers employ force or confrontation to resolve an inter-partner conflict, they may even contribute to conflict escalation instead of resolution.

Response strategies

As alliances progress, partners' firms deploy a wide range of response strategies to solve adverse situations (Ariño and de la Torre 1998). Response strategies entail relationship-focused reactions that managers use to resolve dissatisfying situations, such as economic under-performance and poor working relationships (Tjemkes and Furrer 2010)[1]. Response strategy research provides a particularly deep understanding of a broader range of relationship-destroying and relationship-preserving responses and their antecedents. Therefore, understanding response strategy behaviour is critical for alliance management, as anticipating partners' response behaviour enables alliance managers to allocate resources efficiently and effectively to either restore a relationship or gradually disengage from it.

Hirschman (1970) initially identifies exit, voice and loyalty as three alternative responses to organizational decline, organized along a constructive–destructive dimension. Extending Hirschman's framework with a fourth strategy—namely neglect (Farrell 1983; Rusbult *et al.* 1982)—results in the EVLN (exit–voice–loyalty–neglect) typology. The EVLN typology represents a parsimonious conceptualization of response strategies and derives its strength from the underlying two-dimensional structure into which the four response strategies are organized. This structure contains an active–passive dimension and a constructive–destructive dimension, with the four response strategies located in quadrants: exit as active–destructive, voice as active–constructive, loyalty as passive–constructive and neglect as passive–destructive. More recent alliance research has refined and increased the number of response strategies to the seven listed here (Tjemkes and Furrer 2011):

- Exit indicates a disinclination to continue the current alliance and reflects the most destructive response. Managers using this response do not see any possibility of dealing effectively with the adverse situation.
- Opportunism entails an active intention to increase benefits from the alliance in ways that are explicitly or implicitly prohibited. Managers using this response seek to improve their performance covertly.
- Aggressive voice consists of persistent efforts to solve an adverse situation, regardless of the partner's ideas. Managers using an aggressive voice impose their views forcefully and actively on their counterparts, without necessarily trying to avoid conflict.
- Creative voice refers to voicing novel and potentially useful ideas in an attempt to overcome an adverse situation unilaterally, by proposing constructive solutions.
- Considerate voice represents an attempt to change the situation by communicating in a relationship-preserving manner. Alliance managers consider their own concerns as well as those of their partner by discussing the situation with the intention of developing mutually satisfactory solutions.
- Patience (which replaces loyalty) involves silently abiding the issues, with the hope that things will improve in the future. Alliance managers voluntarily ignore the issue and expect the adverse situation to resolve itself.
- Neglect means allowing an alliance to deteriorate. A neglectful alliance manager expends minimal effort in maintaining the partnership and ignores possible ways to solve the situation, leading to the eventual dissolution of the alliance.

Three distinct factors explain why alliance managers prefer distinct response strategies: individual-level, alliance-level and environmental-level determinants (Tjemkes and Furrer 2011).

At the individual level, alliance managers' personal characteristics influence their decision making in general and their use of response strategy in particular. For example, managers' locus of control and risk aversion tends to influence their response strategy preferences. Internally oriented alliance managers, who believe in their power over events, are likely to adopt active response strategies, whereas externally oriented managers, believing they have little or no control over events, use passive strategies. Risk aversion reflects attitudes towards risk and also influences response strategy preferences. Risk-averse alliance managers might prefer relatively low risks and place greater emphasis on negative consequences, which might lead them to prefer a constructive response (such as the creative voice). In contrast, risk-prone managers facing adverse situations are more likely to engage in more risky response strategies, such as an aggressive voice and opportunism.

Building on social exchange theory (Blau 1964) and interdependence theory (Thibaut and Kelley 1959), response strategy research proposes that response preferences depend on alliance-level exchange variables (Geyskens and Steenkamp 2000; Ping 1993; Tjemkes and Furrer 2010). For example, economic satisfaction pertains to managers' evaluations of the financial outcomes of an alliance. Economic under-performance indicates that alliance managers perceive a discrepancy between prior expectations and desired financial results, which requires an active response (for example, opportunism and the considerate voice) to resolve the adversity rapidly. In contrast, economically satisfied managers prefer passive responses. Social satisfaction, on the other hand, pertains to managers' evaluations of the psycho-social aspects of an alliance. Low social satisfaction creates greater suspicion about a counterpart's intentions and reduces managers' expectations of the relationship's potential future benefits. Therefore, managers who are dissatisfied with relationship quality within the alliance may terminate it rather than try to save it through constructive responses. Managers who are satisfied with the relationship, meanwhile, tend to appreciate contact with their counterparts and are more likely to use constructive response strategies. The presence of exit barriers is also influential; unilateral, alliance-specific investments trigger constructive response strategies and inhibit destructive strategies. This is because constructive responses reduce the risk of losing the investments if the relationship terminates prematurely. In an adverse situation without alternatives, managers have strong incentives to make the current alliance work and are likely to respond actively and constructively to improve the situation.

Competitive intensity and technological change are environmental-level antecedents of response strategy preference. Competitive intensity is the degree of rivalry between competitors in an industry, characterized by industry-wide use of tactics such as aggressive pricing, high levels of advertising, product introductions or adding services to prevent customers from switching to competitors. Firms that operate in industries with high levels of competitive intensity must preserve the quality of their existing alliances in order to secure the resources they provide, which increases the likelihood of constructive strategies, such as the creative voice. In contrast, firms in industries characterized by low competitive intensity are more willing to put the alliance relationship at risk and opt for destructive response strategies, such as exit, opportunism or neglect. Technological turbulence refers to the unpredictability and rate of change of technology in the external environment. In an environment with low turbulence, a firm may benefit from close relationships with alliance partners, so it relies on and preserves these relationships through constructive responses to develop and diffuse innovations. In markets with high technological turbulence, on the other hand, product and process technologies are relatively unstable. Firms have need for emerging capabilities possessed by alternative partners, which means they are more likely to use destructive responses in existing relationships.

In addition to these three levels of determinants, alliance partners may also develop dynamic interaction patterns of actions–reactions in such a way that they use response strategies to address their partner's behaviour. Such patterns are governed by the principle of complementarity, in that correspondence occurs on the constructive–destructive dimension (constructive strategies invite constructive strategies; destructive strategies invite destructive strategies). The active–passive dimension is marked by reciprocity (active strategies invite passive strategies; passive strategies invite active strategies). Although correspondence and reciprocity are distinct interaction patterns, the combination of the two governs strategic alliance development over time. For example, Ariño and de la Torre's (1998) case study of two firms engaged in an international joint venture provides anecdotal evidence that a larger (smaller) discrepancy in efficiency and equity perceptions makes the relationship more (less) likely to deteriorate through reciprocal destructive behaviour. Combining both patterns could lead to either a self-sustaining, reinforcing system of collaborating and commitment, or a downward spiral of conflictual collaboration and alliance termination.

In summary, response strategy research has advanced alliance management by presenting a coherent typology of relationship-destroying and relationship-preserving response strategies, as well as their causes. The typology improves decision making in ongoing alliances, as it enables alliance managers to recognize, and therefore anticipate, partner firms' actions in a timely manner. However, two issues warrant further exploration. In the context of alliances, responses to adversity do not occur in a governance vacuum. Whereas deterrence mechanisms such as contracts, mutual hostages and monitoring are designed to reduce the likelihood of destructive responses, mechanisms such as participative decision making and revenue sharing stimulate constructive responses. The fact that alliance design characteristics are incomplete in nature means they leave room for various response strategy interaction patterns; therefore, the relationship between alliance design and response strategies needs to be better understood. Furthermore, to avoid premature alliance termination and anticipate the impact of response strategy use, there is a need for greater insight into the short- and long-term performance implications of using response strategies.

Inter-partner learning

In the context of alliance management, inter-partner learning refers to the extent to which partner firms create a regular and repeatable pattern of routines that support knowledge and information transfer (Chai 2003). As the relationship unfolds and parties develop and deploy learning processes, they can exchange knowledge and information more easily (Simonin 1999). Learning about and with the partner entails knowledge and information transfers, both of which facilitate alliance management. As firms learn about their alliance partners, they learn how to interface and communicate with them (Cummings and Teng 2003). This type of learning involves the process rather than the content of learning (that is, inter-firm learning), which allows partners to revisit and revise their expectations and to gain a deeper understanding of their counterparts. In removing information-processing barriers between parties, there are three reasons supporting the claim that inter-partner learning fosters alliance success: (1) increased openness, (2) transfer of tacit knowledge and (3) reduced risk of exchange hazards.

Inter-partner learning encourages relationship openness, which is the extent to which parties are willing and able to share information and communicate openly (Inkpen 2000).

Extensive communication contributes to meaningful and timely information sharing. For example, by transferring staff, document exchange, setting up joint teams and developing best practice guidelines, partners' knowledge transfer mechanisms contribute to the quality, variety and amount of information shared (Chai 2003). Openness also helps parties learn about how to work together and increases awareness of their individual interests, which contributes to a climate that eases alliance management.

Inter-partner learning reduces the difficulties implicit in the transfer of tacit knowledge (Simonin 1999). The fact that tacit knowledge is specific to its context makes it difficult to formalize and communicate (Nonaka 1994). The 'sticky' nature of such knowledge means the incremental cost of transferring it in a form that is usable by the recipient is high. Learning enables parties to reduce the costs associated with finding and accessing different types of valuable knowledge and also motivates them to participate and openly share valuable knowledge. Furthermore, learning helps parties to acquire the subjective viewpoints of their partners and develop a common language. Thus, inter-partner learning enhances partners' awareness, which teaches them how to make the alliance work.

As uncertainty about the performance of the alliance grows, so too does the risk of exchange hazards. However, inter-partner learning decreases the likelihood of opportunistic behaviour, goal conflicts, and appropriation and spillover concerns because it constitutes an informal feedback mechanism that provides partners with signals about one another's conduct; in other words, it increases the risk of detection. Inter-partner learning also eases the distribution and interpretation of knowledge and information, which motivates parties to participate and share openly strategic intents, resources and knowledge, thereby pre-emptively reducing the risk of undesirable spillovers, free-riding behaviour and expensive conflict resolution tactics (Dyer and Nobeoka 2000).

In conclusion, as partners learn in collaboration, they become aware and recognize the need to overcome differences in their structure, processes and routines, or ways to combine these resources constructively in order to make cooperation more efficient (Doz 1996). However, inter-partner learning also presents some risks. First, openness constitutes a threat in that the partner firm could take advantage and act opportunistically. For example, it might use acquired information to appropriate proprietary knowledge but withhold its own relevant information. Second, initiating learning processes requires substantial investments, as employee transfers, joint product information sessions and the codification of implicit know-how demand time, energy and resources. There are currently no clear guidelines to inform alliance managers how to seek a balance between the potential benefits and the associated costs.

Alliance design and management

Hennart (2006) argues that crafting an initial alliance structure is both easier and more crucial than its ex-post management. In contrast, de Rond and Bouchikhi (2004) postulate that an understanding of alliance performance requires a rich and detailed account of alliance management. Doz (1996) takes the middle ground, claiming that both alliance design and alliance management are critical to alliance success. Parties in failing alliances were unable to overcome initial design flaws, whereas those in successful alliances made adaptations to the ongoing relationship (Salk 2005). The observation that alliance structure and alliance processes both matter is in line with conclusions from prior alliance research (Contractor

2005). It is likely that structural decisions and management decisions directly and interactively influence alliance outcomes—an observation which is corroborated by the results of a review on alliance governance dynamics conducted by Majchrzak and colleagues (2014). The results suggest that alliance arrangements are inherently instable, that instability does not necessarily contribute to detrimental outcomes and that positive or negative outcomes depend on the pattern of dynamics exhibited as a relationship progresses. For example, in a multi-loop flow pattern, positive outcomes can be expected as changes in contract framing, interaction style, decision-making and organizational structure positively reinforce one another. Although conclusive empirical evidence is not yet available, some relevant insights have emerged regarding alliance dynamics, specifically when focusing on the relationship between alliance design and management.

One stream of studies reflects the ongoing debate about the substitutive or complementary relationship between contractual and relational governance (Albers *et al.* 2016; Krishnan *et al.* 2016). Proponents of substitution assert that relational governance operates as a self-enforcing safeguard that is effective and less costly than contractual governance. When firms work together, they build trust across individual members of the contracting firms, rendering contracts obsolete. In an examination of business alliances, Lee and Cavusgil (2006) find that relational-based governance is more effective than contractual-based governance in strengthening the inter-firm partnership, stabilizing the alliance and facilitating knowledge transfers. The positive effects of relational-based governance increase under the pressure of greater environmental turbulence. Aulakh *et al.* (1996) reveal that monitoring mechanisms and relational norms determine trust and that higher levels of trust positively influence sales growth and market share relative to competitors in cross-border partnerships. In contrast, advocates of complementarity argue that alliance success depends on the alignment between contractual and relational governance, which, if properly aligned, reinforce each other. Poppo and Zenger (2002) report that complementing customized contracts with relational governance results in higher levels of alliance performance. Similarly, Luo (2002) shows that contract completeness guides the course of operations, that ex-post cooperation can overcome the limitations of contracts and that both drive alliance performance independently and interactively. Conducting a study within the biotechnology industry, Kim (2014) reports that alliances characterized by high levels of exchange hazards utilize both formal and informal mechanisms, supporting the complements hypothesis, whereas those alliances with lower levels of exchange hazards utilize only one type of governance mechanism. Reporting on the results of a meta-analysis, Krishnan and colleagues (2016) show, for example, that under conditions of high behavioural uncertainty and low-to-moderate levels of environmental uncertainty, the use of trust-based governance alongside contractual governance might enhance the latter's effectiveness, whereas when both behavioural and environmental uncertainty are high, contractual governance hurts alliance performance while trust-based governance does not function at its best either. Despite these advances, this debate remains unresolved, even as studies consistently suggest that the relationship between contractual and relational governance depends on the type and level of trust (Lui and Ngo 2004), the completeness of the contract (Luo 2002), the alliance development stage (Jap and Ganesan 2000) and environmental dynamics (Lee and Cavusgil 2006). Therefore, alliance managers must seek a balance between contractual and relational governance.

Other studies have noted the relationships among initial formation conditions, post-formation processes and alliance outcomes. In a retailer–supplier setting, Jap and Ganesan

(2000) found that a retailer's specialized investments exert a negative effect on its perceptions of supplier commitment. A supplier's specialized investments and relational norms, on the other hand, increase the retailer's perception of supplier commitment, and explicit contracts are associated with perceptions of low supplier commitment. Furthermore, the retailer's perceptions of supplier commitment increase its evaluations of supplier performance and satisfaction but relate negatively to conflict. Schilke and Cook (2015) suggest that contractual safeguards increase partner trustworthiness because a contract, in which constraints are explicitly written down, encourages partners to act in a trustworthy manner, particularly if an alliance partner lacks a favourable reputation. Ali and Larimo (2016) show that structural (i.e. symmetric dependence and resource dependence) and social mechanisms (i.e. trust, communication and cultural adaptation) reduce opportunism. These findings also correspond with results reported by Doz (1996) and Lane *et al.* (2001) that learning performance benefits are derived from the combination of initial conditions and post-formation processes. However, Tjemkes (2008) reports that the impact of alliance design on alliance performance depends on the alliance objective: a direct effect for financial objectives, a fully mediated effect through relational processes for learning objectives and a partially mediated effect through relational processes for strategic objectives. This suggests that alliance design functions as an architecture for alliance management but also that the more detailed and complex an alliance design is, the less latitude alliance managers have to steer alliance progress. This discussion leads to the three following main conclusions:

1   Alliance management is critical to the effective functioning of alliances in that it compels alliance partners to manage discrepancies, adversities and tensions.
2   Alliance management requires decisions that directly affect alliance continuity expectations, mainly through building and deploying relational governance, engaging in active conflict management, formulating and implementing response strategies to adversity and learning about partners, in order to manage the alliance successfully.
3   The related decisions are not discrete or stand-alone choices; their results are likely to interact. Moreover, alliance management can be constrained and/or facilitated by initial alliance design decisions. Successful alliances overcome alliance design flaws through alliance management.

Alliance management: decision-making steps

Alliances progress across management intervention cycles, instigated by the monitoring of outcome and process discrepancies and by initiatives to deal with these discrepancies, and, if required, to develop, communicate and implement corrective measures. In turn, by monitoring, alliance managers are able to see the effect of these measures. That is, systematic attention should be given to monitoring the alliance's progress, as well as any internal and external conditions that might threaten its success. Using the results of such monitoring, alliance managers can assess the extent to which unforeseen circumstances are, or could become, a threat or an opportunity. Guided by these assessments, the manager then must decide whether to take corrective action. If interventions are required, the manager can decide where to focus those, which mechanisms are appropriate and who is responsible for implementing the corrective measures. To facilitate such complex and difficult activities, we present five steps that should inform decision making during the alliance management stage (see Figure 7.1).

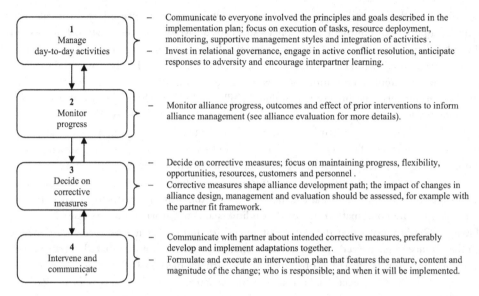

FIGURE 7.1 Decision-making steps: alliance management

Step 1: manage day-to-day activities

The first priority of alliance management is to get the alliance started, mainly by focusing on the daily activities agreed on in the alliance negotiation and design stages. Managers must understand the expectations, the new processes and the activities associated with the alliance. The principles and goals described in the implementation plan therefore should be executed visibly and, if necessary, reviewed or altered. For example, alliance managers are responsible for ensuring that all involved staff members understand their role and tasks in the alliance and that alliance operations are integrated according to plan. Management styles should adopt a 'big picture' attitude, eliminate any 'us versus them' thinking and keep motivation high.

Frequent communication across alliance teams, such as through meetings or joint training, can help encourage their common perceptions. Communications that even go beyond alliance issues also are essential for replenishing the reservoir of relational capital. In addition, emerging tension and conflicts should be dealt with proactively. The impact of destructive conflicts, such as disagreements about appropriation, must be mitigated, but constructive conflict, such as cultural differences, should be exploited effectively. Understanding potential responses should be the goal of any alliance manager because predicting whether partners will respond actively–passively or constructively–destructively will help managers steer their alliances by dealing promptly with expectation discrepancies. Finally, a persistent focus on inter-partner learning enables managers to identify potential hazards and to come to adequate solutions.

Step 2: monitor progress

To identify potential threats to alliance continuity in a timely manner, it is important to monitor alliance outcomes and processes. We elaborate on the design and use of performance metric systems in Chapter 8, but in particular, managers should attend to the following.

- External threats and opportunities. Are there any external developments (e.g. in the partner's organization or broader environment) that might harm or reinforce the alliance's value creation potential?
- Alliance performance. Has the alliance realized outcomes efficiently in terms of financial profits, learning and competitiveness? Is the alliance growing as expected? Is the distribution of outcomes equitable?
- Relational processes. Are partners satisfied with the quality of the working relationship and alliance staff? In the case of conflicts, are they resolved properly? And are the partners flexible in accommodating necessary adaptations?
- Alliance partner. Does the partner still believe in the importance of the alliance? Changes in the partner's environment could have altered its view of the alliance.

Step 3: decide on corrective measure(s)

Based on their assessments, alliance managers must decide if corrective measures should be taken, and if so which, to ensure the alliance continues to operate efficiently and effectively. Consistent with the prescriptions provided through the book, alliance adaptations might target alliance design, such as the board composition of a joint venture, compensation structure, task division, decision making and alliance management itself, including relational governance, conflict resolution and inter-partner learning. In addition, modifications may be required in the performance metric system due to emerging objectives. To overcome identified problem areas (or address opportunities) in the alliance, managers should recognize that discrepancies in outcomes and processes may evoke partner responses ranging from dysfunctional, which ultimately leads to alliance termination, to more functional reactions aimed at minimizing the damage and preventing reoccurrence. When deciding on the nature, content and timing of corrective measures, alliance managers should thus consider the following.

- Flexibility. Any action should preserve the flexibility of the alliance.
- Opportunities. Actions are needed not only to solve problems but also to create new opportunities.
- Resources. Avoid exhausting available resources with actions, and pay close attention to the costs and benefits when making investments.
- Field of intervention. An action in any particular field (e.g. operational unit, team) requires a clear understanding of the effects on other fields.
- Key personnel. Determine who will take the actions and who will be most affected by those actions.

Corrective measures shape the developmental path of an alliance, such that each response to an outcome and/or process discrepancies has multiple repercussions. Assessing the possible implications is important as it provides information to managers whether to proceed to implementation or to abstain from management interventions, such that they continue the alliance but adopt diminished expectations. It is important to recognize that design modifications are likely to affect, for example, alliance processes, thus potential adaptations should be assessed while considering the trade-off between contractual and relational governance. To anticipate the impact of corrective measures, alliance managers could use the partner fit framework (see Chapter 3). For example, managers may ask the following questions:

- To what extent do adaptations affect resource contributions and the alliance's value creation potential (i.e. resource complementarity)?
- To what extent do changes affect partners' strategic visions (i.e. strategic fit)?
- To what extent are decision-making structures, control systems and performance metrics affected by intended changes (i.e. organizational fit)?
- To what extent are cultural differences resolved through managerial intervention (i.e. cultural fit)?
- To what extent do changes influence operational procedures, systems and task allocation (i.e. operational fit)?
- Do interventions affect personal interactions between alliance staff from the partners (i.e. human fit)?

Step 4: intervene and communicate

Building on the prior assessments, it is critical that alliance managers formulate and implement an intervention plan that features at least the nature, content and magnitude of the change, who is responsible and when it will be implemented. Communication processes underlie most alliance functions, so communication behaviour is critical to successful implementation. Providing advance warning of intended adaptations to an alliance partner is important because management interventions that could be viewed as a betrayal of joint interests (whether intentional or circumstantial) must be preceded by ample notice and appropriate explanations. For example, joint decisions to restructure or discontinue alliance activities presumably cause partners to initiate a dialogue about value creation, value appropriation and fairness, considering the value of each partner's contribution. This dialogue could result in a renegotiation of the value appropriation clauses of the alliance, such that it creates a new balance, acceptable to the partners, and reflects changes in the external environment. Moreover, joint participation in decision making, planning and goal setting ensures that required information is timely, accurate, adequate and credible. Alternatively, although under certain circumstances unilateral alliance adaptations signal long-term commitment, more often one-sided enforced modifications trigger an escalating spiral of destructive behaviours ultimately resulting in premature dissolution of the alliance. Therefore, we recommend preparing and implementing modifications jointly, for example by actively engaging the alliance partner in alliance monitoring (i.e. Step 2).

Summary

In this chapter, we have noted the soft side of strategic alliances. Alliance management is responsible for executing the alliance design and governing day-to-day operations. The main objective is to advance alliance progress and, if required, initiate corrective measures. To this end, partner firms may invest in relational governance, use conflict resolution techniques, respond adequately to adversities and stimulate inter-partner learning. However, the bandwidth of the management effort depends on the alliance design because the structural design, such as contractual clauses, decision-making authority and monitoring mechanism, constrain or facilitate a firm's ability to initiate and execute alliance management. Alliance management is also difficult because of its inherently unstable nature; it requires substantial investment in terms of resources, energy and time. To assist alliance managers to maintain viable alliances, we have provided a five-step procedure that enables them to determine the cause of dissatisfaction, develop appropriate responses, assess the impact of potential corrective measures and execute an intervention.

CASE: TNO–HOOGENDOORN[2]

TNO is a Dutch-based knowledge organization that applies scientific knowledge to strengthen the innovative power of industry and government, which it does by assisting in the various stages of product development, from idea generation to implementation and testing. Hoogendoorn is an expert in glasshouse horticulture, and its computers and software have controlled a wide range of climatic conditions for more than 40 years. Hoogendoorn markets its horticultural computers across the world through a global network that is constantly kept up to date with new and innovative product developments. In 2005, TNO and a business unit of Hoogendoorn called Growth Management started to collaborate on a new innovative product: Sensiplant.

Hoogendoorn and TNO signed a letter of intent in July 2005, and expressed their intention to proceed with the product development roadmap, to the point that an agreement between the two parties would be set for further commercialization of the Sensiplant project. Sensiplant is an information system based on wireless technology that measures the soil humidity of pot plants. Sensiplant's self-organizing wireless network makes the system unique, and the communication of the system is based on a self-organizing protocol patented by TNO. Hoogendoorn is responsible for the provision of the required hardware, as well as the sales, marketing and distribution of the product.

Between 2005 and 2007, TNO developed the technology further, and in 2007, the alliance to commercialize the technology became formally effective. A core part of the alliance agreement pertained to TNO licensing its proprietary technology to Hoogendoorn. Some issues however emerged straight away. TNO demanded that Hoogendoorn paid an annual fee, even if sales were below expectations. Although the request was met with resistance, Hoogendoorn complied after extensive negotiations. The development of Sensiplant also had its challenges. Although the hardware seemed to work, the software contained several bugs, which were caused by changes in the initial hardware conditions. To resolve these adversities, a third party, MUCO, was approached. The addition of MUCO to the alliance fixed the hardware and software issues, but also complicated alliance management, as TNO alliance managers perceived that the other two partners were working against it. In addition, tension developed between TNO and Hoogendoorn as the latter decided unilaterally to postpone the release of version 1.0, following initial tests that revealed customers were dissatisfied with Sensiplant's technical performance.

Despite the setbacks, in 2008, version 1.1 of Sensiplant was fully operational, and Hoogendoorn was ready to launch it on the market. The release of the 1.1 version again created conflicts, as Hoogendoorn launched the product internationally, despite contractual clauses stipulating that the Dutch market would be approached first. In addition, the alliance came under pressure as customers provided serious negative feedback about the product. Complaints about cabling, hardware and software reached the partners. However, TNO decided to resolve these issues harmoniously and assist Hoogendoorn in any way it could. This proactive approach and building on customer feedback resulted in the release of version 1.2.

TNO was under the impression that version 1.2 was selling successfully. However, it was unexpectedly informed by Hoogendoorn that it had stopped selling Sensiplant because of customer complaints and a large discrepancy between sales targets and actual outcomes. At this time, two Hoogendoorn managers who had been involved in the project from its inception also left the company. A new team was forged to focus on the future of Sensiplant, and two future directions were identified in early 2009: either the project was to be terminated or the product would undergo an upgrade. Convinced about the product's potential, Hoogendoorn created a crisis team that searched for a solution, and the R&D department of the company started to investigate various technical options.

On the TNO side, however, some frustrations started to emerge as the software had worked well for a while, and TNO was keen to sign the user acceptance: a formal document stating that (1) a group of users who tested Sensiplant confirm it is working properly and (2) that the product is ready to be launched commercially. But, confronted with market uncertainties, Hoogendoorn procrastinated about signing it.

Up until this point, TNO had been very flexible because it was important for them to have a commercially viable product. Thus, TNO imposed some pressure on Hoogendoorn, and the user acceptance was signed at a meeting in mid-2009. Following this meeting, one manager from TNO and one from Hoogendoorn developed a plan to launch Sensiplant version 1.3. However, another setback confronted the partners as the manufacturer of the hardware went bankrupt. Nonetheless, both parties were committed to the product's success, and they agreed to postpone the launch. Despite Hoogendoorn again confronting problems in product development, prior experience gave them sufficient confidence in marketability of the product.

The economic crisis in 2008–2009 made TNO and Hoogendoorn shift their attention to the financial side of the project. The partners decided to adjust the payment scheme to accommodate Hoogendoorn's acute financial needs. TNO complied with this new arrangement as it deemed the long-term relationship with Hoogendoorn more important than immediate financial returns. In 2010, TNO and Hoogendoorn arrived at the conclusion that Sensiplant was not a commercially viable product; it seemed to be a 'nice to have' product but not a 'need to have' one. Furthermore, new and cheaper technologies had entered the market. Consequently, Hoogendoorn decided to stop investing in Sensiplant and to sell the remaining stored products (system modules). TNO and Hoogendoorn decided to dissolve the alliance, and both parties incurred their financial losses.

Questions

1   Explain why TNO and Hoogendoorn continued the alliance, despite dissatisfactory economic performance.
2   Describe the alliance's development. How did alliance management affect the partner interaction pattern?

Notes

1   This section builds on prior research with Olivier Furrer (University of Fribourg), whom we acknowledge for his contribution.
2   Interviews with two senior executives of TNO and two senior executives of Hoogendoorn.

8

ALLIANCE EVALUATION

To maintain effective alliances, alliance partners must evaluate alliance performance continuously; monitoring provides the firms with the necessary information to take appropriate actions, whether doing nothing, adapting the alliance design and management or terminating the relationship. Alliance evaluation is complex, however, owing primarily to the multifaceted nature of alliance performance. Most alliance managers focus on intentional outcomes, but they often neglect assessments of emergent objectives, relational processes and intangible outcomes. Furthermore, they tend to use generic metrics, whereas to be effective, performance metrics should align with unique alliance characteristics. An ill-designed performance metric system increases the risk of erroneous decision making, such that alliances might be continued when they should be terminated, and vice versa. To develop and use performance metric systems, alliance managers must thus understand the nature of alliance performance and the issues associated with metrics (shown in the first section). Obtaining insights into various performance metric approaches supports the development of a balanced performance metric system (second section). What follows provides a systematic framework with a set of decision-making steps for alliance evaluation (third section) and provides a summary before concluding with some case illustrations.

Issues with alliance performance and metrics

How alliance partners assess and react to discrepancies between their expectations and realized outcomes shapes the developmental path of the alliance; alliance evaluation thus is a critical, complex activity (Christoffersen *et al.* 2014; Lunnan and Haugland 2008). To deal with the complexities surrounding alliance evaluation, it is important to understand the multifaceted nature of alliance performance (Ryan-Charleton *et al.* 2022), or the degree of accomplishment of goals—be they common or private, initial or emergent—and the extent to which the pattern of interactions is acceptable to both partners (Ariño 2003). From this definition, we derive seven issues that may impede alliance managers' ability to judge alliance performance (see Table 8.1).

DOI: 10.4324/9781003222187-8

TABLE 8.1 Issues with performance metric

	Description	*Solution*
Common and private benefits	Alliance outcomes pertain to shared and individual objectives.	Use measures that provide a combined picture of alliance partners' shared and individual objectives.
Multifaceted nature	Objectives differ across partners, alliances are forged with multiple objectives and alliance processes affect objective realization.	Use measures that capture both alliance outcomes (e.g. financial, strategic and learning) and alliance processes (e.g. relational).
Time horizon	Objective achievement occurs at different time horizons, and new objectives may emerge.	Identify prospective (input) and output indicators and update performance metrics if necessary.
Intangible outcomes	Intangible outcomes are difficult to value and quantify.	Identify realistic and quantifiable proxies for intangible outcomes; in addition, use prospective and process metrics.
Management control	Management control mechanisms and performance metrics may be disconnected.	When selecting management control mechanism, immediately attribute appropriate metrics.
Alliance types	Different alliance conditions require different types of metric systems.	Use generic performance metric template and adapt to the unique context of the alliance.
Measurement norms	Expectations tend to be unique for each alliance and differ across partners.	Provide a systematic framework for the interpretation of measures.

Sources: Ariño (2003); Kumar and Nti (1998); Perkmann *et al.* (2011).

Common benefits often constitute an important rationale for alliance formation, related to the partners' shared alliance objectives (Khanna 1998). Performance metrics should therefore assess the extent to which partners create value jointly; these objectives might pertain to profits, market share or product innovation. A set of shared metrics helps alliance managers to ensure that both partners address alliance adaptations and continually work to maintain alignment with regard to managing the alliance. Private benefits, on the other hand, depict individual objectives and pertain to the transfer of knowledge and resources from one partner to another with the aim of exploiting activities that may not be part of the initial agreement. Alliances in which partners do not recognize the importance of individual metrics endanger their success in that awareness of individual interests allows the partners to look for ways to add value for their partner. Of course, too much emphasis on individual metrics at the expense of shared metrics will lead to disappointing results, especially if success depends on both partners' contributions. Partners who fail to distinguish between common and private benefits, and forsake metrics in order to capture the extent to which their partners create and appropriate value, will typically find themselves working at cross-purposes.

In the complex organizational arrangements that define alliances, firm objectives often depend on a combination of motives (Christoffersen *et al.* 2014; Kogut 1988). Any performance metric system thus must account for partners attempting to pursue multiple goals. Even if partners' objectives converge, they may forge an alliance to realize multiple objectives simultaneously. Focusing on goals in separation negates the interrelated nature of outcomes, such that resources and activities supporting one goal might undermine the attainment of a different goal (Ryan-Charleton *et al.* 2022). Thus, outcome metrics might entail the extent to which partners achieve economic, strategic and learning objectives. In addition, process metrics relate to the partners' satisfaction with interaction patterns (Kumar and Nti 1998) or to the partner's socially responsible behaviours (Yin and Jamali 2021). Performance metric systems should account for relational processes by explicitly incorporating metrics that capture partner dynamics. Moreover, the presence of multiple objectives may set the stage for conflicts, influencing the way partners interact. Patterns of interaction then influence the ability to realize objectives. That is, due to the interrelatedness between outcomes and process, a performance metric system should account for the multifaceted nature of alliance outcomes and processes.

Given the long-time horizons of most alliances, the benefits of collaborations can be realized only after a considerable time. Therefore, effective performance metric systems should feature prospective indicators that predict the value of benefits over time (Anderson 1990). Outcome measures reflect the intended outcome of a process; prospective indicators reflect the aspects that appear causally related to certain desired outcomes (Perkmann *et al.* 2011). Such input-oriented indicators overcome the disadvantages of outcome metrics, in which the outcomes may be delayed, which implies that information to inform corrective measures arrives too late. In addition, partners often establish alliances with predefined, intentional objectives, but as the alliance progresses, new objectives may emerge, which should be assessed accordingly. For example, if a business alliance transforms into a learning alliance, the metrics should shift from financial to learning metrics. However, knowledge creation is difficult to specify ex ante, so the performance metric system should be supplemented with prospective indicators, such as R&D spending and patenting records.

When alliance outcomes are intangible, as they often are, they are not amenable to direct measurement. For example, R&D alliances focus on generating new knowledge that is relatively far from commercialization, so the value of any project is difficult to assess; it remains uncertain whether the created knowledge will have any future commercial value. Even if it is clear that the knowledge has some value, it remains difficult to quantify. The challenge for performance management, then, is to define metrics that approximate the value of intangible outputs. In addition, the use of prospective and process metrics should result in timely and reliable information.

Management control mechanisms enable alliance partners to monitor each other's behaviours and the alliance's progress. To be effective, alliance control should align with the performance metrics. For example, formalized output control might be captured with outcome metrics. Behavioural control mechanisms can be operationalized through outcome and process metrics; effective social control mechanisms (i.e. relational governance) should be accompanied by process metrics. Setting up a management control system during the alliance design stage without simultaneously defining the nature, content and target of its performance metrics is likely to lead to flawed management decisions.

Alliances also can be classified in different ways, such as exploitation or exploration, cross-border or domestic, and equity or non-equity structures. Accordingly, these various types should be subject to different dynamics that influence the choice of performance metrics. Alliances are also often surrounded by environmental uncertainty, which reduces the meaning and validity of short-term, quantitative indices of performance and hinders the use of outcome metrics. Anderson (1990) argues that manufacturing-based joint ventures operating in stable environments can benefit from outcome metrics, but R&D joint

---

BOX 8.1 DEVELOPMENT AND IMPLEMENTATION METRICS

During alliance formation, firms formulate an alliance strategy, select a partner, engage in alliance negotiations and design the alliance. These stages likely require different sets of metrics than the alliance post-formation stage, when alliance management executes the alliance agreement. During the formation stages, metrics should focus on the vision, strategy alignment, pre-launch development, strategic fit, planning, selection, structuring, negotiation and team selection. These development metrics should give partner firms and stakeholders a clear understanding of why the alliance is valuable. In contrast, the implementation metrics might focus on execution, implementation, remediation, restructuring, re-evaluation, renegotiation, relaunch and termination. These metrics provide systematic and coherent information to the persons responsible for alliance operations, which are often not the same as the persons responsible for its formation.

Source: Segil (1998).

---

ventures operating in dynamic environments will benefit more from input (i.e. prospective) metrics. Thus performance metrics should align with not just alliance strategies (Cravens *et al.* 2000) but also alliance type, governance form and other relevant characteristics (Lunnan and Haugland 2008).

Assessments often rely on subjective evaluations of the alliance partner's satisfaction with the process and outcomes. Even if alliance managers are clear about the alliance objectives, such clarity is difficult to communicate to operational staff if the metrics are not well defined and formalized. Formalized metrics enable better coordination, legitimization, control and learning compared with ad hoc usages (Vlaar *et al.* 2007). Therefore, managers must articulate their goals, set targets and incorporate metrics into their management reports—Patzelt and Shepherd (2008) showed for example how alliances otherwise may extend beyond their productive life-time. Moreover, alliance managers should formulate reference values and targets for comparisons with actual performance metrics. Targets can be based on managerial experience, historical performance or other alliances. Subjective assessment will always have a role, but to measure complex alliance processes, it is sensible to complement it with objective measures.

A useful performance metric system addresses all these features. Performance metrics provide a way to assess the progress of an alliance over time in terms of specific activities that can be quantified in some form (see also Box 8.1). No single measure can represent all the salient aspects, so a set of measures is usually required in an effective performance metric system.

Performance metric approaches

A principal motivation for using performance metrics is the notion that only a collection of conceptually sound measures can properly align firm efforts with its objectives (Christoffersen *et al.* 2014; Kaplan *et al.* 2010). We focus on six performance approaches that together constitute the foundation for a generic performance metric system: (1) economic, (2) strategic, (3) operational, (4) learning, (5) relational and (6) responsible (see Table 8.2).

TABLE 8.2 Six performance metrics approaches

	Economic	Strategic	Operational	Learning	Relational	Responsible
Focus	Economic value	Strategic value	Operational value	Learning outcomes and processes	Relational processes	Code of conduct and societal impact
Characteristics	Easy to specify, short-term, output-oriented.	More difficult to specify, long-term, output-oriented.	Easy to specify, short-term, output- and process-oriented.	Very difficult to specify, medium-term input, output- and process-oriented.	Difficult to specify, medium-term, process-oriented.	Difficult to specify, short-term process-oriented and long-term outcome-oriented.
Indicators	Profits, costs, revenues, return on investments.	Market share, business opportunities, competitive position, risk reduction.	Operating efficiency, production times, product quality, customer retention, satisfaction.	Managerial, market, technological and product know-how, explicit and tacit knowledge exchange.	Trust, commitment, harmony, integrity, opportunism, flexibility, solidarity.	Ethical conduct, disclosing interest, gender equality, labour conditions, ecological impact.

Sources: ASAP (2022); Büchel and Thuy (2001); Segil (1998).

Economic approach

An economic approach provides insights into the economic value of the relationship and the effectiveness of the underlying business processes (Büchel and Thuy 2001). The purpose is to assess whether an alliance is increasing the economic value of the partner firms. The theoretical foundation for this economic approach is founded on the theory of financial and capital markets and involves measures such as return on investment, net yearly profit and increases in shareholder value. Economic metrics reflect the fulfilment of economic goals and enable managers to consider the value of the partnership relative to alternative arrangements. Because of their economic foundation, financial benefits are relatively easy to specify and anticipate ex ante compared with other types of metrics. Furthermore, financial metrics have a short-term time horizon and are outcome-oriented (Anderson 1990), which implies that alliance partners are more likely to anticipate immediate financial returns after the alliance is implemented. Such metrics can be captured with quantitative indicators, including profits, cost reductions, cash flows and revenues.

Under-performance on financial metrics suggests either that the alliance is not realizing its economic potential or that a partner firm is unable to appropriate its share of financial outcomes. To improve financial performance, partners should focus on underlying causes, which may relate to the alliance objectives, design or management, such as when joint product and service offerings fail to meet customer demands. The design of the alliance may hinder profit generation if the costs associated with this negotiation, alliance formation and monitoring outweigh its benefits. In terms of execution, economic under-performance may result from an under-supply of resources, wastefulness, failure to execute specific tasks or withholding of important information. If an alliance is generating economic benefits, however, an inequitable appropriation may also need to be resolved by renegotiating the alliance's compensation structure. A shift in the predetermined distribution rules (e.g. royalty fees) could result in a fairer distribution of financial outcomes.

Strategic approach

Insight into the strategic value of the relationship reflects the long-term viability of the alliance. Akin to financial metrics, a strategic approach emphasizes output criteria, though it considers outputs over a longer timeframe (Büchel and Thuy 2001). Such metrics are more difficult to specify and value because uncertainty increases the time required to achieve these objectives. The metrics offer measures of effectiveness that go beyond the exclusive use of financial metrics and target factors that, if well managed, result in superior strategic performance. They focus on the core competences that a firm possesses or wants to develop, and they seek to provide information about how much the alliance assists in this effort. Strategic metrics can be captured with both qualitative and quantitative indicators, such as new business opportunities, market share or power, reputation, competitive position, resource protection and risk reduction.

Under-performance on strategic metrics suggests that the business logic supporting the alliance is poorly developed and requires adaptation, or even termination, of the partnership. Strategic metrics may also illuminate whether a firm's competitive advantage is at risk through resource leakage. For example, a firm's counterpart could be appropriating proprietary knowhow to strengthen its core competences, or behaving opportunistically and withholding critical information to gain a strategic advantage over its counterparts, which would be explicit through the use of strategic metrics.

Operational approach

Insight into operational performance is important because it taps directly into the alliance's functioning. That is, information obtained through operational metrics provides an indication of the efficiency and effectiveness of the primary processes. An operational approach focuses on output and process criteria but differs from the economic and strategic approaches in that it consists of metrics that capture day-to-day operations. Such metrics are relatively easy to specify because they are output-oriented and can be captured by both qualitative and quantitative indicators. Contingent on the alliance objectives, metrics tapping the production process might describe product lead times, product quality or operational efficiency; marketing efforts can be measured with indicators such as customer retention, customer satisfaction and customer service.

Operational under-performance indicates that alliance partners are not sufficiently committed to making the alliance work on a daily basis. Alternatively, the alliance partners may possess insufficient operational fit, which they can deal with through interventions targeted at aligning the operational processes of the partners. In addition, firms may reconsider the division of operational tasks and adapt their management control mechanisms.

Learning approach

Whereas the first three approaches offer a diverse set of metrics, they are unsuited to capturing inter-firm learning or innovation. Alliances often provide vehicles for creating, acquiring, sharing and exploiting knowledge between partners; learning metrics take account of both learning objectives and learning processes, which support these ends (Büchel and Thuy 2001; Ryan-Charleton *et al.* 2022). Because of their medium- to long-term orientations, learning outcomes are relatively difficult to specify and value (Contractor 2001). For example, an ex-ante assessment of the value of market, technological and production know-how and managerial skills is complicated because their commercial value depends on the exploitation of such knowledge. It is thus difficult, if not impossible, to determine the amount of knowledge creation (e.g. product and market innovation)—let alone formalize parties' claims to this realized knowledge—and distribute it according to a predetermined rule. Learning metrics combine input- and output-oriented notions with a process-oriented approach, and they are best captured by qualitative indicators, such as the transfer of knowledge about production processes, marketing know-how, managerial techniques, technological know-how and product development know-how.

Learning under-performance may be attributed to a poorly designed alliance structure. For example, the initial alliance design might not enhance knowledge creation and/or enable partners to exchange knowledge. Taking the perspective of a single firm, under-performance could also signal that it is leaking valuable knowledge to a partner, without acquiring knowledge in turn. Interventions may target alliance scope in that a broader alliance scope increases opportunities to learn, whereas a narrow alliance scope limits knowledge creation and unwanted transfer. Partners may also reconsider the distribution of tasks and/or redesign their management control system. For example, shared decision making and joint tasks foster learning, but one-sided decision making and task specialization inhibit learning. Partners may invest in relational governance because high-quality working relationships facilitate inter-firm learning while also functioning as a safeguard against misappropriation.

Relational approach

Insight into relational metrics is critical; alliance partners' behaviours function as a lubricant for alliance development. To this end, a relational approach focuses on the conduct of the participants in an alliance. Rather than emphasizing output and results, it addresses behaviours and ongoing processes within the alliance (Büchel and Thuy 2001). These process-oriented metrics enable the firm to evaluate its relationship status, guided by the assumption that high-quality partner interaction patterns will support the firm's alliance success (Kale *et al.* 2000). Measuring the status of the relationship enables the firm to obtain information about its partner's behavioural disposition towards the relationship, such that the firm can take corrective actions to deal with adverse situations, including opportunistic behaviour, asymmetrical inter-partner learning and conflict (Segil 1998). Essential indicators include the development of trust, commitment, transparency, ability to deal with conflicts and harmony between the partners. Such metrics tend to be more subjective and tacit in nature, so they must be captured by qualitative indicators.

Under-performance on relational metrics suggests that partners have not developed sufficient relational norms and/or capital. A primary cause stems from the alliance negotiation and design stages. Distributive negotiation reinforced by hard negotiation tactics may produce a satisfactory negotiation outcome but damage the quality of the working relationship. Similarly, an alliance design could protect one firm's interest (e.g. task specialization) but simultaneously signal distrust to the alliance partner. Repairing damaged working relationships is difficult and demands substantial time and energy. During the alliance management stage, partner firms can demonstrate their commitment with cooperative renegotiations, proactive conflict resolution and constructive responses to adversity.

Responsible approach

Alliance arrangements are increasingly used by firms to enact their societal responsibility (Niesten and Jolink 2020; Yin and Jamali 2021). On the one hand, societal alliances address market opportunities while simultaneously generating positive societal (e.g. environmental) impacts. On the other hand, increasingly organizations include codes of conduct as part of their alliance practices (ASAP 2022). Insight into 'responsibility' metrics is critical as the behaviours and outcomes indicate the extent to which the alliance contributes to partners being socially responsible. Short-term metrics, capturing behavioural responsibility for example, would include ethical conduct, internal and external communication, and disclosing conflicting interests. Long-term metrics, capturing partner's societal impact for example, would include gender equality, ecological imprint and labour conditions. Whereas the former should be integrated into any alliance performance system, the latter could be specifically relevant to public–private partnerships (see Chapter 15) and societal alliances (see Chapter 26).

Under-performance on responsibility metrics suggests that partners are not fulfilling their societal responsibility, or at least are not aware. A cause could be that during alliance negotiation and launch, the partners did not articulate and discuss the code of conduct or conceived societal impact irrelevant (e.g. not discussing the societal ramifications of a new technology). Also, partners may ignore signals from internal and external stakeholders, for example, questioning the alliance's motives. During the alliance negotiation and design stages, the broader societal impact could be a conversational topic. In addition, imposing behavioural guidelines and creating clarity about alliance outcomes are critical tasks during alliance management. Internal and external communication are critical to inform partner firms' stakeholders.

Drawing on the similarities and differences across these six metric approaches, we suggest that together they provide a foundation for a coherent performance metric system, akin to a balanced scorecard (Kaplan *et al.* 2010). Strategic metrics focus on long-term value creation within the alliance and provide important information for various stakeholders, including top management and external parties. The long-term orientation of these metrics enables alliance managers to reconsider the alliance's design and management in light of alternative strategies and other partnerships. Financial metrics provide insights into an alliance's short-term outcomes: is the alliance contributing economic value to the firm? Operational metrics provide information about the day-to-day operations, enabling alliance managers to initiate interventions in the alliance's primary business processes. Learning metrics fulfil a two-fold function: they provide insights into the partners' ability to learn with and from each other, and they reveal the degree to which alliance partners realize their learning objectives. Relational metrics provide insight into the quality of the interpersonal and inter-partner working relationship. Responsibility metrics are critical as they capture the extent to which partners adhere to a code of conduct and/or to which the alliance arrangement effectuates the partners social responsibility. A balanced performance metric system that contains all six approaches would provide alliance managers with a comprehensive, systematic understanding of alliance progress and outcomes (see Box 8.2).

BOX 8.2 BALANCED PERFORMANCE METRICS IN THE DUTCH SHIPBUILDING INDUSTRY

The Dutch shipbuilding industry installed a performance metric programme which aims to enhance its global competitiveness. The primary objective of the programme is the continuous improvement of supply chain performance. By establishing category teams, a shipbuilder clusters all relevant functional domains in the ship-building process to align suppliers with its goals; the key objective is to prevent sub-optimization in the supply chain. A balanced set of performance indicators is used, comprising five pillars of strategic competitiveness: (1) quality, (2) logistics, (3) innovation, (4) flexibility and (5) total cost. During workshops, both the category teams and suppliers participate in designing the key performance indicators. Most key performance indicators tend to be standard, thus the development of the metric system is neither firm nor relationship-specific, ruling out possible competitive interests. Through the co-creation of performance metrics by both the shipbuilders and their suppliers, involvement improves, which offers an important advantage for implementing the change list approach throughout the supply chain. During the implementation, the standard set of performance metrics is made specific to each supplier through the creation of a supplier profile. This profile describes target performance on specific metrics across all five strategic pillars, which provides insight into the performance requests for both shipbuilder and supplier. Actual performance is then measured. The parties together determine improvements to close the gap between required and actual performance. Improvement plans and progress on specific initiatives are discussed regularly in meetings. Through an action learning approach, the performance metric system itself is evaluated regularly by the supply chain members, which results in a culture in which continuous improvement is the norm.

Alliance evaluation: decision-making steps

The main advantage of a comprehensive, balanced performance metric system is that when it is appropriately formulated, implemented and interpreted, it provides alliance partners with relevant, reliable and detailed information about alliance performance. It typically comprises several metrics, standards for performance measurement, measurement techniques, frequency and timing of measurement and reporting, and a reporting format. If metric scores deviate from expectations, partner firms may develop corrective actions to steer the alliance towards its objectives. Although the formulation and implementation of metrics may be lengthy, clear metric procedures actually accelerate alliance development rather than slowing it. However, alliance managers should seek to minimize the administrative burden involved in operating such a system by tailoring their performance metrics to each alliance. Developing and implementing a performance metric system thus consists of four consecutive stages: (1) formulating, (2) implementing, (3) interpreting and (4) assessment (see Figure 8.1).

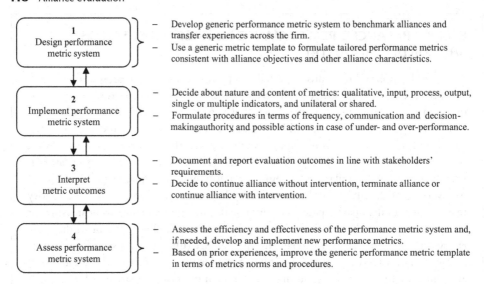

FIGURE 8.1 Decision-making steps: alliance evaluation

Step 1: design performance metric system

A systematic approach to performance metrics enables alliance partners to monitor the alliance's progress and obtain relevant, timely and frequent information that constructively improves the alliance's design and management. In contrast, an unstructured approach will lead to unreliable, inefficient performance metrics. The full burden falls on the alliance manager, who may or may not have experience designing metric systems and is likely to be preoccupied with day-to-day operations. An unstructured approach also misses opportunities to leverage experience and know-how across the firm, which may benefit its other alliances. More important, it keeps firms from comparing their performance across alliances and, thus, from engaging in active alliance portfolio management.

To overcome these issues, firms should adopt a structured approach to performance metrics, including an alliance scorecard template and illustrative metrics. The template should be repeatable, proactive and open to sharing because predetermined metric types allow firms to tailor their metrics to an alliance while still retaining the possibility of comparing performance across partnerships. In addition, guidelines regarding which metrics are most appropriate in different alliance settings are invaluable to alliance managers. Even though standardized performance metric systems require ex-ante investments, the benefits, in terms of benchmarking and learning across alliances, are likely to outweigh the costs.

Building on the performance metric template, the firm can transform its alliance approach into clear, measurable alliance goals and then match performance metrics to them. For example, if a firm aims to realize financial objectives, its performance metric system should incorporate financial metrics, which may include profitability, costs, revenues and returns on investment. If a firm seeks to realize learning objectives, the metric system may contain learning metrics, including output-oriented metrics, such as acquired market know-how, management competences and technological expertise; process-oriented metrics, such as the partner's learning ability and knowledge transfer; and prospective metrics, such as R&D spending.

In addition, a firm should consider other unique alliance characteristics. Learning alliances with exploration objectives tend to achieve superior performance according to learning and relational metrics; business alliances with exploitation objectives, on the other hand, require financial and strategic metrics. Equity-based governance forms often build financial metrics into their very design so as to achieve government approval and meet accounting laws and regulations. However, such regulations do not apply to non-equity-based governance forms, so partner firms in such alliances should build similar metrics into their systems.

Step 2: implement performance metric system

After having developed a tailored performance metric system, the firm should make several decisions in preparation for the implementation step. First, for each type of metric, it should determine the appropriate nature of the metric, and for each indicator, it should make a decision about whether prospective, outcome, process, quantitative or qualitative metrics are preferable. Financial metrics are quantitative in nature and best captured with indicators, such as profitability, that may be part of the firm's accounting system. Relational metrics are subjective in nature and therefore captured with qualitative metrics. For example, perceptual judgements might reveal the degree to which partners trust each other or behave dishonestly and opportunistically. Strategic and learning metrics might be assessed using both quantitative (e.g. market share) and qualitative (e.g. competitive strength) metrics.

Second, procedural decisions involve the frequency of assessment, communication and decision-making authority. Although a performance metric system is preferably comprehensive, partner firms may decide to use single indicators to keep the metric system manageable. That is, multiple metrics may create information overload, which hampers effective decision making. Partner firms also need to decide whether to align their metrics and engage in joint efforts to monitor the alliance, or to implement individual metric systems. Sharing information about metric assessment reduces the magnitude and nature of conflicts because partners engage in mutual sense making. However, individual metric systems may provide more necessary information regarding how to steer the alliance towards the firm's individual objectives. Alliance partners must also decide on the frequency of the evaluation; they might conduct individual assessments once per month but undertake joint assessments on a quarterly basis. Such procedural decisions thus reinforce a comprehensive performance metric system because they stimulate joint sense making, create transparency and signal a willingness to work together in the alliance.

Third, the sources of data must be determined. In many cases, data required for financial, strategic and operational metrics can be retrieved from extant systems, including project management tools and customer relationship systems owned by one partner or the other. If necessary, partners should modify their individual systems and/or build new joint systems to provide the necessary information for assessing the alliance. A questionnaire also might be circulated periodically to all staff involved in the alliance. Learning and relational metrics have a subjective element; the outcomes and processes captured may not be apparent immediately. To address this problem, staff members involved in the alliance might compile qualitative, narrative reports, preferably supplemented by quantitative metrics, although the focus is on linking outcomes directly to inputs. Checking survey and qualitative reports at different time intervals provides a proxy for whether and to what degree outcomes and processes meet their targets.

Step 3: interpret metric outcomes

During the third step, the data obtained should be processed and interpreted. After applying the metrics to an alliance, partner firms can write a report with all relevant information that contains multiple sections with different information for the various stakeholders. Top executives require aggregated information to assess the value of the alliance; operational staff need detailed information to optimize the alliance design and management. The use of reports in combination with a structured agenda and decision-making tools ensures that the information is used adequately to support dialogue, collective sense making and decisions about what to do. It is the responsibility of alliance managers (from both partners) to organize meetings and prepare the metric report.

Using the metric report and progress meetings, these managers can arrive at decisions about corrective measures. A broad range of responses and adaptations is possible, but they consist of three generic types: continue without intervention, continue with intervention and terminate the alliance. If only minimal discrepancies between expectations and actual outcomes emerge, alliance management may decide to continue the alliance in a similar fashion. In contrast, a greater discrepancy between expected and realized profitability may trigger renegotiations about the distribution of costs and revenues; an indication of partner distrust could trigger initiatives to change the management style from task focused to problem solving. If discrepancies between expectations and realized outcomes become substantial and span multiple metrics, alliance partners could decide to terminate the relationship. For example, if the alliance under-performs economically and the partners distrust each other, the preferred alternative may be termination. To anticipate these critical decisions, the alliance manager may explicate the implications of performance discrepancies ex ante, using the following guiding questions:

- What actions will be initiated if the alliance under-performs on some metrics but over-performs on others?
- Is there a minimum level of required performance on certain metrics, regardless of performance on other metrics?
- What conditions will result in the decision to terminate the alliance rather than initiating alliance adaptations (e.g. shift in alliance objectives)?
- If the alliance fulfils its objectives, what actions will be initiated?

Step 4: assess performance metric system

Conversations about the efficiency and effectiveness of the performance metric system are integral to the use of performance metrics, and if necessary, the metric system should be adapted to new circumstances. As an alliance progresses, new objectives may emerge, and assessments of the metric system could indicate the need to incorporate new metrics. Furthermore, based on the firm's experiences, the generic performance template might be improved with the addition of new or reformulated metrics and new reference targets. The procedures surrounding performance metrics also could be altered, such as by changing their frequency and improving the reporting format.

Summary

The ability of an organization to measure the health of its alliances through consistent and appropriate performance assessments is an important predictor of alliance success. Alliances that thrive tend to assess their performance using a balanced performance metric system that includes financial, strategic, operational, learning, relational and responsibility measures and that features milestones that partners can easily evaluate and track to intervene immediately if performance does not live up to expectations. Systematic monitoring also comprises outcome and process metrics that enable alliance managers to monitor alliance progress systematically and retrieve relevant, reliable and timely information to inform decision making. The incorporation of prospective indicators allows for ongoing monitoring and enables timely interventions over the alliance's progress. Although alliance performance, the value it generates and the direct and indirect benefits for individual partners are difficult to capture, balanced performance metrics systems can help alliance managers articulate, explicate and quantify objectives. Especially in situations in which goals vary among the alliance partners, developing and implementing a balanced performance metric system jointly deals preemptively with potential conflicts over alliance progress and outcomes. Armed with a performance metric system, partners can decide whether to continue the relationship and which adaptations to make, or else choose to terminate the relationship.

CASE: DBS SINGAPORE[1]

Singapore-based DBS was established in 1968. DBS wants to help its customers to 'Live More, Bank Less'. DBS believes that banking should be simple and effortless so that customers can spend more time with the people and things that they care about. DBS aims to be 'a different kind of bank for a different kind of world'. Since its inception, DBS has undertaken multiple initiatives to realize the bank's ambitions.

Between 1980–2000, DBS diversified its geographical and product portfolio. The bank launched autosave in Singapore, opened a branch in Taiwan, established a representative office in Jakarta (Indonesia), formed a formal bank branch in India, took lead of a consortium of local banks to exploit Singtel IP, acquired POSB (another Singapore bank) and launched internet banking. Between 2002 and 2010, DBS further strengthened their position in Asia. DBS acquired a 100 per cent interest in Dao Heng Bank, launched CaptaMall Trust, incorporated a fully owned local subsidiary in China, launched an industry-first banking package for social enterprises in Singapore, celebrated their 40th anniversary with a project to help the children in Asia, launched a 'money safe' guarantee for customers worried about transacting over the internet and showed their continued support for social entrepreneurship by launching their flagship community programme, 'DBS Social Enterprise Experience'.

More recently, DBS expressed an ambition to become the world's best bank. In support of this aspiration, DBS launched a new foundation to cement their commitment to social enterprises; implemented a digital transformation agenda to become the best digital bank; launched a full-service digital exchange to support fundraising; launched Digibank India, providing the first mobile-only, paperless, signatureless and branchless bank; and co-launched the Climate Impact X (CIX) initiative—an API-platform for developing solutions that will bring more convenience and value to customers and the planet. In other words, to deliver on their promise, DBS reimagined banking, refusing to be bounded by conventional notions of what a bank should be. DBS is guided by a responsibility towards society and the planet.

Enacting this responsibility, among other initiatives, DBS forged multiple alliances in 2022. DBS has inked a partnership with Sandbox to extend its banking experience into the metaverse. The metaverse experience will be an additional engagement platform for customers visiting the Sandbox. The project consists of a virtual world that is being named DBS BetterWorld, which will be freely available to all members of the public, even to non-customers. In the words, of Sandbox co-founder Sebastien Borget:

> We welcome DBS to The Sandbox as the first bank in Singapore to step into the open metaverse and join our efforts to create the SingaporeVerse, a neighbourhood on our virtual map that will bring the culture of Singapore to life in the metaverse in a very engaging, equitable, inclusive way that is open to all.

Interestingly, Sandbox forged multiple partnerships with financial institutions. In 2022, Standard Chartered bank also teamed up with The Sandbox to create its first metaverse experience. Expanding its offer to (social) enterprises, DBS launched five new platform partnerships featuring the integration of digital and supply-chain capabilities, which are expected to benefit 15,000 small and medium enterprises (SMEs) in Asia. Participating SMEs will benefit from the digital platforms as it will provide them with access to e-commerce, logistics and commodities, amongst others. Reinforcing its societal responsibility aspiration, DBS bank established a partnership with Terrascope. Terrascope is a smart carbon measurement and management platform. By bringing together the ecosystem of real economy stakeholders, financial institutions, reporting platforms and sustainability consultants around a common software platform, Terrascope enables the collaboration between internal teams and external expertise needed for enterprises to translate high-level targets into specific decarbonization action plans.

Together, the partners aim at timely and accurate carbon emissions measurement and management to better assess the bankability of clients and accelerate sustainable financing flows in Singapore and other markets in which DBS Bank operates. As stated by Yulanda Chung (Head of Sustainability at Institutional Banking Group, DBS Bank):

> DBS is committed to achieving scale without compromising the integrity of sustainable finance. Terrascope will help our customers gain a more accurate and comprehensive picture of their carbon footprint, and enable DBS to provide financing to advance their decarbonisation journeys.

DBS also forged a partnership with the National Environment Agency (NEA), a project named the 'Hungry for Change Challenge', which is a nationwide zero food waste challenge to inspire and empower youth from Institutes of Higher Learning. As food waste is one of the huge waste streams in Singapore, accounting for about 12 per cent of the total waste generated in Singapore, the aim of this partnership is to leverage the creativity and energy of Singapore's youth, aiming to engage students in a nationwide competition to ideate, develop and implement impactful solutions to reduce food waste while developing their environmental leadership capabilities. In the words of Karen Ngui (Group Head of Strategic Marketing and Communications at DBS, and Board Member of DBS Foundation):

> Empowering youth and providing opportunities to develop and implement innovative zero food waste solutions is a powerful way to promote sustainability in everyday living. We look forward to partnering NEA and creating greater impact

together in this multi-year programme. It is a privilege to support the next generation in efforts to accelerate and help achieve Singapore's ambition to be a Zero Waste Nation by 2030.

Questions

1   Considering the DBS strategy, what would be appropriate indicators to measure the performance of all alliance arrangements?
2   Considering the four alliance arrangements separately, what would be appropriate indicators to measure alliance performance?
3   Based on the selected indicators, what would an alliance performance dashboard look like, and what interventions could be considered to improve alliance success?

Note

1   Business Times (2022); Cryptoslate (2022); DBS (2022a, 2022b); Globenewswire (2022b); NEA (2022); SBR (2022).

9

ALLIANCE TERMINATION

Because alliance termination is an intrinsic part of the alliance lifecycle, it must be managed actively. Alliances by definition are temporary organizational arrangements, which means alliance management should focus not only on their formation and management but also on their conclusion or termination. Termination creates a complicated burden for alliance managers, who must dismantle financial and organizational relationships, recover alliance-specific investments, value and redistribute tangible and intangible assets, and safeguard their firm against damage to its reputation. Yet many managers still get caught off guard by the prospect of termination and are ill-prepared to deal with the tensions and uncertainties associated with (premature) alliance dissolution. The objective of the alliance termination stage is to organize an exit that offers favourable outcomes to all parties, while simultaneously considering the complexity of the process in terms of key actions and stakeholders, the social and economic costs, and its speed and ease. To inform decision making about alliance termination, the first section suggests that managers should distinguish different types of termination, which enables them to plan the termination during the preceding alliance development stages (shown in the second section). The following sections provide a systematic framework with a set of four decision-making steps for alliance termination and a summary before the chapter concludes with a case illustration.

Alliance termination types, trajectories and motives

An enduring alliance seemingly offers a valid proxy for alliance success, whereas termination is associated with failure. However, this view of termination ignores common situations, such as those in which firms form short-term alliances to achieve specific or immediate goals and then deliberately end them once the alliances fulfil their purposes or reach a pre-set date. Of course, alliance failure may also result when alliances do not or cease to achieve their goals, objectives and/or performance expectations. In this case, alliance termination refers to the dissolution of the relationship because one or more partners withdraws. Before detailing their trajectories, it therefore is important to elaborate on the varied alliance termination types.

DOI: 10.4324/9781003222187-9

Types of alliance termination

Many extant studies inaccurately equate alliance termination with failure and alliance longevity with success (Makino *et al.* 2007; Nemeth and Nippa 2013; Park and Russo 1996). However, we propose that alliance termination could be considered a success when the relationship is ended intentionally, whereas failure relates to unintended termination. An alliance termination is intended and occurs because the initial alliance purposes have been achieved, the aim for which the relationship was established no longer exists, the alliance goals have been met, or the contract date is due. An unintended termination may come about before partner firms achieve the initial purposes of the alliance, in which case the performance expectations have not been met (Reuer and Zollo 2005). Unintended termination also may occur after the alliance has realized its initial purpose, in the sense that the alliance might have continued even though it had ceased to produce value (Patzelt and Shepherd 2008).

Alternatively, alliance termination can be defined as a change in structure, such as when partners switch governance modes (i.e. make, buy or ally) or forms (i.e. non-equity or equity-based) (Makino *et al.* 2007). Some partners internalize alliance activities and acquire complete control, such as when one partner takes over a joint venture and turns it into a wholly owned subsidiary. Other partners divest themselves of alliance activities, perhaps by selling them to their counterpart or through liquidation (Hennart *et al.* 1998). Furthermore, firms may seek new alliance partners or forge new alliances with the same partners. If a firm chooses to take an equity share in its partner, it turns a non-equity-based arrangement into an equity arrangement. In all these situations, the original agreement ceases to exist, but because firms often adopt alternative strategies to realize their performance objectives, the alliance termination does not necessarily constitute failure, especially if the change is in line with the long-term objectives of at least one partner (Peng and Shenkar 2002).

Termination trajectories

Over its trajectory, an alliance termination disconnects former alliance partners by cutting their active links, resource ties and employee bonds. Their business exchanges also start to decline with weaker resource ties. However, interactions in terms of communication, coordination and adaptation may intensify temporarily because firms must adjust to the decline in their exchange activities, as well as negotiating the contract disengagement, proprietary rights and final invoices. These termination discussions often require a great deal of time and considerable adaptations by both parties. The complexity of such disengagement trajectories reflects the status of alliances as strategic and economic arrangements embedded in social relationships; the combination may determine the degree to which partners perceive the termination process and its outcomes favourably (Giller and Matear 2001).

When an alliance is dissolved at a pre-set date or has fulfilled its initial purpose, partners tend to accommodate each other's exit. They agree to the end; therefore, the relatively easy termination trajectory should result in favourable termination outcomes. This natural ending integrates decisions by all parties in the relationship, such that their interests are likely to be taken into account (Halinen and Tahtinen 2002). Even if the alliance termination is unexpected, partners may agree to dissolve the relationship, which reduces any adverse impact of potential conflicts. Rather, the partners tend to facilitate the disintegration of financial and organizational relationships, as well as the recovery of alliance-specific investments and the redistribution of valuable knowledge and resources. The negative impact on the firm's reputation thus is limited.

In contrast, unilateral, unintended termination tends to create tension and conflict. Without mutual involvement, the one-sided decision gets forced onto other parties because the alliance partners do not share the conviction that ending the relationship is in the best interest of everyone. Terminating relationships in these conditions may require a lengthy, expensive process with high risk. The firms involved might be forced to buy out stakes, possibly at a significant premium, pay switching fees or expend significant amounts to safeguard their interests and resources. Moreover, a unilateral ending provides the terminating partner with an advantage because it can prepare for its disengagement in advance (e.g. act opportunistically, exploit alliance-specific investments) before its counterpart can react. However, such a firm would be likely to suffer reputation damages, limiting its access to future alliance relationships. Unilateral exits also impose the risk of conflict escalation and may require arbitration by an outside party.

In some cases, partner disagreements about alliance termination resort to litigation. If one alliance partner violates the alliance contract, the disadvantaged firm may consider a court battle its best alternative. However, litigation means greatly increased termination costs: hiring lawyers, consulting with legal experts and paying for other legal and court costs. In addition, the outcomes of legislative processes are inherently uncertain, and a final decision may be pending for years. Accordingly, many firms turn to voluntary arbitration, using a mediator or independent third party to resolve their conflicts. A mediation procedure offers flexibility and tends to result in tailored solutions, which are rarely feasible through litigation. The use of an outside third party suggests that partners agree ex ante to comply with the provided solutions. Mediation is thus preferable to litigation, for both its time and its cost savings. Mediation procedures also tend to be confidential, so they have limited adverse impacts on the partners' reputations, whereas the probability of favourable termination outcomes increases.

BOX 9.1 THE SKOLTECH PROJECT

The Massachusetts Institute of Technology (MIT) has forged partnerships with partners in countries with repressive governments—including China, Singapore and the United Arab Emirates—as an attempt to use the power of education to modernize. As part of this ambition, in 2011, MIT forged a partnership with the Skolkovo Institute of Science and Technology, also known as the Skoltech project. The main objective of this project was to help build on the western outskirts of Moscow a multi-billion-dollar version of Silicon Valley. According to Professor Reif,

> The programme sprang from a particular historical moment. In 2011, the United States was striving to 'reset' its Russia relationship. At the same time, Russia was seeking to establish an innovation-based economy, and MIT faculty were eager to create new research alliances in areas of shared interest with top colleagues around the world, including Russia, a nation with a pool of exceptional scientific talent.

MIT's work in that direction included extensive efforts at recruiting and sharing students and faculty. In 2019, the agreement was extended with another five years. This was because the partnership served positive societal purpose, even though Russian governmental policies were not supported by MIT. In 2022, however, MIT decided to end this (controversial) decade-long partnership as a protest against the Russian invasion of Ukraine. MIT made the following statement: 'We take it with deep regret because of our great respect for the Russian people and our profound appreciation for the contributions of the many extraordinary Russian colleagues we have worked with'. The emerging reality led to calls throughout Western higher education to reassess and cut off ties to Russia and its people.

Source: Basken (2022).

Motives for premature alliance termination

Although an alliance might end upon pre-set contract dates or objective attainment, reports indicate that 30–90 per cent of alliances are actually dissolved prematurely (Inkpen and Beamish 1997; Makino *et al.* 2007; Park and Ungson 1997). A firm remains in an alliance as long as it perceives the situation as an efficient and equitable organizational form for its purposes (Dan and Zondag 2016). On the one hand, a firm may end an alliance when it creates insufficient value because the firm perceives that it could appropriate more value through an alternative arrangement form. On the other hand, performance differentials between alliance partners could lead a firm to end an alliance when it is not appropriating a fair share of the created value relative to its contribution. In general then, the reasons for premature alliance termination consist of three sets of factors: (1) structural deficiencies, (2) process deficiencies and (3) (unforeseen) external circumstances.

During the alliance formation stage, firms establish alliances to achieve their objectives, select a partner, engage in negotiation and formalize the initial alliance design. A firm may have selected a partner with poor fit, which increases the probability of opportunistic behaviour, knowledge spillovers and goal conflicts (Douma *et al.* 2000), which then foster alliance instability and eventually dissolution. Park and Russo (1996) find that alliances between direct competitors are more likely to fail. Distributive alliance negotiations also increase the risk of dissolution because firms impose unrealistic demands on their counterparts (Rao and Schmidt 1998), and even if such negotiations reach a satisfactory conclusion, they tend to reduce long-term commitment. The alliance structure might offer insufficient coordination or protection against exchange hazards, which also increases the risk of premature alliance termination. For example, unfavourable termination outcomes are more likely if research alliances, which require strong protection against knowledge leakage, are governed by a non-equity arrangement (Reuer and Zollo 2005).

During the execution stages, parties need to focus on managing alliance processes, such that neglecting to invest in relational and learning processes could undermine alliance continuity. For example, relational norms reinforced by a high-quality, trust-based working relationship tend to mitigate the adverse implications of poor economic performance on partners' inclination to end the relationship (Ariño and de la Torre 1998). In addition, alliance studies reveal that learning races by firms that compete to acquire each other's knowledge (Hamel 1991) and the convergence of partners' capabilities over time (Nakamura *et al.* 1996) both adversely affect alliance continuity. Thus mismanaging a partner's learning intentions and outcomes may trigger premature alliance termination (Doz 1996). Taking an economic-resource perspective, Madhok and colleagues (2015) suggest that as the alliance progresses, resources undergo transformation, and this transformation generates new adjustment costs, which, depending on the incentive asymmetry between partners, may cause a change in ownership of resources or a complete dissolution of the alliance.

Beyond structural and process deficiencies, alliance studies have indicated that (unforeseen) external circumstances can trigger dissolution. Dan and Zondag (2016), for example, report that perceptions of higher future returns reduces the probability of alliance termination, but they also demonstrate that the probability of termination is increased by high levels of technological intensity and high market density during alliance formation. Greve *et al.* (2013) investigate alliance withdrawal in the global liner shipping industry and report that, controlling for internal tensions in the alliance, the availability of outside options predicts withdrawal from a relationship; alternative availability reduces the value of an existing arrangement. Changes in the broader environment, such as shifts in foreign direct investment policies or new technologies, may also make the alliance obsolete (Makino *et al.* 2007). According to Kogut (1989), changing partner rivalry, due to shifts in industry concentration, increases the likelihood of joint venture dissolution. Changes within the partner firms' organization can have similar effects (Koza and Lewin 1998). For example, internal reorganization, changing corporate strategies, new resource needs, a weaker financial position or new members on the board of directors may prompt firms to terminate.

Thus research has identified a plethora of factors across levels of analysis that might explain premature alliance termination. (See also Table 9.1 for an overview of theoretical

TABLE 9.1 Theoretical perspectives and alliance termination

Theory	Underlying logic	Rationales for termination
Transaction cost economics	Alliance formation if transaction costs are lower compared to other governance modes.	Unexpected (high) transaction costs, resulting from coordination problems, appropriation hazards and opportunism induce alliance exit.
Organizational learning	Alliance formation to the end of knowledge creation, transfer and exploitation.	Insufficient learning, learning races, lack of knowledge creation and insufficient knowledge appropriation induce alliance exit.
Institutional theory	Alliance formation as a way to gain legitimacy, often in response to external pressures.	Lack of internal or external legitimacy triggers undersupply of resources and insufficient management attention, which bring alliance exit.
Resource-based view	Alliance formation if joint resource combinations are likely to generate superior value.	Partner's failure to supply resources, resources becoming obsolete and one-sided appropriation of resources induce alliance exit.
Network perspective	Alliance formation as a way to obtain access to a repository of resources and information.	Misalignment between network strategy and network position, unsanctioned acts and lack of value creation induce alliance exit.
Social exchange theory	Alliance continuation depends on commitment and on the quality of the relationship.	Conflicts between alliance partners erodes trust and diverts efforts from critical tasks, which brings alliance exit.

Source: Adapted from Nemeth and Nippa (2013).

perspectives and alliance termination.) We suggest, however, that decisions and (in)action by alliance managers at various points during the alliance development stages constitute the main sources. Managers therefore should be advised to prepare a termination trajectory to prevent costly separations and avoid the risk of losing valuable assets due to opportunistic advances by partners to appropriate value at the expense of both counterparts and the alliance. Irrespective of the type of ending, a clear and systematic termination plan is required from the outset.

Planning alliance termination

Although alliance termination is the last stage in the alliance development framework, attention to it should be a priority in the preceding alliance development stages. Such attention often seems contradictory in the honeymoon stages of the alliance. Enamoured of each other and what they can do together, new partners rarely consider breaking up (Gulati *et al.* 2008), leading them to accept vague terms and conditions and develop a false sense of agreement. During the alliance design and negotiation stages, alliance managers should instead take some time to think about the uncertainties that lie ahead and their consequences for the relationship. In addition, as the alliance unfolds, effective evaluations can issue early warnings, provide sufficient time to initiate corrections and avoid premature dissolution.

During the alliance strategy formulation stage, firms should mark out the path for its failure (Wittmann 2007). For example, prematurely formed alliances that represent simply responses to competitors' actions increase the likelihood of premature dissolution. When top management sees competitors forging alliances, they may tend to seek out their own portfolio of alliances, such that the alliance becomes a goal rather than a means to realize performance objectives. Without alliance prioritization strategies, alliance termination also becomes more likely. Rather, firms need to prioritize alliances and allocate resources based on their propensity to contribute to their competitive advantage. The specific prioritization (e.g. strategic, tactical, operational) should match the counterpart's prioritization. Finally, ambiguous performance expectations can foster premature termination. Without performance targets, it is impossible to determine whether the alliance is creating value or simply draining resources.

During the alliance partner selection stage, firms begin screening potential partners. Choosing the right partners based on good partner fit is critical for alliance continuity (Douma *et al.* 2000), but blind spots that fall outside the primary evaluation criteria may also lead to premature alliance termination. The identification of wasteful and surplus resources and their impact on alliance development constitute particularly pertinent hazards. For example, when a firm over-commits its resources to the alliance, managers develop varying perceptions of the equitable distribution of value because they are likely to count both utilized and unutilized resources in their calculations, whereas partners view any surplus and wasteful resources as insignificant with regard to value. These disparate views on value distribution will increase alliance instability. More objective reflection, or taking the partner's perspective, may help managers sharpen their partner selection skills to such an extent that they provide a solid foundation for the collaborative scheme.

The alliance termination planning in the alliance negotiation and design stages preferably entails a broad set of contingency-based exit provisions in the alliance contract to support a well-structured exit. Exit provisions pertain to the conditions in which partners may dissolve the relationship unilaterally, the costs involved in doing so, and the conflict resolution and exit procedures (Gulati *et al.* 2008). A clear and mutually agreed set of exit provisions and the ex-post conditions for activating them can help prevent devastating and opportunistic behaviour, should the alliance need to be terminated. Partners also should work to make the exit easy rather than imposing legal constraints on counterparts. Gulati *et al.* (2008) suggest that symmetric provisions (i.e. no penalties) allow for a smooth exit by both partners because they both can end the relationship without substantial termination costs and then attempt to achieve their objectives through alternative means. Such symmetric exit provisions also are comparatively easier to enforce when all partners involved face substantial termination costs and the alliance is progressing successfully. Another tactic, the buy-out premium, can trigger firms to continue an alliance until it has realized its initial objectives. However, the stipulation of easy exit provisions for only one partner offers no rationale for either partner to avoid jeopardizing their joint value creation. Yet such asymmetric exit provisions may be required if the alliance features dependence asymmetry. The dependent partner is always more exposed to the negative consequences of alliance termination than the independent partner, so inhibiting the latter's exit by imposing an asymmetrical exit provision provides a safety buffer for the dependent partner. In addition, exit provisions should detail situations in which one partner breaches the contract. If in violation, the partner should be penalized accordingly, and specific contractual elements in the alliance contract should stipulate procedures and timelines, and guide partners in any situations in which contract violations are ambiguous. Asymmetric exit provisions should also apply when a firm ends a relationship because it has changed its corporate strategy. If partners are engaged in an alliance and their strategies diverge, they may suffer alliance tensions and disrupted collaborative processes. In this situation, termination blockades result from transition costs. For example, the remaining firm should be compensated if its counterpart unilaterally ends the relationship.

In formulating exit provisions, alliance partners should realize that easy exit provisions provide flexibility, but this free opportunity to exist also could stimulate opportunistic behaviour. In unstable relationships that either partner could exit at any time, neither partner is willing to make relationship-specific investments. Yet challenging exit provisions, even though they signal long-term commitment and can enhance relationship building, pose the risk that partners become locked in to an alliance that is no longer providing value. Finally, irrespective of their nature, exit provisions should be agreed on and embodied in the alliance contract at the outset. However, even with great detail, no alliance contract can capture all unforeseen contingencies, so too much time spent formulating a complete contract might be wasteful or scare away a potential partner. Instead, partners should develop clear consensus performance metrics, monitor them as the alliance progresses and tie the exit provisions to these metrics.

In the alliance management stage, the available alliance contract might include alliance termination provisions—or not. Seldom do alliance managers take part in the preceding negotiations, so they have no insight into the contingencies that led to the specific provisions or ownership of the alliance termination provisions. In general, then, alliance managers should participate early in the alliance formation process so that they gain some ownership of the alliance agreement and the termination provisions. However, as Gulati and colleagues (2008) realize, fierce negotiations can damage relational quality among alliance managers. Instead of active participation, the emphasis should be on involving these alliance managers through active communication. Then the managers can increase the likelihood of a smooth exit by investing their time and effort in building relational norms and capital. When confronted with alliance termination, a good working relationship mitigates conflict because partners expect fair, harmonious communication. These post-formation processes are thus critical for organizing alliance endings with favourable outcomes.

Through alliance evaluation, firms can prepare for alliance termination in several ways. Systematic performance evaluations provide information about outcome and process discrepancies, which informs managers about alliance status (Kumar and Nti 1998). A firm will be well equipped for the future if it remains constantly alert to internal and external events that might threaten alliance continuity. Attending to less noticeable exit communication strategies, such as reduced contacts and investments, enable the partner to determine the danger of break up and take actions to repair the relationship. For example, it may proactively commission legal experts to assess exit provisions or make unilateral investments to demonstrate commitment. A balanced performance metric system enables the firm to anticipate a partner's intention to end the relationship, then prepare an adequate response and economize on termination costs.

Alliance termination: decision-making steps

For the effective management of alliances, managers should know not only how to establish and maintain alliances but also how to end them. Termination costs demand that alliance managers carefully plan and execute their alliance exits. Alliances tend to involve intensive, complex structures that tap the internal organizations of the alliance partners. Their termination therefore requires particular effort and attention from management. Alliance managers might consider a four-step trajectory for a smooth exit: (1) assessment and initiation, (2) dyadic communication, (3) disengagement and (4) aftermath (see Figure 9.1).

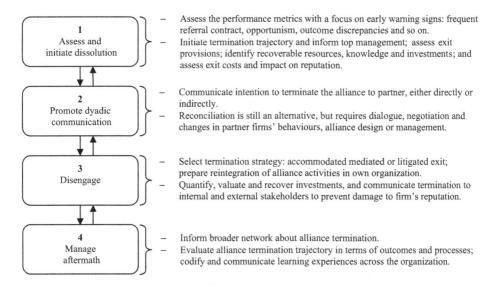

FIGURE 9.1 Decision-making steps: alliance termination

Step 1: assess and initiate dissolution

During the assessment and initiation steps, a partner firm evaluates the alliance, its future and how it might end. We have previously elaborated on the importance of a balanced performance metric system because it alerts managers to early warning signs and symptoms associated with deteriorating relationships. For example, frequent references to alliance contracts, in particular their exit provisions, signal trouble in the relationship. A metric system also details progress towards the initial alliance objectives and thus the appropriate course of action for managers. Because termination is a last resort, managers should assess the conditions creating the current situation and determine whether they might change them. But if the firm perceives the alliance is not as successful as expected, no longer fits with its long-term objectives, includes too many differences between the partners, has realized its objectives or has reached its pre-set ending date, it needs to end. If the termination is unintended, relationship repair through corrective measures could still be viable; however, repeated failed attempts to modify behaviours imply that the relationship is unsalvageable. In this case, the following steps are necessary:

- Inform top management about the intention to end the alliance.
- Intensify monitoring (of partner) to explicate and substantiate rationales behind termination intentions.
- Organize assessment of (contingency) exit provisions by legal experts. Alliance contracts often contain several exit provisions, such that a given clause gets activated in specific situations. Which exit provisions apply to the current situation, and what are its implications in terms of property rights, penalties and so forth?
- Obtain an overview of resources deployed in the alliance and the degree to which they are recoverable.
- Assess the impact of the alliance termination on the internal organization, including required organizational adaptations, transfer of staff and reputation.
- Prepare strategic analyses to organize alliance activities through alternative arrangements, including internalization, merger and acquisition, market exchange or new alliance partners.

Step 2: promote dyadic communication

During the dyadic communication step, a firm communicates the intention to terminate the alliance to the partner. Depending on the quality of the working relationship and the alliance infrastructure, a partner may communicate directly or indirectly. In a disguised exit, the firm hopes to end the alliance but hides its real intentions to coerce the partner into doing the terminating. For example, it might increase the partner's costs so much that it is forced to end the relationship. In a silent exit, the partners achieve an implicit understanding about the ending. Such exits are advised only if the firm realistically anticipates losing vital resources if it notifies its partner of its true intentions. However, in a revocable exit, the disengaging firm notes its willingness to alter its termination decision after a joint discussion. Depending on the communication style and the quality of the working relationship, partners could reach agreement through communication that repairs the relationship. Finally, a firm may communicate its intention to exit directly, presented as a final and irrevocable decision. If some relational capital has built up, most firms notify their partners of their intention prior to the actual exit. At this point, the partners might opt for a chosen termination, in which they agree jointly to end the alliance, or instead engage in a forced ending, in which one partner imposes its decision on the other. This critical distinction affects the likelihood of conflict, although regardless of how they get there, partners next enter the disengagement stage.

Step 3: disengage

The disengagement step often starts concurrently with the dyadic communication step, and induces a fundamental transition in the partners' definition of the relationship. Resource exchange and communication start to decline, and ties begin to weaken. Depending on the quality of the established termination provisions, negotiations may be required to determine the contract end, final invoices, copyrights or intellectual property rights. Disengagement discussions often require time and considerable adaptations by both parties, though if the procedures, terms and conditions already have been agreed on, the process is more predictable and smoother. Some critical issues include the following:

- Quantification and valuation of unilateral and bilateral alliance-specific investments, proprietary knowledge and resources and other resource commitments. Tangible assets and resources are relatively easy to value, but most alliance managers find it difficult to value the in- and outflow of resources and value from and to counterparts. Alliance managers should move beyond the boundaries of the alliance to consider the impact on their firms' other lines of business too.
- Preparation to reintegrate resources and alliance activities into the organization. For example, firms may reorganize internal decision making; relocate staff; realign financial, human resources and operational systems; or redistribute released resources and knowledge.
- Depending on the disengagement process, the need to communicate to internal and external stakeholders that the alliance is about to end. Adequate and timely information is important to limit the possible adverse impact on partner firms' reputations, which strike the path for future alliances.

The alliance disengagement step reveals the level of difficulty of ending the relationship. An uncontested termination suggests the alliance partners do not blame each other but rather acknowledge changed circumstances or needs as the cause. In contrast, a contested termination indicates that one partner refuses to dissolve the alliance, despite its counterpart's desire to do so. It thus appears that alliance managers can follow one of three disengagement trajectories:

1 Accommodated exit: the alliance partners agree that termination is in order and emerging issues and conflicts, if applicable, are resolved using pre-specified procedures.
2 Mediated exit: the alliance partners tend to disagree on alliance termination issues but can reconcile their conflicts. Firms voluntarily submit other conflicts to an independent third party to accelerate the end of the alliance.
3 Litigated exit: the alliance partners fiercely disagree on alliance termination, and conflicts are irreconcilable. Firms, voluntarily or involuntarily, resort to arbitration and litigation to enforce alliance termination.

Each ending has different implications for alliance termination outcomes and processes. The complexity, in terms of conflict resolution and people involved, increases from accommodated exit to litigated exit. Thus internal conflict procedures specifying the time and management level needed to resolve conflicts are sufficient to guide an accommodated exit, whereas a litigated exit demands more time, energy and resources. The termination costs, both economic and social, vary from minimal for accommodated exit to moderate and substantial for mediated and litigated exit, respectively. Uncertainty, procrastination and complexity also tend to increase when alliance partners prefer a litigated exit to mediated and accommodated exits. However, some circumstances (e.g. persistent conflicts, hostility) may make an accommodated exit impossible and a litigated exit unavoidable.

Step 4: manage aftermath

In the aftermath, all resource and personal ties have been disconnected. The partners need an ex-post facto account of the relationship break-up to disseminate, both within the firm and to involved external parties. With this account, the partners can build their alliance capabilities and protect their reputations. Learning from alliance termination, particularly failure, is very important to firms entering into new alliance negotiations; after a failure, many firms tend to be conservative and cautious, seeking better protection. They may also be less likely to trust other parties, or demand more contractual provisions and extensive monitoring. Such excessive controls can increase protection but also jeopardize an alliance before it begins. Through network communications, alliance partners can also inform other parties in the broader network about their efforts, which should reinforce their existing relationships and attract prospective new partners. Thus ex-partners should consider the consequences of their break-up.

Careful planning and execution of the termination process should also acknowledge that termination is not necessarily unavoidable; there are ample opportunities for reconciliation. Yet as dissolution tends to become the primary process, these opportunities diminish rapidly over time. For example, initial monitoring of alliance progress focuses on alliance continuation, but once they enter the process of termination, partners are likely to focus on dissimilarities and discrepancies that prompt termination. Moreover, a public announcement makes the chances of reconciliation and relationship repair slim.

Summary

Unlike extant alliance termination literature that tends to equate termination with alliance failure, we have presented a more fine-grained view: alliance termination can be intended or unintended. An intended termination is in order when the alliance has fulfilled its initial purpose or reached a pre-set termination date. Unintended termination instead indicates that the alliance ends before realizing its objectives or is ended long after it ceased to produce value. In addition, alliance termination may result from structural changes in the alliance governance, such that a plethora of internal deficiencies and external contingencies can prompt alliance termination. Termination suggests some erroneous managerial (in)action, so we also have argued that preparing for alliance termination starts during the alliance strategy formulation stage and proceeds during subsequent stages. Salient issues that managers need to consider include type of termination, termination trajectories, termination planning, the necessity for exit provisions, the importance of relational norms and capital, and continuous monitoring. To guide alliance managers through the complexities surrounding termination, we presented a four-step termination trajectory.

CASE: NOKIA–MICROSOFT[1]

With the introduction of the iPhone in 2007, a revolution took place in the mobile phone industry. With a new user interface and the revolutionary approach of creating an ecosystem to support the phone's functionality through apps, Apple not only took the rest of the industry by surprise but also set a new standard for competition in the mobile industry. In particular, Nokia's leading position in the mobile market, both from a mobile software perspective (Symbian) and a hardware perspective, was endangered. The company rapidly lost ground to Apple, and later to Google from a software perspective thanks to Android, and to Samsung from a hardware perspective.

When Steven Elop, CEO of Nokia, announced the partnership with Microsoft in 2011, it was believed that this would provide Nokia with the opportunity to become competitive again and grow as a smartphone manufacturer. However, by 2013—a little over two years after signing the alliance agreement—the alliance was terminated through the acquisition of Nokia's Devices and Services business by Microsoft. According to Steve Ballmer, CEO of Microsoft, this was 'a bold step into the future—a win–win for employees, shareholders, and consumers of both companies'. However, since that moment, it has been a tragic ride for Nokia; many thousands of employees have been laid off, smartphone production decreased over the years and finally Microsoft wrote off the entire investment in Nokia in an impairment charge. Microsoft abandoned the name Nokia, and everything that was left is being converged in the Microsoft Surface team. The collaboration with Microsoft has been destructive for a company that reigned over the mobile markets for years.

The Finnish company Nokia was founded in 1865 as a ground wood pulp mill and grew to become a global corporation with a prominent position in the global telecommunications industry. The company was able to establish its leading position through easy-to-use phones aimed at individual consumers and businesses. However, the telecommunications industry changed dramatically in 2007 with the introduction of Apple's iPhone. The iPhone revolutionized customer experience and created a market shift. In 2008, Google introduced its open-source Android operating system, which further disrupted the mobile landscape.

During the late 2000s, Nokia was using its own operating system called 'Symbian'; however, it lacked the sleek user experience provided by iPhone and was generally regarded as outdated and old-fashioned. Also Microsoft—which was using Microsoft Mobile platform—was outperformed by the new competitors. Next, Microsoft was taken by surprise when Apple launched the iPad. Both Nokia and Microsoft saw their market shares decreasing steadily, losing it to their new competitors, which outclassed both companies. Both companies realized that this situation could not be sustained for a prolonged period of time.

After the introduction of the iPhone and Android, Nokia began focusing on revitalizing its mobile business. In August 2009, Nokia and Microsoft announced their first step of a strategic partnership by ensuring the porting of Microsoft Office Mobile and Office Communicator to Nokia's Symbian devices (Smart Phones) initially, and then to Nokia's Series 40 devices (Feature Phones). This was followed by a vast array of other Microsoft Office products. The key Microsoft executive sponsor for this initiative was Stephen Elop, then president of Microsoft's business division. In February 2010, Nokia partnered with Intel to develop an entirely new Linux-based platform called MeeGo. This partnership produced the Nokia N9, which used MeeGo as its operating system. However, it took more than two years to develop the Nokia N9, by which time iOS and Android had already secured dominant market positions.

In early 2011, Nokia's new CEO Stephen Elop delivered a 'burning platform' speech to the Nokia employees in which he illustrated that the industry landscape had changed. Instead of device-based competition, the standard had become an ecosystem-based competition. In this, business ecosystems—constellations of hardware and software providers, application developers, social platform partners, etc.—drive industry competition and dynamics. This speech paved the way for the alliance with Microsoft.

Microsoft was looking for ways to re-enter the mobile market. It had developed a new operating system, Windows Phone 7, that had been received reasonably well by critics in 2010, but Microsoft's challenge was to close the gap with its competitors. Although Microsoft forged distribution deals with LG, Samsung and Sony Ericsson, it required a major manufacturer to further commoditize its operating system.

On 11 February 2011, Nokia and Microsoft announced a strategic (contractual) partnership. The main objective of this partnership was to develop a new global mobile ecosystem for smartphones utilizing the Windows platform. This was to be supported by increasing the manufacturing power of Windows smartphones based on the manufacturing capabilities of Nokia. Instead of the Apple strategy of having a single device strategy (the iPhone), Microsoft opted for a strategy in which the Microsoft platform would be available on numerous phones. Therefore, the enlargement of the product portfolio and increased global availability were specific objectives of the alliance.

In April 2011, Nokia and Microsoft signed a definitive agreement. Nokia and Microsoft agreed to exploit their complementary assets to design, develop and market productivity solutions for mobile devices for professionals. Nokia would deliver mapping, navigation and certain location-based services to the Windows Phone system. It would build innovation on top of the Windows Phone platform in areas such as imaging, while also contributing expertise on hardware design and language support, and helping to drive the development of the Windows Phone platform. Microsoft would provide Bing search services across the Nokia device portfolio, as well as contributing strength in productivity, advertising, gaming, social media and a variety of other services. The combination of navigation with advertising and search functions offered opportunities to improve customer value propositions. Through joint developing and the active sourcing of applications, Nokia and Microsoft intended to increase the number of applications. Also, the partners agreed to open a new Nokia-branded global application store that would leverage the Windows Marketplace infrastructure. Nokia was expected to contribute its operator billing system expertise to allow participants of the Windows Phone ecosystem to take advantage of Nokia's billing agreements with numerous operators in more than 30 markets worldwide.

The partnership agreement also contained multiple contractual provisions regarding the financial pay-off. Microsoft would receive a running royalty for the Windows Mobile platform. This fee took into account the predicted volume of phones and joint collaborative efforts, as well as the engineering work done by both companies, with a minimum guaranteed yearly base payment. Although Nokia was not granted exclusivity, the provision would allow Nokia to customize the Windows Phone operating system to differentiate its smartphones from competitor offerings that were also using Windows Phone, such as Samsung, LG and Sony Ericsson. In return, Microsoft would pay Nokia for its contribution to the development of the Microsoft platform and other Microsoft services. Microsoft would also pay Nokia for the right to use its intellectual property, which enabled Nokia to reduce operating expenses. This was covered in the 'platform support payment' of US$250 million that was paid by Microsoft on a quarterly basis.

The partnership agreement also contained a clause related to the division of tasks and co-branding. The companies also reached agreement on Nokia's collaboration with Intel. This would become a long-term open-source project along with Symbian, which would be used on mid-range Nokia phones. Furthermore, Nokia agreed to restructure its organization into two distinct business units: Smart Devices and Mobile Phones. Smart Devices includes Windows Phone, Symbian and MeeGo devices, while Mobile Phones concentrated on Nokia's feature and lower-end phones.

After the initiation of the partnership, Microsoft organized regular training sessions and workshops for Nokia engineers and sales employees. Nokia integrated its technological expertise in Windows-operated Lumia series, such as superb camera and imaging technology. This package persuaded early adopters to buy Microsoft-operated phones. The ecosystem also grew, and Microsoft reported in December 2013 that the number of applications available on the Windows phone platform had surpassed 200,000 apps.

However, the collaboration began to show weaknesses. For Nokia, the partnership with Microsoft was regarded as the company's lifeline to a prolonged future. Its mobile business had been decreasing rapidly in the preceding years. To ensure partnership success, Nokia abandoned its profit-making Symbian platform to focus on the development of the Windows-based platform. Nokia was able to launch ten Lumia smartphones, thereby proving its dedication and earning a leading position in Windows Phone market shares. For Microsoft, however, the mobile phone business was one of the focus areas. At the time, Microsoft's main income was generated by the desktop operating systems, MS Office suites, server software and enterprise solutions. As mentioned, the deal with Nokia was not an exclusive deal, and Microsoft also generated licensing fees from Android smartphone manufacturers. Nokia, anxious to make Windows Phone into a success, became increasingly frustrated with the lack of priority on Microsoft's side in terms of, for instance, developing bug fixes for the Windows Phone platform. Next, Nokia began to work around certain platform issues and differentiate itself from other Windows Phone manufacturers. Microsoft regarded this behaviour as not being transparent. Microsoft felt it was not being informed sufficiently on product developments progressing within Nokia, which denied Microsoft the opportunity to tune its software accordingly. Although the number of apps available was climbing, it did not match the level of apps available for iPhone and Android. This situation, combined with the relatively low market share, created difficulties in retaining and attracting new app developers.

Although Nokia stabilized sales in the lower end of the smartphone market, it had not been able to achieve a market position in the high end smartphone market. Due to the premature termination of the profitable Symbian platform, Nokia was now facing financial difficulties. The platform support payments that it received from Microsoft were not sufficient to alleviate the financial issues Nokia faced. Nokia, aware of its vulnerable position as a non-exclusive Microsoft partner, found itself tentatively exploring the development of Android smartphones to support its financial position and increase its bargaining position with Microsoft. However, Microsoft required a stable hardware manufacturer and, on 3 September 2013, announced it would acquire Nokia's devices and services business for US$7.22 billion.

Questions

1   Explain the extent to which formal and relational alliance governance may have facilitated or hampered the partners' ability to manage alliance termination.
2   Explain whether alliance termination was avoidable in the Microsoft–Nokia alliance, and if so, what the partners could have done to prevent alliance termination.
3   How and to what extent may national cultural differences between Microsoft and Nokia have affected this alliance termination trajectory?

Note

1   Blass (2016); Fried (2011); Microsoft News Center (2001); Nokia (2011); PC World (2009); Today in Windows (2001).

10

SUPPLIER ALLIANCES

In recent decades, the competitive arena of firms has become more dynamic. Markets have become fragmented, technological developments have undermined firms' competitive advantage and customer demands are continuously changing. This has pushed firms to compete not only using their own capabilities, but with their entire supply chain, which has caused a shift from transaction-based exchanges to supplier alliances. A supplier alliance is a collaborative arrangement between a buyer and a supplying firm, formed within a supply chain setting, in which one party (i.e. buyer) transforms the output of another party (i.e. supplier) into end products. These partnerships, also referred to as purchase, vertical or buyer–supplier alliances, are forged to achieve long-term results, including enhanced market offer to customers and reduced channel costs. However, interdependencies between buyers and suppliers increase in supplier alliances, creating coordination issues and the risk of opportunistic behaviour. Accordingly, managers are confronted with a unique challenge. By establishing a supplier alliance instead of conducting a transaction-based exchange, buyers and suppliers sacrifice independence in order to improve their competitive advantage. This requires from (purchase) managers that they become aware, learn and adopt alliance management practices to establish win–win supplier alliances. The first section discusses this supplier challenge, and the following section elaborates on initiatives that managers can use to deal with it. In the third section, a supplier alliance is associated with the alliance development framework in order to develop guidelines for decision making. The chapter concludes with a summary and a case illustration.

The supplier alliance challenge

The literature on buyers and suppliers has traditionally considered exchanges between suppliers and manufacturers, wholesalers and retailers, and producers and distributors as discrete market transactions (Dwyer *et al.* 1987); in other words, a buyer and a supplier exchange a commodity in return for a payment. The actual exchange is price-oriented and short in duration, and negotiations are relatively simple as promises and obligations between the partners are clear. Because no future problems are anticipated, contractual enforcement is usually sufficient to govern the exchange, supported by legislation. However, buyer–supplier exchanges can also be organized through supplier alliances (Grimm *et al.* 2015; Tan 2001).

DOI: 10.4324/9781003222187-10

These are long-term bilateral relationships between buyers and suppliers that aim to create a collaborative advantage, while also enhancing the parties' own competitive position (Nair *et al.* 2011). The exchange in a supplier alliance tends to be an ongoing process, and outcomes are more difficult to specify, as the focus lies on total costs of the relationship rather than price. Along with operational and logistic characteristics, contracts also focus on more tactical and strategic elements and encompass behavioural elements. In short, whereas a traditional buyer–supplier exchange emphasizes sourcing through multiple suppliers, competitive bidding, use of short-term contracts and purchase price and quality, supplier alliances centre on one preferred supplier, the use of contingency contracts, building relational capital and long-term objectives (see Table 10.1).

From a buyer perspective, supplier alliances can yield significant benefits (Lyons *et al.* 1990). Supplier alliances reduce a buyer's uncertainty because forging a preferred supplier relationship secures the continuous supply of critical resources. In addition, supplier alliances may also prevent competitors from obtaining access to the high-quality resources possessed by the preferred supplier. Close and intensive contact with suppliers also improves the effectiveness of R&D, which may result in shortened product development cycles, more innovative products and higher product quality. In addition, intensive collaboration with a supplier may enhance a buyer's reputation as it may evoke positive customer responses. Working with a set of preferred suppliers also reduces operational coordination costs. When parties have increased knowledge

TABLE 10.1 Two views on buyer–supplier exchanges

	Transactional exchange	*Supplier alliance*
Description	Vertical relationship with a supplier with a focus on independence and value appropriation (e.g. costs).	Vertical alliance with a supplier with a focus on interdependence and value creation (e.g. learning).
Power	Bargaining power is exercised by buyers and suppliers to realize individual outcomes.	Bargaining power is managed by buyers and suppliers to realize joint outcomes.
Scope	Narrow; exit is easy due to low termination costs.	Broad; exit is difficult due to high termination costs.
Contractual governance	Contracts have a short duration and are narrow; contingency provisions and litigation are means of resolving disputes.	Contracts have long duration and are broad; broader contingency provisions and mediation are means of resolving disputes.
Relational governance	Relational elements are virtually absent; power and contracts determine outcomes.	Relational elements mitigate adverse implications of power asymmetries, and reduce opportunism and misappropriation.
Knowledge and information	Minimal; buyer provides specifications and supplier provides technological capability.	Extensive and broad; exchange of proprietary information and technological knowledge; inter-partner learning.
Payment	Fixed price per unit; ex ante known; payment upon delivery.	Payment based on revenue; ex ante unknown; payment conditional on success.
Decision making	Mainly autonomous; focus on protecting investments and specifications.	Mainly joint decision making; focus on division of roles authority.

Sources: Dwyer *et al.* (1987); Lyons *et al.* (1990).

about product specifications, production schemes and logistical requirements, this reduces a buyer's administrative overhead costs. The downside, however, is that supplier alliances can function as mobility barriers and reduce a buyer's flexibility because they impose substantial switching costs on a buyer. If a major supplier terminates the relationship, the effects can be significant. Supplier alliances also tend to increase coordination costs in order to deal with diverging objectives and backgrounds. Furthermore, buyers may need to adopt new negotiation styles, reward systems and management skills if they are to accommodate the shift from discrete market transactions to supplier alliances; this often requires changes in the internal organization.

Supplier alliances offer suppliers a stable market for their products and/or services. This, along with their long-term nature, means they enable involved parties to better plan their workforce, production and R&D, with the possibility of technical, managerial or financial assistance from their buyers. In addition, suppliers can exercise influence on a buyer's future decision making and receive insider access on buying decisions. A supplier can become a gatekeeper for a buyer's innovations and may receive and leverage relevant information about its own competitors. However, a supplier alliance also presents costs and risks to a supplier. For example, if a supplier's autonomy decreases, it may involuntarily leak proprietary information, and its personnel mobility may be reduced. In addition, a buyer may pressure a supplier to assume full responsibility for design, quality and costs. A supplier alliance also forces a supplier to become more transparent: for example, the supplier may be required to display cost structures, which undermines the supplier's bargaining position.

All in all, supplier alliances have the potential to contribute to partners' (that is, a buyer and a supplier) competitive positions as they enable the parties to economize on procurement costs while helping realize their long-term objectives (see Table 10.2), such as innovation and

TABLE 10.2 Examples of supplier alliances

	Description
Mercedes-Benz–Luminar Lidar	In 2022, Mercedes-Benz announced a partnership with Luminar Lidar, which is focused on the supply of sensors for the use in luxury vehicles. Luminar Lidar will assist Mercedes-Benz in gathering on-road data to support the Mercedes ambitions for automated driving. As part of the partnership, the German car maker also bought a small stake in Luminar Lidar.
Tesla–Panasonic	In 2013, Panasonic corporation and Tesla Motors formalized a supplier agreement in which Panasonic will expand its supply of automotive-grade lithium-ion battery cells to Tesla. In 2016, they also decided to collaborate on the manufacturing and production of photovoltaic cells and modules. Panasonic operates the Gigafactory in Nevada together with Tesla.
Ernst & Young–Logility Inc.	In 2022, Ernst & Young (EY) announced an alliance with Logility Inc. (Logility). The partnership combines Logility's supply chain planning solutions with the experience of EY US in process management, programme governance, change management and delivery framework. Through this partnership, the partners will have the ability to enhance their supply chain management, leading to better business outcomes such as increased visibility of their supply chains, better demand forecasting, cost and process optimization, sales management, quicker response to market dynamics and improved decision making.

Sources: Mercedes Benz Group Media (2022); Noel (2022); Tesla (2013, 2016).

market share. However, managing supplier alliances is more complicated than discrete market transactions, primarily due to the risks associated with the loss of interdependency, alliance-specific investments and opportunism. Thus managers of a supplier alliance are confronted with a unique challenge: in order to realize their objectives, they must collaborate closely with supply chain partners while simultaneously protecting their firm's long-term interests. This requires a fundamental shift in their management approach of buyer–supplier relationships.

Managing supplier alliances

Various organizational theories, such as transaction cost theory, the resource-based view, the relational view, resource dependence and social exchange theory, provide explanations for the design, management and performance of supplier alliances. As previous chapters have discussed the insights of these theoretical perspectives, this chapter elaborates only on the issues upon which managers responsible for supplier alliances must focus. These are: (1) inter-dependency, (2) scope and intensity, (3) alliance governance, (4) alliance-specific investments and (5) collective identity.

Interdependency

Traditionally, a buyer uses its bargaining power to influence the exchange between a buyer and supplier in order to maximally support its private objectives (Dwyer et al. 1987). However, when buyers exercise bargaining power in supplier alliances without considering long-term implications, the alliance is likely to fail, for two reasons. First, in discrete market transactions, bargaining power can only be exercised until the execution of the transaction. In a supplier alliance, however, the impact of bargaining power stretches from the time the alliance is forged until the relationship is ended because the distribution of benefits continues as long as the partnership progresses. However, excessive and one-sided use of bargaining power undermines the relational capital between partners, which often leads to an increased focus on self-interest and opportunistic behaviour. Second, although extant studies have assumed buyers generally possess a bargaining power advantage, which they use to extract additional concessions from their suppliers, a strong supplier may also face a large number of small buyers, providing the supplier with a bargaining power advantage (Berthon et al. 2003). If a buyer uses bargaining power in a supplier's market, this could lead to retaliation from the supplier that could potentially damage the buyer's interests.

Supplier alliances are unique in that they are embedded in the value chain, though the management implications of mutual dependence and dependency asymmetry are equivalent to those discussed elsewhere (see Chapters 2 and 13). In brief, higher degrees of mutual dependence associate positively with collaborative efforts, serving to foster higher levels of alliance performance (Kumar et al. 1995). More specifically, within a supplier setting, mutual dependence is associated with joint coordination, quality of information exchange, use of non-coercive strategies and less punitive actions. In contrast, dependency asymmetry under-mines collaborative efforts and is associated with increases in conflict, opportunism, the use of coercive strategies and unequal appropriation of benefits. This undermines the ability of a weaker party (either buyer or supplier) to realize its objectives. Parties may attempt to deal with power through offensive tactics (such as alliance-specific investments) and defensive tactics (such as contractual provisions), or they may simply accept a power asymmetry. Thus, as the interplay between mutual dependence and dependency asymmetry affects alliance

TABLE 10.3 Managing supplier alliances

	Description	*Implications*
Interdependency	A shift is required from a focus on autonomy and independence to managing and accepting interdependencies.	Mutual dependence reinforces collaborative efforts; dependence asymmetry reinforces competitive efforts, if not curbed.
Scope and intensity	Scope entails the range of activities in an alliance, whereas intensity refers to the degree of involvement and integration.	A broad scope offers more opportunities for synergy; narrow scope limits opportunism; high involvement enhances information exchange; low involvement facilitates easy exit.
Alliance governance	Pure supplier alliances tend to be non-equity-based; increasing scope and intensity favour equity-based arrangements.	Irrespective of governance form, contractual provisions (e.g. exclusivity) and relational capital (e.g. trust) are critical.
Alliance-specific investments	Supplier alliances benefit from alliance-specific investments in assets, personnel and sites.	Trade-off between unilateral and bilateral investments to reinforce synergies and curb one-sided exploitation and opportunism.
Collective identity	Collective identity between partners stimulates joint-sense making, social cohesiveness and performance.	Boundary-spanning agents are critical in supplier alliances as they function as creators and protectors of collective identity.

development (Gulati and Sytch 2007), managers should consider the timing and content of actions to deal with interdependencies carefully. Table 10.3 provides an overview of how to manage the unique supplier alliance challenges.

Scope and intensity of the alliance

The scope of a supplier alliance is defined by the range of activities it includes. Although the focus in a supplier alliance is on purchasing, the agreement may encompass other activities, such as research and development, production, marketing and sales, and distribution. For example, an automotive supplier providing specialized parts to a car manufacturer can also be involved in innovation activities and after-sales services. Despite the tendency to assume that a larger scope would be preferable to realize a wide-range of synergetic benefits, a relatively narrow scope (i.e. pure purchasing) can be beneficial in that it limits coordination costs and the risk of opportunistic behaviour (Zinn and Parasuraman 1997).

The intensity of an alliance is defined as the degree of direct involvement between partners. The number of direct interactions, the number of people collaborating, the size of investments and joint decision-making structures are all indicators of the intensity of the alliance. High-intensity alliances have a high number of cross-firm connections, which translates into increased communication and information exchange. This enables suppliers to gain insights into the objectives and specific requirements, which can lead to improved customer-specific product and/or service delivery and collaboration that improves overall supply chain performance. However, a higher level of intensity also makes it increasingly difficult for partners to terminate the supplier alliance due to higher switching costs.

Alliance governance

Transactional supplier alliances, typically used for commodity items (e.g. limited scope and intensity), tend to be organized through non-equity-based arrangements (Dwyer *et al.* 1987). Firms then depend on multiple specialized suppliers, reducing incentives to adopt equity-based governance forms. For example, Jaguar Land Rover engaged in more than £2 billion worth of supply contracts to more than 40 key strategic partners to develop its new car model: Evoque. As the scope of a supplier alliance increases, partners may prefer an equity-based arrangement to impose control, secure property rights and obtain long-term benefits. For example, EVO Electric, a pioneer in advanced electric drive solutions for the automotive sector, forged a joint venture with GKN, the world's leading supplier of automotive driveline systems and solutions. The joint venture manufactures and sells drive systems for use in hybrid and all-electric vehicles. Whereas EVO Electric supplies advanced electric drive technology and associated vehicle integration expertise, GKN invested £5m in cash and provides engineering and commercial resources for the development of EVO Electric and the joint venture.

Irrespective of the governance form, contractual and relational governance are critical to supplier alliances to enforce coordination and exploit learning effects. To protect against exchange hazards, buyers and suppliers employ alliance contracts that contain clauses related to matters such as product specifications, exclusivity, financial contributions, specialized investments and logistics. Alliance contracts allow parties to protect themselves against misuse of bargaining power and opportunistic behaviour, as contracts are intended to steer partners' behaviour towards collaboration. However, relational governance (i.e. relational norms and capital) tends to be more effective in supplier alliances because they avoid contracting costs and are better able to anticipate potential opportunistic behaviour. For example, the buyer's dependence and the supplier's opportunism are positively related under low relational norms and inversely related under high relational norms (Joshi and Arnold 1997). Self-enforcement also enables value-creation initiatives, including the sharing of fine-grained tacit knowledge, exchange of resources that are difficult to price, increased responsiveness and participation in innovations.

In terms of management control, assigning joint decision-making authority is critical. Because supplier alliances are often forged in dynamic industry settings, agility and responsiveness within the supply chain demands quick decision making. In addition, supplier alliances benefit from the establishment of cross-functional teams (Lyons *et al.* 1990) because such teams coordinate development and improvement across functional areas and are instrumental in the coordination and integration between a buyer and supplier. In terms of monitoring, parties may install a balanced performance metric system that captures a wide range of output indicators (e.g. price and total cost), process indicators (e.g. logistics) and behavioural indicators (e.g. acting in accordance with standard operating procedures). However, whereas output monitoring decreases partner opportunism in supplier alliances, behaviour monitoring—a more obtrusive form of control—actually increases partner opportunism (Heide *et al.* 2007).

Alliance-specific investments

Productivity gains in a supplier alliance are possible when partners are willing to make alliance-specific investments and combine resources in unique ways (Dyer 1996). Bilateral alliance-specific investments function as a mutual hostage that prompts partners to exploit a collaborative advantage (Jap 1999) as parties voluntarily create and accept mutual dependence. For example, partners might engage in performance improvement programmes, requiring parties to make alliance-specific investments in process, technology and personnel. This translates to increased transparency between parties and a better ability to provide customer-specific performance. For example, manufacturers and suppliers often work together to accommodate stringent just-in-time logistical demands, and specialized technological interfacing ensures the distribution of planning information and forecasts. Within the automotive industry, part suppliers often make physical investments, such as locating their factories in close proximity to an automotive manufacturer. Thus, partners in a supplier alliance tend to benefit from tailored investments in assets, personnel and sites.

When one party makes alliance-specific investments in a supplier alliance, it loses some of its bargaining power and may fall victim to opportunistic behaviour by the other party (Klein *et al.* 1978). Alliance-specific investments cause switching costs to increase, which reduces the likelihood that the relationship might be ended by the party that has to incur those costs (a hold-up situation). For example, suppliers' transaction-specific investments in the physical assets and production facilities jeopardize relationship performance due to hold-up behaviour of the manufacturers (Gurcaylilar-Yenidogan and Windsperger 2014). In an adversarial context, parties make unilateral investments to enhance their own competence selfishly, which usually has a detrimental effect on the relationship (Nair *et al.* 2011). However, unilateral investments may also signal commitment to maintaining the relationship (Gulati *et al.* 1994) as they rebalance a dependence asymmetry by voluntarily creating a hostage situation. For example, Jap and Ganesan (2000) find that, whereas alliance-specific investments made by a buyer influence its perceptions of supplier commitment negatively, specialized investments by a supplier increase the buyer's perception of supplier commitment. Ebers and Semrau (2015) report that buyers or suppliers are more likely to make unilateral specific investments when they can realize positive economic spillover values for other transactions with the same exchange partner as well as for third-party transactions. Thus, buyers and suppliers may expand or limit their degree of alliance-specific investments in order to create favourable exchange conditions. To avoid the adverse implications of potential hold-up situations, alliance partners may install monitoring systems, enforce relational governance and invest in goal congruence.

Collective identity

Creating a collective identity within a supplier alliance can help stimulate alliance performance (Ireland and Webb 2007). A strong collective identity among representatives of buyers and suppliers tends to reduce conflicts. The presence of a collective identity suggests that individuals reduce ambiguity and promote self-enhancement and that partners share goals, visions and working principles. Collective identity creates social cohesion amongst the team members and leads to greater cooperation within the supplier alliance. A higher level of shared identity in supplier alliances allows for increased transparency and knowledge sharing, which results in improved performance, thereby increasing trust. This facilitates further development

---

BOX 10.1 GLOBAL SUPPLY CHAINS

The COVID pandemic exposed the vulnerabilities in global supply chains. Trade restrictions and massive shortages of medical supplies, chips, cloths, toys and other products highlighted the weakness of a globalized world. Ninety-four percent of Fortune 1000 companies have experienced supply-chain disruptions from the pandemic, with three-fourths of them reporting negative or strongly negative impacts on their businesses. Manufacturers are under pressure to become more resilient against external shocks and eliminate their dependence on critical (re)sources. Supply chain partners need to reconsider their (lean) manufacturing and supply strategies. In today's age, firms cannot operate autonomously. Automakers aren't equipped to create touchscreen displays or the countless microprocessors that control the engine, steering and functions such as power windows and lighting. Dependence on niche specialists in a value chain offers flexibility, customization and enhanced offerings but also exposes supply chain partners to vulnerabilities. Production and supply come to a stop when one (niche) supplier is unable to deliver. Firms need to map the full supply chain, including first, second and third tiers to identify and mitigate supply risks. Mitigation can be done by reducing dependence on medium- or high-risk supply partners via adding more sources in more globally dispersed locations. Or by installing safety stocks (i.e. extra inventory) within the global supply chain. Or by pushing process innovations across the value chain (e.g. digitization, reconfiguration, new process technologies and additive manufacturing). Amongst others, these resolutions will boost supply chain resilience against disruptions.

Sources: Accenture (2022); Panwar *et al.* (2022); Shih (2020).

---

of the relationship because firms will feel an intrinsic responsibility to contribute to the well-being of the group. To this end, boundary-spanning agents are critical for the creation of a collective identity. Close interaction between representatives from each party enhances information exchange related to buyers' and suppliers' motivations, strategic direction and supporting visions. Boundary-spanning agents are especially valuable in dynamic situations, which are characterized by a high degree of uncertainty because they allow for faster decision making and act as a network broker within their organizations, allowing the partnership to prosper effectively from the knowledge base and the competences that firms possess. With a collective identity, a supplier alliance may also become a competitive entity in which collaboration is supported, potentially extending beyond the alliance to the entire supply chain.

Supplier alliances: decision-making steps

The increased focus on core competences and greater reliance on more flexible structures has led to suppliers playing a greater role and has changed how suppliers are managed. The emphasis shifts from market transactions to strategic supplier alliances. The key advantages of supplier alliances compared to transaction-oriented exchanges is that they reduce transaction costs; they encourage coordination and communication, which translates into lower manufacturing and labour costs and improved quality, improved predictability and supply assurance;

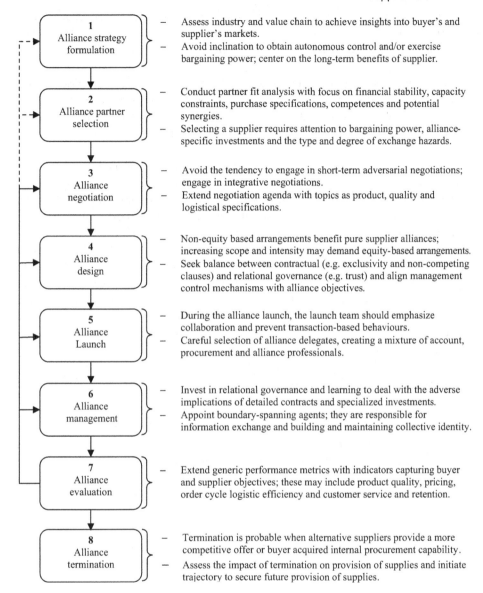

FIGURE 10.1 Alliance development framework: supplier alliances

and they engender a long-term perspective that limits opportunism, exploitation and misappropriation. To provide a coherent set of guidelines for establishing successful supplier alliances (from a buyer's view), decisions at each stage of the alliance development framework are elaborated on next (see Figure 10.1).

Step 1: alliance strategy formulation

During the alliance strategy formulation stage, firms decide whether a supplier alliance depicts an appropriate governance mode to procure critical resources. In addition to the generic rationales discussed in preceding chapters, such as transaction costs, resource complementarity and learning, a firm may focus on buyer–supplier dependence in order to decide whether a supplier alliance is the appropriate governance mode to meet the firm's objectives:

- Internalizing resources and activities (e.g. merger) may appear to be a viable way to reduce uncertainty and secure continued provision of critical supplies. However, firms are often unable to obtain a degree of specialization that is similar to that of autonomous suppliers, which is required to exploit learning effects in terms of efficiency and innovation.
- Commoditized resources can be easily procured through market transactions. In a situation in which reciprocal effects are limited and synergies are not expected, a market transaction constitutes a viable option. Buyers (suppliers) use bargaining power to optimize margins at the expense of suppliers (buyers), which yields short-term benefits.
- Through an alliance, buyers seek to obtain control over the procurement of supplies without internalizing potentially unproductive resources and activities. More specifically, when a supplier contributes directly to the value-creating potential of a buyer, and the latter depends on a stable supply to execute its primary processes, a supplier alliance tends to be a viable option. In these situations (i.e. the presence of a strategic supplier), buyers and suppliers expect reciprocal effects, such as by exploiting complementary resources. Buyers (suppliers) make decisions during the subsequent alliance development stages in order to optimize long-term benefits.

Step 2: alliance partner selection

During the partner selection stage, a firm selects a (preferred) supplier with which to establish a long-term partnership. A buyer should look for a purchasing solution that includes the best products or services to meet the set requirements at an appropriate price level and in keeping with the company's demands for quality, quantity, (speed of) delivery, flexibility and total costs. In this phase, potential partners consider obligations, benefits and burdens, and trial purchases may take place. In addition to generic partner fit criteria, specific questions may help a buyer to select a supplier:

- Financial stability. Is the supplier financially healthy? For example, does it have sufficient working capital to carry out the order, and is it sufficiently solvent to endure a downturn in demand?
- Ability to do the job. Is the supplier capable of providing the agreed product or service? What methods or systems does the supplier use to manage its production process? Is the supplier's quality assurance system sufficient?
- Capacity constraint. Does the supplier have the capacity to carry out the order?
- Clarity of purchase specification. Does the supplier fully understand the product specifications? Misunderstanding in this area can be the greatest cause of delay and extra costs.
- Ease of doing business. Is the supplier easy to deal with and approachable if things go wrong?
- Potential synergies. Do the buyer and the suppliers complement or substitute each other in a manner that could lead to other potentially beneficial synergies? Besides the delivery of a product or a service, the alliance with a supplier or a buyer might build on these potential synergies.

Step 3: alliance negotiation

During the alliance negotiation stage, emphasis is placed on getting the suppliers involved in planning and understanding the buyer's long-term goals (e.g. quality and customer retention). However, there may be some initial resistance to alliance negotiations as supplier alliances tend to threaten the independence that buyers and suppliers value highly. Exercising bargaining power through coercive strategies to enforce a counterpart's compliance could be appropriate in a transactional exchange, but it tends to undermine the joint value creation logic of a supplier alliance and may even result in a premature breakdown. Prompted by purchase experiences, negotiators may be inclined to use bargaining strategies that characterize market transactions and, therefore, do not match the sought-after alliance-type relationship. It is important, however, that short-term adversarial bargaining is supplemented with mutual-benefit bargaining aimed at realizing long-term super-ordinate goals. A supplier alliance is unlikely to develop successfully without bilateral communication of requirements, issues, inputs and priorities, all of which contribute to the development of a collective identity. Negotiators should emphasize their mutual long-term interests and commitments in an open and transparent setting. For example, parties may signal commitment to their channel partners by employing well-trained personnel, participating in buyers' or suppliers' councils, granting exclusive territories, offering exclusive distribution and investing in alliance-specific assets. Non-coercive strategies tend to be more effective. Therefore, accounting for bargaining power differences is critical to achieving favourable individual and joint outcomes during supplier alliance negotiations.

Step 4: alliance design

The design of a supplier alliance is critical to its success or failure. Effective governance mechanisms have the potential to generate favourable outcomes, not only by lowering transaction costs but also by influencing knowledge-sharing activities. Given that supplier alliances often constitute non-equity arrangements, firms must consider the following factors:

- Intensity and scope of the supplier alliance. Suppliers are likely to assume greater responsibilities in supplier alliances, including areas like product design, prototype development, engineering service, manufacturing and assembly. This could lead to an erosion of in-depth knowledge and experience for the buyer, leaving it exposed to potential opportunistic behaviour by the supplier. As the scope and intensity increase, additional coordination and protection is required against exchange hazards.
- The degree of contractual and relational governance. Parties must find a balance between contractual and relational governance mechanisms. Decisions related to designing governance mechanisms tend to be influenced by market characteristics. For example, is the supplier alliance forged in a buyer's market or a supplier's market? In a buyer's market, suppliers will tend to strive for contract completeness, while in a supplier's market, buyers will be inclined to use complete contracts. Depending on the degree of contract completeness, parties must invest in relational norms and capital if they are to curb opportunism.
- The degree of alliance-specific investments. To curb the adverse implications of dependency asymmetry, parties may commit to bilateral or unilateral alliance-specific investments (such as assets, personnel and geographical vicinity). Such investments function as a signal of commitment, as parties voluntarily create and accept a mutual hostage situation.

- The degree of management control. Joint decision making, designated representatives functioning as boundary spanners and the installation of cross-functional and cross-firm teams enables buyers and suppliers to communicate effectively, exchange relevant knowledge and information and develop working routines. Whereas outcome monitoring enables partners to steer the alliance towards their objectives, behavioural monitoring tends to increase opportunistic conduct if it is not accompanied by relational governance.

Step 5: alliance launch

When taking a supplier alliance view, generic alliance launch guidelines are sufficient to attain a successful alliance launch. However, alliance launch managers should be aware of two points. First, the alliance launch team should pay attention to supplier alliance practices that have been built prior to the firm entering. As supplier alliances are distinct from traditional purchase exchanges, launch managers should pay specific attention to team members' backgrounds as procurement managers tend to approach suppliers differently than alliance managers. For example, the former tend to resolve adversities through bargaining, whereas the latter resolve them through dialogue. It is imperative that launch managers advocate a collaborative, instead of a competitive, climate. Second, contracts are of critical importance in supplier alliances as they specify the terms of the delivery. It is part of the launch manager's job to create operational (e.g. logistic and administrative) clarity and ensure all staff involved are updated. However, strict adherence to contractual stipulations (and imposing sanctions in case of non-compliance) during the alliance launch stage may undermine initial initiatives to jointly learn. That is, launch managers should allow for mistakes and offer opportunities to repair mistakes. To accomplish these two tasks, it is critical alliance launch managers familiarize themselves with the supplier and the buyer, for example, through joint (product) trainings and educational programmes.

Step 6: alliance management

Alliance management, in addition to day-to-day operations, should invest in developing a collective identity and mechanisms that enforce relational governance. Boundary-spanning representatives play an important role in establishing a shared identity, which is created by extensive communication and interaction. Furthermore, by investing in relational norms and relational capital, buyers and suppliers establish higher levels of trust, commitment and flexibility. Higher levels of relational capital facilitate knowledge sharing and protect against opportunistic behaviour, enabling the alliance to become increasingly effective and efficient, possibly leading to increased rewards. Joint sense making takes place using cross-firm communicative structures, which also involve discussion and decisions regarding corrective measures to resolve outcome and process discrepancies.

Step 7: alliance evaluation

Supplier alliances are set up to reach certain objectives, and alliance evaluation allows for timely steering of activities or even a decision to terminate the collaborative scheme. As a supplier alliance progresses, the nature of relationship may change. Learning may lead to the development of competences and other resources, thereby changing the power balance between parties, which could impact the distribution of benefits. A shifting power balance may undermine the day-to-day operations and cause alliance performance to deteriorate. This means that adaptability is an important aspect as internal and external forces can strain the relationship, including increased transaction costs, emerging alternative suppliers and changing organizational needs. Effective evaluation and communication structures are required in order for parties to be able to adjust structures with mutual consent. This will reflect the dynamic progression of the alliance and keep the alliance on track to meet its objectives. Indicators that are typical of supplier alliances include price (per unit), total cost (per unit), product and process quality, logistical efficiency, and customer service and retention.

Step 8: alliance termination

A supplier alliance ends if the supplier no longer has strategic value. This could occur (1) because other suppliers have the ability to supply the same products or services or (2) because the buyer has acquired the capability to supply the critical resources for him or herself. Another reason for termination could be if misconduct by either the supplier or the buyer caused damage to the reputation of the other party. Since parties work with each other in one supply chain, their resource provision or usage is likely to be critical for the parties involved. Therefore, ending the alliance may be caused by a halt in supply or demand. This may require buyers to find other sources of supply. If possible, a buyer may use a fall-back scenario in which a dual source strategy can be employed that allows another supplier to take over. For a supplier, the end of an alliance may require it to look for other buyers.

Summary

Increasingly, firms have to be agile in order to respond to continuously changing internal and external conditions. To this end, transaction-based supplier exchanges characterized by market transactions are increasingly being replaced by supplier alliances. Supplier alliances secure the provision of critical resources, and buyers and suppliers use these partnerships to enhance their competitive positions. Alliances allow buyers and suppliers to realize long-term objectives such as improved market offerings, reduced supply channel costs and enhanced opportunities to develop and launch innovations. Unlike traditional bargain-driven supplier exchanges, however, supplier alliances also impose switching costs and reduce flexibility for both suppliers and buyers, and the increased entanglement (that is lock-in) mean that opportunistic behaviour can have much worse repercussions. In addition to generic alliance guidelines, managers can steer supplier alliances to success by paying particular attention to the interdependence relationship, the scope and intensity of the supplier alliance, the balance between contractual and relational governance, the size of alliance-specific investments and to building a collective identity.

CASE: NAM–GLT PLUS[1]

In October 1933, N.V. De Bataafsche Petroleum Maatschappij (now Royal Dutch Shell) offered the Standard Oil Company of New Jersey (now ExxonMobil) the opportunity to pool oil exploitation interests in the Netherlands on a 50:50 basis. The offer was accepted in 1938. However, because of the Second World War, it took until 1947 to formalize the arrangement by forging the Nederlandse Aardolie Maatschappij (NAM). In 1948, NAM discovered natural gas in the Dutch town of Coevorden. Just more than ten years later, NAM discovered the Groningen natural gas field near Slochteren, one of the largest on-shore natural gas fields in the world. That discovery led to the establishment of the so-called Gasgebouw in 1963, the objective of which was to exploit the Groningen gas reserves. Gasgebouw was a partnership between NAM, the Dutch State Mines NV (now Energie Beheer Nederland BV) and the newly formed gas marketing and transportation company Gasunie. Twenty-nine gas locations and six metering stations were developed in the 1960s and 1970s to exploit the Groningen gas field.

After 30 years of operation, renovation of the facilities was necessary to ensure compliance with the latest environmental standards and operational requirements. A major and complex renovation project had to be undertaken while still meeting the Groningen field's contractual production obligations. The competences required to execute the renovation project were not available within the NAM organization, and contractors (that is, suppliers) were considered to play an important role. However, instead of engaging in competitive bidding procedures[2] with multiple parties, NAM decided to opt for an integrated entity that would accept responsibility for execution of the entire project. In so doing, NAM would reduce governance complexity. Furthermore, due to the strategic value of the Groningen gas field and the scope of the programme, NAM also wanted to avoid a 'hit-and-run' mentality as it was important to meet the objectives that had been set for continuous gas production and costs reductions while executing the renovation. One implication was that ongoing maintenance had to be done by the same party responsible for the renovation, although these activities would be organized in two separate agreements. Another implication was that both the NAM and its subcontractor would have to make considerable alliance-specific investments. The upshot was that a long-term supplier alliance was deemed the most viable option.

Partners were pre-selected based on their experience, size and innovative capacity. NAM insisted that consortia would be formed if partners were unable to deliver the project alone. All parties in a consortium had to share liabilities, which stimulated partnership and commitment within the consortium. Three consortia were asked to produce a conceptual design based on a NAM reference case and functional specifications. NAM was pleasantly surprised with the level of innovation in the designs. Based on a functional tender, the consortium Stork GLT was awarded the contract due to having the best performance on quality, integrated approach and costs.

The Stork GLT consortium consisted of Stork Comprimo, Stork Wescon, Delaval Stork, Siemens AG and Yokogawa. Stork Comprimo was later taken over by Jacobs, Stork Wescon was renamed Stork Industry Services and Delaval Stork was taken over by Siemens. The consortium was registered as a separate legal entity. An underlying Heads of Agreement specified the responsibilities and liabilities of the partners involved. Due to the complementary nature of the partners and the clear division of tasks, the consortium opted for a structure in which the five partners were responsible for their own scope of work. Together, they were responsible for renovating the Groningen Gas Field and subsequently maintaining it.

The collaboration between NAM and Stork GLT has been very successful. In terms of performance, nearly all of the renovated facilities have been delivered within time and budget and with zero outstanding items. With the conclusion of the Stork GLT alliance and renovation programme in 2009, NAM initiated a new programme for the continuous maintenance of the Groningen assets. This programme also entailed a second stage gas compression project to counter the further declining gas pressures in the Groningen gas field. Based on the experience with Stork GLT, NAM opted for a similar supplier collaboration scheme. This entailed that NAM again required suppliers to organize in consortia to reduce governance costs. Also, consortia would increase collaboration between the participating companies to further improve the quality and cost of services by providing innovative solutions. The consortium would be responsible for the engineering, procurement, construction and maintenance of the Groningen assets. Using a public tender procedure, numerous parties participated. Through a competitive dialogue procedure, the same consortium was selected as had previously participated in the Stork GLT consortium. The new consortium was named GLT-PLUS.

The two main differences between the STORK GLT and the GLT-PLUS alliance are (1) the type of work and (2) the scope of work. The main assignment of the Stork GLT consortium was the renovation of the 20 production sites of the Groningen gas field. During these projects, the assets were decommissioned by NAM and transferred to the responsibility of the Stork GLT consortium that renovated the sites. Then the newly renovated sites were commissioned and transferred back to NAM to resume production. This allowed Stork GLT to operate in a so-called green field situation. The GLT-PLUS consortium has a maintenance responsibility that requires a much closer collaboration on the operational level between NAM and GLT-PLUS. Sites are not decommissioned and transferred to the consortium. Maintenance needs to be executed in short time frames, while NAM retains the responsibility for a safe working environment. This approach is referred to as a 'brown field' situation. Next, the scope of the GLT-PLUS consortium was enlarged. Besides the 20 production sites, the maintenance responsibility now also entails two underground gas storage facilities, a tank storage facility, a storage facility for by-products and a pipeline. The second-stage gas compression programme is also part of the scope of the partnership between NAM and GLT-PLUS.

To accommodate the new type and scope of work, a layered contract structure was established consisting of four main elements. The first element is a base agreement that describes the terms and conditions. This contract remains static over longer periods of time. Attached to this base agreement are two 'interface manuals' that describe how the collaboration is executed in terms of governance structures, procedures and pricing. The Operational Interface Manual describes the operational requirements and procedures. This also includes extensive health, safety and environmental procedures, escalation procedures and so on. In addition to the Operational Interface Manual, a Commercial Interface Manual describes tariffs, rates and indexations. The interface manuals have a more dynamic character than the base agreement and are updated periodically. The fourth level within the set of agreements is the work orders. The contract specifies that all work is executed in accordance to specific work orders, which are issued for specific work scopes. A work order describes a specific scope, costs and incentives (if required). In establishing this contractual structure, both NAM and GLT-PLUS took advantage of the earlier collaboration and were able to build on previous experience, which allowed for a swift startup.

Given the 'brown field' approach, increased operational interfacing between NAM and the GLT-PLUS consortium is required, which increases the intensity of the relationship. To allow for a smooth collaboration, a thoroughly designed mirror-type governance structure has been put in place, in which representatives of NAM GLT-PLUS participate. In this structure, distinction is made between operations and maintenance. Within NAM, the operational manager has the execution manager as his or her GLT-PLUS counterpart. For maintenance, a similar structure applies in which the maintenance manager of NAM is mirrored by the engineering and modifications manager of GLT-PLUS. Each of the combinations discusses scope of work, timing and costs. Due to the nature of the partnership, NAM specifies in functional terms, while GLT-PLUS performs detailed engineering of the assignment set and thus provides a technical specification that meets the functional requirements. NAM has structured the Groningen assets in various areas. An area team is responsible for each area. In preparation of a work order, the area team is consulted to discuss the scope and timing of the work.

NAM and GLT-PLUS use a 'trust but verify' approach. In this approach, emphasis is placed on transparency. In the Commercial Interface Manual, a tariff structure has been designed to allow for easy calculation of costs. For a specific scope of work, NAM and GLT-PLUS can independently calculate the costs associated with work scope. Partners provide full insight in their calculations. If required, clarifications are requested by NAM. Work may only commence after formal approval and release of the work order by NAM. The transparency not only applies to the partners within GLT-PLUS but also to their subcontractors working on NAM assets. This translates into high levels of trust and an increased effectiveness of the partnership. Within GLT-PLUS, work is divided between the partners according to the competencies required. Work division is facilitated by the fact that the participating organizations within GLT-PLUS are complementary to each other.

The procedure of issuing work orders applies to both maintenance and renovation projects. An important project that has been awarded is the expansion of the underground gas storage facility near the town of Norg. Due to declining pressures in the Groningen Gas Field, NAM is unable to meet the steep increase in gas demands during wintertime. Therefore underground gas storage facilities are used to store gas during the summer, which can be used as a fast deployable resource in wintertime. This project was committed in several stages between 2011–2015 and entailed a total investment of €700 million. The layered contract structure has allowed NAM to issue this significant work order without having to execute a lengthy tendering procedure to select a professional party to execute the work. The high levels of professionalism of all parties involved guarantees NAM to meet gas supply requirements of the Dutch government, also in wintertime.

For both NAM and GLT-PLUS, innovation is important. A well-balanced incentive structure has been designed in order to induce innovative behaviour. Financial benefits from better-than-expected performance by GLT-PLUS are shared between NAM and GLT-PLUS. Incentive structures are dynamic and finalized on Work Order level. During the first years of the collaboration, incentives have been put on timely delivery and complete scope delivery. Later, costs and quality were emphasized in the incentive structures. To further induce collaboration within GLT-PLUS, GLT-PLUS partners decided to position GLT-PLUS as a separate organization, with its own logo, office building and stationery. People who work for GLT-PLUS wear GLT-PLUS clothing and feel part of the GLT-PLUS organization. NAM and GLT-PLUS have been housed in the same offices, although Projects and Maintenance were physically separated. Currently the whole organization is assembled in one office building.

Management of the alliance between NAM and GLT-PLUS has been organized in formal governance structures. On a daily basis, the operations manager and the maintenance manager of NAM have contact with their counterparts of GLT-PLUS. Performance is formally managed on a monthly basis. Performance and outlooks are discussed on a quarterly basis by the CEO board, which is the highest level in the NAM/GLT-PLUS governance structure. In the CEO board, the CEOs of all participating organizations are present, along with high-ranking officials of NAM.

Given the well-designed collaboration and close ties between NAM and GLT-PLUS, future outlooks are shared proactively so that positive or negative outlooks do not come as a surprise. NAM is currently facing significant cut backs in gas production due to falling public support for gas extraction. Specifically, the Dutch Government has decided to reduce gas extraction, and NAM is held accountable for the earthquake damage caused to private infrastructure. This has negative consequences for NAM but also for GLT-PLUS. However, due to the open sharing of information, GLT-PLUS and NAM were able to analyze consequences quickly, and the partners within GLT-PLUS have proactively calculated the consequences of these cut backs. Nonetheless, the future outlook is uncertain.

Questions

1 Explain NAM's motives to forge a supplier alliance instead of using their unique position to play off multiple suppliers against each other.
2 Explain the effectiveness of the supplier alliance's design and management. Also, explain what would change if the alliance would encompass learning and innovation objectives.

Notes

1 Interview with senior executives of NAM; Energy Global (2015).
2 Competitive dialogue is a specific procedure in European public tendering.

11

LEARNING ALLIANCES

In an era characterized by rapid changes and high levels of uncertainty, learning and innovation enable a firm to maintain or improve its competitive advantage. Learning allows a firm to generate new knowledge about markets, technologies, processes, product and service concepts, and business models. However, because firms may lack the internal resources they need to sustain their learning to build new competences, they forge alliances to enhance the breadth and depth of the knowledge available to them, both existing and new. In a learning alliance, two or more firms enter into a collaborative scheme to generate knowledge by sharing and combining their knowledge bases. However, in a learning alliance a firm also provides access to its counterpart, enabling the latter to acquire proprietary or valuable knowledge that is not part of the alliance agreement. Therefore, firms engaged in learning alliances must protect themselves from unwanted knowledge leakage. This situation presents firms with a specific challenge: to strike a balance between learning (i.e. accessing, internalizing and exploiting knowledge), and knowledge protection. The first section of this chapter discusses this challenge in detail. The following sections elaborate on mechanisms that stimulate or hinder learning and knowledge protection, and associate the governance of learning alliances with the alliance development framework. The chapter concludes with a summary and a case illustration.

The learning alliance challenge

A firm is likely to have one or a combination of three generic motives for establishing a learning alliance (Kogut 1988). First, the firm may not possess all of the relevant knowledge and competences it needs to realize its objectives. In such a case, alliances function as learning vehicles that enable the firm to augment its knowledge base with external knowledge. Second, it can be time-consuming and costly to develop knowledge internally. Alliances provide firms with flexible and time-efficient arrangements to develop capabilities beyond their inherited ones, cheaply and more quickly. Third, firms may have fallen into competency traps and lack the ability to develop new knowledge because they have become preoccupied with exploiting their existing knowledge. In this way, alliances enable firms to improve their innovative capacity because exposure to different and externally sourced knowledge enhances their willingness and ability to innovate (Yli-Renko *et al.*

DOI: 10.4324/9781003222187-11

TABLE 11.1 Examples of learning alliances

	Descriptions
Mizuho Financial Group–Cognizant	In 2016, Mizuho Financial Group, one of the largest financial institutions in the world, and Cognizant, a leading provider of information technology, consulting and business process outsourcing services, announced a strategic agreement. As part of the agreement, Cognizant brings together its financial services, consulting and digital technology expertise to design and develop a blockchain solution for Mizuho's customers, counterparties and group companies to exchange and sign sensitive documents in a secure and transparent manner, resulting in faster, more efficient processing and multi-party verification.
Microsoft–Facebook	In 2022, Microsoft announced a partnership with Facebook owner Meta to enhance Metaverse hardware integrations and unveiled three new Surface computers. The partners will collaborate to bring Mesh for Microsoft Teams, the virtual reality overlay for the Microsoft's workplace messaging platform, to the Meta Quest virtual reality (VR) headset.
SotaTek–Dvision Network	In 2022, SotaTek and Dvision Network established a partnership to launch a mutual Blockchain Project. SotaTek is the leading blockchain development company in Vietnam. Dvision Network is a multi-chain metaverse platform, whereby NFT marketplace, meta-space and Meta city are three key platform pillars. The partners have launched a multi-chain metaverse platform based on the Ethereum Network and the Binance Smart Chain. SotaTek continues to support and strengthen the Dvision Network ecosystem by integrating additional technologies into their platform.

Sources: Fintech Finance (2016); Microsoft (2022c); SotaTek (2022).

2001). Therefore, firms have compelling reasons to engage: inter-firm learning enables them to augment their (core) competences (see Table 11.1). In this chapter the focus is on bilateral learning alliances, though firms learn and innovate by forging and managing multiple alliances simultaneously. Consider innovation in alliance portfolios (Chapter 18) and in alliance networks (Chapter 19). Also see Box 11.1 for an illustration on how 'open innovation' builds a focal firm's learning and innovation capacity.

Instead, knowledge protection requires the safeguarding of access to the knowledge a firm possesses so that partner firms cannot access, acquire, imitate, duplicate, expropriate, appropriate or use that knowledge for their own purposes (Lee *et al.* 2007). Knowledge protection can safeguard critical knowledge from involuntarily spillover, which helps the firm sustain its competitive advantage (Norman 2002). The knowledge protection methods a firm employs also function as safeguards against opportunistic behaviour by partners (Simonin 1999). However, knowledge protection implies several hazards. For example, explicit knowledge protection policies and procedures are likely to have negative impacts on relationship quality. If a partner protects (hides) knowledge and information, this suggests an unwillingness to devote resources to the alliance. This perception could create other barriers to the free flow of knowledge and information, such as new contractual provisions, which can increase distrust if partners equate knowledge protection with a greater risk of opportunism. Perhaps even more important, safeguards against unwanted knowledge spillover tend to impede the alliance partners' abilities to learn.

BOX 11.1 OPEN INNOVATION

Open innovation is a term coined by Henry Chesbrough (2003). As in modern times, boundaries between a firm and its environment have become more permeable—knowledge can easily transfer inward and outward—open innovation suggests that firms should identify and exploit external knowledge as well as internal knowledge, and establish internal and external interfaces, to the end of advancing their innovative capability. The central idea behind open innovation is that, in a world of widely distributed knowledge, companies cannot afford to rely entirely on their own R&D departments but should instead buy or license knowledge (i.e. patents) from other companies. Internal inventions not being used should be taken outside the firm, for example, through licensing, joint ventures or spin-offs. Open innovation offers several benefits to firms, including reduced cost of conducting R&D, improvements in development productivity, opportunity to build relationships with customers, potential to enhance market research and potential for creating synergy between internal and external innovations. Proctor and Gamble (P&G) for example embraced and championed open innovation, as it is their aim 'to partner with the world's most innovative minds—from individual inventors and small businesses, to Fortune 500 companies—to deliver on the company's most challenging opportunities'. To this end, P&G forged the 'Connect + Develop' programme, enabling P&G to engage with innovators and patent-holders to meet needs across the P&G business: for products, technology, in-store, ecommerce and the supply chain. In its quest to partner with external resources to drive discontinuous, sustainable innovation and productivity, P&G dedicated a global team working with prospective alliance partners and shepherding breakthrough innovations through the company and into market. Despite the plethora of advantages, implementing a model of open innovation is, however, associated with a number of challenges, including possible knowledge leakage, possibility of revealing intellectual property to a rival, increased coordination complexity and costs, and difficulties associated with developing strategies to identify, align and incentivize external parties in order to maximize the return from external innovation. For example, open innovation is challenging because each new external alliance generates multiple new (internal) relationships as cross-functional teams (e.g. R&D, engineering and marketing) become involved and need to interface internally and externally. In short, to make open innovation work and develop a productive innovation process, firms should purposively manage inbound and outbound knowledge flows across organizational boundaries, using monetary and non-monetary incentives to commit parties in line with the firm's business model.

Source: Chesbrough (2003); Proctor and Gamble (2017).

Therefore, firms that engage in a learning alliance are confronted with a unique challenge. They must design and manage an alliance to enable inter-firm learning, while simultaneously protecting themselves against the unwanted transfer of valuable knowledge (Bamel et al. 2021; Kale et al. 2000). When a firm deals successfully with this challenge, it builds a learning alliance that improves its innovative capacity while also preserving its competitive advantage. However, when a firm is unable to tackle this challenge, its alliance is likely to turn into a learning race (Hamel 1991) in which partners make continuous, opportunistic efforts to outlearn each other. Such races are detrimental to alliance continuation because once a party has achieved its learning objectives, none of the parties has any incentive to maintain the relationship (Khanna *et al.* 1998). Therefore, although learning alliances may help a firm absorb critical knowledge and develop capabilities similar to those of its partner, participation also increases the probability of the unilateral or disproportionate loss of core competences to the partner.

Managing learning alliances

Managing learning alliances requires firms to understand the mechanisms that facilitate inter-firm learning and knowledge protection. Previous literature has emphasized the importance of (1) relative absorptive capacity, (2) governance form, (3) alliance contracts, (4) relational capital, (5) knowledge characteristics, (6) knowledge practices and (7) the role that staff involved in the alliance play in these efforts (see Table 11.2).

TABLE 11.2 Managing learning alliances

	Description	*Implications*
Absorptive capacity	Set of organizational routines and processes that enable a firm to assess and acquire external knowledge; prerequisite to knowledge transfer and creation.	Similar and high level of absorptive capacity enhances learning and reduces need for knowledge protection; protection becomes critical if absorptive capacity is uneven and in alliances between competitors.
Governance form	Equity-based arrangements provide better learning and protection opportunities, but non-equity-based governance may be preferred if relational capital exists.	Conditional on the governance form, supplemental design decisions are required, including alliance scope, task specialization and contractual provisions.
Alliance contracts	Contractual clauses that stipulate knowledge transfer and protection are required, including patents, penalties and non-disclosure agreements.	Contracts provide protection against unwanted knowledge spillover, but over-reliance on contracts tends to damage relational capital.
Relational capital	Influences partners' openness and willingness to exchange knowledge but also functions as safeguard.	Investing in relational capital is critical as it facilitates learning and reduces the risk of learning races and knowledge leakage.
Knowledge characteristics	Tacit knowledge is often key motivation for alliance formation, but higher degrees of tacitness impede knowledge transfer.	Transfer of tacit knowledge requires additional measures; if a firm possesses tacit knowledge, it may need to install protective measures.
Knowledge practices	To manage inter-firm learning, firms need to invest in supportive organizational routines, control and coordination mechanisms.	Training, education, communities of practice, knowledge systems and incentive and reward systems encourage learning.
Alliance staff	Persons involved in the alliance enable learning but also constitute important protection mechanisms.	Involvement of top management, alliance managers and alliance employees is required for knowledge transfer; personnel also need to be aware of their role as gatekeepers.

Absorptive capacity

A firm's absorptive capacity is the organizational routines and processes that enable it to assess and acquire external knowledge and disseminate it internally (Zahra and George 2002). This capacity is the result of a prolonged process of investments and knowledge accumulation within the firm, which makes it a firm characteristic that is shaped incrementally over many years (Mowery et al. 1996). Absorptive capacity also plays an important role for knowledge transfers in learning alliances because it constitutes the firm's ability to recognize the value of new knowledge, assimilate it and apply it to commercial ends (Cohen and Levinthal 1990).

However, Dyer and Singh (1998) argued that absorptive capacity varies as a function of the alliance partner. That is, a firm's ability to absorb knowledge may depend on how much its pre-alliance knowledge overlaps with that of its partner. At the most elemental level, prior knowledge might include basic skills or a shared language, as well as knowledge of the most recent scientific or technological developments in a field. Although a certain degree of overlap in basic knowledge does reinforce inter-firm learning because both alliance partners possess a similar ability to absorb knowledge (Lane and Lubatkin 1998), partners with greater absorptive capacity are likely to learn at a faster pace. Noseleit and De Faria (2013) show that alliance relationships with external partners in related industries (i.e. knowledge complementarity) are more beneficial to a firm's internal R&D efforts for producing innovations compared to collaborating with partners in the same industry (i.e. knowledge overlap). Therefore, firms that perceive the absorptive capacity of their partners as high are more protective of their knowledge (Norman 2002) because absorptive capacity asymmetry between alliance partners increases the threat of knowledge leakage (to the partner with a better ability to absorb knowledge) and learning races (Khanna et al. 1998). This means that awareness of the extent to which partners possess similar or different abilities to absorb knowledge is critical, particularly as it informs alliance decision making.

The issue of relative absorptive capacity becomes even more important in learning alliances between competitors (Khanna et al. 1998). The competitive overlap between partners creates positive and negative incentives to transfer knowledge. High competitive overlap encourages firms to be more protective about their knowledge because unintended knowledge transfer might endanger their own competitive advantage (Khanna et al. 1998). At the same time, it also facilitates knowledge transfers because knowledge bases are likely to resemble one another (Schoenmakers and Duysters 2006), which increases each partner's ability to understand, valuate and assimilate knowledge. For example, Contractor and Woodley (2015) show that firms with stronger technical capabilities (absorptive capacity) benefit more from (technology) alliances. However, such capable partners also depict a potential threat as they may engage in a learning race with the original technology supplying partner. Yang and colleagues (2015) also suggest that a firm's relative capability to learn from its counterpart holds the key to understanding the learning race phenomenon. Specifically, their study shows that firms with a higher learning capability relative to their alliance partner exhibit higher levels of stock performance. However, equity-based arrangements suppress competitive learning, whereas market similarity between the alliance partners aggravates the learning race. Although the empirical evidence is somewhat inconclusive (Chen 2004; Mowery et al. 1996), studies demonstrate that alliances between competitors are likely to fail (Park and Russo 1996). If such alliances are undertaken, they certainly demand more management attention.

Governance form

A firm may derive its ability to assess and acquire knowledge from its governance form decision. Equity-based alliances align the interests of partner firms and offer opportunities for knowledge transfer and protection against unintentional knowledge leakage. For example, Chen (2004) and Mowery *et al.* (1996) reveal that equity-based alliances are superior to non-equity-based alliances in terms of transferring tacit knowledge. Oxley and Wada (2009) corroborate these findings but also found that equity-based alliances (e.g. joint ventures) limit the leakage of knowledge unrelated to the alliance relationship. Reciprocal financial and organizational relationships, which are typical of equity-based arrangements, foster the transfer of knowledge, especially tacit knowledge. However, the degree of protection in an equity-based alliance depends on the overlap between the partner's knowledge bases; knowledge diversity between partners may render an equity form obsolete because firms lack sufficient absorptive capacity (Sampson 2004b).

Decisions pertaining to the alliance design, other than its governance form, can also hinder or reinforce exposure to knowledge that is available through the relationship (Oxley and Sampson 2004; Zeng and Hennart 2002). Partners can reduce their need for knowledge transfer by limiting the alliance scope, allocating specialized tasks among the partners and forging alliances with the purpose of knowledge access rather than knowledge acquisition. For example, two firms that forge a marketing and distribution alliance may be more successful if they exchange market know-how but decide to divide distribution activities to prevent unwanted knowledge transfers. Therefore, alliance governance should retain the option of knowledge exchange, which is necessary to achieve learning objectives, while also controlling knowledge flows in order to protect proprietary know-how and avoid unintended outflows.

Alliance contracts

A firm wishing to protect knowledge may use certain legal mechanisms, such as patents, copyrights and alliance contracts. Intellectual property protection offers legal protection for inventions and processes (Arora and Ceccagnoli 2006). If another party uses a patented product or process without obtaining the proper authority, the patent holder may pursue legal remedies that prevent the use or sale of the product or process and perhaps receive monetary damages for any such infringement. However, intellectual property only provides limited protection against unwanted knowledge transfer. For example, patents do not cover all categories of competitively sensitive knowledge, and over-reliance on them may leave a company vulnerable. For high-tech industries, such as electronics and semiconductors, the patent process discloses information that may enable some competitors to 'invent around' the patent. Therefore, patents have historically been most effective in industries such as pharmaceuticals and chemicals, where the physical composition of the patented products makes them difficult to imitate without violating the patent.

It is also possible to impose certain contractual and legal mechanisms to protect specific knowledge from unwanted appropriation:

• Alliance contracts might explicitly identify knowledge and information that has been designated as proprietary. Such contracts can specify what capabilities can be shared and expressly identify those that are not to be shared.

- A more active approach imposes contractual or legal penalties if an alliance partner deliberately accesses or uses knowledge inappropriately. For example, a contractual clause might specify monetary penalties or contract termination if knowledge protection agreements are violated, such as when one partner establishes itself as a direct competitor by using illegally acquired knowledge to build its own product and discloses protected alliance information to outside parties.
- A widely used approach for implementing contractual protection requires each individual alliance member to sign a non-disclosure agreement (NDA). Each member is then bound to protect designated knowledge from being disclosed to outside parties.
- Partners might reach some kind of exclusivity agreement so that knowledge exploitation is restricted to predefined products and/or markets.
- Another protective mechanism involves employment limitations, which prohibit companies from offering jobs to the employees of an alliance partner. These limitations are usually specified for a given time period and apply to specific employees who have been involved in the alliance or have obtained relevant knowledge.

Relational capital

In a learning alliance, the willingness and ability of partners to communicate freely, share knowledge and risk unintended knowledge transfers is a result of relational capital (Hamel 1991). Trust and commitment signal a willingness to exert effort on behalf of the relationship. Furthermore, these elements increase proximity, frequency of contact and close interactions between partners, which further stimulates openness. Kale *et al.* (2000) find that relational capital based on mutual trust and interactions at the individual level create a basis for learning and know-how transfer across the exchange interface. Relational capital also fosters the accuracy, timeliness, adequacy and credibility of information exchanged. On the prevention side, relational capital mitigates the chance of a learning race because it implies a future orientation in which partners build a relationship that can weather unanticipated problems. Relational capital also protects firms against involuntary transfers of core or proprietary knowledge to partners and restricts opportunistic behaviour by alliance partners to prevent the leakage of critical know-how (Muthusamy and White 2005). For example, Jiang and colleagues (2013) empirically show that competence trust (e.g. trust in partner's capability) and goodwill trust (e.g. trust in partner's benevolence) function as effective safeguards against knowledge leakage, specifically when compared to the effect of formal contracts. In addition, the results suggest that competence trust and formal contracts complement one another, whereas goodwill trust and formal contracts are substitutable in their effect on knowledge leakage prevention.

Knowledge characteristics

The nature of the exchanged knowledge affects each party's ability to assess and acquire knowledge (Simonin 1999). As knowledge ambiguity increases, it becomes more difficult for other firms to absorb that knowledge (Kotabe *et al.* 2003), even though the level of knowledge ambiguity may be different for explicit knowledge and for tacit knowledge. Explicit knowledge, such as checklists and blueprints, is easy to codify and can be absorbed without loss of integrity. In contrast, tacit knowledge is often complex and integrated into organizational routines, technologies and individual experiences in such a way that makes it difficult to transfer across a firm's boundaries. Tacit knowledge is more resistant to appropriation, both within and across firms (Szulanski 1996), because acquiring it requires the active involvement of the knowledge provider. According to Simonin (1999), knowledge ambiguity—which is caused by factors such as tacitness (negative), complexity (positive) and organizational distance (positive)—relates negatively to knowledge transfer. The more tacit the knowledge exchanged in an alliance, the more the firms' potential to assess and acquire the knowledge is hampered, especially if the partners do not take additional measures to facilitate its transfer. Therefore, even though tacit knowledge promises a competitive advantage and represents a key motive for learning alliance formation, it is difficult to transfer, which impedes efforts to capitalize on the alliance.

Knowledge practices

Knowledge practices involve the organizational routines, control and coordination mechanisms, and systems that firms use to manage inter-firm learning (Meier 2011). Firms that engage actively and purposefully in building and deploying such practices are more effective at transferring and creating knowledge as they reinforce partners' motivational orientations towards learning, ensure resource allocations, raise the quality of human assets and stimulate the development of learning-based organizational climates and incentive structures (Chen 2004). The following are some of the forms of knowledge practices that can be used (Inkpen 2000; Lyles and Salk 1996):

- Personnel transfer, delegation of expatriates, training and education programmes and oversight of a partner firm's alliance managers support the transfer of knowledge.
- Proactive technology sharing, articulating goals and aligning learning strategies function as knowledge connections.
- Frequent interaction, active involvement and on-site meetings benefit knowledge exchange.
- Advisory systems, liaison functions, communities of practice and shared ICT systems enhance knowledge exchange.
- Reward and incentive programmes can be structured and implemented in such a way that performance appraisals incorporate measures of employees' efforts to learn and/or protect knowledge.

However, knowledge practices may differ for explicit and tacit knowledge transfer. According to Evangelista and Hau (2009), for example, commitment from senior management reinforces the transfer of explicit knowledge rather than tacit knowledge. Revilla *et al.* (2005) argue that firms must blend different learning approaches with distinct management styles, depending on their knowledge management objectives: a structural approach fits best with both exploitative learning with a focus on existing knowledge and strategic learning with a focus on new knowledge; a social approach fits best with both interactive learning with a focus on existing knowledge and integrative learning with a focus on new knowledge. In addition, Janowicz-Panjaitan and Noorderhaven (2008) demonstrate that informal knowledge practices (such as informal meetings, spontaneous interactions, both during and outside working hours) have a positive influence on knowledge transfer, whereas formal practices (participation in joint projects, joint training sessions, organized events, etc.) have a positive but diminishing effect. These findings are corroborated by Khan and colleagues (2015) reporting that formal socialization mechanisms enhance the comprehension and speed of knowledge transfer from international joint ventures to local partners, whereas informal socialization mechanisms enhance comprehension but not speed.

The role of staff involved in the alliance

Despite not usually being involved in the day-to-day operation of alliances, senior management often plays a significant and vital role in enabling or constraining knowledge flows. Senior managers must identify the firm's core capabilities and determine which knowledge cannot be transferred. Although senior managers may not make all such decisions themselves, they must ensure that adequate management processes exist so that appropriately designated members of the firm can make timely decisions. Senior management must also create awareness by stressing personally the importance of protecting the company's critical capabilities. They should also ensure that the required resources are allocated to protect knowledge and educate the work force. Failure to make these decisions clear and communicate them widely can cause alliance members and other employees to share information inadvertently that could harm the firm's competitive position.

Alliance managers should endorse and strengthen senior management's emphasis on the protection of core capabilities. Alliance managers may appoint or act as knowledge managers, who monitor, survey and scrutinize critical knowledge to ensure it has been classified accurately and that alliance members and other involved employees are properly informed and educated about relevant issues. The role of a knowledge manager is usually an additional duty that is assumed by the overall alliance manager or another key manager (for example, a business coordinator or lead engineer). Alliance managers must also ensure that employees follow the guidelines and procedures established by the knowledge protection system. Finally, alliance managers might also act as consultants if employees believe the circumstances surrounding knowledge protection are vague or unclear.

In turn, these employees constitute an important knowledge protection mechanism. Knowledge leakage is often primarily dependent on the choices of individuals who work daily in the alliance and come in to regular contact with alliance partners. Any point of contact between the firm's employees and its partner's employees represents an information flow that could allow the inappropriate communication of critical knowledge. One way to protect knowledge is to provide employees with education and training programmes, which are usually conducted in conjunction with the alliance manager. For employees who are indirectly involved or may only occasionally come into contact with partner employees, alliance managers must also ensure that they understand the importance of maintaining confidentiality. Firms may also require employees to report any contact with alliance partners if they believe an information issue exists. Such a report would be advisable, for example, if an employee believed an alliance partner was 'fishing around' for critical knowledge that had been marked as off-limits.

Learning alliances: decision-making steps

A high-quality knowledge interface creates the potential for alliance partners to evaluate each other's competences, strengths and weaknesses. Such an interface enables a firm to assess the value of new knowledge and integrate this knowledge into its existing knowledge base. However, a high-quality knowledge interface also increases the degree of openness, which exposes alliance partners to the danger of losing valuable knowledge, thus creating the need for knowledge protection. To steer learning alliances towards success, we connect the governance of learning alliances to the stages of our alliance development framework (see Figure 11.1).

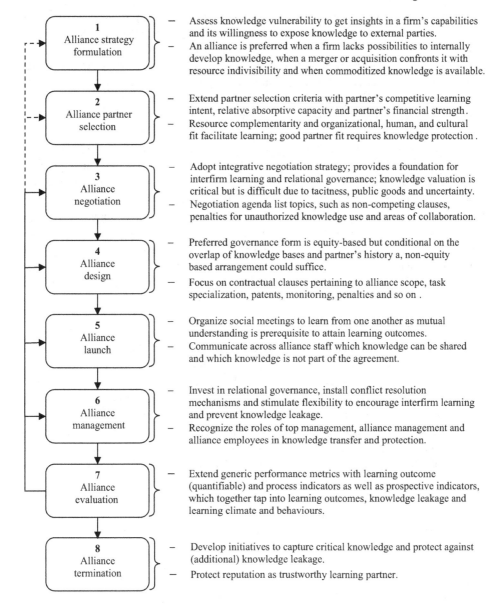

1
Alliance strategy formulation
- Assess knowledge vulnerability to get insights in a firm's capabilities and its willingness to expose knowledge to external parties.
- An alliance is preferred when a firm lacks possibilities to internally develop knowledge, when a merger or acquisition confronts it with resource indivisibility and when commoditized knowledge is available.

2
Alliance partner selection
- Extend partner selection criteria with partner's competitive learning intent, relative absorptive capacity and partner's financial strength.
- Resource complementarity and organizational, human, and cultural fit facilitate learning; good partner fit requires knowledge protection.

3
Alliance negotiation
- Adopt integrative negotiation strategy; provides a foundation for interfirm learning and relational governance; knowledge valuation is critical but is difficult due to tacitness, public goods and uncertainty.
- Negotiation agenda list topics, such as non-competing clauses, penalties for unauthorized knowledge use and areas of collaboration.

4
Alliance design
- Preferred governance form is equity-based but conditional on the overlap of knowledge bases and partner's history a, non-equity based arrangement could suffice.
- Focus on contractual clauses pertaining to alliance scope, task specialization, patents, monitoring, penalties and so on.

5
Alliance launch
- Organize social meetings to learn from one another as mutual understanding is prerequisite to attain learning outcomes.
- Communicate across alliance staff which knowledge can be shared and which knowledge is not part of the agreement.

6
Alliance management
- Invest in relational governance, install conflict resolution mechanisms and stimulate flexibility to encourage interfirm learning and prevent knowledge leakage.
- Recognize the roles of top management, alliance management and alliance employees in knowledge transfer and protection.

7
Alliance evaluation
- Extend generic performance metrics with learning outcome (quantifiable) and process indicators as well as prospective indicators, which together tap into learning outcomes, knowledge leakage and learning climate and behaviours.

8
Alliance termination
- Develop initiatives to capture critical knowledge and protect against (additional) knowledge leakage.
- Protect reputation as trustworthy learning partner.

FIGURE 11.1 Alliance development framework: learning alliances

Step 1: alliance strategy formulation

During the alliance strategy formulation stage, firms decide whether an alliance is an appropriate governance mode for acquiring and/or developing new knowledge, technology and capabilities. From a learning alliance perspective, the objective is to obtain or access knowledge that reinforces the firm's knowledge base. To this end, a market exchange is unsuited as it means that the desired knowledge is readily available to rivals as well; commoditized knowledge is not likely to contribute to a firm's competitive advantage. When a firm recognizes that it both lacks the desired knowledge and the possibility to develop it internally (e.g. lack of know-how or too expensive), a merger or acquisition could be a viable alternative. But in most instances, resource indivisibility impedes this governance mode as a firm is often only interested in accessing and obtaining specific knowledge, not a target's complete knowledge endowment. Alternatively, an alliance constitutes an appropriate option as it grants access to desired knowledge while offering flexibility. For example, pharmaceuticals forge alliances with a wide range of small bio-tech firms to access their knowledge and only acquire a bio-tech firm when it has developed a commercial viable particle for a drug.

However, exposing critical knowledge to external parties through an alliance increases the risk of unwanted spillovers, which can directly undermine a firm's competitive position. During their strategic analysis, therefore, firms must also assess their vulnerability by analyzing the knowledge resources they possess, as well as the strategic relevance and transferability of that knowledge. If a firm's knowledge has strategic value and the risk of knowledge leakage is relatively high, internal development and mergers and acquisitions might become preferred alternatives because these governance modes provide better protection. However, if the potential risks of an alliance are outweighed by its benefits, the firm should consider taking steps to protect itself. The firm must consider its decisions at the subsequent stages with great care.

Step 2: alliance partner selection

During the partner selection stage, a firm selects the partner(s) with which it can establish the learning alliance. Partner fit must enable inter-firm learning, and resource complementarity between partners is also important. The partners' knowledge foundations should have sufficient overlap to enable knowledge transfer, but the partners should also be different enough to capitalize on learning opportunities. Organizational fit is particularly relevant because it enables partners to build an adequate knowledge interface through compatible organizational structures and systems. Human and cultural fit, which suggest similarity between employees in terms of experience, background, education, and professional and cultural identities, are also important because they foster learning at the micro level between individuals. However, firms must be aware that, as partner fit increases, so does the need for knowledge protection.

Partner selection criteria may also include relative absorptive capacity, the learning intent of potential partners and financial resources. If partners have differing abilities to evaluate, assess and assimilate external knowledge, this could create learning races, which are likely to lead to a premature dissolution of the alliance. Relevant indicators of absorptive capacity include existing knowledge resources, learning structures, staff competences and knowledge practices. When a potential partner has high absorptive capacity, protective measures may be required, specifically if an alliance is formed with a competitor. Knowledge leakage to a rival usually jeopardizes a firm's competitive position. Furthermore, the assessment of a partner's learning intent should reveal whether possible knowledge spillovers are likely to be exploited. However, although indirect sources of information can provide important clues about learning intent, firms must remain aware that this intent may be hidden, misrepresented or denied. For example, a systematic pattern of alliances focused on an emerging technology implies competitive learning intent. If a potential partner has such a competitive learning intent (i.e. is a direct competitor), detrimental learning races are more likely. To prevent such races, a firm should consider whether it can impose knowledge protection mechanisms on its partner without destroying the value creation potential of the alliance. In addition, financial strength of a partner may constitute a selection criterion as building and maintaining successful learning alliances often require substantial financial investments in, for example, research centres and patenting.

Step 3: alliance negotiation

This stage involves negotiations between alliance partners regarding scope and conditions; if the parties reach a consensus, they can formalize the outcomes in an alliance contract. When parties adopt integrative negotiation strategies, they are likely to create openness, build transparency, engage in mutual information exchange and stimulate joint problem solving, which increases the chances that they will achieve aligned interests. Furthermore, this negotiation strategy creates a solid foundation for learning alliances, which tend to have uncertain learning outcomes and depend on cooperative alliance processes. Distributive negotiation strategies, on the other hand, prevent mutually beneficial solutions and require withholding or distorting information to secure and protect individual interests. Though possessing valuable knowledge may provide a firm with a bargaining power advantage, using it to support distributive negotiation strategies undermines the knowledge creation potential of a learning alliance.

Furthermore, in order for a learning alliance to succeed, each partner must contribute some knowledge, whether it is in the form of basic research capability, product development skills, manufacturing capabilities or market know-how. An ex-ante assessment of the value of knowledge is cumbersome; it is easier to attach value to tangibles than to measure the value of intellectual capital. However, as competitive abilities increasingly come to rely on firm competences, efforts to assess their value are necessary. Firms should assess investments made in building skills that are central to their competitive advantage and should judge the competitive consequences of a partner's development of those same skills. However, the knowledge created in an alliance often constitutes a public good, meaning that parties can appropriate knowledge and information without depleting the source during different stages of alliance development. This makes it difficult, if not impossible, to determine the amount of knowledge creation, let alone formalize parties' claims to this realized knowledge and distribute it according to a predetermined rule. In addition, a negotiation agenda may contain topics, such as noncompeting provisions, penalties for unauthorized acquisition and exploitation of knowledge and the knowledge scope (i.e. the areas in which knowledge is shared).

Step 4: alliance design

An alliance design shapes the flow of knowledge, the breadth and depth of the interaction between the two firms and the incentives for inter-firm learning. Decisions about the knowledge interface should aim to enhance inter-firm learning by directly affecting the partners' ability to absorb knowledge and the rate of knowledge dissemination. As a result, parties should have little difficulty assessing the value and relevance of new knowledge or assimilating that knowledge into their existing knowledge stores. In addition, because an alliance design functions as a first and critical protection mechanism against knowledge leakage, it should incorporate incentives to learn and barriers to avoid knowledge leakage.

The decision regarding governance form is likely to indicate some preference for equity arrangements because such arrangements stimulate knowledge exchanges but still safeguard against knowledge leakages. If the partner firms have already built relational capital, perhaps through their prior collaborations, the flexibility and lower coordination costs of non-equity-based arrangements may outweigh the benefits of an equity-based form. In addition, firms must formalize contractual decisions. Contractual clauses should state that knowledge exchange is tied exclusively to non-competitive activities, is protected by patents and copyrights, or is subject to shared ownership by partners. Such restrictions limit the likelihood of competitive and opportunistic behaviour. Furthermore, partners may reduce the alliance scope (that is, market overlap in alliance and firm activities), which also minimizes the risk of leaking sensitive knowledge to another partner. Therefore, the scope of the alliance may only involve precompetitive cooperation. Contractual clauses specifying how and when partners are supposed to contribute financial resources are also critical.

In learning alliances, the potential outflow of proprietary technology is partially controlled by partitioning tasks between partners, but in turn, co-specialization also impedes knowledge transfer. Sequential knowledge sharing may also help build partner trust before the partners share sensitive knowledge that could harm either firm's competitive position. For example, a firm might start by sharing older technologies and gradually start sharing newer ones over time; this approach enables firms to observe partner behaviour and secure intent. Control over human resources is also a means of protecting intellectual capital. For example, agreeing to involve senior management and operating managers in alliance formation should stimulate learning and prevent post-formation opportunistic behaviour. Because knowledge flows over learning interfaces, staff members who are directly involved in the alliance should be allocated in such a way that they constitute a collaborative membrane, maximizing the inflow of necessary knowledge while minimizing unintended outflows. Agreement on the location of the alliance is also important as it affects partners' ability to control knowledge flows. For example, a neutral location offers partners equal opportunities to learn, whereas research activities located at one of the partner's facilities offers its counterpart a learning advantage.

Step 5: alliance launch

During the alliance launch stage, the partner firms evolve from negotiation and design to executing the alliance contract. Systemically organizing the alliance implementation in a learning alliance is critical as joint learning is surrounded by ambiguity. First, although partners may have agreed upon joint learning objectives (e.g. development and commoditization of an innovative service), operational staff may have questions, possess different views about innovation and may have a natural disposition against the rival partner to share key knowledge. As part of the alliance launch strategy, the launch manager should develop initiatives, such as kick-off meetings, joint training programmes and communities of practice, to inform, motivate and provide clear directions to involved staff. As part of operational plans, communication should also focus on informing staff about motives for the learning alliance and also about what skills and technologies are off-limits to the partner and how learning processes are to be monitored. Second, as learning thrives on relational capital, the launch manager should invest in trust-building and provide a context in which strong social networks between staff members can emerge and flourish. Such networks enhance learning, stimulate creativity and provide protection against unwanted knowledge leakage. To accomplish these two tasks, it is critical that alliance launch managers find a balance between relational governance and formal governance. The former facilitates learning efforts, and the latter enables monitoring and detecting deviant (learning) behaviours via tailored performance metric systems.

Step 6: alliance management

Within the setting of learning alliances, the alliance management stage initiates day-to-day operations that enable partner firms to create and exchange enough knowledge to obtain advantages over rivals outside the alliance but still prevent the wholesale transfer of core skills to a partner. A critical task for management is to build relational capital, which serves two main purposes:

1   Relational capital increases proximity, frequency of contact and close interactions between partners, which enables them to overcome learning barriers and embrace transparency and receptivity. Joint information processing makes partners better able to evaluate each other's competences, strengths and weaknesses, which facilitates the integration of new knowledge within a firm's existing knowledge base.
2   Relational capital reduces the probability of distributive-oriented learning strategies that focus on securing individual interests, transfer of knowledge that is not part of the agreement, protecting proprietary knowledge and appropriating knowledge without considering the alliance's value-creation potential.

Step 7: alliance evaluation

This stage requires a performance metric system that should include learning and relational metrics. Learning metrics should comprise metrics capturing learning processes and outcomes, which are pivotal to steering learning alliances. Whereas process metrics, such as the learning behaviour of researchers and the number of documents exchanged, provide information about the quality and working of the knowledge infrastructure, outcome metrics, such as degree of knowledge leakage and number of commercially viable product innovations, are indicative of the alliance's success. In addition, prospective indicators, such as the patenting rate and R&D spending, are required to obtain information about the alliance's progress. Relational metrics capture the quality of the relationship and entail trust and commitment metrics. Because relational processes are critical to learning alliances, the insights that related metrics provide enable firms to enhance the alliance's learning climate: to stimulate inter-firm learning while enforcing relational protection against leakage. Taken together, learning and relational metrics provide alliance managers with relevant information to initiate adaptations to their alliance design and management.

Step 8: alliance termination

If partners have reached this stage, it means they have decided to dissolve the alliance. Depending on the alliance contract, each firm must capture knowledge and secure it against loss. Using the performance metric system, a firm can assess the extent to which it has achieved its learning objectives. If the outcome is not satisfactory, the firm should explore possibilities to internalize critical knowledge as well as erect additional knowledge protection barriers, if possible, to prevent the other partner from appropriating valuable knowledge. A firm also might examine contractual clauses and, if required, confront the other partner. However, for the sake of its future alliance efforts, the firm must protect its reputation as a trustworthy learning alliance partner.

Summary

Learning alliances provide platforms for the creation and application of knowledge; their essential purpose is to create, transfer, assemble, integrate and exploit knowledge assets. As such, learning alliances function as vehicles to enhance a firm's competitive advantage. However, learning alliances also present risks for a firm as they provide partner firms with an opportunity to obtain access to knowledge that is not part of the initial alliance agreement. The risk of unwanted knowledge leakage creates the need for knowledge protection. To this end, this chapter has elaborated on mechanisms that enable or impede inter-firm learning, including absorptive capacity, alliance governance, contracts, relational capital, knowledge practices and alliance staff. In a learning alliance, the primary task of alliance management is to achieve the delicate balance between exploiting learning opportunities and curbing learning risks. To guide decision making, we presented managerial guidelines for each alliance development stage.

CASE: HOLST CENTRE[1]

The Holst Centre is an independent open-innovation centre for R&D that develops generic technologies for wireless autonomous sensor technologies and flexible electronics. A key feature of the Holst Centre is its partnership model with industry and academia, which is based on shared development roadmaps and programmes. This kind of cross-fertilization enables the Holst Centre to tune its scientific strategy to industrial needs. The Holst Centre was set up in 2005 by IMEC (Flanders, Belgium) and TNO (the Netherlands), with support from the Dutch Ministry of Economic Affairs and the Government of Flanders. The centre is named after Gilles Holst, a Dutch pioneer in research and development and the first director of Philips Research. Located on High-Tech Campus Eindhoven, the Holst Centre benefits from the state-of-the-art on-site facilities and has more than 170 employees, representing roughly 25 nationalities and commitments from approximately 35 industrial partners.

During the 1990s and the early 2000s, Philips Research (formerly Natlab) found it increasingly difficult to provide cutting-edge but affordable R&D services to the Philips product divisions. Rapid technological developments made it increasingly difficult for Philips Research to remain a front-runner in all of the necessary technology domains using only its in-house R&D resources. The future was in combining knowledge that was developed and owned by Philips with knowledge of other firms and research institutions in a more open environment. To this end, the closed 'Philips Research Campus' was transformed into the open 'High-Tech Campus Eindhoven'. Moreover, many of the Philips-owned laboratories on this campus were made accessible to third parties through a separate organization called 'MiPlaza'. Supporting activities and facilities such as restaurants, sports facilities and shops were centralized in a building called 'the Strip', which became the central meeting place of the High-Tech Campus and a vital element in open communication and exchanging information. Independent organizations were set up to facilitate and orchestrate open innovation. The primary role of these organizations is to bring people and organizations together and facilitate active communication, information sharing and co-research. The most important facilitator is the Holst Centre.

At the Holst Centre, leading scientists work on research programmes together with scientists of partner companies and universities. These parties participate in research programmes facilitated by the Holst Centre to share ideas, costs and risks. Conducting the type of research in which the Holst Centre is involved requires significant investment, which may not be affordable for many firms individually. The Dutch government provides subsidies, which creates more favourable conditions for partners to join the research programmes. Another important motivation for joining research programmes at the Holst Centre is the availability of research competences that are complementary to those available at one's own organization. The Holst Centre facilitates and expands its research programmes by actively managing the partnerships. For example, in 2022, TNO and Imec (two independent research institutes) signed a letter of intent committing to work together on integrated photonics. Both research centres have been working on photonics innovations for some time, but they have now joined forces to accelerate the development of the photonics industry in the Netherlands, Belgium and Europe. The collaboration will start in 2023 within Holst Centre. Holst Centre plays an active role in PhotonDelta's National Growth Fund proposal and will further strengthen its position as a knowledge centre with this agreement.

In other words, the Holst Centre plays an active role in facilitating knowledge creation and knowledge sharing, while respecting the fact that the background knowledge of each of the participating firms may not be affected. Therefore, the Holst Centre focuses its research programmes on generic technologies for 'wireless autonomous transducer' solutions and 'systems in foil'. The Holst Centre does not engage in product development, which is left to the participating companies. The focus on this so-called pre-competitive research reduces the threat of competitive interests jeopardizing the open research model. The Holst Centre also engages in active partner portfolio management. Traditional alliances tend to focus on single goals and typically consist of a fixed number of specific partners, which team up during a fixed period. Since technology development is so dynamic, various competences are required at various stages of the research programme. This might require partners to phase in or out of the research programmes. The Holst Centre has implemented effective partner portfolio management structures by using research roadmaps, knowledge mapping and partner selection strategies.

The research programmes are managed by roadmaps. Research roadmaps typically describe goals that can be realized in five to ten years, and for each roadmap, work breakdown structures are provided that describe how the long-term goals are to be achieved. These research roadmaps allow the necessary research competences to be identified. The Holst Centre then approaches appropriate partners that will benefit from the shared results, are able to deliver the required competences and fit the open innovation culture within the Holst Centre. In order to build the strongest knowledge and value chains in the Holst Centre, partners must be leading players in their field. Diversity is also considered a vital asset to the research community active within the Holst Centre. This refers not only to diversity in research competences and knowledge areas but also diversity in culture and nationality. As well as large corporations, small companies and startups are also partners of the Holst Centre. Research benefits from the dynamic atmosphere within the consortium.

Individual participating organizations do not have a blocking vote regarding the admission of a new partner. However, the Holst Centre communicates closely with existing participants about the admission of new participants in order to maintain the required motivation and provide reassurance that appropriate choices will be made. The Holst Centre charges entrance and participation fees, which entitle partners to non-exclusive access to the research results. When new partners step into an existing research programme, they must pay an entrance fee that increases over time to maintain a fair situation between earlier and later entrants. By paying the entrance fee, the new partners receive access to the background knowledge that was created in the research programme prior to their involvement. However, this access is limited to background knowledge that is required to exploit newly created foreground knowledge (the intended results achieved during participation).

The Holst Centre also actively helps organizations that are considering joining the consortium to establish what should be exclusive and what can be brought into the consortium. The Holst Centre provides an important assurance to participating organizations that collaboration will not endanger in-house research activities and intellectual property. Each research programme is managed by a programme manager (a Holst Centre representative), who plays an important role in preventing participation imbalances. Research contributions and transfer of research results are actively monitored. Parties are confronted if any imbalances between knowledge contributions and knowledge acquisitions are detected or suspected. Partners receive only access to the knowledge resulting from the specific programme(s) in which they participate, and the Holst Centre's open innovation works only within secure environments. Not all knowledge is open to all participants, and participation does involve certain obligations. In other words, the Holst Centre's open innovation is not 'public innovation'.

Questions

1   Explain why the mechanisms the Holst Centre uses to facilitate knowledge exchange and guarantee knowledge protection are effective.
2   Explain why the Holst centre promotes pre-emptive research and openness among participants but does not consider marketization a primary task.
3   How would these mechanisms operate in a single alliance between two partners?

Note

1   Interview with a senior executive of the Holst Centre; HSD (2022).

12

CO-BRANDING ALLIANCES

Co-branding, co-partnering or dual branding are all terms to refer to the act of presenting two established brand names, owned by different companies, simultaneously to customers. Such tactics have made inroads into nearly every industry, from automotive and high-tech internet firms to banking and fast food providers. Co-branding alliances constitute a weapon for firms as they attempt to transfer the positive associations of their partners' products or brands to the newly formed co-brand, or composite brand, create synergy between existing brands, or even build up (or change) an existing brand. This avenue draws in new customers, increases brand awareness, supports customer loyalty, offers signals of quality and an image of success and binds the brand with certain emotions. Although a co-branding strategy thus can be a win–win proposition for alliance partners, even when those brands have unequal standing or brand equity in the marketplace, co-branding alliances present their own set of unique risks. For example, actions by one partner firm may damage the other's reputation, established co-brands are difficult to dismantle and brand spillover effects may be distributed unevenly across the partners. This tension—between reaping the benefits of co-branding and simultaneously protecting firms from negative repercussions—confronts alliance managers with a unique challenge. Therefore, our first section discusses this co-branding alliance challenge, and the following section elaborates mechanisms for dealing with it. We use the alliance development framework to develop managerial guidelines for co-branding alliances in the third section, and the chapter concludes with a summary and a case illustration.

The co-branding alliance challenge

A brand is the personality that identifies a product, service or company and its relationship with key constituencies, such as customers, staff, partners and investors (Kotler 1991). In addition to a brand name, a brand may be a term, sign, symbol or drawing or some combination of these elements. The brand translates the organizational identity—the internal perception of organizations and their product and services—into terms that external stakeholders can understand, with the goal of creating a positive image. The brand also cues customers to recall images they have formed through their past experiences with brands or information they obtained about it (Swait *et al.* 1993). When further information is not available, customers

DOI: 10.4324/9781003222187-12

can use the brand (or brand names) to make judgements about the product. Consequently, a firm hopes to position its brand in a way that makes its uniqueness and value apparent to customers. As a form of communication, brands effectively communicate, consistent with firms' actions, which gives customers deeper and more meaningful consumption experiences.

To build strong brand reputations, firms increasingly employ co-branding alliances, which pair two (or more) individual brands and present them simultaneously to customers (Geylani et al. 2008), often in the form of a single, unique product or service (Chang and Chang 2008). Co-branding alliances link the participating brands in the mind of consumers to enable the transfer of thoughts and feelings from one brand to another. This use of two or more brand names to introduce new products helps the partners capitalize on their combined reputations in an attempt to achieve immediate recognition and positive evaluations by potential buyers (see Table 12.1). These immediate attitudes towards a particular co-branded alliance also influence subsequent attitudes towards the individual brands in that alliance. For example, the presence of a second brand on a product reinforces the perception of high product quality and thus higher product evaluations. Most co-branding relationships include brands with an obvious or natural relationship that has the potential to be commercially beneficial for both parties. When the target customers of each firm match, at least to some extent, customers also should accept this connection and thereby formulate associations easily.

Several motives underpin firms' decisions to forge co-branding alliances (Chang and Chang 2008; Erevelles et al. 2008). First, firms may find themselves unable to reach new customer segments with their individual marketing apparatus. A co-branding alliance provides access to the partner firm's marketing infrastructure, which is likely to reach somewhat different customer segments, or reaches them in a different way, increasing sales revenues. Second, marketing activities are costly, especially when they include new product development and launches. A co-branding partnership shares such marketing costs across the partners. Third, marketing activities often pose risk to individual firms, again especially when their scope includes new

TABLE 12.1 Examples of co-branding alliances

	Description
Kellogg–Nickelodeon	In 2022, Kellogg established a co-brand partnership with Nickelodeon. The partners intend to co-create a new green apple flavoured cereal inspired by Nickelodeon's green slime. The cereal contains green and orange coloured loops and green pieces that turn milk the colour of Nickelodeon's famous green slime.
GoPro–Red Bull	In 2016, GoPro and RedBull announced they were joining forces on a multi-year, global partnership that includes content production, distribution, cross-promotion and product innovation. As part of the agreement, Red Bull received equity in GoPro, and GoPro became Red Bull's exclusive provider of point-of-view imaging technology for capturing immersive footage of Red Bull's media productions and events.
Heineken–The Shoe Surgeon	In 2022, Heineken, a beer brewer, teamed up with The Shoe Surgeon, a celebrated sneaker designer. To support the launch of Heineken Silver, the brewer's lighter, low-alcohol beer, the partners introduced a limited edition Heinekicks.

Sources: GoPro (2016); Kiefer (2022); Kellogg (2022).

product development. Relying on the strength of a partner brand through a co-branding alliance, each member has a better chance of reaching its marketing goals. Fourth, a firm that aligns its brand with another is often seeking to enhance its product image and credibility, which can then improve customer confidence. These motives reflect the promise of positive spillover effects (Park *et al.* 1996): reinforcing positive reciprocal effects of co-branding on alliance partners' brands. However, co-branding alliances also may result in image impairment if combining the two brands causes brand meaning to transfer in ways that were never intended.

In particular, a negative brand spillover effect, which represents an adverse impact of co-branding on the perceptions of stakeholders, including customers' perceptions (Park *et al.* 1996), results when firms that are incompatible in some way forge a co-branding alliance. For example, inconsistency between customers' associations for the two brands leads to a negative response if the alliance forces the customer to transfer the association of one brand to the other. A potential repositioning of a brand also could adversely influence the other party's brand. Furthermore, such negative spillover effects often get unevenly distributed, such that one partner experiences positive repercussions, while its counterpart suffers the negative outcomes. Such an unbalanced spillover effect creates a free-riding problem; the partner experiencing positive effects lacks the incentive to accommodate any changes to address the negative effects suffered by its partner.

In addition to potential negative spillover effects, a co-branding alliance can reduce a firm's flexibility because once this association becomes rooted in stakeholders' perceptions, it is difficult to end the partnership without incurring substantial costs. When a co-brand achieves a particular position in a market, it is difficult to knock it out of that place—and even more difficult to re-establish a single brand on its own. Furthermore, customers do not just accept that things can go wrong, and rebuilding a damaged reputation requires substantial investment. In particular, inappropriate actions by one alliance partner may have severe repercussions on its counterpart's brand, though reputation damage is also possible owing to events beyond the alliance, such as when interest groups bring pressure to bear on one of the alliance partners.

Firms engaged in a co-branding alliance thus confront unique challenges. On the one hand, they need to collaborate to strengthen their brand reputations and achieve positive spillover effects. On the other hand, these partners risk damaging their brand reputations through negative spillover effects and the potential for harmful actions by partners. Alliance partners that can deal effectively with such challenges have an opportunity to create powerful synergies that not only improve reputations but also accelerate performance. Those that fail to do so, however, are likely to damage the alliance's progress, the partners' reputations and their own brands.

Managing co-branding alliances

A wide range of co-branding alliance activities take place in the marketplace (Geylani *et al.* 2008), ranging from touting several brands in a single advertisement (e.g. joint Shell–Ferrari ads, messages about the complementary consumption of McDonald's fries and Coca-Cola) to jointly branded products (e.g. the Lexus Coach Edition, Kellogg's Healthy Choice cereal; see Box 12.1 for some other examples). Because customers seek consistency and internal harmony in their attitudes, but their evaluations of one brand are influenced by the context of another co-brand, it is important to distinguish these various types of co-branding alliances. In general, co-branding consists of four types (Chang and Chang 2008; Washburn *et al.* 2000).

First, in a joint promotion, two brands promote their products together, usually because one or both of them hopes to secure a corporate endorsement that will improve its market position. For example, cross-marketing co-branding involves the mutual promotion by two companies, such as when one company includes coupons for another company in its packaging, in return for which the other company features a promotion from the first company in its direct mailing to its client base.

Second, joint advertising occurs when a specific product owned by one firm appears in the advertising campaign or product of another firm. In *Austin Powers: The Spy Who Shagged Me*, a woman in a photo shoot uses a Powerbook G3 Lombard; in *Mission Impossible 2*, Anthony Hopkins' character describes the mission on a Powerbook G3 Wallstreet. Unlike joint promotion, in joint advertising, partners avoid long-term or repetitive campaigns. However, both joint promotion and joint advertising are relatively easy to design and manage as the effort is limited mainly to the firms' marketing departments.

Third, when promoting the complementary use of their products, firms endorse the brands of a distinct yet complementary product. In addition to aligning the brands, such efforts can evoke favourable responses from consumers. For example, Nike and Apple suggest using an iPod with running shoes to encourage faster times, further distances and personal coaching. Such complementary uses again constitute a less intensive form of collaboration because the partner firms turn to existing products to endorse their brands.

Fourth, physical product integration or ingredient co-branding involves actual product integration. One brand, which is usually the market leader for its product, supplies that product as a component in another branded product. In one example, Bacardi and Coca-Cola provide mixers with both brand names that suggest combining their flagship products to make a rum-and-cola drink. Ingredient co-branding alliance is thus the most intensive form of collaboration because it involves multiple departments, including product design, production and marketing. It appears particularly common when a supplier comes under the threat of entry by a competitor because the incumbent supplier can reduce the probability of this entry while rewarding its downstream partner with a lower price.

BOX 12.1 ALTERNATIVE FORMS OF CO-BRANDING

Partnering charitable causes with brands has become a common practice, referred to as cause–brand alliances. Allying a cause with a familiar brand improves attitudes towards the cause if the cause is relatively unfamiliar, but it also tends to result in more favourable brand associations. Firms might also sponsor sports or the arts in an attempt to associate their brands with renowned events, athletes, artists and celebrities. Adidas' long track record of alliances with famous athletes features partnerships with David Beckham and Lionel Messi. In addition, firms forge global co-branding alliances to obtain global coverage for their brands or use co-branding alliances to extend the number of product categories in which they are active. Philips and Nivea combined their brand names and product to mass market the Cool Skin: an electric razor that dispenses shaving lotion; Gillette M3 power shaving equipment is co-branded with Duracell batteries, both brands owned by Proctor & Gamble; the BMW–Rover alliance to develop the new Mini constituted a brand extension strategy. Although they differ in nature, these alternative forms of co-branding alliances all seek to improve competitive positions through an alignment with a prestigious partner brand.

Managing spillover effects in co-branding alliances

The main principle behind co-branding alliances, irrespective of the type of alliance, is that the allying firms help each other to exploit their brands. The purpose of their double appeal is to capitalize on the brand value of the partner brand to achieve immediate recognition and a positive evaluation from potential buyers. In managing co-branding alliances, firms may focus on five instruments that influence the emergence of positive—and prevent the creation of negative—spillover effects (Simonin and Ruth 1998): (1) brand and product fit, (2) preexisting brand attitudes, (3) brand equity, (4) alliance partner behaviour and (5) contractual provisions (see Table 12.2).

Brand and product fit

The success of co-branding alliances primarily depends on associations that (potential) customers have with the involved brands. That is, the likelihood that consumers will purchase the new product increases when two brands fit together (Moon and Sprott 2016; Nabec *et al.* 2016). Co-branding alliances form to increase positive perceptions of at least one of the brands involved; the presence of a second brand creates the possibility that the two brands will be perceived as similar in quality. For example, if one brand is less well known than the other, a co-branding alliance can increase assimilation, such that the image of the less well-known brand comes to align with the image of the better known brand and its values, in the minds of consumers. The existence of overall cohesiveness between the two brands makes evaluations of the brand alliance more positive and favourable than they would be if the brands and their associations were regarded as incompatible and inconsistent. Whereas perceived fit between the two brands, products or services thus offers a predictor of alliance success, brand misfit impedes alliance performance (Chang and Chang 2008).

TABLE 12.2 Managing co-branding alliances

	Description	*Implications*
Brand and product fit	The extent to which brands and/or products are perceived by customers to possess similar attributes.	Overall cohesiveness between brands and/or products results in more favourable perceptions of the co-brand.
Pre-existing brand attitudes	Initial attitudes towards an individual brand affect dispositions towards the co-branding alliance.	Negative and positive pre-existing brand attitudes impact the direction and nature of brand-spillover effects.
Brand equity	Set of assets and liabilities linked to a brand's name or symbol, which adds to or subtracts from the perceived brand value.	Brand equity management enables partners to reinforce positive and mitigate negative brand-spillover effects.
Partner's behaviour	Perceptions of partner's competence and morals are critical, as they affect perceptions of the co-brand.	Incompetent (e.g. low-quality) or immoral (e.g. dishonest) behaviour results in negative brand-spillover effects.
Contractual provisions	Contracts help to reduce the adverse repercussions of negative brand-spillover effects.	Contracts may contain clauses related to licensing, trademarks, intellectual property, liability and exclusivity.

Brand misfit arises when customers perceive incompatibility between the alliance partners' brands. For example, if a high-quality brand partners with a low-cost brand, customers of the high-quality brand will perceive a misfit and experience more uncertainty towards their brand because the association allows for a transfer of uncertainty from the less reliable to the more reliable brand (Geylani *et al.* 2008). In the late 1990s, the financial services provider H&R Block partnered with Bristol-Myers Squibb in a joint promotion of tax services and Excedrin pain relievers. No one got it. That is, the co-branding alliance failed because customers did not recognize any association between the two brands. On paper, the message seemed to make sense: both Excedrin and H&R Block could relieve the headaches associated with completing taxes. Unfortunately, customers instead perceived that H&R Block would cause migraines that only Excedrin could cure. This difference between actual and perceived meanings may have seemed difficult to anticipate in advance, but the overall lack of product or brand fit contributed to the failure of the alliance. Poor fit offers less positive attitude changes than co-branding with strong fit; it can also induce deteriorating quality perceptions and a costly erosion of brand equity. If a firm, however, decides to opt for a low-fitting co-branding alliance, beneficial behavioural consequences might still be expected. For example, if partners forge an alliance with unrelated brand concepts but develop a strong and persuasive argument, the co-branding arrangement could be perceived as relevant (Samuelsen *et al.* 2015). This is because 'misfit' co-branding alliances may trigger curiosity, which could lead to elaboration to resolve the low-fit perceptions.

In addition to brand fit, product fit reflects perceived compatibility in terms of the function or quality of the products offered by the alliance firms. Two brands working together should provide greater assurance about product quality than one brand on its own, and attitudes towards the brand alliance should improve even more at higher degrees of product fit. Customers see that another firm is willing to put its reputation on the line, so they develop greater trust in the product (Park *et al.* 1996). However, if no natural logic aligns the combined products, customers cannot understand the reason for the partnership. In addition, product fit matters more when the alliance lacks brand fit. That is, consumers look first for image congruence, and if it is missing, they try to find congruence on the product category level.

The selection of co-branding partners accordingly must take brand and product fit into consideration. A firm might seek a complementary partner; Park and colleagues (1996) show that the combination of two brands with complementary attribute levels leads to a composite brand extension with a better attribute profile than either a direct extension of the dominant brand or an extension with two favourable but non-complementary brands. Alternatively, a firm might seek a partner with similar brand associations because the brands then evoke equivalent responses from customers. For example, alliance managers in the mobile telephone industry might forge co-branding alliances based on brand personality, such as sincerity, excitement, competence, sophistication and ruggedness (Chang 2009). If a firm appears exciting and competent, it might search out a partner that is sincere, sophisticated and rugged because the resulting complementary alliance would cover all the dimensions. Or it could find another exciting and competent partner to forge a co-branding alliance with similar attributes.

Pre-existing brand attitudes

Attitudes are relatively stable psychological constructs, so pre-existing brand attitudes tend to relate closely to post-exposure attitudes towards that same brand (Simonin and Ruth 1998). Consequently, initial negative or positive attitudes towards an individual brand often transfer to a co-brand, and vice versa. A firm with a favourable perceived brand image might thus forge a co-branding alliance with a firm that suffers from a less favourable perceived brand image, assuming brand and product fit exist, to reconcile customers sympathetic with their adverse perceptions. Positive attitudes towards individual brands get reinforced even further when customers process favourable information about a co-branding alliance (e.g. advertisements) or enjoy positive experiences with a co-branded product. Thus a well-known, well-liked firm such as McDonald's might signal the quality of a lesser-known brand, but it must do so carefully because, in some cases, a low-quality image can have negative spillover effects on its partner. McDonald's needs thus to take great care in selecting which partners will provide co-branded foods or beverages. Aligning with a perceived low-quality brand such as Faygo could have negative effects on the McDonald's brand, so instead, it allies with Coca-Cola. Thus the negative or positive pre-existing brand attitudes of consumers determine the likelihood and direction of potential spillover effects in a co-branding alliance.

Brand equity

Brand equity refers to the set of assets and liabilities linked to a brand's name or symbol, which add to or subtract from the value provided by the branded product or service. These associations define the product in customers' minds and have powerful effects on their buying behaviour. Co-branding alliances might increase the alliance partners' brand equity. In particular, pairing a well-known brand with a less-known brand will enhance the less-known product's equity (Washburn *et al.* 2000). However, such effects demand active management if the co-branding alliance is to succeed because brand equity is associated with critical outcomes, including sales revenue, market growth and customer retention. Through careful brand equity management, firms can capitalize on positive brand spillover effects and prevent negative implications. Management attention should focus particularly on four major elements of brand equity, each of which has a powerful influence on customer perceptions:

- Brand awareness refers to the strength of the brand presence in customers' minds. It can vary from recognizing the brand to associating the brand actively with a product or product family.
- Brand loyalty refers to the tendency to be loyal to the brand, demonstrated in the form of an intention to buy the brand whenever possible. High brand loyalty also means a reduced tendency to switch between brands. This outcome is cost-effective because it is much more difficult and expensive to attract new customers than to keep existing ones.
- Perceived brand quality indicates customers' perceptions of the overall quality or superiority of a brand relative to alternative products and influences their buying behaviours.
- Brand associations reflect non-product-related associations evoked by the brand and can be actively influenced by marketers. For example, to encourage a sporty, youthful image, Nike frequently employs celebrity spokespersons such as Michael Jordan and Rafael Nadal, but it also establishes alliances with Apple that grant it a technical, intelligent image.

In managing brand equity, a firm needs insight into the manner in which stakeholders construct perceptions; the alliance partners could execute targeted marketing initiatives to enhance those perceptions. For example, to increase brand equity, they might provide customers with greater value to ensure the value they perceive exceeds the price they paid. In addition, high-quality support services are likely to enhance brand equity; the provision of timely, reliable, accurate information, perhaps through brochures, salespeople and online channels, also tends to increase customers' perceptions. In service contexts, customers often associate employees who have superior skills with better service quality. Such management initiatives become even more important when there are differences in brand equity between the partners. In particular, a co-branding alliance may pose a potential risk for the stronger brand, whereas the weaker brand can enjoy improved product quality perceptions without having to invest in the provision of better product quality. Neglecting such inequalities over time may result in long-lasting damage to reputations.

Partners' behaviour

Brand spillover effects often reflect two primary attributes of partners' behaviour (Votolato and Unnava 2006): competence and morality. Competence is a firm's ability to deliver information about the brand promise it makes to the customer. Negative information that arises in this category might pertain to the failure to meet quality standards, according to consumers. In a co-branding alliance, such failures adversely affect both partners' reputations, but they also often are due to the deliberate actions of managers. For example, partners might demand cost savings and use substandard raw materials, such that they undermine product quality.

Morality is the representation of the firm's ethics and principles. Negative outcomes emerge when behaviours (such as dishonesty) conflict with consumers' established ethical standards. For example, the use of child labour is perceived to be immoral, so companies that engage in such methods suffer damaged reputations. When customers receive signals of such immorality, they tend to dissociate from the brand; in co-branding alliances, partners must continuously monitor their partner's behaviours and initiate behaviour changes if necessary to prevent negative spillover effects. In the mid-1990s, Intel's poorly designed microprocessors diluted its brand quality, which then spilled over to its partners Gateway and Dell, tarnishing their quality images as well. A few years later, after Intel corrected the problem, it was able to rebuild its quality image and allow Gateway and Dell to see a return on their investment in partnering with the microprocessor manufacturer.

Research on negative information has suggested that information about companies' morality and competence affect customers' responses in different ways. Customers are more willing to forgive competence failures than moral failures because moral standards represent hygiene factors that should be respected by every individual (Brown and Dacin 1997). Wojciszke *et al.* (1993) also argue that consumers are less forgiving of moral failures when the negative information pertains to a particular person. Votolato and Unnava (2006) find similarly that a brand may be impervious to negative publicity surrounding its partner; it suffers ill effects only if consumers come to believe that the focal brand knew of and condoned its partner's behaviour.

Contractual provisions

In co-branding alliances, licensing of one or more trademarks between the parties is common. This approach helps reduce the adverse repercussions of negative spillover effects on a firm's brand and reputation. For example, licensing provisions may include guidelines for the use of the respective brands, trademarks or other intellectual property, including the partners' proprietary rights, quality controls, continuing rights upon termination, policing and enforcement. The licensing terms generally are reciprocal, specifying that the parties may use each other's trademarks, trade names, logos and copyrights solely to perform the obligations of the co-branding alliance agreement. They also usually contain a clause that states that the use of the respective marks must be in accordance with established policies and procedures.

In addition, any trademark licensing deal embodies a contractual provision regarding the potential of product defect liability. Each company involved in a co-branding alliance deal must know that affixing their brands to the product makes them liable for product failures. Indemnification, warranty and termination clauses should be specified carefully if they are to provide any protections in worst-case product defect and liability scenarios. Furthermore, exclusivity provisions may restrict co-branding partners' rights to enter into other third-party agreements. Such provisions typically prohibit any co-branding, co-marketing or other alliance with direct competitors in an attempt to avoid any unwanted transfer of customers' brand associations. Some co-branding alliance agreements also include restrictions on affiliations with categories of services, products or industries. The exit provisions then specify the conditions for ending the alliance by one of the partners, which might include damaging actions that lead to possible negative spillover effects. Finally, an alliance contract might include penalties for broken conditions, varying from limiting or correcting the damage to active communication or even rectification. Penalties also can be specified in monetary terms, such as settling for damages of negative spillovers.

Co-branding alliances: decision-making steps

The core logic underpinning co-branding alliances is that alliance partners combine their brands, occasionally augmented with an existing product or service, to realize objectives such as sales revenue and market share. However, unawareness of brand and product quality misfits, preexisting brand attitudes, brand equity asymmetry and partner's misconduct may cause serious damage to a firm's brand. Alliance managers thus need to find a way to exploit positive spillover effects while preventing the emergence of negative spillover effects. To provide guidelines for forging win–win co-branding alliances, we next elaborate on specific decisions in each stage of the alliance development framework (see Figure 12.1).

Step 1: alliance strategy formulation

During their strategic analyses, firms should decide whether a co-branding alliance is an appropriate governance mode to realize their branding strategy. In addition to generic rationales, such as transaction costs, resource complementarity, resource dependence and learning, a firm may consider improved brand equity as its primary motive. The analysis then should focus on the value of the existing brand, stakeholder perceptions and the anticipated benefits of co-branding. If the sole purpose of the branding strategy is to exploit the combination of two brands, such as through a joint promotion, an alliance generally suffices. However, if the physical integration of products is involved, firms may prefer more hierarchical control (e.g. merger or acquisition) as a means to govern the design, production and marketing processes.

If a firm decides to forge a co-branding alliance, it must make decisions about whether it will undertake joint promotion, joint advertisement, complementary use of products and/or physical product integration. In developing their co-branding strategy, the partners should be aware that familiar brands are better stimuli in brand alliance relationships because they have a relatively higher degree of likeability among consumers due to their pre-existing associations and possibly positive previous experiences. In addition, high awareness brands are recalled more easily and generally signal high product quality and trustworthiness.

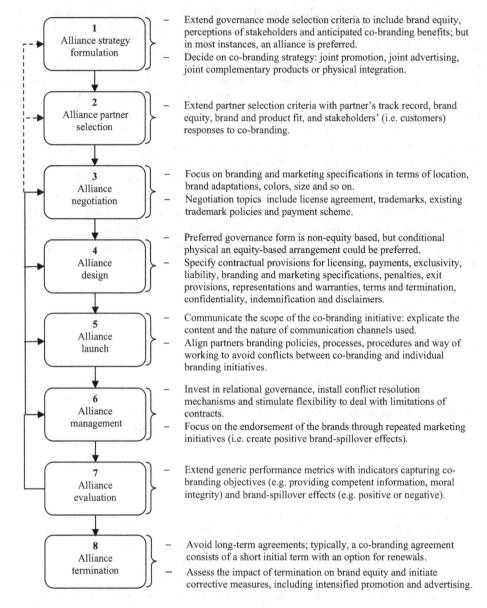

FIGURE 12.1 Alliance development framework: co-branding alliances

Step 2: alliance partner selection

During the partner selection stage, a firm selects a partner to establish a co-branding alliance. The partner chosen should be reliable and responsible. Both companies should represent the partnership responsibly, without scandals or public relations problems. For example, each firm should be comfortable with its counterpart's product-safety track records and original equipment manufacturer relationships, especially if it is responsible for manufacturing or bringing goods to market. When the co-branded product features brands with inconsistent images, customers tend to regard it as inconsistent with the brands' existing products and only slightly revise their prior beliefs. The acts of each partner thus influence customer bases powerfully; a poor decision will result in failure and increase negative brand images. Anticipating both positive and negative potential spillover effects can prevent costly mistakes, which implies that partnering firms must evaluate both the actual monetary expenses involved in an alliance and the potential costs associated with the possible negative effect on their brand. Brands tell consumers who made a product and therefore whom to punish if the product fails to perform up to their expectations. The more positive the equity associated with a brand prior to the alliance, the higher the downside risk if the alliance partner proves to be a poor-quality provider. Firms must carefully weigh the costs and benefits of any alliance and consider both best- and worst-case scenarios during their due diligence process. Several questions can assist a firm in its efforts to identify and select an appropriate partner:

- What is the track record of this potential partner? Its existing brand may have prompted some association in the past, which could limit the co-branding alliance possibilities. In addition, partnering with a firm that has exhibited moral failures is likely to have negative repercussions.
- What is the brand equity of the potential partner, in terms of brand awareness, quality, loyalty and association? Partnering with a low-equity brand may create an uneven distribution of positive and negative spillover effects.
- Which brand personality dimensions are most important in a potential partner? Does the potential brand combination constitute a complementary or supplementary brand fit?
- How will customers react to the combination? Are customers able to associate the brands? If (potential) customers fail to see the connection between two brands, they will not understand the logic behind the partnership, which can ultimately lead to confusion and damage to the brand.
- If products are involved, how will customers react to product fit, and to what extent do product designs need to be altered to develop a valuable market proposition?

Step 3: alliance negotiation

Consistent with generic guidelines, alliance negotiations should be integrative and rely on soft tactics. However, any firm might want to add branding and marketing specifications to the agenda to ensure they determine the appearance and positioning of the respective brands in terms of location, colour, size and proximity, as well as any needed modification to existing brands. Other important topics to cover include the types of marketing initiatives employed (e.g. direct marketing), the use of each party's customer data and media campaign planning (e.g. television, print advertising, promotions). In addition, negotiations need to focus on the content and nature of licence and trademark provisions; co-branding alliances generally involve the licensing of at least one of the trademarks between the parties. Additional topics might cover payment schemes, existing licence and trademark policies, or the partner's marketing contributions.

Step 4: alliance design

A co-branding alliance design can be the key to alliance success or failure. If the sole purpose of the branding strategy is to exploit the combination of two brands, perhaps through joint promotion, a non-equity arrangement generally suffices. However, if a physical integration of products is needed, alliance partners could prefer more hierarchical control, such as through equity arrangements. The alliance governance form and management control mechanism should be consistent with generic guidelines, though the partners should place a particular focus on contractual provisions seeking to limit the adverse impact of negative spillover effects. Finally, the following contractual provisions are preferable ingredients of a successful co-branding alliance contract:

- Licensing provisions that cover guidelines for the use of the respective brands, trademarks and other intellectual property, including those for proprietary rights, quality control, continuing rights upon termination and policing and enforcement of rights.
- Product defect liability provisions, such as indemnification and warranty and termination clauses that provide protection in worst-case scenarios.
- Exclusivity provisions prohibiting co-branding, co-marketing or alliances with direct competitors.
- Penalty provisions, varying from limitations to or corrections of damage to public reputation through active communication, rectification and financial compensation.
- Exit provisions that specify the conditions in which alliance can be ended, such as when one partner engages in damaging actions and induces negative spillover effects.

Step 5: alliance launch

When taking a branding alliance view, general alliance launch guidelines are sufficient to attain an efficient and effective alliance launch. However, alliance launch managers should be aware of two points. First, the alliance launch team should pay attention to specific branding practices that have been built prior to the firm entering. The partners may have developed specific branding requirements, and the alliance launch managers should create clarity and reconcile any operational differences. For example, the partner may have different procedures and templates to communicate their brand. Second, staff involved may identify strongly with their own brands and resist efforts to co-brand, or not be convinced that co-branding may lead to synergetic effects. The launch managers should deal with these hostile dispositions through dialogue and convey the motives for co-branding. To accomplish these two tasks, it is critical alliance launch managers act as advocates of the co-branding alliance, set up liaisons between marketing and sales staff, and work with them to define and fine-tune the partners' co-branding proposition.

Step 6: alliance management

Although alliance contracts can increase the predictability of partner behaviour, detailed contracts also signal distrust, such that they may become a liability in co-branding alliances. Extensive contracts undermine initial trust building, reduce moral entanglements between partners and allow for opportunism. Investing in relational norms and capital is therefore critical once the co-branding alliance has been executed. In addition, interdependency between the collaborating organizations is greater than the initial scope of an alliance might reveal. For example, acts undertaken elsewhere in a partnering firm might have adverse effects on public awareness and stimulate conflicts. A closer interaction between collaborating parties can help ensure that they communicate a consistent message. However, their different organizational and cultural backgrounds are likely to give rise to varying views on the activities needed to strengthen reputations. Thus the managerial climate must leave room for active communication and sense making.

During the course of the co-branding alliance, partners may initiate joint efforts to endorse the endeavour. However, managing public awareness and strengthening reputation is not an exact science. To increase positive effects, the co-branding connection needs the benefits of repetition, appearing several times in advertising. Advertisers also should be aware of the special features of this strategy, such as the appropriate timing of the co-branding presentation or the proper ordering of images to achieve maximum brand association formulation. For example, to increase the chance of positive associations, a (joint) product should be presented before the brand(s) in a joint advertisement.

Step 7: alliance evaluation

Co-branding alliances are established to reach certain goals; alliance evaluation supports the timely revision of activities or even the decision to terminate before negative effects become overwhelming. A performance metric system might be augmented with indicators that also tap the positive and negative effects of brand spillovers. For example, some indicators might determine customers' perceptions of the co-brand, satisfaction, loyalty and retention. In addition, performance metric systems could feature indicators of the partner firms' behaviour in terms of their morality and information competence. Another set of metrics could capture changes in partners' brand equity elements: brand name awareness, brand loyalty, perceived quality and brand associations.

Step 8: alliance termination

The length of the agreement and the termination provisions are important because they affect the parties' ability to escape from co-branding alliance arrangements that turn out to be harmful or that simply are not as effective or profitable as expected. Typically, a co-branding alliance agreement consists of an initial term and the option for renewal. The initial term should be relatively short (e.g. two to three years), so that the brands are not tied together for an excessive period, but long enough to establish the co-branding strategy and realize its success or potential. Incorporating exit provisions in the alliance contract also enables partners to end the alliance without creating anger or unfavourable conditions.

Summary

Co-branding alliances combine brands and often the products of allying firms in an attempt to realize marketing objectives such as market share, sales revenue and customer retention. Such marketing solutions may stimulate quality perceptions and provide reassurances about the true quality of a product because brand names communicate a certain level of quality to consumers. A combination of one brand name with a reliable partner in a co-branding alliance reduces the risk to customers of buying a product. However, an ill-designed co-branding alliance will have severe repercussions for alliance partners, especially if customers transfer their negative associations to each of the partner brands. Such associations fail primarily because the value is not equitable for both brands in the relationship, the brands' values do not match or consumers have trouble understanding the alliance strategy. Through careful partner selection and contractual provisions though, partner firms can reduce the risks associated with co-branding alliances. Selecting partners with good brand and product fit and pursuing continuous investments in brand equity increase the chances of success, even as licence agreements, exclusivity provisions and termination clauses help protect the firm from liability issues and reputational damage.

CASE: HEINEKEN–JAMES BOND[1]

On 15 February 1864, Gerard Adriaan Heineken (1841–1893) purchased 'De Hooiberg' ('The Haystack') brewery in Amsterdam, which would become the Heineken brewery. In 1875, Heineken won the Medaille D'Or at the International Maritime Exposition in Paris and became the biggest beer exporter from the Netherlands to France. After Prohibition was lifted in 1933, Heineken became the first European beer to be imported to the United States. Since then, Heineken has grown to become the third largest brewer in the world, owning more than 165 breweries in more than 70 countries. Heineken produces more than 180 million hectolitres of beer annually.

Almost directly after its foundation, Heineken deployed an active marketing and sales strategy. Premium quality has always been one of the core features of Heineken. Given the poor general hygiene in the mid-1800s, Gerard Adriaan Heineken pledged to clients that he would supply them with a clean and safe product. This provided him and his new company with its first peak of growth. Marketing became exceptionally important when Freddy Heineken took control of the company. After learning the trades of marketing and sales in the United States, Freddy Heineken returned to the Netherlands. In the late 1940s, Heineken set up a 'publicity department' to persuade consumers to drink Heineken beer. Freddy Heineken understood that marketing had to be simple and consistent. He introduced well-known and short slogans and started updating Heineken's packaging to be more in tune with the company's vision.

While Heineken had become a global company, it had not become a global brand. In the 1980s and 1990s, local trademarks were available in many markets, and Heineken's positioning as a premium lager required further support. In many places in the world, beer was still considered a bestial product, and wine was considered too 'decent'. To support Heineken's global positioning, interest was devoted to using James Bond as an advertising platform. Based on the novels of Ian Fleming, James Bond movies started to be produced regularly, starting with *Dr. No* in 1962. This represented the start of the most successful series of movies in history and attracted the attention of advertisers. Although marketing effectiveness is exceptionally hard to measure, companies are increasingly defined by their reputation. This, combined with a strong brand, differentiates companies in the eyes of the public. For Heineken, James Bond offered a global advertising platform reaching the desired target groups: cosmopolitan males who could identify with James Bond. James Bond is synonymous with high-quality goods, which underlines Heineken's reputation as a premium lager. Heineken is a logical partner for James Bond since the character James Bond enjoys the occasional alcoholic beverage, although this was generally a vodka martini, famously 'shaken, not stirred'. Brand cohesiveness between Heineken and James Bond was less obvious and posed a risk in the partnership between James Bond and Heineken.

The partnership between Heineken and James Bond dates back to 1997, when Heineken participated in the movie *Tomorrow Never Dies*. In this movie, James Bond uses a truck loaded with Heineken crates as a ramp to get his bike back on street level. Heineken commercials have been produced in which John Cleese participates as Q, receiving a phone call through a Heineken bottle. Heineken was again involved in the movie *The World Is Not Enough*. This was the company's first global campaign, and it introduced the slogan 'not everything should be shaken or stirred'. Satisfied with the results, Heineken has participated in all subsequent Bond movies, although it wasn't until 2012 that James Bond himself enjoyed a Heineken, in the movie *Skyfall*, causing disturbance with James Bond purists who argued that the stylish character of James Bond could not be combined with 'ordinary lager'. However, the risks of limited brand cohesiveness were effectively managed by Heineken. Using a keen marketing strategy, the movie *Skyfall* coincided with the London Olympics of 2012, of which Heineken was the official lager supplier. Heineken sales reportedly increased by 5.3 per cent.

The production of the James Bond film *Spectre* required a budget of US$350 million. To finance the film, reliance on sponsorship was crucial. According to the film's star, Daniel Craig, 'the simple fact is that without them [advertisers], we couldn't do it'. Heineken's partnership with *Spectre* implied an investment of US$167 million. The vast majority of this amount was a countertrade in joint promotion: Heineken does not pay the film producers but invests in movie marketing, which translates into free publicity for the film makers. For Heineken, the *Spectre* campaign was the brand's largest global marketing platform of 2015. Part of this campaign involved James Bond again enjoying a Heineken in the film itself. Next, Heineken was allowed exclusive rights to using Daniel Craig in a commercial. For its digital *Spectre* campaign, Heineken took the world's first ever selfie from space. For the 'Spyfie', Heineken partnered with Urthecast to take ultra-HD imagery using its camera on the Deimos satellite, which was orbiting 600 kilometres above the Earth's surface. Via a relay of technology, Heineken created a selfie for attendees who had been recruited from around the world. The Spyfie content was customized for each attendee of the top-secret experiential event, sending the material directly to their mobile devices for use on social media. Heineken also allowed Bond fans to get exclusive access to *Spectre* content through the estimated half a billion bottles bearing the *Spectre* logo that were sold around the world. By scanning the Heineken logo, fans could unlock content with Daniel Craig and behind-the-scenes footage. The Heineken 'limited editions' all had James Bond–style packaging. However, product placement and co-branding arrangements in films are not without risks. Audiences are increasingly sceptical about such strategies. Research suggests that when product placement becomes too prominent, it affects attitudes negatively because viewers become aware of a deliberate selling attempt. Product placement can also lower audiences' evaluations of the focal entertainment product (the film or the show). Active management of the portfolio of partners ensures that brand cohesiveness is guaranteed and the partnership delivers its intended value. With regard to the collaboration between Heineken and James Bond, the introduction of Heineken in the movie *Skyfall* created a surge of complaints. However, according to Heineken officials, the campaign was successful. The movie was also highly successful, making US$1.1 billion in ticket sales compared to costs of $200 million. In 2021, the latest James Bond movie was released: *No Time to Die*. The promotion activities included a commercial featuring Daniel Craig, who slowly pours a glass of Heineken extending the gratification of the first sip. The rationale behind the commercial originated in an experiment, where participants would be offered a Heineken 0.0 (i.e. alcohol free), but were served with time delays varying from 0 to 30 minutes. The results suggested that participants experienced extreme satisfaction after a 20-minute wait.

As for Heineken, for many companies, association with James Bond bears significant value in terms of reputation and positioning of their brand. Examples of iconic brands that have been associated with James bond include Omega watches, Aston Martin and Tom Ford. These companies have been willing to invest significant amounts of money to further increase their promotional effects.

Questions

1   Explain how the Heineken and James Bond brands reinforce one another positively (e.g. have brand and product fit).
2   Explain what risks this alliance entails for Heineken with regard to negative brand spillovers.
3   Heineken received complaints about this co-branding alliance. Explain why they decided to continue and expand it?

Note

1   Cooper (2012); Engbers (2021); McCann (2013); Zagt (2015).

13

INTERNATIONAL ALLIANCES

Global markets, which represent the convergence of consumer demand across different societies; lowered barriers to trade and investment; the alignment of government policies; and key technological developments in information processing, communications and transportation have prompted firms to adopt internationalization strategies to maintain their competitive advantage. Within the portfolio of competitive instruments a firm can use to discover and exploit international opportunities, international alliances have become quite prominent (Beamish and Lupton 2016). They often enable firms to produce goods less expensively but with the same quality level, which improves their cost structure and/or helps them penetrate new markets to improve their profits. Although international alliances thus have grown increasingly popular, their failure rate also is extremely high. Clashing cultures are the most widely cited reasons for such failures, though cultural tensions often intertwine with other deal breakers, such as unrealistic expectations or distrust. That is, the international environments in which international alliances operate may exacerbate adverse situations or create great opportunities; in either case, their management is critical. The first section details this unique challenge. Then we elaborate on the nature of national culture (second section) and discuss cross-cultural management approaches (third section). In the fourth section, we use our alliance development framework to highlight key management issues before concluding with a summary and a case illustration.

The international alliance challenge

International alliances (see Table 13.1), which refer to partnerships between parties located in different countries, are forged for multiple reasons (Beamish and Lupton 2016; Glaister and Buckley 1996; Li *et al.* 2013; Zahoor *et al.* 2023). They offer firms opportunities to gain access to knowledge and capabilities not currently controlled or available within their home country. International alliances also function as vehicles to enable firms to enter developing markets that may have restrictive conditions for foreign investment or gain a significant presence and greater market penetration more rapidly in new markets. Through international alliances, the partners create common and global platforms for products and services, as well as supplementing their knowledge bases with the new knowledge possessed by the foreign partner, such

DOI: 10.4324/9781003222187-13

TABLE 13.1 Examples of international alliances

	Description
Tokio Marine–Bolttech	In 2022, Japan's largest non-life insurance group Tokio Marine formed a capital and business alliance with Singapore-headquartered InsurTech company, Bolttech. The partners aim is to realize the global expansion of embedded insurance and innovative insurance binding processes through a unique digital platform. In collaboration with Bolttech, Tokio Marine will provide new products and services on a global scale.
DSM–Padang & Co	In 2019, DSM powered by Padang & Co, established the Bright Science Hub in order to connect technology startups, entrepreneurs and other partners to foster innovation that can deliver positive impact in the Asia-Pacific region.
Lendico–PostFinance	In 2016, the Germany-based Lendico and the Swizz PostFinance launched a joint venture, established in Switzerland. The aim of the joint venture is to provide Swiss small businesses with a modern alternative to traditional bank financing. The two partners are contributing their complementary expertise in customer contact and lending and repayment processes.

Sources: DSM (2020); Martino (2010); PRNewswire (2016); Tokio Marine (2022).

as when they integrate knowledge from different areas of science and technology to develop more radical innovations (Lane *et al.* 2001). It is important to note, however, that motives for international alliances may vary with the type of alliance. Whereas, for example, Li *et al.* (2013) show that low-tech firms use international alliances to share resources, costs and risks, in contrast to high-tech firms who use such arrangements to mitigate environmental dynamism, Choi and Yeniyurt (2015) report that firms are more likely to form R&D alliances where there are similar levels of innovation infrastructure between countries of partnering firms.

Despite the good reasons for forging international alliances, they are inherently unstable because the partners lack shared cultural norms and values (Christoffersen 2013; Meschi 2005; Park and Ungson 1997)—that is, these alliances feature cultural distance. Increasing cultural distance undermines the partners' interpretation of each other's strategic intents and tends to hamper their effective communication during alliance negotiations (Rao and Schmidt 1998). Many firms thus adopt alliance designs characterized by excessive governance and control to deal with the uncertainties related to different regulations, work-related values or management practices (Steensma *et al.* 2000). Even when the firms focus on governance, however, they often fail to establish effective control processes and procedures to encourage cooperation or mitigate resistance to change (Inkpen and Beamish 1997). Moreover, cultural distance tends to impede the building of trust as the partnership develops, along with inter-firm learning and knowledge sharing (Aulakh *et al.* 1996; Parkhe 1991). In general, cultural distance thus appears to affect negatively the strategic, tactical and operational processes that underlie the formation and maintenance of international alliances.

Yet some studies paint a rosier picture, in which international alliances develop into long-lasting, productive partnerships. Park and Ungson (1997) find that international joint ventures between Japanese and US parents survived longer than those between two US parents, perhaps because their prior relationships had already stimulated trust and enabled inter-firm learning, which counter-balanced any cross-cultural differences. Aulakh *et al.* (1996) show that investing in relational norms and mutual trust increases the likelihood of high-performing international partnerships. Brouthers and Bamossy (2006) reaffirm these findings and reveal that alliance processes, such as trust and commitment, constitute an important condition for developing successful international joint ventures. Although cultural distance is thus a prominent and potentially destructive factor, cross-cultural experience and management can also help firms overcome their cultural adversities and enable them to exploit cultural differences. Insights into the nature of national cultures and cross-cultural management are thus critical for successful international alliances (López-Duartea et al. 2016).

The nature of national culture

National culture is ubiquitous, multi-dimensional, complex and pervasive. It consists of values, behavioural norms, beliefs, language, rituals governing behaviour, patterns of action, shared expectations and responses to the environment by a group that constitutes the nation. Deeply set values, norms and priorities are thus common to members of a nation (Hofstede 1991), acquired early in life through a person's primary socialization in families, schools and social interactions. A country's culture permeates all aspects of life within that society—including the norms, values and behaviours of managers in its companies. It also constitutes an ethical habit, nurtured by repetition, tradition and example, which is manifested through images, habits and social opinions. In this role, it regulates the behaviour of people, often through communication and decision making. Because national culture is learned, however, people should be able to adapt their mental programming, regardless of their national culture. This point is important because forging international alliances requires the managers involved to adapt their cultural dispositions to deal with cultural differences. National cultural frameworks can assist managers in this endeavour.

National cultural dimensions

Of the various national culture frameworks, including those by Trompenaars (1993) and the GLOBE study (House 2004), we turn to Hofstede's (1991) well-known framework for this chapter. Hofstede's framework has been criticized as outdated and specific to the context in which data was collected, but recent studies still maintain that the positions of the countries he established are relatively stable (Taras et al. 2009). Furthermore, although the development and application of various cultural frameworks remain constantly subject to controversy, they make similar contributions: namely, a better understanding of the relationship between people's cultural dispositions and their behaviour. Hofstede (1991) initially identified four cultural dimensions—individualism–collectivism, masculinity–femininity, power distance and uncertainty avoidance—to which he later added a fifth (Hofstede and Bond 1988), time orientation (Table 13.2).

Individualism–collectivism indicates the relative closeness of interpersonal relationships. It thus anticipates fundamental issues about individual motivation and place (and the management thereof), as well as about the organization and functioning of society as a whole. It pertains to people's attitudes towards relationships. People from individualistic countries, characterized by loose interpersonal ties, tend to emphasize their self-interest. But when the ties among individuals are tight (i.e. collectivism), their concern lies with the group interest. Thus alliance managers from collectivistic countries tend to be more loyal to the alliance, whereas those from individualistic countries consider the alliance as a means to an end.

The masculinity–femininity cultural dimension pertains to norms regarding an achievement motivation versus quality of life. Masculine cultures convey norms that emphasize the

TABLE 13.2 Hofstede's five cultural dimensions

Description	Characteristics	Example
Individualism–collectivism	In individualistic cultures, relations with others should be rational, based on personal goals and governed by cost–benefit calculations. In collectivistic cultures, relations are organized to protect group harmony and save face and avoid embarrassment.	Alliance managers from individualistic countries (e.g. US) tend to focus on individual achievements and rights; their counterparts from collectivistic cultures (e.g. Turkey) tend to emphasize joint achievements.
Masculinity–femininity	Masculine societies convey norms that emphasize the need for autonomy, competitiveness and assertive actions to achieve materialistic goals with a preference for extrinsic rewards. Feminine cultures convey norms that emphasize the need for collaboration and relationships. The dominant norms are caring for others and quality of life, with preference granted to intrinsic rewards.	Alliance managers from masculine countries (e.g. Italy) tend to focus on decisive and daring behaviours and resolve conflicts through fighting; their counterparts from feminine-oriented cultures (e.g. Netherlands) tend to emphasize consensus behaviour and resolve conflicts through compromising.
Uncertainty avoidance	In cultures with high uncertainty avoidance, people seek to reduce uncertainty by planning everything carefully and relying on rules and regulations. In countries with low uncertainty avoidance, people are more willing to accept uncertainty and not afraid to take risks.	Alliance managers from high uncertainty avoidance countries (e.g. Belgium) tend to focus on incremental improvement steps guided by blueprints; their counterparts from low uncertainty avoidance cultures (e.g. Singapore) tend to accept uncertainty.
Power distance	In cultures with high power distance, a belief exists that power should govern relationships; inequality in power is the basis of societal order. In cultures with low power distance, the belief is that power is a necessary evil that should be minimized, and people should treat one another as equals.	Alliance managers from high power distance countries (e.g. France) tend to focus on centralized decision making; their counterparts from low power distance cultures (e.g. Denmark) tend to focus on empowerment and subscribe to management by consensus.
Time orientation	In cultures with a long-term time orientation, ordering relationships by status and observing this order, thrift and a sense of shame are important. In cultures with a short-term orientation, personal stability, protecting face, quick results and unimportance of status are typical.	Alliance managers from short-term-oriented countries (e.g. US) tend to focus on immediate (financial) results; their counterparts from long-term-oriented cultures (e.g. China) tend to focus on long-term (strategic) outcomes.

Sources: Hofstede (1991); Hofstede and Bond (1988).

need for autonomy, competitiveness and assertiveness to achieve materialistic goals. In contrast, in countries with a feminine culture, the dominant norms emphasize sympathy, collaboration, the importance of relationships and helping others. Alliance managers from masculine countries tend to be more proactive in imposing their alliance solutions, if necessary with the risk of conflicts, on their counterparts, whereas managers from feminine countries tend to propose consensus-based solutions.

Power distance refers to the distribution of power within a country, as well as how societies deal with inequalities in social status. In countries with high power distance, citizens tend to accept such power inequality, whereas in low power distance countries, they emphasize equality. Therefore alliance managers from countries with high power distance tend to prefer centralization, whereas managers from low power distance countries tend to focus on empowerment.

Uncertainty avoidance pertains to people's inclination to reduce or cope with uncertainty about the future and deal with risk. High uncertainty avoidance indicates that the future is viewed as a threat, so alliance managers from these countries are less inclined to take risks. Managers from low uncertainty avoidance countries, however, tend to engage in more risky endeavours.

Finally, the time dimension entails a long- versus short-term orientation distinction, or the degree to which a society embraces a persistent devotion to traditional, forward-thinking values. With a long-term orientation, a society tends to focus on the future, but a short-term focus indicates that people focus on the present. Thus alliance managers from long-term-oriented countries tend to be more patient with alliance progress, but their counterparts from short-term-oriented countries demand immediate results.

When people from different countries work together, conflicts and opportunities are likely. For example, an alliance manager with an individualistic orientation might make decisions to prioritize the protection of individual profits, as justified by utilitarian principles. His or her counterpart from a collectivist culture recognizes the group as the dominant structure and therefore makes decisions to achieve consensus, protect group harmony and save face. In an international alliance, an individualistic alliance manager tends to be less concerned about process discrepancies (i.e. distrust) than the collectivist counterpart. The former manager also exhibits a low desire to understand the causes for distrust or initiate corrective measures. The collectivist manager in the meantime is viewing the process discrepancy as a barrier to alliance progress that must be resolved. These contrasting views might result in decision-making conflicts or, if properly managed, constructive dialogues. In an alliance, cultural differences therefore can function as (1) barriers to cooperation, (2) challenges to be addressed or (3) windows to unexpected opportunities (Child and Faulkner 1998; Christoffersen 2013).

Culture as a barrier

An international alliance brings people from different countries together in a working relationship. If they identify strongly with their national cultures, collaborating with members of other nations may constitute a threat. The participants in the international alliance may then resist changes to their structures and practices, especially those initiated to advance the alliance's progress. For example, considerable difficulties arise in international alliances featuring firms that manage and organize their employees according to masculine versus feminine orientations. In the former, managers emphasize goal achievement, completion and management action. In the latter, they will focus on mutual collaboration and a supportive working climate. It is difficult to reconcile these contrasting orientations. In turn, the cultural differences signal a loss or low level of control and a source of fundamental conflict, which leads to misunderstanding and disagreements. At a superficial level, cultural differences may entail simple misunderstandings, originating in language and behaviour differences (Joshi and Lahiri 2015), which are relatively easy to address as long as people are sensitive and aware. Even if a foreign alliance partner recommends different management practices, joint, open communication and dialogue can help resolve any cultural differences. At a more fundamental level though, such differences reflect conflicts in values and thus may bar the development of successful international alliances. If socially embedded values clash, they can seriously damage interpersonal collaboration.

Culture as a challenge

Beyond their roles as barriers to cooperation, cultural differences confront managers with unique challenges, including the very design of the alliance. Firms that face seemingly incomprehensible cultural differences tend to adopt excessive governance forms to obtain protection and safeguards against exchange hazards. Gulati and Singh (1998) report that the country of origin often determines the choice between minority-equity investment and joint ventures, according to the partners' different perceptions of time. For example, Japanese partners tend to adopt long time horizons when dealing with exchange hazards, in contrast with their European and US counterparts. Choi and Contractor (2016) show that whereas the likelihood of using a more-integrated alliance governance mode decreases as the difference or 'distance' between nations of the partner firms increases in terms of human capital and cultural distance, greater geographic and institutional difference is positively associated with the selection of more integrated alliance governance modes. Brouthers and Bamossy (2006) find that initial formal control by a foreign partner often benefits alliance progress, particularly if supplemented with social controls, but then as the alliance progresses, management control must be shared. Moreover, maintaining dominant formal control tends to result in underperformance by the international alliance (Fryxell *et al.* 2002).

Other challenges pertain to alliance negotiation and execution; cultural distance increases the likelihood of premature breakdown due to cultural conflicts. Developing a negotiation climate characterized by mutual trust is difficult for negotiators from different countries because the probability of mutual misunderstandings, miscommunications, erroneous interpretations of proposals and personal offence tends to increase. For example, US managers might adopt soft negotiation tactics when dealing with foreign partners, but as their cultural distance increases, the likelihood of the use of hard tactics increases because the managers perceive higher risks of opportunistic conduct and non-compliance (Rao and Schmidt 1998). In the alliance execution stage, cultural differences may result in considerable operational problems. If people involved in the alliance focus on different priorities, as reflecting their cultural orientations, any breakdown in relational norms and capital, interpersonal communication, or inter-firm learning will inhibit these partners' ability to work together. Many alliance managers just assume that their counterparts will respond similarly to a problem, but managers from masculine Japan are quick to adopt destructive response strategies, whereas managers from collectivist Turkey prefer more passive responses (Furrer *et al.* 2012). Similarly, managers from individualistic cultures perceive conflict as a constructive and inevitable part of alliances, so they use dialectical inquiry and play the devil's advocate to improve decision making (Parkhe 1991). Managers from collectivistic countries would never embrace such tactics, which reduce their ability to save face and lead to vigorous and inappropriate-seeming conflicts. Furthermore, developing and implementing performance metric systems that accommodate both partners' interests is difficult in the face of vast cultural differences (Büchel and Thuy 2001).

Culture as opportunity

Differences in national culture also may constitute an opportunity. Cultural diversity enables alliance partners to build on their cultural strengths by combining the advantageous aspects of their existing cultures into a new, improved culture. The establishment of NUMMI by Toyota and General Motors is a well-known example of the US car manufacturer's attempt to learn about the lean manufacturing methods being used so successfully in Japan. Meanwhile, Toyota gained access to information about the competitive strategies of its partner and developments within the US auto industry (Doz and Hamel 1998). Yeheskel and colleagues (2001) find that certain cultural differences (e.g. in masculinity and power distance) have negative impacts on joint venture performance, whereas others, such as individualism and uncertainty avoidance, produce positive impacts. To explain this divergence, they argue that if perceived properly, cultural differences offer a valuable asset. If alliance managers recognize the potential challenges of working with foreign partners, they should be more willing to expend effort to avoid misunderstandings, such that differences in national culture then lead to high-level communication and more sustained collaboration (Shenkar and Zeira 1992). When regarding cultural differences as an opportunity, the partners aim to harvest the benefits of the diversity in alliance partners' cultures while also building effective bridges between them.

Exploiting cultural opportunities is not always an appropriate course of action, however. Culture provides people with a sense of social cohesion (i.e. reference point) and makes them accept shared goals. Firms must therefore consider carefully the form of their international alliance. If it will entail a stand-alone entity (e.g. joint venture), partners may benefit from building a separate alliance identity that intentionally aims to meld the strengths of both partners' national cultures. However, if an alliance represents an investment opportunity, the transfer of cultural values and norms may not outweigh the potential benefits of cultural integration. Furthermore, even if alliance partners are willing to accommodate their partners' national cultures, they still need the opportunity to maintain their own identity.

Firms engaged in international alliances thus confront a unique challenge: they must counter the negative consequences of cultural differences, such as the greater risk of opportunistic conduct, by first recognizing the potential for cultural barriers and thereby initiating measures to avoid detrimental implications. Simultaneously, they should identify opportunities to exploit cultural diversity. To this end, alliance managers need to understand the extent to which cultural differences exist (see Box 13.1), identify whether they

BOX 13.1 HIGH AND LOW CONTEXT CULTURES

A more parsimonious classification of national cultures entails the distinction between high and low context cultures. In a high context culture, information remains tacit, and interpretation requires an understanding of the situational context. In a low context culture, information is primarily communicated in codified form, and the burden of interpretation is placed on the receiver. Most Asian cultures fall at the high context end of this continuum; North American cultures fall at the low context end. International alliances between partners that are both from either high or low context cultures are likely to experience only minor cultural adversities, but partnerships that span these categories will tend to suffer substantial cultural conflicts. In the latter case, alliance managers must adapt their communication styles to accommodate the partners.

constitute a threat or opportunity and assess the degree of influence of alliance acculturation. That is, partner firms need to decide to create a hybrid culture in which the partner's cultures are melted into a new cultural construction, build a cooperative culture in which the partners' cultures coexist alongside one another or create a new culture from scratch (Dasi-Rodriguez and Pardo-del-Val 2015). Following this decision, appropriate cross-cultural management can then transform cultural differences into assets, which increase the probability of alliance success.

Managing international alliances

The management of international alliances includes activities designed to reconcile differences in the alliance partners' cultures—a prerequisite of the long-term viability of an international alliance. When different national cultures enter into a workable relationship, the alliance partners can realize their objectives with minimal tension, conflict or disagreement. This point does imply, however, that the original cultures should be reconciled. The more national cultures differ, the greater their impact on alliance development, and the more difficult and time-consuming management becomes. If national cultures in an alliance are deeply embedded, their attempted reconciliation with other cultures will result in resistance to change. Therefore, the active management of cultural diversity is important in alliances, and managerial attention should focus on (1) building cultural competence, (2) partner selection, (3) alliance manager selection and (4) the work climate.

Cultural competence

In an alliance context, cultural competence refers to the ability to interact effectively with people of different cultures, and it comprises three components. First, alliance managers must become aware of their own cultural worldview; such consciousness of their personal reactions to people who are different improves their attitudes towards cultural differences. Prior to forging an international alliance, managers must make an effort to assess the nature of their partner's cultures and the potential for adversities. Second, knowledge of different cultural practices helps alliance managers maintain consistency between their attitudes and behaviours. With cultural awareness, they can identify the implications of their (unintended) actions. Third, cross-cultural skills, such as developing cultural competences, result in an ability to understand, communicate with and effectively interact with people across cultures. Neglecting cultural differences instead results in highly unpredictable consequences. The active and constructive interaction between counterparts eases cultural harmonization and integration because a firm with a good cultural competence can diagnose and remedy cultural differences, which enables cultural integration.

Cultural competences might be built through training or education in cross-cultural management. Training should improve managers' cultural awareness, sensitizing them to their own interpretive schemes, as well as those of their partner. It also reduces managers' natural tendency to process information automatically so that they do not make instantaneous judgements about their partner's intentions. Cross-cultural sensitivity and language competence in particular can increase managers' understanding of partner needs and interests, resulting in high-quality cross-cultural interactions. Other forms of beneficial education include training in the partner's country for both sides, or personnel exchanges between the alliance partners. In addition, a firm may learn from its prior international alliances and coach other alliance managers using these prior experiences. Once firms gain more experience in international business, they are more confident about operating abroad, more willing to take risks and better able to manage international alliances, even to the extent that enhanced international alliance experiences dissuade (SME) firms to forge international alliances (Arranz *et al.* 2016). Yet, host country–specific experience is especially useful when it comes to strategic decisions, managing local labour and communicating with customers, suppliers and stakeholders. Rewards are key when building and using such cultural competences. Firms often provide training but never mandate full participation or reward employees who apply the training to their work. To manage international alliances successfully, it is utterly necessary that the involved staff and management gain sufficient understanding of their partner's cultural dispositions and recognize the value of cultural diversity.

Partner selection

Partner selection confronts firms with a dilemma (Meschi 1997): is it better to collaborate with a partner with a compatible national culture, or seize an opportunity with a partner that is less compatible but immediately available? Investing too much time in seeking out a compatible partner may allow the motivation underpinning the alliance to expire. But collaborating with a partner with an incompatible culture could jeopardize any alliance outcomes anyway. For example, the immediate realization of short-term financial benefits is often difficult when cultural differences exist. Harmonizing cultural differences requires time and devoted management attention, but when the partners share at least certain aspects, their cultural integration can be accelerated. During partner selection, alliance managers thus might consider other partner selection motives. Foreign partners tend to contribute distinctive resources (Hitt *et al.* 2000), increasing the risk of exchange hazards (i.e. unwanted knowledge leakage), and greater cultural distance increases the likely preference for a marketing or supplier alliance over an innovation-oriented alliance (Kaufmann and O'Neill 2007). International alliances thus demand extensive protection against exchange hazards, which is possible through effective partner selection. A firm should select a partner by making trust and commitment the foremost priorities because alliance partners must believe that they can depend on each other before they can possibly deal with the adverse consequences of cultural differences (Cullen *et al.* 1995).

Alliance manager selection

National cultural differences may inhibit alliance managers' ability to interact. To resolve this issue, a firm preferably should select alliance staff with open minds and flexible personalities, as well as those who demonstrate positive approaches during previous experiences in alliances or international business settings. Schneider and Barsoux (1997) propose a set of behavioural competences needed for effective intercultural performance, including linguistic ability, interpersonal (relationship) skills, cultural curiosity, ability to tolerate uncertainty and ambiguity, flexibility and patience, cultural empathy, a strong sense of self and a sense of humour. If managers lack these abilities, they need cultural training and education to help them adjust to the different national cultures. The content of such training should be up to date and realistic, with an added focus on language proficiency—insufficient comprehension of another language often creates conflicts. Trainers should preferably include native speakers of the language who maintain regular contact with their country of origin. These anticipatory trainings are both costly and time-consuming, so some firms designate alliance staff with hands-on cultural experience to conduct it. In another approach, an alliance partner sets up a team of experienced managers who take responsibility for the alliance execution in an attempt to absorb initial cultural shocks. As soon as the alliance operation is functioning smoothly, they hand it over to others who continue their work.

Finally, when evaluating employees for staffing decisions, competency models provide useful guidance that can increase the organization's ability to staff its alliances with employees who will easily adjust to and enjoy cultural diversity.

The work climate

International alliance failure often results from the execution of the venture, rather than the rationale and resources used to form it. The parties involved might fail to develop or implement post-formation processes to overcome international barriers to success. Furthermore, a healthy working climate is critical to successful international alliances, which means partners must be able to acknowledge their differences to avoid fatal conflicts. For example, Japanese firms and foreign partners may follow similar paths to develop trust, commitment, credibility, reciprocity and benevolence, but trust tends to be more important for the former (Cullen *et al.* 1995). In this sense, cultural differences between partners tend to inhibit open and prompt communication, which is necessary to spur a process in which parties are able to examine one another's credibility and trustworthiness. Although partners with similar cultural backgrounds also tend to use similar trust forms (e.g. cognitive versus affective), they are more opportunistic when they embrace dissimilar trust forms. If cultural differences are great, partners should invest in building a high-quality working climate to prevent the emergence of inter-partner conflicts and tensions. Similarly, norms that govern giving and receiving feedback differ greatly across cultures, but regardless of culture, some feedback is necessary to achieve effective relationships. Cultural differences leave feedback communications particularly prone to misunderstandings and misinterpretations, so well-designed performance management practices should be in place to ensure that employees receive the feedback they need in a culturally appropriate way. Investing in intensive cross-cultural programmes can reduce the adverse impact of cultural differences overall, as well as improve relational norms and capital, which positively influence alliance performance (Brouthers and Bamossy 2006).

International alliances: decision-making steps

Whereas international alliances enable companies to share risks and investments, as well as obtain access to new technologies and markets, the international environments in which they operate also exacerbate the likelihood of dissatisfying economic performance, distrust between parties and premature termination. Therefore, the improper management of cultural adversities contributes to high failure rates; decision making is critical in such situations to avoid premature termination. To help steer international alliances towards greater chances for success, we next present managerial guidelines for each stage of the alliance development framework (see Figure 13.1).

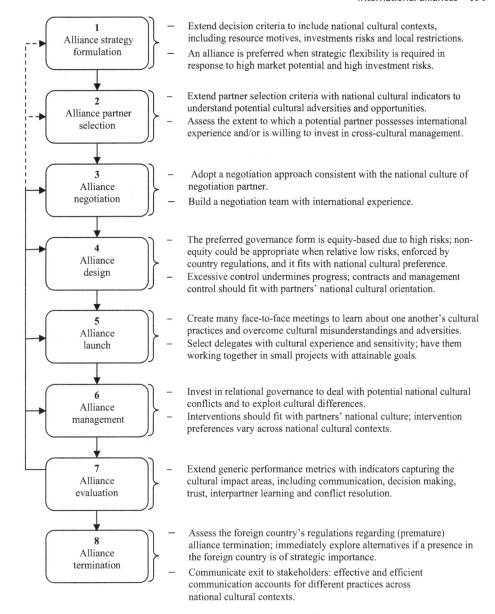

FIGURE 13.1 Alliance development framework: international alliances

Step 1: alliance strategy formulation

During its strategic analysis, a firm decides whether an international alliance is even an appropriate governance mode, compared with international mergers and acquisitions or other forms, to realize its objectives (see Box 13.2). Before selecting a governance mode, the firm should analyze whether it possesses sufficient know-how and know-what (i.e. cultural competence) to engage in an international endeavour. Detailed preparations in the form of cross-cultural management efforts are required in order to guarantee that the international alliance

---

BOX 13.2 MARKET ENTRY GOVERNANCE MODES

During the formulation of an alliance strategy, a firm decides which governance mode—make, buy or ally—is appropriate for realizing its objectives. Though traditional theoretical perspectives, such as transaction cost economics (TCE) and resource-based view (RBV), offer explanations (see Chapter 2), within the context of international alliances, extant studies have investigated the impact of cultural distance on entry mode choice, focussing on specific governance modes, including wholly owned subsidiaries, joint ventures, export alliances and acquisitions. Though contingencies (i.e. industry and firm-level) may affect governance mode choice, some empirical support has highlighted a preference of wholly owned subsidiaries (i.e. full ownership) over joint ventures (i.e. shared ownership) when cultural distance increases. Focusing on the choice between equity and non-equity alliance arrangements, research shows that managers' preferences for an alliance governance is biased by cultural orientation. Managers from countries with high uncertainty avoidance scores, for example, tend to prefer equity-based governance and complete alliance contracts, unlike managers from countries with low scores, who tend to prefer non-equity alliances. The choice between minority-equity investment and joint ventures also varies with alliance managers' different perceptions of time. For example, Japanese partners tend to adopt longer time horizons when dealing with exchange hazards, in contrast to their European and US counterparts, who adopt shorter time horizons. International alliances may also pose additional risks, such as country-specific regulations, opportunistic behaviour, knowledge leakage and misappropriation, which necessitate the choice of a governance form which provides additional protection. Consequently, equity arrangements (i.e. international joint ventures) supplemented with extensive contractual clauses and management control are often used in cross-cultural alliances requiring superior safeguards, such as when there is a large cultural distance between the partners.

Sources: Ang *et al.* (2015); Nippa and Reuer (2019).

---

delivers on its promise. In addition to various general considerations, firms must recognize that forging an international alliance necessitates some additional, specific analyses:

- Partners of different countries often have different resource needs and offer different resources and capabilities. For example, conditional on its resource alignment, an international alliance may have a low (high) degree of resource similarity and a high (low) level of resource heterogeneity, which would suggest the appropriateness of (non) equity-based governance modes.
- Distinct countries pose different risks and challenges due to their unique appropriation regimes, regulations and industry conditions. Collaboration then may constitute an investment risk and induce additional transaction costs, which must be carefully analyzed. For example, wholly owned subsidiaries are preferable to joint ventures when market potential is high, investment risks are low and local legal restrictions are comparable for both partners.

Step 2: alliance partner selection

Differences in national culture between alliance partners could be an opportunity for or a threat to joint value creation. The partner fit framework needs sufficient indicators to be able to identify fit (or misfit) between national cultures. Against the background of a generic framework, firms also need to acquire information about the national culture of their potential partners and assess the possibility of adverse implications, as well as of potential synergies. A cultural misfit suggests that partner firms' cultures are potentially incompatible, which could be detrimental to alliance success. Being aware of possible cultural misfits is critical as they tend to relate to differences in communication and language, decision-making styles and problem-solving approaches. The greater the cultural distance, the more measures are necessary to deal with cultural barriers, which may adjust cost–benefit calculations downward. Furthermore, it is important to know upfront whether a potential partner has sufficient experience and know-how to participate in an international alliance: has the partner been involved in prior (successful) international alliances, does it offer cultural training programmes and is it willing to appoint experienced managers?

Step 3: alliance negotiation

During the alliance negotiation stage, the firm needs to consider not only its negotiation approach but also cultural dynamics. The national culture of the partners may determine the right composition of the negotiation team, which topics are to be discussed and with whom, and how to codify the results of the negotiation. Negotiators may want to adapt their strategy and tactics to the cultural context of the alliance negotiation. For example, negotiators from collectivist countries (e.g. Japan) are likely to respond adversely to hard negotiation tactics because direct conflicts cause them to become embarrassed, whereas their counterparts from individualistic countries (e.g. United States) are better able to deal with open confrontation.

Step 4: alliance design

International alliances may also pose additional risks, such as country-specific regulations, opportunistic behaviour, knowledge leakage and misappropriation, which necessitate additional protection. Consequently, equity arrangements (i.e. international joint ventures) supplemented with extensive contractual clauses and management control can offer a preferred governance form by functioning as a superior safeguard. However, not all international alliances include learning objectives, so sometimes excessive protections are unnecessary. Furthermore, excessive, prolonged control by a single partner tends to result in poor performance because the costs associated with alliance design outweigh the benefits. Dominant control also reduces incentives for active participation by the counterpart in the alliance. Efforts to impose controls on a foreign partner might provoke resistance and hostility, thus undermining the development of the relational norms and capital that are so critical to success and the resolution of cultural tensions. Thus, during the alliance design stage, partners need to resolve a dilemma: how to include enough governance to secure individual interests without undermining the working relationship. Although clear-cut prescriptions are virtually impossible, some guidelines can inform the related decision making:

- Extend generic rationales for alliance design with contextual factors, such as country-specific regulations and investment risks. Some countries have strict laws and regulations that dictate acceptable alliance designs (e.g. China). Economic and social uncertainty within a country will also influence alliance design decisions.

- Alliance design preferences are likely biased by cultural orientation. Managers from countries with high uncertainty avoidance scores will focus on equity-based governance and complete alliance contracts (to reduce uncertainty), unlike managers from countries with low scores.
- Even if dominant control appears appealing (e.g. a majority joint venture), alternative design arrangements should be considered, such as non-equity-based alliances with supplemental contractual provisions and management control.

Step 5: alliance launch

When taking an international alliance view, general alliance launch guidelines need to be tailored to attain an efficient and effective alliance launch. First, the alliance launch team should pay attention to the specific cultural backgrounds of the partners. Initial cultural conflicts may escalate quickly and become an integral part of alliance development (e.g. via story telling). To deal with cultural differences, launch managers should assess and use cultural experiences that have been built prior to the partners entering the relationship. In addition, social meetings, training and joint experiences need to be organized to make staff aware of cultural differences and how to deal with them. As part of the alliance launch strategy, extensive communication becomes very important. The launch manager should inform employees at all levels about the motives for and importance of the alliance relationship. As part of operational plans, communication should focus on overcoming cultural adversities and transforming differences in synergetic opportunities (i.e. creative solutions). To overcome the 'we-versus-us' schism, kick-off meetings are critical at and across hierarchical levels. To accomplish these two tasks, it is critical that alliance launch managers act as cross-cultural competent managers skilled to deal with a variety of cultural backgrounds.

Step 6: alliance management

An important task during the alliance management stage is to harmonize actively the national cultural differences between the partners, to the extent desired. Appropriate alliance designs and launch management initiatives should have reduced the adverse impacts of cultural distance, but these differences remain manifest in the ongoing behaviour and thinking of the people involved. Culturally specific behaviours thus can produce misunderstanding, conflicts, limited trust and learning barriers. For example, the developmental path of the international alliance depends on whether collectivist partners try to manage process discrepancies, and then the resulting response of individualist partners to these interventions as they focus instead on outcome discrepancies. In principle, the interaction could lead to the resolution of the crisis or intensify it further. To avoid such cultural-based adversities, alliance management should focus on the following:

- Building collaborative communication patterns and, if necessary, undertaking management interventions to improve cultural awareness through training and education.
- Interpreting constructive and destructive conflicts consistently with cultural orientations and using resolution techniques that fit the cultural context.

- Avoiding breakdowns in relational norms and capital (e.g. trust) and investing time, energy and resources to rebuild them because strong working relationships are critical.
- Understanding that responses to adverse situations vary across countries and thus considering partners' cultural orientations while making response strategy decisions to prevent destructive spirals of partner interactions.

Step 7: alliance evaluation

In international alliances, specific consideration should be granted to performance metrics that imply cross-cultural problems, such as communication, conflict, trust, decision making and learning. With such attention, the firm can monitor the process of working together and outcomes, which are pivotal for steering the international alliance. If alliance partners also intend to combine the strengths of their national cultures, they need measures that facilitate cultural integration. Also important is a consistent focus on shared goals and objectives. Certain training programmes can inform employees about the shared goals of alliance partners, but performance management systems must convince employees that the rhetoric fits the reality. Ideally, in each development stage, all involved employees will understand how their performance is being assessed and how those performance assessments relate to the overall goals for the alliance.

Step 8: alliance termination

Finally, and conditional on the alliance design (i.e. governance form and exit provisions) and cultural orientation of the partners, firms must decide how to terminate their international alliance to ensure favourable outcomes for all involved. Issues that the partners may need to consider include the following.

- Irrespective of whether the termination is intended or unintended, country-specific regulations may affect the termination trajectory. For example, legal restrictions may inhibit the acquisition or divestment of equity stakes.
- If it is of strategic importance for one partner to be present in the foreign country, it should explore alliance alternatives immediately and ensure that it capitalizes on its learning experiences.
- Cultural orientations tend to influence the effectiveness of communication strategies. For example, in collectivistic countries, saving face is critical; an abrupt, premature alliance termination will thus have serious repercussions for all parties.

Summary

International alliances confront managers with a unique challenge: the international environments in which they operate can either exacerbate adverse situations or create a new opportunity. This challenge can be addressed using time-consuming processes associated with becoming acquainted with others' cultural dispositions. To reconcile cultural differences effectively, each partner must make an effort to learn the ideologies and values of its counterpart. Developing mutual understanding prompts tolerance and a proactive approach to the reconciliation. In particular, it requires a systematic assessment of the characteristics of potential international partners, a programme to deal with these cultural differences and attention to key alliance design and management dimensions, depending on the partner's nationality.

CASE: DAMEN SHIPYARDS[1]

Damen Shipyards was established in 1927. In 1969, Mr Kommer Damen took over the company from his father and introduced a revolutionary concept of modular construction to build small boats and launches. This concept of standardization (known today as the Damen Standard) generated clear advantages: fast delivery times, reduced costs and proven designs. Today, with more than 9,000 employees, the Damen Shipyards Group has earned a leading position in the shipbuilding world. However, the concept of standardization and industrialization remains very much at the heart of the company. Partnerships have always formed a strategic cornerstone of Damen Shipyards. The company actively collaborates with its clients, research institutes and suppliers to continuously innovate its ship designs and associated products and service offerings and pursue state-of-the-art manufacturing capabilities. Being a family-owned company, partners tend to be engaged with high intensity and a long-term focus. This is especially true for shipyards, with which Damen Shipyards has many partnerships. Damen Shipyards actively partners with shipyards in order to gain access to well-equipped production capacity with competitive capabilities. Next, shipyards can provide access to local markets because local governments often regard shipbuilding as having strategic importance to local and regional economies, especially in developing countries.

An important region for Damen Shipyards is South East Asia. Due to political reforms in South East Asia, the business landscape has changed considerably since the 1980s. Damen Shipyards was early to venture into China. In 1994, Damen Shipyards established a joint venture with Changde Shipyards, which was followed by the acquisition by Damen Shipyards in 2002. In Vietnam, political changes allowed for new business activity. From 1986 on, the Vietnamese government initiated the Doi Moi policies. These policies changed the country from a traditional communist, centrally led state economy to a 'socialist-oriented market economy'. This was followed by reforms in legal frameworks in the private sector. In 1990, the Law on Private Enterprises, which provided a legal basis to private firms, was enacted, while the Companies Law acknowledged joint-stock companies and private limited liability companies. The constitution established in 1992 officially recognized the role of the private sector. By 1994, the Netherlands had established an Embassy in Vietnam, and this embassy has played an important role in stimulating trade between the Netherlands and Vietnam. One of the first companies to become active in Vietnam was Damen Shipyards. Along with an attractive domestic and regional market, the highly motivated and well-trained Vietnamese labour force provided the strategic foundation for Damen Shipyards to start venturing in Vietnam.

Before venturing into Asia, Damen Shipyards was selling ships that were most often being built in the Netherlands. This proved to be a difficult commercial concept. Ships were too expensive, and Asian customers disliked the fact that their ships were being constructed on the other side of the world. In 2002, Damen Shipyards won a Vietnamese tender for six search and rescue (SAR) vessels. The Vietnamese requested that these ships be built in Vietnam in order to support the local economy. Damen Shipyards was willing to do this and decided that five of the six vessels would be built in Vietnam. To select the appropriate shipyard in Vietnam, a tender was released for the construction of these five vessels. Numerous yards were visited by Damen Shipyards staff. The general impression was that most yards did not meet the high standards that Damen Shipyards required. However, next to the focus on the yards' 'hardware' and current capabilities, Damen Shipyards looked closely at the human resources and management mindset. If these yards were to build ships according to the Damen Shipyards standard, both yard management and personnel had to be eager to learn and engage in an active collaboration for the construction of the SAR ships. The management team of Song Cam Shipyard in Haiphong had the eagerness Damen Shipyards was looking for. The management team of Song Cam Shipyard realized that collaboration with Damen Shipyards would enable them to learn state-of-the-art shipbuilding practices and increase competitiveness. The two parties collaborated to build the five SAR vessels. The cooperation left Damen Shipyards very satisfied with the building quality and costs. Song Cam Shipyards had received technical and management support, enabling it to further improve its shipbuilding standards. Both parties were very satisfied with the quality of the cooperation.

During that same period, Australia had a high demand for powerful but simple tug boats that could be operated by a two-man crew. The development and construction of these vessels progressed slowly partly due to the fact that these ships were being built in a crowded yard in the Netherlands. This led to an experiment in which Damen Shipyards allowed Song Cam Shipyard to construct two of these ships. The construction of these ships commenced in a very smooth manner. Costs were far lower than expected, while similar quality was delivered as in the Netherlands. This led to a following assignment involving the construction of four vessels. This represented the start of a more durable alliance between Song Cam Shipyard in Vietnam and Damen Shipyards in the Netherlands.

Damen Shipyards began to regard Song Cam Shipyard as one of the primary production locations for Damen Shipyards in South East Asia. Damen increased the amount of ships that were to be built at Song Cam Shipyards. Since a high level of trust existed between the two parties, the level of formality was initially kept low. A minimum quantity of production value was never agreed. Prices were not agreed up front; the only obligation that Song Cam had was to offer sharp prices, while remaining profitable. This required Damen Shipyards to actively monitor the sharing of profits between Damen Shipyards and Song Cam Shipyards. The amount of ships subcontracted to Song Cam Shipyard grew quickly due to the attractive cost price and good quality. This led to further formalization of the relationship between Damen Shipyards and Song Cam Shipyards to counterbalance potential business risks.

The formal agreements not only entailed the initial requirement on profitability but also required Song Cam Shipyard to grant exclusivity to Damen Shipyards. Song Cam Shipyards also had to abandon its sales activities. In exchange, Damen Shipyards would share technical and management knowledge, increasing the yard's competitiveness. Damen Shipyards would also ensure a reasonable utilization of the yard. Damen Shipyards would be responsible for sales, product development, engineering and after-sales, while Song Cam Shipyards would be responsible for the construction of the vessels.

The cultural distance between the Netherlands-based Damen Shipyards and Vietnam-based Song Cam Shipyards was significant. The Netherlands is characterized by a low power distance and high levels of individualism, while Vietnam has a high power distance and is a highly collectivist culture. High cultural awareness of Damen Shipyards staff was important for a successful outcome. Damen Shipyards employees knew the Vietnamese culture due to their pioneering activities in the years before the partnership was established.

Damen Shipyards uses a simple but effective model in which the various stages are described in building a business relationship. The model describes the following four phases: (1) getting acquainted, (2) earning respect, (3) building trust and (4) granting business. In Vietnam, moving from one phase to the next requires time and collective decision making. Damen Shipyards was willing to invest time and refrained from a 'hit-and-run' mentality. From 1994 on, Damen Shipyards was already pioneering the Vietnamese shipbuilding market. Damen Shipyards representatives visited Vietnam frequently. This illustrated the endurance and willingness of Damen Shipyards to build sincere business relations with Vietnamese companies, which helped move from making acquaintance to building respect. The building of trust requires a company to stay true to its word, even when it makes no sense from a business model point of view.

At one point, a project in Vietnam failed, causing considerable risk for loss of face for Vietnamese management and officials involved. Damen Shipyards assigned its resources to turning the project around and making it into a success. This had a lasting positive effect on the impression the Vietnamese had of Damen Shipyards. This event was an important contributor to building the required trust. An important element in the collectivist culture is that decision making takes place in groups and committees. This meant that numerous people knew Damen Shipyards and were able to translate the positive reputation in their respective communities. Therefore, the positive behaviour of Damen Shipyards became quickly known by a larger group of people. Within the Vietnamese shipbuilding community and associated political levels within Vietnam, Damen Shipyards became known as a trustworthy party. Avoiding shame is also important in Vietnam. As Damen Shipyards takes responsibility for handling complex projects, these projects are turned into a success. These aspects, combined with ORET (the Dutch Development Aid Fund), meant that Damen Shipyards was finally offered a business opportunity through the tender of six SAR vessels. This initiated the relationship between Damen Shipyards and Song Cam Shipyard.

Since 2002, the relationship between Damen Shipyards and Song Cam Shipyards has been very successful. Damen Shipyards has also set up similar collaborations with other shipyards; in the meantime, more than 250 ships have been produced at these locations. However, bridging the cultural distance remains challenging. To ensure the durability of this relationship, a management structure has been designed in which both representatives of Damen Shipyards and Song Cam Shipyards are positioned. Next, due to the increased strategic nature of the alliance, Damen Shipyards and Song Cam Shipyards have decided to move on to an equity-based relationship by setting up a joint venture called Damen Song Cam Shipyards. A result of this joint venture is the construction of a modern, state-of-the-art shipyard in the city of Haiphong. Although Damen Shipyards has a majority stake in the joint venture, the partners treat each other as equals, which is also represented in the governance structures. Both Damen Shipyards, as a family-owned business, and Song Cam Shipyards, as part of the collectivist Vietnamese culture, regard each other as being part of the same family. This level of trust and sincerity provides the foundation of the alliance and allows both parties to effectively bridge their cultural differences.

Questions

1   Explain how cross-cultural differences between Dutch-based Damen Shipyard and Vietnamese-based Song Cam Shipyards without careful cross-cultural management may have led to adversities between the partners.
2   Explain how cross-cultural differences may have affected the decision to opt for a joint venture and what post-formation initiatives may have been developed to steer the joint venture towards success.

Note

1   Interview with a senior executive of Damen Shipyard.

14

ASYMMETRICAL ALLIANCES

Alliances tend to be asymmetrical in nature, such that a dominant partner has a bargaining power advantage due to its superior resource endowments.[1] When such power asymmetries characterize the relationship, alliance partners are engaged in an asymmetrical alliance; the dominant firm can exert power, and the weaker firm risks being taken advantage of. In turn, dominant firms might appropriate the lion's share of the alliance benefits. Without proper management, power asymmetries create an eminent risk of inequitable value appropriation and sub-optimal alliance performance. Thus partners—especially weaker ones—face a unique challenge: finding the balance between exploiting resource asymmetries to create value while still preventing the escalation that can result from power asymmetries. This chapter focuses on this asymmetrical alliance challenge (first section) and elaborates on the mechanisms that managers might use to deal with it (second section). Connecting asymmetrical alliances with the alliance development framework offers some guidelines for decision making (third section). We conclude the chapter with a summary and a case illustration.

The asymmetrical alliance challenge

Alliances are forged from resource interdependencies between firms, which provide them with an opportunity to create value jointly. However, interdependency between firms is rarely equal, so an asymmetrical alliance results (see Table 14.1), in which one (dominant) partner possesses a net bargaining power advantage, and the other (weaker) partner possesses a net bargaining power disadvantage. By combining the partners' unique resources, the alliance might enable significant advantages. However, a dominant firm with a bargaining power advantage could exercise or even just threaten to use its power to coerce the weaker firm to comply with its demands, which reduces the weaker firm's motivation to continue the alliance (Gulati and Sytch 2007) and probably diminishes alliance performance. Even though asymmetry often offers advantages for both partners (e.g. resource asymmetry; see Chapter 3), the presence of power asymmetries (one specific form of asymmetry) tends to influence partners' commitment to value-creating activities.

DOI: 10.4324/9781003222187-14

TABLE 14.1 Examples of asymmetrical alliances

	Description
Amazon–ATDC	In 2022, Amazon Robotics invested in the Georgia Institute of Technology's Advanced Technology Development Center (ATDC). ATDC is a startup incubator that helps technology entrepreneurs in Georgia build, launch and scale successful companies. The goal of the investment is to accelerate growth of automation and robotics by leveraging staff and resources at ATDC in collaboration with Amazon. They also work with Amazon to identify specific areas of technical interest with the aim of developing virtual and physical events to attract relevant startups.
Garmin–iSpot TV	Garmin and iSpot TV have an active Technology Partnership. iSpot TV is a medium-sized organization which helps advertisers measure the brand and business impact of TV and streaming advertising, from concept to airing to conversion. Garmin is multinational and wants to be a sustainable company that makes superior products that can be used in cars, planes, boats, nature and sports, and play an important role in the lives of their customers.
MasterCard: StartPath™	MasterCard initiated StartPath™ to demonstrate its commitment to innovation through partnerships with early stage startups. MasterCard partners with startups from around the world to help scale their businesses, to develop new products and solutions and to accelerate the future of eCommerce. The programme enables startups to gain access to MasterCard's global ecosystem and to break new markets through relationships with MasterCard and its customers. Some key features include a six-month virtual program, two immersion weeks at different cities and no upfront equity in exchange for participation.
Coca Cola–Kol and TeleRetail	In 2019, Coca-Cola European Partners (CCEP) invested in two startups (Kol and TeleRetail) to explore how on-demand delivery and self-driving technologies can transform the customer experience. Coca Cola would share their experience with Kol and TeleRetail and learn from each business's innovation. Through these partnerships, they can ensure that they are continually adapting their own established model for a digital-first world and have an innovative new approach to getting their drinks into the hands of their customers faster.
JP Morgan Chase & Co.: In-Residence	In 2016, JPMorgan Chase & Co. started a new programme, In-Residence. The objective was to foster fintech startup companies in-house as they try to find ways to operate faster, with more security at a lower cost. The programme offers fintech startups access to facilities, systems and expertise to enhance their ability to create technology-led solutions that can be put into practical use for the industry. Fintechs with potential may receive continued support after the official six month period ends.

Sources: Amazon (2022a); Coca-Cola (2019); iSpotTV (2022); Mittelman (2016); StartPath (2016); Garmin (2021).

We warn, however, against the common misconception that power asymmetries always reflect firm size (see Box 14.1). Small firms often have strong motives to forge an alliance with larger firms (Street and Cameron 2007), but they are not necessarily the weaker partner. Certainly larger firms tend to have more resources, can draw on more extensive partnership experience and possess more (financial) stamina to endure negative alliance outcomes or conflicts. Furthermore, alliances with larger firms tend to increase the legitimacy of smaller firms and offer them an opportunity to tap into a broader resource base, which implies a faster time to market, better ability to serve new and geographically dispersed markets and market expansion (Alvarez and Barney 2001). These trends often lead to the presumption that larger firms are always more powerful than smaller firms. But smaller firms can possess specific resources (e.g. need for radical innovations) with great value to a larger firm, and their organizational characteristics (e.g. an innovation and entrepreneurial focus) may appeal greatly to that larger partner. Thus a smaller firm can dominate an alliance if it provides crucial, unique resources that the larger firm must have. In forging asymmetrical alliances, firms must therefore resist the temptation to attribute power solely on the basis of the partner's size.

A weaker firm forges an asymmetrical alliance because it hopes to gain access to valuable resources owned by the dominant firm. For example, manufacturers might enter into a

---

BOX 14.1 SMALL FIRMS AND ALLIANCES

In successfully realizing their objectives, small and medium sized enterprises (SMEs) often have a resource dependency on other firms. SMEs can gain substantially from forging alliance relationships. Resources that are shared allow SMEs to develop market propositions, gain scale advantages or penetrate new markets. Next, through these collaborations, SMEs are also provided with learning opportunities, which are particularly useful when structuring a growing organization (see Table 14.1 for examples). Alliances are also pivotal to enable an SME to accelerate its (international) growth and market performance. International growth is strongest when relationships are forged with noncompeting partners. In contrast to the benefits, alliance research also shows that alliances pose risks and challenges for SMEs. SMEs must be aware of the fact that partnering with large-scale firms imposes power imbalances, which might jeopardize the SME viability. In addition, other partner misfits are likely to exist—often confused with symptoms of power asymmetry—and partners should take adequate alliance design and management precautions to curb inevitable adversities (e.g. decision making and cultural conflicts). Developing alliance management capabilities is thus important to attain SME alliance success. Next, research has shown that SMEs have to be careful not to embrace too many alliances. Establishing a moderate number of alliances provides SMEs with the resources (e.g. capital, reputation and technology) required to grow. Establishing too many will cause a dilution in management attention.

Sources: Franco and Haase (2015); Moghaddam *et al.* (2016); Mohr *et al.* (2014).

partnership with more powerful integrators, distributors and retailers to market their products. For the dominant firm, access to the specific resources possessed by the weaker firm also constitutes a primary motivator for establishing the alliance. Pharmaceutical firms with large and established R&D centres, for example, could ally with smaller biotechnological firms that have less bargaining power but offer state-of-the-art, commercially unexploited knowledge. The weaker biotechnology firms in turn receive financing for their high-risk research programmes, and the dominant firms can continue to expand their competitive advantage. If this setting entails a low risk of misappropriation, the asymmetrical alliance represents a viable strategy for both partners.

But regardless of these strong motives for asymmetrical alliance formation, a power asymmetry inherently represents a source of alliance friction that poses a particularly stringent risk on the weaker party. That is, because the dominant partner can appropriate an unequal share of the value created by the alliance, it enjoys a better position relative to, and at the expense of, its weaker counterpart. Vandaie and Zaheer (2014) provide indirect support for this claim as they show that small movie studios that engage in higher levels of alliance activity with large (dominant) partners, i.e. the major studios, realize lower growth benefits from their internal capability. Although dominant firms may not use this power advantage to exploit their partners, weaker firms remain subject to the threat of exploitation. The very threat is likely to increase conflicts and reduce relationship proclivity. Moreover, the presence of this threat may cause the weaker firm to react preemptively to defend itself, which creates the further risk of retaliation by its dominant counterpart, perhaps in the form of the threatened misappropriation. Thus even when both partners are fully aware of the value generated by an alliance, the asymmetrical dynamic gives rise to frustration and tension, undermines joint value creation and can harm both the weaker and the dominant firm.

Whereas asymmetrical alliances may offer significant advantages for both partners, the realization of benefits requires cooperative behaviour. Power asymmetry creates the risk of misappropriation by the dominant firm, which will evoke dysfunctional conflicts and translates into alliance under-performance. To deal with this challenge, managers involved in asymmetrical alliances, especially those who represent the weaker party, must learn how to defend against or neutralize the adverse impacts of power asymmetry to ensure that their initiatives do not interfere with the collaborative efforts and benefits of the alliance.

Managing asymmetrical alliances

Bargaining power implies an ability to change multi-party agreements in one's own favour, such that individual benefits are maximized. By using their bargaining power, firms influence both the scope of activities within the alliance and the appropriation of the resulting alliance benefits (Pfeffer and Salancik 1978). Dominant firms enjoy an advantageous position; with their bargaining power, they can deploy various strategies, from non-coercive to coercive, and reap the benefits. The weaker firm suffers a great risk because of its lack of bargaining power, which minimizes its ability to prevent exploitation. A weaker firm must take a reactive position to secure its share of the value generated, and these strategies are relatively limited. Because a fair distribution of value (i.e. outcomes relative to contributions) between partner firms is crucial to build stable alliances, we propose three sets of tactics that weaker firms might use to deal with dominant partners: (1) offensive, (2) defensive and (3) acceptance (see Table 14.2).

TABLE 14.2 Managing asymmetrical alliances

	(1) Offensive tactics	*(2) Defensive tactics*	*(3) Acceptance tactics*
Logic	Seeking to (re)balance power relationship between partners; mutual dependence offers incentives to preserve alliance.	Installing protection against misappropriation; being protected offers parties incentives to preserve alliance.	Accepting power asymmetry and using non-power-based tactics; equitable outcome offers incentives to preserve alliance.
Goal	Change in resource–need balance.	Change in alliance governance.	Accepting power asymmetry.
Mechanisms (examples)	Provide additional and/or intangible resources; make relationship-specific investments, inter-firm learning.	Equity arrangement, contractual provisions, residual sharing, task specialization, relational capital.	Trade off relative share for absolute outcome, trade off objectives, exploit spillover and information asymmetry.
Downside	May trigger retaliation by dominant firm, undermines weaker firm's position.	May require extensive resources, difficult to impose contractual clauses on dominant partner.	Exposure to exploitation by dominant firm as alliance progresses.

Offensive tactics

Weaker firms may take a proactive stance to reduce the threat of misappropriation (Wang *et al.* 2016). In this case, their offensive tactics aim to shift the resource–need asymmetry to enhance their own relative bargaining power position (Makhija and Ganesh 1997). For example, they might proactively contribute more valuable resources to the alliance, which would increase the dependence of the dominant firm on them (Blodgett 1991b). Contributing additional or intangible resources should also enhance their bargaining position. It is unlikely that intangible resources, which are more difficult to transfer, can be seized by a dominant, more powerful firm, so the provider of these resources can protect itself from this form of opportunism (Coff 1999). Proactively redefining market boundaries may enable weaker firms to opt for substitute partners, which reduces their dependence on new partners and therefore offers strategic options in terms of negotiating with a dominant counterpart (Chiambaretto 2015). Weaker firms can also increase the dependence of their dominant counterparts (i.e. reduce the dominant firm's power) by convincing them to make specialized, relationship-specific investments to signal their commitment to the relationship (Gulati *et al.* 1994). If a firm is tied to the alliance through specialized investments, it cannot easily dissolve that alliance without incurring significant costs and the loss of non-recoverable investments (Klein *et al.* 1978). In addition, (supplier) customization and bonding through managerial ties tend to mitigate the detrimental effect of (buyer) power advantage on long-term collaboration (Wang *et al.* 2016). Finally, learning can help a weaker firm improve its bargaining power (Hamel 1991) because acquiring knowledge from a dominant partner expands its resource base and thus reduces its dependency over time.

Yet offensive tactics also can be counter-productive in that they ultimately decrease the weaker firm's relative power, leading eventually to a greater risk of exploitation by a dominant partner. In particular, offensive tactics can trigger retaliation because the dominant firm is motivated to retain its strong ability to appropriate value. Furthermore, by increasing their resource contributions, weaker firms might enter into even more vulnerable positions because they are likely to commit substantial expenditures that are open to retaliatory actions by the dominant firm. Such contributions also make the weaker firms more dependent because they have increased their alliance-specific stake. If weaker firms instead choose a learning race (Hamel 1991), they undermine the relationship's value-creation potential. Moreover, without some partner-specific absorptive capacity to acquire socially and organizationally embedded skills, expertise or tacit knowledge, learning tactics also are not particularly effective. Even when offensive tactics enhance a weaker firm's bargaining power by reducing the power asymmetry, their use ultimately may provide the dominant firm with more leverage to exploit its overall bargaining power advantage.

Defensive tactics

Defensive tactics serve rather as mechanisms to protect the firm against value misappropriation (Oxley 1997). Such tactics build on the logic that firms with superior power seek to exploit their power, so weaker partners must try to limit that exploitation by adopting a defensive, protective stance. Forms of such protection include a governance structure that prohibits the use of bargaining power or rules that guarantee an appropriate division of alliance benefits. Compared with non-equity arrangements, equity-based alliances (e.g. joint ventures) offer better protection against misappropriation (Gulati and Singh 1998) because they guarantee the weaker partner a pre-specified share of the value created, depending on their equity stake. For example, Yang and colleagues (2014) show that weaker firms (i.e. small) are more likely to appropriate value from an exploration-based alliance, if governed by an equity-based structure, whereas a non-equity arrangement suffices for exploitation-based objectives. Contractual provisions such as royalties and transfer prices offer another form of protection against misappropriation because they summarize firms' ex-ante agreement about the ex-post distribution of value (Hagedoorn and Hesen 2007). Detailed contracts that specify, for example, the use of patents, the nondisclosure of trade secrets, exclusivity conditions and task specialization protect the firm from partner misappropriation, such as the unwanted transfer of proprietary resources or knowledge (Katila et al. 2008). In addition, firms can invest in trust- and commitment-building efforts because relational capital tends to reduce the risk of exploitative behaviour (Kale et al. 2000).

Similarly, defensive tactics have their own limitations. Weaker firms may expose themselves to exchange hazards by using contract-based defensive tactics in that they lack the power to coerce a dominant firm to comply. In this case, the dominant firms are more likely to obtain formal controls to reinforce their power imbalance (Yan and Gray 2001). Moreover, weaker firms tend to prefer simpler contracts, which lack the clauses necessary to deal with unforeseen misappropriation (Ariño and Reuer 2004). More complete contracts increase contract monitoring burdens, and many weaker firms lack the resources and opportunities to monitor contract fulfilment actively. In contrast, incomplete contracts are less of a concern for dominant firms, which can just substitute their bargaining power. Relational-based defensive tactics also entail risks. A high-quality working relationship could substitute for an alliance contract (Lui and Ngo 2004), but over-reliance on relational governance leaves the weaker firm exposed to exploitation (Barney and Hansen 1994). Relationship building also is expensive and time-consuming: if it stretches its limited resources to focus on better relationships, the weaker firm could undermine its vulnerable position even further. In summary, defensive tactics may seem appealing to weaker firms to protect themselves against misappropriation by the dominant firm, but they also have serious potential repercussions.

Acceptance tactics

As the name suggests, acceptance tactics acknowledge upfront that dominant firms are better positioned to extract value. However, they also assume that weaker firms can contribute best to establishing stable asymmetrical relationships if they accept this power difference, rather than actively addressing the power differences as the offensive and defensive tactics do. To avoid direct conflicts, weaker firms simply accept the power asymmetry and use careful tactics to appropriate value, which increases the likelihood of alliance stability. During alliance negotiations, partner firms bargain about the distribution of anticipated value, and the allocation depends primarily on the partners' relative bargaining power. The weaker firm may purposefully accept a relative smaller share in this negotiation to stimulate joint value creation, with the belief that doing so will eventually provide a larger absolute (not relative) share. In addition, it may trade off some alliance objectives, such that its financial loss is compensated by an opportunity to acquire knowledge. Finally, the weaker firm might increase its pay-off by focusing on forms of value that are difficult to specify ex ante in an alliance contract, such as knowledge spillover. If it possesses information about future circumstances, the weaker firm could strategically wait patiently to exploit its information asymmetry.

Of course, acceptance tactics also have their own limitations. Weaker firms expose themselves to future (unforeseen) exchange hazards because the effectiveness of these tactics partially depends on the success of the alliance. For example, reaping a large absolute share, trading off between alliance objectives and exploiting information asymmetries all require that the alliance create value first. The weaker firm therefore needs to demonstrate its commitment before it can appropriate its share of value, although as the alliance progresses, the dominant firm could exploit its advantage to secure its individual interests. Despite this disadvantage, acceptance tactics help the weaker firm increase its individual benefits, just not at the expense of the dominant firm. It thus can avoid direct conflicts, prompt cooperation, focus on value creation and appropriate value without jeopardizing alliance stability.

The different properties tied to each type of tactic thus have varying implications. Offensive and defensive tactics require some bargaining power to appropriate value, and their use can clearly initiate conflicts. Acceptance tactics suggest that bargaining power is just one of multiple ways to appropriate value, and conflicts can be avoided. Acceptance of power imbalances also encourages cooperation without imposing a cost on the dominant firm, unlike tactics to manage power, which prompt competition. Although firms preferably select partners with which they can achieve a net bargaining power balance, which would reduce the need for protection, acceptance tactics make bargaining power a somewhat less important selection criteria. In turn, the degree of contractual specification can be minimized, unlike offensive and defensive tactics, which often require formalized alliance contracts (e.g. specifying resource contributions) if they are to avoid and resolve ex-post conflicts. Investing in relational norms and contributing capital increases alliance stability, especially in the context of offensive and defensive tactics, in that their effectiveness depends partially on the degree of trust and support offered by the dominant partner. In contrast, acceptance tactics require less trust and commitment because implementation can be unilateral and without partner support. In practice though, weaker firms might use offensive, defensive and acceptance tactics simultaneously and interchangeably.

Asymmetrical alliances: decision-making steps

Although asymmetrical alliances are common, they are also inherently unstable. In addition to generic guidelines, we identify several specific managerial guidelines that will enable alliance managers to turn potentially unstable asymmetrical alliances into stable ones. To this end, we discuss asymmetrical alliances in light of our alliance development framework (see Figure 14.1).

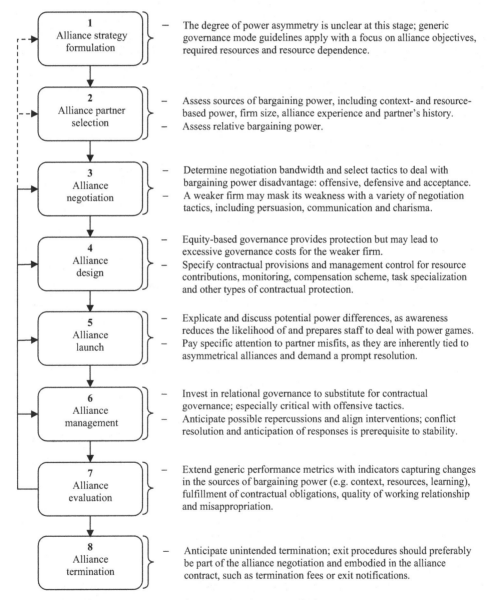

1 Alliance strategy formulation
- The degree of power asymmetry is unclear at this stage; generic governance mode guidelines apply with a focus on alliance objectives, required resources and resource dependence.

2 Alliance partner selection
- Assess sources of bargaining power, including context- and resource-based power, firm size, alliance experience and partner's history.
- Assess relative bargaining power.

3 Alliance negotiation
- Determine negotiation bandwidth and select tactics to deal with bargaining power disadvantage: offensive, defensive and acceptance.
- A weaker firm may mask its weakness with a variety of negotiation tactics, including persuasion, communication and charisma.

4 Alliance design
- Equity-based governance provides protection but may lead to excessive governance costs for the weaker firm.
- Specify contractual provisions and management control for resource contributions, monitoring, compensation scheme, task specialization and other types of contractual protection.

5 Alliance launch
- Explicate and discuss potential power differences, as awareness reduces the likelihood of and prepares staff to deal with power games.
- Pay specific attention to partner misfits, as they are inherently tied to asymmetrical alliances and demand a prompt resolution.

6 Alliance management
- Invest in relational governance to substitute for contractual governance; especially critical with offensive tactics.
- Anticipate possible repercussions and align interventions; conflict resolution and anticipation of responses is prerequisite to stability.

7 Alliance evaluation
- Extend generic performance metrics with indicators capturing changes in the sources of bargaining power (e.g. context, resources, learning), fulfillment of contractual obligations, quality of working relationship and misappropriation.

8 Alliance termination
- Anticipate unintended termination; exit procedures should preferably be part of the alliance negotiation and embodied in the alliance contract, such as termination fees or exit notifications.

FIGURE 14.1 Alliance development framework: asymmetrical alliances

Step 1: alliance strategy formulation

During the strategic analysis, firms decide whether an alliance is an appropriate governance mode for realizing their objectives. At this point, firms do not have any understanding of whether the potential alliance will be symmetric or not because their relative bargaining power is a function solely of the potential partner's bargaining power. Nevertheless, given their objectives, firms identify the required resources and determine the nature and severity of interdependencies with other firms to gain access to resources that cannot be provided autonomously. Interdependency provides strong collaboration motives to capture synergies; however, increasing dependence on a potential partner could also suggest the benefits of internalizing an activity to secure the focal resources. If a firm is willing to accept some power asymmetry, however, the alliance could be the preferred alternative because the costs of internalization might outweigh the potential benefits. For weaker firms, these benefits probably involve access to deeper, broader resource bases and potentially advantageous reputation effects. For dominant firms, the benefits primarily pertain to specific resources that extend and enhance their competitive advantage. By allying rather than internalizing, dominant firms also minimize divestment, coordination and integration costs.

Step 2: alliance partner selection

During the partner selection phase, power asymmetries should be identified and analyzed prior to the actual selection. Specific attention should centre on assessing the sources of bargaining power and levels of power asymmetry. In addition to partners' characteristics and motives for establishing the alliance, each firm should consider the following topics:

- Sources of partners' bargaining power, including context-based (e.g. possessing more scope to form an alliance than a potential partner) and resource-based (e.g. possessing more valuable and scarce sources than a potential partner) power.
- Other indicators of power, such as firm size (because the relative importance of alliances tends to be greater for small firms), alliance experience (which improves firms' ability to exploit power) and cultural background (because national cultural orientations may favour power use).
- The relative bargaining power of each potential partner, which reveals whether the intended alliance is asymmetrical. Such information is necessary to develop the most effective negotiation approach.
- The possibility of partnering beyond the narrow boundaries of an existing market/industry. Forging global and cross-border alliances allows weaker firms to escape from dominant industry incumbents.

Step 3: alliance negotiation

As the introduction to this chapter noted, asymmetrical alliances confront weaker partners with a unique challenge: to negotiate a favourable outcome without any bargaining power to make demands. Formulating a negotiation approach therefore requires substantial thought and consideration about the various tactics available, including offensive, defensive and acceptance tactics. Each tactic has unique and specific implications for the negotiation span and alliance stages. Offensive tactics demand additional resource contributions, which will increase the weaker firm's stake in the alliance. Unilateral or mutual relationship-specific investments both increase the commitments of the partnering firms and function as exit barriers. However, they also demand precise, careful negotiations and contractual specification to avoid ex-post exploitation. Similarly, defensive tactics require ex-ante agreements about ex-post benefit sharing, and their use often requires formal alliance contracts that might specify, for example, equity exchanges, royalties and trade secret protections. Acceptance tactics require that negotiators consider trade-offs between short- and long-term interests (common and private), thereby avoiding conflict with a dominant partner.

In addition, a weaker firm may use negotiation tactics to mask its weaknesses. Through communication and persuasion, a good negotiator might coerce its counterpart to accept outcomes that conflict with its own interests. A negotiator also might present information to make the outcomes seem like a win–win situation—whether they are or not. A charismatic, skilled negotiator who can build strong personal relationships may function as another influence tactic, as can consistent advocacy of normative conformity (i.e. convincing claims that a particular position is correct, legitimate or principled). However, excessive negotiation may jeopardize relational norms and capital, which are necessary to protect weaker partners from exploitation by their dominant counterparts.

Step 4: alliance design

Equity-based arrangements provide protection against exploitation; they also can create excessive governance costs, depending on the partners' actual objectives. Partner firms should follow generic guidelines to select an appropriate governance form. Irrespective of the form they adopt, though, the alliance design stage should emphasize the alliance contract and supplemental coordination mechanisms. The preferred tactic also influences the protective measures that should be embodied in an alliance contract. Agreements about partners' resource contributions and mechanisms to monitor the fulfilment of their obligations should nearly always be specified. Formalizing their task specialization can prevent leaks of vital knowledge between partners by limiting access to strategically important competences and capabilities. Each firm thus should define which activities and processes are most vulnerable to unwanted leakage and the degree to which its partner would be able to absorb that knowledge. Provisions specifying exclusivity and non-disclosure of trade secrets should also be incorporated in any contract. By setting up incentive structures that continually reward cooperation (i.e. residual sharing), partners can develop the foundation for a stable asymmetrical alliance. Finally, alliance design should allow for intensive inter-firm contact because strong working relationships reduce the tendency to resort to bargaining power. High-quality working relationships are generally characterized by strong bonds between the individual representatives of partnering firms, which enhances mutual trust. Thus overall the alliance contract should formalize ex-ante decisions that aim to reduce ex-post ambiguities related to the division of benefits between partners and help mitigate ex-post repercussions of the use of bargaining power.

Step 5: alliance launch

When taking an asymmetrical alliance view, generic alliance launch guidelines are sufficient to attain an efficient and effective alliance launch. However, alliance launch managers should be aware of two points. First, although the partners contractually agreed on how to deal with asymmetry (i.e. curb the threat of exploitation), it is imperative they establish a collaborative climate from the start. To overcome the 'we-versus-us' schism, kick-off meetings are important at and across hierarchical levels. The purpose is to induce collective sense-making processes that signal that they are mutually dependent on one another to attain the collective alliance objectives. Second, based on the partner fit analysis, they should address partner misfits and align, for example, differences in decision-making authority (e.g. organize mandates), differences in organizational culture (e.g. organize social meetings) and differences in performance systems (e.g. develop a new system). To accomplish these two tasks, it is critical alliance launch managers act as neutral mediators between the partners, advocating both dominant and weaker firms' interests.

Step 6: alliance management

The risk of exploitation represents a continuous threat. At any given point, a dominant firm may to decide to exploit its bargaining power advantage. Therefore, according to their alliance monitoring and evaluation efforts, weaker firms should focus on building relational norms and capital. Regardless of the governance structure or management control, partners' ability to influence each other in a relational sense is critical to effective interaction, learning, knowledge transfer and joint decision making. Because relational influence becomes manifest as mutual support, forbearance and power sharing, it may be more effective than contractual governance as a means to avoid misappropriation. Moreover, it facilitates conflict resolution and joint decision making. Other alliance processes, such as responses to adversity and inter-firm learning, also demand attention. Partners may develop an interaction pattern in response to adversity that stimulates power use, such as when dominant firms engage in opportunistic behaviour or aggressively impose solutions onto their weaker counterparts, which prompts the weaker firms to respond with similar tactics. In contrast, more constructive responses, such as seeking compromises and creative solutions, imply power avoidance. When partners organize and monitor learning processes, they also acknowledge knowledge transfer as an important source of shifts in bargaining power and conflict. Thus in addition to the generic alliance management guidelines, weaker firms should focus on conflict avoidance so as to develop stable relationships, particularly by adopting acceptance tactics.

Step 7: alliance evaluation

In addition to generic metrics, asymmetrical alliances need a performance metric system that features metrics to capture the sources of bargaining power, including resource contributions and alternatives. For example, partner contributions may change due to learning, which directly influences the power relationship. A weaker firm needs to be aware of such shifts. Depending on the type of tactic used, weaker firms may also employ different metrics. For example, offensive tactics require active monitoring of contractual fulfilment, defensive tactics need metrics to capture relationship quality and acceptance tactics require output metrics that can capture the degree of objective achievement over time. Alliance performance metrics should also centre on alliance process execution, which may be more qualitative and thus more unambiguous than objective inputs, though these still provide valuable insights into the actual functioning of the alliance and the extent to which a firm is exploiting its counterpart. The inherently unstable nature of asymmetrical alliances means that performance metric systems should also include indicators that capture and regulate communication. Representatives of both organizations would preferably come together to evaluate performance, decide on corrective actions and communicate decisions across their organizations.

Step 8: alliance termination

Finally, alliance termination still tends to favour the dominant party, which can use its power advantage to secure exit provisions, explore alternatives and reap the remaining value of the alliance. In an unintended termination, weaker firms might protect themselves from unilateral termination with contractual provisions that demand a termination fee if the alliance is dissolved prematurely. Advance notice agreements in an alliance contract can also postpone any effective termination for a pre-set period of time, which allows the parties to recoup their contributions and stimulate learning to maximize the alliance benefits. Another prevention of premature, one-sided alliance termination demands relationship-specific investments by all parties. The costs of such investments should arise only with alliance termination, such that they erect a potential exit barrier. Because these precautions against unintended alliance terminations often require formalization, weaker firms should ensure that the type and content of exit provisions represent part of their negotiation agenda.

Summary

The danger of misappropriation and sub-optimal value creation makes an interesting challenge for partners in an asymmetrical alliance. They need to exploit their resource asymmetries to create value, but at the same time, they must prevent exploitative moves that often result from power asymmetries. By taking the dominant firm's perspective, most mainstream alliance research focuses on value attainment, but weaker firms can also use offensive and defensive tactics to secure their share of jointly created value—though not without some risk. These tactics demand resource commitments and increase conflict (i.e. they induce power use by the dominant firm), which may make acceptance tactics more attractive to the weaker firms. With such strategies, weaker firms acknowledge their weakness but still extract satisfactory value and thus have good incentives to maintain their asymmetrical alliance relationships. In practice, however, most firms use some combination of these tactics.

CASE: DISNEY–PIXAR[2]

In the past two decades, the world of computer animation has witnessed rapid developments. In particular, increasing technological possibilities have radically changed the style and complexity of animated films. Furthermore, the markets for these offerings keep changing too, providing great opportunities for new entrants and significant potential threats to existing industry players—such as Walt Disney, the king of the animated movie industry. Familiar characters such as Oswald the Rabbit, Mickey Mouse, Donald Duck and Goofy helped Walt Disney build a business empire held up by four pillars: (1) production and distribution of animated and live-action motion pictures, (2) parks and resorts, (3) consumer products (i.e. merchandising) and (4) media networks, including ABC and ESPN.

Despite the expansion of the Disney enterprise, its core remained the production of animated films. The competence underlying this core contributor also was well set: hand-drawn animated figures. In the face of a technical revolution, however, Disney found it was lacking competences to generate the sophisticated look and creative approaches that consumers were demanding. To overcome these challenges, it sought alliance partners to incorporate new animation technologies into its film production; Pixar appeared to be an excellent alliance candidate.

Begun in 1979 as the Graphics Group, Pixar was part of the Computer Division of Lucasfilm before being acquired by Apple co-founder Steve Jobs in 1986 for approximately $16 million. Pixar focused on the development of computer-animated feature films that would target all layers of a society. Its key strengths, creativity and technological ability to produce computer-animated characters and feature films helped Pixar develop its first short film in 1987, called *Red's Dream*.

Although the companies were about to become partners with closely aligned goals, they were quite different. Pixar was a young, relatively unknown entrepreneurial company with a culture renowned for its friendly working environment. Disney was an established multinational with a strongly hierarchical management style and a consistently financial focus. But perhaps the biggest difference was the two firms' size. Disney was a far bigger company than Pixar.

The year 1991 started poorly for Pixar, which laid off 30 employees from its computer department. But the $26 million deal it made with Disney that year to produce three computer-animated feature films improved the outlook. Despite strong income, however, the company was still losing money, and Jobs often considered selling it. As late as 1994, Jobs contemplated selling Pixar to other companies, including Microsoft. Only after confirming that Disney would distribute *Toy Story*, the first feature movie developed by the alliance, for the 1995 holiday season did he decide to give it another chance. And the film went on to gross more than $350 million worldwide.

Following this success, Pixar and Disney signed a co-production–distribution partnership in 1997, agreeing to co-produce five feature films. Disney obtained access to Pixar's technological competences and creative drive. Beyond reinvigorating the animation genre with a new visual style, the alliance allowed for more cost-efficient and easy repurposing of digital content. But perhaps most important, Pixar's films provided great storytelling, the very foundation of Disney's long-held dominance in the market. Furthermore, with its functioning alliance, Disney could neutralize potential competitors. For Pixar, the partnership with Disney meant access to the vast Disney production and distribution resources. Pixar thus could focus on its core competence: producing computer-animated films. In addition, Disney offered access to its merchandising knowledge and distribution network, so Pixar could develop and sell toys, apparel and so on.

Profits and costs were split 50:50. Disney owned all story and sequel rights and also collected a distribution fee. Pixar lived up to its end of the agreement by creating and releasing *A Bug's Life*, *Monsters Inc.*, *Finding Nemo*, *The Incredibles* and *Cars*. The alliance thus provided production capital to Pixar and distribution fees to Disney. Soon enough, however, the success of these animated films shifted Pixar's position; it no longer needed capital because it could source production and distribution capital more cost efficiently if it worked with other studios. The disagreement that arose surrounding the release of *Toy Story 2* exemplified the deteriorating alliance conditions.

Originally, *Toy Story 2* did not fall under the alliance agreement because the intention was to release it straight to video rather than in the theatres. But Disney decided to release *Toy Story 2* as a motion picture in theatres, prompting Pixar to demand that *Toy Story 2* be counted as one of its contracted films. Disney refused. Then Pixar began questioning the equitability of its arrangements. The distribution fee was growing into an increasing problem for Pixar in that the distribution and merchandising fees ultimately resulted in a 68:32 split of profits in Disney's favour. As Pixar voiced its concerns, Disney insisted on maintaining the initial contractual agreement, and the relationship grew more contentious.

The two companies attempted to reach a new agreement in early 2004. The new deal would cover only distribution: Pixar proposed that in the revised alliance contract, it would provide full financing for its films but also be entitled to the full benefits. Disney would receive only a distribution fee of approximately 10 to 15 per cent of the gross sales. Disney rejected the proposal. In preparation for the potential fallout, Jobs announced in late 2004 that Pixar would no longer release movies in November, as Disney dictated, but would rather pursue the more lucrative early summer months, which would enable it to release the DVD versions just in time for the Christmas shopping season. The possibility that Pixar would find a more cost-efficient distribution arrangement with another studio became too great a risk for Disney, even if the new distribution arrangement yielded much lower distribution fees for it. By the time Disney came to this recognition, however, the personal relationship between Steve Jobs (owner of Pixar) and Michael Eisner (Disney CEO) had deteriorated to the point that the negotiation ultimately wound up a failure.

Pixar had grown so much by now that it could be self-supporting even after the demise of its alliance with Disney. Jobs admitted he would be on the lookout for other partners. In 2006, Disney headed off this possibility by acquiring Pixar for $7.4 billion in an all-stock deal. The acquisition was of the utmost strategic importance to Disney, not only because of where the distribution relationship with Pixar seemed headed, but also because of Pixar's potential value to Disney's entertainment brand and assets, such as its theme parks and television, that it needed to keep feeding off this valuable brand.

Questions

1   What asymmetries appear in the Disney–Pixar alliance? How do they change? To what extent do they affect the alliance's power relationship?
2   In which ways did the dynamic power relationship between Disney and Pixar, and its management, influence the alliance development?
3   Disney paid a high price to acquire Pixar. Could it have done something differently?

Notes

1   This section builds on prior research with Anoop Madhok (Schulich School of Business), whom we acknowledge for his contribution.
2   Amazon (2022b); CNNMoney (2004); Fonda (2006); IBS Center for Management Research (2006); Pixar Planet forum (2008); corporate website: www.pixar.com/companyinfo/ (accessed 2 August 2011).

15

CROSS-SECTOR ALLIANCES

The challenges that societies currently face are highly complex and unprecedented. Many of these challenges, such as climate change, scarcity of natural resources, increasing globalization, terrorism, poverty and food shortages, cannot be resolved within the public sector alone. Consequently, collaboration between private firms and public organizations, such as governments, universities and non-governmental organizations (NGOs), has become increasingly important. These cross-sector alliances (or public–private partnerships) provide opportunities for partners to share resources and expertise, which allows more effective solutions in keeping with individual and communal objectives. However, private firms and public organizations vary in many ways, including societal function, profit and non-profit orientation, accountability and organizational backgrounds, all of which are major causes of alliance instability. If these differences are not controlled, they will negatively affect the partners' ability to realize their individual and collective alliance objectives. Thus, although cross-sector alliances can enhance a firm's competitive position, they also present a unique challenge in that firms wishing to realize their private objectives must reconcile a wide range of differences that give rise to conflicts. The first section discusses this cross-sector alliance challenge, and the second section elaborates on the mechanisms that managers can use to deal with it. Next, a cross-sector alliance is associated with the alliance development framework to develop guidelines for decision making (described in the third section). The chapter concludes with a summary and a case illustration.

The cross-sector alliance challenge

The literature covers a wide range of cross-sector alliances (see Table 15.1), including business–community partnerships, union relationships, NGO–business partnerships, fund-raising alliances, ethical responsibility networks, voluntary corporate code agreements and cause–brand alliances (Rondinelli and London 2003; Wood 2002). Each type of cross-sector alliance is unique and poses distinct barriers to alliance formation and management. For the sake of brevity, however, this chapter focuses on three prototypical cross-sector alliances: (1) university–industry partnership, (2) public–private partnership and (3) non-governmental organization-business partnership (see Chapter 26 for emerging cross-sector alliances).

DOI: 10.4324/9781003222187-15

TABLE 15.1 Examples of cross-sector alliances

	Description
Inditex–Coruna University	In 2016, Inditex and the University of Coruna signed a collaboration agreement for the creation of a programme for the recruitment and promotion of international scientific researchers. The programme, called InTalent, enables scientists with a proven track record abroad to carry on their research projects at the University's facilities, thereby improving the latter's faculty and research capabilities while boosting students' chances of finding work and enterprising.
World Wide Fund for Nature–Bolton Food	In 2016, the World Wide Fund for Nature (WWF) and Bolton Food entered into a four-year partnership aimed at helping safeguard a healthy ocean and the livelihoods of communities that depend on it. In 2020, Bolton Food (with its brands Rio Mare, Saupiquet, and Isabel) and WWF renewed their transformational partnership for another four years (2021–2024) to promote more sustainable fishing activities. In addition, phase II of the partnership will strengthen advocacy efforts for responsible management of tuna stocks globally.
CARE–Cargill	CARE and Cargill formed an innovative partnership to fight poverty and long-term hunger in the developing world. CARE is a leading humanitarian organization fighting global poverty. Cargill is a multinational corporation that specializes in agriculture, food and beverage ingredients, meat products, industrial agricultural and steel products. CARE and Cargill leverage their respective strengths to improve livelihoods while at the same time improving Cargill's competitive advantage. For example, CARE partners with local Cargill teams provide training, skills development and market access for farmers; enhance education and nutritional support for children; and organize health care and safe drinking water for rural communities.

Sources: CSIS News (2011); Inditex.com (2016); Oneworld Trust (2009); WWF (2020).

A university–industry partnership depicts a collaborative agreement between a private firm and a university that combines resources to create and exchange academic and experience-based knowledge (Perkmann *et al.* 2011), often to develop innovative products and services and/or develop new technologies. For example, pharmaceutical companies, such as GlaxoSmithKline and Novartis, leverage academic knowledge to acquire fundamental expertise in specific disease areas. Engineering-based companies such as Rolls Royce work with academic departments in a variety of fields, including combustion aerodynamics and systems software engineering. Firms establish alliances with universities for a variety of reasons, all of which relate directly to their competitive position, including the ability to gain access to scientific breakthroughs, state-of-the-art information and training and support for building in-house skills, as well as to recruit highly qualified staff, to save costs by delegating research and development activities and to economize on investments in internal facilities (Bonaccorsi and Piccaluga 2000). In contrast, universities benefit from partnerships with industry through the additional funding, direct access to hands-on knowledge and expertise, access to case material and facilities (for example, laboratory facilities) and references for future public projects (Meyer-Krahmer and Smoch 1998).

Public–private partnerships are cooperative institutional arrangements between private firms and government agencies (Kwak *et al.* 2009). Governments are challenged to act effectively in an increasingly complex society that puts a strain on available resources, while gradually reducing funding. To realize their objectives, governments depend more and more on the corporate sector. Public–private partnerships enable government agencies and private firms to work together on such projects as developing and maintaining large infrastructural projects, including roads, bridges and tunnels. Firms supply specialist construction knowledge, management skills and funding in long-term infrastructure projects commissioned by governments. In return, private sector actors agree on the commercial exploitation of the project through which they receive revenues. Public–private partnerships rebalance the division of government and private responsibilities, allowing governments to reduce spending and implement their policies simultaneously. When firms in the corporate sector assume responsibilities that were previously executed by government agencies, they tap into new markets, which leads to extra revenues.

An NGO–business partnership refers to a cooperative arrangement between an NGO and a private firm that aims to strengthen the firm's efforts to support its corporate social responsibility policies (Austin 2000) and to improve the NGO's ability to achieve its idealistic and communal objectives. The profit-oriented nature and competences of private firms makes them relatively incapable of dealing with the social and environmental demands of customers, shareholders and other stakeholders on their own. Consequently, firms forge NGO–business partnerships to develop a green image; prevent boycotts and protests and circumvent public pressure; enhance their credibility through voluntary codes of conduct; avoid adverse publicity; improve staff morale, public affairs and public relations; and improve their credibility and positive reputation (Arya and Salk 2006; Loza 2004). NGOs, on the other hand, rely on the corporate sector primarily for funding and critical resources.

Although these three types of cross-sector alliances differ from business-to-business alliances in terms of their objectives and partner characteristics (see Table 15.2), they have three types of conflict in common that jeopardize alliance stability without adequate management. First, institutional conflicts are likely to emerge that originate in the different functions parties fulfil in society. The objectives of a firm primarily concern profit, while universities are mainly focused on knowledge production and dissemination. NGOs tend to focus on social issues (such as poverty and the suppression of minorities), while governments serve the

TABLE 15.2 Cross-sector alliance partners

	Government agency	University	Non-governmental organization	Private firm
Main interest	Public	Intellectual	Charity	Profit
Main source of income	Community	Government	Donations	Customers
Time horizon	Long term	Long term	Short term	Short term
Focus	Societal and economic situation of a country or region	Knowledge production and dissemination	Societal and economic situation of a country, region and minority groups	Discovering and exploiting market opportunities
Ranking of conflict	Accountability Institutional Intellectual	Intellectual Institutional Accountability	Institutional Accountability Intellectual	Competitive

Sources: Austin (2000); Kwak *et al.* (2009); Stafford *et al.* (2000); Wood (2002).

community. In other words, there is a distinction between profit and non-profit orientation and between private and public interests. These diverging orientations affect the way representatives perceive themselves and their behaviour. Consider a large infrastructural project, such as the construction of a highway. Private firms get involved and support the construction of a highway so as to generate revenue; motorists participate constructively because such projects tend to reduce travel times, but environmentalists are likely to resist because highways often imply negative consequences for ecosystems. Thus, decision-making in cross-sector alliances is impeded owing to different institutional backgrounds.

Second, an accountability conflict may emerge, referring to differences in how partners need to deal with financial responsibilities and reporting. Universities, government agencies and NGOs rely primarily on a variety of stakeholders to provide funding. Such variety in the sources of (public) funding, along with the social pressures imposed on public organizations, increases the need for accountability and transparency but also makes it complicated to assign accountability. In contrast, private firms are primarily accountable to owners, shareholders and external regulative entities. Partners in cross-sector alliances have varying requirements for accountability, which means that their stance towards the partnership is likely to differ in that they demand different financial infrastructures. The need to comply with distinct internal and external requirements complicates alliance design decisions as well as ex-post modifications. This disparity in funding and accountability can lead to tensions between partners.

The third type of conflict is the intellectual conflict that often exists between partners in cross-sector alliances. Research institutes, in keeping with their role in society, attempt to share their research findings with a larger audience, whereas a private firm that shares intellectual property could lose its competitive edge. Similarly, knowledge and technology developed through public funding, such as is the case in public–private partnerships, should be openly available (sometimes free) to the public; firms, on the other hand, would prefer to acquire and protect unique assets to strengthen their position in the market. For example, intellectual conflicts tend to characterize cross-sector alliances between pharmaceuticals and universities. Due to the high costs of R&D activities and the increasing speed of technological change, pharmaceutical companies collaborate with research institutions that possess state-of-the-art knowledge and facilities. Whereas firms strive to protect intellectual capital, specifically if research output undermines claims about the effectiveness of new medicines, universities are inclined to disseminate knowledge—sometimes having been forced to do so by specific legislation. Similarly, intellectual conflicts may arise in NGO–business and public–private partnerships.

In summary, partners in a cross-sector alliance face challenges that are inherently tied to this type of partnering. Differences in partners' societal functions, profit orientation, organization design and culture, and incentive systems form critical obstacles for win–win cross-sector alliances. The repercussions of these dissimilarities manifest themselves in divergent objectives, different time horizons and context-specific languages that, if left unresolved, can lead to institutional, accountability and intellectual conflicts. For example, whereas universities are supposed to act as independent societal institutes with a long-term orientation to generate high-quality knowledge in relatively stable environments, firms operate in highly competitive environments with short-term orientations and a focus on profit making, knowledge protection and the commercial value of knowledge. Due to these differences, the objectives of all parties can be met only to a limited extent, and the challenge for alliance management is to find an optimal trade-off solution in which each party can improve its pay-off without damaging the interests of its counterpart. In other words, partners in cross-sector alliances face the challenge of reconciling private interests with communal interests.

Managing cross-sector alliances

The management of cross-sector alliances requires partners to identify differences proactively and to understand how these differences give rise to conflicts and what initiatives they can develop to reconcile these differences in order to reduce the probability of conflicts (London *et al.* 2006). This section presents three areas that managers may focus on in order to steer their cross-sector alliance towards success. These are (1) enforcing power neutrality, (2) creating autonomy and transparency and (3) building a culture of collaborative commitment.

Power neutrality

Heterogeneous resources, competences and alternatives make it unlikely that partners in a cross-sector alliance will have balanced power positions. However, successful cross-sector alliances are often characterized by power neutrality, which means that partners' participation in communication is democratic. All parties involved in discussions about the partnership must have an equal voice in determining the outcomes, even if one of them (often the private firm) possesses a power advantage. In order to achieve commitment and constructive collaboration, partners must create a context that is free of coercion and the fear of retaliation. To develop a platform for power-neutral discussions, partners may use defensive, offensive and acceptance tactics (see Chapter 14). However, whereas the first two tactics are likely to ignite a power struggle, the use of acceptance tactics is more likely to contribute to a stable partnership; by using acceptance tactics, partners recognize that all interests are best served on egalitarian grounds. For example, Starbucks and Conservation International formed an alliance to encourage environmentally friendly coffee. Although Starbucks' strong position in the coffee market provided it with a power advantage, it did not exercise (or threaten to exercise) this power in an attempt to hinder Conservation International's attempts to achieve its own objective (Austin 2000). Failure by any partner to realize and accept some degree of power neutrality is likely to hamper the performance of the alliance.

Autonomy and transparency

Autonomy of the partners and transparency in cross-sector alliances is important for creating a climate in which parties can deal actively with potential conflicts. Autonomy refers to the extent to which a participant should have an equal opportunity to express its interests and be able to question the assertions made by any other participant. When a partner cannot participate fully in the discussion, its autonomy becomes jeopardized, which constrains its efforts to advocate its individual or communal interests. For example, Macdonald and Chrisp (2005) described an alliance between a pharmaceutical firm and a charity organization that encouraged teenagers to lead healthier lives. One reason the alliance failed is because the pharmaceutical firm gained dominance and suppressed the charity, driving the partnership towards the achievement of its own private interests rather than being concerned with the interests of the partnership or the charity. Recognizing the need for autonomy requires managers to plan and invest resources carefully to enable and facilitate dialogue and discussion. A win–win cross-sector alliance can only be established when all partners are equally able to express their interests fully.

Transparency suggests that partners are able to communicate in such a way that makes other members aware of their positions, goals and interests. This applies not only to the partners involved in the alliances but also to external stakeholders. Although there is no clear way of guaranteeing transparency within a single discussion, ongoing interaction over time can provide the conditions in which the true motives of the stakeholders become exposed (Reynolds and Yuthas 2008). This notion of transparency conflicts somewhat with alliance practices within business-to-business settings. During alliance negotiations, for example, companies tend to withhold critical information to secure private interests. In the pharmaceutical–charity alliance described previously, partners agreed openly on certain private interests (the pharmaceutical sought public relations and the charity sought funding), but the parties did not acknowledge the fact that their fundamental intentions were causing conflicts as the alliance progressed. Transparency requires an ongoing, iterative dialogue between partners and their stakeholders as discussion exposes each partner's position, interests and intentions.

A culture of collaborative commitment

In the context of cross-sector alliances, it is important that partners share fundamental values and beliefs if they are to reduce the risk of potential conflicts, or to resolve them effectively once they have emerged (Barroso-Méndez *et al*. 2016). A culture of collaborative commitment enables partners to become aware of and reconcile diverging values. However, it can be difficult to build and maintain a culture of collaborative commitment because it requires staff to be aware of individual dispositions and those of their counterparts. Developing and maintaining a collaborative commitment culture does not happen by organizational decree alone. It must be interwoven into all aspects of the partners' organizations and into the alliance. This new or modified culture must start with a focus on internal and external stakeholders as it is they who must embrace the alliance's intended direction. For example, if a firm and a university acknowledge different time horizons, they may agree to postpone publication of research output in order to provide the firm with an opportunity to exploit this knowledge by staying ahead of its competitors. Building a culture of collaborative commitment in a cross-cultural alliance requires partners to focus on the following factors.

Employees and senior management from partner organizations should support the alliance's objectives. Management plays a powerful role in the process of establishing a collaborative culture within a cross-sector alliance as it ensures the credibility of the push for collaborative behaviour (Noble and Jones 2006). Management must be perceived to support the collaboration both publicly and privately. A project champion who supports the alliance may serve as an example to other members of the staff. In addition, designating boundary spanners enables a firm to lay a foundation for collective sense-making activities that reinforce the development of a collaborate culture. Partners should use an employment selection process for participating in the alliance in order to prevent the inclusion of people who are unsupportive of the alliance's objectives. For example, staff can be selected by conducting a test that taps into the congruency between their value systems and that of the alliance. Furthermore, the initial stage of involvement in the alliance is the best time to start instilling the collaborative commitment culture into alliance staff. It is not enough simply to impart information about the existence of collaborative values. Through training and education, alliance staff must be made aware that collaborative behaviour is the foundation for the alliance and should be manifested in all its activities. An education programme designed to understand and subsume fully the alliance philosophy on collaborative commitment practices and behaviour may fulfil this purpose. This programme should be formally endorsed by the alliance and should explain to all levels of alliance participants the importance in being collaborative, not only for the benefit of their organizations but also to enhance alliance performance. Hence, it is desirable to establish an 'education committee' that can not only coordinate but also monitor the level of education and the subsequent exposure to and awareness of collaborative issues.

In addition, partners may introduce a code of conduct that serves as an instrument to enhance awareness and helps organizations reduce and/or deal with conflicts of interest in a constructive manner (Harrington 1991). Within the context of a cross-sector alliance, a code of conduct should be developed that has both an internal and external focus. An external code of collaborative commitment provides guidelines for how to interact with various stakeholders connected with the partners and the alliance. This also contributes to transparency in their communication to other members outside the alliance. An internal code targets employees who work at all levels within the alliance and aims to provide guidance to staff when they face conflicts of interest during day-to-day operations. The process of developing a collaborative culture can be enhanced only if all parties are consulted and agree on the collaborative stance of the alliance.

Cross-sector alliances: decision-making steps

Cross-sector alliances are unique because the partners are likely to have noticeable differences in terms of their societal functions, incentive systems, organization cultures, decision-making styles, time horizons and professional languages. Cross-sector alliances are difficult to realize and tend to result in minimal joint decision making and continuity in cooperation owing to inherent conflicts between the partners. To assist alliance managers, the next section provides guidelines for each stage of the alliance development framework when forging successful cross-sector alliances (see Figure 15.1).

Step 1: alliance strategy formulation

During the strategic analysis stage, a firm will decide whether a cross-sector alliance is an appropriate governance mode to realize its objectives. Although generic rationales such as transaction costs, resource complementarities and resource dependence inform governance mode choice, an alliance is most likely to be the preferred alternative owing to the partners' distinct backgrounds. For example, a merger between a university and a private firm is unlikely because the two parties fulfil different functions in society. A market exchange is also improbable because state-of-the-art academic knowledge is often not commoditized.

Alternatively, a cross-sector alliance enables a firm to exploit efficiently the synergies obtained through collaboration with a public organization. However, to complete its strategic analysis a firm may wish to include a stakeholder analysis. An effective cross-sector alliance strategy fits with a firm's environment to accommodate the demands of external stakeholders, comply with social pressures and capitalize on contextual opportunities. This requires conscious decision-making, both from the private firm and from the public organization considering a cross-sector alliance. Whereas a private firm must assess the extent to which a partnership strengthens its competitive position, a public organization must evaluate whether its interests are best served by a cross-sector alliance. Moreover, public organizations must often adhere to laws and regulations that limit the room in which they can manoeuvre. Private firms must also take certain risks into account, such as changes in law, public acceptance and government. These could impact such areas as increased operating costs to comply with new laws, adverse effects on quality and service delivery and/or additional operating costs and time delay. These aspects need to be incorporated in the strategic analysis.

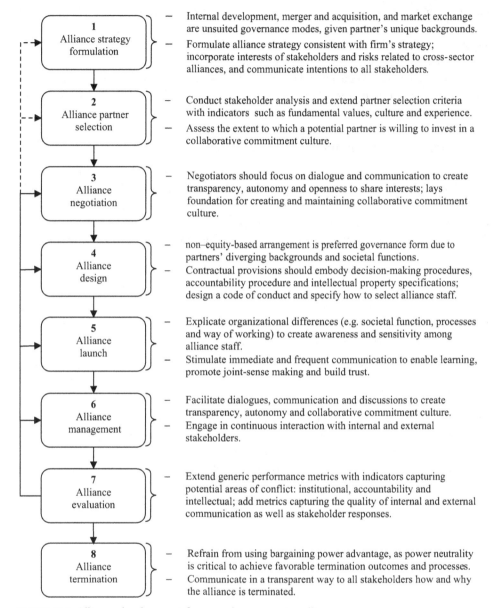

1 Alliance strategy formulation	– Internal development, merger and acquisition, and market exchange are unsuited governance modes, given partner's unique backgrounds. – Formulate alliance strategy consistent with firm's strategy; incorporate interests of stakeholders and risks related to cross-sector alliances, and communicate intentions to all stakeholders.
2 Alliance partner selection	– Conduct stakeholder analysis and extend partner selection criteria with indicators such as fundamental values, culture and experience. – Assess the extent to which a potential partner is willing to invest in a collaborative commitment culture.
3 Alliance negotiation	– Negotiators should focus on dialogue and communication to create transparency, autonomy and openness to share interests; lays foundation for creating and maintaining collaborative commitment culture.
4 Alliance design	– non–equity-based arrangement is preferred governance form due to partners' diverging backgrounds and societal functions. – Contractual provisions should embody decision-making procedures, accountability procedure and intellectual property specifications; design a code of conduct and specify how to select alliance staff.
5 Alliance launch	– Explicate organizational differences (e.g. societal function, processes and way of working) to create awareness and sensitivity among alliance staff. – Stimulate immediate and frequent communication to enable learning, promote joint-sense making and build trust.
6 Alliance management	– Facilitate dialogues, communication and discussions to create transparency, autonomy and collaborative commitment culture. – Engage in continuous interaction with internal and external stakeholders.
7 Alliance evaluation	– Extend generic performance metrics with indicators capturing potential areas of conflict: institutional, accountability and intellectual; add metrics capturing the quality of internal and external communication as well as stakeholder responses.
8 Alliance termination	– Refrain from using bargaining power advantage, as power neutrality is critical to achieve favorable termination outcomes and processes. – Communicate in a transparent way to all stakeholders how and why the alliance is terminated.

FIGURE 15.1 Alliance development framework: cross-sector alliances

Step 2: alliance partner selection

Owing to varying interests, objectives and organizational backgrounds, partner fit can be deemed low in most cross-sector alliances. Consequently, partner selection becomes a critical activity as recognizing areas of incompatibility—which include strategic, organizational, cultural, operational and human areas—allows partners to develop corrective measures. For example, managers must consider whether the partners' organizational missions match, whether the alliance is equally important to both partners, whether partners' needs and capabilities can be integrated and whether the partners share values. In addition, partner analysis may focus on earlier partnership experience and partnering culture as prior successful cross-sector alliances are indicative for future successes. An existing collaborative commitment culture or a willingness to build will reduce the likelihood of conflicts. More specifically, the cultural ability to appreciate different environments and the ability to adapt accordingly is an important partnering criterion. In addition, partner analysis may focus on flexibility, as the willingness of partners to adapt to existing and unforeseen circumstances is an important condition to success.

Step 3: alliance negotiation

In order to achieve mutual collaborative commitment, partners in a cross-sector alliance must recognize the problems within their power relationship and also take precautions to neutralize power imbalances that may affect the fundamental purposes of their alliance. Thus, in addition to the generic negotiation guidelines, the negotiation approach should preferably be integrative and accompanied by soft tactics. It is important to obtain agreement on how to stimulate all participants and reward them for expressing their interests and objectives openly, as well as to make assertions and question the assertions of others. Moreover, the partners should openly explain their positions, goals and interests, both to each other and to the 'outside world'. Such transparency and openness during alliance negotiations foster alliance progress and performance, and firms must suppress the pressure to engage in distributive tactics. This means that partners should use acceptance tactics that recognize the fact that all interests are best served on egalitarian grounds.

Step 4: alliance design

Like the rationale of avoiding mergers and acquisitions, cross-sector alliances tend to be most efficiently governed through non-equity-based arrangements that are supplemented with specific contractual provisions and management control. Whereas the alliance's governance form and management control mechanism should be consistent with generic guidelines in cross-sector alliance, particular focus should be given to contractual provisions and control mechanisms that deal with potential conflicts. More specifically, the following elements should be embodied in an alliance design if possible:

- Agreement on the decision-making procedures. For example, decision-making speed is critical as public and private organizations often have different requirements. Failure to manage these differences can translate into high levels of frustration, possibly damaging collaborative efforts.
- Agreement on accountability. Whereas public organizations are under public scrutiny and must adhere to laws and regulations, private firms must satisfy shareholders and other regulatory requirements.
- Contractual provisions, including communication structures, escalation procedures and conflict management structures, must be designed to deal with relational risks in order to prevent potential damage to the partnership.
- Agreement on how to select and monitor employees involved in the alliance. The dispositions of these employees should match the desired collaborative commitment culture. If necessary, partners should develop and implement a collaborative commitment culture programme to train and educate staff.

- The design of operational procedures must reflect the need for interaction and sense making. Therefore, working in mixed teams is preferable to working in separated teams that remain organization-specific.
- Constructing a code of collaborative commitment culture, as well as communicating and discussing this with all participants in the alliance. Besides internal communication, it is also important to communicate the code to other stakeholders in the environment.
- Measures to ensure sufficient power neutrality. Selecting coordinators and staff who are aware of power-based behaviour makes it possible to deploy adequate countermeasures. It is also important to educate staff to be aware of the consequences of power abuse.

Step 5: alliance launch

Partnering with a non-profit organization can involve uncertainty for a firm because it requires working with institutions (e.g. government agencies) that may have complex decision-making systems and a complex set of interests and objectives. Consequently, within a cross-sector alliance, employees are challenged to deviate from their normal intra-organizational routine life and confront a situation that often involves a new and potentially complex inter-organizational experience. Systemically organizing the alliance launch is thus critical with regard to a cross-sector alliance as employees may possess a naturally hostile disposition towards the rival partner. Often the cross-sector partner has been portrayed as an adversary, and suddenly it is expected of staff to collaborate. The various motivations, organizational cultures and value patterns of the public and private sectors would be expected to give rise to management challenges that are not normally associated with private–private or public–public partnerships. As part of the alliance launch strategy, launch managers should attempt to remove any misconceptions and prejudices. Launch managers should provide employees with sufficient time to become familiar with the collaborative commitment culture. In addition, they should inform staff at all levels about the motives for the alliance relationship. As part of operational plans, organizing efforts should focus on aligning the partners (e.g. based on partner fit analysis) and on creating clarity about what is expected from staff with regard to skills, communication, interaction and collaborative behaviours.

Step 6: alliance management

In managing a cross-sector alliance, continued understanding of the backgrounds and interests of one's partners allows participants to act and react better, which improves the management interventions and quality of the working relationship. This is also the perfect time to try and mould employees into the alliance's culture. In addition to generic management guidelines, alliance managers should therefore facilitate and monitor dialogue and discussion between the partners in order to create an environment that fosters autonomous behaviour. During progress meetings, for instance, the chair should ensure that participants are able to express their interests and question claims made by others. It is also important to stimulate continuous interaction with external stakeholders based on transparency and openness. Partners may create a common website about the alliance that presents the goals, participants, their roles, events and news on a regular basis.

Step 7: alliance evaluation

Cross-sector alliances are established to reach certain objectives. The performance metric system can be augmented with additional indicators that tap into these objectives, such as customers' awareness and funding. In addition, metrics may capture the potential conflicts that are likely to emerge. For example, indicators may concern the extent to which participants are satisfied with how they dealt with intellectual and accountability issues, how they cope with or respect each other's interests and how they handle external stakeholders. Performance metric systems may also include indicators that capture the collaborative culture, such as partner firms' behaviour, in terms of the extent to which management and employees behave according to the collaborative commitment culture; how open communication is; and whether partners have the opportunity to express their interests and objectives. Metrics may also ascertain the extent to which partners are sufficiently transparent about their position, goals and interests to external stakeholders, and whether potential power differences have been neutralized.

Step 8: alliance termination

The duration of the agreement and the termination provisions are important because such items affect the parties' ability to escape from cross-sector alliance arrangements that turn out to be harmful to the business, or simply not as effective or profitable as other stakeholders might have expected. Because of the desire for transparency, it is important to communicate to the external environment why and how the alliance is being terminated. It is important to refrain from using power to attain favourable termination outcomes as retaining power neutrality will increase the likelihood of avoiding barriers for future cross-sector alliances.

Summary

Alliances between private firms and public organizations, such as governments, universities and non-governmental organizations, have become increasingly important for dealing with society's challenges. These cross-sector alliances provide opportunities to align resources to achieve individual and communal objectives. However, uncertainty and ambiguity can be expected to increase when people with different backgrounds and cultures interact with each other. A lack of mutual understanding, varying interpretations and different ways of doing things might lead to frustration that could ultimately damage and possibly jeopardize the partnership. Managers may deal with the promises and perils of cross-sector alliances by adopting a power-neutral stance, emphasizing autonomy and transparency and building a culture of collaborative commitment.

CASE: MARKS & SPENCER–OXFAM[1]

The average UK household has about £4,000 of garments hanging in the wardrobe. Approximately 30 per cent of this clothing has not been worn for over a year, mostly due to the fact that it no longer fits. This amounts up to £30 billion of unused clothing. Roughly 31 per cent of these clothes are thrown away and end up as landfill, amounting to roughly £10 billion of good-quality clothes. At the same time, there is a high demand for good-quality second-hand clothing, both in the UK and abroad, especially in developing countries. The ability to get access to good-quality second-hand clothing can fulfil demand at the same time as reducing pollution. That is why Marks & Spencer and Oxfam joined forces in their alliance called Shwopping.

Oxfam was established in 1942 as the Oxford Committee for Famine Relief by a group of Quakers, social activists and Oxford academics. This group campaigned for food supplies to be sent through the allied naval blockage in order to feed the starving population of Greece. After the Second World War, the organization started to expand, and its first overseas Oxfam was founded in Canada in 1963. The organization changed its name to Oxfam in 1965. Oxfam is currently an international confederation of 18 organizations, working together with partners and local communities in more than 90 countries. The mission of Oxfam is to relieve people from poverty. To do so, Oxfam finds practical and innovative ways to enable people to lift themselves out of poverty.

Marks & Spencer (M&S) is a major British multinational retailer. Founded in Leeds in 1884 by Michael Marks and Thomas Spencer, the company grew quickly, focusing mainly on the sale of clothes and food. Offering fair value for money was always a key feature for M&S, which established long-lasting partnerships with suppliers in order to do this. The company experienced healthy growth but went through tough times in the late 1990s. In 2004, a hostile takeover bid was made, which led to a change in leadership and a rebalanced strategy. Although the takeover bid was fought off, the new strategy also incorporated setting higher standards with regard to environmental and societal consciousness. Due to growing pressure on natural resources and poor global stewardship, M&S risked an increased cost base, growing difficulties in getting access to raw materials and increased volatility in the M&S global supply chain. To counter these threats, M&S launched its 'Plan A' in 2007. The goal of Plan A is to make M&S the world's most sustainable retailer and improve the protection of the planet and its communities.

An important part of Plan A is to work with partners in order to realize the ethical and environmental goals that have been set. One such partner is Oxfam. Oxfam aspires to make a positive impact on relieving the world from poverty. It believes that this goal can only be achieved through the collective efforts of many actors. Therefore, partnerships are pivotal in this strategy. Oxfam seeks partners that are effective at alleviating the root causes of poverty. It is important for Oxfam that partnerships are built on a shared vision of a fair world that is free of poverty and injustice.

Oxfam sells second-hand clothing in the UK to attract finances to fund its activities across the globe. However, the supply of good-quality clothes has become a problem. Good-quality clothes are essential for Oxfam. Approximately 80 per cent of Oxfam's income is generated from income received from items sold in its stores. Good-quality clothes generate regular visiting customers for Oxfam, ensuring a stable cash flow.

Following the Plan A principles, M&S formulated the ambition to recycle one piece of clothing for each item it sells. Oxfam and M&S were already in contact about opportunities to improve the supply chain and ensure that the clothing it sold was meeting the highest ethical and environmental standards. In 2008, the two parties decided to embark on a partnership called 'Shwopping'. Shwopping aims to change consumer behaviour by emphasizing recycling in a very consumer-friendly manner.

In practice, Shwopping works in two ways. First, consumers can take any type of clothing to Oxfam stores. If the donated clothes are from M&S, customers receive a £5 voucher, which can be spent at M&S to buy new clothes. This gets potential customers back to M&S, ensuring the 'traffic' that is highly important for M&S. The second trajectory is that customers can donate any type or brand of clothes directly at M&S stores, and M&S guarantees that these clothes will be recycled. Good-quality clothes are sent to Oxfam stores. If these items are not sold at Oxfam stores, Oxfam sends these clothes to developing countries to support local projects. These local projects drive the local economies and ensure that people receive income, housing and opportunities to further build on a better future. If the clothes donated at M&S stores are not fit for sale at Oxfam, M&S will recycle those items.

M&S and Oxfam actively generate attention to Shwopping by having Joanna Lumley, a well-known British actress, illustrate the relevance of the initiative. By conducting interviews and travelling to developing countries, Lumley demonstrates the effects of Shwopping. For M&S, this is effective marketing and helps potential customers into their shops; for this, Oxfam increases the public awareness for the organization and its ambitions.

In creating and managing partnerships, Oxfam uses clear principles that guide all of its partnerships with stakeholders and, therefore, also applies to the partnership it has with M&S. First, Oxfam emphasizes the relevance of a shared vision and shared belief. Partnerships between Oxfam and other organizations need to be built on a shared vision of a fair world that is free of poverty and injustice. According to Oxfam, this implies solidarity beyond the implementation of specific programmes or activities. M&S's Plan A provides a solid basis and an institutionalization of the willingness M&S has to contribute to a better world. Oxfam's second principle is the complementarity of purpose and added value. Whether it is a short- or long-term partnership, the goals of the partnership should be clear, as should the contribution and benefits for all partners involved. In the partnership with M&S, the partnering structures and activities have been articulated well and are monitored by both M&S and Oxfam. Oxfam realizes that partnerships pose challenges with regard to aligning interests and views. Therefore, Oxfam has stated that partners must remain autonomous and independent. Through active communication and alignment in partnership structures, common ground needs to be found upon which the partnership can be based. This emphasizes a thorough partnership design. The clear and simple structure of the partnership between M&S and Oxfam ensures clarity regarding what they share mutually, while both partners remain independent entities.

The partnership has been very successful. Since the partnership began in 2008, right up to 2021, more than 35 million garments have been donated in M&S and Oxfam Shops, worth an estimated £22 million for Oxfam. In 2022, as part of the retailer's Plan A sustainability programme, M&S is calling on customers to donate their used clothing to Oxfam via its recently refreshed Shwopping scheme. For M&S, the Shwopping concept has generated increased traffic into its stores; however, it has also ignited other kinds of innovations. Prior to the launch of the Shwopping concept, M&S had no real reverse supply chain in place to get clothing back from M&S stores. Also, the clothing recycling industry was still small in scale and poorly structured. With the Shwopping concept, M&S created new infrastructure that has enabled M&S to reduce costs by sourcing recycled wool and cashmere at lower prices than new. With Shwopping, M&S has made significant steps in realizing its Plan A ambitions and becoming part of the circular economy.

Questions

1. Describe the company interests of both Marks & Spencer and Oxfam to participate in the Shwopping alliance, and compare these to their joint interests. Which tension(s) do you observe, and how did (or may) the alliance partners deal with them?
2. Provide a systematic overview of management initiatives Marks & Spencer and Oxfam implemented to avoid and resolve conflicts.
3. Explain why it would be difficult for competitors and other non-governmental organizations to mimic the success of the Shwopping alliance.

Note

1   Bardsley (2013); M&S (2022); Oxfam (2016a, 2016b, 2021).

16

COOPETITION ALLIANCES

Forging alliance arrangements between competitor firms has become increasingly popular. These so-called 'coopetition' alliances, despite their inherent risks, provide partner firms with market opportunities and operational synergies extending beyond what partners could have achieved individually. The risks however, such as loss of proprietary knowledge and escalating conflicts, require specific alliance designs and adequate alliance management. Whereas alliance relationships between non-rival partners bring forth a tension between cooperation and competition, this tension amplifies when rival firms collaborate (Ryan-Charleton and Gnyawali 2022). This tension, however, is not unlike the challenges and management practices associated with learning alliances (see Chapter 11). This is because most coopetition alliances involve, or are exclusively focused on, R&D collaboration. If partners decide to extend their collaboration beyond pre-competitive co-creation and innovation initiatives, the potential synergies increase greatly, but these are paralleled by increases in competitive pressure on the relationship. Without preemptive considerations of these risks, alliance instability and ultimately premature termination is imminent. This chapter first details coopetition and its unique challenge (first section). In the second section, the governance mechanisms typically associated with coopetition are discussed. Connecting coopetition alliances with the alliance development framework, we also offer some guidelines for managerial decision making (third section). We conclude the chapter with a summary (fourthsection) and a case illustration (fifth section).

The coopetition alliance challenge

We define *coopetition* as a business situation in which independent firms collaborate with one another and co-coordinate activities to achieve mutual goals but simultaneously compete with one another in markets, as well as with other firms (Bengtsson and Kock 2000; Dorn *et al.* 2016). Coopetition alliances, also known as horizontal alliances, thus entail mutually beneficial partnerships with competitors (see Table 16.1 for examples). To reap the benefits of economies of scale and scope and to seize market opportunities related to innovations, competitors may collaborate to set new standards and/or integrate existing

DOI: 10.4324/9781003222187-16

TABLE 16.1 Examples of coopetition alliances

	Description
Pfizer–BioNtech	In 2020, Pfizer and BioNTech announced a partnership to develop vaccines to counter the effects of a COVID-19 infection. This vaccine is based on BioNTech's mRNA vaccine program. Pfizer paid BioNTech $185 million upfront and will prefund the development costs. BioNtech will refund their 50% stake of the development costs during the commercialization of the vaccine. The vaccine was introduced in the course of 2020 and received formal FDA approval on August 23, 2021.
Alliance for open media	In 2015, Amazon, Cisco, Google, Intel, Microsoft, Mozilla and Netflix announced that they had formed a new open source alliance—the Alliance for Open Media—with the goal of developing the next generation of royalty-free video formats, codecs and other related technologies.
Toyota–Team Japan	In contrary to the fast increasing electrification of cars, Toyota Motor Corporation is seeking carbon neutrality by expanding fuel options for internal combustion engines. Toyota is partnering with Subaru, Kawasaki, Mazda and Yamaha to pursue three initiatives: (1) participating in races using carbon-neutral fuels, (2) exploring the use of hydrogen engines in two-wheeled and other vehicles and (3) continuing to race with hydrogen engines. By doing this, the companies want to provide customers with greater choice.

Sources: Alliance for Open Media (2015); Lardinois (2015); Pfizer (2020); Toyota (2021).

businesses through complementary technologies. Coopetition is therefore frequently undertaken in industries in which firms have to deal with emerging technologies (i.e. bio-technologies, information and communication technologies, electronics, semiconductors, etc.). The emerging technologies increase the level of uncertainty on market opportunities and technology developments, and firms involved in businesses affected by these technologies can manage uncertainty by cooperating with competitors for sharing resources and spreading risk. Moreover, in industries affected by continued innovation, cooperation among competitors frequently turns into competition among different 'networks of innovators' (Bengtsson and Raza-Ullah 2016) or 'group-to-group' competition (Gnyawali and Park 2011). For example, within the airline industry, multiple groups comprising industry incumbents are engaged in intense competition. The three dominant groups are Oneworld, established in 1999, composed of 14 members including British Airways, American Airlines and Cathay Pacific; SkyTeam, founded in 2000, composed of 19 members, including KLM, AirFrance and China Airlines; and (3) the Star Alliance, founded in 1997, composed of 26 members, including Air China, Lufthansa and TAP Portugal. Such rival groups emerge as partners who are able to share funding and research skills related to technology development and to join efforts to get access to the marketplace. As becomes evident, despite competitive pressures, the motives for collaborating with competitors are pressing as well as divers (Bamford *et al.* 2003; Bengtsson and Kock 2000; Gnyawali and Park 2011; Meena *et al.* 2022; Zineldin 2004).

Motives

Coopetition may result in economies of scale and enhanced product/service offerings (Gnyawali and Park 2011). Coopetition between market leaders for example may allow consumers to enjoy multi-feature products at a reasonable price due to economies of scale, pooling of complementary resources to develop more integrative technologies, reduction of duplication efforts, as well as intensified competition. Further economies of scale are attained as rivals combine similar assets and resources. Examples of economies of scale motives for partnering can be found in the airline industry as airline companies opt for code-sharing and joint luggage handling. Coopetition is also a way to establish an industry standard. Besides competing to develop new technologies, companies try to shape emerging industry structures and standards required to support their development and diffusion (Garud 1994). As technological standards and platforms lay the foundation for new products and services (Geurts et al. 2022; Lei 2003), competitors cooperate with each other to win battles for industry standards and to create industry-wide norms (Gomes-Casseres 1994). For example, the Flexiblepower Alliance Network wants to contribute to a renewable energy future by promoting open-source standards for flexible energy demand, matching the variations in renewable energy, paving the way for a fully renewable energy future and bringing together seven market-leading partners (Flexiblepower Alliance Network 2016). All partners add their specific knowledge/area-of-expertise, market connections and influence to co-develop solutions in order to realize their mission. Coopetition may also foster innovation and learning (Teece 1992). As competitors collaborate, they combine resources and knowledge, they share risks and R&D funding, and they can bundle their sales and distribution power to market their innovative products and services. As a result of co-innovation, partners may learn from one another and thus facilitate their own product/technological development and leverage the knowledge across related businesses within the firms (Gnyawali and Park 2011). Extant coopetition alliances are forged to achieve economies of scope. These partnerships often provide opportunities to expand product portfolios and (geographical) markets. For example, integrated solutions offered by ICT-based alliance partners extend the scope of their service, enhance the quality of the service offer and improve customer experience. As a consequence, coopetition alliances tend to reduce market uncertainty, increase market share, generate network effects and unite critical suppliers (Chiambaretto and Fernandez 2016).

In addition to strategic and economic motives, coopetition alliances provide an excellent opportunity for competitive benchmarking (Hamel et al. 1989). That is, via an alliance a firm may obtain information to conduct a legitimate and detailed analysis; systematically calibrate performance against external targets; learn to use rough estimates to determine where a competitor (or partner) is better, faster or cheaper; translate those estimates into new internal targets; and recalibrate to establish the rate of improvement in a competitor's performance. The great advantage of competitive collaboration is that proximity makes benchmarking easier. Competitive collaboration also provides a way of getting close enough to rivals to predict how they will behave when the alliance unravels or runs its course (Hamel et al. 1989). How does the partner respond to price changes? How does it measure and reward executives? How does it prepare to launch a new product? By revealing a competitor's management orthodoxies, collaboration can increase the chances of success in future head-to-head battles. Because of the interaction between alliance partners, information can flow about future directions and plans and the strengths and weakness of the organizations. A partner could, for example, predict future moves and could take advantage of its counterpart's weaknesses. A coopetition alliance thus provides a way of getting close to rivals without raising suspicion.

Barriers

Besides the potential benefits, coopetition alliances are inherently tied to burdens, adversities and conflicts (Bamford *et al.* 2003). In non-rival alliances, the cooperation–competition dilemma is always present, yet in coopetition alliances the impact of the dilemma is amplified (Geurts *et al.* 2022). Enacting rivalry is what partners have been doing before they forged an alliance relationship. Despite strong motives to collaborate, partners may find it difficult to view their rival counterparts differently. It is the common and continued practice of competitive acts that potentially jeopardizes alliance stability and performance. Another barrier preventing partners from attaining their objectives pertains to the threat of leaking unique knowledge and technology. For example, through coopetition core technologies, processes or knowledge may fall into your competitor's hand. Because of this, this competitor can use it in his competition against you. However, this 'being out-learned and out-competed' barrier is multifaceted (Hamel *et al.* 1989). Whereas top management puts together strategic alliances and sets the legal parameters for exchange, the nature and degree of knowledge exchange is determined by day-to-day interactions of engineers, marketers and product developers. Whereas managers operating at the organizational level, for example, squabble over sharing and protecting financial data, at the operational team level, critical and technical information is exchanged. That is, the most important deals may be struck four or five organizational levels below where the deal was signed, and it is here where a coopetition alliance is challenged. Coopetition may also generate lock-in effects and reduce flexibility and adaptability (Zineldin 2004). For example, if two competitors are committed to an existing technology and new technologies emerge, coopetition acts as a barrier to withdrawing from the relationship. Decision-making tends to slow down to deal with the adversity, which implies that the partners' flexibility and adaptability diminishes. If one of the partners decides to withdraw from the (unproductive) relationship, its counterpart may feel betrayed by the prospect of losing the investments made in the relationship, and thus reputational damages are created (Gnyawali and Park 2011). Coopetition may also act as a signal to customers (Bamford *et al.* 2003). When participating in an alliance with a competitor, current and potential customers of the organization can switch to the counterpart. Contact moments may occur, customer information may be exchanged, and a risk exists that the partner will use its increased brand awareness, customer understanding and direct personal relationship to steal customers away at some future date.

To effectively and efficiently deal with these barriers—and capture synergies—coordination costs need to be incurred. Given coopetition experience levels, the costs for managing a partnership between rivals may outweigh the possible benefits (Zineldin 2004). A coopetition strategy may incur too many costs in coordinating and controlling the cooperation and competition tensions, adversities and conflicts (Bengtsson and Kock 2000). Time and resources have to be devoted to learning about each other, coordinating activities with the potential partner and carrying out the adaptations needed to maintain and enhance the relationship. Those adaptations—technological, economic, cultural, psychological or administrative—also require resource mobilization. The predicted return on such investment is, however, highly uncertain. A coopetition relationship may be managed so poorly that a strategic opportunity is lost. If organizations become more dependent on other parties, their vulnerability may increase.

To conclude, coopetition alliances are complex as they consist of two diametrically different logics of interaction (Bengtsson and Kock 2000; Geurts *et al.* 2022). Parties on the one hand engage in a competitive logic due to conflicting interests within and outside the partnership, and on the other hand, they embrace a cooperative logic due to shared and common interests

(Rai 2016). These two logics of interaction are in conflict with each other. For example, a rival partner may invest in an alliance relationship to promote joint innovation but simultaneously enact aggressive competitive acts outside the partnership. A rival partner may act collaboratively but simultaneously seek to obtain private benefits (i.e. market knowledge) to enhance its competitive position. Or, a rival partner may promote joint learning while simultaneously enacting a learning race. If not properly managed (i.e. separated from one another), these tensions may culminate in dysfunctional process and outcomes and thus undermine alliance continuity. Simultaneously sharing and protecting the drivers of competitive advantages (e.g. resources and knowledge) is critical in coopetition alliances. The main issue is how competitors within an alliance can resist acting in conflict with each other to get the alliance to work. In order to succeed in terms of coopetition, partners must wisely manage the risks of coopetition.

Managing coopetition alliances

The management of coopetition alliances includes activities designed to reconcile the tensions between collaboration and competition—a prerequisite of the long-term viability of a coopetition alliance (Dorn *et al.* 2016; Stadtler and Van Wassenhove 2016). Taking a parsimonious view, managerial attention may focus on two sets of pre-emptive measures: alliance and organization-based measures. See Table 16.2 for an overview.

Alliance-based measures

Alliance design measures pertain to mechanisms that are part of alliance governance yet employed in such a way that they stimulate cooperative behaviour and mitigate the risk of competitive behaviour. One critical measure which a rival partner can use to organize the alliance's activities pertains to formalizing the alliance scope. Scope refers to the boundaries of alliance of geography, product categories, customer segments, brands, technologies and fixed assets (Khanna *et al.* 1998). Partners must identify the activities in which the alliance may engage (Gnyawali and Park 2011). A narrow alliance scope implies that rival partners have sufficient overlapping and complementary activities to generate common benefits but that (unwanted) appropriation of private benefits (i.e. spillovers) is constrained. For example, the alliance might cover a single technology rather than an entire range of technologies, involve part of a product line rather than the entire line and distribute in a limited number of markets or for a limited period of time. As part of scoping, rival partners may also opt to work with a black box (Bamford *et al.* 2003). That is, one partner provides a finished component to its counterpart who agrees to not reverse engineer the component (i.e. not to open the black box). A related approach is to contribute competencies or a bundle of skills rather than disaggregated skills or assets. Bundles of competencies are extremely hard for partners to replicate. Alternatively, rival partners may stipulate that the objective of the partnership is strictly pre-competitive and thus, for example, limited to research and development activities. Once the partners have developed the product/ service, they are allowed to approach the market individually. How the alliance is scoped (i.e. broad or narrow) may have implications for specific contractual stipulations. Clauses about present and future intellectual propriety rights are critical as they specify which partner contributes what knowledge, how this knowledge can be used and, if new knowledge is generated, who the proprietary owner is. Also, it implies that contractual clauses about market exclusivity (e.g. product and geography) are relevant to avoid future adversities. Limiting the alliance scope is thus a means to obtain control over information, knowledge and resource flows (Khanna 1998).

TABLE 16.2 Managing coopetition alliances

Focus	Measure	Example application
Alliance		
Design	Alliance scope	Limit collaborative activities to pre-competitive R&D and/or specific geographical areas, product categories and technologies.
	Incentive scheme	Create a hybrid compensation structure: provide incentives for long-term collaboration, and reduce incentives for short-term competition.
	Decision making	Install decision-making and monitoring structures aligned with joint interests to reduce information asymmetry between alliance partners.
	Behavioural rules	Create guidelines for alliance staff describing what they can and cannot share with their counterparts.
Management	Alliance climate	Develop a climate of psychological safety in which partners openly collaborate and proactively deal with competitive tensions and adversities.
	Management support	Enact partners' top management support to set exemplary behaviour and reduce partners' proclivity to attribute more weight to private than to common interests.
	Third-party mediation	Resolve conflicts and tensions between rival partners in a neutral and objective manner via third parties.
	Prospecting	Continue to search for (new) win–win synergies as capturing such emergent opportunities extends the viability and longevity of the coopetition alliance.
Organization		
Design	Chinese wall	Compartmentalization of alliance and non-alliance activities protects against unwanted knowledge and resource loss while securing contributions to alliance.
	Gate keeper	Appoint boundary-spanning agents who monitor information sharing, track resource flow and inform alliance management in case of adversities.
Management	Selection & training	Selection and training of staff assigned to the alliance is critical to generate a collective understanding about what can and cannot be exchanged.
	Coopetition capability	Learn from prior coopetition experiences to develop a coopetition capability; a capability which in turn enhances the efficacy of alliance management initiatives.

As part of alliance design, it is also critical to create an adequate incentive scheme (Bamford *et al.* 2003). That is, a hybrid compensation structure—inherently part of an equity arrangement or formalized in a non-equity arrangement—provides partners with incentives for long-term collaboration and reduces their incentives for short-term competition.

For example, in the Samsung–Sony alliance, partners agreed to cross-license patents, which in addition to offering mutual incentives, stimulated knowledge sharing and product development, while protecting their core proprietary technology (Gnyawali and Park 2011). Moreover, as part of the alliance contract, formal (financial) sanctions may be applied if a partner violates contractual stipulations. As part of the design, clarity in the decision-making structure is critical. Without this decision making, everything procrastinates, contributing to a slow deterioration of the relationship. During alliance design, it is thus important to identify the set of the most important decisions the alliance will encounter and then define which decision makers participate in the formulation and execution of these decisions. The monitoring structure needs to be aligned with the decision-making structure. Rival partners may also create guidelines and rules for employees working in the alliance that describe what they can and cannot share/discuss with the partners. This is a way to reduce unwanted information leakage.

Alliance management measures pertaining to activities form part of formal and informal governance, used in such a way that they mitigate competitive and stimulate cooperative behaviours. Of utmost importance to creating a successful coopetition alliance is to build a constructive alliance climate (Gnyawali and Park 2011; Hamel *et al.* 1989). That is, for mutual benefits and interests to be achieved, it is imperative that partners communicate, cooperate and compete in an atmosphere of frank debate, trust, interdependence and mutual positive expectation. Such a climate enables partners to anticipate tensions, handle conflicts and deal with adversities to create value together and appropriate an equitable share (Stadtler and Van Wassenhove 2016). A win–win approach of open-minded executives is critical for success (Hamel *et al.* 1989). Organizing top management support is a way to show the organization the importance of the alliance (Gnyawali and Park 2011). This in turn could reduce opportunistic behaviour of employees. Appointing a third party to oversee the alliance signals neutrality and objectivity. Alternatively, an independent facilitator could be assigned to manage tensions between the partners. To enhance the value of the alliance, prospecting, the continuing search for win–win synergies and opportunities, depicts a powerful management tool. The creation of new areas of collaboration as the relationship progresses implies that the rival partners are able to create more value together, which reduces competitive pressures.

Organization-based measures

When engaged in a coopetition alliance, it is critical that a firm keeps developing resource and capabilities internally to maintain its competitive position relative to its competitors (Gnyawali and Park 2011). For example, Samsung developed LED technology, which was a critical factor in solidifying its competitive position. Ownership and continued development of the technology enabled Samsung to effectively collaborate with its rival Sony. In addition, firms may install a variety of structural measures to adapt their internal structure in such a way that competitive forces are mitigated and cooperation is stimulated. Internally building a Chinese wall for example depicts an effective design solution to separate the management of a coopetition alliance from other parts of the organization. It allows an organization to scope information (Hamel *et al.* 1989) such that it determines which information can be shared with a rival and which not. Ultimately, this compartmentalization protects against unwanted information and resource leakage to the competitors, while simultaneously relevant assets are contributed to the alliance. Appointing a gate keeper, whose main task is to monitor information and knowledge exchange (Hamel *et al.* 1989), is one way to internally deal effectively with coopetition alliances (Bamford *et al.* 2003). A gate keeper is acting as an information funnel to and from the partner. Limiting unintended transfers at the operating level requires careful attention to the role of gatekeepers, the people who control what information flows to a partner. A gatekeeper can be effective only if there are a limited number of gateways through which a partner can access people and facilities. Collegiality is a prerequisite for collaborative success, but too much collegiality should set off warning bells to senior managers. CEOs or division presidents should expect occasional complaints from their counterparts about the reluctance of lower level employees to share information. That's a sign that the gatekeepers are doing their jobs. It is also part of the gatekeeper's task to update senior management regularly and to debrief operating personnel to find out what information the partner is requesting and what requests are being granted.

To support gatekeepers, some organizations establish a clearinghouse to collect and disseminate acquired information from the partner and the alliance (Hamel *et al.* 1989). In a clearing house, gatekeepers regularly contact all employees involved in alliances in order to identify what information has been collected by whom and then pass it on to appropriate departments. Furthermore, regular meetings where employees share new (alliance) knowledge enable gatekeepers to determine who is best positioned to acquire additional information. Organization management measures pertain to activities an organization initiates to deal internally with coopetition alliances. Organizations may develop specific selection and training practices. For example, they may limit the number of employees working in an alliance and only select employees with a profound understanding of coopetition hazards. Firms successfully collaborating with rivals inform employees at all levels about what skills and technologies are off-limits to the partner and monitor what the partner requests and receives (Hamel *et al.* 1989). Therefore, tailored training programmes targeting employees participating in a coopetition alliance may, for example, detail how to deal with coopetition challenges, how to enact the rules of engagement and how to deal with privileged information. In addition to selection and training, building and leveraging prior coopetition experience depicts a critical management task (Gnyawali and Park 2011). Such experience enables a firm to develop coopetition capabilities in order to create value and capture a greater share from the created value. For example, Samsung has a long track record in partnering with rivals, and they leveraged this experience in their transition from a firm producing key parts such as semiconductors to a major manufacturer of consumer electronics. To be able to learn from a coopetition alliance, learning begins at the top. Senior management must be committed to enhancing their companies' skills as well as avoiding financial risk. But most learning takes place at the lower levels of an alliance. Employees not only represent the front lines in an effective defence but also play a critical role in acquiring knowledge. They must be instructed on the partner's strengths and weaknesses and understand how acquiring particular skills will reinforce their firm's competitive position. A coopetition capability also enhances a firm's ability to decide how and when to communicate coopetition ventures to internal and external stakeholders as well as a firm's ability to assess and appropriate external knowledge.

Taken together, in light of the potential synergies and challenges, partner firms may deploy a wide range of organizational and alliance-based governance mechanisms to curb the negative repercussions of working together with a competitor. However, instead of adopting all possible measures, partner firms should tailor governance to the specific context. For example, providing access to one another's markets demands different measures (i.e. exclusivity) compared to when two rivals merge distribution channels (i.e. transfer pricing). In case multiple rivals are participating in an alliance (i.e. multi-lateral coopetition), the cooperation–competition tension amplifies further, yet the mechanisms remain effective. Though, additional attention has to be given to resource orchestration and safeguarding rewards for individual participants (Geurts *et al.* 2022). If measures are not tailored to alliance objective and context, the coordination costs are likely to outweigh the benefits. To enable effective management, it is thus critical to capture experiences, develop best practices and share success stories.

Coopetition alliances: decision-making steps

Once competitors decide to forge a coopetition alliance, establishing an infrastructure that promotes cooperative behaviour and mitigates the threat of unwarranted competitive acts is the foremost critical activity. That is, alliance launch, management and evaluation deserve managerial attention as well once the alliance becomes operational. If alliance objectives incorporate learning and innovation, the learning alliance guidelines are informative as well, and we suggest reading Chapter 11. Next, we present several managerial guidelines, in addition to generic guidelines, that enable alliance managers to turn potentially unstable coopetition alliances into viable and stable ones. To this end, we use our alliance development framework (see Figure 16.1).

Step 1: alliance strategy formulation

During the strategic analysis, firms decide whether an alliance is an appropriate governance mode for realizing their objectives. Taking a coopetition lens, the objective is to obtain or access competitors' resources, which, combined with the firm's resource endowment, generate value beyond what would have been possible individually. A market exchange is a less likely alternative as this would suggest that the desired resources have been commoditized and are available to all industry incumbents. A merger or acquisition could be a viable alternative if the acquirer's and target's resources combined create a superior competitive position, without (too many) issues of resource indivisibility and divestments. But in most instances, a coopetition alliance could become the preferred governance mode, specifically if the alliance provides access to critical resources while offering a firm sufficient flexibility. For example, in the airline industry, companies forge alliance relationships with competitors to strengthen their hub and spokes systems (i.e. destinations), engage in code-sharing and other activities to achieve economies of scale and scope. But if potential synergies extend beyond a threshold and shareholders impose pressure on boards, mergers and acquisitions become a viable alternative to partnering.

If the decision is made to establish a partnership with a rival firm, it is important that top management initiates an internal assessment of the organization. During their strategic analysis, therefore, firms must assess their vulnerability by identifying potential sources for conflicts. For example, if a large ICT firm sells integrated solutions directly to their customers but also decides to forge a coopetition alliance to offer their ICT solutions indirectly through its rival partners, it becomes important that the organization structure is adapted to accommodate this situation. Without a Chinese wall, for example, customers and the rival partner may question this firm's integrity. Thus, coopetition alliances may warrant that a firm adapts the internal organization structure and management practices to avoid a destabilizing impact on the alliances.

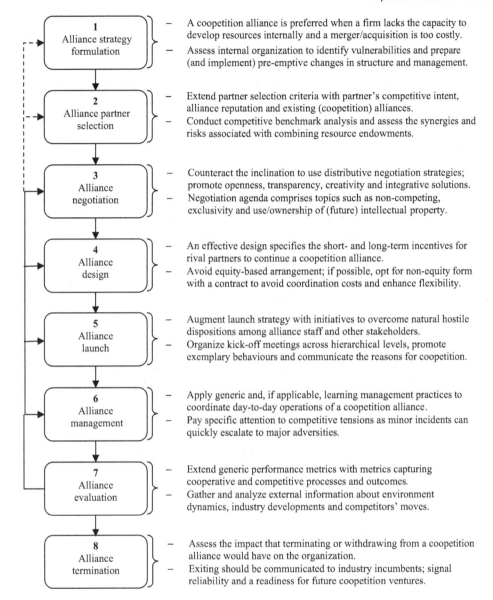

FIGURE 16.1 Alliance development framework: coopetition alliances

Step 2: alliance partner selection

During the partner selection phase, a firm selects the partner(s) with which it can forge a coopetition alliance. A thorough analysis of partner fit and resource complementarity is critical for multiple reasons. With regard to partner fit, if rivals are of similar size and operate in the same markets, the inner workings are more likely to mimic one another, reducing concerns about organizational, cultural, human and operational fit. If misfit occurs, generic guidelines should be sufficient to overcome the consequences of misfit. However, firms must be aware that increasing levels of partner fit also increase the need for protective measures because high fit facilitates competitive benchmarking and inter-organizational learning. In addition, despite high levels of partner fit, coopetition alliances have failed because partners have neither shared information nor allocated their best people and have given low priority to sustaining the relationship. In other words, strategic fit—partner's compatibility in strategic vision and direction—is essential to build successful coopetition alliances. A comprehensive understanding (and in later stages even an agreement) about how and to what extent the coopetition alliance may strengthen the partner's resource and competitive positions is an important partner selection criterion. A firm should not select and forge an alliance with a rival firm who benefits more (strategically) from the alliance than the firm itself.

In addition to a fit analysis, a firm should conduct an analysis of resource complementarity. Often alliance partners claim that the motive for the coopetition alliance originates in the combination of their resource endowments; which may pertain for example to R&D facilities, manufacturing, distribution channels and brands. Despite these synergetic motives, resource complementarity also imposes risks on partners, specifically in coopetition alliances. The extent to which resources overlap may offer economies of scale but also may increase the likelihood of unwanted spillovers. Resource combinations may enable partners to obtain dominant market positions, but unexpected legal consequences may unfold (see Box 16.1). The extent to which firms' resource endowments are complementary is indicative of their relative dependence on one another. Because partners have a common long-term goal and want to make the relationship work to achieve it, they accept an increasing level of interdependence. However, as dependence is the inverse of power, specific attention should be given during partner selection to interdependency asymmetry, particularly if a potential rival partner is part of a larger strategic group. In such groups, mutual forbearance is the guiding rule, which implies that members forsake competition and may target non-members jointly. Concerns about these adversities tend to be mitigated if rival partners have successfully collaborated before or build a reputation as a preferred and reliable alliance partner.

BOX 16.1 COMPETITION LAW[1]

Most markets in the free world are regulated to ensure undistorted competition and to prevent the abuse of a dominant market position. Concentrations of undertakings—including alliance arrangements—that meet certain turnover thresholds must be appraised beforehand by the authorities because such concentrations diminish competition and can lead to a dominant market position. In the Netherlands, the Competitive Trading Act (Mededingingswet) applies; in the EU, both the Treaty on the Functioning of the European Union and the Merger Regulation 39/2004/EC set competition rules; while in the US, the Sherman Antitrust Act must be adhered to. Particularly, if alliance partners consider adopting an equity-based arrangement to govern their alliance, the arrangement may be subject to this type of merger control. Equity alliances may allow companies to spread and diversify risks and bring together sufficient equity for projects that require high investment. Equity alliances usually have a more permanent effect on competition and are scrutinized beforehand by way of merger control. For that purpose, intended equity alliances with a potentially profound effect on competition must be notified to the competent authorities and may not be carried out without prior approval. Examination of the intended concentration focuses on the need to maintain sufficient competition in the relevant market and to prevent disadvantages for customers. If the concentration significantly impedes competition, this may be remedied, for instance, by selling one or more business units or by ensuring that services or supplies will remain available to competitors. Non-equity alliance arrangements are not subject to merger control. Nevertheless, competition law dictates these alliances may not distort competition otherwise and must comply with the prohibition of cartels. Non-equity alliances may for instance be formed to facilitate costly research and development. Especially if the market fails to provide for such R&D by individual companies and the consumer ultimately benefits from combined R&D, such an alliance may be in compliance with competition law. For both equity and non-equity arrangements, partner firms need to monitor growth and assess changes in market position and corporate governance to ensure continued compliance with competition law. A successful alliance may obtain a dominant market position in which case its actions are monitored closely by authorities to prevent the abuse of such dominance, e.g. by predatory pricing. When establishing an alliance, competition law must thus be taken into consideration. If merger control is undesirable, a non-equity alliance is recommendable, while an equity-based alliance will need to ensure it stays below the relevant thresholds to rule out merger control. If merger control is unavoidable, parties will need to enter into a comprehensive letter of intent that sets out their desired cooperation in order to allow the authorities to perform a detailed appraisal. Failure to comply with competition law can result in hefty fines in order to deter undertakings from non-compliance. Violations of competition law cannot be undone, so it pays to engage legal advice at an early stage to prevent unnecessary risks when structuring the alliance.

Step 3: alliance negotiation

The alliance negotiation stage involves partners in achieving agreement on the alliance objectives, scope and governance; if they achieve consensus, the outcomes are formalized in the alliance contract. Akin to other alliance types, a mixture of integrative and distributive most likely results in favourable negotiation process and outcomes. Appointing savvy negotiators is, however, critical because competitors tend to prefer to use distributive negotiation strategies as such an approach enables them to protect their stakes and interests. Actively using integrative negotiation strategies to promote openness, transparency and creativity is thus critical to overcome this disposition and to achieve integrative solutions that extend above and beyond individual interests. With regard to the outcomes of the negotiations, coopetition alliances may demand specific governance and contractual mechanism to invoke cooperative behaviour. Setting the negotiation agenda first is therefore a critical task. Before the negotiations begin, partners thus need to prioritize topics; identify communalities, differences and specific risks; and explicate the objectives of the coopetition alliances. For example, it is important that negotiators on both sides of the table have insight in the areas where the partners are competing, including products, services, markets and technology. Negotiation topics may then refer to scope, non-competing, exclusivity and use/ownership of (future) intellectual property. Also negotiators must achieve agreement on how to deal with each other's clients, specifically if the collaboration extends beyond pre-competitive R&D. That is, to what extent are customer contact details exchanged, who is allowed to approach customers and is the market divided between the competitors? During this stage it also becomes critical to assess whether the coopetition alliance (with regard to objectives, scope and governance form) infringes on antitrust laws and regulations. If so, the initial agreement may need to be renegotiated.

Step 4: alliance design

An alliance design specifies the nature and scope of the alliance, shapes the breadth and depth of the interaction between the two firms and outlines the short- and long-term incentives for the rival partner to continue the relationship. Decisions about the formal governance should aim to enhance cooperative behaviours by directly developing linkages and shared modes of operating. The decision regarding governance form is likely to indicate some preference for an equity-based arrangement because such arrangements stimulate long-term collaboration but still safeguard against opportunistic acts. However, a relatively small company should perhaps avoid an equity-based arrangement, such as a joint venture, with large and established competitors because whereas the smaller party puts its core business into the venture, the alliance may be only a short-term distraction and learning opportunity for the larger partner. Equity-based arrangements may also increase coordination costs and promote rigidity, which may render a coopetition alliance inefficient. Also equity-arrangements may violate anti-trust laws, or at least draw governmental attention. Non-equity arrangements offer more flexibility, and via tailored alliance contracts, similar degrees of protection may be achieved.

Because the alliance design functions as a first critical deterrent against unwanted competitive behaviours, the contract should incorporate hybrid compensation schemes to provide sufficient incentives to the partner firms. It should also specify how the alliance relationship is protected from external competitive acts (in other markets) that may be continued even if the alliance becomes operational. In addition, partners may formally agree to reduce the scope of the alliance relationship to circumscribe a partner's opportunities to learn. That is, partners must identify the activities in which the alliance may engage and set boundaries of the alliance, to include or exclude specific geographical markets, product categories, customer segments, brands, technologies and fixed assets. Such restrictions limit the likelihood of competitive and opportunistic behaviours. The partners should also define responsibilities clearly and agree on an effective dispute-resolution mechanism so that the first problem to emerge will not sour the atmosphere and lead to a decline in trust. Effective communication systems should be installed between many people at many organizational levels. They do not abuse the information they gain. They are flexible, and they respect each other. They show mutual integrity and act in honourable ways that justify, enhance and sustain mutual trust and commitment. In addition to governance form and contractual decisions, during the design stage partners may erect other mechanisms. Within their organizations, partners may award the relationship with a formal status and organized responsibilities such that conflicts are less likely to emerge and, if they do, are quickly resolved.

Step 5: alliance launch

During the alliance launch stage, the partner firms transition from negotiation and design to preparing and implementing the alliance contract. Systemically organizing the alliance execution is critical with regard to a coopetition alliance as employees may have a naturally hostile disposition towards the rival partner. Specifically, the partner has been portrayed as an enemy, and suddenly it is expected that staff will collaborate. As part of the alliance launch strategy, internal communication thus becomes very important. Partners should inform employees at all levels about the motives for the alliance relationship. As part of operational plans, communication should not only focus on informing involved staff about motives for the coopetition alliances but also on what skills and technologies are off-limits to the partner, and how to monitor what the partner requests and receives. To overcome the 'we-versus-us' schism, kick-off meetings are critical at and across hierarchical levels. If applicable, before executing the alliance, check whether governmental approval has been given to avoid post hoc sanctions and penalties.

Step 6: alliance management

Within the setting of a coopetition alliance, the alliance management stage initiates day-to-day operations that enable partners to leverage the foundation that has been laid by the alliance negotiation and launch teams. It is imperative that management continues to invest in the quality of the working relationship. Trust building and learning about one another is critical to overcome natural inclinations to resort to a competitive logic. Also, ongoing monitoring of alliance progress and assessment of whether partners comply with agreed-upon stipulations is critical. For example, early detection of unwanted (and perhaps unintended) knowledge exchange enables alliance management to take necessary precautions. Also, swift conflict resolution is imperative in coopetition alliances. Due to the competitive nature, conflicts are likely to emerge—if not caused by internal actions, external competitor moves may cause conflicts—and without adequate resolutions, conflicts may spread through the alliance, destabilizing the relationship. In short, the main task of alliance management is to create a climate in which knowledge can be exchanged, while simultaneously securing the protection of knowledge not part of the alliance agreement.

Step 7: alliance evaluation

This stage requires a performance metric system that accounts for the idiosyncrasies tied to a coopetition alliance (see Rai 2016 for a measure of value creation in coopetition alliances). In addition to generic metrics, the system may comprise metrics capturing cooperative and competitive processes and outcomes with regard to the alliance and the individual partner organizations. Alliance-level metrics entail (generic) relational metrics with a focus on harmony, conflicts and commitment but also metrics that capture unwanted spillovers, knowledge leakage and other competitive acts. Within the partner organizations, metrics may be deployed to capture the functioning of gatekeepers, the effectiveness of a Chinese wall and other aspects of organizational alignment. External monitoring is also critical as, for example, an unexpected move by an outside competitor or the entry of a new competitor may render a coopetition alliance obsolete (or demand radical structural adaptations). This implies that the performance metric system should account for environmental and industry dynamics. In addition, as the alliance grows (and outperforms other rivals), anti-trust laws may become salient, particularly if the partner firms together obtain a dominant market position. The performance system should be able to identify such hazards promptly.

Step 8: alliance termination

If partners have reached this stage, it means that they have decided to dissolve the alliance. Depending on contractual agreements, each firm must secure its presents and future interests. Depending on the scope of the alliance, a termination plan may also involve procedures and guidelines for disintegration. For example, withdrawal from a pre-competitive R&D alliance is usually easier than pulling out of a multi-objective coopetition alliance. In both instances, however, alliance partners should seek to recoup critical resources and knowledge, as neither partner wants to provide its rival with a (free) advantage. Communication strategies must also be developed because termination of the alliance or the departure of one partner may have serious repercussions for the other partners. Operating in similar industries and markets, future alliance opportunities depend on the partners' reputations; hence, making a constructive exit is the preferred option.

Summary

Coopetition refers to a collaboration between competitors and thus depicts a paradoxical relationship that emerges when two or more firms cooperate in some activities and, at the same time, compete with each other in other activities. In coopetition alliances, learning from rival partners is paramount, and successful companies view such arrangements as a window to explore and capture their partners' capabilities. They use the alliance to build skills in areas outside the formal agreement and systematically diffuse new knowledge throughout their organizations. However, effective coopetition alliances also offer safeguards, organization- and alliance-based, against unwillingly transferring competitive advantages to ambitious partners. Taken together, though coopetition alliances are inherently tied to risk and uncertainty, in the contemporary competitive landscape they are of critical importance to firms to maintain their competitive edge.

CASE: RECKITT BENCKISER[2]

Reckitt Benckiser Group (RB) is a British multinational consumer goods company headquartered in Slough, England. It is a producer of health, hygiene and home products. It was formed in 1999 by the merger of the UK-based Reckitt & Colman plc and the Netherlands-based Benckiser NV. RB's brands are segmented into Health, Hygiene and Home brands. Examples are Neurofen, Strepsils, Gaviscon and Durex (Health); Finish, Dettol, Lysol, Veet, Harpic and Cillit Bang (Hygiene); Vanish, Woolite, Calgon and Airwick (Home). RB has operations in around 60 countries, and its products are sold in almost 200 countries. RB is the global market leader in automatic dishwashing detergents through the brand Finish.

One of the most time-consuming household chores is washing dirty dishes by hand. To make this process more convenient, the appliance industry introduced automatic dishwashers in the 1960s. Instead of washing dirty dishes by hand, consumers could now put them in the dishwasher, add chemical products (dishwashing detergent, rinse aid and salt) and the machine would clean and dry the dishes. Furthermore, a dishwasher consumes less water and energy than hand-washing. However, the household adaption of automatic dishwashers was significantly slower than the household adaption rate of washing machines. Even today, only two out of ten households globally wash dishes in a dishwasher.

Consequently, RB decided to form 'Automatic Dishwashing Market Creation Alliances' with leading automatic dishwasher manufacturers in order to set up consumer education marketing programmes. The objective of those programmes was to make consumers aware of the automatic dishwasher category and to create the desirability of purchasing an automatic dishwasher. The content of the marketing programmes was intended to communicate the emotional and rational benefits of automatic dishwashing compared to manual dishwashing, such as more time for yourself and your family, better cleaning results and less water and energy use. The programmes started in Western Europe in the 1970s and were then extended in the next decades to Southern Europe, Eastern Europe, Turkey, Russia, Middle East, South Africa, Brazil, China and other developing markets.

RB initially collaborated with two rival manufacturers: BSH and Electrolux. As the programmes expanded geographically, the number of participating rival manufacturers increased, and companies like Arcelik, Whirlpool, LG, Haier and Samsung joined the market creation programmes as well. The alliance partner selection criteria were based on strategic and cultural fit; for example, the strategic intention of the partners to invest in creating the automatic dishwasher category and the capability of the partners to work together in a strategic alliance.

Consider the alliance between Finish and Bosch (BSH Group). In 2010, in an attempt to vitalize the dishwasher market in Singapore, Finish and Bosch launched an island-wide marketing campaign. The campaign communicated to consumers about the benefits of washing dishes in a dishwasher compared to washing dishes by hand and a call to action to buy a dishwasher for a special introductory price with free delivery and installation, and with a month's supply of the detergent Finish. In the words of Mr Cheok Kian Sheong, strategic alliances manager at RB,

> Bosch is our global partner in creating awareness on the benefits of dishwasher use. We are very excited to be able to bring this concept to Asia and to Singapore, and as Bosch is the market leader of dishwashers in Singapore, we are confident that once consumers experience the benefits of the dishwasher, they will soon be telling their family and friends about it.

In the beginning, the programmes were managed on a country-by-country basis. With the globalization of the programmes, however, a central alliance group was introduced to coordinate the overall programme. The coordination consists of strategy and marketing plan alignment with the global Finish marketing team and the global marketing teams of the partners, and the execution of the programmes with the country teams of RB and the partners.

Each market creation alliance with a dishwasher manufacturer is managed by Finish on an individual and bilateral basis, without direct interaction between the different (rival) machine manufacturer partners. Thus, Finish aligns the overall programme objectives and manages the execution with competing dishwasher manufacturers. In this context, the key is to set up clear rules; for example, the market creation programmes in each country are carried out sequentially with the partners. An important lesson is that early planning of the entire marketing plan is very important to avoid overlap of programmes.

The 'Automatic Dishwashing Market Creation Alliances' approach has been very successful as a clear positive correlation can be shown between investments in the joint marketing programmes and an accelerated household adaption rate to automatic dishwashers. The programmes has expanded to more countries in developing markets. In 2019, Finish and Bosch partnered to launch dishwashing products in the Indian market using the '#NoMore-DishStress' campaign.

Questions

1 Explain why the household adaption rate of washing machines was faster than the household adaption rate of automatic dishwashers.
2 Explain why the described alliances can be termed 'star-type alliances'. Consider that the participating competitor dishwasher manufacturers are not directly engaged in a cooperative arrangement.
3 Explain where you see the main challenges in the execution of the described market creation alliances.

Notes

1 Text by Henk Raven, Habraken Rutten Advocaten.
2 Interview with a senior executive of Reckitt Benckiser.

17

MULTI-PARTNER ALLIANCES

Multi-partner alliances (or multi-lateral alliances) are partnerships formed by more than two parties. A multi-partner alliance enables firms to align multiple sets of complementary resources, often with the aim of creating additional synergies or complying with increasing customer demands. Examples of multi-partner alliances can be found in a variety of industries, from the semiconductor and airline industries to agri-food industries. If properly managed, a multi-partner alliance strategy can be a win–win situation for all parties involved. However, whereas dealing with adversity is relatively straightforward in an alliance with only two partners, governance within a multi-partner alliance becomes more complex as the one-to-one relationship is replaced by a one-to-many relationship. The increasing number of parties presents the managers involved with a particular challenge. In order to capture the potential synergies that come with a multi-partner alliance, these managers must prevent and control free-riding behaviour by their counterparts. The opening sections of this chapter explore this multi-partner alliance challenge and elaborate on the mechanisms that managers can use to deal with it. The alliance development framework is used in the following section to present specific managerial guidelines for multi-partner alliances. The chapter concludes with a summary and a case illustration.

The multi-partner alliance challenge

A multi-partner alliance is defined as a collective, voluntary organizational arrangement between more than two parties, with common objectives, joint decision-making and shared risks. These parties engage interactively in multi-lateral activities, such as collaborative research, development, sourcing, production, marketing and commercialization of technologies, products and/or services (Lavie *et al.* 2007; Rochemont 2010). Multi-partner alliances are typical in areas such as the airline industry. Through code-sharing, joint network coverage and joint marketing initiatives (such as frequent flyer programmes), airlines are able to increase their utilization rates and offer an increased number of destinations. Although a multi-partner alliance can be organized through an alliance contract, parties often establish a separate organizational structure in which the alliance activities are executed. Such entities are usually non-profit-oriented, and participating firms pay a cost-covering fee. The main advantage of this arrangement

DOI: 10.4324/9781003222187-17

is that it allows the partnership to enlarge easily if other parties are interested in joining. A consortium is another specific type of multi-partner alliance in which multiple parties collaborate to achieve a common goal, often related to research and development, economies of scale and setting industry standards. See Table 17.1 for examples of multi-partner alliances.

Similar to the motives behind bilateral alliances, firms form multi-partner alliances to access and complement each other's resources (García-Canal *et al*. 2003). By sharing resources across multiple partners, participants are better able to use their resources and improve their ability to serve a larger part of the value chain. For example, partners within co-development multi-partner alliances exchange knowledge to develop new products and/or services, thereby increasing customer value and competitive advantage. Sharing research and development activities also enables partners to divide investments over a larger number of participants and to realize economies of scale. In addition, shared procurement with multiple partners provides an opportunity to bundle volume, which translates into increased bargaining power and, consequently, lower purchase prices. Multi-partner alliances also offer opportunities in terms of network connections as participating parties join a network that becomes a repository of resources and information about the availability and reliability of prospective partners. Multi-partner alliances are sometimes forged to enable collective lobbying to guard the interests of multiple firms or even entire industries. Through a multi-partner lobbying alliance, firms can influence political decision making that affects a group of firms or entire industries. Multi-partner alliances also arise when industry standards are to be set. Setting an industry standard often involves substantial investments and is beyond the ability of a single firm. By participating in a multi-partner alliance, firms reduce individual costs and risks, while increasing the chance of successful market introductions.

TABLE 17.1 Examples of multi-partner alliances

	Description
Sematech	SEMATECH (Semiconductor Manufacturing Technology) is a consortium of American semiconductor manufacturers which was founded in 1987. The motivation for establishing the alliance was the loss of American market share due to increased competition among Japanese manufacturers. Between 1987 and 1992, SEMATECH generated 15 patents and 36 patent applications, helped enact more than 300 industry standards, participated in 110 equipment improvement projects and joint development programmes and published more than 1,100 technical documents. In 1993, American semiconductor producers recaptured the top position in worldwide sales with 45.3% of the chip market.
Deutscher Robotik Association	In 2020, the Deutscher Robotik Verband was founded in Nuremberg. The aim of the robotics association is to promote the use of robot technology, especially in small and medium sized enterprises. Manufacturers and users are expressly encouraged to become members in order to make experience from the operator's point of view usable within the network.
DiTek cluster	DiTek is known as the Lithuania's Artificial Intelligence Technology Cluster. It was created to boost the market position of its members by exploiting their collective AI knowledge base and skill sets. The cluster aims for value-added by developing new AI-based products and services or improving existing ones. The dual use and defence sectors represent some 60% of its members' activities, which range across electronics, energy, ICT and robotics.

Sources: Browning *et al.* (1995); Ditek Cluster (2017); German Robotic Association (2020).

Despite the potential advantages of multi-partner alliances, they are inherently more complex to manage than two-party alliances. A growing number of partners increases the risk of opportunistic behaviour because the number of dyadic relationships increases geometrically as the number of partners becomes larger (García-Canal *et al.* 2003). One critical hazard concerns the danger of free-riding behaviour by partner firms, whereby a member of a group obtains benefits from group membership but does not bear a proportional share of the costs (Albanese and Van Fleet 1985). A multi-partner alliance may generate 'collective' or 'public' goods, such as knowledge, that are accessible to all partners involved, even when they fail to fulfil their resource contributions and other obligations (Dyer and Nobeoka 2000). For example, a partner firm may willingly participate in knowledge-sharing activities to acquire knowledge and then exit the multi-partner alliance or refuse to contribute its own knowledge. The multi-partner setting reduces the guilt that a partner feels towards its counterparts when it chooses not to cooperate. This causes the risk of internal competition and conflicts between partners to increase due to diverging interests and the possibility of unsanctioned free riding (Zeng and Chen 2003).

To deal effectively with free riding, multi-partner alliances need specific governance mechanisms that pertain to areas such as coordination, communication and incentives schemes. Partners must strike the right balance between under-investing and over-investing in multi-partner alliances. Whereas some firms seek to free ride on their partners' investments, others end up subsidizing their partners and fail to earn an appropriate return on their investments. It is also important to identify the right time to exit a multi-partner alliance given that, unlike one-to-one alliances, a multi-partner alliance can maintain its operations even after certain members have left. Therefore, alliance managers must invest in the partnership to increase the probability of value creation, while also preventing and controlling free riding by their counterparts to avoid asymmetrical contributions and appropriation.

Managing multi-partner alliances

The main motivation behind multi-partner alliances is to capitalize on resources supplied by multiple partners, with the aim of achieving synergies that can only be realized with multiple partners. Simultaneously, however, partners must eliminate the risk of free riding preemptively and, if necessary, resolve (for example, through sanctions) the adverse impact of this behaviour. There are five mechanisms by which participants can achieve this two-fold objective: (1) resource complementarity, (2) task organization, (3) contractual governance, (4) relational governance and (5) orchestrator role (see Table 17.2).

Resource complementarity

The precise amount of resources that each alliance partner contributes to a multi-partner alliance depends on the competences of each partner. Preferably, each partner would contribute resources to the multi-partner alliance that their counterparts cannot provide. Partners ideally bring something unique and non-redundant to the alliance so that the overall resource base of the alliance becomes stronger. At the same time, the fact that partners depend on each other helps prevent internal competition (Hill and Hellriegel 1994). For example, whereas one partner may provide a financial contribution, its counterparts may supply non-financial resources, such as specific material assets or tacit capabilities, deployment of personnel, machines or

TABLE 17.2 Managing multi-partner alliances

	Description	Implications
Resource complementarity	Multiple partners contribute resources to the purpose of generating synergy.	Unique resource contributions reduce the risk of free riding, whereas overlapping resource contributions encourage free riding.
Task organization	Multiple partners make it more difficult to distinguish between individual tasks and outcomes.	Designating identifiable, unique and transparent tasks to partners reduces the risk of free riding.
Contractual governance	Multi-partner alliances tend to be organized through a non-equity-based arrangement, implying a need for clear contractual specifications.	Developing a transparent incentive system, demanding an entrance fee and installing a clear decision-making and monitoring structure reduce the risk of free riding.
Relational governance	Multi-partner alliances demand high-quality relational governance.	Investing in relational norms to guide collaborative behaviour is imperative.
Orchestrator role	An orchestrator is responsible for the proactive management of a multi-partner alliance.	Orchestrators create stability, align interests, encourage communication and execute brand management.

production facilities and technical skills. In addition, when each party provides a unique contribution, any failure to fulfil obligations is quickly noticed and subject to immediate sanctioning. Unique contributions also reduce the risk of surplus and wasteful resources. In contrast, the presence of resource substitutes within a multi-partner alliance may cause tension. Resource substitution undermines power relations because partners that provide similar resources may lose their justification for being a member of the alliance. Consequently, a firm may either increase its resource contribution to signal its commitment or economize on its resource contribution and engage in free-riding behaviour. However, alliance continuity is not necessarily jeopardized as resource contributions made by free-riding partners are substituted by the resource contributions of other partners. Nonetheless, if management does not effectively control free-riding behaviour, free-riding partners will illegitimately reap the benefits of a multi-partner alliance. Therefore, a successful multi-partner alliance is dependent on having a precise mix of partners with resources that are complementary to one another and required to realize alliance objectives.

Task organization

Increased group size reduces the perceptibility of individual contributions and tasks, which makes it more difficult to distinguish free-riding partners (Albanese and Van Fleet 1985). Therefore, it is important to translate a multi-partner alliance strategy into identifiable, unique and transparent tasks in order to prevent free riding in multi-partner alliances. Identifiable tasks are those in which the output of the specific tasks can be identified and tied to a specific partner. According to Davis (2016), one effective way to organize complex tasks (i.e. innovation) is to decompose activities in a series of interlinked tasks between multiple subsets of partners, overseen by a third party. By temporarily restricting participation to subsets, multi-partner alliance managers can optimize local output and in turn choose how local output is incorporated in the broader whole.

A lack of clear task definitions results in weak contracts, which allows partners to make use of ambiguity about duties and responsibilities and behave in an opportunistic manner. However, as the number of partners increases, identifying and allocating specific tasks for each member may become more hazardous, and tasks may overlap across partners. The more partners involved in an alliance, the more difficult it is to formulate a specific role for each alliance partner. The risk of free riding increases if similar tasks are delegated to more than one partner as the failure of one partner to execute a task is most likely to remain unnoticed. Moreover, this partner can still enjoy the benefits because other parties may have completed similar tasks. Free riding may also result from a lack of transparency in the objectives and related tasks. When tasks are not made transparent, it is difficult to monitor progress, which increases the opportunity for partners to exploit this ambiguity. Designating identifiable, unique and transparent tasks in a multi-partner alliance prevents free riding, reduces conflicts and stimulates collective value creation.

Contractual governance

Owing to the larger number of parties involved, multi-partner alliances are often organized through non-equity-based arrangements. To reduce the likelihood of premature dissolution, homogeneity in governance forms between partners in a multi-partner alliance is preferable over heterogeneity in governance forms (Heidl *et al*. 2014). However, if the number of partners increases, supplemental governance in the form of contractual provisions and management control is required (García-Canal *et al*. 2003). An effective and formalized incentive system can prompt parties in a multi-partner alliance to act in the interests of the collaborative arrangement (Zeng and Chen 2003). Since free-riding behaviour is essentially a result of an individual's unfavourable comparisons of benefits to costs, one major way of reducing or preventing free riding is either to improve a party's perceptions of its pay-off by increasing its share of benefits of public goods or to decrease its costs. For example, special incentives can be offered to encourage the provision of public goods. Extrinsic incentives include additional compensation, extra time off, assignment to preferred projects, extra released time, a larger share in the public good and recognition from superiors or peers. Intrinsic incentives include the sense of achievement or satisfaction that results from completing a difficult or unique task. Another way to build long-term commitment is to ask participating firms for an entrance fee. High entrance fees represent incentives to solve any emerging adversities as participating firms are locked into the partnership.

Effective monitoring of partner behaviour (contributions and compensation) is also vital for effective management of multi-partner arrangements. These monitoring systems can act as early warning systems since deviations are detected promptly and allow partners to impose (economic) sanctions, such as penalties. Clarity in decision-making processes is also important in order to prevent opportunistic behaviour because a lack of clarity increases ambiguity among parties and provides opportunities to pursue separate interests covertly (Rochemont 2010). Decision-making procedures, including majority voting, consensus, blocking votes and lead partners, describe how decisions are made within the alliance. It should be clear who has the authority to make decisions and what decision-making procedures are being used or will be implemented. Without a clear decision-making structure, partners may feel isolated or ignored and may start to question whether their influence is sufficient to achieve the alliance's objectives. Financial investments may also function as a signal of commitment. In the SEMATECH alliance, for example, companies were obliged not only to contribute R&D knowledge but also to bring financial resources. These financial resources were necessary to develop an industry standard successfully, but they also had the effect of locking in the members of the network, which can act as glue for the cooperation (Hwang and Burgers 1997). Preferably, agreements about these and other governance mechanisms should be embodied in an alliance contract.

Relational governance

A multi-partner alliance demands strong relational governance. It is impossible to safeguard every action through formal contracts, and a strong collaborative climate represents a powerful tool for managing the free-riding problem. Relational norms comprise unwritten rules that depict how parties collaborate with each other and pertain to flexibility, solidarity and continuity expectations. Relational norms reduce self-interested behaviour and help parties understand the congruency of individual goals more easily, thereby reducing the need to resort to close formal monitoring. These norms also reduce uncertainty about potentially destructive behaviours (such as free riding) and encourage partners to act in accordance with alliance objectives. In the presence of such norms, the partnership will develop based on the principles of solidarity and fair exchange, suggesting that all partners believe that the benefits they receive from the relationship are equivalent to their contributions. Relational norms also stimulate the building of a relational capital. Based on the belief that partners will be dealt with in an equitable manner, even in ambiguous situations, relational capital will guide partners' behaviour to trust one another. They will act for the best performance of the alliance, which will lead to optimal contributions. When free-riding parties deviate from relational norms, they can be forced to leave the alliance or change their behaviour. Socialization within multi-partner alliances increases the likelihood of collective success.

Apart from formal sanctions, free-riding behaviour can be prevented by social sanctions or the threat thereof (Albanese and Van Fleet 1985). This form of sanctioning does not involve formal policies and procedures, management directives and controls; instead, it uses relational and or behavioural persuasion to enforce the conduct of partners by the other partners. In a multi-partner alliance, social sanctions are a powerful instrument with which to guide partner behaviour since they can have significant implications for an individual partner, especially in situations in which the partner is dependent on the multi-partner network. Collective group sanctions may then be an effective measure for resolving conflicts as they affect a firm's opportunities negatively over a longer period of time. Social sanctions become more effective if the group size increases as the possible damage to a member's reputation is greater if more partners spread negative word of mouth.

The orchestrator role

Maintaining a group of partners can be difficult due to the risk of conflicting interests. This requires active management. Whatever the governance structure, the group of firms must have some way to coordinate actions. Without leadership, a multi-partner alliance cannot expect to formulate and execute a consistent strategy (Bamford and Ernst 2003). In large multi-partner alliances, this function can be performed by orchestrators (Rochemont 2010), an active network manager (Doz and Hamel 1998) or a strategic centre (Lorenzoni and Baden-Fuller

1995). Effective orchestrators foster group stability by minimizing internal competition among member firms. Having a larger number of parties in an alliance implies diverging interests, and a key task of an orchestrator is to align members' interests and prevent free riding by stressing the importance of collective objectives over individual objectives. In addition, the orchestrator needs to proactively manage alliance entry and exit as alliance reconfiguration may destabilize the partnership, particularly if they are a member with a comparatively large resource-based exit (Bakker 2016). Orchestrators also engage in brand management as many multi-partner alliances create a unified brand in order to increase the awareness of potential consumers. An orchestrator can promote the network brand and ensure that all marketing activities are consistent to create a uniform appearance.

Multi-partner alliances: decision-making steps

Value appropriation in multi-partner alliances must be considered jointly with the value-creating strategy because the quality of the collaboration and value-sharing rules both determine how much value the partnership can create. Alignment of complementary resources may provide strong motivation to forge a multi-partner alliance, but the issue of value appropriation is more salient owing to the higher governance costs caused by the risk of free riding. In order to provide guidelines for establishing win–win multi-partner alliances, this section elaborates on specific decisions for multi-partner alliances at each stage of the alliance development framework (see Figure 17.1).

Step 1: alliance strategy formulation

During the strategic analysis, firms decide whether a multi-partner alliance is an appropriate governance mode to realize their goals. Their focus at this stage should be to analyze the benefits of a multi-partner alliance in comparison to alternative governance modes, including autonomous growth, mergers and bilateral alliances. A multi-partner alliance is a preferred governance mode when the type and magnitude of required resources extends beyond the focal firm and an alliance with a single partner. Internalization would only be a preferred alternative if a firm were able to integrate and exploit a variety of external resources efficiently; yet most firms lack this ability. In addition, desired resources are often not readily available in markets, making market exchange inappropriate. For example, developing an industry standard requires substantial investments, involves high risks and depends on the participation and commitment of parties across the value chain. It is beyond the scope of one or two firms to develop such a standard. In such circumstances, multi-partner alliance strategies are appropriate because the probability of one firm's success depends on the resource contributions of multiple parties, including suppliers, competitors and customers. Analysis should focus on resource availability and the potential strengths, weaknesses, opportunities and threats related to participation in a multi-partner alliance.

Step 2: alliance partner selection

During the partner selection stage, a firm either selects multiple partners to forge a multi-partner alliance or decides to participate in an existing multi-partner alliance. A key issue in both situations is assessing partner fit as a misfit may encourage free-riding behaviour. Furthermore, it is important that partners have some degree of common objectives and shared visions on

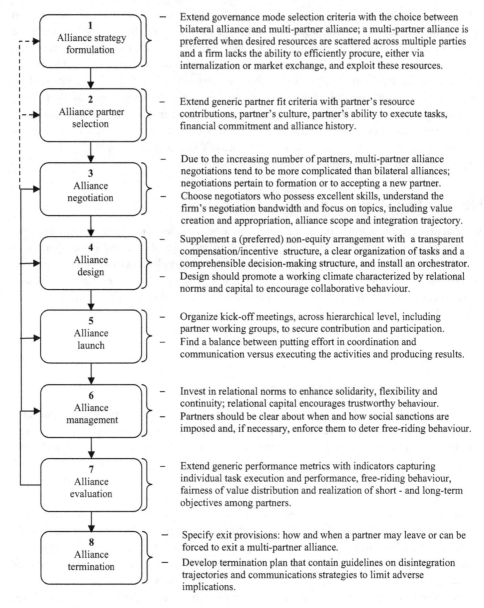

1 Alliance strategy formulation

- Extend governance mode selection criteria with the choice between bilateral alliance and multi-partner alliance; a multi-partner alliance is preferred when desired resources are scattered across multiple parties and a firm lacks the ability to efficiently procure, either via internalization or market exchange, and exploit these resources.

2 Alliance partner selection

- Extend generic partner fit criteria with partner's resource contributions, partner's culture, partner's ability to execute tasks, financial commitment and alliance history.

3 Alliance negotiation

- Due to the increasing number of partners, multi-partner alliance negotiations tend to be more complicated than bilateral alliances; negotiations pertain to formation or to accepting a new partner.
- Choose negotiators who possess excellent skills, understand the firm's negotiation bandwidth and focus on topics, including value creation and appropriation, alliance scope and integration trajectory.

4 Alliance design

- Supplement a (preferred) non-equity arrangement with a transparent compensation/incentive structure, a clear organization of tasks and a comprehensible decision-making structure, and install an orchestrator.
- Design should promote a working climate characterized by relational norms and capital to encourage collaborative behaviour.

5 Alliance launch

- Organize kick-off meetings, across hierarchical level, including partner working groups, to secure contribution and participation.
- Find a balance between putting effort in coordination and communication versus executing the activities and producing results.

6 Alliance management

- Invest in relational norms to enhance solidarity, flexibility and continuity; relational capital encourages trustworthy behaviour.
- Partners should be clear about when and how social sanctions are imposed and, if necessary, enforce them to deter free-riding behaviour.

7 Alliance evaluation

- Extend generic performance metrics with indicators capturing individual task execution and performance, free-riding behaviour, fairness of value distribution and realization of short - and long-term objectives among partners.

8 Alliance termination

- Specify exit provisions: how and when a partner may leave or can be forced to exit a multi-partner alliance.
- Develop termination plan that contain guidelines on disintegration trajectories and communications strategies to limit adverse implications.

FIGURE 17.1 Alliance development framework: multi–partner alliances

industry development; otherwise, the multi–partner alliance is likely to collapse. Next, attention should be given to resource complementarities. In a multi-partner setting, partners prefer to contribute varying resources as the level of resource uniqueness is inversely correlated with free-riding behaviour. In other words, resource substitution should be minimized as overlap tends to lead to free-riding behaviour and dysfunctional conflicts. If overlap is inevitable, analysis of the partner firms' market positions could reveal that they serve different markets, which reduces the risk that the overlap will actually translate to dysfunctional conflicts or competition. Cultural fit between partners stimulates a collaborative culture, whereas misfit prompts a competitive culture that fuels the chance of free riding. Therefore, a cultural assessment of the potential partners is required. Another important selection criterion relates to a party's willingness to pay an entrance fee. By complying with this requirement, new partners express commitment by providing a certain contribution to a collaborative platform.

Step 3: alliance negotiation

Negotiations in multi-partner alliances tend to be more complicated than in bilateral alliance negotiations. Because more parties are involved within the alliance, it can be more difficult to develop a collective value creation strategy and agree on the fair distribution of benefits. To this end, the role of an orchestrator becomes important. By demonstrating leadership, an orchestrator is able to influence partners positively and in a functional manner by providing a clear and enthusiastic vision, emphasizing the importance of the collective over the pursuit of individual interests. In addition to these qualities, the role of the orchestrator is critical in two separate negotiation situations that are typical for multi-partner alliances. If the multi-partner alliance is newly established, negotiating partners may benefit from appointing an orchestrator directly (or a group of people fulfilling an orchestrator's role). An orchestrator's task is to introduce the parties involved, disentangle private interests, create a shared understanding of the alliance's objectives and individual roles and responsibilities, and create common ground from which to launch the partnership. If the alliance has been operating for a while, the orchestrator represents the collective and is tasked with negotiating with any new partners and initially ascertaining the desirability of the new partner (for example, identifying the unique contribution the partner will make to realize the collective objectives). In addition, because accepting a new partner involves enlarging the group, negotiation topics and approaches may differ from the former situation. For example, negotiations may split in several phases, enabling a new partner to integrate slowly. In this way, a new partner can be brought up to standard; this prevents disturbances in the existing alliance, and existing partners postpone a definitive entry decision until the final negotiations.

Step 4: alliance design

The focus during the alliance design stage should be on installing governance mechanisms to supplement the non-equity-based governance form through which multi-partner alliances tend to be organized. Even if partners exchange equity, these additional coordination mechanisms are necessitated, as equity alone is insufficient to protect against free riding and other types of exchange hazards. Specifically, in addition to generic guidelines, managers responsible for forging multi-partner alliances may focus on the following areas:

- A compensation structure that specifies partners' tangible (financial) and intangible (knowledge) outcomes in the short and long term. A clear compensation structure helps prevent different expectations among partners as the alliance progresses and functions as an incentive system. It preferably involves some form of advance payments (such as an entrance fee) and rules about the ex-post distribution of outcomes (for example, royalties and transfer prices). Incentives include financial benefits, a larger share in the public good and bonuses for completing tasks. The absence of a clear incentive system increases ambiguity, which encourages free-riding behaviour.

- Task organization in terms of allocating identifiable and unique tasks to specific partners. Clear responsibility and transparency prompts responsibility and prevents free riding.
- Ideally, decision-making and communication structures and processes are designed to stimulate a collaborative working climate that provides sufficient incentives for each partner to remain committed. However, because the relative weight of one partner might differ from the next, responsibilities and authority should be adapted consistently. Voting rights can be distributed consistently with contributions, but excessive dominant control by one partner undermines collective efforts.
- Preferably, an orchestrator's function will be formalized. This could constitute a person or a team of representatives that aims to resolve conflicts originating from diverging interests, contributions, outcomes and expectations. An orchestrator is also responsible for the entrance and integration of new members.
- The monitoring of outcomes, processes and behaviours is critical for advancing the progress of multi-partner alliances. Rules and procedures should be formalized regarding how and when to act if discrepancies are detected.
- Clear exit provisions, to avoid partners being able to exit the alliance without having fulfilled their contractual obligations, which could include elements such as sharing knowledge and technologies. The absence of such provisions may lead to free-riding behaviour from the exiting partner, which could decrease the trust and commitment of the remaining partners.

Step 5: alliance launch

When taking a multi-partner alliance view, general alliance launch guidelines are sufficient to attain an efficient and effective alliance launch. However, alliance launch managers should be aware of two points. First, launch managers, acting as orchestrators representing the collective, should attempt to build and maintain a healthy collaborative climate. These managers are responsible for enhancing the development of relational norms and capital between the parties involved in a multi-partner alliance. They must create a climate for building trust and be aware of possible feelings of distrust among members in order to prevent or resolve free riding or other forms of opportunism. Second, acting as orchestrators, it is the launch manager's task to create clarity and sufficient detail in partners' goals and contributions; such clarity is prerequisite to formulate operational plans. It also allows them to observe promptly whether all partners are sufficiently committed to the alliance and are not withholding effort, information or resources. To accomplish these two tasks, it is critical that alliance launch managers act as orchestrator, set up liaisons with and between partners, and work with them to define and fine-tune the multi-partner alliance's value proposition.

Step 6: alliance management

When alliance management takes over leadership from the launch managers, it is their main task to continue building a collaborative climate. For example, promoting face-to-face communication prior to formal decision making ensures that partners are motivated to participate in such meetings. In addition, management should focus on the use of social sanctions to deter partners from behaving dysfunctionally. It is the role of the management team to advance a system of social sanctions and a shared understanding of when these social sanctions are to be used and by whom. Social sanctions serve to weaken the reputation of the penalized parties and limit their access to vital resources, particularly when partner reputation is connected with the alliance or when there is strong partner dependency on the alliance. As the partnership progresses, under-performance might justify modifications to the alliance design, including the incentive scheme, the sanction system and group size. Clear procedures are required in order to prevent conflict, stating when procedures may become effective, who can make the appropriate decisions and what the consequences will be.

Step 7: alliance evaluation

Although the perspective of managing partners individually, using unique tasks and measuring individual contributions looks promising, the inherent danger is that the overall alliance performance may be overlooked, along with the potential synergies that can be realized through the collaborations between partners. Therefore, evaluation must also apply to alliance-wide performance indicators for which all partners, or a subset of partners, have specific responsibility. To this end, in addition to generic indicators, the performance metric system will preferably be augmented with indicators that capture the following factors:

- Objective and subjective indicators of multi-partner performance.
- Short- and long-term performance objectives of individual partners and the partnership.
- Fairness of value distribution across partners.
- Individual partners' task execution and performance.
- Behavioural aspects, including free-riding behaviour and other forms of opportunism.

Step 8: alliance termination

The length of the term of the agreement is important, as are exit provisions specifying how and when partners may exit or be forced to exit. Such clauses affect parties' ability to leave a multi-partner alliance that has become unproductive. Depending on the degree of integration, a termination plan may also involve procedures and guidelines for disintegration. For example, withdrawal from a research consortium that has more than 100 members is usually easier than pulling out of a highly integrated airline multi-partner alliance. Communication strategies must also be developed because termination of the alliance or the departure of one partner may have serious repercussions for the other partners.

Summary

A multi-partner alliance can be a win–win situation for all parties involved. However, multi-partner alliances present their own set of unique risks. Whereas the likelihood of detecting free-riding behaviour is relatively high in a bilateral alliance, within a multi-partner alliance, the one-to-one relationship is replaced by a one-to-many relationship, which increases the risk of undetected free-riding behaviour. Free riding occurs when partners act opportunistically by not contributing to the alliance, while benefitting unequally from the outcomes of the alliance. In order to deal effectively with this challenge, firms may require (new) partners to supply unique resources, design alliances with sufficient protection (e.g. task organization), invest in relational governance and install an orchestrator function to coordinate alliance activities.

CASE: SKYTEAM[1]

The airline industry is characterized by fierce competition between airlines and high levels of regionalization, owing to national ties between airlines and their country of origin. This translates into restrictions on landing rights and routes. Despite the deregulation of recent decades, no single airline in the world is able to provide a global network. In order to build and maintain a competitive advantage, airlines circumvent these strict regulations through collaboration. For example, bilateral agreements, such as code sharing, allow airlines to share their network, which enables passengers to complete a journey involving multiple airlines using just one ticket. However, having recognized that bilateral agreements were insufficient to maintain their growth strategies, airlines started to initiate and participate in multi-partner alliances.

The establishment of the Star Alliance in 1997 by United Airlines, Lufthansa, Air Canada, Thai Airways and Scandinavian Airline System (SAS) constituted the first global airline network. The Star Alliance example was soon to be followed by the Oneworld alliance in 1999. SkyTeam was the third alliance to be created in 2000.[1] The primary motivation for SkyTeam was to create a globe-spanning network of routes and airports. Therefore, the most important contribution that partners within the SkyTeam alliance make is their network of routes and airports. Initially, SkyTeam consisted of four founding airlines: Aeroméxico, Air France, Delta Airlines and Korean Air. In 2001, KLM merged with Air France, while in the North American market, Northwest and Continental airlines had already formed a partnership. This partnership was expanded with Delta Airlines forming an important North American bloc. Within Europe, Air France and Alitalia were part of the SkyTeam alliance. The merger between KLM and Air France strengthened the European bloc. Combining both blocs within SkyTeam provided SkyTeam with a key asset: transatlantic routes. SkyTeam currently consists of Aeroflot, Aeroméxico, Air Europa, Air France, Alitalia, China Southern Airlines, Czech Airlines, Delta Airlines, Kenya Airways, KLM, Korean Air, TAROM and Vietnam Airlines, offering a worldwide network. This constellation of multiple airlines presented SkyTeam with the challenge of aligning varying interests and preventing dysfunctional behaviour such as free riding. By carefully selecting its partners and requiring them to pay a membership fee, and incorporating active alliance management and specific decision-making structures, SkyTeam was able to ensure alliance viability.

SkyTeam developed an extensive partner recruitment policy consisting of multiple stages. The primary criteria for selecting potential partners are (1) the network the potential partners can contribute to the alliance and (2) the access a partner can provide to new markets in, for instance, developing regions and countries. In other words, SkyTeam reduced internal competition by minimizing substitution of routes and airports within the alliance. Guided by these criteria and building on the results of preliminary assessments, SkyTeam may decide to proceed to the next stage, introducing a new member of the SkyTeam alliance. During this next phase, the alliance terms and conditions are discussed. An important factor in this negotiation phase is the partner's ability to meet SkyTeam's requirements. These requirements cover aspects concerning flight safety, airline organization and IT infrastructure. The time it takes to fulfil these requirements means the negotiation phase typically takes between one and two years. Meeting these requirements sometimes requires airlines to make significant changes and investments within their organization and operations. Becoming a member of an airline alliance is often critical for long-term airline viability, so airlines are willing to make these investments. In most cases, SkyTeam appoints a buddy airline (sponsor) that helps the airline meet the SkyTeam requirements. Through this buddy system, new partnership members are introduced to partnership rules and routines, translating into easier integration within the alliance. In addition to the process of becoming a member of SkyTeam, partners must also agree to pay an alliance fee. This fee covers general alliance expenses such as marketing, communication and management costs.

SkyTeam has seen its alliance management structure develop, and a transition was made from a decentralized to a centralized management structure. During the first decade of the alliance, SkyTeam employed a decentralized management structure. Coordination of alliance activities was designated to airline managers. Whereas Oneworld and the Star Alliance opted for a more costly centralized alliance office, SkyTeam was able to economize on overhead costs. Having a limited number of partners, a decentralized management model fulfilled SkyTeam purposes. However, the increased complexity, which was mainly caused by the increased number of partners, increased the need for more centralized control. To this end, a specialized alliance office was established. Acting as an orchestrator, this office was made responsible for managing airline contributions, overall performance, collective decision making and managing projects and analyses to identify and incorporate potential new partners.

Decision making was formalized by securing a collective competitive advantage and managing the pluralistic interests within SkyTeam. At the strategic level, the governing board consists of the CEOs of each airline, who meet twice a year and discuss general alliance developments and its strategic direction. The potential for new partners to join is also a responsibility of the governing board. Accepting a new partner requires a 'super majority' of 85 per cent, and blocking votes are not allowed. The supervisory board acts as a steering committee and is occupied with more daily affairs within the alliance, and it monitors the activities of the central alliance office. This board meets six times each year and decides on specific projects that will be executed. The alliance office is in charge of the daily monitoring of project execution and reports to the supervisory board. The chair of the alliance office is also the chair of the governing board. The alliance office monitors general airline performance and keeps track of customer complaints. If airlines are not in compliance with SkyTeam standards, the supervisory board discusses measures that will be taken to ensure airline compliance. SkyTeam has an elaborate compensation structure; based on each airline's performance, size and position, that airline receives an appropriate share of the benefits. The alliance office is responsible for maintaining the compensation structures for each airline but also for developing and implementing new initiatives.

In 2020, Skyteam launched 'SkyCare&Protect', for example. A hygiene and safety initiative in response to rapidly changing regulations, targeting customers and employees across its global network of 19 members. Through this initiative, SkyTeam provides customers with all the information they need—including the latest travel restrictions and how and where to book pre-travel COVID tests—so customers comply before they fly. In addition to digital enhancements, health and hygiene protocols include intense aircraft sanitizing, mandatory mask wearing, frequent access to hand sanitizer stations at hubs, safe distancing, onboard service adjustments and more. In 2022, airlines Delta and Aeromexico were the first two members to implement the alliance-first technology powered by SkyTeam's Digital Spine. This technology enables digital check-in for multi-airline travel via airlines' existing apps or websites. SkyTeam's seamless check-in forms a key part of the alliance's SkyCare&Protect program.

SkyTeam is flourishing. Although the alliance is becoming increasingly complex as a result of its new members and a collective strategy to integrate the partner airlines further to further exploit synergies, recent reorganization of the management structure and the high maturity level of alliance procedures and relational capital have increased the chances that SkyTeam will prosper in the future.

Questions

1   Explain how competition is different in the airline industry for autonomous firms than for groups of firms connected through a multi-partner alliance.
2   Why is free riding a typical exchange hazard for multi-partner alliances? Assess the quality of the measures that SkyTeam took to prevent it.
3   Under what conditions is decentralized or centralized governance more likely to result in superior performance for individual alliance members and the multi-partner alliance?

Note

1   Interview with a senior executive of KLM; SkyTeam (2021, 2022).

18

ALLIANCE PORTFOLIOS

A firm may maintain multiple alliance relationships that, together, constitute a firm's alliance portfolio. By extending their focus beyond the management of single alliances to one that incorporates their alliance portfolios, firms gain additional opportunities to enhance their competitive advantage. A central issue then becomes how a firm can generate, configure and develop a high-performing alliance portfolio, as firm performance depends not only on the success or failure of single alliances, but also on the firm's bundle of alliances. To realize portfolio synergies, firms must proactively design and manage the linkages and interdependencies between their partners of different alliances. However, alliance portfolios also tend to increase management complexity, coordination costs and the risk of conflicts. To be able to realize superior portfolio performance, it is important for managers to understand what an alliance portfolio is (first section) and how to design and manage a high-performing alliance portfolio (second section). The next section of this chapter also provides a set of guidelines that explain how alliance portfolio management impacts the governance of single alliances. The chapter concludes with a summary and a case illustration.

The meaning of an alliance portfolio

Firms wishing to successfully implement strategies cannot rely on a single alliance and are increasingly using different kinds of alliances, including contractual alliances, joint ventures and consortia, to improve their competitive advantage. In addition, many firms have established alliances with customers, suppliers, competitors and other kinds of public and private organizations. The way that a focal firm organizes these intertwined relationships has a notable influence on its competitiveness, which means that a goal-oriented alliance portfolio approach could play a decisive role in firm performance (Hoffmann 2007). By adopting an alliance portfolio approach, a firm shifts its focus from single-alliance governance to systematic governance of its bundle of alliances (see Table 18.1 for examples). The argument is that firms can benefit from engaging in multiple simultaneous alliances that may not be available if the firm had only one alliance at a given point in time. In other words, the linkages and interdependencies between a firm's alliance partners provide additional opportunities for synergy.

DOI: 10.4324/9781003222187-18

TABLE 18.1 Examples of alliance portfolios

TerraVia Holdings Inc

Before being acquired by Corbion in 2017, TerraVia Holdings Inc. (formerly known as Solazyme), was a renewable oil and bioproducts company and a leader in industrial biotechnology. Founded in 2003 and headquartered in San Francisco, its technology allows microbes to produce oil and biomaterials in standard fermentation facilities quickly, efficiently and at large scale. In 2003, they allied with Bunge. Bunge buys, sells, stores and transports oilseeds and grains; processes oilseeds to make protein meal for animal feed and edible oil products; and produces sugar and ethanol from sugarcane. In 2010, the partners extended the alliance to develop microbe-derived oils utilizing Brazilian sugar cane feedstock. In 2011, a partnership with Dow Chemical Company was forged to develop bio-based dielectric fluids. Dow signed a letter of intent to use up to 20 million gallons of TerraVia's algal derived oils in 2013 and up to 60 million gallons in 2015. In 2017, Corbion, a food and specialty ingredients company, acquired TerraVia. Whereas TerraVia's IP portfolio and R&D pipeline, as well as its partnerships with industry leaders, provide high-growth opportunities for the new division, Cobrion continued to forge partnerships in support of TerraVia's goals. For example, Corbion teamed up with Cargill and other food manufacturers to promote adoption of regenerative agriculture practices that lower CO2 emissions, preserve agricultural productivity and enable long-term food security.

Starbucks Coffee Company

Starbuck Coffee Company was founded in 1971. Their mission is to inspire and nurture the human spirit—one person, one cup and one neighbourhood at a time. From the beginning, Starbuck's purpose extends beyond profit. It would like to be (1) leading in sustainability, (2) strengthening communities and (3) creating opportunities. To realize its objectives, they depend on multiple partnerships. For example in 2021, Starbuck Coffee Company launched a new store concept in New York City, together with Amazon. The new store integrates the digital and physical retail experience, bringing together the connection and comfort of a Starbucks café and convenience of Amazon Go's Just Walk Out Shopping experience. Ahead of its 30th Annual Meeting of Shareholders in 2022, Starbucks affirmed its bold aspiration to be a resource positive company—giving back more than it takes from the planet. They announced a new pilot programme with Volvo to help electrify a driving route from the Colorado Rockies to Seattle. Moreover in 2022, Starbucks Coffee Company announced partnership with Delta Air Lines that will offer members of Delta SkyMiles and Starbucks® Rewards, two of America's most highly regarded loyalty programmes, the ability to unlock even more ways to earn rewards at Delta and Starbucks.

Sources: Algeanews (2011); Business Wire (2011a); Corbion (2017); Energyboom (2011); Grooms (2008); PR Web (2011); SBMC (2022a, 2022b); Starbuck Coffee Company (2021, 2022a, 2022b, 2022c).

Firms build and maintain alliance portfolios for purposes that go beyond those of entering into individual alliances. By pursuing multiple goals through a number of simultaneous alliances, firms mitigate risk and uncertainty and may obtain greater alliance benefits overall (Chiambaretto and Fernandez 2016; Hoffmann 2007; van Wijk and Nadolska 2020). For example, when suppliers provide complementary offerings, managing proactively the connections between them enables a firm to achieve economies of scale. In addition, whereas single alliances are generally considered critical mechanisms for accessing valuable resources, an alliance portfolio, and thus the simultaneous access to a broad range of valuable resources from different partners, can be an effective means of enhancing a firm's resource endowment (Lavie 2006). For example, synergies occur in an alliance portfolio when partners from different alliances are stimulated to create and exchange knowledge. Furthermore, by drawing on the social network perspective, firms can use alliance portfolios to capitalize on information advantages (Parise and Casher 2003). Examples include existing portfolio partners providing valuable information about existing and potential partners. A history of joint collaboration across the portfolio reduces transaction costs and reinforces partners' reputations. Next, alliance portfolios can reinforce firms' internationalization efforts (García-Canal *et al.* 2002). Having international partners in the alliance portfolio could provide additional benefits, such as access to new resources, information and capabilities, that may not be available from local partners. Multiple simultaneous alliances with different partners can also help firms to create a more substantial experience base with which to accelerate institutionalization of best practices for governing alliances (Anand and Khanna 2000). Thus, a proactive alliance portfolio approach involves the creation of tighter coordination among alliance partners by exploiting interdependencies between them to achieve portfolio synergies.

However, portfolio management is more complex and demanding than governing single alliances (Parise and Casher 2003). Whereas facilitating interdependencies between partners in different alliances presents certain opportunities, it may also constrain a firm's value creation potential because these linkages expose a firm to unique hazards. Any attempt at collaboration between partners from two different alliances with opposing objectives, such as competitors in the same industry, is likely to meet resistance. The firms are probably unwilling to share valuable product, customer and market information, or new business opportunities, for fear that this information would become available to their rival. Similarly, when partners are members of competing networks or promote competing technologies, attempts by any firm to capitalize on interdependencies are most likely to cause conflict and tension. In addition, one single alliance may exhibit such high exclusivity that it prevents a firm from working effectively with other partners. For example, an alliance with a market leader may impede alliances with smaller niche players in the same product space. The partnership with the market leader is most likely to use the majority of the firm's resources, including the time of the dedicated sales force. In turn, the smaller partners may become dissatisfied with their inability to expand the alliance because of the rival partner. Thus, constraining interdependencies lead to distrust, lower transparency and decreased commitment. However, alliance portfolios with constraining interdependencies are not unheard of; a well-formulated alliance approach can curb the negative consequences.

In summary, a portfolio approach is unlike single-alliance governance in that it includes explicitly the design and management that facilitates and constrains interdependencies between partners of different alliances. Firms that embrace an alliance portfolio approach can enhance their competitiveness as the overall value created by an alliance portfolio with adequate governance is greater than the sum of the values created by each individual alliance in the portfolio (see Box 18.1). However, whereas a proactive alliance portfolio approach involves facilitating interdependencies between partners, constraining interdependencies can undermine the realization of portfolio synergies. Firms can use portfolio design and management to deal effectively with this unique challenge.

Alliance portfolio governance

The issue of alliance portfolio design and management revolves around what type of partners to incorporate in the portfolio (Ozmel and Guler 2015) and, in connection with this, what type of portfolio management is necessary (Zheng and Yang 2015). A first fundamental task is then formulating a portfolio strategy to the end of a goal-oriented alliance portfolio approach.

BOX 18.1 TOYOTA'S SUPPLIERS' PORTFOLIO

In 1988, Toyota started producing cars in the United States. At this time, Toyota's suppliers had virtually no contact with each other, so Toyota formed the core of a network with bilateral arm's-length supplier relationships. Each party pursued its own individual objectives while maintaining its independence, and relationships were organized through formal contracts, the outcomes of which were determined through power. Toyota faced the challenge of how it could improve efficiency and innovation to respond to shifting customer demands. Over the next few years, Toyota implemented a learning plan consisting of three phases. Phase 1 was to develop weak ties among suppliers. In 1989, Toyota initiated a supplier association (BAMA). Phase 2 was to develop strong ties between the suppliers and Toyota. To this end, the company offered trained consultants to BAMA members at no cost. In Phase 3, to develop strong ties among suppliers, Toyota divided its suppliers into small learning teams. After the completion of its plan, Toyota had built an effective knowledge-sharing network of suppliers consisting of multi-lateral relationships with strong direct and indirect ties, through which explicit and tacit knowledge was exchanged. Trust between participants governed the relationship through fairness, interdependence and open informal contracts. Toyota's network solution increased its knowledge-sharing by devising methods that would motivate members to share valuable knowledge openly (while preventing undesirable spillovers to competitors), prevent free riders and reduce the costs associated with finding and accessing different types of valuable knowledge. Toyota's network, which is characterized by a variety of institutionalized routines and a collective identity, facilitates multi-directional knowledge flows among its suppliers.

Sources: Dyer (1996); Dyer and Nobeoka (2000).

Essentially, firms can use one of two different alliance portfolio strategies (Hoffmann 2007; Yang *et al.* 2014). First, firms may focus on exploration, which then makes the purpose of an alliance portfolio to acquire new resources and capabilities through alliance relationships. For example, adopting an exploration strategy suggests that alliances are used to develop new technologies, fundamentally improve product lines and develop new service offerings to meet changing customer needs. Second, an exploitation strategy relies on using existing resources efficiently and protecting competitive advantages as much as possible. An alliance portfolio then functions as a vehicle to stabilize the environment, and alliances are used to refine and leverage built-up resources. The composition of alliance portfolios (i.e. functional heterogeneity) has also been associated with liquidating events, such as IPO and acquisitions (Hoehn-Weiss and Karim 2014). Firms can also use their alliance portfolios to seek a balance between exploration and exploitation strategies. A portfolio can provide quick and flexible access to different kinds of resources, while also reducing environmental uncertainty by developing long-term stable alliances (Bakker and Knoben 2014). The key is not the success or failure of a single alliance but whether a firm reaches its exploration and/or exploitation objectives by means of its alliance portfolio. Therefore, the design and management of the alliance portfolio is at the centre of interest (see Table 18.2).

TABLE 18.2 Alliance portfolio governance

	Portfolio design	*Portfolio management*
Objective	An efficient portfolio configuration in support of the alliance portfolio strategy.	Management of inter-partner linkages between set of alliance partners.
Focus	A firm's configuration of intertwined alliances in which facilitating interdependencies are maximized and constraining interdependencies minimized.	Capturing portfolio synergies through active management of alliance formation and termination and coordination of inter-partner knowledge and resource flows.
Mechanisms	Portfolio size • Large or small portfolios Structural • Redundancy or non-redundancy Governance • Weak or strong ties Partner • Heterogeneous or homogeneous	Knowledge management • Develop knowledge infrastructure between alliance partners. Internal coordination • Orchestration and alignment of internal organization with alliance portfolio.

Sources: Parise and Casher (2003); Wassmer (2008).

Alliance portfolio design

The challenge of portfolio design is to configure a set of intertwined alliances in such a way that maximizes portfolio synergies (that is, exploits facilitating interdependencies) and minimizes coordination costs (that is, controls constraining interdependencies). An efficient portfolio design determines the quality, quantity and diversity of information and resources to which the focal company has access, the efficiency of getting access to these resources and the flexibility or stability of the firm's position in the industry (Baum *et al.* 2000). Prior studies on alliance portfolio design have identified various design parameters, including (1) a size dimension, (2) a structural dimension, (3) a governance dimension, (4) functional dimensions and (5) a partner diversity dimension (Golonka 2015; Hoehn-Weiss and Karim 2014; Jiang *et al.* 2010; Wassmer 2008, 2010).

The size dimension pertains to characteristics such as the number of alliances and partners. Some studies, primarily those that have examined entrepreneurial biotechnology firms and technological performance, suggest that larger alliance portfolios are more likely to result in portfolio synergies, such as innovation output rates (Shan *et al.* 1994). However, other studies report that once a firm's alliance portfolio has reached a certain size, any additional alliance will provide diminishing returns. For example, Deeds and Hill (1998) report a curvilinear relationship between the number of alliances held by an entrepreneurial biotechnology firm and the firm's rate of new product development. Lahiri and Narayanan (2013) report that highly innovative firms benefit less from increasing alliance portfolio size than less innovative firms with respect to financial performance. Contrary to studies that focus solely on portfolio size, this book suggests that portfolio size alone is not a sufficient predictor of portfolio performance and is outweighed by other design parameters (Yoon *et al.* 2015). For example, Castiglioni and Galán González (2020) show that portfolio size in combination with portfolio coordination enables firms to yield superior value from their alliance portfolio.

The structural dimension pertains to the level of redundancy across alliances within the portfolio. Redundancy within an alliance portfolio is the result of a firm collaborating with multiple partners that make similar contributions. The main advantage is that redundancy provides a firm with multiple access points to critical resources, valuable knowledge and information about existing and potential partners. A firm itself is also more visible for firms seeking partnering opportunities (Ahuja 2000). In contrast, an alliance portfolio character-ized by non-redundant relationships (that is, where each alliance makes a unique contribu-tion) enables firms to enhance portfolio performance by leveraging and exploiting resources obtained through the few specialized alliances they have. Koka and Prescott (2008) show that, when confronted with a radical change in the environment, an entrepreneurial alliance portfolio (redundant) outperforms both a prominent alliance portfolio (non-redundant) and a hybrid configuration. This suggests that distinct structural configurations can enhance port-folio performance, yet the impact of portfolio structure is likely to be conditioned by other factors, including governance form and partner characteristics (Wassmer 2008).

The governance dimension pertains to the level of commitment, degree of integration and learning of alliances in the portfolio (Jiang *et al.* 2010); this is also referred to as tie strength. Strong ties, such as equity-based arrangements, serve as vehicles for learning and information exchange, as partners are highly interconnected through reciprocal financial and organiza-tional relationships (Hoffmann 2007). An alliance portfolio composed of primarily strong ties has a positive effect on a focal firm's innovative capabilities, especially if they are trust-based, knowledge-intensive and reinforced through relationship-specific investments (Capaldo 2007; Yang *et al.* 2014). Alternatively, an alliance portfolio composed of primarily weak ties, such as non-equity-based arrangements, provides firms with strategic flexibility as these relation-ships are more easily established and terminated (Bakker and Knoben 2014). Such portfolio configurations tend to support exploitation strategies (Yang *et al.* 2014). Firms that build a homogeneous portfolio of governance forms tend to experience higher performance (Jiang *et al.* 2010) as repeated experience with a specific governance form often translates into institutionalized knowledge that can be readily applied to future alliances, thereby reducing managerial costs (Sampson 2005). However, a homogenous portfolio with primarily strong ties can also have a negative effect on a focal firm's innovative capabilities by stimulating a vicious circle in which a reduced number of contacts, decreased flexibility for collaboration with new partners and diminishing responsiveness to new market trends reinforce each other. In a similar fashion, firms are more likely to opt for a prespecified short-term alliance than for a long-term alliance when environmental factors increase the need for strategic flexibility in managing their alliance portfolio (Bakker and Knoben 2014). Thus, whereas heterogeneity in governance forms (and time horizon) within an alliance portfolio enables a firm to realize multiple objectives simultaneously, homogeneity tends to reduce coordination costs.

The partner diversity dimension refers to partner-related characteristics, among which include partner industry (e.g. convergence/divergence), organizational characteristics (e.g. similar/dissimilar), nationality (e.g. focal/foreign) and functional orientation (e.g. upstream/downstream) (Golonka 2015; Jiang *et al.* 2010; Sukoco 2015; Wassmer 2010). Because no single firm can possess all of the critical resources required for long-term success, an effective means of achieving a firm's objectives is to ally with partners operating in different indus-tries. Partners from the same industry are often competitors whose overlapping backgrounds, experiences, knowledge and technological bases may provide learning in the form of imita-tion and greater absorptive capacity. However, conflicts of interest do exist, and learning races can happen, which increases monitoring and safeguarding costs. For example, Lavie (2007) finds that the relative bargaining power of partners in the alliance portfolio constrains the firm's appropriation capacity, especially when many of these partners compete in the focal firm's industry. However, the firm's market performance (e.g. market share) improves with the intensity of competition among partners in its alliance portfolio. Thus a holistic approach towards alliance portfolios to prevent competition among portfolio partners is pivotal for sustainable alliance strategies and beneficial portfolio outcomes (Park *et al.* 2015). In contrast, although collaboration with partners from different industries tends to increase coordination costs, owing to different routines and processes that can make collaboration difficult, it also leads to novel resources, knowledge and information. In support of these insights, Sukoco (2015) reports that compared to convergent learning (portfolio proximate to industry domain), divergence learning (i.e. portfolio distant from industry domain) contributes greater to market performance, particularly when partners are relatively independent from one another. Golonka (2015) corroborates these findings and suggests that proactively searching for and selecting strangers, as opposed to friends and acquaintances, as potential partners positively affects the complexity of alliance portfolios (e.g. functional, geographical and governance); complexity in turn is expected to enhance a firm's innovativeness. Like industry diversity within an alliance portfolio, organizational characteristics, nationality and functional orientation all have positive and negative performance implications. Consider functional orientation for example: firms employ a mixture of marketing, manufacturing and distribution alliances to broaden their market reach and enhance value creation, and for further exploitation of core competences; a primary focus on R&D alliances, on the other hand, enables firms to build new capabilities and competences. Thus, variation in partners' characteristics plays a role in determining the benefits and costs that firms derive from their alliance portfolios.

It is clear from the earlier discussion that each portfolio design parameter associates positively or negatively with (different types of) performance; though empirical evidence tends to inhibit conclusive comparisons as studies tend to be fragmented in their use of portfolio configuration and performance measures. To explain the effects of portfolio diversity for example, Goerzen and Beamish (2005) focus on the effect of geographical, product and partner diversity on MNE's economic performance, whereas Yoon and colleagues (2015) focus on portfolio size and organizational diversity to explain knowledge creation in small bio-tech firms. Nevertheless, we proffer that the portfolio design dimensions combined constitute an alliance portfolio configuration and that a configuration is 'high performing' when it supports an alliance portfolio strategy (Castiglioni and Galán González 2020). In additive portfolio approach, firms refrain from any systematic approach, since each alliance is managed individually, without any strategic intent for the set of alliances. A strategic portfolio approach adds a strategic component to the portfolio, guided by a firm's strategic objectives (Hoffmann 2005). More specifically, contrasting exploration and exploitation strategies with distinct portfolio designs leads to two generic implications:

- An exploration strategy is more likely to be effectuated when an alliance portfolio has a set of redundant alliances, primarily weak ties and diverse partner characteristics. The resulting heterogeneity increases the richness of information and resources, broadens search options, improves a firm's ability to develop new capabilities and increase its visibility in the broader industry network, which in turn enhances performance. The downside is that a firm may fall into a learning trap, and the coordination costs are very high.

- An exploitation strategy is more likely to be effectuated when an alliance portfolio has a set of non-redundant alliances, strong ties and uniform partner characteristics. The resulting homogeneity enables a firm to build and leverage a specialized resource pool, exploit existing capabilities and react flexibly and quickly to changing circumstances. This may cause a firm to fall into a competence trap, but the coordination costs are relatively low.

The implications outlined earlier are generic (see Figure 18.1), and firms may seek alternative configurations (i.e. different combinations of design parameters) in support of their objectives. For example, when a firm adopts an exploration strategy but seeks some degree of flexibility in its research efforts, weak ties are preferable to strong ties. However, a firm can replace weak ties with strong ties when more stability is required during the development stage. Alternatively, if an exploitation strategy requires multiple sources of resources, partner diversity is preferable to uniformity. Critical is that the design parameters are internally consistent as, for example, shown in a study by Castro *et al.* (2015) who report that portfolio capital mediates the relationship between portfolio configuration and market share growth. Irrespective of strategy and configuration, however, obtaining a high standing (i.e. firm's rank in expected returns compared to other portfolio partners) in an alliance portfolio positively associates with the firm's access to the partner's resources and the firm's performance (Ozmel and Guler 2015).

When seeking a balance between exploration and exploitation strategies, firms may also seek to establish an integrated or hybrid configuration (i.e. parallel), thereby simultaneously accommodating exploration and exploitation requirements. Alternatively, a firm may use a structural configuration in which an organization develops two separate portfolio configurations to accommodate exploration and exploitation requirements, respectively. A firm may also use a temporal configuration in which an alliance portfolio is restructured over time to accommodate subsequent exploration and exploitation requirements; for example, a portfolio configuration may evolve with a product life cycle.

The configuration of an alliance portfolio is generally not static and may actually change over time through the formation of new alliances and the termination of existing ones. Firms are often forced to change the configuration of their alliance portfolios if they are to improve their competitive position vis-à-vis their rivals in an industry, or simply to secure their competitive advantage. Adding, replacing or removing alliance partners may influence the facilitating and constraining interdependencies within the alliance portfolio. Therefore, instead of

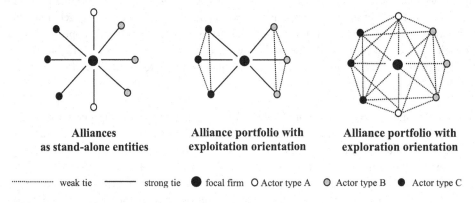

Alliances as stand-alone entities	**Alliance portfolio with exploitation orientation**	**Alliance portfolio with exploration orientation**

·············· weak tie　——— strong tie　● focal firm　○ Actor type A　○ Actor type B　● Actor type C

FIGURE 18.1 Generic alliance portfolio configurations

adding and removing partners opportunistically, conveniently or randomly, firms should adopt a proactive alliance portfolio approach. For example, a pharmaceutical company may envision a portfolio that consists of research and development alliances with biotech companies during the discovery stage of a drug's product life cycle, but a dramatically different portfolio involving marketing alliances with drug delivery or other pharmaceutical companies during the commercialization stages of the product's life cycle. Whereas an efficient alliance portfolio configuration can provide a firm with the desired synergetic effects, constraining interdependencies will limit willingness to share knowledge, decrease transparency, undermine communication and adversely affect trust building. To overcome these negative repercussions, firms must complement portfolio design with portfolio management (Castiglioni and Galán González 2020).

Portfolio management

Portfolio management (or coordination) pertains to governance of the set of alliances and the linkages between partners. The design and management of single-alliance relationships are critical; however, to secure a competitive advantage, firms must extend single-alliance governance with portfolio management (Haider and Mariotti 2016). Research has shown, for example, that the relation between alliance portfolio size and alliance portfolio benefits lies at a higher level for firms coordinating their alliance portfolios (Wijk and Nadolska 2020). The two management factors that allow firms to maximize their return on their alliance portfolio are knowledge management and internal coordination (Parise and Casher 2003; Wassmer 2008, 2010).

When managing an alliance portfolio, it is critical to initiate some form of knowledge management targeted at knowledge creation and exchange between partners. The degree to which a firm captures, shares and leverages information and knowledge across its alliance portfolio, as well as the mechanisms it has in place to promote communication among its partners' alliance managers, has a direct effect on its performance. Zheng and Yang (2015) show for example that familiarity about the inter-organizational routines between partners in an alliance portfolio facilitates knowledge integration, which stimulates new knowledge discovery. However, the repeatedness of same-partner R&D projects within a firm's alliance portfolio has a negative effect on breakthrough innovations. Examples of knowledge practices include designated project teams, a secure extranet, a directory that contains contact details, a virtual team room, joint training and education and a repository with important alliance documents. For example, Dyer and Nobeoka (2000) showed that intentionally facilitating knowledge transfer between Toyota's suppliers increased those companies' commitment to share valuable knowledge, prevented free riding and reduced the costs associating with finding and accessing knowledge. Thus, knowledge management targeted at knowledge exchange between partners in an alliance portfolio increases awareness of partners' abilities, enables inter-firm knowledge creation and stimulates partner referral. In addition, knowledge management practices may involve intra-firm knowledge sharing, which improves insights in alliance portfolio opportunities as well as professionalism in alliance management. Instruments that can be deployed include the creation of best practices, formal and informal communication structures, the creation of communities of practice and the implementation of IT infrastructure. Knowledge management is important, therefore, as it enables firms to overcome constraining interdependencies by increasing the cohesion between partners in the alliance portfolio, which in turn allows them to exploit facilitating interdependencies.

Managing an alliance portfolio requires the internal coordination of alliance activities, which will enable a firm to orchestrate the linkages between alliance partners. Internal coordination helps firms to align the alliance portfolio strategy with the separate parts of the organization (such as corporate and business units). Most alliances are initiated on an operational level as ad hoc responses to local business issues. A business unit will forge an alliance that serves its own (business unit) objectives, often without realizing the impact this has on other parts of the organization or firm as a whole. This silo-thinking approach could create situations that are not only conflicting but also costly. For example, when a newly formed alliance overlaps in products and markets with existing partners' businesses, a firm may not only incur increased conflict resolution costs but also have to bear the consequences associated with dissolving pre-existing alliances. Communication structures and information exchange between managers operating at different levels and businesses allows managers to keep up to date with latest developments in strategy and adapt their alliances accordingly. Managers become informed about alliance initiatives outside their responsibility, which reduces the risk of forging alliances that undermine portfolio performance. Internal coordination also involves a systematic approach to defining and measuring portfolio performance. In addition to metrics that capture the performance of single alliances, a performance metric system should include measures of the entire portfolio's performance. Although alliance metrics may indicate that a single alliance generates superior performance, portfolio metrics may reveal that it undermines portfolio performance. Taken together, internal coordination provides a holistic approach to a firm's set of alliances, which enables the firm to identify and resolve opportunities and threats within the alliance portfolio. Some firms may establish a separate department to coordinate all these alliance-related activities.

Alliance portfolio dynamics

With respect to alliance portfolio dynamics, little attention has been directed at the question of how and why firms change the configuration of their alliance portfolio over time (Cui 2013; Wassmer 2010). Most studies describe portfolio evolution as driven by endogenous path-dependent alliance formation decisions that take a unidirectional causal effect on portfolio evolutionary trajectories, where decisions to alter the alliance portfolio are guided by a combination of internal inducements and the availability of alliance opportunities (Lavie and Singh 2012). For example, Gulati (1995a) suggests that a firm's decision to engage in new alliances is significantly based on the accumulation of its prior alliance ties, which forms a social context in which the focal firm finds itself embedded when deciding with whom to partner now and in the near future. Focusing on alliance termination, Cui (2013) reports that resource dissimilarity between partners in an alliance portfolio may be less supportive of, or even detrimental to, the continuity of an alliance; this negative effect may, however, be countered for example through strong inter-partner linkages.

An alternative approach towards portfolio development takes a life-cycle perspective, focusing on how alliance portfolios develop over time and on their configurative evolution as a result of firm action and coordination. Dyer and Nobeoka (2000) report on their study of the Toyota case and suggest that Toyota produced a knowledge network that evolved 'from weak ties, to strong bilateral ties with the convener (Toyota), to strong multi-lateral ties among suppliers'. Likewise, Hite and Hesterly (2001) suggest that a firm's portfolio develops from primarily dense, cohesive, and path dependent at a firm's emergence into a network that consists of both embedded and arm's-length ties, structural holes and being intentionally managed.

Lavie and Singh (2012) complement the previous with the inclusion of co-evolutionary mechanisms as a potential driver of portfolio evolution. Studying the case of Unisys Corporation, a US-based technology company, they find four idiosyncratic interacting processes that influenced portfolio evolution, namely (1) co-evolution, referring to the process of adjusting the alliance portfolio configuration as a result of changes in the focal firm's strategic orientation, while changes to its alliance portfolio would support or constrain the implementation of strategies; (2) external stimuli, referring to stimuli that instigate the (co-)evolutionary process referred to earlier, such as changes in the technological environment; (3) inertial pressures, referring to internal crises and processes of resistance to change that would delay or alter the portfolio evolution; and (4) restructuring and realignment, referring to organizational structural changes that would promote changes in the alliance organization in order to realign portfolio configuration and strategy. Taken together, the foregoing makes clear that alliance portfolio evolution is a phenomenon that must be considered from a range of perspectives when seeking to understand its drivers as well as its course of development. Future research may take on this endeavour.

Alliance portfolio: decision-making steps

A traditional perspective considers alliances as isolated transactions. However, firms that adopt an alliance portfolio approach create new opportunities to improve their competitive advantage (Wassmer and Dussauge 2012). Many firms' alliance portfolios are configured and managed inefficiently and often represent nothing more than a random mix of strategic alliances that sometimes even have conflicting demands. In contrast, managers in firms with high-performing alliance portfolios visualize their portfolio in the context of the entire network rather than as a series of single partnerships. These managers have a holistic visualization of the possible interdependencies among (potential) partners, which broadens their range of strategic actions. The next section connects alliance portfolio thinking to the stages of the alliance development framework depicted in Figure 18.2 in order to provide insights into the efficient governance of single alliances in light of the broader alliance portfolio.

Step 1: alliance strategy formulation

Before managers decide which governance mode (make, ally or buy) suits their objectives, an alliance portfolio approach helps them assess the extent to which an alliance will strengthen the alliance portfolio (that is, facilitate interdependencies) or weaken it (that is, constrain interdependencies). Taking the alliance portfolio as a departure point, a clear alliance portfolio strategy that is consistent with a firm's corporate and/or business strategy will enable managers to determine the preferred portfolio configuration. Periodic scenario-planning exercises can be a useful tool for analyzing the effects of adding, removing and replacing specific alliance partners in the alliance portfolio. Communicating the portfolio strategy across business units increases transparency and allows expectations to be managed accordingly. Managers will understand the changes being made in portfolio composition as they will fit the portfolio strategy that has been communicated. By incorporating a portfolio approach (that is, considering the linkages between partners) in the strategic analysis, firms become aware of synergies and constraints among multiple alliance partners, which in turn inform their governance mode decision making. That is, they understand the degree to which an alliance depicts an alternative that is preferable to internalization or market exchange.

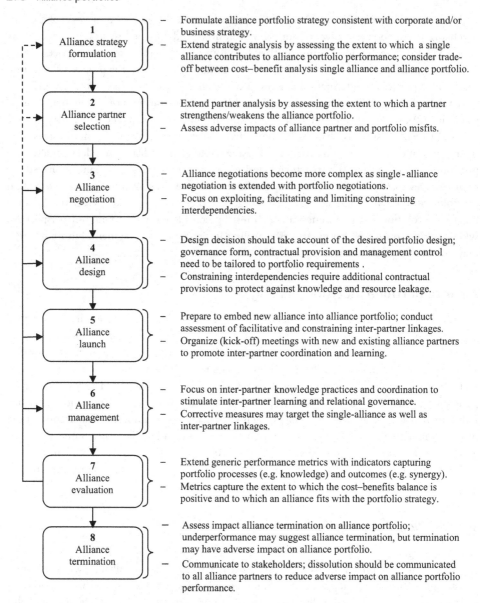

FIGURE 18.2 Alliance development framework: alliance portfolios

Step 2: alliance partner selection

Partner fit is critical when selecting a new partner. However, firms must be aware that the positive implications of good partner fit could be offset if that partner creates constraining interdependencies in the alliance portfolio. For example, although a firm and a potential partner may serve distinct markets indicative of resource complementarity, the preferred partner may possess market overlap with an existing partner in the alliance portfolio. This new partnership is therefore likely to create conflicts as the existing partner may start to decline to share resources and knowledge. A firm that wishes to be aware of such adverse consequences asks the following questions during the partner selection phase, in addition to generic partner selection criteria:

- To what extent does a potential partner reinforce an exploration or exploitation portfolio strategy? The firm assesses whether the intended alliance needs to be integrated in the alliance portfolio or whether it can be considered as a stand-alone alliance.
- To what extent does a potential partner create facilitating interdependencies (that is, synergy) in the alliance portfolio? The firm assesses the extent to which existing partners and the potential partner are part of the same collaborative network, provide complementary offerings, promote similar standards or infrastructure, are willing to learn from each other and view the presence of other partners in the portfolio as a way to mitigate risks.
- To what extent does a potential alliance partner create constraining interdependencies (that is, conflicts) in the alliance portfolio? The firm assesses the extent to which existing partners and the potential partner are members of competing collaborative networks, are strong rivals in an industry, promote competing technologies or infrastructures and create conflict as one alliance relationship becomes so exclusive that it prevents the firm from working effectively with the new partner (or vice versa).
- The firm compares the results of the assessments. What are the potential benefits and costs of this potential partner from a portfolio perspective? If the benefits are higher than the costs, the firm then proceeds with the alliance. If the costs are higher than the benefits, continuation depends on the cost–benefit analysis of the single alliance.

Step 3: alliance negotiation

During the alliance negotiation stage, negotiators seek agreement on the initial alliance conditions, including topics such as compensation, contribution and coordination. By embracing an alliance portfolio approach, however, single-alliance negotiation strategies tend to become more complex as a firm is confronted with multiple trade-offs (e.g. knowledge exchange and protection) that can be resolved by using integrative and distributive negotiation strategies interchangeably. Furthermore, the negotiation bandwidth is extended as a firm's total value creation potential comprises the value of the single alliance and the value derived from this single alliance's embeddedness in the alliance portfolio. Transparency and openness are critical as potential partners must understand that part of their value is generated through collaboration with other alliance partners. Awareness of potential facilitating and constraining interdependencies may also affect the negotiation process and outcomes. For example, whereas jointly identifying and discussing opportunities to create portfolio synergies creates a constructive dialogue, attempts to resolve a partner's conflicting interests with other partners may result in resistance, conflict and tension. Therefore, alliance negotiations must centre on both the alliance and the alliance portfolio.

Step 4: alliance design

Against the background of facilitating and constraining interdependencies, managers should design alliances in such a way that maximizes potential portfolio synergy and minimizes additional governance costs. To this end, the generic guidelines for alliance design are extended with guidelines that follow from an alliance portfolio approach. If an alliance is forged to support an exploration strategy, an equity-based arrangement is preferred in order to support knowledge transfer, such that the learning from one alliance or partner can be applied to other alliances. In contrast, if an alliance is forged to support an exploitation strategy, a non-equity-based arrangement is preferred to support flexibility. In addition, an alliance design may include provisions that specify how and when a partner will collaborate with other partners in a firm's portfolio. For example, there may be a clause stating the circumstances under which partners will exchange product information and specifications. However, constraining interdependencies (such as competitors) will necessitate additional contractual provisions to protect against knowledge and resource leakage. Furthermore, an alliance design may stipulate the nature and content of knowledge management practices.

Step 5: alliance launch

When taking an alliance portfolio view, generic alliance launch guidelines are sufficient to attain an efficient and effective alliance launch. However, alliance launch managers should be aware of two points. First, launch managers should develop assessment activities to embed the (new) partner(s) into the existing alliance portfolio. Assessments may focus on the extent to which facilitative or constraining inter-partner linkages emerge. Mutual introductions between partners may help to capitalize on facilitative linkages, whereas communication should reduce concerns about possible competitive adversities between partners. Second, acting as the linking pin between portfolio partners, it is the launch manager's task to clarify each partner's contribution as well as to create a climate in which inter-partner coordination and mutual knowledge exchange can thrive. To accomplish these two tasks, it is critical alliance launch managers proactively involve all partners, set up liaisons with and between partners, and work with them to work towards the firm's objectives.

Step 6: alliance management

During the alliance management stage, managers focus on the day-to-day operations that enable them to realize the alliance's value creation potential. In addition to stimulating inter-firm learning, resolving conflicts and initiating appropriate responses to adversities, managers must pay continuous attention to the management of inter-firm linkages. For example, Microsoft, IBM and Oracle all provide some type of infrastructure (for example, research centres, testing facilities, training, online communities) to support knowledge exchange between developer partners. Another critical task is to build relational capital between portfolio partners. This facilitates knowledge exchange, functions as a safeguard against misappropriation and reduces the risk of opportunism. In addition, managers can fulfil the role of mediator if conflicts emerge between their alliance partners. Furthermore, based on performance assessment, managers may initiate modifications in order to enhance the performance of a single alliance as well as the portfolio.

Step 7: alliance evaluation

Defining and measuring performance objectives for a single alliance can be a challenge for many firms. However, by adopting an alliance portfolio approach, the performance metric system should be supplemented by metrics that capture portfolio process and outcomes. For example, it is informative to look for patterns of high or low performance across alliances, which can expose areas of strength or weakness in the alliance portfolio. In addition, portfolio metrics ideally capture portfolio synergies, including learning, financial, strategic and coordination costs pertaining to contracting, monitoring and safeguarding. A comprehensive performance metric system including milestones that allow partners to evaluate and track alliance and portfolio performance easily enables managers to intervene immediately if expectations are not met.

Step 8: alliance termination

An alliance portfolio approach complicates alliance termination. Consistent with generic guidelines, under-performance of a single alliance may prompt premature termination. However, the dissolution of a single alliance may adversely impact portfolio performance, which suggests that a termination decision should be postponed until the negative repercussions have been resolved appropriately. For example, a partner may provide critical knowledge to other high-performing partners. In this case, the provision of knowledge needs to be secured before dissolving the relationship. If the termination trajectory is continued, firms need to communicate the termination to other partners in the portfolio in a timely manner if they are to avoid damaging their own reputations.

Summary

Driven by the proliferation and increasing diversity of alliances, firms that embrace an alliance portfolio approach often find themselves in a tangled web of interdependent alliances. Whereas governance of single alliances can be challenging, governance of the partners embedded in an alliance portfolio that encompasses multiple alliance relationships tends to be more complex and demanding. A proactive alliance portfolio approach enables firms to exploit interdependencies between partners and generate synergies beyond what would have been possible through single alliances. However, these interdependencies may also constrain a firm's ability to create portfolio synergies as some partners are unwilling to collaborate with other partners under certain circumstances. Firms can resolve this situation through efficient alliance portfolio design and active portfolio management. In other words, an alliance portfolio can enhance a firm's competitive advantage only when the portfolio design fits with the portfolio strategy and is supported by portfolio management.

CASE: GENERAL ELECTRIC[1]

General Electric (GE) is a diversified infrastructure, finance and media company. With products and services ranging from aircraft engines and power generation to financial services, healthcare solutions and television programming, GE operates in more than 100 countries and employs more than 300,000 people worldwide. The company is also active in the energy market. Until 2013, GE energy incorporated all business activities in one unit, but to provide further focus, three new GE businesses were created: GE Energy Management, GE Oil & Gas and GE Power and Water. With these businesses, GE has become one of the world's leading suppliers of power generation and energy delivery technologies. The businesses work together to provide integrated product and service solutions in all areas of the energy industry, including coal, oil, natural gas and nuclear energy; renewable resources such as water, wind, solar and biogas; and other alternative fuels. Collaboration with a variety of partners is an important building block in GE's long-term growth strategy. Some of GE's alliance initiatives in recent years are outlined next.

GE energy has built on its growing technology presence in China's thriving chemical production industry by signing new agreements to licence its gasification technology to five Chinese companies for a variety of applications. The licence agreements grant customers the right to utilize GE's proprietary gasification technology, which converts coal and other carbon-based fuels into synthesis gas (syngas) for use in chemical production and other applications. GE's gasification technology is one of the most widely applied technologies of its kind in China, with more than 50 licensed facilities.

GE Energy signed a service alliance with the Tennessee Valley Authority (TVA), the largest public power provider in the United States, which covers four TVA power plants and is valued at $116 million over the next five years. The alliance helps the TVA meet its strategic needs by ensuring the long-term reliability, efficiency and cost-effective operation of its power generation equipment. Under the agreement, GE provides a core team that offers on-site expertise and experience at the various plant locations to help TVA manage outages and respond quickly to specific project requirements. In 2015, it was announced that TVA would grant GE a contract to supply high-efficiency gas turbines for a new combined-cycle plant. This plant will replace three coal-fired units to further reduce coal emissions.

In 2010, GE signed a cooperation agreement with Norwegian energy companies Statoil and Lyse to carry out technical and environmental feasibility studies jointly regarding the construction of an offshore wind demonstration project in Rogaland County, off the southwest coast of Norway. The agreement includes the installation of up to four 4.0-megawatt offshore, direct-drive wind turbines. In 2015, GE initiated a collaboration with Statoil in what has been called the Powering Collaboration programme. This programme entails finding solutions to meet the global challenges that energy producers are facing, including CO_2 and methane emissions and water usage. Utilizing the capabilities of both companies, the programme aims to develop new approaches to create efficient and low-cost technologies that can be implemented globally. Some 20 projects have already been initiated, covering a wide portfolio of potential solutions. The partnership utilized open innovation and crowdsourcing to get access to new ideas and support the development of new technologies.

GE and Indian-based Ramky signed emergency water and industrial wastewater treatment agreements designed to address India's industrial wastewater treatment and recycling needs. Such water reuse initiatives can play a major role in helping improve overall water supplies in areas where water issues are critical, such as India. The agreement involves Ramky using GE's industry-leading ultra-filtration (UF) and membrane bioreactor (MBR) technology for wastewater treatment and recycling in India's industrial sector. Ramky and GE will also bring the innovative concept of mobile water treatment plants to the Indian water sector.

GE Energy and wind energy developer Iberwind Group SA have signed a 10-year operational and maintenance (O&M) services agreement to cover two Iberwind wind farms in Portugal. Following a complete service agreement for the units that began in 2005, Iberwind chose to continue using GE as its preferred service provider for the next ten years. Working closely with Iberwind, GE has customized a complete service programme that will offer Iberwind operational and maintenance support and technology and engineering expertise, while GE Energy will deliver parts to support corrective maintenance activities.

An $18 million outsourcing agreement and facility upgrade for Yara S.p.A.'s Ferrara (Italy) plant with industrial water treatment leader GE Oil & Gas has helped Yara meet increasing customer demands. The Ferrara plant supplies ammonia and urea liquid fertilizers to agricultural markets. While production of these products requires large amounts of clean water, the plant must rely on brackish, low-quality surface water sources. Yara outsourced its Ferrara water treatment operations to GE in 2005 to reduce costs, increase reliability and focus on its main businesses. With the recent contract expansion, GE will continue to build, own and operate the water treatment plant with onsite GE personnel until 2020. The facility currently produces up to 320 m^3/hr of demineralized water using two proprietary GE technologies: brackish water reverse osmosis filtration (BWRO) and electro-deionization (EDI). The partnership with Yara was further extended in 2013, when it was announced that GE and Yara had signed a 12-year contractual service agreement to maintain an array of rotating GE equipment at Yara's fertilizer plant in the Netherlands.

Since 2015 GE Digital Energy is collaborating with AT&T to create the next generation of smart energy solutions for the Industrial Internet of Things. The collaboration should result in technology that improves the way that the energy industry works. The combination of the GE capabilities with regard to secure wireless technologies and utility software solutions, and the AT&T capabilities with regard to extensive connectivity, will drive development forward to a more cohesive energy network. The alliance is focusing on solution development that can be marketed and sold to customers. This partnership builds on a global alliance that AT&T and GE signed in 2013, which resulted in the incorporation of AT&T connectivity technology on many GE products and solutions. In 2021, AT&T and GE announced further collaboration on 5G connection for healthcare solutions. As part of this collaboration AT&T will deliver both high and low-band 5G connectivity to the GE research campus, allowing the partners to actively explore ways to use 5G connectivity to improve patient care and outcomes.

Questions

1   Given GE Energy's objective to build and maintain a competitive advantage in the global energy industry (i.e. demanding exploration and exploitation strategies), what are the important considerations in designing and improving GE Energy's alliance portfolio?
2   What portfolio management initiatives can GE Energy develop to ensure inter-firm learning and coordination between its alliance partners?
3   What recommendations would you offer GE Energy with regard to alliance portfolio development and its embeddedness in the internal organization?

Note

1   AT&T (2021); Business Wire (2011b); Capgemini (2007); Deutsch (2007); Genewsroom (2017a, 2017b), PRNewswire (2015).

19

ALLIANCE NETWORKS

The network view on alliances states that firms are embedded in a set of inter-firm linkages between multiple parties. Whereas alliance portfolios only consider the set of direct relationships between a firm and its partners, alliance networks also involve indirect relationships: the set of relationships between a firm and third parties intermediated by the firm's alliance partners. An alliance network functions as a repository of knowledge, resources and information and can potentially enhance a firm's competitive advantage. However, an alliance network also involves (social) obligations, interdependencies and lock-in effects, which threaten a firm's autonomy and control. Therefore, from the perspective of a focal firm, an alliance network increases management complexity and coordination costs. The extent to which network benefits outweigh costs depends on a firm's strategic intent, its position in the alliance network and its ability to influence network processes and outcomes. As the opening two sections of this chapter explain, this cost–benefit balance makes it critical to understand the nature of alliance networks, as well as the role of a firm's network position and how a firm can leverage its position to its advantage. Taking the alliance network view as a reference point, the third section also presents managerial guidelines, and the chapter concludes with a summary and a case illustration.

The meaning of an alliance network

An alliance network view comprises a firm's direct alliances and its indirect relationships (see Table 19.1). Whereas a direct relationship entails a single alliance between partners, an indirect relationship connects two parties (such as firms) through a third party. For example, a supplier alliance directly connects a manufacturer to a supplier, but the supplier can also be indirectly connected to a manufacturer's wholesaler if the manufacturer and the wholesaler are connected through an alliance of their own. According to alliance network logic, despite the lack of a formal partnership between the supplier and the wholesaler, all three firms may possess relevant technologies, knowledge and/or expertise that could be beneficial to all of them. Essentially, these relationships could take multiple forms, such as informal relationships (for example, regular meetings at professional associations) and formal relationships (such as supplier alliances). However, to stay consistent with the scope of this book, the focus here is on alliance relationships.

DOI: 10.4324/9781003222187-19

TABLE 19.1 Examples of alliance networks

Focal firm	Description	Network type*
General Motors	General Motors is organized through internal market units, each of which is expected to have expertise in an area related to an automotive system and be able to sell its products on the open market.	Internal market network with interdependent profit centres; compliance with firm policies and collaborative culture.
Nike	Nike's core competence is the design of sport shoes and equipment. It maintains an extensive network of suppliers and retailers, which enables it to reduce manufacturing costs and respond flexibly to customer demands.	Vertical market network with independent organizations; upstream suppliers and downstream distributors around one company (integrator).
Toshiba	Toshiba is a diversified manufacturer and marketer consisting of more than 200 companies, 600 'grandchild' companies and numerous direct and indirect exchange relationships across markets, products and countries.	Inter-market network with independent organizations; institutionalized affiliation among firms in unrelated industries and linked in vertical direct and indirect relationships.
Tata Group	The Tata Group is a conglomerate operating in a wide range of industries, such as consumer products, steel, financial services and is embedded in a large network of direct and indirect exchange relationships.	Opportunity network with independent organizations; organized around a central broker and temporal productions and services to execute particular projects.

Note: * Taking a focal firm as reference point, firms can participate in different types of alliance networks.

Source: Achrol (1997).

An alliance network can enhance a firm's competitive advantage as its set of direct relationships provides access to a pool of resources that might not otherwise be easily available (Gulati 1998), including financial capital, research and development facilities and human resources. The network also functions as a source of valuable information through its indirect relationships by means of referrals, contacts and knowledge and reputational spillovers (Baum *et al.* 2000). Firms can use this access to resources and information to compete more effectively, to access markets with high entry barriers, to lower their reliance on others, to create innovative products and services, to realize economies of scale and scope and to obtain legitimization. An alliance network also provides a firm with strategic manoeuvrability (Powell 1990). It represents a more efficient form of governance than hierarchies and markets, particularly in uncertain and competitive environments, as it allows a firm to be more flexible and enhance its control over external parties. For example, an alliance network enriches a firm's repertoire of strategic actions as it provides managers with greater access to industrial intelligence and other types of information than they would generate operating autonomously. Moreover, an alliance network reduces behavioural uncertainty concerning a firm's network partners. Although not all network partners are formally connected through an alliance, the presence of indirect relationships may promote solidarity and collective norms regarding how to operate within an alliance network.

However, alliance networks also present firms with risks and hazards (Gulati and Gargiulo 1999). First, the exchange of resources, information and knowledge in an alliance network often entails obligations for future transactions as network members may expect receiving firms to reciprocate their efforts. Expected obligations from network partners, as well as the resulting costs for switching to other partners, could cause a firm to be locked-in, which hinders the firm's strategic manoeuvrability. Second, an alliance network creates interdependencies between network members, which reduces their autonomy and therefore constrains their decision making. A firm whose partners have extensive control of key resources cannot exclude those partners from its alliance network without jeopardizing access to those resources; this is a resource constraint that enhances the partners' power over the firm. As other parties in an alliance network obtain more power, concerns also arise over the extent to which value is equally and equitably distributed. Third, firms that are not part of the core of an alliance network may not receive new information or may receive it too late and may be subject to blind-spot biases. For example, when technological changes occur frequently in an industry, access to new and/or different types of information becomes critical. Consequently, firms that are disconnected from the alliance network are at a considerable disadvantage.

In summary, an alliance network can provide a firm with substantial benefits. However, it also brings a degree of managerial complexity that extends beyond the governance of single alliances and alliance portfolios. The challenge for one firm participating in an alliance network is to capture network benefits while curbing the negative implications of alliance networks. This requires a holistic approach that encompasses an understanding of the effectiveness of a firm's position in an alliance network and the degree to which a firm can exercise influence over network processes and outcomes.

Alliance network governance

The governance of alliance networks (from a focal firm perspective) is more complex than the governance of single alliances and alliance portfolios, owing to the greater number of direct and indirect relationships to be considered. With regard to alliance formation, studies have shown that new alliance formation is not only influenced by firm- and alliance-level factors (e.g. resource motives and partner fit) but also by repeated experiences with the same alliance partners (Gulati 1995a). For example, Ghosh and colleagues (2016) demonstrate that new alliances may be predicted by both the technical, geographic and product-market fit of potential partners as well as by prior ties between partners, but only when these industries are less mature. Nevertheless, as with alliance portfolio governance, firms can control their network position in light of their network strategy and initiate corrective actions by creating, changing and maintaining their set of alliances (see Table 19.2). Hence, we next discuss network position and management.

Alliance network position

A firm's network position refers to the number and pattern of structural linkages between a firm and other parties in a network (Gulati and Gargiulo 1999). Prior studies have assessed a firm's network position by focusing on the structural configuration of an alliance network; their key argument was that a firm's position influences its resources and information availability, as well as how much control a firm has over resource flows in the network (Yli-Renko and Autio 1998). An alliance network view extends beyond an alliance portfolio view (also referred

TABLE 19.2 Alliance network governance

	Network position	*Network management*
Objective	Achieve a position in the alliance network in support of a firm's strategic intent.	Capitalize on network position and execute network functions and roles.
Approach	Support exploration intent with a closure position; support exploitation intent with a structural hole position; or reconcile strategic intents via temporal separation, structural separation or parallel configuration.	Engage in framing, activating, mobilizing and/or synthesizing functions supported by network management roles, including information-broker, coordinator, relationship broker and network structuring agent.
Concern	Trade-off between strengths and weaknesses of network position.	Trade-off between costs and benefits of network management.

Sources: Burt (1982); Coleman (1990); Jarvensivu and Moller (2009).

to as an egocentric alliance network) by encompassing indirect relationships. Consequently, the alliance portfolio design parameters can be extended to include indirect relationships in order to explain the relationship between a firm's network position and its performance.

The size dimension pertains to the boundary of the alliance network. Academic studies often set this boundary arbitrarily, which implies that their results need to be interpreted with caution (Scott 2000). The key advantage of larger networks is that they tend to improve a firm's innovative performance as partners within an alliance network can align resources and information more easily, while created knowledge becomes more easily available to all partners. However, it is also more difficult for a firm to influence resource and information flows in a larger network because of its greater complexity. The partner dimension pertains to partner characteristics within the alliance network, including the partner's industries, functional orientation and countries of origin. The greater the partner diversity in an alliance network (e.g. different kinds of resources, information, technologies, etc.), the better the access a firm generates to more sources of critical resources (Yli-Renko and Autio 1998). However, indirect relationships mean that firms have less control over the adverse impact of constraining interdependencies, or are less able to leverage facilitating interdependencies than they would be in an alliance portfolio. The governance (or relational) dimension pertains to the strength of the relationship (Granovetter 1973). From an alliance network point of view, strong ties (e.g. equity-based) suggest that a firm is embedded in a web of highly integrated direct and indirect relationships. The reciprocal nature of these relationships means that information flows easily through the alliance network. However, whereas partners may initially supply novel information, their contributions may become known over time, thereby reducing the benefits of strong ties. In contrast, weak ties (e.g. non-equity-based) suggest that a firm is connected loosely to the other firms in the alliance network. Although the distribution of information is less predictable, weak ties are better suited to the rapid diffusion of new ideas between a variety of parties. The structural dimension pertains to the level of redundancy (that is, overlap) between direct and indirect relationships within an alliance network. To capture redundancy in an alliance network, multiple parameters have been identified. However, it is beyond the scope of this book to discuss them all; therefore, the two prominent parameters in the alliance network literature that are discussed are (1) density and (2) centrality.

Network density (or closure) refers to the extent to which firms in an alliance network are directly connected as opposed to being connected through a series of indirect relationships (Coleman 1990). Density tends to make inter-party interactions observable to others because those parties have known and common contacts, which increases their willingness to share information freely amongst each other. Firms participating in a dense alliance network can rely on relational norms to promote collaboration and social sanctions (that is, negative reputation) to reduce opportunism. Consequently, network density enhances a firm's performance because it reduces monitoring costs, spreads risk and encourages collective risk-taking. It also enhances reputation, facilitates rapid dissemination of information, improves direct access to resources and facilitates collaboration between network members. However, the fact that partners in the network have similar expectations means that a dense network also decreases a firm's flexibility. For example, social obligations and operating rules may constrain a firm from forging new alliances outside the network.

Network centrality is the relative proximity of firms to the core of the alliance network's inter-firm linkages (Coleman 1990) and is regarded as a measure of network power. A central position in a network is a strategic location because it enables a firm to exercise influence over resource flows and the diffusion of information. For example, obtaining some control over network processes and outcomes provides a firm with preferential access to resources, such as market information, customer information and technological developments. A case in point is Super Bakery, a food service broker that maintains control over its order-filling cycle, not by direct supervision of the work of the contractors but by maintaining control over communication with its customers and serving as a communications and coordination centre for the contractors (Williams 2005). Consequently, network centrality enhances a firm's performance because it provides a firm with control over resource and information flows.

When the network dimensions are considered together, it follows that a firm can occupy different network positions, each of which enables the firm to acquire different types of network benefits (Ahuja 2000). This heterogeneity in various network positions also indicates that a network position is only beneficial to a firm when it is aligned with the firm's strategy. The next section draws on two prominent views on alliance networks, those of Burt (1982) and Coleman (1990), to present two prototypical network positions that, respectively, support a firm's exploitation and exploration intents (see Figure 19.1).

In terms of a firm's exploitation intent, favourable outcomes (that is, performance) stem from occupying a structural hole position in an alliance network that is characterized by centrality, relatively few strong direct and indirect relationships, non-redundant relationships and partner homogeneity. A structural hole position suggests that a firm functions as a broker between two otherwise disconnected groups of intertwined parties. Although the two disconnected groups that are connected by a broker are not necessarily unaware of one another, information, resources and knowledge are exchanged through the intermediate firm. Because different information flows within each group, a broker firm has the opportunity to control exchanges between the groups providing it with informational advantages. For example, brokers have the advantage of being able to bring together disconnected firms, which provides them with an opportunity to determine whose interests are served and when contact is established. The structural hole position is best suited to an exploitation strategy as it enables a firm to organize the flow of resources in an efficient manner. That is, a broker's function in an alliance network supports the exploitation of existing resource endowments to reduce variety, increase stability and enhance performance. For ease of coordination, a firm will also preferably occupy a prominent position in the centre of the alliance network.

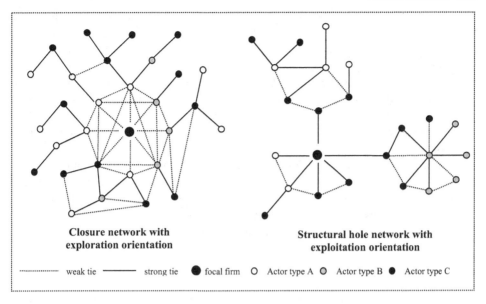

Closure network with exploration orientation   Structural hole network with exploitation orientation

··········· weak tie ——— strong tie ● focal firm ○ Actor type A ◯ Actor type B ● Actor type C

FIGURE 19.1 Alliance network configurations

In terms of a firm's exploration intent, favourable outcomes (that is, innovation) stem from the firm's closure position in an alliance network that is characterized by density, multiple weak direct and indirect relationships, redundant relationships and a high diversity of partners. Closure suggests that a firm is embedded in a network of highly coupled, yet loosely coupled, interconnected parties. Closure provides a firm with informational advantages as it possesses access to multiple sources increasing reliability, timing and early acquisition of information. In addition, network parties tend to interact based on a set of relational norms, which stimulates collaborative behaviour. These network characteristics best suit an exploration strategy. This is because a firm in a network position that is loosely connected to a variety of parties with diverse organizational backgrounds and resources is well positioned to develop new knowledge, see new opportunities and create those capabilities necessary for survival. Furthermore, the rapid diffusion of information in closure networks, and diversity in the cognitive focus of network partners, reinforces innovation. The openness in a closure network also reduces the risk of uneven distribution of network outcomes. For example, closure offers protection against misappropriation because a firm and its counterparts are better able to act together against a party that violates relational norms and conduct.

The closure and structural hole positions depict two prototypical network positions. As exploitation and exploration can be considered opposing strategies, a firm may seek to obtain either a closure or structural hole position. However, high-performing firms tend to reconcile exploration and exploitation intents, which requires them to adjust their network position accordingly. Despite the absence of any universal prescriptions, the following three implications can be offered, building on the logic that the optimal network position of a firm is contingent on its strategic intent:

- A firm may alternate between exploration and exploitation intents over time, suggesting that its network position also needs to be adapted. A focus on exploration requires a closure network to obtain informational benefits, whereas a focus on exploitation requires a structural hole network to obtain resource benefits. By entering and exiting alliances, a firm can change its network position over time in accordance with its strategic focus.

- A firm may seek to realize its exploration and exploitation intents concurrently, suggesting that its network position needs to accommodate both strategic intents at the same time. Although the closure and the structural hole views on alliance networks have opposing implications, a firm may attempt to configure a position that combines both perspectives.

- A firm may accommodate both strategic intents by separating the organization into two 'parts', each of which pursues its own strategy. For example, by dividing research and development and production into two different business units, the R&D business unit with a focus on exploration may benefit from a closure position, whereas the production business unit with a focus on exploitation may benefit from a structural hole position.

Network management

Firms engage in network management in order to attain and support their position in an alliance network (McGuire 2002). Network management involves restructuring the existing network and improving the conditions of cooperation within the existing structure. Whereas restructuring involves adding or removing alliances, improving the conditions of cooperation involves various network activities to facilitate cooperation between network partners. However, there is a degree of controversy regarding the extent to which alliance networks can be intentionally managed (Jarvensivu and Moller 2009). On one hand, building on the logic that alliance networks constitute a source of a firm's competitive advantage, one view suggests that firms can and should manage an alliance network actively and purposefully. On the other hand, another view indicates that, from a focal firm's perspective, alliance networks are surrounded by uncertainty as firms cannot manage the behaviour of other parties in the network. The position of this book is that although firms can manage their direct alliance relationships and their alliance portfolios, they can at best, and only to a certain degree, influence network processes and outcomes. To realize network management, we suggest that a firm must fulfil the four functions described later and take on associated network management roles (Jarvensivu and Moller 2009; Knight and Harland 2005).

Framing entails a firm's attempts to influence the roles that each participant may play at any given time and perceptions about the common purpose of the alliance network. Separate missions, distinct constituencies and competition for resources in alliance networks make it increasingly difficult to achieve some form of overall coordination. A firm may set an agenda and develop initiatives to support joint value creation in an alliance network. Its task is then to create awareness about the agenda and plans among key participants within the alliance network. In order for parties to collaborate and not compete, they should recognize the complementarity of their needs and have mutually understood definitions of the issues to be addressed. To this end, a firm may adopt the role of an information broker, which means that it gathers, analyzes and disseminates information to various parties in the network; sometimes this is in response to a request, but it is usually done proactively. A firm may seek to establish an identity and culture for the alliance network, even if it is temporary. Collective sense making helps to develop a working structure for the network and aligns the perceptions of participants without mechanisms based on authority relations. An alliance network does not need to have completely aligned goals in order to create value, but a certain level of shared planning is required among at least some of the networked actors. If actors believe that they can achieve greater value as network members, then they may be willing to share part of their autonomy to the network and operate like a quasi-organization.

Activating involves identifying potential network participants and assessing the extent to which their skills, knowledge and resources improve network performance. It also includes the process of structuring the alliance network. Building on the overall network objectives, required partners, resources and activities are identified and an attempt is made to install some form of coordination. For example, a firm may fulfil a coordinator role and engage in activities such as facilitating inter-partner activities, bringing together representatives of the different firms and facilitating communication and other network practices. A firm can organize meetings between all relevant network participants in order to align perceptions and strengthen linkages. Coordination in alliance networks is maintained increasingly through informal open-ended contracts rather than hierarchical control and authority. Thus, the interactions between network members are neither random nor uniform but patterned so that they engage in a complicated dance of mutual alignment and adjustment.

Mobilizing involves building commitment among parties in an alliance network to carry out the necessary activities. This is a common and ongoing task for achieving network outcomes. A firm may fulfil the role of advisor, which involves advising parties in the network on various topics, such as policies and alliance activities. In addition, a firm may act as a relationship broker, attempting to initiate and facilitate new alliances between different parties in order to create new opportunities, and, if needed, it may mediate in conflicts. In addition, a firm acting as an innovation sponsor tries to mobilize organizations in the network to innovate, with the goal of motivating and stimulating parties to recognize new opportunities for innovation and facilitate potential alliances.

Synthesizing relates to organizing and controlling, and it involves creating conditions for productive interaction while preventing, minimizing and removing obstacles to collaboration. The activities are carried out so as to produce effective and efficient network outcomes vis-à-vis expectations. If this does not occur, corrective measures are taken to improve the alliance network. Synthesizing entails facilitating and furthering interaction, facilitating linkages among participants and reducing complexity and uncertainty by promoting information exchange. For example, a firm may fulfil the role of a network-structuring agent, which monitors and influences the structure of alliance relationships. In this role, a firm may focus on such areas as restructuring the alliance network by initiating new alliances, seeking ways to reduce the costs of resource exchange and enforcing protection mechanisms against misappropriation. The objective is to achieve cooperation among actors while minimizing and removing informational and interactional blockages to the cooperation. This steering of network processes is inherently difficult in that the result of the network process is derived from the interaction between the strategies of all actors involved.

The way in which a firm can fulfil these management functions depends partially on the intent and structural configuration of an alliance network (Jarvensivu and Moller 2009). First, while some alliance networks are based on more emergent cooperation, others are based on a more deliberately set strategic intent. In emergent alliance networks, management tasks tend to be characterized by ongoing negotiation and renegotiation, adaptation and re-adaptation.

In contrast, alliance networks with a few strong players are more likely to set clear strategies based on the strategy of these players, which means that coordination is more likely to be imposed on other network participants. Second, the distribution of power in an alliance network (that is, centrality) impacts a firm's ability to influence network processes and outcomes. As a firm occupies a central position in an alliance network, it may adopt a more power-driven, hierarchical-type managing style. In contrast, a firm with low centrality must adopt more subtle negotiation approaches. Third, the density of inter-partner linkages affects how well network participants are able to make sense of the current, potential and future partners in their alliance network. High density suggests that network partners frequently interact, which requires less managerial effort to negotiate the framing of the network and allows efforts to focus on activating, mobilizing and synthesizing the network. In contrast, low density indicates that network partners are more distant, which demands more effort to align parties' perceptions and interests.

To conclude, extending beyond (formal) network management functions, networks may also be governed through social mechanisms (Capaldo 2014). Such mechanisms refer to governance efforts that support coordination of economic action across partnered organizations. Generally, a distinction can be made between relational mechanisms, such as interpersonal relationships, inter-organizational trust, and reciprocity and structural mechanisms, including restricted access, collective sanctions and reputation concerns. Both types of social mechanisms influence partners' behaviour and sustain inter-organizational coordination in alliance networks. Alliance networks can thus provide firms with knowledge resources that enhance the firms' ability to compete. However, in order to exploit the potential for competitive advantage embodied in inter-organizational collaboration, the processes of network governance need to be carefully managed. Therefore it is important to diagnose and intervene in the formal functions and social mechanisms affecting the behaviour of the partners in the alliance network.

Network dynamics

Studies have investigated how alliance networks develop over time. Traditionally, studies adopted static approaches and assumed that the informational and resource value of an alliance network remains constant over time or evolves from carrying low value to progressively higher value (Gilsing et al. 2016). Despite inconclusive evidence on the evolutionary path—from closure to structural hole or vice versa—early studies adopt the (implicit) assumption of a linear process of network evolution. Akin to alliance portfolio dynamics, however, more recently, by investigating network evolution along development phases of birth, growth and maturation, new insights into network dynamics have been generated. Lipparini et al. (2014) show that core firms took charge of the processes of inter-firm learning from firms to dyads, and from dyads to networks, and of knowledge-enhancing practices all needed to nurture the transfer, recombination and creation of specialized knowledge. Gilsing and colleagues (2016) show that the evolution of both structural and positional embeddedness strongly exhibits nonlinearity by resembling a fluctuating pattern that is induced by changes in technological uncertainty. Networks evolve from an initially low level of structural and positional embeddedness to a progressively higher level, through patterns of network expansion and network strengthening, though with different structural and positional configurations. Despite these insights, understanding how alliance networks evolve is at an embryonic stage, thus requiring more (empirical) research (Agostini and Nosella 2019).

Alliance network: decision-making steps

Many firms are unaware of their network positions, let alone the fact that they engage intentionally in network management activities. In contrast, high-performing firms tend to recognize the importance of their alliance networks and consider the formation and management of single alliances in the context of the entire alliance network. Their holistic visualization of the alliance network broadens their range of strategic actions. This section connects the stages of the alliance development framework to an alliance network view (see Figure 19.2) in order to provide insights into the efficient governance of single alliances in an alliance network.

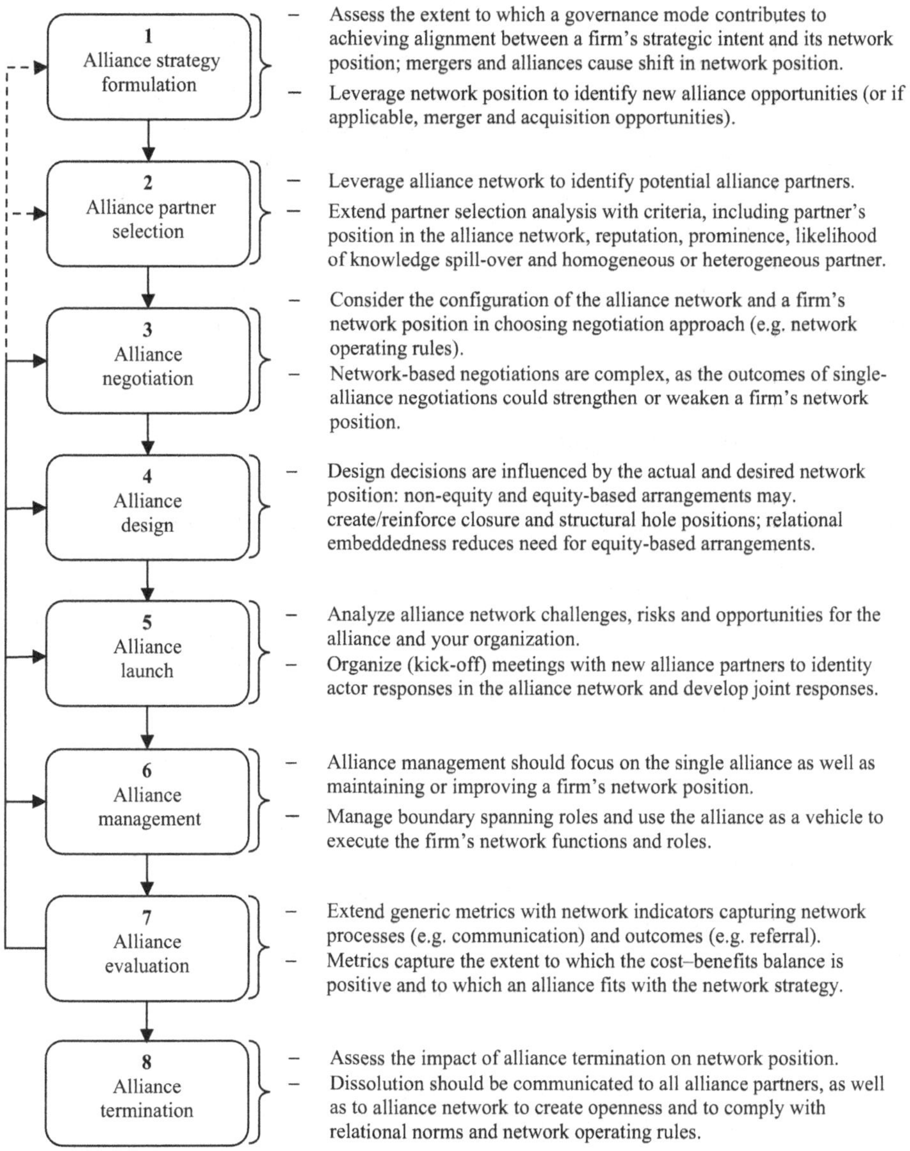
1
Alliance strategy formulation
– Assess the extent to which a governance mode contributes to achieving alignment between a firm's strategic intent and its network position; mergers and alliances cause shift in network position.
– Leverage network position to identify new alliance opportunities (or if applicable, merger and acquisition opportunities).
2
Alliance partner selection
– Leverage alliance network to identify potential alliance partners.
– Extend partner selection analysis with criteria, including partner's position in the alliance network, reputation, prominence, likelihood of knowledge spill-over and homogeneous or heterogeneous partner.
3
Alliance negotiation
– Consider the configuration of the alliance network and a firm's network position in choosing negotiation approach (e.g. network operating rules).
– Network-based negotiations are complex, as the outcomes of single-alliance negotiations could strengthen or weaken a firm's network position.
4
Alliance design
– Design decisions are influenced by the actual and desired network position: non-equity and equity-based arrangements may. create/reinforce closure and structural hole positions; relational embeddedness reduces need for equity-based arrangements.
5
Alliance launch
– Analyze alliance network challenges, risks and opportunities for the alliance and your organization.
– Organize (kick-off) meetings with new alliance partners to identity actor responses in the alliance network and develop joint responses.
6
Alliance management
– Alliance management should focus on the single alliance as well as maintaining or improving a firm's network position.
– Manage boundary spanning roles and use the alliance as a vehicle to execute the firm's network functions and roles.
7
Alliance evaluation
– Extend generic metrics with network indicators capturing network processes (e.g. communication) and outcomes (e.g. referral).
– Metrics capture the extent to which the cost–benefits balance is positive and to which an alliance fits with the network strategy.
8
Alliance termination
– Assess the impact of alliance termination on network position.
– Dissolution should be communicated to all alliance partners, as well as to alliance network to create openness and to comply with relational norms and network operating rules.

FIGURE 19.2 Alliance development framework: alliance networks

Step 1: alliance strategy formulation

The decision to establish an alliance is not only influenced by strategic, resource-led and economic imperatives but also by how a firm is embedded in an alliance network. In addition to generic guidelines, a governance mode decision should thus also incorporate the extent to which certain governance modes help to align a firm's strategic intent to its network position. Where market exchange and internal development are unlikely to affect a firm's network position, mergers and acquisitions and alliances may. For example, merging with a prominent party in the alliance network may enhance a firm's centrality, whereas acquiring a competitor may create a structural hole position. Similarly, entering (or exiting) an alliance causes a shift in a firm's network position from closure to structural hole and vice versa.

In addition, the firm's position in an alliance network either helps or hinders its identification of new opportunities. For example, through its indirect relationships, a firm receives information about potential alliance partners (or merger and acquisition targets), which may affect its ability to forge viable alliances. A network position may also constrain the extent to which potential partners are aware of potential partner firms, thereby limiting its set of choices. For example, informational advantages tend to enable firms with more central and prominent network positions to establish more new alliances and to do so with greater frequency. As the available information grows, firms seeking to forge alliances become less reliant on external conditions and more influenced by the alliance network in which they are embedded.

Step 2: alliance partner selection

An alliance network can reduce what it costs a firm to find and select partners. Through indirect relationships, an alliance network may provide a firm with information about the availability and reliability of potential partners. Moreover, alliance network partners may have a certain status and reputation, which makes them more attractive as partners. Specifically, status and reputation are critical in uncertain environments because they signal that a potential partner has valuable resources and unique skills and is able to maintain alliance relationships successfully. An alliance network also provides information about the predictability of a potential partner's behaviour. Prior successful experiences with other alliance partners may increase a partner's trustworthiness, which is disseminated in an alliance network through referrals. Within an alliance network, firms with prior alliances tend to forge new alliances with the same partner. The alliance partners have established prior working relationships, are aware of their skills and needs and are therefore more likely to realize high performance levels. In addition, unconnected firms are more likely to ally if they have common partners or are closer in an alliance network. Thus, a firm that leverages its alliance networks actively may reduce costs related to partner search, selection and monitoring. However, a firm may wish to consider the following questions when selecting a partner:

- To what extent does a potential partner enhance or undermine the network position?
- To what extent does a potential partner change the power position of a firm?
- To what extent do network-operating rules tolerate an alliance partner outside the existing alliance network?

Step 3: alliance negotiation

When taking an alliance network view, generic alliance negotiation guidelines are sufficient to realize favourable negotiation processes and outcomes. However, negotiators should be aware of two points. First, when starting alliance negotiations with a partner that is embedded in a firm's alliance network, a negotiator should be aware that the alliance network itself might function as a safeguard against unbalanced negotiation outcomes. If the partners have a history of shared experiences, negotiations are more likely to be characterized by integrative negotiation strategies. In addition, to avoid negative reputational spillovers, negotiations are more likely to occur in a collaborative climate. Second, single-alliance negotiations tend to become more complex when the alliance network view is incorporated. The negotiation bandwidth becomes extended as a firm's value creation potential comprises the value of the single alliance and the value of the single alliance within the alliance network. Awareness of potential network contributions and constraints may affect negotiation processes and outcomes. For example, while identifying and discussing opportunities to create a joint business proposition generates constructive interactions, attempts to resolve opposing interests within the alliance network may result in resistance, conflicts and tensions. In addition, when network-level decisions are part of the negotiation, multi-lateral negotiations (that is, multiple partners) require a careful negotiation approach.

Step 4: alliance design

Firms tend to approach alliances as stand-alone transactions, which means that they often neglect the influence of a firm's alliance network on alliance design decisions. That is, a firm changes the configuration of the alliance network through alliance design decisions. Whereas partner selection constitutes a critical decision as it affects the homogeneity or heterogeneity of partner diversity, the adopted governance form affects the strength of the tie and thus the network position. For example, forging a non-equity-based learning alliance with a university may strengthen a closure position, whereas establishing a joint venture with a supplier may reinforce a structural hole position.

An important implication of relational embeddedness in an alliance network is the enhanced relational capital between firms. Relational capital promotes collaborative behaviour and increases a partner's awareness that the other has a lot to lose from behaving opportunistically. Social sanctions extend beyond the alliance and may include loss of reputation, loss of business with the alliance partner and deteriorated relationships with other network partners. Consequently, rather than relying on equity-based arrangements and complete contracts, firms may opt for self-enforcing safeguards, which mitigates the risk of opportunism, misappropriation and unpredictable partner behaviour. In other words, familiarity between alliance partners generates relational capital, which enables the partners to use less quasi-hierarchical structures (i.e. non-equity) in the design of the partnership.

Step 5: alliance launch

During the alliance launch stage, the partner firms transition from alliance formation to preparing and implementing the alliance contract. Organizing alliance execution is pivotal with regard to the firm's alliance network. With the formation of a new alliance, a firm's network position may change (substantially). Launch managers should make detailed assessment on how the firm's position changes and what initiatives are required to curb adversities and leverage synergies. For example, a new alliance may create a linkage through which a firm obtains access to previously unattainable knowledge sources, or it may become part of a referral network. In contrast, new alliance relationships in a network may violate implicit behavioural rules, thus necessitating corrective actions. In addition, the launch of a new alliance may provide the launch manager with an opportunity to assemble existing partners. Together they may discuss actions to act upon new network opportunities and formulate joint responses to network actors' (defensive/offensive) responses to the alliance announcement. To accomplish these tasks, it is critical alliance launch managers adopt a helicopter view, thus understanding how their actions may have repercussions extending beyond narrow organizational boundaries.

Step 6: alliance management

When firms embrace a proactive approach towards alliance network management, the management of a single alliance extends beyond regular activities, which include building relational norms and capital, initiating corrective measures, resolving conflicts and stimulating inter-firm learning. More specifically, boundary-spanning individuals become critical as they have a crucial impact on information exchange and decision making in their own organization and that of their counterparts. Building on the groundwork laid by the launch managers, alliance management may focus on boundary-spanning agents to enhance information exchange and obtain control over network benefits (such as referrals). In addition, management may focus on the role the alliance plays in fulfilling its network management efforts. Examples of such roles include the following:

- An information-broker role (framing) in the network: a firm uses the alliance as a vehicle to disseminate information to various parties in the network.
- A coordinator role (activating): a firm uses the alliance as a vehicle to bring together representatives of the different firms in the alliance network.
- A relationship broker or innovation role (mobilizing): a firm may use the alliance as a vehicle to initiate and facilitate new alliances between different parties.
- A network structuring agent role (synthesizing): a firm uses the alliance as a vehicle to monitor and influence the structure of relationships in the alliance network.

Step 7: alliance evaluation

By adopting an alliance network view, the performance metric system should be supplemented by metrics that capture alliance network processes and outcomes. Network processes can be captured through metrics that measure the extent to which information is exchanged within the alliance network. Examples could include the number and quality of referrals and contacts an alliance partner provides. In addition, alliance network metrics may capture outcomes associated with the direct relationship, such as the extent to which an alliance generates knowledge, and outcomes associated with indirect relationships, such as the extent to which third-party resources have been used. Metrics should also capture the network maintenance costs imposed on a firm. A comprehensive performance metric system enables a firm to evaluate and track alliance and network performance, and, if necessary, it can intervene immediately if expectations are not met.

Step 8: alliance termination

From an alliance network view, an alliance termination decision becomes more complex. Consistent with generic guidelines, the under-performance of a single alliance may prompt a premature termination. However, because the dissolution of a single alliance may adversely impact a firm's network positions, any decision to dissolve the alliance should perhaps be postponed until the negative repercussions are resolved. For example, a firm's alliance partner may be connected to a prominent network partner, and terminating the partnership may have serious negative knowledge and reputational spillovers. If a termination trajectory is continued, a firm must communicate this decision to other partners in the network in a timely manner. If exiting an alliance violates the relational norms established in an alliance network, a firm's relational capital may be seriously damaged unless it can provide an explanation.

Summary

A network view on alliances states that firms are embedded in a set of inter-firm linkages between multiple parties. The functions of an alliance network can potentially enhance a firm's competitive advantage by providing resource advantages through direct relationships and information advantages through indirect relationships. However, an alliance network also increases management complexity and coordination costs because it imposes (social) obligations, interdependencies and lock-in effects on a firm. Although we have questioned the extent to which a single firm can manage its alliance networks, such networks can enhance a firm's performance when its network position is aligned with its strategic intent. In general, a closure network enables a firm to realize its exploration objectives, whereas a structural hole network favours exploitation objectives. Furthermore, a firm can fulfil different network functions and roles to support an alliance network. As firms can restructure their network position by means of entering and exiting alliances, this chapter has also discussed how an alliance network view impacts the formation and management of single alliances.

CASE: IBM[1]

International Business Machines (IBM) is a multinational US technology and consulting firm. It manufactures and sells computer hardware and software and offers infrastructure, hosting and consulting services in areas ranging from mainframe computers to nanotechnology. Throughout its history, IBM has operated at the forefront of computing technology. In the 1930s, IBM's tabulating equipment enabled its customers to process unprecedented amounts of data. In the 1950s and 1960s, IBM developed self-learning programmes to play draughts (IBM 704). It also developed FORTRAN, a scientific programming language, and built a reservation system for American Airlines called SABRE. IBM's computing power even helped NASA track space flights and provided support to the NASA moon missions. In 1973, IBM developed the Universal Product Code, also known as the barcode, which can still be found on virtually every product in the world. The development of mainframe computing, which allowed businesses to upgrade their computing power and run more sophisticated applications, proved pivotal to IBM's performance. IBM was able to build a strong and virtually unchallenged competitive position, primarily due to its innovative capacity, its focus on process optimization and its control over the supply chain.

Due to its internal focus, IBM failed to recognize the change in the markets in the 1980s. One critical threat to IBM's position was the partnership between Sun and Hewlett Packard, which developed an alternative operating system called UNIX; this was the first real alternative to IBM's mainframe operating systems. The public started to become interested in personal computers, and, despite IBM's conviction that mainframes would remain the primary source of computing power for business and enterprises, the company entered the 'microcomputer' market in 1981. IBM did not enter the PC market using its standard vertically integrated approach; instead, it used external sources to provide components and operating software that fit IBM requirements. However, due to their open architecture, Intel and Microsoft were able to achieve market dominance. In addition, Intel and Microsoft both supplied new hardware manufacturers like Fujitsu and Compaq in the early 1990s. In addition, in response to increasing complexity, customers were looking for system integration, which was an indication that the IT market was about to change from being technology-oriented to service-oriented. IBM's once comfortable competitive position was fading rapidly. This required IBM to change its internal focus and adopt an external focus.

In 1991/1992, IBM forged a total of 55 alliances, 23 of which focused on further developing its operating system and another 23 of which focused on improving its microprocessor technology. In addition, 42 of the 55 alliances were related to research and development activities, whereas nine partnerships involved joint ventures and research consortia. An example was IBM's long-term alliance with Intel to develop microprocessors and its collaboration with Microsoft to cross-license Windows New Technology. IBM also developed software for third parties, including a flight reservation system and CAD/CAM applications. IBM was also engaged in ten alliances with Apple, primarily aimed at developing microprocessors and software architecture. These bilateral partnerships enabled IBM to advance its existing technologies. However, to remain competitive, IBM had to discover new markets and technologies.

From 1996 onwards, IBM engaged increasingly in multi-partner collaboration, the objectives of which changed from further development of existing technologies to development of new areas of expertise. For example, the pioneering work of the IBM Internet group was reinforced by its partnering strategies. An initial joint venture with parties such as Netscape and Oracle to develop internet browsing software was followed by the introduction of various internet-related products (such as ThinkPad), which were generated through IBM's alliance network. The relatively strong market position that IBM established in 2000 resulted from alliances in the telecom and ICT consultancy industries. By the end of the 1990s, IBM had transformed itself from a hardware manufacturer to a global service provider by changing its internal organizations.

During the first years of the new millennium, IBM further intensified its focus on software development and service provision. Whereas alliances with hardware manufacturers Motorola and Sun had enabled IBM to exploit existing technologies, partnerships with Microsoft, PeopleSoft and Citrix enabled IBM to explore a wide variety of software development projects. IBM also explored the telecommunications industry through network developers and phone manufacturers, such as Cisco and Nokia. IBM has also released code under various open-source licences, such as the platform-independent software framework Eclipse, the three-sentence International Components for Unicode (ICU) licence and the Java-based relational database management system (RDBMS) Apache Derby. By 2001, IBM's revenue stream from its global services outstripped its traditional revenue stream from hardware.

Following these successes, IBM continued its network-based service strategy. For example, IBM sold its hardware division to Lenovo in 2005 but forged a multi-year agreement whereby Lenovo is the leading provider of personal computers to IBM clients, and IBM provides financing and end-user support services for those PC solutions. Building on this success, the agreement was expanded into a global alliance to develop and deliver industry-specific, integrated technology solutions for enterprises, small- and mid-market businesses and individuals. In addition, virtually all of the latest-generation console gaming systems use microprocessors developed by IBM. The Xbox 360 contains a PowerPC tri-core processor, which IBM designed and produced in less than 24 months. In 2014, IBM sold its chip-manufacturing business to GlobalFoundries. GlobalFoundries will be the sole provider of IBM's server processor chips until 2025.

Currently, IBM is focusing on cloud computing, cognitive computing, Internet of Things, Big Data and other business domains. In these businesses, the reliance on a broad alliance network remains vital to provide breakthrough innovations. In 2022, IBM forged a partnership with Sierra Space on the Next Generation of Space Technology and Software Platforms. IBM's platform facilitates Sierra Space's efforts for automating business operations to achieve better performance, automate IT operations to deliver actionable insights, automate application and data flows to improve client experiences, automate networks to deliver zero-touch operations and generate deeper insights into threats, orchestration actions and automatic responses. IBM also teamed up with VMware, providing clients new ways to modernize hybrid cloud environments in regulated industries. Their intention is to develop and market jointly engineered IBM and VMware Cloud solutions. This will help clients in regulated industries such as financial services, healthcare and the public sector address the cost, complexity and risk of migrating and modernizing mission-critical workloads in the cloud. Building on a long-standing relationship, in 2022, IBM initiated one of the world's largest corporate transformation projects based on SAP® ERP software, designed to fuel the company's growth and better support its clients. The SAP arrangement will enable IBM to accelerate its business transformation in the cloud and fuel its future growth. Following the introduction of different partnerships in the field of hybrid cloud computing, IBM also has announced different partnerships in the field of Quantum computing. For instance, IBM joined forces with Vodafone in exploration quantum technology and quantumsafe cryptography, forged a partnership with Cleveland to start with the installation of IBM quantum system one, and started a partnership with Bosch on strategic quantum computing materials science engagement.

Questions

1   Explain how IBM's network and partnering strategy and position changed as a result of changes in its strategy (e.g. hardware, service, cloud).
2   Explain how, at different points in time, IBM's alliance network helped or hindered it in realizing its strategic objectives.

Note

1   Adapted from Dittrich *et al.* (2007). See also IBM (2007, 2011a, 2011b, 2022a, 2022b, 2022c, 2022d); TechScoop (2011).

20

BUSINESS ECOSYSTEMS

Customers are increasingly demanding complex, integrated solutions rather than standardized products and services delivered in homogenous volume (Williamson and De Meyer 2012). Internal knowledge and capabilities, even if supplemented with alliance relationships, are no longer sufficient to meet these demands. Effective companies develop business advantages by abandoning the vertically integrated firm as the preferred organizational structure, participating together with a variety of partners in innovation communities and actively engaging in processes of co-evolution and learning (Adner 2017; Iansiti and Levien 2004). Competitive advantage in the new world stems from knowing when and how to build profitable business ecosystems and from being able to steer them to lasting growth and continuous improvement. Successful firms act in new economic wholes from which new businesses, new non-profit organizations, new rules of competition and cooperation, and new complete industries emerge (Adner and Kapoor 2010; Moore 1998). Business ecosystems depict a dynamic co-evolving constellation of diverse players, uniting around a particular, occasionally social, challenge (Moore 1996). The key challenge for firms participating in an ecosystem is therefore to identify and develop opportunities to create value while ensuring that they appropriate a fair share in light of their contributions (Adner 2017). This chapter starts by exploring this business ecosystem challenge in some detail in the first section and then elaborates on types of business ecosystems and roles participating firms may fulfil (second section). Subsequently, insights are provided on activities associated with the management of business ecosystems (third section). The alliance development framework is then used to present specific managerial guidelines for firms participating in business ecosystems (fourth section). The chapter concludes with a summary and a case illustration.

The business ecosystem challenge

The concept of ecosystem as coined by Moore (1993) described the interdependence and co-evolutionary nature of business activities. Gaining prominence, the strategic management, marketing and innovation literature further conceptualized business ecosystems to include, for example, innovation, entrepreneurial, industry, platform and service ecosystems (Aarikka-Stenroos and Ritala 2017). Across these perspectives, a business ecosystem is defined as a

DOI: 10.4324/9781003222187-20

constellation of organizations that co-evolve their capabilities and roles, align their investments so as to create additional value and/or improve efficiency, and share a set of dependencies as they produce the goods, technologies and services customers need (Moore 1993; Williamson and De Meyer 2012; Adner 2017). A business ecosystem comprises all of the organizations, governmental entities and regulations with whom a business interacts, including customers, competitors and media (Cobben *et al.* 2022; Kelly 2015). These communities come together in a partially intentional, highly self-organizing manner, such that members provide contributions that fill out and complement those of the others (Moore 1998). Business ecosystems create, scale and serve markets and possess a collective ability to learn, adapt and innovate (Adner 2017) (see Table 20.1 for examples).

TABLE 20.1 Examples of business ecosystems

	Description
The Hague Security Delta	The Hague Security Delta (HSD) is the largest security cluster in Europe with strong bonds with the security clusters in the USA, Canada, Singapore and South Africa. In the HSD ecosystem, businesses, governments and knowledge institutions work together on innovations and knowledge in the field of cyber security, national and urban security, protection of critical infrastructure and forensics. They share a common goal: more business activity, more jobs and a secure world.
Drupal	A non-profit business ecosystem organized around a free and open-source content-management framework to design and build web applications (i.e. websites). Because of continued interaction and learning between Drupal users, Drupal developers and Drupal service providers, the Drupal community continuously contributes modules to the core web application framework. Such modules alter and extend the core capabilities, behaviour and appearance of a Drupal site. In January 2022, Drupal celebrated 20 years of ecosystem-driven innovation. One in 30 sites on the web is powered by Drupal. That means that most users of the web have experienced Drupal—even if they don't know it. Success at this scale is possible because the Drupal ecosystem exemplifies the values of open source and proves that innovation is sustained by healthy communities.
Cisco Hyperinnovation Living Labs	Cisco Hyperinnovation Living Labs (CHILL) is helping Cisco redefine how ideas come to fruition. CHILL takes a vertical perspective and creates an environment where a handful of Cisco's biggest (non-competing) customers come together, collaborate and build prototypes to drive rapid results without complicated intellectual property agreement. In 2019, they focused on 'Industry 4.0': the application of machine learning and IoT technology into the industrial revolution. CHILL focuses on five areas—informed decision making, autonomous automation, enhancing human senses, upskilling and safety, and supply chain. Since 2018, CHILL has led to two startups, seven patent applications, and more than 20 internal growth initiatives. Next, Cisco Systems Inc. has merged CHILL into its global innovation centre programme and together with thingQbators, they are housed in the Centoni's group of Cisco in 2020.

Sources: Cisco (2019, 2020); Drupal (2016, 2022); Furr *et al.* (2016); HSD (2016).

Several contextual drivers caused the rise of ecosystems in management practice (Gulati and Kletter 2005; Williamson and De Meyer 2012). First, to remain competitive, firms are forced to focus on fewer core activities to cope with rising investment costs and increased coordination costs due to complexity. Business ecosystems are specifically attuned to deliver such complex solutions. Second, the knowledge content of many business activities is rising, and knowledge management becomes increasingly central to competitive advantage. The model of an extensive ecosystem will become more critical to success as it allows knowledge and innovation to be rapidly generated and translated in opportunities for growth. Third, as companies face increasing uncertainty, ecosystems, where the partners can collaborate flexibly through loosely coordinated development and experimentation, can absorb this uncertainty more effectively than traditional hierarchies or subcontracting relationships, where deliverables have to be precisely specified in advance and structures are more difficult to reconfigure. Fourth, advanced information and communications technology (ICT) is becoming more powerful and cost-effective. This enables business ecosystems to economically marshal diverse resources and knowledge scattered across the globe. Technological advances and falling unit costs are enabling more complex and dispersed ecosystems to become economical.

Business ecosystems possess unique attributes—(1) core and complements, (2) accelerated innovation and (3) continuous co-evolution—that make it different from other relationship-based organizational arrangements. A business ecosystem is generally built around a core product/service and complements to increase value to the user (Adner 2017; Moore 1993). The core product/service constitutes the basis for providing value to end customers, enabling a firm to obtain economies of scale and large volume sizes. Complementary products and services ensure that the customer receives a 'total experience' (Moore 1998), an experience that cannot be created by the core product/service alone. A business ecosystem thus combines a core product with a network of specialist niches (Moore 2006) in which parties make unique contributions to enhance customer value and create critical mass (Adner 2017). To be effective, on the one hand the system's logic is based on an access-and-usage instead of transaction-and-ownership logic (Williamson and De Meyer 2012). On the other hand, firms reinvest profits from the core products and services in further additions to capabilities and in developing future generations of offers. Competition is not the sole driver of success; actors are incentivized by shared goals and values, as well as by the need to collaborate (Moore 1996). Thus, the key to a healthy ecosystem is a network of mutually rewarding relationships (Zahra and Nambisan 2012).

The imperative for businesses to learn and innovate has never been greater. Business ecosystems provide businesses with access to people and resources, whether they are located with suppliers, customers or competitors. Innovation is the result of connecting and integrating knowledge across different fields and industries and is therefore accelerated in the fluid, permeable, exchange-oriented and co-creative communities that are forged by ecosystems (Kelly 2015). Thus, innovation drives value creation, opens up niche markets and may trigger processes of creative destruction. Yet, key to a healthy business ecosystem is that parties within the system adopt these innovations and create critical mass to leverage resources and stimulate commoditization.

Business ecosystems are the product of a long and evolutionary process that defines the relationships among industry players (Zahra and Nambisan 2012). Specifically, akin to biological ecosystems, members of ecosystem communities co-evolve their capabilities (Moore 1998). Each member must improve and transform itself while paying attention to, and actively relating to, other members of the community. Companies thus must pay attention to their core business and ensure performance improvement but also ally with others to ensure the required complementarity in contributions and offerings. Connectivity across specialized capabilities enables actors to co-create solutions and new business models (Moore 1996). These continuous processes of co-evolution and renewal ensure the viability of an ecosystem but also may render an ecosystem obsolete as new business ecosystems emerge.

Despite the potential advantages of business ecosystems, among which are innovation, market access, renewal and profitability, the challenge for a firm participating in a business ecosystem is to identify and develop opportunities to create value while ensuring that they appropriate a fair share in light of their contributions. In dealing with this challenge strategically, parties should acknowledge that their performance (and that of other members) is dependent upon the health and performance of the whole ecosystem. Building strong and interdependent linkages among ecosystem members is thus critical but also may impose risks, including loss of proprietary knowledge, lock-in effects, competence trap and inertia (Moore 1996; Zahra and Nambisan 2012).

Before we proceed, we deem it important to discuss a critique on the business ecosystem concept. First, some ambiguity surrounds the concept of business ecosystems (Aarikka-Stenroos and Ritala 2017). Specifically, other concepts with a focus on interdependency and innovation have been coined, such as open innovation (Chesbrough 2003), triple helix (Etzkowitz and Leydesdorff 1995, 1997) and multi-partner alliances (see Chapter 17). These conceptions share characteristics with business ecosystems, however, the latter are different to the extent that the underlying theoretical logics—core-complement, accelerated innovation and co-evolution—depict an alternative way of organizing external relationships (see Table 20.2 for a comparison). Restated, viewing a corporate network as an ecosystem requires more than connecting the innovation funnel to the outside world, monetizing unused IP, or tapping into cash-strapped but idea-rich ventures (Van Dyck 2012).

Business ecosystem attributes

Business ecosystems are viable in competitive environments where customers demand complex integrated solutions, where knowledge is a key resource and tends to be dispersed among parties and locations, and where uncertainty demands flexibility in how value is created (Moore 1996). Their success depends on three critical attributes: (1) ecosystem members, (2) ecosystem types and (3) evolution.

Business ecosystem members

Within a business ecosystem, different types of members can be identified, including ecosystem leader (i.e. providing core technology), suppliers (i.e. offering technology enhancements), complementors (i.e. providing add-on offerings) and customers (i.e. procuring integrated solutions) (Adner and Kapoor 2010; Dedehayir et al. 2016; Iansiti and Levien 2004; Moore 1998). To establish and develop a business ecosystem, an ecosystem leader is indispensable. The ecosystem leader sets the roles of other members and coordinates the interactions between them. Also the leader orchestrates the resource flows, attracts new ecosystem members, orchestrates collective action, stimulates the discovery of complementarities and sets the rules for value creation and capturing (Dedehayir et al. 2016). Lead firms may take on the role of ecosystem frontrunner, either as keystone or dominant leader. An effective keystone leader ensures the survival and prosperity of the ecosystem, by improving the health of the

TABLE 20.2 What is a business ecosystem, and not?

Characteristics	Business ecosystem	Open innovation	Triple helix	Multi-partner alliance
Description	Constellation of parties, collaborating on a core product/ service and competing on complements	Commercialization of external and internal ideas by developing outside (and inside) paths to a market	Constellation of university, industry and government, organized in a meta-innovation system	Constellation of parties, collaborating in a partnership to attain private and common objectives
Organizational priority	Creation and exploitation of market opportunities	Creation and exploitation of innovations	Contribute and partake in an innovative region	Creation and exploitation of shared resources
Organizational boundaries	Open, member by choice	Open, partner by selection	Open, member by location	Open, partner by selection
Attributes				
Customer focus	To offer integrated, innovative solutions	To offer new products/services	No direct customer focus	To offer best products/services
Management	Self-organizing, or lead firm	High levels of internal control	Self-organizing, or lead partner	High levels of internal control
Financial	Optimize financial return through the ecosystem	Optimize financial return from innovation	Optimize financial return from presence in region	Optimize financial return from alliance relationship
Performance	Firm performance depends on eco-system's performance	Firm's performance depends on its innovative ability	Firm's performance depends on its ability to capture synergies	Firm's performance depends on its ability to appropriate value
Examples	Amazon, Microsoft, Google, Drupal	Proctor & Gamble, Hewlett Packard	Amsterdam Economic Board, Joint Venture Silicon Valley	Sky team, One World, SEMATECH, WiFi-alliance

Sources: Chesbrough (2003); Etzkowitz and Leydesdorff (1995); Moore (1998).

ecosystem as a whole, and creates and shares value with ecosystem members. That is, keystone leaders exercise a system-wide regulator role despite their small part in the ecosystem's mass. In contrast to this open approach, a dominant leader favours a closed approach and aims to integrate horizontally or vertically to exercise control, or even directly own, a large proportion of the ecosystem. It attempts to dominate all niche markets, for example, by leveraging and controlling access to the technological platform. Even if a dominant firm relinquishes direct control over the ecosystem, its main goal remains to extract as much value as possible. Niche players represent the bulk of the ecosystem and play a critical role in value creation and innovation. Niche players develop specialized capabilities that differentiate them from other members. They focus on a narrow domain and seek to improve their position while leveraging complementary resources.

Other roles in an ecosystem relate to value creators (Dedehayir *et al.* 2016). In their upstream position, suppliers for example coordinate the inflow of resources and deliver materials, technologies and services to other ecosystem members. Assemblers aggregate received resources and information received by others to deliver products and services that result from this assembly. Complementors extend the core offering of the ecosystem, and, as such, their offering needs to function in conjunction with the contributions made by other ecosystem members. However, a complementor's offering must meet customer demands as to generate value. The user (i.e. customer) contributes to the ecosystem by indicating a demand, which invokes the emergence of the ecosystem. In addition to value creation roles, other actors fulfil supportive and entrepreneurial roles. Universities and research organizations contribute knowledge necessitated to enhance the ecosystem's value proposition. Entrepreneurial firms contribute to an ecosystem's renewal ability; through investments, sponsors are critical to safeguard an ecosystems growth; and regulators enable or inhibit ecosystems by loosening or tightening regulatory restrictions. Though each ecosystem encompasses these roles, their involvement varies with ecosystem development. For example, an ecosystem leader may initially focus on building a collective understanding among initial members, a role which transitions into the formal coordination of resource flows. Users participate in ideation during the early stages, but as the ecosystem matures, their role shifts towards purchase and use.

In addition to different roles, within business ecosystems members may vary with regard to their organizational origin (Zahra and Nambisan 2012). Established firms may initiate the building of business ecosystems and take on a leadership role. Ecosystems offer established firms several advantages. The ecosystem enables them to offer integrated solutions to customers, reduces the need to own complementary resources and offers flexibility and access to a repository of knowledge and leverage to entry barriers (i.e. entrants have to duplicate the core product and compete against the whole system). Another way for an established firm to participate in an ecosystem is to launch a corporate-sponsored venture to probe or exploit opportunities. Although these corporate ventures can benefit from the resources, skills and connection of their parent corporations, they also face the dual challenge of building credibility with their parents and establishing market legitimacy. Though better funded than independent ventures, their ability to capture and exploit opportunities might be constrained by their parents' goals and controls placed on them. New ventures may also enter the ecosystem and occupy a niche position with a complementary service to a core product. These entrepreneurial ventures tend to be adept in reconfiguring their business models, and over time, they may develop into ecosystem leaders. Their advantage stems from their ability to learn quickly, share knowledge and anticipate rival moves and a lack of path-dependent constraints (e.g. sunk costs and prior relationships). Limitations may result from entrepreneurial overconfidence and optimism, first mover disadvantages and organizational constraints, such as a lack of time and funding.

Business ecosystem types

Value-creating business ecosystems exhibit strong linkages between members of the ecosystem. These relationships develop because of specialization in different skill areas, historical ties among members and personal relationships among people working in different parts of the ecosystem (Zahra and Nambisan 2012). The long-term success of an ecosystem hinges on understanding, managing and effectively and creatively exploiting these linkages. Members thus work on building relationships, cultivating them and recognizing their importance in transforming the ecosystem with regards to introducing new business models and capturing market opportunities. Although linkages constitute the cornerstone of any business ecosystem, different types of business ecosystems exist with distinct relational attributes, advantages and disadvantages: (1) business ecosystem, (2) innovation ecosystem, (3) entrepreneurial ecosystem, (4) platform ecosystem and (5) service ecosystem (Aarikka-Stenroos and Ritala 2017; Cobben *et al.* 2022).

The business ecosystem model involves a group of firms coming together to exploit a market opportunity based on an explicit (product/service) architecture that is defined by a dominant firm, or the keystone leader (Adner 2017). The ecosystem leader, who often holds proprietary rights of the technology, provides strong leadership by envisioning and clarifying the organizational architecture, which offers a basis for structuring the activities of members. For example, ICT companies such as Microsoft, Intel and IBM use technology to build and maintain an orchestra-model ecosystem (Zahra and Nambisan 2012). New entrants and corporate ventures create new products and services that complement the core technology or become part of an integral solution when combined with the core product or service. The orchestra model thrives if the leader considers benefits of all ecosystem members before making decisions and makes sure that members operate within a fair playing field; an equal opportunity to become profitable. The primary challenge for the keystone leader is to maintain the relevance of its organizational architecture. Changing customer preferences, competitor moves and technological developments may cause the core product or service to become obsolete. The keystone leader needs to adjust, adapt and, if necessary, reinvent its offering. Such modifications tend to be inhibited by the leader's inability to change as it may demand that they challenge competences they have developed over the years. To enable this, some leaders may use corporate ventures to explore new technological frontiers and help them build new competences, while preserving existing ones.

In the innovation ecosystem, a dominant firm shops for innovation in a 'global bazaar' of new ideas, products and technologies (Zahra and Nambisan 2012). In pursuit of (technological) innovation, the ecosystem leader uses its proprietary infrastructure to build on these ideas and commercialize them (Gomes *et al.* 2018). Regardless of the source of ideas, the dominant company offers its infrastructure, including design capabilities, brands, capital and distribution channels, for developing and getting innovative products/services to market. It implies that, for example, a keystone leader redefines the openness of its organization, and innovation ecosystems typically comprise of societal actors as well as public organizations to support innovation (Aarikka-Stenroos and Ritala 2017). The more closed, the more difficult to absorb and exploit external ideas and get them to market quickly. The more open may require a cultural change as well as a need to adopt a long-term perspective in sharing the (innovation) profits with partners. To accomplish commercialization objectives, members need to openly exchange proprietary information at the risk of losing valuable knowledge. Corporate ventures may be used to accomplish these goals as it enables established firms to sidestep bureaucracy and corporate routines. In contract, new ventures, or entrepreneurial firms, may focus on the front-end innovation of keystone or dominant leading members. The identification of knowledge areas may be limiting to a certain extent but can enhance the probability that innovative ideas are embraced by the leader firm.

In the entrepreneurial ecosystem, members seek to improve and exploit an (existing) innovation architecture or technological platform by developing and contributing modifications, and make these available in integrated solutions to customers (Aarikka-Stenroos and Ritala 2017). Independent new ventures function as the creative engine, albeit within the boundaries of the existing innovative architecture offered by the leading firms. Soliciting the support of investors and governments, for example, the aim is to explore alternative applications for an existing product in new markets, often accompanied by some level of knowledge creation. This implies not only creating unique value-added modifications of the product/platform but also generating new business models to capture value from these efforts. For established (leading) firms, orchestrating an entrepreneurial ecosystem implies that they need to develop and provide access to tools and capabilities, enabling other members to make cost-effective modifications to the end of attracting a wider range of partners. It also means that these firms need to adopt a long-term perspective as new ventures may capture some of the rewards. This is because these new ventures enhance value to the firm's customers, increase the life cycle of existing products and/or widen the reach of product/technologies to new markets.

In the platform ecosystem, members coalesce around a technological platform—owned by a focal organization—connecting multiple sides of markets together (Aarikka-Stenroos and Ritala 2017). Seeking to attain economies of scale and network effects, the shape of a platform ecosystem is predominantly oriented towards making connections between suppliers and complementary firms in an integrator business model (see also Box 26.1). Traditional industry leaders embrace platform ecosystems, and platforms can be found in social media (e.g. TikTok), entertainment (e.g. Netflix) and telecom (e.g. Wifi) industries, for example. The success of platform ecosystems hinges in a large part on the number and quality of ecosystem members involved as external partners offer the platform credibility. Reputable partners mitigate concerns regarding data ownership, coopetition, switching costs and security and interoperability, but they are also critical in attracting new customers by developing innovative (complementary) value propositions (Khanagha 2021). Establishing and advancing a platform ecosystem requires a balance between openness and control. Openness allows for new partners to become involved in the platform and reinforce its value proposition through complementary products and services. Control seeks to harness these second-movers, who may seek to take advantage, capturing value or creating new business models (rendering the old one obsolete).

Service ecosystems are oriented towards solution adoption (Zhang et al. 2021). With a service ecosystem, members seek to create and capture value through asset optimization around the services offered and enhance customer experience. Airline carriers are experimenting with partnerships to create new joint services, banks are contracting with data-processing firms to offer new financial services and mobile communications firms and entertainment companies are teaming-up to offer electronic news services. Service ecosystems bring additional complexity regarding co-branding (i.e. customer brand perceptions), performance evaluation (i.e. evaluating intangible services) and mutual interdependence (i.e. matching service quality). Extending beyond co-branding and co-sharing of assets, service ecosystems entail a constellation of service offerings, where the multiple actors' service systems develop many-to-many relationships, and customers increasingly co-create value through the combination of service offerings from multiple firms (Vink et al. 2021). By extending and diversifying the services offered in a well-integrated seamless experience, the delivery of a combined service by a service integrator supposes tight collaborative activities between service partners and necessitates a lead company to align tasks and contributions derived from the cooperation agreements. Within service ecosystems, to appropriate value, customers interact with service providers at different stages of the service process. Customer involvement is critical as the achievement of a critical mass of interacting actors determines the value of the network. Lead

TABLE 20.3 Ecosystem types

Elements	Main goal	Main actors	Orchestration	Value creation and capture
Business ecosystem	Competitive advantage	Focal firm, suppliers, complementors	Focal firm orchestrator	Focus on firm-level value capture
Innovation ecosystem	Innovation	Technology leader, government	Focal firm orchestrator	Focus on firm-level value creation and capture
Entrepreneurial ecosystem	Growth	New ventures, investors	Collective orchestration	Focus on ecosystem value creation
Platform ecosystem	Technological advantage	Technology leader	Focal firm orchestrator	Focus on ecosystem value creation
Service ecosystem	Integrative service offering	Service provider	Collective orchestration	Focus on ecosystem value creation

Sources: Aarikka-Stenroos and Ritala (2017); Cobben *et al.* (2022).

service firms, such as platform owners, serve as typical 'orchestrators' in that they create the necessary organizational systems and conditions for resource integration among other actors to take place (Fu *et al.* 2017).

A business ecosystem could be considered an overarching concept for distinct types of interdependent and co-evolving systems of actors, technologies and institutions (Aarikka-Stenroos and Ritala 2017), among which include innovation, platform, entrepreneurial and service ecosystems. More recently, however, other manifestations of business ecosystems emerged (Van Dyck 2012). For example, science ecosystems are geared towards the front-end of the innovation-conversion cycle (i.e. idea generation). In such an ecosystem, value is created and captured by building critical mass when pushing the scientific frontier in an applied field. The shift towards better disease understanding after the cracking of the human genome made ecosystems a viable alternative in the pharmaceutical industry. Pharmaceutical firms use ecosystems, comprised of universities, biotech and rivals, to develop and market personalized medicine approaches in such a manner that they obtain sufficient critical mass to make it profitable. Business ecosystems tend to become increasingly omnipresent across industries, typically combining elements of the various ecosystems types. For example, firms like Apple and Amazon take on leading roles in business ecosystems to innovate and market their devices. Lego, however, the Danish plastic building blocks company, provides a perfect example of a merged, service- and technology-based ecosystem with its use of customer crowdsourcing but also with its toy robotics platforms developed with the help of MIT. But, even though managing a retail or banking ecosystem is different from managing an Intel semiconductor or Pfizer's pharmaceutical ecosystem, generic management implications can be identified.

Business ecosystem dynamics

The challenge to deliver more complex solutions to customers while simultaneously limiting capital expenditures and costs has extended beyond high-tech industries into other industries, promoting the rise of business ecosystems (Tjemkes 2021). Activating, catalyzing, guiding and promoting collaboration within ecosystems enable ecosystem members to innovate, reconfigure and create added value to the customer base. As such, business ecosystems evolve, and transformation stems from the internal and external environment, materializing through processes of lifecycle stages, teleological purpose, dialectical tensions and co-evolution, thereby showing an intricate interaction among external, organizational and strategic stimuli that leads to business ecosystem dynamics.

Conceiving ecosystem evolution to follow a stylized lifecycle, ecosystems progress through four phases—birth, expansion, leadership and self-renewal (or death) (Moore 1993). In Stage 1 (birth), an ecosystem leader establishes a value chain for creating value for customers; in Stage 2 (expansion), emerging business models capture value for a larger number of customers. Members are able to scale up. In Stage 3 (authority), ecosystem leaders set the future direction to encourage partners to work together and secure stability within the ecosystem. In Stage 4 (renewal), via learning and adaptation, a new business ecosystem emerges from the incumbent business community by bringing new ideas and innovations. Alternatively, in the absence of self-renewal, the business ecosystem dissolves. Drawing on a teleological view, Adner (2017) proposed an ecosystem-as-structure approach, stipulating that an ecosystem represents an 'alignment structure of the multilateral set of partners that need to interact in order for a focal value proposition to materialize' (p. 40). That is, different actors may have different end states and end goals in mind and initiate action to attain these goals. A dialectical view stipulates ecosystems change as conflicts emerge between opposing forces (thesis and antithesis) that collide to produce a new organizational form (synthesis) (de Rond and Bouchikhi 2004). For example, Beltagui et al. (2020) investigated a digital innovation ecosystem and indicated that ecosystem members cooperate to develop and deliver a joint value proposition; within the ecosystem, however, members compete for market niches, and the ecosystem as a whole competes with rival ecosystems, offering a similar value proposition to end-customers. A key feature of business ecosystem conceptualizations is that they are, by nature, co-evolutionary (Moore 1996): ecosystems engage in continuous and interrelated self-renewal processes in an attempt to seek and maintain fit. Beltagui et al. (2020) also indicated, for example, that within digital innovation ecosystems, internal disruption, resulting from competition for niches within an ecosystem, and external disruption, introduced by an actor external to an ecosystem, invoke learning and adaptation processes.

Managing business ecosystems

According to Moore (1998), strong business ecosystems enact a virtuous cycle of investment and return in which improvements target the ecosystem's core and the community of allies. This demands that ecosystem members couple strategic thinking with entrepreneurial insight to create, shape, navigate and exploit business ecosystems (Dedehayir et al. 2016; Zahra and Nambisan 2012). Strong ecosystem members are able to simultaneously create and discover opportunities while creatively and profitably exploiting other opportunities. As such they are able to collaborate with other members, while competing with them when required (Kapoor and Lee 2013). Although the majority of business ecosystem studies take the perspective of an ecosystem leader (e.g. Moore 1998; Williamson and De Meyer 2012), the managerial insights presented may apply to all parties involved in the ecosystem; the extent, however, may vary with the type of ecosystem and the position a firm occupies. Nevertheless, once a company's senior management has adopted the business ecosystem perspective, it may deploy six mechanisms by which they may accomplish their objectives and build a profitable

TABLE 20.4 Business ecosystem management

Key to advantage	Focus	Implementation
Pinpoint added value	Enhance customer value by improving functionality, offering innovative solutions and offering higher levels of customization.	By identifying primary sources of value creation, ecosystem members are able to target the required complementarities and hence the right partners.
Structuring partner roles	Organize ecosystem members' roles to achieve benefits of specialization, provide focus and promote cooperation over competition.	By differentiating roles, ecosystem members (leaders and niche) can keep the burden of partner interaction to manageable levels.
Stimulate co-investments	Enables ecosystem members to amplify the impact of their investments and create potential for increasing returns to scale.	By making co-investments, members together develop value propositions, reduce uncertainty and encourage (new) members to participate.
Reduce transaction costs	Systemize interactions between parties as to reduce (unnecessary) bargaining, coordinating and monitoring costs.	By granting access to knowledge, resources and tools, ecosystem members establish flexible arrangements with a high degree of transparency.
Enable flexibility and co-learning	Enable a mix of formal and informal knowledge sharing to flexibly promote knowledge creation.	By stimulating continuous interaction and learning between ecosystem members, they and the system as a whole become adaptive and resilient.
Engineer value capture mechanisms	Creatively engineer value capture mechanisms to monetize members' contributions, incentivize them and counter free riding.	By leveraging proprietary knowledge, reaping economies of scale and acquiring access to new markets, members optimize their value.

Source: Adapted from Adner (2017); Williamson and De Meyer (2012).

business model (Williamson and De Meyer 2012): (1) pinpoint added value, (2) partner roles, (3) co-investments, (4) transaction costs, (5) flexibility and co-learning and (6) value capture mechanisms (see Table 20.4).

The first step towards creating a sustainable business ecosystem is to pinpoint why the ecosystem will create added value to the customer. To have parties involved in an ecosystem, it is prerequisite that the system is attractive to them as well as to customers (Khademi 2020). Customers' willingness to pay depends on the recognition of incremental value from the ecosystem over and above that offered by alternatives. A large and diverse ecosystem can create additional value for the customer by improving functionality, promoting faster innovation or enabling higher levels of customization. This analysis enables new and participating (lead) firms to assess resource complementarities and opportunities for co-learning.

To deliver customer value, the activities of parties with complementary capabilities need to be aligned in a business ecosystem (Kapoor and Lee 2013). The lead firm (or parties together) needs to create a structure and incentives for attracting partners and managing overlap and possible conflicts between them. Such a structure may entail different roles for different parties (Moore 1996; Williamson and De Meyer 2012). If an ecosystem has a lead firm (e.g. innovation and platform), it is the responsibility of this firm to establish a core capability that can become the basis for providing real value to end customers. It needs to seek and align a combination of players and contributions. The leader must invest in and generate returns from an ever-expanding community of allies. The ecosystem leader must rediscover and reinforce his/her own strongholds and strive to establish business ecosystems around them. In addition to a leader role, parties may fulfil the role of knowledge source and provide, for example, access to technology, competences and customers. They could act as market maker and may help to gain acceptance of complementary products and services in the market by pursuing sales of their own products and services. Parties may act as niche players who enhance customer value by offering specialist products and services. For example, the set of niches composing the ecosystem needs to be complete; all of the necessary tasks to deliver value need to be covered. Structuring an ecosystem and partner roles is an ambitious task, but if successful, the designed architecture is likely to attract valuable parties (Adner 2017). Moreover, a well-designed ecosystem achieves the benefits of specialization and focus of individual partners and promises cooperation over competition.

Partners in an ecosystem will only co-invest if they see the prospect of building a profitable business. Clear value proposition will invite partners to invest, implying that (lead) firms identify profitable market (niches) and reduce uncertainty. In a healthy ecosystem, (lead) firms refrain from encroaching on profitable niches as such action reduces parties' propensities to investment. In turn, (lead) firms proactively stimulate joint investments to generate and capture market opportunities. To reduce uncertainty, parties may work with a roadmap for innovation, enabling them to make sense of unforeseen events and make investments to strengthen the ecosystem. This is, for example, particularly salient in fast-moving industries with rapidly changing technologies.

One disadvantage of an ecosystem, compared to a vertically integrated firm, is the relatively high transaction costs that result from having a multitude of relationships. If transaction costs are not managed, they can quickly outweigh the customer value generated by the ecosystem. To systematize interactions between partners, a (lead) firm may develop and share a set of tools, protocols and contracts. Alternatively, firms may invest in relational governance. The mechanisms used depend on the nature of the interdependencies and risks to which partners are exposed. For example, contracts may be used in situations of asymmetric dependence, but co-branding (i.e. reputational enforcement) is an informal mechanism. In general, within an ecosystem, flexible arrangement and transparency are key to create a healthy system. Whereas flexibility is required to deal with contingencies and unforeseen events, transparency reduces risks associated with moral hazard (e.g. free riding or renegotiation). If well managed, parties' behaviours will generate a self-reinforcing cycle of collaboration and trust, reducing transaction costs.

Few ecosystems can expect to be static in terms of their structure, partner roles and relationships. An inherent advantage of an ecosystem, compared to single organizations, is the potential for dynamic re-configuration and accelerated learning. Flexibility and learning are a prerequisite for healthy business ecosystems because efforts to align and organize a diversity of partners with different backgrounds and experiences are thwarted by inflexible structures. Rather, in an ecosystem, the objective is to design an architecture that can be changed and adapted in response to development in the market and technological environment. A healthy ecosystem, therefore, is a highly malleable structure combined with specifications with regards to roles, contributions and performance. One way to enable continued learning and interaction is through a tier-system in which parties obtain different privileges (i.e. analogous to a club membership). For example, startup ventures are loosely coupled, whereas founders make up the core of the ecosystem. This mixture of formal and informal knowledge sharing and creation based on continuous interaction within formal and informal relationship arrangements invokes flexibility and learning.

A critical issue in business ecosystems pertains to the mechanism deployed to share value between the parties involved. Amid the hype around 'openness', one might forget that a healthy business ecosystem must be contributing to a firm's performance. Even if a firm is the lead company controlling the architecture (e.g. management of intellectual property), it is not a sufficient guarantee that it will capture sufficient value. One mechanism to capture value entails that a firm contributes a unique component or activity to the ecosystem, one that cannot be easily replaced with an alternative (or procured through an open market, or imitated). The firm needs to engineer a mechanism to monetize the value of this contribution, which may include licence fees, royalties, expanded margins or profits on higher sales volumes. Though transparency fosters a healthy ecosystem, it may impede a firm's ability to maximize value capture. Information asymmetry constitutes a source of power and competitive advantage, particularly in knowledge-intensive businesses. At the same time, withholding critical information may undermine the ecosystem's overall profit pool. A useful principle to achieve the right balance is to share information on the interfaces but keep the inner workings of your contribution proprietary and non-transparent.

To conclude, although the mechanisms discussed apply to all firms, ecosystem-savvy incumbents have an advantage over new entrants and are likely to remain in power (Moore 1998). This is because members of the ecosystem are reluctant to switch to new (leader) entrants, particularly if the ecosystem is creating value. The uncertainty that comes with a new entrant raises the question of whether it will equate volumes, offer protection, resolve disputes and build a thriving ecosystem. Sustainable ecosystems demand a certain degree of ecosystem-entrenched incumbents (Moore 1998), which explains (in part) why some business ecosystems have failed to establish themselves. If members do not see an architectural alliance as the only way to obtain and sustain a competitive advantage, business ecosystems are likely to be unable to bring value to large numbers of customers.

Business ecosystems: decision-making steps

Firms participating in business ecosystems are confronted with tension between creating and capturing value. Excessive value appropriation undermines collective value creation as well as a partner firm's individual ability to appropriate their fair share of the value. In order to provide guidelines for successfully leading or participating in business ecosystems, the next section elaborates on specific decisions for business ecosystems at each stage of the alliance development framework (see Figure 20.1).

Step 1: alliance strategy formulation

The decision to establish an alliance is not only influenced by firm-specific imperatives, such as resources and strategic opportunities, but also how a firm is, or desires to be, involved in a business ecosystem. In addition to generic guidelines on alliance strategizing, a governance mode decision should also incorporate decisions about the role the firm aspires to in the business ecosystem (i.e. lead firm or niche player), the extent to which the firm possesses the required resources (e.g. technological leadership or complement technologies) and its disposition towards other ecosystem members (e.g. collaborative or competitive). As such, before partaking in a (new) business ecosystem, a firm needs to make a comprehensive analysis of the

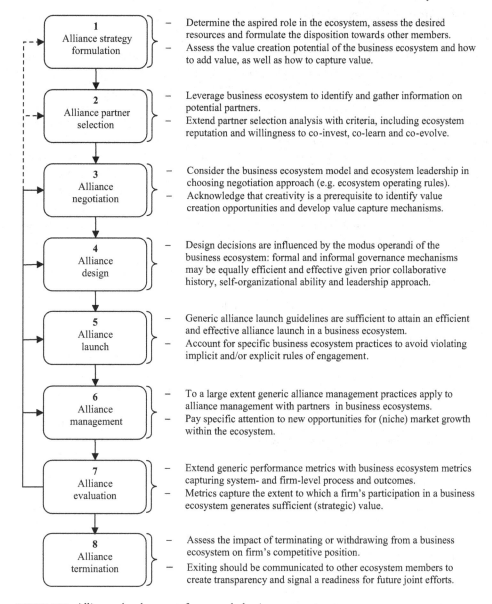

1 Alliance strategy formulation	– Determine the aspired role in the ecosystem, assess the desired resources and formulate the disposition towards other members. – Assess the value creation potential of the business ecosystem and how to add value, as well as how to capture value.
2 Alliance partner selection	– Leverage business ecosystem to identify and gather information on potential partners. – Extend partner selection analysis with criteria, including ecosystem reputation and willingness to co-invest, co-learn and co-evolve.
3 Alliance negotiation	– Consider the business ecosystem model and ecosystem leadership in choosing negotiation approach (e.g. ecosystem operating rules). – Acknowledge that creativity is a prerequisite to identify value creation opportunities and develop value capture mechanisms.
4 Alliance design	– Design decisions are influenced by the modus operandi of the business ecosystem: formal and informal governance mechanisms may be equally efficient and effective given prior collaborative history, self-organizational ability and leadership approach.
5 Alliance launch	– Generic alliance launch guidelines are sufficient to attain an efficient and effective alliance launch in a business ecosystem. – Account for specific business ecosystem practices to avoid violating implicit and/or explicit rules of engagement.
6 Alliance management	– To a large extent generic alliance management practices apply to alliance management with partners in business ecosystems. – Pay specific attention to new opportunities for (niche) market growth within the ecosystem.
7 Alliance evaluation	– Extend generic performance metrics with business ecosystem metrics capturing system- and firm-level process and outcomes. – Metrics capture the extent to which a firm's participation in a business ecosystem generates sufficient (strategic) value.
8 Alliance termination	– Assess the impact of terminating or withdrawing from a business ecosystem on firm's competitive position. – Exiting should be communicated to other ecosystem members to create transparency and signal a readiness for future joint efforts.

FIGURE 20.1 Alliance development framework: business ecosystems

value-creation potential of the system and how it may contribute, as well as how the firm will appropriate value from the ecosystem to legitimize its participation. Based on the results of these assessments, a firm may decide to abandon a business ecosystem strategy, establish a new business ecosystem, participate in an existing business ecosystem or enhance or change their role/position in their existing business ecosystem. As part of the strategy, firms may also decide to participate in multiple business ecosystems in various stages of ecosystem development. For example, companies such as Google, Microsoft and IBM develop and invest in different business ecosystems simultaneously.

Step 2: alliance partner selection

Once the decision has been made to participate in a business ecosystem, firms need to assess which partners are likely candidates to forge alliance relationships. Partner selection depends on the role a firm aspires to play in the system. For example, a niche player may need to establish a formal relationship with a keystone leader, who owns proprietary rights of a technological platform. For example, a game developer, representing a niche player, needs to choose between different technological systems, including Xbox, PlayStation or Nintendo. Similarly, leading firms need to select partners that complement their core offer. As such, a resource analysis focusing on complementarities is critical, as well as a competitor analysis with a focus on interdependencies between ecosystem members. Critical questions guiding partner selection may include the following: to what extent does a potential partner add value to the business ecosystem? To what extent is a potential partner embedded in other (rival) business ecosystems? To what extent is a potential partner likely to disrupt, positively or negatively, the modus operandi of the business ecosystem?

Step 3: alliance negotiation

The manner in which alliance negotiations unfold, for example, formalized or informal, largely depends on the business ecosystem model. In a tightly controlled ecosystem with a dominant leader, negotiation bandwidth tends to be limited and the outcome pre-determined (e.g. if you are an Apple IOS platform application developer). In contrast, in a more flexibly coordinated ecosystem with a keystone leader, alternative opportunities to create and capture value could become part of the negotiation agenda (e.g. if you are an Amazon Fire platform application developer). In setting the negotiation agenda, it is also important to acknowledge that, as business ecosystems are complex organizational arrangements, creativity is a prerequisite to identify value-creation opportunities and develop value-capture mechanisms.

Step 4: alliance design

Generic alliance design guidelines take an 'alliance as stand-alone arrangement' view, which means that they neglect the influence of the business ecosystem on design decisions. In a business ecosystem, the product and service requirements of the customer must be well understood by all members of the ecosystem. This understanding guarantees the collaboration of members towards common objectives, and, if applicable, an ecosystem leader assumes a central position by securing and organizing the cooperation of (potential) members, which collectively deliver value to the customer. In addition, it is also important for members to protect the new innovation idea from competitors, while at the same time forging strong ties with lead customers and important channels of delivery. To accomplish these objectives, business ecosystems tend to use standardized alliance structures, primarily to economize on transaction costs, enact flexibility and accommodate a need for co-learning and co-evolution. As such, equity-based arrangements are less likely to be adopted as non-equity-based arrangements fit better with these requirements. As with alliance networks (see Chapter 19), relational capital between ecosystem members promotes collaborative behaviour and increases members' awareness that free riding may not only damage bilateral alliance relationships but also the whole ecosystem. For example, as business ecosystem members meet during informal encounters, including conferences, dinners and social events, and during more formal meetings to set agendas, develop innovation roadmaps and organize lobby activities, relational capital is likely to be created. Such activities create behavioural norms and stimulate co-learning as relational capital mitigates the threat of unwanted knowledge appropriation and allows parties to collaborate with different ecosystem members.

Step 5: alliance launch

When taking a business ecosystem view, general alliance launch guidelines are sufficient to attain an efficient and effective alliance launch. However, alliance launch managers should be aware of two points. First, the alliance launch team should pay attention to specific business ecosystem practices that have been built prior to the firm entering. Formal and relational sanctions may befall the firm if they have violated the implicit and explicit rules of engagement. For example, it is imperative for an ecosystem entrant (or creator) to obtain an understanding of how peers in the ecosystem defined what customers want, what the value is of a proposed product or service and how the offer is best delivered. Short-term success often goes to those members who best understand customer requirements. Second, if new members get involved in the ecosystem and forge an alliance relationship with a firm, alliance launch managers should pay specific attention to the development of a common view, promote collective sense making and facilitate the learning process. This means they are not only learning from the individual firm but also from and about the alliance and the whole business ecosystem. To accomplish these two tasks, it is critical alliance launch managers act as a boundary spanner, set up liaisons with other members and work with them to define and fine-tune the firm's value proposition.

Step 6: alliance management

Alliance management practices in business ecosystems are to a large extent similar to practices adopted in bilateral alliance arrangements, which include building relational capital, stimulating learning, dealing with tensions and conflicts and enacting change to enhance performance. Specifically, management activities may focus on maintaining alignment between alliance partners but also with the ecosystem. Also, management should organize frequent meetings to discuss the future of the alliance, within the context of the ecosystem, to enhance the commitment of the partners (and other ecosystem members). Specific attention should be given to changing conditions that may alter a firm's bargaining power in the alliance; it is critical to maintain strong bargaining power in relation to the partner but also other players in the ecosystem, including key customers and valued suppliers. In addition, to maintain the viability of the ecosystem, and thus alliance relationships, alliance management should continuously explore new territories of ecosystem growth. It is possible that rival firms, part of competing ecosystems, seek to capture similar market opportunities. These battles are more likely to be won by a given ecosystem if members maintain strong alliance relationships and apply their expertise in complementary resources.

Step 7: alliance evaluation

By adopting a business ecosystem perspective, the generic performance metric system should be supplemented with metrics that capture system- and firm-level business ecosystem process and outcomes. System-level measures pertain to the viability and health of the system (e.g. number of product offers), the resilience and robustness of the system (e.g. threat of competitive ecosystems), the adaptability of the system (e.g. leader change initiatives) and, for example, the extent to which the business ecosystem is able to renew itself and to generate (niche) spin-offs. Firm-level metrics for example capture the extent to which membership reduces transaction costs (e.g. selection, negotiation, monitoring), offers new opportunities for value creation (e.g. new markets) and enables access to knowledge (e.g. technology). These firm-level metrics together should provide a firm insight into the extent to which its participation in an ecosystem generates sufficient (strategic) value to continue without changes, to intervene or to withdraw from the ecosystem. Together, these business ecosystem metrics enable a firm to capture emerging threats from new ecosystems and innovations, or upheavals in the ecosystem's environment, such as those pertaining to government regulations and business chances, which create opportunities for new ecosystems to emerge. It also implies that in addition to an alliance score card (i.e. performance system), a firm may develop a business ecosystem dashboard, which comprises metrics that support business ecosystem decision making and strategy. For example, such a dashboard may provide insight into ecosystem spin-offs, renewal or death. With regard to alliance evaluation outcomes, there are three possible responses: continuation with, renewal of or withdrawal from the alliance.

Step 8: alliance termination

From a business ecosystem perspective, an alliance termination decision is more multifaceted when compared to the decision to dissolve a bilateral alliance relationship. Before finalizing a termination decision, it is critical to assess the impact of this decision on the firm's competitive position. This is because a premature decision to dissolve an alliance relationship may have unforeseen and adverse consequences. For example, a premature termination of an alliance may also mean withdrawal from the business ecosystem. This could imply that access to valuable resources is blocked, a firm is not able to capture the benefits from innovation, and it may negatively alter customer perceptions. Any decision to withdraw from the business ecosystem should perhaps be postponed until the negative repercussions are resolved. In the case of a formal exit, the decision should be communicated to other ecosystem members to create transparency and openness. It also acts as a signal that the firm is reliable and ready for future (business ecosystem) endeavours.

Summary

Vibrant business ecosystems depict a new form of organizing economic activities and constitute a powerful, and according to some the only, source of competitive advantage. The challenge to deliver more complex solutions to customers while simultaneously limiting capital expenditures and costs has extended beyond hi-tech industries into other industries. Activating, catalyzing, guiding and promoting partners in an ecosystem will enable the system to innovate, reconfigure and create added value to the customer base. Despite the advantages, a business ecosystem is not always the optimal and most viable strategy. Firms should avoid the inclination to hop on the bandwagon and participate or lead ecosystems without value potential. Nevertheless, a company in pursuit of value may attain interests in multiple business ecosystems, which means it should coordinate its cross-ecosystem activities. Two challenges are awareness and identification of inter-ecosystem synergies and decisiveness to organize a timely entry or exit from a business ecosystem.

CASE: APPLE VS AMAZON[1]

Since the industrial era, companies that have had the best assets have usually been the most competitive. However, this situation has changed over the last decade. In today's competitive environment, companies are constantly looking for new sources of customer value. Organizations are often unable to generate this value on their own and therefore have to rely on an ecosystem of organizations that helps and supports them in finding this new value. The ability to collaborate with an increasing number of varying stakeholders, which are more and more loosely connected to the company, is essential in meeting ever-changing customer demands. This is especially true in the hi-tech industry, but it is notable how two giants are choosing very different strategies.

Apple Computer Inc. (Apple) was founded in 1976 by Steven Jobs and Steve Wozniak. For almost three decades, Apple focused on the design and manufacturing of personal computers, including revolutionary models like the Apple II, which institutionalized the home computer market; the Macintosh, which revolutionized the DTP market; and the Power Mac. In the mid-1990s, Apple was struggling because of an ill-controlled product portfolio that enabled other hardware manufacturers to use Apple Operating Systems, products that were too expensive and competition that was not sitting still. The introduction of Microsoft's Windows95 further reduced Apple's competitive advantage. In 1997, Apple bought NeXT, the company Steve Jobs had founded in 1985 after he was forced to leave Apple. Steve Jobs regained control of Apple and ended the possibility of Apple clones; Apple itself introduced the translucent plastic iMac in 1998. This marked the turnaround of the company. In 2001, Apple introduced iTunes and the iPod. With iTunes, Apple created a media management system that acted as a front layer for devices that were introduced in the following months and years. In 2001, Apple shocked the world with the introduction of the first iPod. Through the iPod, users could listen to music and later also videos using a cleverly designed device. In 2007, Apple introduced the iPhone, which revolutionized the smart-phone industry. The year 2010 saw the release of the iPad, which basically defined the tablet market. Apple knew that it required an ecosystem approach to differentiate itself from a traditional appliance manufacturer.

With the introduction of the iPhone in 2007, Apple allowed third-party software developers to develop software for Apple devices. Third-party developers could download a software development kit for free to develop applications for the iPod and iPhone and later the iPad. Publishing the applications in the App Store is only possible after paying an Apple Developer Connection membership fee; then the apps go 'on sale' in the App Store. The software developer is free to set a price for the app, but Apple receives a 30 per cent fee. The App Store was launched in 2008, which fuelled the success of the iPhone and iPod. The App Store set the standard in the smart-phone market, which has been followed by Google's Play Store and Microsoft's Windows App store. In the business ecosystem that Apple has created, Apple is the dominant player. It holds firm control over its ecosystem. For one thing, Apple has to first sell its devices, with high margins, before publishers in the App Store can sell their products. This latency in earning models requires publishers to be fully dependent on the ability of Apple to develop and market an attractive platform. Next, Apple has the final authority to decide what it will and will not publish on the App Store. In 2022, Apple and Mercedes-Benz announced that Apple Music's highly acclaimed Spatial Audio with support for Dolby Atmos is now available as a native experience in Mercedes-Benz vehicles for the first time, delivering on a shared commitment to provide customers worldwide with the very best music experience. Also in 2022, Apple accelerated its work with suppliers to decarbonize Apple-related production and expand investments in clean energy and climate solutions around the world. Apple requires from their suppliers to report on progress towards these goals—specifically Scope 1 and Scope 2 emissions reductions—and will track and audit annual progress. Apple also encourages suppliers to address the greenhouse gas emissions beyond their Apple production, prioritizing clean energy.

Amazon has taken a very different approach in managing its business ecosystem. Amazon was founded in 1994 by Jeff Bezos as an online bookshop. Bezos quickly realized that the company could increase its footprint in the retail industry by increasing the width of the assortment. Therefore, collaboration with other markets was required, ranging from video and music to gaming. Next, Amazon realized that it could benefit from other entrepreneurs selling products on the internet if it was able to cross sell through the Amazon retail engine. By the end of 1996, Amazon had launched the Amazon Associates Program. Amazon associates could place an Amazon banner or a link on their website or link directly to the Amazon homepage. When a visitor clicked on the Associate's website and landed on the Amazon website and purchased a book, the associate would receive a commission fee.

Through this programme, Amazon enabled third-party website owners to build their business through the advertising of Amazon products. When a purchase is made at such a third-party website, the purchaser is actually buying Amazon products. The website owners earn referral fees at the moment a purchase takes place. In the following years, Amazon began to increase its service offerings to affiliates by developing technology to support the startup of web shops, thereby lowering the entry barriers for entrepreneurs to start web shops and subsequently increasing traffic to Amazon websites. With the introduction of the eReader Kindle Fire, it required the availability of content and a very affordable consumer price. It sacrificed hardware profits in order to subsidize book publishers and movie studios to publish their content on the Amazon Kindle. Given that affiliate marketing is performance based and financially motivated, Amazon uses a clever and well-balanced system. Amazon and its partners benefit directly from an online purchase from the Amazon platform. Amazon enables writers and booksellers to proactively participate in the ecosystem, as well as those that want to sell to the Amazon community. Given the fact that both the objective and financial reimbursement are aligned, partner collaboration is easier to orchestrate. Amazon continuously forges partnership to support its ecosystem. For example, in 2022, Amazon helped Disney fans worldwide to get excited about the D23 fan expo. The partnership with Walt Disney Archives offers Amazon a unique opportunity to showcase Walt Disney's iconic Grumman Gulfstream company airplane. The plane will be displayed for guests at the D23 Expo as part of the exhibit Mickey Mouse One: 'Walt's Plane, presented by Amazon'. The plane serves as the central inspiration for Amazon's custom merchandise.

Apple and Amazon have taken very different approaches to managing their respective business ecosystems. Apple has created an Apple community in which Apple is the cornerstone and has a dominant position. Amazon positions itself as a facilitator of retail business using its retailing platform. Retailers have a high liberty of use and have an equitable stake in the ecosystem, unlike in the Apple ecosystem. However, both models have been very successful. Apple has become the most valuable company in the world and has sold more than 140 billion apps in its App Store. Amazon has attracted millions of affiliates and has become the biggest online retailer in the world.

Questions

1   Applying a business ecosystem lens, provide a systematic comparison of Apple's and Amazon's ecosystems. Explain why both ecosystems are successful.
2   Taking the viewpoint of developers, explain why they would participate in either the Apple and/or Amazon business ecosystem.
3   Identify the future hazards and adversities that are most likely to undermine the success of both business ecosystems.

Note

1   Amazon (2022a); Adner (2012); Apple (2022a, 2022b); Isckia and Lescop (2009).

21

ALLIANCE PROFESSIONALS

Managing alliances to achieve a shared objective is not for the faint of heart. Alliance professionals have the responsibility to ensure effective governance of the relationship, protect their firm's interests and maximize long-term value for the partner firms. Alliance management thus requires multifaceted individuals that possess abilities to be flexible and adaptive to the role necessary, and with a set of characteristics that enhances, not detracts, from the alliance objectives (Isabella and Spekman 2001). One of the issues with alliance professionals however is that there is no consistent academic or managerial definition of what an alliance professional is or does. For some firms it may mean an exclusive executive position, whereas for other firms it pertains to middle management or operational functions. In addition, for one firm alliance professionals associate with procurement and sourcing, for another with learning innovation and business development, and for other firms, with distribution channels, or a combination of these functions. Depending on the nature of the alliance and the organizational structure of the partners, alliance professionals may thus occupy different hierarchical positions, fulfil different roles and require distinct competences. Despite this variety, one common denominator stands out. Successful alliance relationships demand dedicated and effective alliance professionals (Bruner et al. 2003) with skills and competences that transcend traditional organizational functions (Spekman et al. 1998). This chapter starts by exploring the uniqueness of alliance professionals and then elaborates in the second section on hierarchal positions and alliance roles. Subsequently, in the third section, insights are provided on alliance managers' traits and competences. The fourth section presents managerial guidelines. The chapter concludes with some points of interest and a case illustration of an Alliance Director.

Alliance professionals: a unique job

Given the complexity and idiosyncrasy of alliance arrangements, hierarchical positions, role definitions and job titles with regard to alliance arrangements vary across firms and regions in the world (see Table 21.1 for examples). Despite this diversity, academics and practitioners alike share the idea that alliance professionals possess a unique function within organizations (Bamford et al. 2003; Simoons 2016). When compared to CEOs, for example, alliance

DOI: 10.4324/9781003222187-21

TABLE 21.1 Alliance professionals job advertisements (excerpts)

Job	Description	Responsibilities	Qualifications
Alliance manager at Cisco	To work in collaboration with various stakeholders to contribute to the achievement of revenue targets by implementing alliance/vendor partnership plans that are robust and competitive.	To identify appropriate contacts and target businesses/organizations, cultivate interest, nurture leads. To develop the ability to provide leadership, develop trust, negotiate objectives and work directly with a broad group of senior executives across industry verticals. To work cross-functionally. To create alliance marketing plans, train sales teams and develop initiatives to strengthen alliance results. To hold quarterly business roadmap sessions with partners, aligning on strategies for mutual growth.	Good interpersonal, communication, and organizational skills. Good analytical skills and display good business acumen. Good relationship-building skills with the ability to engage with a variety of internal and external stakeholders. Good team players and maintain the integrity and display. Good attention to detail. Great presentation, verbal and writing skills; ability to communicate complex ideas effectively across a wide range of audience levels and functions. Demonstrable network of industry contacts.
Alliance partner manager—Phoenix Market at Slalom	Slalom takes a new approach to the traditional channel sales, partner sales position and evolves the role to a position that helps combine sales, local market enablement, strategic forecasting and global delivery.	Co-creates a partner strategy for the market with local leadership, builds brand awareness, aligns sales and client teams with partners, such as Salesforce, AWS, Snowflake, Microsoft and Google Cloud, and is a technology enthusiast through and through.	Building strong, trusted relationships within Slalom's strategic partner ecosystem. Generating sales pipeline through partner relationships. Working with local market leaders to co-create a strategic partner road map. Evangelizing local market wins, both internally across Slalom and externally with partners.

(Continued)

TABLE 2.1 (Continued)

Job	Description	Responsibilities	Qualifications
Alliance manager sustainability and trust at Deloitte	Help Deloitte lead the development of capabilities in priority solution areas with alliance partners. Alliance partners are a critical component to win work in our emerging markets.	In the field area of strategy: To articulate how the alliance partnership aligns with and elevates Deloitte emerging market opportunities, capabilities and firm strategy. To lead and participate in multi-disciplinary discussions regarding the alliance relationship and ongoing development needs. To relay marketplace signals shared by alliance partners with firm leadership to inform ongoing strategic planning, prioritization sales and subsequently deepen the relationship. In the field of Operations: To maintain a strategic alliance plan, coordinating with Deloitte and the alliance, to keep a current view of a go-to-market approach, priorities, sales and pursuit targets, and other financial and non-financial goals.	Minimum 5+ years of related professional experience with 2+ years focused on alliance management or equivalent experience working with external vendors. Experience articulating value propositions for alliance products. Experience navigating a complex ecosystem of stakeholders with demonstration of creating and maintaining relationships internally and externally. Outstanding interpersonal and communication skills that foster and build relationships at all levels. Ability to travel 20–60%, on average, based on the work you do and the clients and industries/sectors you serve.

Sources: LinkedIn (2022a, 2022b, 2022c)

professionals share with the former that both span the entire product/service life cycle with a clear focus on value creation, the main difference being that an alliance professional has limited budget, resources and formal decision-making power. Account managers and alliance professionals both deal with an external relationship. However, sales and procurement type relationships are typically about value-exchange with near-term results, suggesting that account managers may overlook long-term value-creation opportunities and lack the experience in spanning all functional areas of an organization and up to executive level required to create long-term value. When compared to project managers, alliance professionals are alike in that task and team coordination are critical. They are different in that project managers tend to focus on managing the task and team, whereas alliance managers need to deal with shared decision making, shared responsibility and accountability, shared resource commitment and shared risk and reward.

Alliance professionals focus on the 'collaborative' work of alliance relationships and can be considered as its choreographers or orchestrators (Kittel 2013). Successful alliance professionals simultaneously operate on the inter-organizational, intra-organizational and interpersonal levels (Bruner *et al.* 2003). On the inter-organizational level, alliance professionals must balance the needs, resources and desires of the partner firms. On the intra-organizational level, alliance professionals must manage the needs, resources and desires of their own firm. On the interpersonal level, alliance professionals must manage relationships with peers, supervisors and subordinates not only in their own firm but across the boundaries of their partner firms. Confronted with this balancing act, the rules that apply to bureaucratic, hierarchical organizations are likely to fail when imposed on alliance professionals (Spekman *et al.* 1998).

The complex linkages among strategies, structure and systems of partner firms and the alliance require a perspective that is different and unique, specifically when compared with more traditional structures and coordination mechanisms in organizations. Alliance professionals must gain their counterpart's agreement on mutually achievable goals and must enact relationship building and interactional processes to achieve these goals. In alliance arrangements, the people involved struggle with balancing the demands of formal and informal governance. Although role demands are affected by the hierarchal system, effective alliance management depends on one's ability to work outside of prescribed routes and routines. Successful managers rely on persuasion and influence, which are bound by the social fabric of the alliance relationship (Hutt *et al.* 2000). Simply, command and control and/or management by fiat will not work, as partner firms remain autonomous. Compromise, influence and trust emerge as key operative terms, as one simply cannot dictate how colleagues in the alliance should work.

High-performing alliance professionals possess a unique mixture of functional skill sets, interpersonal skill sets and alliance mindsets (Bruner *et al.* 2003). Functional skill sets can be considered the tools that a manager calls upon to accomplish specific objectives throughout the business cycle. These skills are similar to skills of business and line managers. Interpersonal skill sets can be considered the tools an alliance professional uses to initiate, cultivate and maintain relationships throughout alliance development. Alliance mindsets are an overarching perspective that frames how a manager approaches alliance problems and creates order from ambiguity and chaos (see Chapter 24). In other words, alliance professionals hold a strong disposition towards long- and near-term value creation through external relationships; possess skills that pertain to value-discovering, curiosity, interpersonal focus, creativity and out-of-the-box thinking; and act as agents of growth and transformation (Kittel 2013). People whose perspectives accentuate creativity and learning, in addition to business savvy, would make the strongest alliance professionals.

Strong alliance professionals are able to deal with the tension between acting according to the spirit of the collaboration and acting in pursuit of the firm's interests (Vangen and Huxham 2003). It seems thus reasonable to conclude that, when compared to more traditional organizational functions, alliance professionals possess unique responsibilities, skills and perspectives that transcend, for example, the capabilities required to be a strong line or project manager. Is also implies that it is risky to assume that successful business, functional or line managers can be promoted to alliance professional positions and adopt an inspiring and motivating leadership role (Spekman et al. 1998). Although the skills and traits discussed are important, how they become manifest varies with alliance professionals' positions and roles and the alliance development stage (Isabella and Spekman 2001).

Hierarchical positions and alliance roles

Despite the complexity of alliance arrangements and idiosyncratic use of alliance professionals within firms, it appears that firms consistently assign tasks and responsibilities to alliance professionals operating at different hierarchical levels. Here, we distinguish between three hierarchical levels—operational, middle management and executive level—and detail three associated alliance jobs: (1) alliance manager, (2) senior alliance manager (3) and the alliance director. In addition to these positions, firms assign and designate personnel to fulfil different roles, either part-time or full-time tied to the alliance, among which are alliance team member, governance committee member, alliance coordinator and various supportive roles (see Table 21.2). Although positions and roles may overlap, for the sake of clarity, we discuss them separately.

TABLE 21.2 Examples of alliance professionals' roles

	Role description	Critical because . . .
Alliance team member	Individual who works directly with firm and partner colleagues in the alliance and is engaged in activities such as R&D, manufacturing, marketing, distribution, etc.	Without alliance team members, the alliance would become an empty shell; an executive agreement without clear operational alliance tasks and activities.
Executive sponsor/ alliance champion	Member of the focal firm's top management, who assumes responsibility for the development of the alliance at the executive level and is the contact for top management of the partner.	Without sponsorship, top management sends an internal signal indicating a lack of importance and commitment, which will undermine value creation. Escalation of conflicts continues without executive involvement and resolution.
Governance committee member	Individual who represents the alliance and the firm on a joint committee responsible for working with the partner on strategic and organizational issues.	Steering committees set the alliance strategy and supervise its execution. Tasks pertain to budgeting, forecasting, approving plans developed by sub-committees and reconciling conflicts.

	Role description	*Critical because . . .*
Alliance coordinator	Internal contact person for a specific alliance or internal coordinator of all cooperation activities in a specific field or business.	Alliance coordinators create internal alignment between and across functions and offer cross-functional input to the alliance manager. Alliance coordinators understand and communicate the implications of alliance decisions on respective functions.
Internal consultant	Pool of internal specialists who provide technical support for individual alliance management tasks.	Without internal consultants, opportunities to enhance effectiveness and efficiency of alliance arrangements may be missed. Internal consultants stimulate internal learning and cross-fertilization of alliance best practices.
Relationship manager	Contact person for a specific alliance partner at the operative level who co-ordinates all co-operation activities with this partner.	Without relationships managers, early warning signs about adversities and conflicts may go unobserved. Building strong and resilient working relationships demands specialized skills and knowledge.
Supportive staff	Personnel assigned to the alliance to provide assistance to make the alliance work; examples include lawyers, legal specialists, administrative support, launch managers and innovation experts.	Without support staff, alliance development tends to be inhibited, and successful continuation is at risk. Legal specialists are critical during alliance design, launch manager during startup and innovation experts during management.
Launch manager	Individual who is solely responsible to successfully implement and execute the alliance, consistent with the alliance contract.	Without a launch manager, the transition from design to management is impeded. Launch managers organize launch meetings, set feasible milestones, build relational capital, secure resources and steer the alliance towards its objectives.

Sources: Bamford *et al.* (2003); Hoffmann (2005); Isabella and Spekman (2001); The Rhythm of Business (2016).

Positions

An alliance manager is responsible for ensuring that day-to-day operating requirements for assigned alliances are effectively managed and performance objectives are achieved (ASAP 2016). The alliance manager serves as the primary point of contact with the alliance partner and is responsible for attaining alliance objectives. The tasks and activities an alliance manager may initiate involve, but are not restricted to, supervising the alliance management team, organizing appropriate communications, coordinating activities, anticipating and resolving adversities, facilitating conflict resolution, managing escalation, solving business problems, negotiating with the partner on ongoing agreements and winding down the relationship. Alliance managers also develop and maintain relationships with all individuals involved in the alliance, either working internally or at the partner level. Furthermore, a key task is to establish performance standards, use scorecards and gather data to evaluate and manage the performance of an alliance. The results of these assessments are reported to the senior alliance manager. As a rule of thumb, an alliance manager is often responsible for one major alliance or several secondary alliances.

A senior alliance manager is responsible for directing all the activities for assigned alliances (ASAP 2016). In addition to the operational tasks required of an alliance manager, the senior manager is expected to contribute to the development of tools, processes and strategies employed by alliance managers to ensure effective coordination across the portfolio of alliances. That is, he/she directs and supervises activities across the complete alliance life cycle and ensures that sufficient and appropriate resources are allocated to alliance activities. A senior alliance manager may have mentoring and/or supervisory responsibility for alliance manager-level individuals and is committed to improve competence levels of individuals working in the alliance. The senior alliance manager will report to the director of alliance management and is typically responsible for one or more major alliances or (part of) the alliance portfolio.

The director of alliances is responsible for the performance of alliance relationships and thus coordinates overall alliance management resources to ensure appropriate coverage across the organization's portfolio of alliances (ASAP 2016). His/her tasks encompass the design and management of the alliance portfolio, coordinating activities between internal functional departments and providing support for activities initiated by partners. Administrative responsibilities include staffing of the alliance management function and overall the credentials of people involved. The alliance director is often responsible for a team of alliance managers and/or senior alliance managers and reports to a divisional or organizational executive. If multiple alliance directors are appointed, a vice president of alliances has an executive function and may supervise them.

When compared with one another, the alliance manager, the senior alliance managers and the alliance director (or VP of alliances) differ, in addition to hierarchical position, with regard to two job elements. First, an alliance manager is primarily engaged in single alliance management: the efficiency and effectiveness of a designated alliance relationship. In contrast, the senior alliance manager and the alliance director are engaged in multi-alliance management, the supervision of alliance portfolios, networks and ecosystems. Second, and not surprisingly, to qualify as an alliance manager, in general, less experience is required, and one may fulfil different roles when compared to more senior positions.

Roles

A first critical role an alliance professional may fulfil is that of alliance team member. An alliance team member works directly with the firm and partner colleagues in the work of the alliance (Hoffmann 2005), such as the development, manufacturing or commercializing of a product. As such, they are part of an alliance project team or working group. As a team member, responsibilities include but are not limited to having a general understanding of the purpose and limits of the contract, being knowledgeable about the firm's position on issues that impact their function, monitoring project budget and forecasts as applicable to team member's function and working collaboratively with their counterparts (*The Rhythm of Business* 2016).

Senior alliance managers or the director of alliance may become a member of the alliance steering committee and thus fulfil the role of governance committee member (Hoffmann 2005). Governance committee members represent the alliance and the partner firms in a joint committee responsible for steering the alliance towards its objectives. Specifically, the committee members set the alliance strategy and decide how it is achieved, recommend budgets and forecasts relevant to the partner firms, approve plans and supervise sub-committees, reconcile and resolve differences between the partners and represent the alliance internally and externally (*The Rhythm of Business* 2016). In sum, governance committee members provide oversight to keep the alliance on track.

A critical role which contributes to the successful management of an alliance relationship pertains to that of executive sponsor or alliance champion (Hoffmann 2005). Usually, this role is assumed by a senior executive, and his/her involvement encompasses more than appointing alliance managers (Hutt *et al.* 2000). Executive sponsors define the meaning of the alliance and assume a critical role in communicating the strategic role of the alliance in creating an identity for the alliance within the organization. He/she provides the alliance managers with support, such that he/she ensures the alliance has the necessary resources, endorses requests made by the alliance manager, provides advice to the alliance manager and mediates if internal conflicts occur (*The Rhythm of Business* 2016). Without an executive sponsor, the alliance is less likely to succeed.

A unique role, which preferably is executed by a senior staff member with experience and knowledge about the organization, is that of alliance coordinator (Hoffmann 2005). To ensure that the collaboration among functions (or business and fields) and affiliates is effective and efficient, alliance professionals, such as governance committee members, also have an internal role to work with the alliance manager. These alliance coordinators enable communication between functions, update functional leadership, ensure functional resources to achieve (intermediate) alliance objectives, provide cross-functional input to the alliance manager and help to foster internal alignment. In some instances, a governance committee member may appoint a deputy to serve this role, provided that the deputy has sufficient authority to carry it out.

The alliance roles discussed, and the other roles listed in Table 21.2 (e.g. internal consultant and supportive roles), share the belief that to successfully fulfil a role, the person responsible should possess appropriate skills and an alliance mindset. However, the roles differ with regard to work-orientation and leadership. First, some roles, such as internal consultant and supportive roles, operate more on the intra-organizational level (e.g. company focus), whereas others focus more on the inter-organizational level (e.g. relationship focus), such as governance committee members. Some roles, such as alliance champions, operate on multiple levels, the intra-organizational level (e.g. providing internal support), the inter-organizational level (e.g. preemptively deal with relationship tensions) and the inter-personal level (e.g. building strong personal relationships), whereas other roles are less demanding, such as team member and internal consultant. Second, some roles (and positions) demand alliance leadership. Leadership in alliance arrangements demands that he/she engages in processes of embracing, empowering, involving and mobilizing individuals partaking in the alliance arrangement (Vangen and Huxham 2003). This particularly applies to alliance directors and senior alliance managers, but alliance managers also need to inspire personnel (from both sides) to actively partake in the relationship, even if their assigned role is limited in time and constrained to a specific alliance developmental stage.

Alliance manager: attributes and competences

Research investigating the importance of roles and positions of alliance management showed that the alliance manager function, relative to other alliance professionals, is most critical to generate value-creating alliance relationships (Hoffmann 2005). Alliance managers can be described as choreographers or orchestrators acting within or to support an alliance arrangement (Canter and Twombly 2016; Kittel 2013). They have deep knowledge of the business, are politically savvy, possess diplomatic skills and excel in interpersonal communication. They also possess great amounts of both tenacity and empathy and tend to challenge traditional hierarchies, lines of authority and existing ways of working within each partner organization. Strong alliance professionals embrace creativity and learning (Spekman *et al.* 1998). Taken together, alliance managers possess unique cognitive attributes and competences.

Cognitive attributes

Personality traits often associated with alliance managers include being a risk taker, reflective, a careful listener and open to new ideas (Kittel 2013). Other traits that have been attributed to alliance managers pertain to diplomacy and analytic mindsets (Simoons 2016). These traits together suggest that an alliance manager is able to operate as diplomat and lobbyist, connect people and information, and get things done, primarily based on sound analysis, experience, out-of-the-box thinking and creative strategies. That is, strong alliance managers see and think differently when compared to other more traditional functions (Spekman *et al.* 1998).

An alliance manager's unique perspective has been asserted to originate from unique cognitive attributes (Isabella and Spekman 2001). Strong alliance managers recognize and attend to multiple points of view simultaneously. They use this information to build creative solutions, serving the interests of partner firms. For example, an alliance manager may propose a creative business model with hybrid compensation to align partners' interests. In addition, strong alliance managers learn from past experiences but are not constrained by them. They use their own experiences, but also those of others outside their company, to build generalizable principles and best practices and apply them creatively to resolve a current problem. In doing so, they use imagination and intuition to think across time and see into the future. Good alliance managers are creative and ever curious and questioning. They have an ability to recognize patterns in disorganized data and disorder in apparently orderly circumstances. They also see what is possible and have an innate talent for improvisation, managerial qualities which are all necessary to operate successfully in a hierarchical vacuum surrounded by uncertainty; that is what an alliance is.

Competences

All-round and high-performing alliance managers possess a specific set of competences (ASAP 2016; Isabella and Spekman 2001). Strong alliance managers possess functional or context competences. These competences pertain to the foundational elements that enable an alliance manager to perform his or her job duties effectively but are not exclusive or unique to alliance management. These skills are important to perform the work job but do not in themselves ensure that the alliance management group is fulfilling its strategic mission for the company. Such skills include communications skills, time management, conflict resolution, contract negotiation, financial management, interpersonal skills and project management. Critical among these competences are interpersonal skills (Isabella and Spekman 2001), which enable an alliance manager to build strong relationships, act comfortably in social business settings, interact across cultures and with people, use verbal and non-verbal communication techniques and affect the mood of individuals and groups. Alliance managers also need to possess core competences (ASAP 2016). Core competences are functionally critical skills; they are key to the success of the alliance manager in defining and driving an alliance. Such skills include intimate knowledge of the alliance life cycle, alliance governance, alliance

---

BOX 21.1 ASAP CERTIFICATION

The Association of Strategic Alliance Professionals (ASAP) offers an alliance management certification programme providing ASAP members with the opportunity to demonstrate their mastery of core alliance skills and the management of all forms of collaborative business relationships. The programme features two levels of certification:

1. Certification of Achievement—Alliance Management (CA-AM)—the first level of certification for up-and-coming alliance professionals.
2. Certified Strategic Alliance Professional (CSAP)—the advanced level of certification for seasoned practitioners with a command of the full alliance life cycle from inception to termination.

ASAP has established the following skill sets for alliance management professionals: context competencies, core competences, business and industry knowledge, and company-specific competences (see section on attributes and competencies for details). These competencies are skills that can be learned or developed through experience. Individuals seeking certification will be tested on ASAP's Context & Core Competencies. In addition to being a successful alliance manager, individuals should have a complete knowledge of their organization's business and industry and their company's specific competencies. Becoming certified demonstrates a commitment to the profession. Just as important, certified alliance management professionals are recognized leaders and serve as role models within the alliance management profession. Certification thus not only brings value to the organization but also to the alliance professional.

Source: ASAP (2016).

---

management, professional development of alliance managers, collaborative climate, alliance portfolios and collaborative network and ecosystem. These are all competences that are used by the Association of Strategic Alliance Professionals to certify alliance managers' credentials (see Box 21.1).

In addition, strong alliance managers possess company-specific knowledge and skills. Knowledge, which is very specific to the company and its strategy (ASAP 2016), enables an alliance manager to understand the role and the mission of the strategic alliance group and the role and mission of the particular alliance to be managed. Knowledge includes company general market priorities and overview, company partnering culture, company-specific market and partnering strategy, and company technology initiatives. It also pertains to the extent to which an alliance manager develops an extensive network in the company and in the industry, solid relationships within the firm and credibility among superiors, peers and subordinates (Isabella and Spekman 2001). Business and industry knowledge pertain to the unique demands that business models and industry differences place on alliances. It is believed that such differences will require alliance managers to adopt and master different practices as a result. They include, for example, business/financial analysis skills, understanding of business models of different types of partners, partners' industry knowledge and industry/market value chains.

Taken together, strong alliance managers tend to be unique personalities with tailored competences. Developing good alliance managers, therefore, takes time and effort. One of the reasons why training and educating alliance managers is difficult is because many of the traits, skills and competences required are difficult to learn and perhaps are natural talents. Firms with short-term time horizons may be reluctant to invest in alliance managers; the pressure to perform in the present conflicts with rewards from training that will come but only in time. Instead, firms need to act strategically as increasingly alliance managers become a critical cornerstone of executive decisions and successful business models. Therefore, alliance managers may become the future leaders!

Alliance professionals: decision-making steps

Successfully deploying alliance professionals as the alliance relationship progresses is complex and challenging (Spekman *et al.* 1998). To provide a more fine-grained insight, we next discuss some generic guidelines to manage alliance professionals (see Figure 21.1).

Step 1: alliance professional criticality

Firms that proactively assign and develop alliance professionals are likely to outperform their rival peers. But prior to that, initiating programmes to select, appoint and educate alliance professionals, it is salient to assess the criticality of alliance professionals to the organization. Undeniably alliances are becoming more critical to firms, but firms must understand how and to what extent alliance professionals are necessitated. Staffing depends on the firm's business model and the nature of the alliances within it. For example, as alliance arrangements become increasingly critical to a firm's competitive position, and thus a firm engages in more and different types of alliance relationships, staffing hierarchical positions and securing the fulfilment of different roles becomes critical. As such, alliance management, and thus alliance professionals, obtain a legitimate role in an organization. Consequently, a firm needs to develop career paths, initiate programmes to attract top talent to alliance management and develop criteria to assign staff to positions, roles and alliance relationships.

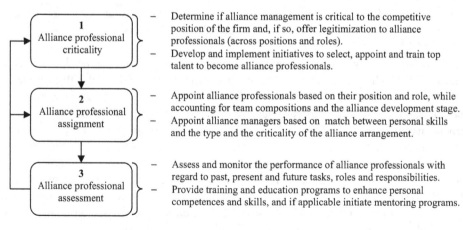

FIGURE 21.1 Decision-making steps: alliance professionals

Step 2: alliance professionalassignment

Choosing an alliance manager is a critical decision to creating a successful alliance. Different alliance professional positions and roles associate with different stages of alliance development (Isabella and Spekman 2001). During alliance formation, firms decide whether an alliance is an appropriate governance mode for realizing their objectives. At this point, decision makers have limited or little understanding whether an alliance arrangement is the solution to their strategic conundrum. Pre-alliance competitive needs and motivation emerges, and the top management team need to conduct assessment on how to organize activities and generate desired resources. The alliance director may act as visionary and envision the possibilities and opportunities associated with alliance relationships. A (senior) alliance manager may begin to articulate the strategic intent for the alliance, create a sense of urgency, start to develop a business plan and begin to form the requisite criteria for a partner selection. Involved managers must be able to communicate how an alliance fits within the firm's corporate strategy. Their aim is to ensure that the collective effort is coherent and that initiatives are communicated vertically and horizontally throughout the organization. In addition, they should be able to translate a firm's requirements into a coherent alliance strategy and create constructive perceptions about the alliance's future. During this stage, business skills are important to formulate a sound alliance strategy, whereas interpersonal skills enable alliance managers to build strong (internal) relationships and obtain sponsorship. But as the alliance takes shape, networking and advocating the relationship to internal and external stakeholders becomes important, and when the alliance solidifies, managing and mediating conflicts become key activities (Bruner *et al.* 2003).

The next steps—negotiation and designing—require competences pertaining to advocacy and facilitation. Involved managers must sell the alliance internally to senior and operational managers. In addition, they must sell the potential partnership to their counterparts. A manager during these stages thus acts as a networker who oversees boundary conditions and disseminates information, both internally and externally. A manager also needs negotiation and political skills to align conflicting interests and explore potential tensions creatively to find common ground and solutions.

Stabilizing and solidifying defines the stage in which the alliance becomes an ongoing and viable organizational arrangement. Alliance managers dedicate effort to managing the alliance with the adjustments and fine-tuning needed to keep it on track. Their main focus is on smooth operation of the alliance and attending to those issues and adversities that may bog down its workflows. The manager acts as facilitator and honest broker who is respected by people involved in the relationship. It is the responsibility of alliance managers to measure performance against intentional and emergent objectives, financial targets and operational milestones. A manager must be flexible enough to accommodate partners' interests, possess competences to rebuild damaged interpersonal relations and have tolerance for unfamiliar or uncomfortable situations. Endurance and patience will help managers build the honest and reliable personal relationships needed to foster relationship progress. Sensitivity, defined as an ability to listen and observe, is also important with regard to building relational norms and capital. Curiosity is vital: an interest in others contributes to an open climate. In the management stage, an alliance manager needs the competences to act as both an operational manager and a disturbance handler.

The alliance termination stage demands, yet again, different skills to extract value from the relationship and avoid unintended repercussions. A manager should be able to communicate the termination intention and possess mediation skills to deal effectively with the virtually inevitable conflicts. As in the negotiation and design stages, negotiation and political skills are required to organize an exit with favourable outcomes.

Taken together, the precise position and role of an alliance professional must reflect the scope, potential value and likely duration of the relationship that needs to be managed. Any individual alliance manager is unlikely to have such a comprehensive set of competences, which leads many firms to set up alliance teams. Such teams comprise a group of diverse people who together personify the managerial competences required for each alliance development stage (see Chapter 22).

Step 3: alliance professional assessment

How do you know a good alliance professional when you see one? To sustain superior alliance professional performance levels, managers must continuously monitor the development and performance of alliance professionals. Annual performance appraisals provide the necessary information to take appropriate actions, whether this means to replace, educate or promote an alliance professional. The criticality of evaluating alliance professionals means that appraisal criteria should fit with the present and possible future position, roles, skills and competences of an individual. The appraisal results are also important as they depict an important input for alliance training and education. New alliance managers working together with more experienced managers in mentoring programmes help to ensure that corporate practices and knowledge are passed on. Furthermore, if unexpected management transitions occur, new alliance managers are prepared to take over activities.

Following the three steps for alliance professional deployment and development does not provide a clear-cut recipe for instant success. But, by using the guidelines, alliance professionals can contribute to alliance success.

Summary

Because an alliance is a dynamic interaction of business and people whose purpose is to achieve mutually beneficial goals, superior alliance performance not only depends on the rigour of the business case but also on the people who make decisions and support the alliance relationships. Although the work of alliance professionals varies from alliance to alliance, consistently, academic and professional literature reports that dedicated alliance managers are pivotal to success. The alliance manager is the key contact point for partner firms and possesses diplomatic skills to keep the partner aligned, entrepreneurial skills to identify and capture new opportunities, project management skills to meet deadlines and keep the alliance on track, and inter-personal skills to mobilize and motivate personnel involved. Thus, as a final note, we warn again against the common misconception and practice to promote business or line managers to become alliance managers. Alliance managers are creators of value, and becoming one without training, experience and perhaps an innate talent is doomed to result in alliance failure.

CASE: IVAN VOGELS[1]

After obtaining a master's degree in international economics at the University of Utre-cht, Ivan Vogels travelled and worked for two years in Asia and North America before he became junior product manager at NavTeq (later Nokia). Since then, Ivan has worked for various international IT companies, initially with a strong focus on sales, but as his career progressed, his key responsibilities shifted towards the management of alliances and part-nerships. In his words: 'I realized after having worked at Marketing, Pre-sales and Sales for say eight years that working with alliances depicted a challenge to combine marketing and sales and it promised to be a great area to work in'. According to his LinkedIn profile, he is result-driven, has an aptitude for international business, is a good communicator, is reliable and independent, a team player and has an ability to bring 'structure to chaos'. According to Ivan: 'the latter is exactly what companies need when professionalizing their alliances department'.

In his first 'alliance job', Ivan became Director Alliances and Partnership at eVision. eVi-sion Industry Software, established in 2008, is the global leader in Control of Work software. Companies in the oil and gas, (petro)chemical and other high-risk and critical infrastruc-ture industries turn to eVision to improve control over their operational processes, resulting in fully auditable, real-time corporate risk management as well as increased operational efficiency. eVision's headquarters are based in The Hague, the Netherlands, with regional offices located in Aberdeen, Stavanger, Houston and Qatar. eVision has a global partner network and clients covering five continents. Its single purpose is to empower its clients to be 'in control' of their operations. eVision strive to make it easier for the users to access information and knowledge that helps them to work safely and efficiently. eVision Indus-try Software is used by some of the largest companies in the world to help them man-age risk and achieve operational excellence. eVision's flagship product Permit Vision is the market-leading Integrated Safe System of Work, which integrates permit to work software, risk assessment, isolations management processes and external work order systems into one user-friendly system.

In general, as an Alliance Director, it is Ivan's responsibility to establish alliance relation-ships enabling eVision to increase economies of scope and scale. Specifically, eVision distin-guishes between three types of alliance relationships. Business partnerships enable eVision to boost and scale sales. That is, these relationships accelerate market growth by creating new product/service offers in existing markets and by entering new markets, geographical and customer. In addition, service partnerships are forged to boost and scale implementa-tions trajectories, as they increase flexibility and scalability of offers, and to enhance sales resources and delivery capacity. With regard to the third type, technology partnerships, these are used to innovate the software (e.g. integration and features), for example, by establishing co-development projects and enabling integration with third-party solutions. Across these different responsibilities, it is also Ivan's task to leverage eVision's brand via the partners. With regard to accountability, Ivan provides monthly updates to the board of directors (specifically the CCO and COO); reports will contain information, for example, on product development progress, lead generation, secured deals and alliance status.

Over time, Ivan's job has become more complex as a result of eVision's successful growth strategy. First, a shift occurred from tailor-made client projects to standardized product offerings, imposing a strong need for partnerships with technology developers and hardware suppliers. That is, eVision collaborates with IT companies, such as SAP, Dasault Systèmes, Intergraph, Oracle and Osisoft, to further improve existing and possibly create new software products. For example, by integrating with graphic software of Intergraph, eVision can bring the correct plans and drawings to the field workers. In the first seven years of its existence, eVision primarily grew via a direct sales model. It relied on direct sales to market their products and services and used a team of sales representatives, business consultants, deal makers and bid managers to secure profitable deals. However, to further scale-up looking at geography and new industries, eVision has been contracting business partners to increase its addressable market and generating growth via indirect sales through a portfolio of (international) resellers, among which are business and service partnerships. Business partners, for example, such as L&T Infotech and Neon Infotech, act as resellers and support eVision in the local marketing, sales and delivery of the products. Service partners are mostly Global System Integrators such as Accenture, Infosys and Atos, which operate globally and act as full-service delivery partners and thus generate sales and offer training and on-site support to clients. Three companies encompass all activities—Oracle, Intergraph and Accenture—and are therefore considered strategic alliance relationships. As an alliance director, it is Ivan's main task to oversee all three partner categories, oversee on-boarding of new partners, work on a daily basis with the alliances and generate good leads with all active partners.

To successfully execute this alliance strategy, in support of the corporate strategy, Ivan required various skills and competences. To be able to interact and deal with a variety of (potential) partners, he depended heavily on past and present work experiences. For example, his familiarity with international business, marketing and sales, and B2B channels, all within the context of IT services, made him a credible counterpart for technological, business and service partners. To adequately deal with internal pressure and resistance—originating because some employees perceived that the shift from direct sales to indirect sales may threaten their job—Ivan needed to use his inter-personal communication skills and emphatically explain to internal stakeholders that alliance partners may be beneficial to their performance. This is because alliance partners may enhance the quality of the product, may generate more direct sales, may improve the product experience and may boost brand exposure.

To manage the alliance team, comprised of four members, Ivan used generic management skills, such as administrative, project, leadership, pipeline management and financial skills. In addition, he acted as the spider in a web (1) to obtain internal support from the board as well as functional managers, (2) to coordinate alliance managers and connect them internally and externally to counterparts and (3) to align alliance partners with eVision's internal organization. More importantly, as eVision was growing, changing and experimenting, Ivan's know-how of successfully managing change and transformation processes was critical. Within eVision, alliances are both a cause and consequence of organizational change. Managing alliances thus demands a creative and open mindset but also visibility and credibility within the organization.

To accomplish these and other alliance director tasks, Ivan deemed it important to be perceived as a trustworthy and knowledgeable partner, both internally and externally. According to him, to act as a successful alliance director, it is critical to reconcile a business focus with a collaborative mindset. He considered it his task to reconcile eVision's emphasis on sales and deal making with a mindset comprising cooperation, openness and transparency.

To enact this process, he proactively built bridges between functional specialists, develops creative solutions to deal with adversities and secures the commitment and participation of relevant staff. The partnering strategy has led to an explosion of partner-related and driven events where eVision was asked to present itself, and the value of partner-related opportunities in the pipeline went up from less than 5 per cent to 30 per cent in about 12 months.

In his subsequent 'alliance job', Ivan has become Strategic Alliances Director in Market Unit NL at SAP. SAP is one of the world's leading producers of software for the management of business processes, developing solutions that facilitate effective data processing and information flow across organizations. The company's integrated applications connect all parts of a business into an intelligent suite on a fully digital platform, thereby replacing the process-driven, legacy platform. Today, SAP has more than 230 million cloud users, more than 100 solutions covering all business functions and the largest cloud portfolio of any provider. Globally, SAP operates 19 global alliances, and Ivan is responsible for 9 of those within the Dutch market, among which include Accenture, Capgemini, and PWC. In his role, he is responsible for proactively developing the partner's SAP business by driving sales, demand generation and partner capabilities with a strong focus on mid-term perspective. Furthermore, he acts as the central advisor to the partner, owning the partner relationship end to end and responsible for coordinating all SAP interactions (with executives, working groups, etc.) in order to drive partner investments and growth in SAP's solutions portfolio. Regarding long-term development, Ivan's task is to safeguard health-of-business and effectuate transformation to new solutions, technologies and business models. In a summary statement, Ivan describes his work as 'connecting people, connecting business, and find win–win solutions'. To this end, his role demands deep knowledge about the software industry, partnering and leadership skills, experience with cloud/SaaS solutions, strong analytics competences, an ability to lead teams and executive-level interpersonal skills. The key performance indicators (KPI) are joint partner revenue, indirect channel revenue, number of new (certified) partnerships and number of marketing and sales leads, amongst others.

Questions

1 Does the entrepreneurial background and strategy of eVision require unique skills and competences of an alliance director, specifically when compared to alliance director positions in more established, mature and bureaucratically organized companies, such as SAP?

2 Alliance arrangements are becoming increasingly critical to the execution of eVision and SAP's corporate strategy. How will this development impact and change the tasks, responsibilities and required competences of Ivan Vogels?

Note

1 Interview with Ivan Vogels; SAP (2022).

22

ALLIANCE TEAMS

The FIFA World Cup, NASA's Mars Rover and hydro water engines would not exist without alliance teams. Alliance teams allow the combination of specialized resources and expertise over organizational boundaries and occasionally national boundaries and are, as such, a key driver of alliance performance (Li and Hambrick 2005; van der Kamp *et al.* 2022). While critical to alliance success, alliance teams are also particularly prone to under-performance. The tensions in bringing a partner firm's representatives together and having them work on individual and shared tasks are immense (Drach-Zahavy 2011). As a result, team members may struggle with communication, face identification issues and form conflicting subgroups (Joshi and Lahiri 2015; Ring 2000). Furthermore, team functioning in alliances is complicated; as in most alliance arrangements, teams face the hardships of teamwork, next to working with other teams that also consist of delegates of partnering organizations (Marks and Luvison 2012). While alliance-level factors are certainly at play, alliance failure is as much a team (member) problem as an organizational problem. This chapter starts by exploring the alliance team challenge in some detail (first section) and then elaborates on alliance team types (second section).[1] Subsequently, insights are provided on activities associated with the management of alliance teams as a stand-alone entity and as part of a multi-team system (third section). Next, we present some managerial guidelines (fourth section), and the chapter concludes with a summary (fifth section) and a case illustration (sixth section).

The alliance team challenge

Alliance teams are temporary collectives of delegates from two or more organizations with a shared responsibility to coordinate and integrate resources across organizational boundaries to accomplish individual and common goals at the team, organizational and alliance levels (Drach-Zahavy 2011; Li and Hambrick 2005). Alliance teams integrate resources from partner organizations and team members within an alliance context that sets boundaries, constrains and enables the team and influences exchanges with other entities in the alliance. Alliance teams face challenges common to other types of teams. They are temporary structures set up to deal with uncertain and complex environments; a characteristic they share with project teams, for example. Alliance teams often are diverse in nationalities and are geographically

DOI: 10.4324/9781003222187-22

dispersed—characteristics they share with global and virtual teams. Alliance team composition is fluid because when the alliance develops and changes, team members move in and out of the team—a characteristic shared with R&D and product development teams. In addition to these shared attributes, alliance teams and their members, however, face a unique challenge.

Alliance team members need to resolve a mixed motive task while operating in a hierarchical vacuum. That is, alliance team members as representatives are expected to serve the needs of their firm while at the same time focusing on the success of the alliance (Hambrick *et al*. 2001). For example, team members work towards a shared objective that asks for cooperation in integrating resources such as knowledge, finances and IT systems, yet at the same time they are expected to compete to appropriate maximum returns for their organization. This tension between cooperative and competitive pressures depicts a source of conflict and disintegration of alliance teams (Li and Hambrick 2005), and team members often find themselves conflicted in their commitment (Johnson *et al*. 2002). To complicate matters, alliance teams tend to start with a blank slate; no formal hierarchical or authoritative structure is in place at the start of an alliance, though governance mechanisms and authority are installed as the alliance progresses. Without a degree of hierarchy and authoritative structure, it is very hard to coordinate alliance activities over teams. Moreover, different alliance teams are necessary to setup, maintain and adapt the alliance governance structure, which may include management and operational teams. It is thus important to understand how alliance teams can improve team and alliance performance, while resolving cooperation–competition pressures and navigating a hierarchical vacuum.

Alliance team types

The literature on alliance teams tends to be fragmented in terms of field and theory, most likely the result of an attempt to acknowledge the variety in alliance teams (van der Kamp *et al*. 2022). Strategy scholars, for example, took an interest in the composition of joint venture (board) teams to explain joint venture performance (Hambrick *et al*. 2001; Li and Hambrick 2005). Focusing on supplier relationships, other scholars examined the role of customers, boundary spanning and communication in inter-organizational teams to explain new product development (Stock 2006; Stock 2014). Studies also emphasized the complexities that arise when teams are composed of multiple nationalities, such as in international alliance teams (Li *et al*. 2002). In these teams, cultural differences complicate effective team functioning, and without cross-cultural management, these teams will break into factions. Furthermore, alliance teams have been used as a specific context for studies in the areas of negotiation, engineering, project management, health care and information systems. When comparing alliance team studies, two observations stand out. See Table 22.1 for an overview.

First, team composition and task change according to the hierarchical level. Typically, an alliance has strategic (board), tactical (steering committee) and (multiple) operational teams with very specific tasks that require different inputs, processes and outputs (Luvison and Marks 2013). At the strategic level, alliance board teams, or joint venture board teams, play an active role in formulating and implementing the strategy and governance of alliance arrangements. Their main tasks are to secure the attainment of strategic and financial objectives, protect shareholder interest, secure capital and resource allocation, and enact risk and performance management. These teams act as role models, signal relationships' importance to partners' organizations, lend support at key points, spot new opportunities and determine the appropriate degree of governance and partner involvement. Beckman and colleagues (2014),

TABLE 22.1 Examples of alliance team types

Category	Teams (examples)	Typical team members	Tasks and responsibilities
Hierarchical			
Strategic	Alliance board Joint venture board	Board members, VP alliances, alliance directors	The board plays an active role in three areas critical to drive alliance performance and protect partners' interests: capital allocation, risk management and performance management.
Tactical	Alliance steering committee Joint venture management team	Alliance director, senior alliance managers, insourced third-party managers	The management team focuses on planning, coordinating and monitoring organizational and operational activities. The team sets (project) priorities and milestones, assigns staff, resolves conflicts and tracks progress.
Operational	Working groups Project teams Operational teams	Research staff, engineers, procurement managers, marketers, account managers, alliance managers	Operational teams focus on the day-to-day operations of designated activities, which may pertain to any of the value-chain or support activities, among which are R&D, manufacturing, marketing, sales and distribution.
Development			
Pre-formation	Top management team Alliance team	Board members, alliance director, business unit managers	A firm's top management team proactively scans for partnering opportunities and consults with the alliance director. Alliance director develops partnering opportunities and business cases.
Formation	Alliance team Negotiation team	Senior alliance managers, operational managers, expert negotiators, juridical and financial advisors	Formation team builds business case, initiates partner selection, whereas negotiation team interacts and deals with counterpart's negotiation team in order to set the governance structure and formalize the alliance agreements.
Management	Launch team Management team	Launch managers, alliance managers	The launch team's main task is to execute the alliance relationship, and after the initial execution, management is transferred to the management team.

for example, show that when a board includes members with heterogeneous, multiplex relationships, as well as central network positions, diverse alliance portfolios emerge faster. With regard to decision making and conflict resolution, these teams have a definitive authority. The alliance steering committee, or alliance management team, coordinates organizational and operational processes, including staffing, project prioritization, milestone setting and interventions. Their task is to establish a collaborative climate, craft strategy, manage execution and discuss and set levels of confidentiality for different categories of information. Management of boundary-spanning agents is also part of their task as alignment of interrelated project goals and task is critical. Operational teams, also labelled as working groups, are responsible for executing specific alliance activities and tasks on a day-to-day basis. For example, operational teams' activities may pertain to new product design, building a product line or developing a marketing campaign. The main task of these teams is to execute tasks and attain short-term goals and milestones, which implies that they require timely access to information and resources. Together, the strategic, tactical and operational alliance teams represent the governance architecture of any alliance arrangement.

Second, team composition and task change according to the alliance development stage; it is thus critical to distinguish between the role different alliance teams may play during the alliance development stages (Büchel 2000). Before the alliance is initiated, the top-management team of a firm may approach potential partners informally to assess whether an alliance arrangement is feasible (Lee and Park 2008). Such pre-formation interactions between partners' representatives increases the likelihood of reaching a formal agreement. If the top-management team proceeds, an initial alliance team, for example, needs to shape the alliance; think about goals, tasks and criteria for evaluation (Ring 2000). Often this team is composed of senior managers, operational managers and alliance managers who are responsible for obtaining top-management support, developing a business case and initiating partner selection. With regard to alliance formation, for example, negotiations teams are critical as negotiators have a task to defend and advocate the interests of their firm while concluding an alliance deal. Negotiations teams are often composed of top managers, negotiation experts, alliance managers, lawyers and operational delegates who, depending on the negotiation stage, may be more or less involved in the negotiations. Once negotiations have been concluded, team members' roles may change as, for example, lawyers withdraw, whereas alliance launch managers become responsible for alliance execution, and as the alliance develops, alliance managers become responsible for day-to-day management and the supervision of operational teams. If the alliance is terminated, new team members may be appointed, for example, to handle juridical and financial issues between the partners. Taken together, 'the' alliance team does not exist, but rather within alliance arrangements, multiple alliance teams are required, and they are jointly responsible for alliance success.

BOX 22.1 MULTI-DIMENSIONAL CONCEPTUALIZATION OF ALLIANCE TEAMS

Research on alliance teams exhibits a lack of consensus among researchers on how to conceptualize an alliance team, which inhibits the development of a coherent body of knowledge on alliance teams. Building on the results of a review of alliance team research, van der Kamp and colleagues advance a multi-dimensional conceptualization of alliance teams. Alliance teams can be positioned in a multi-dimensional landscape along three dimensions: factionalism, team scope of responsibility and team entitativity. Factionalism is the extent to which interests compete between (groups of) partner representatives in relation to finite resources, such as materials, authority and status within the team. Scope of responsibility includes the range of team tasks and the responsibility and decision-making authority that come with these tasks over functions, people, processes and resources across the alliance and partner organizations. Team entitativity can be defined as the property of a group, resting on clear boundaries and clear internal structure, and making a group 'groupy'. The three-dimensional landscape can conceptually distinguish a joint venture working group from a joint venture management team. Joint venture working groups often have pre-defined short-term tasks (narrow *scope of responsibility*) and team members with aligned interests (weak *factionalism*) who work together coherently in an entity on its own (high *entitativity*). However, a joint venture management team can be defined by vested interests between representatives (strong *factionalism*) who face a range of complex and ill-defined tasks across organizational boundaries (broad *scope of responsibility)* as part of a larger constellation of teams (low *entitativity*). Based on this, the performance drivers of a joint venture working group might have more similarities to other alliance teams with similar attributes than to a joint venture management team. The proposed conceptualization furthers the understanding of how alliance teams differ from intra-organizational teams by focusing on the inter-organizational characteristics of alliance teams. It also allows for advancing insights on the formation, functioning and outcomes of (different) alliance teams.

Source: van der Kamp *et al.* (2022).

Managing alliance teams

The literature on alliance teams is permeated with different theoretical perspectives, all of which provide partial explanations for alliance team functioning and performance (van der Kamp *et al.* 2022). Most research relied on micro-level social psychological and small group theories, such as social identification and categorization, to explain team processes and outcomes (e.g. Li and Hambrick 2005; Luvison and Marks 2013). Meso-level theories on boundary spanning (Büchel 2000; Drach-Zahavy 2011) and systems approaches (Luvison and Marks 2013) have proven helpful to point out that alliance teams operate in a larger environment that affects their performance. Other studies adopted macro-level theories, such as transaction cost and exchange theories, to examine strategic and structural components of alliances and teams to explain, for example, bargaining costs in alliance negotiations (e.g. Johnson *et al.* 2002; Pearce 2001). While it is insightful that many theories apply to alliance teams, it is beyond the scope of this chapter to provide a full account. Therefore, we briefly detail two alliance team perspectives: (1) stand alone and (2) multi-team system. See Table 22.2 for an overview.

Alliance team: stand-alone perspective

The majority of alliance team studies viewed alliance teams as stand-alone entities. These studies sought to explain alliance and alliance team outcomes by focusing on the effect of team-level variables. Specifically, the effects of team formation and functioning on a variety of outcome measures, including behavioural disintegration (Li and Hambrick 2005), team identification (Salk and Shenkar 2001), alliance profitability (Luo 2005) and JV performance (López-Navarro and Camisón-Zornoza 2003), were examined. The forming stage pertains to the early stages of alliance team development. This stage is critical as the architectural foundation of the team is established, which comprises input variables that explain how teams

TABLE 22.2 Alliance team management

Perspective	Point of attention	Example
Stand-alone		
Composition	Team diversity may accentuate 'us-vs-them' perceptions and enforce factions, or diversity may function as a basis for informational synergies.	A joint venture board composed of members with heterogeneous functional backgrounds and experiences invokes constructive decision making.
Coordination	To obtain effective team coordination, a team leader should set team tasks, organize decision making, stimulate participation and create incentives.	Goal clarity, task interdependency and strong team leadership in a R&D team enhances joint learning, knowledge sharing and overall team effectiveness.
Identification	Team members identify with the team, the alliance or their organization; identification may stimulate or impede intra-team collaboration and team effectiveness.	Strong identification by a steering committee member with his/her individual organization may lead to decisions that favour partner interests over collective interests.
Relational	Relational practices in the form of intra-team cooperation, communication and conflict resolution strengthen the social fabric of an alliance team and positively affect team effectiveness.	Distrust in an operational team inhibits the progress of joint work, invokes opportunistic acts and undermines the team's ability to attain its goals.
Multi-team system		
Goal hierarchy	A clear goal hierarchy aligns proximate alliance team goals with distal alliance objectives, such that it enables alliance leadership to set team tasks and organize activity sequencing.	Alignment between joint design, manufacturing and marketing teams with regard to tasks and goals enables the partners to successfully develop and market an innovative product or service.
Multi-team membership	Multi-team membership may be used as a stabilizing governance mechanism as it promotes multi-tasking, productivity and learning; though it demands team members capable to work under high pressure.	When an alliance manager is involved in each stage of alliance development (e.g. strategizing, negotiation, execution and management), the social fabric of the alliance is strengthened over time.
Hand-offs	The timing, quality and accuracy of between-team hand-offs are critical to attain team goals and, more importantly, to accomplish alliance objectives.	Organizing a hand-off between the negotiation and the launch team secures that strategic intent is clear, formal agreements are correctly installed and constructive relational practices are continued.

operate and perform. Following the forming stage, alliance teams proceed to the functioning stage. In this stage, the team becomes operational and hence the focus shifts from designing the team to actual team functioning and processes. Next, we detail team composition and coordination as critical forming conditions and identification and relational practices as functioning processes.

Team composition is one of the most expansive research topics to date on alliance teams. Diversity is inherently part of alliance teams as team members bring distinct demographics, experiences, cultural values and backgrounds to the alliance team. Studies draw on social categorization theory to point out that team members act as representatives for organizations which they are loyal to and identify with because these organizations provide them with safety, and they are familiar with them (e.g. Li *et al.* 2015). Based on a series of interviews, Li and Xin propose that international joint venture (IJV) team members' identification with their parent organization leads to factionalism, which negatively affects communication, commitment and alliance performance. Li and Hambrick (2005) coined the concept of factional groups to capture these phenomena and report that demographic fault lines between factions (i.e. delegate groups) engender task conflict, emotional conflict and behavioural disintegration. In contrast, technical competence, the ability to cope with ambiguity and the cooperative disposition of individuals in alliance teams can increase a team's social cohesion. Together these studies suggest that alliance teams easily break down into conflicting subgroups, factions or coalitions that inhibit the team to accomplish its tasks.

Coordination and control in the context of alliance teams is extremely prevalent because the coordination of alliance activities occurs in the absence of structures and systems available in conventional organizational contexts (Zoogah *et al.* 2011). Although across hierarchical levels coordination activities may vary, coordination tends to focus on task setting, decision-making, participation and incentives. To be effective, alliance teams need to have clear tasks. In a study of JV management teams, Adobor (2004) finds that task complexity negatively impacts the evolution of the team but also that goal clarity and mandate of the JV management team increases team effectiveness. Pearce (2001) finds that task interdependence not only diminishes the effect of factionalism on hard influence tactics but also stimulates team members to use persuasion, consultation, coalition and legitimating tactics. Decision making in alliance teams entails clear procedures about who has the authority to make decisions. For example, board members' decisions pertain to budgeting and staffing, whereas management team members focus on project prioritization and budgets. Reuer *et al.* (2014) recognize the coordinative function of joint venture boards and report that involvement by the IJV board can be beneficial when the partners are engaged in collaborative R&D activities that tend to be subject to contractual incompleteness as well as opportunism. With regard to participation, team coordination entails the instalment of integrative mechanisms between team members, such as initiating direct contact between executives and initiating socialization processes (e.g. training and meetings). The goal is to obtain commitment and involve team members in planning and performance management. Incentives to team members, such as economic and career development paths, depict a control mechanism to steer team members' behaviour towards attainment of team tasks. Economic incentive alignment between representatives is a necessary condition for alliances to succeed, with an uneven alliance benefit for partners resulting in less success (Agarwal *et al.* 2010). In addition, team level rewards (as opposed individual level) tend to increase joint venture team effectiveness (Adobor 2004). Taken together, effective teams depend on team managers' ability to reduce parent companies' uncertainty and solve incentive and coordination problems, an effect that is reinforced if (JV) managers have more decision-making autonomy (López-Navarro and Camisón-Zornoza 2003).

In the setting of an alliance team, a team member may identify with the alliance team, the alliance, the organization or even the team within the partner that they represent. Team members' identification is a critical driver of team processes, such that identification with factions in the alliance team can lead to team conflicts and team disintegration (Li and Hambrick

2005). Identification received specific attention in studies investigating teams in international joint ventures where nationality and organizational boundaries depict strong identifiers (Li *et al.* 2002; Salk and Shenkar 2001). In a study of a Japanese–German joint venture, Salk and Brannen (2000) found that nationality is an important antecedent of individual influence in the joint venture, such that ingroup–outgroup discrimination persisted despite convergence of shared norms. Reporting on a case study of an international joint venture, Salk and Shenkar (2001) unravelled that subgroup boundaries may exist, organized along cultural values (i.e. British–Italian), parent differences (i.e. firm origin) and parent–IJV. The results indicate that national-based subgroups persisted as the IJV progressed, despite structural and contextual offsetting mechanisms (e.g. language and resource dependence). Taken together, identification depicts a critical sense-making vehicle in alliance teams. Perceived similarity, proximity, shared goals and common perceived enemies or threats affect identification with a team.

As alliance team members interact, a variety of relational practices may unfold that directly affect team and possibly alliance outcomes. Team members initiate and engage in collaborative processes to pursue shared or complementary goals. This form of team cooperation is often characterized by intensive communication, trust building and socialization practices between team members. Cooperation tends to improve when team members work together under non-binding contracts when compared to binding contracts (Malhotra and Murnighan 2002), and cooperation (in JV teams) tends to result in improved alliance performance ratings (Luo and Park 2004). Alliance team studies also reported on the positive effects of intra-team communication and how communication mitigates barriers to team effectiveness. For example, Agarwal and colleagues (2010) report that intra-team communication reinforces the positive effect of economic incentives alignment between team members on team performance. Rockmann and colleagues (2007) show that rich communication reinforces team identification, specifically if team members do not strongly identify with their own organizations. Informal socialization mechanisms, such as communication guidelines and social events, can further aid information sharing between team members. Conflicts are part of alliance teams and may endanger alliance team effectiveness (Lumineau *et al.* 2015). For example, Li and Hambrick (2005), investigating joint venture management teams, report that emotional and task conflicts both result from factional fault lines but that only emotional conflicts negatively affect subsequent behavioural disintegration and alliance performance. Agreement exists in the alliance team literature that conflicts form an integral part of alliance teams, however, depending on how they are managed (see Box 22.2), conflicts may be formidable partners or dangerous adversaries.

BOX 22.2 ALLIANCE TEAM LEADERSHIP

One recurring theme across alliance team research pertains to the role alliance team leadership fulfils in driving team functioning and effectiveness. For example, focusing on diversity, studies show how team leadership may resolve diversity challenges (Li *et al.* 1999); focusing on ambiguity, studies show how leadership enables knowledge sharing and creativity (Gu *et al.* 2018); and focusing on connectivity, studies show how team leadership shapes social networks across team boundaries (Bjørkeng *et al.* 2009). Regarding diversity, when team members consider themselves part of an in-group, and thus strongly identify with team members in the alliance team, they are more likely to unify and pursue activities favouring team effectiveness. Effective team leadership then requires team leaders to focus on leadership practices aimed to reinforce a relational identity in support of collective behaviours, enabling team members to capture synergies originating in their diverse backgrounds. By contrast, when team members consider themselves part of out-groups, and thus strongly identify with their (organizational) sub-groups, the alliance team is prone to polarization and behavioural disintegration. Effective team leadership then rests on the ability to construct an intergroup relational identity across organizational boundaries. Such leadership practices ensure that all team members' interests are recognized and all team members are treated respectfully and fairly, thus advancing team effectiveness. To resolve (goal) ambiguity, leadership practices in an alliance team may seek to reinforce the effects of formal and/or relational governance mechanisms. Formal governance, such as contracts, procedures and incentives, provides coordination and control to the team, enabling team members to collectively work towards goals. Effective leadership then reinforces the formalized team structure and is more likely to be centralized and task-driven. In contrast, relational governance, such as trust-building, knowledge sharing and socialization, invites team members to collectively make sense of team processes and goals. Effective leadership practices invest then in enhancing the social fabric of team and are more likely to enhance team process through decentralized and person-driven leadership practices. Taken together, a wide-range of leadership practices can be effective, but the applicability depends on alliance team objectives and composition.

Sources: Hogg *et al.* (2012); Kramer *et al.* (2019); Smith *et al.* (2018); van der Kamp *et al.* (2022).

Alliance team: a multi-team system perspective

A multi-team system perspective proffers that organizational arrangements, such as alliance relationships, are best described as organizational collectives that consist of two or more teams that interface directly and interdependently to accomplish collective goals (Zaccaro *et al.* 2012). The system's boundaries are defined by virtue of the fact that all teams within the system, while pursuing different proximal goals, share at least one common distal goal and, in doing so, exhibit input, process and outcome interdependence with at least one other team in the system (Marks and Luvison 2012). For example, within an alliance, multiple teams simultaneously work on specific team tasks, such as product innovation, setting-up manufacturing and coordinating distribution channels, to accomplish an overarching alliance objective: the commoditization of a new product. In alliance arrangements, team members thus continuously shift attention between team and cross-team activities, which in combination with the strong interdependencies between teams, influences not only their team outcomes but also the extent to which the alliance attains its objectives (Luvison and Marks 2013). As visualized in Figure 22.1, with the introduction of the multi-team system perspective, three topics deserve attention: goal hierarchy, hand-offs and multi-team membership.

Establishing a goal hierarchy and sequencing of interdependent team activities represents a fruitful manner to orchestrate performance in alliance arrangements. A goal hierarchy is an overview of team goals that ensures that all teams pursue goals that align with the common

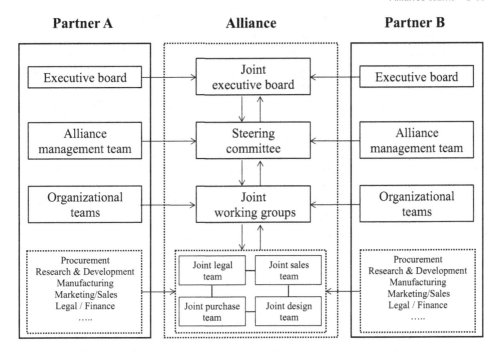

FIGURE 22.1 Alliance multi-team system

alliance objective. In building a goal hierarchy, it is important to consider that the overarching alliance objective can be different from objectives set by the individual partners. As such, an effective goal hierarchy comprises alignment between team goals, partner firm goals and alliance objectives. Consider an example. Two firms forged an alliance to develop and market a new product. A goal hierarchy first specifies the overarching alliance objective—increase market share and profitability by launching an innovative product. Then, derived from the overarching objective, specific individual team goals are formulated, which may include new product development for the R&D team, setting up equipment for the engineering team and developing and negotiating access to a new distribution channel for the sales team. In a perfect world, these teams may work perfectly together; however, without a clear goal hierarchy, inter-team adversities are likely to emerge. The R&D team may develop a high-end product, which the sales team views as unmarketable and which according to the engineers is too expensive to mass produce. A goal hierarchy prevents a waste of resources as it enables management to prioritize and sequence team tasks and activities in such a way that alliance objectives are attained efficiently and effectively. Another important implication of establishing a goal hierarchy is that performance trade-offs become explicit. A performance trade-off implies that although teams in a multi-team system are collaboratively working towards an overarching objective, simultaneously they are competing for the time, resources and funding required to attain their team goals. Explicating and resolving these performance trade-offs is critical. This is because the presence of trade-offs implies that temporary team under-performance may be accepted for the greater good: superior alliance performance. For example, in the previous example, priority could have been given to the marketing and sales team to better understand customer requirements, which implies that the R&D and engineering teams were asked to postpone their activities. Although empirical evidence is lacking, it is reasonable to assume that misspecification of goal hierarchies and task sequencing (i.e. lack of coordination) depicts a cause of alliance instability and under-performance.

Understanding the complexities surrounding hand-offs becomes explicit with a multi-team system perspective. Whereas within-team hand-offs are required when team members are replaced or work is divided among team members, between-team hand-offs facilitate the transfer and completion of tasks in multi-team systems. These between-team hand-offs are even more complex in alliance arrangements as multiple and different teams over time are critical to alliance progress, and it is the quality of the hand-offs that determines whether alliance objectives are attained (Luvison and Marks 2013). For example, as management pushes for progress but does not provide a feasible time planning, it may occur that a R&D team provides the engineering team with erroneous product specifications too late. Across-team hand-offs potentially work like the childhood game of 'Chinese whispers' in which errors accumulate as hand-offs become less accurate over time. Moreover, when some teams exit and others remain, the required hand-off knowledge often remains implicit or assumed by remaining teams. Also, the knowledge and expertise of different teams (regarding hierarchical level and task) makes hand-offs more difficult because team members often use jargon and approach the task from their own perspectives.

By viewing alliance arrangements as multi-team systems, the issue of multi-team membership also becomes salient (Boyer O'Leary et al. 2012). While teams are often considered stable in their team membership, in most alliances, representatives take part in multiple teams, and alliance staff thus may be assigned to multiple teams, over time, across hierarchy and with different tasks. An engineer, for example, can be part of the alliance negotiation team and provide input about operations, can be part of the engineering team working on a new product, can be part of the management team as he/she operates at management level and could be involved in other operational teams. Multiple team membership enables advantages such as multi-tasking, increased productivity and learning. Take how marketers, for example, often have knowledge about business development that enables them to take up some business development tasks, enabling a smoother workflow and shorter throughput time, while on the flip side there might be a conflicting interest with other team goals. Team members with multiple team memberships, however, may face difficulties such as with spreading their time and attention among teams, scheduling and the required discipline to make it all work.

Taken together, the stand-alone perspective emphasizes that alliance teams function as a critical coordination mechanism necessary to steer alliances towards their objectives. Forming conditions and team functioning are critical, but how each alliance team interacts with other teams as part of the multi-team system also represents an important driver of alliance stability and performance. Coordinating alliance teams, alone or as part of a system, therefore necessitates strong boundary agents. Boundary agents in an alliance arrangement play a critical role in the development of a common understanding within and across teams; these agents often initiate the development of shared social meaning across alliance team members (Drach-Zahavy 2011). They gather and interpret information from the partners and transfer their interpretation to other representatives. In addition, they aid alliance leadership in building and maintaining strong ties between teams and partner organizations, ties critical to initiate knowledge, information and resources flows.

Alliance teams: decision-making steps

To steer an alliance arrangement towards its short- and long-term objectives, strong alliance leadership establishes and orchestrates a network of interdependent teams. Moreover, it continuously needs to shift between the individual, team and organizational level in the alliance

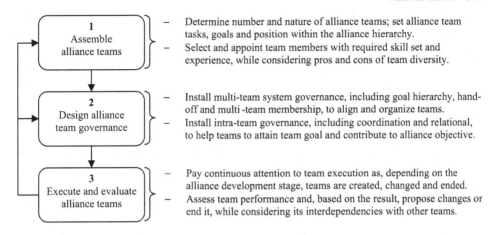

FIGURE 22.2 Decision-making steps: alliance teams

and exhibit strong multi-team leadership. In order to provide guidelines for successfully using teams as the alliance relationship progresses, the next section elaborates on specific decisions for alliance teams at each stage of the alliance development framework (see Figure 22.2).

Step 1: assemble alliance teams

When a firm forges an alliance relationship, among the first critical tasks is to determine the required number of alliance teams, the task for each alliance team and to designate the hierarchical level at which the team operates. A distinction between pre-formation, formation and management activities could be helpful in designing the team governance structure. With regard to pre-formation activities, a firm may set up a team (or alliance function) to explore alliance opportunities and coordinate the portfolio of alliance relationships (see Chapter 23), whereas the top-management team, as part of their job, may champion various alliance initiatives. During the formation stage, partners' negotiation teams interact and lay the foundation for the alliance, whereas launch teams take over and are responsible for alliance execution. Once operational, alliance management teams become responsible for coordinating resource exchange, knowledge transfer and political manoeuvring across organizational boundaries. As part of their task, this team may coordinate and align the activities of multiple project teams or working groups. Documenting team governance could be beneficial as it allows alliance leadership to proactively deal with changes in team membership, caused by alliance development transitions (e.g. from formation to management), under-performance (e.g. team member replacement) and task completion (e.g. intended dissolution).

Each alliance team has a specific task, and delegate selection constitutes a critical activity as the people staffing an alliance team form a major input factor that affects team processes and outcomes. In general, partners should select and appoint team members with the required skill set and experience for the task at hand. For example, the negotiation team may include skilled negotiators, senior alliance managers, operational managers and juridical and financial advisors. The launch team may comprise savvy alliance managers with experience in alliance and change management and a deep understanding of the partner organizations. Accounting for diversity is important as, on the one hand, alliance teams, across hierarchical levels, may break into subgroups, and on the other hand, diversity between team members may facilitate information exchange and creativity. Representative selection may thus, in addition to personal skills and experiences, focus on a team member's ability to work in factional teams.

Step 2: design alliance team governance

Alliance team governance entails the design of the multi-team system as well as the design of the different alliance teams. With regard to the design of the multi-team system, alliance leadership's main task is to establish a governance structure that contributes to alliance stability and enables the partners to accomplish their objectives. To this end, the first task is to establish a goal hierarchy, which represents an overview of the alliance objectives, derived sub-goals per team and insight into how the attainment of these goals is interdependent. Specifically, a goal hierarchy explicates the sequencing of activities between teams and thus allows alliance management to organize smooth hand-offs. Without a clear hand-off between teams, alliance processes are likely to become obstructed. One way to organize hand-offs is to formalize multi-team membership, which allows team members to create alignment between team tasks and processes.

With regard to intra-team governance, formal and relational coordination mechanisms help teams to attain goals and allow them to make their contribution to alliance objectives. Specifically, team managers must carefully choose team members who will match their counterparts in the partnering organization in rank and experience. Asymmetry in decision-making authority (e.g. seasoned senior versus less experienced junior managers) may inhibit decision-making speed and also function as a signal of low commitment. In addition to formal governance, it is imperative to develop and build the social fabric of the team. Early communications between team members tend to be frequent and intense, yet occasionally issues are confusing. To build social ties and stimulate joint sense making, team-building sessions, field trips and other social activities should be organized.

Step 3: execute and evaluate alliance teams

Given the plethora of teams involved in an alliance arrangement, alliance leadership should pay continuous attention to team execution. During each alliance development stage, teams are created, changed and dissolved. Team execution is thus a continuous and dynamic process with multiple potential hazards. During team execution, hand-off and transition hazards may emerge that demand quick resolutions. For example, once negotiations are successfully concluded, negotiation teams need to provide the (joint) launch team with all relevant information; procrastination, neglecting to provide information about relational quality or forgetting to explain important contractual details may all impede a smooth alliance execution. Similarly, steering committees may withhold information from operational teams, direction and resources. As the alliance progresses, it becomes more likely that critical interpersonal links between team members are built, which can be broken as delegates change positions or jobs. A decision to reassign personnel that makes sense from a partner firm's perspective can inflict severe penalties and trigger a major setback to an alliance. Dismantling a team, intended or unintended, may also undermine alliance progress as the social fabric of the alliance is changed. Thus, to achieve alliance objectives, well-integrated communication and workflows among managers and teams within and across firms are required.

Team leaders are expected to assess team performance and, based on the result, propose changes, while considering its relationship with other teams. For example, without clear product specifications, engineering teams cannot set up production lines. In other words, underperformance of the engineering team could be caused by intra-team conditions, but poor performance may also result from mismanagement of the interdependencies between teams. The alliance management team therefore should not only receive reports on team performance, but it should also conduct a regular audit of evolving social, work and communication ties within and between teams as it is valuable for managers to gauge the health of the alliance and spot problem areas. It is their responsibility that the multi-team system functions. As such, a generic performance metric system should be extended with metrics capturing team performance (tailored to the specific team) and metrics capturing processes and outcomes pertaining to the multi-team system.

Summary

The 'alliance team' does not exist. Within alliance arrangements, multiple teams interact in a multi-team system spanning across hierarchical levels and over time. The development of an alliance entails continual changes in the composition of teams because of part-time team members, team-member turnover and teams that are only involved in the alliance for a specific short-term task. To attain alliance objectives, alliance leadership therefore should direct its attention to the composition and functioning of various teams involved in an alliance arrangement. In addition, alliance leadership needs to consider that teams in an alliance arrangement operate in a network of interdependent teams, such that the accomplishment of more distal alliance objectives originates in alliance teams attaining more proximate team goals.

CASE: DUTCH OPTICS CENTRE[2]

In October 2016, the Dutch Organization for Applied Sciences (TNO) and the Technical University of Delft (TU Delft) signed an alliance agreement for the initiation of Dutch Optic Centre (DOC). Against the background of internal development at TNO (for example, stagnation of financing existing RD activities in this field) and external development (such as SMEs' need to get affordable access to fundamental knowledge to realize their product innovation, and increased use of field labs and government pressure to do more in public–private partnerships), TNO decided to explore the possibilities of realizing their ambition by setting the DOC alliance together with TU Delft.

The DOC aims to boost Dutch industry in the field of optics and opto-mechatronics by increasing the utilization of Dutch science through joint R&D. The Netherlands is unmatched in the field of optics and opto-mechatronics, holding a leading position in science and industry. The DOC is an innovation-oriented alliance consisting of knowledge institutes and more than 20 hi-tech companies from all over the Netherlands. The objective of DOC is to become an ambitious public–private partnership in the field of optics and opto-mechatronics by 2020. It strives to realize three objectives. The first is to develop (fundamental) knowledge focused on the long-term needs of companies. Second, it seeks to support and collaborate with companies to develop new products up to the highest technology readiness level and to introduce products on the markets. Finally, DOC aims to promote the DOC brand in order to attract new R&D partners and also create an interesting environment for students and PhDs. TNO and TU Delft fulfil the leadership role and will be guided by the needs of the industry.

Before focusing on the functioning of the alliance set-up team, we will briefly explain the set-up process. In 2014, TNO started the process of setting up the DOC alliance. The period between 2014 and the start of 2016 can be characterized as the exploration phase. TNO and TU Delft explored the possibilities of creating a viable DOC alliance. This was done by holding meetings with internal and external stakeholders such as SMEs and the Ministry of Economic Affairs. During that period, more and more people started to believe in the power of concepts like field labs, test beds, ecosystem thinking and joint innovation centres. This fostered the creation of a viable DOC alliance. Between the start of 2016 and October of that year, the alliance set-up team created a DOC website, defined the set of potential products/ service of the alliance, organized two network meetings with SMEs, aligned the interests of the Ministry of Economic Affairs and RVO with those of the DOC alliance partners and other stakeholders (such as SMEs), and developed a DOC business plan and a contract supported by top management of each partner. This resulted in the signing of a DOC alliance agreement on 19 October 2016.

An alliance formation team was created in early 2014, led by the managing director of TNO industry and a full professor and head of the Optics Research Group at TU Delft. The objective of this team was to create a feasible and executable DOC business plan, including a business model (cost–revenue structure), an assigned collaboration agreement and the first step in the execution (for example, a website and initial projects with SMEs).

This team consists of a research manager of expertise and a business developer from TNO, and a professor and some members of the valorization centre of TU Delft. Both organizations put someone in place with knowledge of this field of expertise, as well as someone who is external and more business-oriented. The employees of TNO and TU Delft had worked together for a long period of time and therefore had a good understanding of each other's interests and capabilities. This helped the process of creating a common ambition and plan. Moreover, the set-up team was located in the same building, which supported communication between the members: a lot of informal, face-to-face communication. They spoke to each other frequently (almost daily) and held a meeting every Friday to discuss progress and set new actions.

At the beginning of 2016, a new person entered the alliance set-up team. This person was also externally oriented and pragmatic but also more entrepreneurially oriented and had no background in this field of knowledge and no prior collaboration experience with the individuals from TU Delft. This had consequences for the team dynamic. For example, there was uncertainty about whether this person understood the interests of the other organization well enough. This resulted in constructive debate but also conflicts, which were resolved as alliance preparations continued.

The basic attitude of alliance team members was pragmatic; that is, it was not about making plans first and then doing, but more about 'thinking–doing' and dealing with obstacles as they appeared. The advantage of this mindset was that they made a lot of progress in terms of making plans and actions (examples included constructing a website, defining first projects inclusive of SME partners, and finding funding). Because of this, higher management saw the immediate consequences of setting up this alliance. This provided energy but also internal friction and questions. For instance: is this what we want, for example, working on a higher technology readiness level than we used to do? What is the relationship between my 'technology road map' and the roadmap of the alliance? Is this sufficiently aligned? What does it mean for the relationship between TNO and SMEs and for the DOC alliance and their stakeholders (also including SMEs)? Would we cannibalize our own initiatives or not?

In order to acquire and maintain support from their own organizations, the alliance setup team communicates frequently, via a newsletter, to their internal stakeholders regarding the status, actions and questions concerning DOC. This helps the team to speed up the progress, and the internal organization feels that they have to be alert; otherwise, the situation is set. The fact that more internal people see consequences (both positive and negative) of this alliance for their work also creates internal tensions. Moreover, TNO has a unique (legal) position in the market and is still learning how to collaborate with external partners within the legal framework.

Finally, the collaboration agreement was created with support from the legal department at TNO as well as TU Delft and signed by the chief executive officer of TNO and the rector magnificus of TU Delft. Moreover, a detailed business plan and business model has been developed. From July till October 2017, DOC alliance transitioned to a fully operational arrangement. This is the result of this team, with support of management of TNO and TU Delft, and great help from the various secretaries and legal support. Since then, the DOC alliance has broadened it scope and developed activities in the area of agri food, energy and environment, health, ICT and manufacturing. In addition, the DOC offers training and education, bringing together academic and industrial partners.

Questions

1   The team representatives of TNO and TU Delft were primarily focused on continuing to make progress. They did take a little time to engage in team building. Explain why team building during the (pre)launch stage is critical to overcome post-launch impediments to alliance development.
2   Team composition changed over time as a new team member was added to the (pre) launch team. Explain how team composition (and team-member skills) may affect alliance launch team functioning and how changes in team membership may positively or negatively affect team functioning.

Notes

1   We acknowledge Martijn van der Kamp for his contribution to this chapter.
2   Interview with a senior executive of TNO; for more information see: www.dutchopticscentre.com/

23

ALLIANCE CAPABILITIES

A firm's alliance capability refers to its ability to design, manage and terminate alliances successfully. An alliance capability thus can enhance the overall performance of a firm's alliances in that it enables the firm to purposefully create, extend or modify the routines it uses to inform its alliance decision making. Firms develop alliance capabilities over time, but they also tend to capture only minimal knowledge or develop just a few best practices. In an environment with few alliances, such an ad hoc approach may be effective; however, the increasing importance of alliances implies that an unstructured approach will ultimately produce frustrating, unsatisfactory results. In contrast, a structured approach that embeds the alliance capability in the organizational design, culture and minds of employees enables the firm to build and deploy its expansive alliance capabilities more effectively. To adopt such a structured approach, alliance managers first need to understand what alliance capabilities are (first section) before they can gain insights into capability building and deployment (second section). In the next two sections we provide a systematic framework with a set of decision-making steps regarding alliance capabilities and a summary. We conclude with a case illustration.

The meaning of alliance capabilities

One of the main factors contributing to strong alliance performance is the development of specific managerial routines to address (sets of) alliances—that is, a firm's alliance capability (Kale and Singh 2007). Extant studies have shown that building, possessing and deploying such an alliance capability enables firms, compared to peers without an alliance capability, to better generate and appropriate value from their alliance arrangements. One set of studies focused on 'learning from alliances' and explored the effects of alliance experience. In general, these studies show that having forged alliances in the past positively affects the performance of future alliances (Liu and Ravichandran 2015; Simonin 1997). Lee *et al.* (2015), for example, show that firms with more alliance experience are better able to protect their interests under any given alliance structure, making the choice of structure less consequential to them. Ariño *et al.* (2014) show that the length of prior relationships has a U-shaped effect on negotiation time, suggesting that partner firms learn from prior encounters. Pangarkar (2009) demonstrates that firms that have experienced prior terminations are less likely to have their future alliance

DOI: 10.4324/9781003222187-23

dissolved as prior termination experiences will enable them to design better alliances and adopt more appropriate alliance management strategies. Some studies distinguished between generic and partner-specific experiences (Zollo *et al.* 2002). Rahman and Korn (2014) demonstrate positive performance consequences, such that generic alliance experience breeds dynamic routines, which facilitate better alliance management and increased the likelihood of alliance survival, whereas partner-specific experience substitutes for coordination and control mechanisms as prior encounters generate trust and promote learning from past mistakes.

Extending beyond the effect of experience, other studies focus on institutionalization of alliance practices. In general, these studies report positive effects of alliance capabilities on alliance and alliance portfolio performance (Heimeriks and Duysters 2007; Heimeriks *et al.* 2009). For example, Zheng and Yang (2015) demonstrate that the benefits and liabilities of inter-organizational routines, arising from alliance partner repeatedness at a firm's alliance portfolio level, lead to an inverted U-shaped relationship between alliance partner repeatedness and breakthrough innovations. de Man and Luvison (2014) report that an alliance-supportive culture was found to mediate the relationship between alliance experience and performance, suggesting that experience with alliances leads to better alliance performance when this experience is institutionalized into the organizational culture.

Taken together, with alliance capabilities, firms can standardize and optimize the partner selection process, then make appropriate alliance design and management decisions. A highly developed alliance capability also assists firms in choosing performance indicators that are consistent with their specific alliance strategy, then evaluate and, if needed, terminate under-performing alliances while still ensuring favourable outcomes. In addition to augmenting the performance of bilateral alliance arrangements, alliance capabilities may enable a firm to optimize alliance portfolio design and coordination (Haider and Mariotti 2016). Beyond the direct effect of alliance capabilities, firms also vary in their degree of capability, such that those with superior competences have a competitive edge over their peers (see e.g. Bouncken and Fredrich 2016; Simonin 1997). To comprehend the performance implications of possessing alliance capabilities, and their varying levels, it becomes important to distinguish between (1) alliance capability routines and (2) alliance capability instruments.

Alliance capability routines

The dynamic capability view (Teece *et al.* 1997) suggests that alliance capabilities constitute a set of managerial routines designed to improve firm performance by optimizing the governance of its alliance. Thus routines relate to the governance of a single alliance, in the form of coordination and transformation routines, or else target the management of a firm's alliance portfolio through alliance proactiveness and alliance portfolio coordination.

Alliance coordination routines coordinate activities and resources with a specific alliance partner (Schilke and Goerzen 2010). They thus provide firms with the ability to formulate an alliance strategy, select an alliance partner, negotiate and design an efficient structure and then manage, evaluate and terminate that specific alliance. If a firm possesses alliance coordination routines, it will also have developed a standardized approach to guide and inform its decisions about each new alliance. Each alliance development stage demands different alliance capabilities, but their coordination routines enable firms to deal readily with potential deal breakers as the alliance progresses. For example, the routines might centre on developing partner profiles, building long and short lists of potential partners and formulating a partner fit framework to support partner fit analyses. In contrast, in the alliance management stage, the routines pertain to the firm's ability to coordinate, communicate and bond with its counterpart (Schreiner *et al.* 2009). Thus they ensure that any single alliance is governed as efficiently as possible and that the legitimacy of the transaction is maximized.

Alliance transformation routines instead pertain to a firm's ability to modify alliances over the course of the alliance process (Niederkofler 1991). Where alliance coordination routines inform decision making, transformation routines reflect the recognition that it is unrealistic to expect a perfect fit between partners from the very beginning (Schilke and Goerzen 2010). Interaction and adaptation between partners are prerequisites as the alliance develops for establishing and maintaining high partner fit; the transformation routines include contract amendments, fluctuations in alliance-related personnel or changes in alliance-related governance mechanisms that encourage such adaptations. Flexibility in alliance design is frequently mentioned as a critical element of win–win alliances, but transformation routines actually facilitate firms' ability to act flexibly and initiate timely corrective measures during the progression of their partnerships.

Alliance proactiveness pertains to a firm's ability to discover and act on new alliance opportunities before its competitors can (Sarkar *et al.* 2009); it therefore applies beyond individual alliances. By institutionalizing sensing routines, firms can readily identify potential partners and enjoy first-mover advantages over their competitors. The potential scarcity of suitable alliance candidates may leave late movers with sub-optimal partnering options; firms with proactiveness routines enjoy an advantageous position in the market for partners. In a market with limited high-quality partnering options, routines to identify potentially valuable partnering opportunities constitute a source of strategic advantage.

Finally, the potential interdependencies between individual alliances may enable the firm to develop routines for coordinating its alliance portfolio. An alliance portfolio coordination capability helps the firm identify interdependencies, avoid duplicate actions and produce synergies among its individual alliances (Castro and Roldan 2015; Schilke and Goerzen 2010). By systematically identifying and creating synergies, alliance portfolio coordination can also turn an alliance portfolio into more than just the sum of its parts. These routines minimize risks by lowering the resource investments needed to achieve gains and diminish conflicts across different relationships in the firm's alliance portfolio. Supplemental benefits may derive from the firm's ability to identify, assimilate and use knowledge within and across alliance partners. Alliance portfolio coordination also improves the firm's performance because it implies the coordination of knowledge across otherwise disconnected alliance partners. Routines and practices targeted at knowledge management across alliance partners provide firms with a competitive advantage.

Alliance capability instruments

The performance-enhancing qualities of an alliance capability depend not just on routines (Zollo *et al.* 2002) or a supportive organizational culture (de Man and Luvison 2014) but also on the instruments that are at the disposal of the firm (see Table 23.1). An alliance function refers to all systems of communication, authority and workflow surrounding the alliance. It identifies the effective and ineffective alliance practices and refines the experience-based data to highly useful information. It provides a focal point for capturing and storing alliance management lessons and best practices, whether in the form of a part- or full-time position or even a specialized department. Thus, the alliance function serves as a reservoir as well as a refinery of alliance management knowhow. Firms such as Hewlett-Packard, Eli Lilly and Philips have established separate organizational units to manage their alliances. The alliance

TABLE 23.1 Alliance capability instruments

Instruments	Description	Tools
Alliance function	Specialized support staff offers (standardized) know-how and know-what, contributing to efficient alliance design, management and assessment.	Alliance department, specialists, designated top executives, designated alliance managers, gatekeepers.
Alliance training	Training and learning enable managers to identify problems, develop solutions and implement them skilfully and responsibly.	Internal training, external training, alliance handbooks, alliance best practices, cross-alliance evaluation, formal learning structures, training in intercultural management.
Alliance managers	Integrating the function of alliance managers with human resource management practices provides alliance managers with incentives to achieve excellence.	Management programmes, competency framework, rewards and bonuses.
Alliance tools	Developing supportive decision-making tools helps alliance managers make better-informed decisions.	Alliance database, intranet, generic template alliance metrics, standardized tools, joint business planning, joint alliance evaluation, country-specific management, partner programmes.
Third parties	Overcoming deficiencies in alliance capabilities by hiring external parties increases the chances of alliance success.	Consultants, financial/legal experts, mediators for conflict resolution.

Sources: Heimeriks and Duysters (2007); Heimeriks et al. (2009).

department thus functions as a link, a coordinator and a bond within the organization that supports the extensive use and development of alliance capabilities.

Generally an alliance function fulfils five roles: expert, advisor, knowledge manager, coach and network facilitator (Kale et al. 2001). The expert role means it identifies potential partners and governs the ins and outs of the alliance relationships. The advisor role refers to providing line management with expertise, tools and operating procedures and, when necessary, mediating in alliances that are suffering escalating conflicts. The knowledge management role requires collecting, codifying and communicating alliance best practices. The role of coach develops and offers training, education and advice to alliance managers and partner firms. Finally, as a network facilitator, the function initiates gatherings to enable alliance managers to meet and share experiences. Firms with such an alliance function tend to enjoy superior performance (Dyer et al. 2001). Interestingly, Rahman and Korn (2014) show that the presence of a formal alliance unit negatively associates with alliance longevity. This is because firms with a specialized alliance function are better able to manage their alliance arrangements. That is, such firms are able to quickly assess the usefulness of an alliance, expedite the completion of alliance tasks, quickly identify under-performance and allocate scarce resources efficiently.

Alliance training refers specifically to managers' acquisition of the knowledge, skills and mindset required to perform different activities related to each distinct alliance development stage (Heimeriks *et al.* 2009). Firms may engage in different forms of training and learning, including in-house and external alliance training, developing an alliance handbook, cross-alliance evaluations or inter-departmental learning. For example, Hewlett-Packard (HP) developed a two-day course on alliance management, which it offers three times a year. The company also provides shorter, three-hour courses on alliance management and makes all its alliance materials available on the internal HP alliance website. Such offerings are not trivial when it comes to the success of the partnership because alliance governance often does not come naturally to traditional managers, who prefer decision autonomy.

To effectuate alliance capabilities among alliance managers, firms may develop management development programmes (Lambe *et al.* 2002) to organize alliance manager competences systematically in a competency framework that also includes reward and bonus systems. Participating in such programmes enhances managers' ability to keep track of and coordinate a vast number of partners, and as alliances grow increasingly important for business, such practical alliance management experience is likely to become a standard criterion for managerial careers. Thus HP created opportunities for internal networking among its managers, not just through internal training programmes but also through company-wide alliance summits and virtual meetings with executives. The company also regularly sends alliance managers to alliance management programmes at various business schools to develop their competences.

The standardized alliance tools that firms might develop include alliance databases, intranet access, performance metrics and tools tailored to each alliance development stage (see Table 23.2). The application of alliance tools indicates that firms have codified and leveraged methodically their alliance knowledge and best practices gained from previous alliances (Kale and Singh 2007). A database provides access to others' past experiences, tools, checklists and information about partners, all of which can support alliance managers in their daily functions. Hewlett-Packard again offers a prime example: it has developed 60 different tools and templates, all of which are included in a 300-page manual for decision making in specific alliance situations. The manual includes, for example, a template for making a business case for an alliance, a partner evaluation form, a negotiation template that outlines the roles and responsibilities of different departments, a list of ways to measure alliance performance and an alliance termination checklist (Dyer *et al.* 2001). Such alliance tools not only support managerial decision making but also enhance alliance performance.

Firms may also use third parties, such as consultants, legal/financial experts and mediators, who provide specialized knowledge related to legal issues, conflict resolution, financing and alliance governance. Because alliance capabilities foster firms' alliance (portfolio) performance, third parties might be helpful for developing and supplementing internal alliance capabilities (Heimeriks and Duysters 2007). For example, during the alliance design stage, firms are likely to rely on outside financial, legal and alliance specialists to secure their investments. They often use external financial experts to perform due diligence or valuation services, as well as to give them advice on investment structures. Legal experts might substitute for a firm's lack of knowledge regarding contractual agreements, especially if the firm is relatively small. When conflicts arise, external experts can assist in conflict resolution by acting as independent mediators. Thus, access to external knowledge decreases the constraints imposed on firms by a scarcity of internal resources and enables them to deal better with their capability deficiencies.

Overall then, firms with alliance capabilities (i.e. routines and instruments) tend to outperform their peers who lack those capabilities (Niesten and Jolink 2015). In particular, they experience more positive effects on their stock prices after alliance announcements (Anand and Khanna 2000), enjoy stronger value creation and profit generation in single alliances

TABLE 23.2 Alliance tools

Alliance strategy formulation	Alliance launch	Alliance partner selection	Alliance negotiation	Alliance design	Alliance management	Alliance evaluation	Alliance termination
Value chain analysis	Generic alliance execution roadmap	Partner screening form	Negotiation matrix	Alliance governance form guidelines	Alliance contact list	Generic performance metric template	Termination checklist
Resource need checklist	(Early) Healthcheck diagnosis tool	Partner selection protocol	Needs-vs-wants checklist	Alliance contract template	Alliance communication infrastructure	Evaluation form	Termination planning work sheet
Resource vulnerability checklist	Kick-off meeting template	Partner fit framework Partner database	Negotiation procedure checklist Negotiation team checklist	Alliance management control guidelines	Trust building worksheet Response strategy framework	Checklist metric procedures	Best practice template

Sources: Dyer *et al.* (2001); Kale and Singh (2009).

(Lambe *et al.* 2002) and achieve higher overall rates of goal achievement (Heimeriks and Duysters 2007; Ziggers and Tjemkes 2010). Firms with well-established alliance management capabilities are better able to generate relational assets from complementary resources (Leischnig *et al.* 2014), whereas institutionalized management processes aimed at coordinating, communicating and bonding the alliance partners positively affects performance at both alliance and firm levels (Schreiner *et al.* 2009). Furthermore, processes related to alliance proactiveness, relational governance and strategy or resource coordination by the alliance partners enhance alliance portfolio performance (Sarkar *et al.* 2009). Most companies engage in multiple alliances, so a firm's capability to govern its portfolio of alliances constitutes another important competitive advantage.

Building and deploying alliance capabilities

Before a firm can deploy its alliance capabilities, it must obtain access to or develop them. Although firms learn by doing, alliance experience cannot ensure superior alliance performance by itself (Simonin 1997). Lessons must be translated into know-how, which needs to be actively managed and dispersed throughout the organization (Anand and Khanna 2000). Alliance learning processes provide a key mechanism for enabling the alliance function to lead to greater alliance success (Kale and Singh 2007). Deliberate learning mechanisms allow alliance experience to produce enhanced performance in future alliances (Kale *et al.* 2002).

Developing alliance capabilities in particular requires four learning mechanisms: (1) capture, (2) codify, (3) communication and (4) coaching (Dyer *et al.* 2001; Kale and Singh 2007). Drawing on prior experience with alliance relationships, a firm should initiate activities to capture its managers' experiences. For example, debriefing can reveal managers' tacit know-how about the design, management and termination of an alliance. Furthermore, a firm might stimulate the codification or recording of experiences by providing guidelines, checklists and worksheets and encouraging managers to revise them; though working with codified knowledge appears to be beneficial for the alliance formation and termination stages, its use may be detrimental during the management stage (Heimeriks *et al.* 2015). Prescribed templates for example increase rigour yet reduce relational adaptability. With such codified knowledge, the firm can encourage activities that facilitate communication among staff members. Knowledge sharing in the form of networks and fora contributes to the development of routines and new insights. Routinization and increasing know-how enable managers to provide coaching that further diffuses alliance knowledge. When these learning mechanisms are employed simultaneously, alliance capabilities become institutionalized.

However, depending on the number and purposes of the alliances they undertake, firms might work to achieve varying competence levels (see Table 23.3). A Level 1 competence suggests that a firm primarily uses a reactive alliance strategy that excludes efforts to build partnerships. Alliances get stimulated by single champions with limited responsibilities. Initial alliance management is chaotic and ad hoc; alliance problems get solved as they arise. No tools support diagnoses or solutions, even if some of these Level 1 firms build on their prior experience to make decisions.

A Level 2 competence suggests that firms recognize that alliances represent viable growth alternatives, so they have standardized their important alliance processes. For example, a firm might have developed a partner fit tool to select the right alliance partner(s) and use it systematically throughout the organization. In addition, it works to develop its efforts in different functional areas, such as R&D, production, marketing or distribution. Firm-wide,

TABLE 23.3 Alliance capability competence levels

	Level 1: Ad hoc	Level 2: Extended	Level 3: Institutionalized
Alliance	Few alliances; reactive approach disconnected from corporate strategy.	Reasonable number of alliances; alliance are strategic alternatives; becoming a partner of choice.	Large number of alliances; systematic reengineering of the value chain/ecosystem to develop and sustain competitive advantage.
Learning	Non-deliberate and ad hoc.	Informal knowledge sharing and codification of best practices.	Creation of knowledge structure, processes and routines to build and leverage alliance capabilities.
Champion	Individual, single champion with a vision.	Alliance team, responsible for capability building and deployment.	Organization, company-wide awareness to build and leverage alliance capabilities.
Authority	Line management.	Middle management.	Top management.
Activities	Legal and financial skills; hands-on tools; partner selection; performance assessment.	Develop alliance community; standardization of tools across alliance development stages; training, best practice handbook; balanced metrics.	Corporate strategy-driven; integrate with firm's strategic analysis, alliance portfolio management; alliance function, alliance programmes; intranet.

Sources: Harbison and Pekar (1998); Pekar and Allio (1994).

management invests in a corporate architecture and strategy, so to some degree, a Level 2 firm can measure, monitor and perhaps even manage the quality of the alliance process.

A Level 3 competence suggests that firms systematically reengineer the value chain (or ecosystem) to achieve the close integration of their operational activities. The coherent, integrated alliance strategy gets embedded in the corporate strategy. The firm possesses widespread alliance capabilities and thus can obtain and leverage a competitive advantage through partnerships. Procedures are standardized, often with dedicated staff that engages in significant sharing to develop best practices. Some repository of knowledge has been established for future use; alliance knowledge gets periodically disseminated through training and education. To exploit their alliance knowledge, these firms commit to process discipline; that is, their alliance processes, methods and tools are well organized and finely tuned. On this level, alliance management tools are used consistently and developed systemically. At this high level of alliance maturity, one or more specialists are at work within the organization; with greater maturity, this specialist takes a greater role, and the criteria for selecting the specialist become more stringent.

Effective alliance capability building and deploying is conditional on the firms' need and ability to forge alliances. Resource allocation decisions must reflect the size of the firm and its tendency to use alliances as a competitive strategy. Moreover, a sole emphasis on possessing and deploying alliance management capabilities may result in inertia and rigid applications of tools and templates (Kauppila 2015). Competence levels therefore need to be tailored to alliance requirements. For relatively small firms with few alliances, Level 1 alliance capabilities are sufficient. To enhance their alliance capability over time, however, these firms might search for partners with institutionalized alliance capabilities or hire third parties. Relatively large firms with numerous alliances may want to invest to develop a Level 2 competence and eventually progress to Level 3 because, for them, alliance capabilities constitute a source of significant competitive advantage. Learning implications pertaining to heterogeneity in competence levels are that, (1) to enhance their alliance capability, less-experienced firms may seek to ally with partners at a higher competence levels, whereas the latter may decide to invest in the former to enhance the likelihood of alliance success (Howard *et al.* 2016), and (2) entrepreneurial firms, often operating at competence level 1, are better off entering a select number of strategic alliances and focusing on enhancing the outcomes of those select alliances as well as developing a dynamic alliance management capability rather than depending on a small number of alliances or becoming overwhelmed with a great number of alliances (Moghaddam *et al.* 2016).

Alliance capabilities: decision-making steps

To develop and use alliance capabilities effectively, firms need a systematic, structured approach that allows them to consider a variety of issues. For example, firms must decide on the importance of alliance activity for realizing their strategic objectives and consistently organizing their alliance capabilities. Conditional on this decision, other choices that inform alliance (portfolio) success follow: the use of advanced management techniques, formalization of procedures, dedicated staff, establishment of knowledge repositories, dedicated alliance functions, best practices and alliance training. To facilitate these choices, we organize them into three decision-making steps (see Figure 23.1).

Step 1: alliance capability criticality

To determine the criticality of an alliance capability, firms must understand how and to what extent their alliances contribute to their competitive advantages. For example, if realizing its long-term strategy depends primarily on a firm's autonomous growth, alliances and alliance capabilities will play a limited role. In contrast, if a firm focuses on its core competences and perceives alliances as strategic instruments that help it remain competitive and flexible, building and using alliance capabilities becomes critical. In the latter case, alliances are integral to

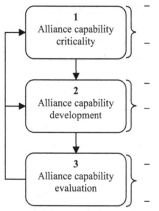

1 Alliance capability criticality	– Assess the criticality of alliance capabilities; determine the role alliances play in executing a firm's strategy taking account of firm size and industry conditions; determine desired competence level. – Firms operating in industries with widespread alliance activity require a Level 3 competence.
2 Alliance capability development	– Compare existing alliance capabilities and desired alliance capabilities to develop an alliance capability development plan. – Invest in routines and tools that improve alliance (portfolio) governance; invest in learning mechanisms that enable a firm to capture, codify, communicate and coach alliance best practices.
3 Alliance capability evaluation	– Assess and monitor alliance development trajectory and, when necessary, implement corrective measures, including modification of development goals and approach. – Extend generic performance metrics with metrics tapping into alliance learning and best practices.

FIGURE 23.1 Decision-making steps: alliance capabilities

firms' corporate strategies and embodied in their corporate strategies and policies. That is, even if modern alliances tend to underpin a firm's competitive advantage, the actual alliance capabilities may fulfil three roles:

- Critical success factor: an alliance capability is a critical success factor if it contributes to alliance success, but alliances themselves are not key to gaining competitive advantages. To make these alliances work, firms require a Level 1 alliance competence.
- Core competence: an alliance capability constitutes a core competence when the firm obtains a distinctive competitive position through its smart alliance management. Firms leverage their alliance capability to outperform that of their competitors; therefore, they should invest in obtaining Level 2 alliance competence.
- Qualifier: in many industries, allying has become so pervasive that it is virtually impossible to operate successfully without alliances—such as the automotive industry with its manufacturer—supplier dyads, the pharmaceutical industry with its biotechnology links, and the airline industry with its multi-partner coalitions. Thus an alliance capability is a prerequisite for firm survival, and failing to attain Level 3 competences will impose a severe disadvantage on a firm.

Step 2: alliance capability development

Depending on the criticality of its alliance capabilities, a firm should formulate and execute an alliance capability development plan. First, it should identify which alliance capability routines are required to achieve its desired competence level. For example, a firm may develop routines to optimize the governance of single alliances, such as alliance coordination and transformation routines. It also could invest in alliance portfolio routines, including alliance proactiveness and alliance portfolio coordination, or it might seek a combination of single and portfolio alliance routines. Second, the firm should decide which alliance capability instruments are required: is it really necessary to establish an alliance function (see Box 23.1), offer alliance training, initiate a management development programme, build alliance tools and source third parties? Third, by comparing the desired routines and instruments with its existing alliance capabilities, the firm's managers can formulate alliance capability development goals and plan to organize and manage the development trajectory. In other words, managers determine how to capture experience with existing alliances, codify it, communicate the information throughout the organization and coach and facilitate appropriate processes.

BOX 23.1 DESIGNING AN ALLIANCE OFFICE

When an alliance office is centralized, it often represents an integral part of the firm's top management team. The key advantages of centralization include the following:

- Clustered know-how.
- Diffusion throughout operational departments.
- Development of best practices.
- Specialized expertise and routines.
- Ongoing repetition of standardized processes.

Thus a centralized office requires senior executive champions, relationship managers, well-defined tools and practices, consistent and sufficient assistance to business units, coordination across partners, centralized knowledge, and monitoring and management. The contributions of a centralized alliance office to value creation, as perceived by business units, can be limited.

It might be useful instead to consider integrating an alliance office into the operational structure, such that alliance activity is organized within a business unit, which reports to headquarters. The key advantages of such decentralization are the following:

- Integration into the operational/business strategy.
- Ability to adapt to local knowledge of customers and partners.
- Direct accountability.
- Flexibility and speed in design, decision making and execution.

In terms of organizational design, decentralization requires informal cross-linkages, limited formalization and bureaucracy, and fast decision making. However, it also makes building and leveraging alliance know-how and know-what across the company more difficult.

Step 3: alliance capability evaluation

To sustain effective alliance capability developments, managers must continuously monitor the development process. Monitoring provides the necessary information to take appropriate actions, whether that means changing alliance capability development goals, altering the development approach, or organizing and managing the learning processes differently. The criticality of evaluating alliance-learning processes means that firms often should extend their alliance performance metric system with indicators that capture the degree to which they engage in alliance learning and develop and use best practices.

Following the three steps for alliance capability development and deployment does not provide a clear-cut recipe for instant success, but by adopting these insights, alliance managers can enhance their firm's long-term alliance capabilities.

Summary

Firms that possess an alliance capability tend to outperform those that lack institutionalized alliance know-how and know-what. An alliance capability can enhance the performance of a firm's (portfolio of) alliances because it leads to the purposeful creation, extension or modification of the routines and tools that inform alliance decision making. In this context, routines pertain to alliances and alliance portfolio practices that inform decision making; tools constitute the instruments that firms can deploy to manage their partnerships. Conditional on achieving a required level of alliance capabilities—determined by the contribution of the alliance activity to the firm's competitive advantage—firms should engage in a more or less structured approach to build and deploy their alliance capabilities. In short, the firm articulates a clear alliance strategy that is supported by senior management, establishes a dedicated structure to manage and coordinate alliances, facilitates decision making and learning in alliances, invests in building a culture that encourages growth through alliances and provides training to create partnership mindsets and skills. To conclude, alliance capabilities are a means to an end. The various routines, tools and practices are not designed to impose rigid standardization or corporate dictates, nor should they be objectives in and of themselves. Rather, these practices are intended to improve management skills.

CASE: PHILIPS[1]

Founded in 1891 as an electric lamp manufacturer, Royal Philips (Philips) has become a global player in the consumer electronics, healthcare and lighting industries. Throughout its successful history, Philips has been known for its innovative capacity to introduce industry- and market-changing products. During the late 1990s, Philips engaged increasingly in various partnerships in its attempts to respond to changing global markets. Alliances with companies such as Sara Lee, InBev and Nike enabled Philips to create new product categories that fuelled its growth. Philips also forged multiple alliances with similar partners; companies like Dell, Nokia and Sony were not only Philips customers but also supplied it with many of their own products and services. To deal with the increasing complexity of its relationships and take a more structured approach to dealing with them, Philips established an Alliance Office: a dedicated department tasked with developing and implementing a proactive, systematic, company-wide approach to managing alliances.

The Alliance Office started as a centre of expertise on alliance management and then became a vehicle for developing, spreading and institutionalizing alliance know-how and know-what. To prioritize its work, the Alliance Office classified Philips' alliances into four categories, based on the level of synergy with the alliance partner and the alliance's potential value. Alliances with low synergy and low potential value represented business alliances, whereas corporate alliances had high value and high synergy. Philips thus focused initially on the management of its most important alliances; for each corporate alliance, it assigned a dedicated alliance manager, created a 'corporate partner team' across divisions with executive sponsorship and organized support by the managerial board. This alliance team interacted frequently to exchange information and develop plans for approaching the partner company.

After enjoying some initial successes, the Alliance Office moved on to tackle strategic alliances, characterized by their high potential value but little apparent synergy with Philips. Strategic alliances typically implied the development of a new product or service and thus demanded high involvement by operational managers. The Alliance Office refrained from active alliance management in this case; instead, it offered support for any consideration of new strategic alliances. Operations and Alliance Office delegates worked together to evaluate systematically the business rationales for each alliance and the extent of partner fit. If the alliance was executed, the Alliance Office provided support, advice and tools for managing it.

The Alliance Office also developed multiple alliance tools to enhance alliance management throughout the organization. For example, its partner selection tool tapped the degree of partner fit between Philips and any potential partner. The tool emphasized the importance of cultural fit: even if partners contributed complementary resources and shared the same strategic vision, their alliance could still fail if they simply could not work effectively together due to the huge or insurmountable differences in their cultures. The alliance office created other tools for individual managers; for example, a Health Check tool evaluated the performance of any alliance using both hard and soft metrics. The logic behind all these tools was not to prescribe decisions but rather to generate systematic analyses, debate and dialogue to support the decisions that managers must make at every stage of an alliance.

In line with Philips' decentralized management structure, each alliance was formed and managed independently by various divisions or businesses. In this setting, however, it was difficult to share best practices, which led to some repeated alliance mistakes. Therefore, a main objective of the Alliance Office was to institutionalize alliance capabilities and lead the implementation of systematic processes that would guide alliance management decisions. In addition to developing routines, providing tools and advocating their use in individual alliances, the Alliance Office sought to capture and disseminate knowledge to improve the competences of alliance managers. To this end, it organized quarterly alliance meetings and pushed for periodic alliance reviews.

Since establishing the Alliance Office, Philips has entered into several successful alliances with companies from a variety of industries, including but not limited to fast-moving consumer goods, telecom, IT and pharmaceuticals. Although initially business managers resisted asking the Alliance Office for help, they quickly acknowledged the value it offered to their business and its performance.

Questions

1   To what extent has the structured approach Philips adopted to govern its alliances contributed to its competitive position?
2   During the establishment of the Alliance Office, Philips' management structure was decentralized. How might this management structure have impeded and/or reinforced the effectiveness of the Alliance Office?

Note

1   Bell and Lemmens (2007); Bell *et al.* (2010); Singh *et al.* (2008).

24

ALLIANCE MINDSET

Organizational complexity within alliance arrangements, derived from the co-occurring and entanglement of multiple tensions, represents a key characteristic of alliances and a source of potential collaborative advantage. It is also one of the causes of friction and underperformance. Whereas prior alliance literature emphasized instrumental approaches to deal with this complexity, one key driver of alliance performance originates in the alliance mindset. An alliance mindset refers to the frame that alliance managers use to interpret situations and make decisions. A critical aspect of an alliance mindset pertains to identifying and dealing with tensions, a practice which is inherently associated with alliance management (first section). To inform their alliance management decisions, managers must understand the tensions between cooperation and competition (second section), structure versus process (third section), deliberate versus emergent (fourth section), and corporate versus societal (fifth section). We conclude this chapter with a summary (sixth section) and a case illustration.

The meaning of alliance mindset

Research in managerial cognition and interpretation has suggested that the job of decision makers is also one of interpretation (Weick 1979). As interpreters, managers bring a mindset through which they view the world and translate events into managerial reality. A mindset helps explain how a manager interprets the world, solves problems and, in particular, manages uncertainty. In other words, an alliance mindset informs the way of thinking that alliance managers have towards the complex linkages among strategies, structure and systems within alliance arrangements (Spekman et al. 1998). Traditional approaches towards alliance management promote mindsets that aim for simplicity and consistency; they aim to reduce complexity by advancing 'linear' and 'pre-set' solutions to deal with the alliance challenges they encounter (see also Box 24.1). However, a traditional—i.e. instrumental—alliance mindset blinds alliance managers as it tends to negate the prevalence of tensions in alliance arrangements (Das and Teng 2000a). A non-traditional alliance mindset, in contrast, enables alliance managers to build and leverage an ability to identify opposing forces, reconcile contradictions (tensions), articulate creative solutions and implement them responsibly and effectively. Framing alliance challenges as a tension holds promise for alliances managers as dealing with

DOI: 10.4324/9781003222187-24

tensions will help managers make sense of an apparently unexplainable and often seemingly irrational contemporary world (Smith *et al.* 2018). A tension-informed alliance mindset enables managers to shift between interests and views. Moreover, dealing with contradictory forces within alliance relationships requires leadership practices that have a focus on seeking imaginative, reconciliatory solutions that can enable fast-paced, adaptable decision making. This type of decision guides alliances towards success.

To engage in successful alliance management, managers need to shift their mindsets from an either/or mindset to a both/and mindset; the latter being a source of creative solutions (Yin and Jamali 2021). An either/or mindset is associated with a puzzle-solving or a trade-off frame. As alliance managers adopt the notions of planning and predictability, they assume a mechanistic worldview. For example, using a partner selection instrument suggests that partner firms attain superior performance as they choose partners based on appropriate selection criteria (see Chapter 3), or sticking to a contract design template will safeguard partner firms against contingencies (see Chapter 5). In a mechanistic world, alliances managers put the pieces of the puzzle together, or resolve a trade-off by allocating resources to one activity (Ryan-Charleton *et al.* 2022), knowing that a suboptimal resource allocation may have adverse consequences (De Wit and Meyer 2004). However, alliance managers function in unpredictable and dynamic environments; they frequently lack information, and instrumental approaches are ineffective (Tjemkes and Mihalache 2021). A both/and mindset allows alliance managers to operate effectively in situations in which two seemingly contradictory, or even mutually exclusive, forces appear to be in effect at the same time (De Wit and Meyer 2004). Such a problem that is a tension has no easy solution. Tensions bring about cognitive and emotional stress experienced by alliance managers, directly resulting from contradictory yet interrelated elements that persist over time (Ryan-Charleton and Gnyawali 2022). Rather, resolving a tension requires decisions that aim to achieve one of many possible creative reconciliations of the two opposing forces as there is no logical way to integrate the two opposites into an internally consistent understanding (Poole and van de Ven 1989). Nonetheless, extending beyond semantics, a tension refers to opposing forces that appear irreconcilable, although we also argue that such tension may be resolved through intelligent and creative alliance management (Wit and Meyer 2004).

A tension-based perspective on alliance mindsets brings about three possible ways of dealing with tensions. First, alliance managers may negate the prevalence of tensions and consider alliances as organizational arrangements depicting complex puzzles. Guiding by alliance management tools and frameworks (see Chapter 23), managers put the pieces together in pursuit of success. Not understanding or neglecting to seek creative solutions may upset the status quo, leading to premature alliance dissolution. Second, alliance managers may adopt an either/or mindset and adopt a substitution logic (such as a trade-off). The pursuit of two opposing objectives will be resolved by separation of activities, either physical or temporal. For example, through task specialization and setting up separate alliance working groups, alliance partners separate exploitation and exploration objectives. Although such an approach could be effective, the two opposing forces are still considered irreconcilable. Third, alliance managers may opt for synthesis (i.e. a both/and mindset) when dealing with tensions and seek complementarity between opposing forces. This synthesis of two opposing forces typically generates creative solutions because alliance managers take collective ownership of the tension and integrate it into their joint decision-making. For example, to cope with the need for stability and adaptation, alliance managers could resort to contracts (e.g. providing stability), yet use

TABLE 24.1 Two examples of tensions in alliances

Description	Tension	Solutions
Alliance to End Plastic Waste • With 92 alliance partners, the collaboration aims to end plastic waste in the environment and protect the planet.	Internal ambition versus external credibility • Internal ambitions are driving and delivering transformational change. • External credibility is questioned as external stakeholders (e.g. Greenpeace) claim that the alliance is a marketing ploy (i.e. green washing).	Partner constellation • Partners from across the plastic value-chain, with members from the petrochemical, converter, enabler and brands segments of the value chain. Communication • Conveying that the result and impact of one (failing) project does not provide a fair picture of what is to be a long-term campaign investing in many different waste projects.
Swiss Re–Oxfam alliance • Swiss Re, a leading global insurance company collaborates with Oxfam to develop and implement a new insurance for Ethiopian farmers against risks to crops from climate change.	Resistance versus interests • Internal resistance, as Swiss Re seeks to expand its market to developing countries while being committed to addressing climate change. • Internal resistance, as Oxfam participated to safeguard Ethiopian farmers against risks to their crops from climate change by offering them an insurance policy.	Inclusive leadership • Inclusive leadership allowed the project to go forward. The project champion was respected by other employees, and the project had backing from executive leadership. Empowerment • Champions who involved both business and philanthropic units, linking the project clearly to business strategy. Learning together • Partners gradually developed confidence in each other and their approach to the issue, and they continually explored ways that the collaboration could best suit the two organizations' needs.

Sources: Endplastic (2019); GreenPeace (2021); NBS (2022); Packaginginsights (2021).

stipulations to engage in collaborative problem solving (e.g. effectuating change). In sum, an alliance manager's mindset (that is, the framing of tension) directly influences alliance progress and performance (see Table 24.1 for examples).

Alliance tensions

Prior alliance research identified a variety of tensions. Ryan-Charleton and colleagues (2022), for example, make a distinction between trade-offs (such as the balance between cost and benefits) and tensions (for example, rigidity versus flexibility). The latter being different from the former as tensions demand continuous alliance managers' attention, whereas trade-offs dissipate once a choice has been made. de Rond and Bouchikhi (2004, p. 66) provide an over-view, including tensions between cooperation versus competition, design versus emergence, innovation versus replication, and collectivism versus individualism. These tensions have been discussed (to some extent) in this book. Coopetition alliances—partnerships between rival firms—are replete with tensions centring on the interplay between cooperation in pursuit of common goals and competition in pursuit of individual goals (see Chapter 16). While the literature on alliance design has provided insights into how contracts drive alliance success, contract adaptability is necessitated to deal with unforeseen circumstances (see Chapter 5). Partners establish alliances to effectuate exploration and exploitation learning strategies; strat-egies when pursued in combination require specific structural and processual solutions to be effectuated (see Chapters 11, 18 and 19). Also within international alliances, tensions tend to emerge as partners with different cultural backgrounds work together (see Chapter 13). The common denominator across these topics is that alliance arrangements are inherently associ-ated with tensions, and, with the 'right' mindset, alliance managers are able to identify and effectively deal with tensions.

Recognizing the salience of tensions, several alliances studies have advanced insights into how to manage alliance tensions. Das and Teng (2000a) present a tension-based framework comprising cooperation versus competition, rigidity versus flexibility and short-term versus long-term orientation, and alliance managers need to find a balance between forces, account-ing for (changes in) alliance conditions. de Rond and Bouchikhi (2004) report on a longi-tudinal case study, showing how alliance managers (socially) construct and resolve tensions regarding cooperation and competition, trust and vigilance, expansion and contraction, and control and autonomy. Niesten and Stefan (2019) present the results of a literature review on value creation (cooperation) and value capture (competition) in inter-organizational relation-ships and indicate that tensions associated with value creation and capture spur virtuous cycles (such as balancing trust and contracts) and vicious cycles (for example, myopia of learning). Jarzabkowski and colleagues (2021) show how partners in an inter-organizational systems balance between equilibrium and disequilibrium while identifying and resolving tensions (that is, paradoxes) to secure the availability of capital to respond to natural disasters. These studies consistently suggest that tension identification and management is critical, otherwise conflicts are bound to occur. Next, we detail on four alliance tensions that are an integral part of a 'tension-based' alliance mindset: (1) cooperative versus competitive tension, (2) economic versus social tension, (3) deliberate versus emergent tension and (4) corporate versus societal tension (see Table 24.2).

Cooperative versus competitive tension

Cooperation and competition are opposing forces (Das and Teng 2000a). Throughout the alliance development process, any collaboration between partners balances against the com-petitive aspects of their partnership (Niesten and Stefan 2019). That is, each partner seeks to reconcile joint alliance activities with its own interests. Cooperation consists of the parties' efforts to implement value-creating conditions and processes (Das and Teng 2003). For exam-ple, as the alliance progresses, partners may contribute complementary resources (Das and Teng 2000b), make alliance-specific investments (Madhok and Tallman 1998), initiate recipro-cal learning (Lubatkin *et al.* 2001) or invest in relational capital (Ariño and de la Torre 1998) to support the collaborative logic. In contrast, competition implies efforts to appropriate value

TABLE 24.2 Four key tensions in alliances

Tension	Description	Trigger (examples)	Reconciliation (examples)
Cooperative vs competitive	Collectively creating value versus individually appropriating value.	Power imbalance, internal change, inequity, partner asymmetry.	Hybrid compensation mechanisms, contingency-based contracts, contract-trust complementarity.
Structure vs process	Efficiency via formal governance versus viability via informal governance.	Cultural differences, resource asymmetry, different risk perceptions.	Comprehensive performance assessment, contract-trust complementarity, balanced governance designs.
Deliberate vs emergent	Execution based on planning versus openness to adaptation.	Managers' preferences, sectoral differences, strategic misfit.	Separation of activities in units, delegation of activities, temporal organizing.
Corporate vs societal	Firm-centred (economic) logic versus societal responsibility of a firm.	Clash between partner firm cultures, stakeholders' voices, code of conduct violation.	Assume joint ownership, transparency, separation of activities, narrow alliance scope, specialized resource contributions.

Sources: Das and Teng (2000a); Faems et al. (2008); Koza and Lewin (2000); Yin and Jamali (2021).

from the alliance, if necessary, at the expense of the partner firm (Dyer et al. 2008). As the alliance evolves, the partners' focus shifts to realizing a favourable pay-off structure (Parkhe 1993), opportunism (Wathne and Heide 2000), knowledge acquisition (Hamel 1991) and the use of bargaining power (Lax and Sebenius 1986) to support their individual interests. Typically, partners become aware of the tension when they are rivals (e.g. coopetition), resources are scarce (e.g. small versus large partners) or internal and external changes (e.g. new technologies or new market entrant) occur. Also, distrust, learning races and learning myopia may cause competition (e.g. value appropriation) to be prioritized over cooperation (e.g. value creation), jeopardizing the health of the collaboration. Cooperative and competitive forces are at odds, differing in both philosophy and spirit. To realize high-performing, sustainable alliances, such forces are indispensable and must be reconciled.

A traditional way to approach alliances involves considering value creation and appropriation as unrelated so that the alliance depicts a zero-sum situation. Attempts to appropriate more value from the alliance have no effect on value creation. This logic can apply to pure transaction-based alliances with financial objectives, but it appears less valid for more complex alliance relationships that pursue multiple objectives (Tjemkes 2008). Alternatively, considering alliances as positive-sum situations and acknowledging their temporal interrelatedness can help resolve the cooperative–competitive alliance tension. Initiatives to appropriate excessive value from the alliance hinder subsequent value creation, and superior value creation reduces incentives to appropriate excessive value; therefore, value creation and appropriation are interrelated. For example, exercising a bargaining power advantage to reap additional financial benefits may increase a firm's performance temporarily, but it also undermines the counterpart's collaborative effort and jeopardizes joint value creation. Similarly, exploiting an absorptive capacity advantage to obtain additional knowledge may enhance a firm's resource endowment, but it may also ignite a learning race that undermines the alliance's long-term knowledge creation. In contrast, when a firm refrains from exploiting a bargaining power and/or absorptive capacity advantage, it signals commitment to its partner, which increases the chances of greater value creation. The firm may then appropriate more absolute value because it focuses on cooperation rather than solely pursuing competition. In other words, to reinforce a constructive interplay between cooperation and competition, alliance managers must establish balanced governance designs (such as contracts and trust), build and deploy collaboration capabilities (for instance, relative absorptive capacity) and opt for hybrid compensation schemes (residual sharing, for example).

BOX 24.1 ALLIANCE MINDSET: THEORETICAL PERSPECTIVES

Though more established theoretical perspectives, such as transaction cost economics, resource-based view and institutional theory, encompass behavioural assumptions (e.g. bounded rationality), other theoretical perspectives centring on 'mindsets' have been introduced to the alliance field. Regulatory focus theory (RFT) states that decision-maker behaviour is induced by dispositional and situational regulatory focus. One's dispositional focus can be focused on avoiding negative outcomes (prevention focus) or gaining positive outcomes (promotion focus). Situational regulatory focus is defined by the situation in which an action takes place, which can also represent a setting in which people are framed to work towards a gain (promotion focus) or to avoid a loss (prevention focus). Within an alliance setting, RFT has been primarily used to provide insight in alliance contracting (e.g. Weber and Mayer 2011). Different contractual clauses can have different psychological impacts on the parties and how they perceive their alliance arrangement. For example, promotion- and prevention-framed contracts interpreted by managers with promotion and prevention dispositions induce different emotions, behaviours and expectations; even if economic incentives are equivalent. In turn these discrepancies may lead to different relationship repair approaches and exchange outcomes (Kumar 2016). Signalling Theory is useful for describing behaviour when two parties have access to different sets of information (Connelly et al. 2011). The core logic of theory stipulates that one party, the sender, must choose whether and how to communicate (or signal) that information, and the other party, the receiver, must choose how to interpret the signal. Within an alliance setting, signalling theory has been used in different ways, including investors' responses to alliance announcements, executive board's prestige, entrepreneurs seeking endorsement of alliance relationships and international alliances as signals of organizational legitimacy. Whereas prior alliance studies primarily focused on alliance formation, signalling theory may also provide valuable insights in post-formation and termination inter-partner dynamics.

Sources: Connelly et al. (2011); Kumar (2016); Weber and Mayer (2011).

Structure versus process alliance tension

Another alliance tension comprises the opposing pair of structure (centring on economic efficiency) and process (centring on social embeddedness) forces (Faems *et al.* 2008). An economic exchange view focuses on the structural design of single transactions and emphasizes the importance of alliance design (governance form and contracts) as an effective and efficient governance mechanism. Thus, alliance managers appear rational, purposeful and calculative. In contrast, a social exchange view centres on relational processes in ongoing alliances and emphasizes the importance of relational norms and capital for coordinating alliances and safeguarding partners' interests. Social bonds and individual entanglements act as social control mechanisms that encourage managers to reciprocate cooperative behaviours (Ring and Van de Ven 1994). Although both structural and process forces drive alliance development and permeate all development stages, they constitute contending forces. Typically, alliance managers experience the structure–process tension when they have different cultural backgrounds (for example, cultural preference for structure or process), contribute different resources (for example, financial versus knowledge) or interpret contractual stipulations differently (such as risk-prone or risk-averse interpretation). Also, when alliance managers perceive a high risk of opportunism, observe opportunities for misappropriation and anticipate coordination complexity, they may prioritize alliance structure over alliance processes, jeopardizing the health of the collaboration. Thus, a primary focus on the structural aspects of an alliance implies an under-socialized view of managerial action, which is problematic because social interactions in an alliance constitute a critical prerequisite of win–win partnerships (see Chapter 7). A primary focus on alliance processes is also undesirable in that an over-socialized view neglects the function of an alliance structure (see Chapter 5). To create a high-performance alliance, the contrasting forces must be reconciled.

Because alliances serve to contribute to firm performance, one way to approach this tension would be simply to ignore the social (that is, process) side of alliances. Here again, however, the logic applies better to simple transactions (market exchanges) than to complex alliance relationships (Dwyer *et al.* 1987). Economic exchanges are embedded in social relationships (Granovetter 1985), and the way in which alliance managers reconcile the structure–process tension determines alliance outcomes. Alternatively, resolutions of the alliance tension could focus on temporal interrelatedness between alliance structure and processes. For example, Faems and colleagues (2008) showed that contracts (that is, structure) that have a similar degree but different nature of formalization trigger different kinds of trust dynamics (that is, processes). Tjemkes (2008) demonstrated that, depending on the alliance's objective, alliance design influences performance, either directly or indirectly through relational governance. Therefore, initial alliance design functions as an architecture that either catalyzes or impedes social interactions. However, structure and process forces may also become manifest in unison in various distinct development stages. Poppo and Zenger (2002) found that formal contracts and relational governance reinforce each other in effective explanations of alliance performance. According to Kumar and Nti (1998), combined assessments of outcome and process discrepancies shape the developmental path of alliances, such that each combination requires different managerial actions. To resolve the alliance tension, it is critical to consider structural and processual forces simultaneously. Alliance managers must establish balanced governance designs (such as complementarity between contracts and trust), use comprehensive performance measurement systems (such as capturing output and process) and opt for contingency clauses in contracts (stipulations on how to deal with unforeseen events, for example). That is, alliance managers need—in addition to an in-depth understanding of how structure and processes forces interrelate, the contingencies that affect them, and their direct and combined impacts on alliance progress—to make use of their experience, expertise and creativity to develop viable solutions.

Deliberate versus emergent alliance tension

In this third alliance tension, deliberate and emergent forces come into apparent conflict (Wit and Meyer 2004). Deliberateness suggests that alliances are organizational arrangements that can be designed and managed purposively. Firms can impose controls on and generate predictable patterns of behaviours and actions: they can formulate a set alliance strategy and then develop a plan to execute it. This results in an alliance contract, and firms expect partners to behave consistently with the stipulations in that contract. However, unforeseen events often prompt learning, change and adaptation, which generate necessary patterns of emergent (strategic) actions to recover the relationship (see Chapter 25). For example, the introduction of a new product by a competitor may prompt partners to re-evaluate their initial plans and develop an alternative course of action. Thus, a primary focus on deliberate forces suggests that alliance managers have an instrumental understanding of alliance management, which conflicts with the inherently unstable nature of these relationships. A primary focus on emergent forces implies a reactive approach to alliance management, which is likely to result in under-performance due to a lack of direction. The deliberate–emergent tension typically becomes manifest when alliance managers have different cultural backgrounds (for example, cultural preference for planning or flexibility), operate in different sectors (for example, public versus private) or differ in their strategic ambitions (for example, exploitation or exploration).

To resolve this tension, alliance partners could simply ignore one force. If they ignore emergence, partners depend solely on a blueprint to form and execute their alliance, which often creates structural and contractual rigidities and restrains partners from responding to internal and external unforeseen circumstances (Das and Teng 2000a). Moreover, partners may become locked into a repeated mode of interaction, with little learning, which initiates greater frustration for both partners in terms of the lack of progress. In contrast, when emergent forces receive too much emphasis, the alliance tends to evolve without direction or control. Even if the alliance objectives have been planned intentionally, progress in the alliance allows new objectives to emerge (Ariño 2003). Without a clear strategy and aligned system, it is difficult to evaluate the potential value of each new objective. Thus, another option arises: to focus on the temporal interrelatedness between deliberate and emergent forces. To achieve short-term results, decision makers set milestones and execute a straightforward project plan, while they also consider their formulated long-term objectives. As the alliance progresses, they use their new insights to deal with emergent circumstances. However, deliberateness and emergence may appear simultaneously, in which case the solution requires some form of separation. For example, it may be beneficial to disconnect exploration and exploitation activities in the alliance (Koza and Lewin 2000). Exploration requires flexibility, whereas exploitation benefits from a more rigid approach. Similarly, the alliance might distinguish decision making at strategic versus operational levels. In the former, decision-making processes should account for emergent circumstances, whereas in the latter, deliberateness helps the partners achieve efficiency. In any case, there is a need for skilful, experienced alliance managers to reconcile the tension between deliberate 'stick to the plan' and emergent 'open to adaptation' approaches.

Corporate versus social tension

In this fourth alliance tension, corporate and societal forces come into apparent conflict. A corporate logic suggests that alliances are organizational arrangements that firms use to attain corporate goals, including economic, strategic and innovation motives. With the exception of detailing on cross-sector partnerships (Chapter 15) and societal alliances (Chapter 26), this book conveys a corporate logic—forming, managing, and evaluating alliances, accounting for contingencies, in support of corporate goals. However, more and more firms are conceived of fulfilling a societal role, extending beyond shareholders' interests. Specifically, challenges pertaining to common public goods (that is, grand challenges), such as environmental pollution, healthcare and labour conditions, extend beyond the social responsibility of a single firm (Yin and Jamali 2021). Increasingly, firms forge societal alliances in support of this societal responsibility (Sadovnikova and Pujari 2017). This focus suggests that alliance managers devote time and energy to form and manage alliances in support of a firm's corporate societal responsibility, which may conflict with the inherently economic nature of alliance relationships. Alliance managers experience this tension, for example, when institutional logics embedded in the partner organizations clash (for example, public versus private), internal and external stakeholders voice concerns (for example, social movements) or codes of conduct are violated (for example, transparency).

Acknowledging that firms have a dual responsibility—both corporate and societal—alliance managers must understand that this tension is a fundamental part of any alliance arrangement. To resolve this tension, alliance partners could simply ignore one force and, for example, favour a corporate logic over a societal logic. A primary focus on corporate goals implies a firm-centred (economic) approach to alliance management, which is likely to undermine a firm's (corporate) social responsibility practices. A primary focus on alliances in support of a firm's societal role is also counter-productive in that a firm with a profit goal would be typically criticized for green-washing. Nonetheless, favouring a corporate logic could work for certain alliances, such as (simple) learning and supplier alliances, but in more visible alliances, such as co-branding partnerships, stakeholders may voice concerns. One way to deal with the tension could be to separate the corporate and societal activities. By narrowing the scope of their collective activities, for example, partners only contribute specialized resources. It would also allow them to understand how both the corporate and societal logics could advance a firm's competitive advantage. For example, together with public partners, a firm could use its resources to develop and market a new sustainable technology. In addition, transparency and clear communication about motives, contributions and goals tends to mitigate concerns. Yin and Jamali (2021) showed that within successful societal partnerships, all partners assume ownership of the societal issue, integrate it into their main activities and frame challenges as an opportunity to collectively develop creative solutions. In other words, reconciling the corporate–societal tension requires alliance managers with a flexible alliance mindset.

Summary

Although strategic alliances can improve a firm's competitive advantage, they are also inherently fragile, unstable, and difficult to manage. Whereas deep knowledge of strategic alliance management advances informed and systematic decision making, alliance managers' mindsets are critical for building successful partnerships. Alliance managers must however recognize that tensions are embedded in any collaborative arrangement, within and between alliance development stages. Thus, strategic alliance management consists of consecutive and repetitive decisions propelled by interactive forces; namely, cooperative versus competitive, structure versus process, deliberate versus emergent, and corporate versus societal. An in-depth understanding of these contending forces, obtained from extensive experience, will help alliance managers better predict, prevent and even deal with specific tensions in their own alliance situations. By combining knowledge with managerial experience, expertise and creativity, alliance managers can formulate and implement the right decisions for each unique alliance situation they confront. In short, to navigate alliance tensions, an alliance mindset encompassing an either/and logic will promote joint ownership of the tension, invoke creative solutions and enable alliance managers to steer the partnership towards success.

CASE: MICROSOFT[1]

Microsoft's mission is to enable people and businesses throughout the world to realize their full potential by creating technology that transforms the way people work, play and communicate. The company develops and markets software, services and hardware devices that deliver new opportunities, greater convenience and enhanced value to people's lives. Microsoft's products include operating systems for computing devices, servers, phones and other intelligent devices; server applications for distributed computing environments; productivity applications; business solution applications; desktop and server management tools; software development tools; video games; and online advertising. The company also designs and sells hardware devices, including Surface RT and Surface Pro, the Xbox 360 gaming and entertainment console, Kinect for Xbox 360, Xbox 360 accessories and Microsoft PC accessories. Furthermore, Microsoft offers cloud-based solutions that provide customers with software, services and content over the internet by way of shared computing resources located in centralized data centres. Examples of cloud-based computing services include Microsoft Office 365, Microsoft Dynamics CRM Online, Windows Azure, Bing, Skype, Xbox LIVE and Yammer. Across its business, Microsoft earns revenue from usage fees, advertising and subscriptions. The company also provides consulting and product and solution support services, and training and certification. In support of this business model, Microsoft establishes alliance arrangements with a variety of partners, though with a singular expectation.

Microsoft expects that alliance partners embrace and continually improve and uphold Microsoft's ethical and integrity standards and operate in full compliance with all applicable laws and regulations while conducting business with Microsoft and its customers. Microsoft strives to be more than just a good company—they want to be a great company. Microsoft is committed to their mission of empowering every person and every organization on the planet to achieve more. This mission reflects who they are as a company, how they manage their business internally and how Microsoft works externally with customers, partners, governments and suppliers. Microsoft's partners are responsible for training all employees who work on behalf of Microsoft and need to ensure that all staff members involved in a partnership adhere to the 'Partner Code of Conduct', a document stipulating how alliance staff members should behave.

The code of conduct details on values, for example. Microsoft's values are the foundation of their success and reflect the company's continued commitment to ethical and responsible business practices. The core values are respect, integrity and accountability. While conducting business with Microsoft customers, alliance partners will conduct their business practices and activities in accordance with applicable law, with integrity, fairness, respect and in an ethical manner. For instance, partners will not commit fraud or violate anti-trust laws, and they will promote fair competition and comply with tender regulatory requirements. Furthermore, alliance staff will conduct themselves in a professional manner at all times, helping Microsoft to create an inclusive, productive, respectful and professional environment, free from any forms of discrimination or harassment. Also, partners will respect intellectual property rights, protect confidential information and comply with privacy rules and regulations. If issues arise, partners are encouraged to work with their primary Microsoft contact in resolving a business practice or compliance concerns. At times when this is not possible, partners should report any concerns about violation of the code of conduct or applicable laws to their legal department and/or their ethics and compliance officer.

In 2022, Microsoft and Meta (i.e. owner of Facebook and WhatsApp) teamed up to deliver immersive experiences for the future of work and play. Meta's mission is giving people the power to build communities. Meta is building innovative new ways to help people feel closer to each other, and the makeup of the company reflects the diverse perspectives of the people who use our technologies. Meta's main principles are as follows: build connection and community, serve everyone, keep people safe, protect privacy and promote economy opportunity. The Microsoft–Meta alliance seeks to provide customers with more choice and security as they venture into the metaverse. For example, Mesh for Microsoft Teams and Microsoft 365 apps will be made available on Meta Quest devices This enables, for instance, users to join a Teams meeting from inside Meta Horizon Workrooms. The partners will also explore together ways to bring Xbox Cloud Gaming to Meta Quest Store. This partnership enables Microsoft to continue evolving their mixed-reality devices roadmap, whereas Meta obtains access to new services. Together, the partners establish the foundations of a responsible metaverse with security, compliance and enterprise-grade experiences. Together, they will continue to unlock new possibilities for the future of work.

Questions

1   Tensions typically originate in values, such as those that are articulated in Microsoft's 'Partner Code of Conduct'. Explain what tensions are inherently associated with the code of conduct.
2   How does the 'Partner Code of Conduct' imprint Microsoft's alliance managers' mindset?
3   What tensions exists in the Microsoft–Meta alliance, and how can alliance managers cope with these tensions?

Note

1   Microsoft (2022a, 2022b, 2022c, 2022d); Meta (2022a, 2022b).

25

ALLIANCE SYSTEM

As organizational entities, alliances are inherently complex to manage, and they are continually under threat from external contingencies that originate either in the partners' own organization or in the external environment. The preceding chapters have discussed how these internal and external forces drive alliance development and the instruments alliance managers can use to develop win–win alliances. However, establishing and maintaining alliances also cause changes in partners' organizations and environments, which in turn could force managers to modify their alliance design and management in an effort to maintain fit between the alliance, the alliance partners and the environment. A misfit could lead to deteriorating efficiency or effectiveness and, in an extreme situation, could decrease the viability of the alliance or even decrease the viability of one or all alliance partners in the environment. Together, these relationships between the alliance, the alliance partner organizations and the environment constitute an alliance system. The dynamic interaction within an alliance system has been referred to as alliance co-evolution. This chapter starts by explaining what is meant by a co-evolutionary view on alliances, as well as why, when and how alliance co-evolution occurs. The third section uses the alliance development framework to present managerial guidelines, and the chapter concludes with a summary and a case illustration.

A co-evolutionary view

The idea of co-evolution is rooted in the tradition of population ecology and evolutionary theory (Hannan and Freeman 1977) and refers to the simultaneous development of organizations and their environment, both independently and interactively (Wilson and Hynes 2009). Co-evolution assumes that change may occur in all interacting populations of organizations, which allows changes to be driven by direct interaction and by feedback. The theory of alliance co-evolution suggests that natural selection (that is, the argument that an alliance that fits with its environment has a greater chance of survival) does take place but that the simultaneous change in organizations connected through an alliance results in favourable inherited traits that bestow certain advantages, both at an individual level and at a dyadic level. Alliance co-evolution occurs in a population consisting of heterogeneous firms that have adaptive learning capability and are able to interact and

DOI: 10.4324/9781003222187-25

TABLE 25.1 Driving and inhibiting forces of alliance adaptation

	Driving forces	Inhibiting forces
Alliance environment	Governments changing foreign direct investment policies, competitors introducing new technologies and companies entering or exiting industries may prompt adaptation.	Governments raising legal and other barriers to exit or entry markets, competitors forming multi-partner alliances and a lack of legitimacy in an environment may create inertia.
Partner firms	Internal reorganizations, a shift in corporate strategy, a shift in resource needs, a shift in financial position and changes to the board of directors may prompt adaptation.	Existing alliances with other firms, lack of necessary resources, internal political games and administrative policies and procedures may create inertia.
Alliance	Worse-than-expected performance, partners updating their expectations, the governance form appearing to be inefficient and differential learning may prompt adaptation.	Sunk costs due to non-recoverable investments in technology, machinery and personnel; the dynamics of political coalitions; and a lack of partner interactions may create inertia.

mutually influence each other, and where at least two firms have formed an alliance (Volberda and Lewin 2003). In addition, some initiating event, which can either be internal (within the alliance) or external (within one or both alliance partner organizations and or the environment), is present to trigger the co-evolutionary process (see Table 25.1). This dynamic interaction between alliance, partner organizations and environment implies that organizations and the alliance itself represent adaptive entities that, based on learning and experience, engage in a continuous and interrelated self-renewal processes in an attempt to seek and maintain fit.

In order to understand why alliance co-evolution occurs, it is important to elaborate on three overarching principles that underpin co-evolution (Volberda and Lewin 2003). First, self-renewing organizations focus on managing variety by regulating internal rates of change so that they equal or exceed relevant external rates of change. For example, firms reorganize their organizations in response to unforeseen moves by competitors, changes in technology and customers' demands. Second, self-renewing organizations seek to optimize self-organization, which suggests that they are continuously engaged in learning and adaptive processes to improve their ability to maintain a fit between themselves and their environment. Third, self-renewing organizations synchronize concurrent exploitation and exploration. In this context, exploitation refers to the strategic intention to enhance performance by leveraging existing capabilities, while exploration refers to the strategic intent to enhance performance by discovering new potential useful capabilities. Alliances represent a way of evoking organizational self-renewal; they enable firms to align flexibly with environmental requirements; they trigger internal optimization, and firms contemplating an alliance may use it to exploit and explore while avoiding competence traps (too much exploitation) and learning traps (too much exploration) (March 1991).

Though four co-evolutionary generative mechanisms have been distinguished (see Table 25.2) to illustrate the wide range of evolutionary paths that can occur, within the context of alliances, managed selection provides the foundation for the underlying principles of coevolving in an alliance system (Volberda and Lewin 2003). Managed selection suggests that self-renewing organizations can use alliances to manage internal rates of change, optimize self-organization and balance concurrent exploration and exploitation. Moreover, managed selection implies that alliance governance is a mixture of market selection mechanisms and managerial adaptation processes, which makes this view less path-dependent and deterministic than, say, the naïve selection mechanism. More specifically, when selection is applied to alliance management, it suggests that devising partnerships is one way that firms adapt to a changing environment.

Whereas evolution suggests that change initially occurs at the firm level, co-evolution considers simultaneous changes with firms and their environment, or dyadic pairs of firms. In addition, a co-evolutionary view captures multi-directional causalities over a long period of time, in which the outcomes of co-evolution are emergent and in which changes in any one variable (for example, at the micro or macro level) may be caused endogenously by changes in the other (Das and Teng 2002). Consequently, a co-evolutionary view is made up of dynamic trajectories evoked by drivers that enable and restrict change within an alliance system. For

TABLE 25.2 Four co-evolutionary trajectories

	Description
Naïve selection	Co-evolution through naïve selection proceeds through a continuous cycle of variation, selection and retention and causes a firm (or organization) to evolve towards a better fit with the environment. Variations emerge through blind or random change initiatives, while selection occurs principally through competition for scarce resources, and retention involves forces that perpetuate and maintain selected initiatives.
Managed selection	Co-evolution through managed selection suggests that managers develop preferences for certain responses or variations. Instead of blind variations, variations become more deliberate or intelligent, based on past experience. Management may develop forms of anticipatory control system in which prior knowledge functions as a selector, blocking perceived dangerous or inadequate actions before they are executed.
Hierarchical renewal	Co-evolution through hierarchical renewal suggests that managers can shape their environment and that strategy making involves multiple levels of management. In this context, co-evolution is driven primarily by the strategic intent of senior management. Adaptation results from the top-down administrative decisions, and the resulting outcomes are highly idiosyncratic. Successful trajectories are highly dependent on senior management's decision rationality and industry foresight.
Holistic renewal	Co-evolution through holistic renewal focuses on collective sense making and suggests a close link between collective cognitions processes of co-evolution. Periods of stability and convergence, as opposed to those of upheaval and change, are mirrored in similar changes in beliefs and ideologies. Interpretations give meaning to data and precede learning and action.

Source: Volberda and Lewin (2003).

example, economic, social, technological, environmental and political macro-variables may change over time and influence firms' micro-level alliance decisions. This, in turn, influences the broader alliance environment, including alliance partners' organizations (Wilson and Hynes 2009). Because firms are able to change themselves proactively, their alliances and, to a certain degree, their environment (that is, they can select the 'best' alternative), alliance co-evolution occurs through a deliberate approach rather than via random chance-like processes.

Drivers of alliance co-evolution

The literature on alliance co-evolution has emerged only recently, which means that conclusive evidence on alliance co-evolution is virtually non-existent (Volberda and Lewin 2003). However, the alliance studies that examined alliance co-evolution did identify drivers of alliance co-evolution operating at three levels of analysis: the alliance, the partner organizations and the alliance environment.

Alliance level

At the alliance level, outcome and process discrepancies may prompt adaptation in alliance conditions and processes (Kumar and Nti 1998), including changes in the governance, the alliance contract, the division of activities, decision making and performance expectations. In turn, these modifications affect the development and outcomes of the alliance, which creates a continuous cycle of learning and adaptation (Büchel 2002). Although multiple drivers of adaptation have been identified (see Table 25.1), these tend to operate through three key mechanisms (Koza and Lewin 1998): (1) relative absorptive capacity, (2) control and (3) identity.

A partner's relative absorptive capacity is a critical driver of alliance adaptation and development (Koza and Lewin 1998). Relative absorptive capacity refers to the extent to which partners have a similar ability to value, assimilate and commercialize knowledge within their own organization (Lane and Lubatkin 1998). The extent to which alliance partners are similar (or different) in their ability to learn from and with one another may cause partners' 'resource endowments' to diverge or converge over time, which creates different managerial responses (Nakamura *et al.* 1996). Resource convergence eliminates the initial motives to establish the alliance, which requires managers to dissolve the alliance or seek alternative ways to create value. In contrast, resource divergence increases partners' dependence on one another, which encourages them to increase efforts to acquire each other's valuable resources. In addition, learning about each other's capabilities may cause partners' strategic intentions to diverge or converge (see Box 25.1). For example, examining co-evolution in the banking industry, Ul-Haq (p. 154 2005) identifies three development patterns: (1) 'differential parallel co-evolution', in which the evolution of the strategic intents of the two firms are at different rates but in a broadly similar direction; (2) 'differential convergent co-evolution', in which the strategic intents of the two firms evolve at different rates but in a convergent direction; and (3) 'differential divergent co-evolution', where the strategic intents of the two firms evolve at different rates but in a divergent direction. Although partners' absorptive capacity functions as a driver for alliance adaptation, the impact is, to a certain degree, conditioned by the exploitation or exploration intent of the alliance. In exploration alliances, partners' ability to acquire knowledge is critical, whereas the role of absorptive capacity is of minor concern in exploitation alliances. Therefore, asymmetry between partners in terms of absorptive capacity is likely to trigger adaptation in exploration alliances to control the emergence of learning races (Hamel 1991).

BOX 25.1 NEXIA'S CO-EVOLUTION

Nexia is a professional service network in the public accounting industry and was intentionally forged and formally organized in order to produce cross-border referrals. It selected members by means of two criteria: potential members are independent national players, and they lack the ability or desire to internationalize. However, as time passed, some members discovered and became attracted to opportunities beyond their national market. In addition, unfair distribution of outcomes led individual members to bypass the original intention of the network by entering each other's markets independently. To cope with this unintended consequence, Nexia developed two initiatives. First, it imposed a variety of coordinating, integrating and formalizing mechanisms to support its referral work, and it invested in building a collective network identity. The expectation was that enhancing a network identity would attenuate the member firms' incentives to defect. However, as tensions rose, Nexia realized that nurturing and institutionalizing one's identity was not enough to deal with competitive behaviours. Second, Nexia's control mechanisms were not highly elaborated initially because of the perceived need to minimize overhead costs. The controls were primarily developed to facilitate cooperation in international referrals. However, as the potentially opportunistic intent of some member firms began to emerge, Nexia developed more stringent mechanisms and procedures to counteract and control the behaviour of participants.

Source: Koza and Lewin (1999).

Control mechanisms enable alliance partners to monitor alliance progress and emerging outcome and process discrepancies (Kumar 2010). These mechanisms function as an important driver of alliance adaptation and development (Koza and Lewin 1998). For example, Ariño and de la Torre's (1998) detailed account of the development of an international joint venture suggests that assessments of efficiency and equity conditions prompt partner firms to address dissatisfying situations in various manners, such as by improving relational governance, engaging in contractual renegotiations, doing nothing and terminating the alliance. However, alliances vary in their use of control mechanisms and, for example, match the choice of output and behaviour control with the exploration and exploitation intents (Koza and Lewin 1998). In exploitation alliances, output controls are predominantly used to capture short-term results, whereas exploration alliances employ behavioural and process control to tap into time-dependent activities such as learning. When the intended outcome is uncertain or vague, as is the case in exploration-oriented alliances, an alliance is more receptive to adaptation as managers change their initial conditions once the outcomes become clearer.

Identity also functions as a mechanism that enables alliance learning and adaptation (Koza and Lewin 1998). Identity may prompt processes of collective sense making, which creates a sense of shared fate among alliance members. For example, creating a common identity in a joint venture eases decision making, conflict resolution and learning as individuals share similar values and norms. In contrast, identifying with one's partners could be counter-productive due to identity conflicts. Therefore, identification with the alliance functions as an integrating mechanism within the alliance and as a differentiating mechanism that demarcates the alliance itself from the partners. Identity integration is more critical in exploitation alliances because it enables partners to exploit existing capabilities jointly. In exploration alliances, identification tends to be with the partners as identifying with an alliance partner may inhibit knowledge acquisition and result in alliances that extend beyond the intended time horizon. However, a certain degree of identification can serve to moderate conflict.

Partner firm level

Changes in partner organizations, both foreseen and unforeseen, may prompt alliance adaptations (Koza and Lewin 1998). A shift in corporate strategy, internal reorganizations, changing resource requirements, a shift in financial position, changes in required technology and even a change in the board of directors may encourage managers to modify alliance design and management (Blodgett 1992; Shortell and Zajac 1988). For example, the alliance between Liz Claiborne and Avon encountered difficulty when Avon acquired an upscale cosmetics company in an effort to enhance its image (Stafford 1994). Because the acquisition increased the market commonality of the two partners, Liz Claiborne began to view Avon more as a competitor than a partner, which led to the termination of the alliance. To deal with conflicting pressures for exploration and exploitation, a firm's alliance portfolio is likely to evolve continuously (Lavie and Rosenkopf 2006), with existing alliances terminated and new ones established. In addition, the pursuit of exploration and exploitation may cause alliance partners to impose changes to their alliances, such as modifications in governance form, incentive systems and monitoring systems, in an attempt to maintain consistency between their corporate/business strategies and the alliance objectives. A shift in a partner firm's experience managing alliances as an alliance progresses may also trigger alliance adaptations (Das and Teng 2002). A firm that increases its institutionalized alliance experience may enhance its reputation and function as a signal for trustworthiness, which reduces the need for (costly) contractual governance.

As an alliance develops, it may also cause changes within the partner firms' organizations. Alliance outcomes and processes are likely to affect alliance partners as, in most cases, the alliance is at least partially integrated into the organization. Reciprocal financial and organizational relationships facilitate the transfer of resources, information and routines, which are not necessarily part of the alliance agreement, from the alliance to the partner organizations. An exploration alliance designed to develop new products is often organized through an equity-based arrangement that is characterized by high levels of involvement and integration. Consequently, an alliance partner is likely to absorb valuable knowledge elements of the initial alliance agreement and may also acquire additional knowledge and information about areas such as markets, production technologies and operating procedures. The assimilation of this knowledge changes a firm's resource endowment, which means it is also likely to cause changes in a firm's strategy, systems and operations. Although exploitation alliances tend to be organized through non-equity-based arrangements (that is, with relatively little integration), a similar transfer of resources, information and routines may occur. For example, successful supplier alliances are characterized by alliance-specific investments, such as co-production locations, which often require partner organizations to adjust their operations to accommodate one another's needs. For example, Wilson and Hynes (2009) show that a firm seeking access to the fresh produce market in the UK through an international alliance experienced changes in its technical skills, new product development and networking opportunities as a result of the alliance.

Alliance environment level

The alliance environment affects a firm's decisions to form and manage alliances (Koza and Lewin 1998). In a stable environment, a firm may enhance its competitive position by establishing exploitation alliances to use existing capabilities with the aim of achieving cost reductions and economies of scale, for example. Exploration alliances are more suitable in a dynamic environment as a heterogeneous resource endowment contributes to a firm's ability to respond in an appropriate and timely manner to new circumstances. For example, the results of Lampel and Shamsie's (2003) study of the US motion picture industry indicate that changes in the environment caused a transition to flexible hub organizations supported by alliances. Practices and routines that speed up mobilizing capabilities became more important to box office success than practices and routines that make up the transforming capabilities associated with a studio era dominated by integrated hierarchies. Jacobides and Winter (2005) report on co-evolution trajectories in American mortgage banking and Swiss watch manufacturing. Their results indicate that, within an industry, differential profitability, arising from heterogeneous capabilities across firms, promotes distinct vertical structures. Whereas incremental innovation provides access to specialization gains and produces a secular drift towards vertical disintegration, radical changes in technology require new and integrated capabilities, leading to a phase of vertical reintegration. Therefore, firms are sensitive to changing environmental conditions, such as shifts in customer preferences and technological developments, and this prompts them to adapt their alliance strategies.

Changes in the alliance environment may also require partners to adapt alliance design and management and to renew the conditions under which the collaboration takes place. For example, if competitors intend to introduce a new technology that renders existing technologies obsolete, partners engaged in a learning alliance may need to speed up their own development process, search for possibilities to collaborate with these competitors or decide to dissolve the alliance. Tjemkes and Furrer (2011) argue that industry conditions also affect managerial responses to adversity within alliances. Firms that operate in industries with high technological turbulence tend to prefer destructive response strategies, unlike those firms that operate in industries characterized by low technological turbulence, whose response strategies aim to maintain and preserve their alliance relationships. In contrast, when firms operate in industries characterized by low competitive intensity, the relative importance of preserving existing alliances diminishes as alternative suppliers could be required to respond satisfactorily to customers' preferences. Consequently, these firms are more willing to put the alliance relationship at risk and more likely to prefer destructive response strategies, such as exit, opportunism and neglect.

In turn, an alliance may impact its environment as alliance formation and outcomes could impact industry and market dynamics. For example, the announcement of the Star Alliance, a multi-partner airline alliance involving United Airlines, Lufthansa, Scandinavian Airlines, Air Canada and Thai Airways, led non-members to immediately look for partners, such as Air France with Air India and American Airlines with Aerolineas Argentinas (Guidice *et al.* 2003). Firms respond to alliance competition by seeking and forming countervailing alliances with similar partners as a way of duplicating the benefits their rivals are gaining (Gimeno 2004). A firm could seek entry into its rivals' networks by creating alliances with its rivals' partner, or it could seek to match the rivals' advantage by creating countervailing alliances with other partners that also face the same competitive threat. For example, Wilson and Hynes (2009) report that the formation of alliances within the fresh produce industry in the UK changed the power dynamics across the value chain, which prompted other parties in the value chain to form new alliances.

Alliance system

The linkages between alliance, alliance partner organizations and alliance environment create an alliance system in which alliance co-evolutionary processes occur (see Figure 25.1). Each level represents a unit of change but also depicts the object of change (Wilson and Hynes 2009). Therefore, drivers associated with each level generate learning and adaptation directly, interactively and reciprocally within the alliance system. This dynamic pattern of interactions, both within and between different levels of the system, generates co-evolutionary alliance processes in which all elements progress. However, a state of equilibrium is never likely to be achieved owing to converging and diverging patterns of positive and negative feedback and the extent to which learning occurs. van der Meer-Kooistra and Kamminga (2015), for

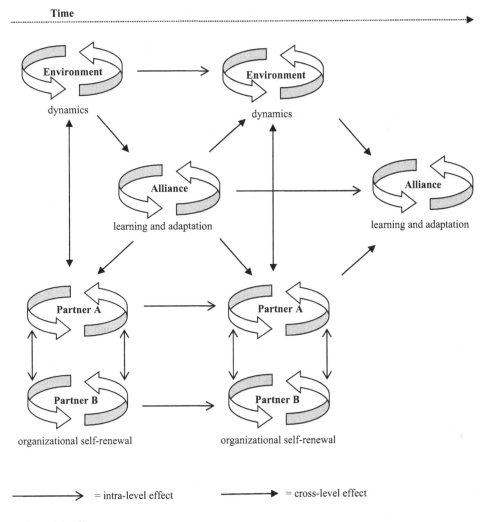

FIGURE 25.1 Alliance system

example, show how antecedents within the parent company, within the JV relationship, in the environment of the JV relationship and in the environment of the parent company, led to decisions made within the parent company, and how these decisions in turn affected the JV relationship and responses by the parent companies.

Taking the perspective of one firm participating in an alliance system, this chapter also proposes that proactive management of an alliance system is beyond the ability of any manager. Owing to bounded rationality and cognitive limitations, it is unlikely that a single alliance manager could comprehend the relationships between drivers of change, intermediary mechanisms or the consequences of change across the alliance, partner firm and environmental levels of analysis. Nevertheless, we suggest that when firms are viewed as self-renewal entities, they have a certain degree of managerial control over co-evolutionary processes:

- Based on continuous assessment of efficiency and equity conditions, alliance partners may initiate modifications to alliance design and alliance management, thereby generating continuous cycles of learning and adaptation.
- Based on continuous assessment of alliance (portfolio) outcomes, alliance partners may experience and initiate modifications to their firm's strategy and organization.
- Based on continuous assessment of alliance environment, alliance partners may experience and initiate modifications to their firm's strategy and organization, as well as to alliance design and management.

A firm can enhance the viability of an alliance system by installing buffering mechanisms and boundary-spanning agents. Buffering refers to the regulation and/or insulation of alliance activities, functions, resources and individuals from the effects of changes in environment and/or partner organization (Lynn 2005). Different buffering mechanisms can be integrated into the core activities of the alliance. A buffer of financial resources within an alliance functions as a cushion when unforeseen circumstances threaten the alliance's viability. Appointing a manager who is responsible for finding, hiring and training new alliance employees can reduce the potential uncertainty of not having the right experts with the right collaborative mindset. Another example of buffering is allocating surplus resources to stimulate radical innovation in response to anticipated external changes, while simultaneously allocating resources to achieve the immediate alliance objectives. Boundary-spanning agents link and coordinate alliance activities with key elements of the environment and partner organizations (Jemison 1984). These agents are concerned primarily with the exchange of information to detect and bring into the alliance information about changes in the environment and alliance partner organizations, as well as send information into the environment that presents the alliance in a favourable light. For example, in order to detect and bring relevant information about alliance partner organizations, an agent could hold regular meetings with people from relevant parts of the corporate and business levels of each alliance partner organization.

Navigating an alliance system

Drawing on a co-evolutionary view, alliances are complex adaptive systems that have far from optimal performance. Changes at the alliance, partner firm and alliance environment level require managers to learn and adapt their alliances continuously if they aim to navigate the alliance system successfully.

In addition to factors such as economic, strategic and learning motivations, a co-evolutionary view stresses the importance of environmental conditions as firms consider to establish an alliance. For example, a firm may prefer an alliance when resources are not readily available in a market and its environment is volatile as it provides a firm with the required strategic flexibility. An alliance then functions as a strategic way for a firm to cope with external uncertainties. However, when developing an alliance strategy, it is important to consider implications that extend beyond the alliance's direct value creation potential. Forging an alliance may affect environmental dynamics, which may have positive or negative consequences for the firm. For example, allying with a competitor to achieve economies of scale may prompt other rivals to form partnerships. An alliance may also trigger changes in the firm's organization as knowledge, resources and organizational routines are transformed through the alliance relationship.

When co-evolutionary processes in an alliance system are taken as a reference point, alliance formation activities (i.e. selection, negotiation, and design) constitute a crucial activity. Though it is critical to select a partner with similar resource and organizational attributes, as partner misfit is a primary source of alliance adaptation. For example, a differential ability to learn combined with diverging organizational identities, specifically in exploration alliances, may trigger a learning race and an escalating cycle of modifications that could potentially lead to the termination of the alliance. In addition, different perceptions about internal and external developments must be reconciled before alliance negotiators are likely to agree on the nature, the timing and the cause of an alliance adaptation. For example, a partner's vulnerability to changes in the environment, which may include financial strength, portfolio of alliances and innovative capacity, is likely to disrupt the alliance (system). Co-evolutionary alliance processes involve repetitive cycles of learning and adaptation. This means that an alliance design shapes how learning and adaptation in response to unforeseen circumstances occurs as the alliance progresses. More specifically, partners designing an alliance must consider, to the best of their ability, the impact and consequences of co-evolutionary processes within the alliance system. For example, a learning alliance could be organized through a non-equity-based arrangement (as opposed to an equity-based one) and supplemented with process and behavioural control mechanisms as partners operate in a relative dynamic environment, which increases the need for flexibility. In other words, governance form, alliance contracts and control mechanisms need to be tailored to the (expected) alliance environment, the partner firms' conditions and the alliance objectives.

The significance of relational adaptability increases as the alliance progresses towards the alliance launch, management and assessment stages. Adaptability refers to the willingness and ability of partners to be flexible when conducting the relationship, above and beyond the constraints posed by alliance design (if necessary). This causes partners to treat the relationship as an adjustable framework in which changes will occur to redress imbalances in the relationship if either party is adversely affected by changing circumstances. Moreover, partners are willing to make these adaptations without resorting to expensive and time-consuming contractual renegotiations. For example, a new alliance may induce changes in the partners' organization, which adversely affect the effectiveness of existing alliance arrangements. Adaptability enables the partners to formulate and implement solutions (e.g. exclusivity). Alliance managers must also pay attention to changes in their partner's organization, as well as the environment, and their potential impact on alliance design and management. While the performance metric system should be tailored to the objectives of the alliance, additional metrics could include indicators that tap into a partner firm's organization (such as shifts in strategy; shifts in organizational structure, culture and routines; new product and service) and indicators that tap into the alliance environment (such as technological advancements, industry dynamics, political and economic developments). Information about changes in the alliance system is critical to prepare adaptations in alliance design and management.

From an alliance system perspective, exiting an alliance is as critical as forging one. Although a firm may shift its focus away from the single transaction, termination could cause a series of changes within an alliance system. The firm and its partner must act and secure the provision of resources via alternative arrangements, which may include a new alliance, an acquisition or a market exchange. In addition, competitors, suppliers and customers may respond as the termination may either present new opportunities or restrict their range of strategic actions. Paradoxically, terminating one under-performing alliance to improve a firm's performance may actually harm the firm due to unpredictable alliance system processes.

Summary

Alliance co-evolution occurs when different parts of an alliance system evolve simultaneously and interact with each other in such a way that learning and adaptations in the alliance, the partners' organization and the alliance environment influence interactively the performance of the alliance, and thus the performance of the partner firms. As such, alliances depict the outcome, object and trigger of change in the alliance system. However, it is most likely that a state of equilibrium will never be achieved, owing to the converging and diverging patterns of positive and negative feedback across the alliance system levels. Owing to ongoing co-evolutionary processes, the purposeful management of an alliance system is beyond the ability of any manager. However, taking the viewpoint of a single alliance, managers should attempt to take account of the triggers and consequences of co-evolutionary processes in alliance decision making.

CASE: ORAL CARE APPLIANCES[1]

The world market for oral care appliances is forecast to grow to $99.78 billion in 2030. This growth is due to improving economic conditions, an ageing Western population, increasing awareness with regard to personal wellness, growing online sales and a further increasing level of automation. There is intense competition in the personal care electrical appliances market due to the presence of a limited number of players, including Colgate-Palmolive, Helen of Troy, Johnson & Johnson, Matsushita Electric Industrial Company, Royal Philips Electronics, Procter and Gamble, Braun, Sanyo Electric Company and Wahl Clipper Corporation. A sub-segment in the personal care market is oral care appliances.

Proctor & Gamble (P&G) is an important player in the oral care market. In 2000, P&G was facing declining innovation payoffs. With the company gradually losing its grip on the market and losing more than half its market capitalization along the way, the new CEO Lafley called for a reinvention of the company's innovation model. Instead of nurturing innovation from inside the company, Langley set a target to acquire 50 per cent of P&G innovations from outside of the company. In order to facilitate this, the Connect+Develop innovation model was created, which produced successful results.

With Crest, P&G had a strong name in the oral care market in the 1990s. However, it got surpassed by Colgate. Looking for a comeback, P&G focused on disruptive innovation through the C+D programme. This resulted in Crest Whitestrips, which allowed customers to whiten their teeth in an easy and affordable manner. In 2006, P&G introduced Crest Pro-Health, which is a toothpaste that deals with the most common threats to dental health. Next, in 2010, P&G introduced Crest 3D White, which is an advanced line of oral care products that focuses on improving dental health and aesthetics by the introduction of a product that whitens teeth in less than two hours. By introducing these products, P&G was able to retain the lead in the oral care market. With regard to electric toothbrushes, P&G was anxious to introduce a pulsating toothbrush. However, the development was forecast to last over five years. Through the C+D programme, P&G established a partnership with a classified Japanese firm which was producing products that met the needs of P&G. This partnership resulted in the introduction of the Oral-B Pulsonic toothbrush in less than one year.

Like P&G, its competitors also found new ways to innovate their product offerings in the oral care market. During the 1990s, Philips also found itself in decline. Innovation was organized in a fragmented way and did not yield the required results. In 1999, the principles of open innovation were adopted and resulted in the establishment of the world renowned 'High Tech Campus'. Philips was able to develop appealing new products by setting up alliances with various companies. In 2004, Philips and P&G crossed paths when they announced a joint venture to co-develop and co-market the IntelliClean System. With IntelliClean, both companies wanted to attack their largest competitors in the US oral care market: Gillette and its Oral-B brand. The alliance combined the best companies in the oral health industry, the technological competence of Philips and P&G in the area of oral care, and added Crest's toothpaste expertise. Initially, the IntelliClean was available only through the American Dental Association (ADA), but it was launched in the US consumer market in 2005.

In 2005, P&G embarked on its largest acquisition to date: a $57 billion deal for Gillette that would create the world's largest consumer-products company. P&G added Duracell batteries, Right Guard deodorant and Gillette razors to its more than 300 consumer brands. P&G's acquisition of Gillette further intensified competition in the oral care market. In 2005, the SpinBrush product line was acquired by Church & Dwight from P&G, the latter divesting its SpinBrush toothbrush business because it competed with Gillette's Oral-B brand, which had a better position in the electric toothbrush market. In addition, Gillette was very competitive and probably had the best power-brushes in the world at that time. However, P&G's acquisition of Gillette conflicted with its partnership with Philips for the IntelliClean brand, as Oral-B and IntelliClean competed heavily. Moreover, the US market for rechargeable toothbrushes was highly concentrated, with Gillette and Philips accounting for virtually all sales of these products. The acquisition would have allowed P&G to acquire the only significant competitor to its joint venture partner—Philips—which would have reduced P&G's incentives to support the IntelliClean product. Therefore, the agreement between Philips and P&G was revised to contain non-compete provisions to protect customers' interests. For example, P&G and Philips agreed to limit joint activities to the US market only.

Since the Gillette acquisition, P&G has continued its proactive marketing of the Oral-B brand. For example, it has established multiple relationships with professional dentists and associated organizations that endorsed the Oral-B brand. In turn, in 2008, Philips Sonicare partnered with Oral Health America (OHA) to conduct a public opinion survey to reveal the state of oral health in America. In 2010, Philips Sonicare also formed an alliance with Susan G. Komen to raise funds for the fight against breast cancer. The power-toothbrush brand donated $100,000 to the organization and agreed to release a commemorative Sonicare toothbrush with a pink power button (pink is the official colour of the Komen organization).

In recent years, advancing technology with regard to connectivity has launched a new era in the development of oral care. P&G launched the interactive toothbrush in 2015, which uses Bluetooth 4.0 connectivity to help consumers to improve oral care. Oral-B has successfully developed a strategy in which it connects its toothbrush with a mobile app. This technology has been developed in partnership with Iconmobile. Philips has taken a similar path. It has produced an electric toothbrush that has the ability to track areas of the mouth that have been missed during the brushing routine. Through Bluetooth connectivity, this data is synchronized with the Philips Sonicare App to help users to improve their brushing techniques. Especially for children, Philips has developed an app to establish oral care habits in children. Philips is partnering with 20th Century Fox, allowing children to brush their teeth with their favourite characters from the Ice Age movie. In 2022, Oral-B Europe teamed up with the International Association of Disability and Oral Health (iADH) to make oral care more inclusive and accessible for people with disabilities. Through a joint programme, called 'Positive practices', the partners aim to make oral care more accessible and positive for all. This partnership also offered Oral-B with an opportunity to enhance its brand to signal 'inclusiveness' to its customers. Benjamin (P&G Europe Oral Care Senior Vice President) said, 'As a brand, we recognize our responsibility to help ensure that oral care is accessible to all and we are proud to partner with the iADH to work to improve the experience for people living with disabilities'.

Co-evolution of partner relationships is of crucial importance in the highly competitive oral care market. Companies active in the oral care market continuously respond to new developments and opportunities. This reflects in continuously changing partners and partnering structures.

Questions

1   Explain how Proctor & Gamble and Philips use acquisitions and alliances to enhance their competitive positions. What are their different motives?
2   What changes took place on the alliance, partner firm and alliance environment levels, and how do they affect the alliance system?

Note

1   Brown and Anthony (2011); Businessweek Online (2002); Federal Trade Commission (2006); HFN Daily News (2010); Oral Health America (2008); PG (2022); Philips (2004); PR Web (2008); Statista (2017).

26

CONTEMPORARY ALLIANCES

Technological innovation and societal developments are reshaping the business environment and changing the rules of the alliance game. Because markets change continuously, firms are pushed to continuously innovate. Industry incumbents focus on technological innovation (such as blockchain, artificial intelligence and cloud computing) to improve their products and services, whereas market entrants take advantage of new technologies to gain a foothold by delivering enhanced offerings (Christensen *et al.* 2018). To this end, firms use alliances and participate in various alliance constellations to formulate and execute innovation strategies (first section). In response to societal developments, firms also increasingly participate in alliance arrangements seeking to enact their social responsibility. Whereas some firms opt for 'green-washing' to show their social responsibility, others are intrinsically motivated to reconcile a corporate profit-logic with social responsibility practices. To this end, firms establish and participate in various alliance constellations to effectively navigate and accommodate societal interests (second section). The emergence of new alliance constellations (see Table 26.1 for illustrations) raises questions about the relevance of traditional strategic alliance management explanations. Therefore, we discuss mainstream theoretical perspectives and how they advance (or not) insight about contemporary alliance manifestations (third section). We end the chapter with concluding insights (fourth section) and a case illustration.

Technological innovation

Technological innovation has become a key driver of a firm's competitive advantage (Duysters and de Man 2003). Firms operate in a world characterized by high levels of volatility, uncertainty, complexity and ambiguity (VUCA) (Bennis and Nanus 1985). Environments are changing quickly, drastically and unpredictably. To remain competitive, firms need to formulate and effectuate collaborative strategies that allow them the flexibility to deal with unexpected and unpredictable changes in their environments (He *et al.* 2020; Yang *et al.* 2007). Being innovative allows firms to take on these challenges. Unsurprisingly, most firms have adopted open innovation practices—a shift from in-house innovation to leveraging external parties to accelerate a firm's innovation (Chesbrough 2003). In contrast to traditional business strategy, which has guided firms to construct barriers to competition, open innovation

DOI: 10.4324/9781003222187-26

TABLE 26.1 Examples of contemporary alliance arrangements

Alliance	Description
Crowd-sourcing alliance	Quirky and General Electric (GE) forged a crowd-sourcing alliance. Quirky, offering a social network platform for inventors, helps startup ventures turn ideas to marketable offerings. GE provides access to patents, improving the offer while capturing value on unused intellectual property.
Blockchain alliance	IBM, AIG and Standard Chartered Bank initiated an alliance aimed at devising a multinational insurance policy based on a blockchain. The blockchain technology enables a shared, real-time view of policy data and documentation to all partners involved. The blockchain permits the recording and tracking of events in each country related to the insurance policy and the automatic execution of payments if prespecified conditions are met.
Poverty alliance	The Scottish-based poverty alliance brings together grassroots community groups, large national NGOs, voluntary organizations, statutory organizations, trade unions and faith groups to rebalance the distribution of power and resources. Partners seek to influence policy and practice, support communities to reduce poverty, build the anti-poverty movement, and change attitudes through evidence-based interventions.
Global Energy Alliance	The Global Energy Alliance for People and Planet (GEAPP) is working in partnership with countries across Africa, Asia, Latin America and the Caribbean to operationalize renewable energy transitions and expansions, which will reduce greenhouse gases, extend clean power to underserved people and enable green jobs. The partners have built a collective action platform with a radically collaborative approach, working hand-in-hand with national governments and global partners and bringing together stakeholders that would otherwise remain fragmented to enable our country programmes to flourish.

Sources: Bloomberg (2017); Global Energy Alliance (2022); PovertyAlliance (2022); Sterling (2013).

promotes openness beyond immediate firm boundaries and the use of partnerships, even between competitors. Open innovation, for example, enables firms to become disruptors as open innovation enables them to enhance their offerings for their existing customers and/or gain a foothold in new markets by delivering more suitable functionality, frequently at a lower price. Open innovation in combination with emerging technological developments offers even more new opportunities as technological advances help firms to transform business activities, processes and competencies. Consequently, these developments give rise to new alliance practices and constellations (see Box 26.1 for an illustration).

The emergence of blockchain technology has also changed the alliance landscape. 'A blockchain is a cryptography-based decentralized system consisting of an ongoing list of digital records that are shared within a peer-to-peer network (i.e. a chain of blocks of digital records)' (Lumineau *et al*. 2020, p. 500). Blockchain is used to establish integration over the internet and can be understood as a many-to-many decentralized integration model, deployed in the public cloud to conduct secured transactions rapidly and at low cost (He *et al*. 2020). Blockchain minimizes unnecessary use of third-party intermediaries and is capable of providing security and flexibility at a lower cost than 'third party' transactions. Although blockchain needs further development (for example, to meet the need for international standardization of documents), it is regarded as a promising future means of business-to-business transactions.

BOX 26.1 MULTI-SIDED PLATFORMS

Companies such as Facebook, Alibaba and Uber are competing in a new multi-sided platform (MSP) world; the primary focus of firms leading a MSP, from their inception, is to provide digital infrastructure, information and technology-intangible assets that enable direct interaction or value creation across (global) platforms by linking different user group and complementors. The platform typically offers a combination of a core technology and a subset of complementary components, which enrich the functionalities offered (i.e. ecosystem). Compared to bilateral alliances, value creation is not exclusively dependent on dyadic resource exchange, it is mainly based on external customer input to drive demand and direct customer interaction to generate economic value. The platform functions as a broker between a group of end users and one (or more) group of suppliers which hold the ownership of the products sold or the resources to deliver services (through the platform). Another unique feature of MSPs pertains to network externalities: a customer's utility of using a product or service through the platform increases with the number of suppliers and customers using the platform. Furthermore, the platform leader (i.e. actor operating the platform) may generate additional income by processing data—collected via monitoring platform transactions—which customers have consented to as they typically have a formal affiliation with the platform (i.e. a subscription). Consider Uber, as it has been frequently used as an example of a MSP. Established in 2009, Uber is a tech-company that connects the physical and digital worlds to offer mobility as a service at the tap of a button. Initially using a platform to connect self-enrolled suppliers (i.e. cars with chauffeurs) and customers (i.e. users), Uber diversified in food delivery (e.g. Uber Eats), package delivery and freight transportation. Leveraging the platform's functionality, Uber forged partnerships with complementors to enhance service value, delivery and quality, as well as to attract supplier and customers. For example, alliances were forged with Italian-based IT Taxi (a cab dispatcher) and Cornershop (grocery delivery). That is, the success of Uber depends on continuously improving the platform's value to attract and connect new drivers and customers. Despite several adversities, among which are concerns about the quality of drivers, security breaches and non-compliance with local regulations, Uber's growth remains unchanged.

Sources: Poniatowski *et al.* (2022); Zeng *et al.* (2019).

Blockchain will enable many-to-many business transactions, such that short-term and even ad hoc interfirm partnerships will be feasible. Blockchain holds the promise to solve alliance governance issues, including contractual and relational governance, in making collaborations both more reliable and faster (Lumineau *et al.* 2020). This is because Blockchain bypasses humans' unpredictability and biases and exploits the benefits of automation. Moreover, in a decentralized blockchain configuration, consensus is achieved such that no party owns all of the decision rights. Taken together, instead of contractual enforcement by laws and regulations (that is, use of third parties), or relational enforcement by social norms (partners), blockchain enforces alliances (i.e. transactions) by a self-contained and automated set of rules (codification) (Lumineau *et al.* 2020).

Industry 4.0 is likely to reshape (global) value chains, competition rules and structure of industries (Dalenogare *et al.* 2018); it will also fundamentally change the mechanisms of interfirm relationships. Industry 4.0 is an emerging technology framework based on cyber–physical systems, coordinated by wireless and internet-based protocols and standards. Industry 4.0 is enabled by some foundational technology advances, such as adaptive robotics, artificial intelligence (AI), big data analytics, embedded systems, Internet of Things (IoT), Industrial Internet, cloud systems, additive manufacturing, and simulation and virtualization technologies (Xu *et al.* 2018). Industry 4.0 will feature horizontal integration via value chains, vertical integration and networking of manufacturing or service systems, and end-to-end engineering of the overall value chain. These developments suggest that the existing business models of companies will be increasingly data-driven, and new business models will rapidly emerge to redefine how companies create and deliver value. In addition, digital transformation opens new networking possibilities and enables cooperation between different actors. For example, the supply chain network of future firms is likely to be much shorter than it is now, and supply chain partnerships can be extremely short-term and dynamic. For example, in the field of urban management, cities are seeking to become smart at dealing with challenges such as air pollution, traffic congestion, cyber security and fresh food supply. This has encouraged alliances of IT firms possessing specialized knowledge with public authorities.

Blockchain and Industry 4.0 will result in the emergence of new modes of interfirm collaboration, driven by new business models moving towards digitalization and decentralization of information processing (He *et al.* 2020). Whereas traditional strategic alliance management assumes long-term arrangements to create value, guided by technological advances (such as cloud computing and smart contracts), future alliances will be designed to encompass flexibility and agility, typically with shorter lifecycles. Furthermore, it is unlikely that a single firm can develop and marketize a new technology—doing so is not economically viable—so constellations in various forms are likely to emerge, contributing to further industry specialization and division of labour. For example, alliances between auto manufacturers and AI firms, between oil exploration companies and high-tech companies, between medical device specialists and IT companies are to be expected. These constellations will also further intensify coopetition, that is, cooperation between competitors (see Chapter 16). Developments in new technologies, from cloud computing to blockchain, are making such coopetitive and hybrid collaborations possible. For example, it is likely that more and more horizontal collaborations, such as facilities and human resource sharing, will be common practice among (groups of) competitors (Geurts *et al.* 2022). As firms participate in multiple technological solutions (such as digital platforms), alliance partners will occupy different roles simultaneously (for example, lead firm, complementor or market entrant). Alliance management becomes an ability to continuously redefine and reposition themselves in the value creation system, finding suitable partners, building capabilities and switching between partners when appropriate.

Societal responsibility

Social responsibility means that firms, in addition to maximizing shareholder value, must act in a manner that contributes to the welfare of society (Tjemkes and Mihalache 2021). Acting responsibly has become increasingly important to investors, employees, customers and other stakeholders. For example, the scope of corporate social responsibility (CSR) is no longer constrained to company headquarters (Agudelo *et al.* 2019) but instead stretches along its entire, and often global, supply chain and production network (Wickert 2021). Responding to political, social and economic forces, such as environmental laws and regulations, the United Nations' Societal Development Goals (SDGs) and resource depletion, firms have become increasingly aware that the scope for a business extends beyond making a profit. Specifically, more and more firms are conceiving of how to contribute to societal (grand) challenges, including the achievement of gender equality, safeguarding food supply, contributing to biodiversity and other environmental issues. Resolving societal challenges would require acknowledgement of the tensions originating in the vested interests of stakeholders (see Chapter 24). If these are not identified and resolved, problems such as the climate crisis will persist, as favouring one stakeholder's interest above the other will invoke resistance and conflict. One way to enact social responsibility is through alliances (Dentoni *et al.* 2021). Successful collaborative projects are omnipresent. Local communities collectively work together with businesses and municipalities to reduce the local ecological footprint while securing economic stability. Global corporations collaborate with transnational non-governmental organizations and other stakeholders to develop global solutions to cross-border challenges. New ways of organizing emerge, and the emergence of societal alliances has changed the alliance landscape.

Societal alliances are voluntary collaborative efforts of actors from business and non-profit sectors in which partners attempt to address a social and/or environmental problem of mutual concern (Yin and Jamali 2021). Particularly essential here are problems pertaining to common public goods (such as poverty, environmental protection, healthcare and education) or social issues, which are recognized to have spillover effects on multiple constituencies and stakeholders, going beyond the scope of a single organization (Yin and Jamali 2021). Societal alliances typically involve two or more diametrically different institutional logics (see Chapter 15). An institutional logic, usually value- and norm-based, provides the assumptions, rules and beliefs that shape decision making and actions. The business and non-profit actors coming from different sectors to collaborate on the social and environmental cause not only face conflicting organizational values and beliefs that reflect broader cultural templates but must also overcome unfamiliarity to develop a solid level of trust and comfort for shared goals. For example, Yin and Jamali (2021) showed that successful societal alliances can reconcile opposing institutional logics, such that the partners frame societal challenges as an opportunity and collectively assume ownership to enact practices in support of women's empowerment, improved employee engagement and social innovation, among others. Since the scope of the challenge, the identities of the partners and the interactions between them are often influenced by one or more shared institutional logics; creating and maintaining a societal alliance requires partners to integrate multiple and potentially incompatible logics.

Environmental alliances are a common response to societal sustainability demands (Wassmer *et al.* 2014). In environmental alliances, firms collaboratively exploit and explore environmental technologies to address market opportunities while simultaneously generating positive environmental impacts (Lin 2012). These alliance arrangements typically involve actors from the private sector, the public sector and non-governmental organizations who collectively (or bilaterally) generate positive environmental value and/or knowledge value from innovations in environmental technologies (Niesten and Jolink 2020). For example, environmental alliances seek to create a positive (or mitigate negative) impact on domains of climate change, energy efficiency, forestry renewal, decarbonization, clean water and so on. Furthermore, the knowledge gained from an environmental innovation spills over to other firms and society at large that benefit from the R&D investments of the alliance. For example, Sadovnikova and

Pujari (2017) showed that announcements of green marketing partnerships have an immediate positive and significant effect on shareholder value, whereas announcements of green technology partnerships produce an immediate negative and significant effect (with a delayed positive effect). By contrast, Sanzo-Pérez and Álvarez-González (2022) showed that social enterprises partnering with firms that support their goals are more likely to attain sustainability and transformational impact of the innovation, countervailing the short-term orientation of firms.

A circular economy pertains to a zero-waste economic system. Transitioning from linear to circular production systems requires interactions that include cross-sectoral collaboration in ecosystems (Panwar and Niesten 2022). Although the number of individual businesses adopting principles of the circular economy has been growing globally, economy-wide transformations have not yet emerged. It is important to note that circularity-oriented practices are more likely to become effective when companies adopt circular business models rather than marginally updating their existing business models. A key element for circular business models is to build a closed-loop supply chain. It requires that firms closely monitor their supply chains, which may sometimes be achieved through using such tracing techniques as blockchain. In other cases, firms may have to take more radical actions, such as developing local production and consumption networks. Lead firms can aid this transformation from linear to circular by taking an ecosystem approach and by cultivating collective capacities of their ecosystem partners, including suppliers, customers, local communities and regulators. Alliances are thus crucial to system-wide improvements that the circular economy entails (Niesten and Jolink 2020). For example, Köhler and colleagues (2022) report on the Circle House project, a lighthouse project in the Danish construction sector, and showed that open innovation supports circular value creation, while collaborative capabilities enable partners to remain an innovative frontrunner through quick adaptations to a dynamic environment. Ho and colleagues (2022) develop a boundary framework for understanding the interplay between business and civil society in circular economy transitions. For example, in campaign-based boundary work, civil society organizations exert pressure on firms to deal with end-of-use products, and firms respond with low-level circular economy innovations such as better recycling mechanisms, whereas in resource-efficiency-based boundary work, civil society organizations collaborate more closely with firms to jointly implement 'reduce and reuse' strategies that not only reduce pollution but also deliver cost savings. Taken together, in the environmental realm, the value manifests in the form of eco-efficiency, waste removal and reduction in pollution and resource use. These gains occur due in large part to open communication among alliance partners (or ecosystem members) that aids in effectively closing the loop and redesigning business processes. Partners are also able to generate economic rent for themselves mainly in the form of cost savings and competitive advantage. The emergence of complex alliance constellations, such as purpose ecosystems (Stubbs *et al.* 2022), enables all private, public and societal partners to reconcile economic goals with societal impact (Table 26.2).

Theoretical implications for strategic alliance management

Technological innovation and social responsibility will reshape the way companies collaborate with partners, either vertically, horizontally or concentrically, as well as how alliances operate and are managed. Unmistakably, these developments affect the alliance landscape, which raises the question whether traditional notions of strategic alliance management will become obsolete. Next, we use the resource-based view (RBV), transaction cost economics (TCE)

TABLE 26.2 Contemporary alliances: description and implications

	Description	*Drivers (examples)*	*Implications for alliance management*
Technological innovation	Multi-lateral and multi-sector alliances to develop and marketize technological innovation.	Blockchain, cloud computing, artificial intelligence, digital platforms.	• Increasing levels of ambidexterity, decentralization and openness. • Emergence of new (automated) governance mechanisms.
Societal responsibility	Multi-lateral and multi-sector alliances to mitigate societal threats and capture (business) opportunities.	UN-SDG, circular economy, climate crisis, inequality, social movements.	• Increasing levels of conflict, opposing interests and coordination complexity. • Emergence of new mechanisms to internalize external value.

Sources: He *et al.* (2020); Niesten and Jolink (2020).

and institutional theory (IT) to highlight implications (see Chapter 2 for details on these theoretical perspectives).

Drawing on the RBV, technological and societal alliances enable alliance partners to share resources (such as blockchain technology and waste and by-products), capabilities and information. According to RBV logic, firms use alliances to develop new technology or to advance environmental sustainability business models, which enhances their competitive advantage (He *et al.* 2020). In other words, firms can economically profit from technological and societal alliances as alliance partners share value resources, reduce risks, respond to external pressures and invest in co-development of resources. But, changing customer expectations of firms in terms of technological innovation and social responsibility, while providing products and services at lower cost, greater speed and with better customization, implies that firms need to collaborate more widely to continuously enhance their resource endowments. This implies that the RBV's imperfect mobility assumption is challenged (He *et al.* 2020) as the transfer of information and knowledge is becoming highly dynamic and open, enabled by new business models and seamless technology solutions. Technological and societal developments may render existing resource endowments obsolete. As a firm's future competitive advantage originates in resource sharing between alliance partners, protection of key resources will be increasingly important, for example, via enhanced cyber security and intellectual property regarding sustainability initiatives.

Drawing on TCE, one inference is that technological and societal developments enable alliance partners to reduce transaction costs, rendering alternative governance modes and forms efficient (see Chapters 2 and 5). Although design costs (such as automation and algorithms) could come with substantial investments, blockchain governance, for example, may reduce searching, monitoring and enforcement costs, specifically when transactions are codifiable and verifiable (for example, selling insurance). Also, investments in specific assets for sustainability enhance cooperation between alliance partners and generate environmental value (Niesten and Jolink 2020). Asset-specific investments provide partners with incentives to avoid misappropriation of societal value while promoting the development of joint activities. However, TCE explanations fall short in terms of explaining how efficient transactions interrelate with collectively created value. For example, in an open society, technology is not only more likely to be codified and disclosed via patents, but, because of the desirability of (green) technologies, firms might be under pressure to share those in the public domain to facilitate the diffusion of technological and social innovations.

Taking IT as reference, firms form technological and societal alliances to generate value to deal with external pressures from customers, regulators and other stakeholders. For example, environmental activism and lawsuits, mobilizing public sentiment, altering accepted norms, withdrawing important resources and lobbying governments prompt firms to enter into environmental alliances to offer greener products, inform consumers on sustainability and motivate suppliers to adopt more sustainable practices (Niesten and Jolink 2020). Technical and societal alliances create new industry norms and standards and lobby for new rules and regulations to promote the digital and societal transition. IT analyzes the build-up of partners' legitimacy as they collaborate. However, legitimization of initiatives can only be expected when alliance partners communicate about their technological and societal improvements.

Because these traditional theoretical perspectives tend to negate the dynamics invoked by technological and societal forces, alternative explanations are needed to explain the motives and management of emerging dynamic and flexible alliance constellations. For example, the relevance of the RBV has become partly superseded by the dynamic capability view (Teece *et al.* 1997) as the latter offers insights into a firm's alliance capability building and deployment, which is needed when a firm is confronted with technological and market disruption. A firm's ability to combine heterogeneous sources of knowledge and to mobilize such knowledge to commercial ends will become a defining success factor. In addition, the multi-stakeholder involvement in the business ecosystem suggests the need to integrate stakeholder theory (Freeman 1984) into strategic alliance management explanations. For example, emerging alliance constellations encompass various stakeholders, and a better understanding is needed to reflect the changing role of stakeholders in technological and societal alliances and ecosystems. Such advances would also require a reconceptualization of alliance performance to include not only stakeholders' interests (e.g. economic, ecological, technological and societal) but also agility and adaptation to the changing environment and expectations. In sum, new perspectives will need to explain the emerging motives behind emerging alliance forms and the cost–benefit balance between switching to new alliances and alliance ecosystems driven by new opportunities and the maintenance of relationships (Leipämaa-Leskinen *et al.* 2022).

Summary

Technological innovation and social responsibility increase the level of uncertainty and complexity that firms need to consider when developing and executing their alliance strategies. Firms are challenged to proactively seek collaboration with a wide range of (new) partners. These emergent alliance forms embody a shift from competition to cooperation, from firm-centred to multi-centred, from closedness to openness, and from control to orchestration. Understanding of these new alliance constellations, which are established in environments in which organizational boundaries become increasingly blurred, demands understanding of collaborative engagement. It requires decision makers to be able to manage decentralized cross-sector alliances, lead and participate in virtual collaborations, and navigate coopetitive and hybrid partnerships, either as bilateral arrangements or as part of a multi-layered ecosystem.

CASE: TORVALD KLAVENESS[1]

Shipping is a vital source for economic development. Approximately 80 per cent of the world's trade volume and about 70 per cent of trade value are transported by ships. The true importance of shipping became apparent in 2021 when the 'Ever Given' got stuck in the Suez Canal, resulting in a blockage that lasted for six full days. Analysts have calculated that this blockage resulted in economic damages of roughly $400 million per hour. Shipping is a vital link in world trade and will remain in the years to come. At the same time, shipping is also polluting. At the time of writing, the shipping industry accounts for 3.5 to 4 per cent of all climate change emissions, primarily by emitting carbon dioxides. These exhaust gasses also result in local atmospheric pollution. Next, the discharge of ballast water can negatively impact local ecosystems as ballast water contains biological elements which are foreign to those ecosystems. Shipping also impacts wildlife, whether through propellors' collisions with marine mammals or sound pollution from engines, which can impact species who rely on sound for navigation and orientation. Shipping companies are increasingly aware of these problems, and some are actively striving to improve environmental performance.

One such company is the Norwegian Torvald Klaveness (TK). In 1946, Torvald Klaveness founded the company aiming at providing technical management and Norwegian seafarers to the American shipping industry. Shortly after, he started in ship brokering and contracted its first vessel, the MV Bilbao, in 1950. The company moved further into bulk carriers in the 1950s and 1960s, using innovative ships and the ability to establish long-lasting relationships with customers and partners. Today that same pioneering character is still part of the culture. TK's vision is to improve the 'nature' of shipping. Decarbonization, improving cost effectiveness and increasing resilience are the main themes supporting that vision, and within those themes, the adoption of new technologies and services to increase shipping efficiency and reduce its environmental footprint is vital. This vision is very much carried by the company's owners and leadership team. The relevance of shipping companies will be determined by their ability to offer their services while taking account of their environmental impact. The company now exists of five business units, one of them being ZeroLab, which was established in 2021.

ZeroLab's ambition is to make decarbonization of seaborne supply chains a reality for cargo customers. Specifically, ZeroLab partners with ambitious cargo owners who want to lead the way in creating a market for low-carbon deep sea shipping. In setting up this business unit, the company could build on the experiences it already had gained setting up Klaveness Digital. Guided by customer centricity, ZeroLab used an internally validated approach to develop a business around decarbonization. For example, understanding the challenges which lie further down the supply chain was crucial in focusing the activities of both Klaveness Digital and ZeroLab. Cargo owners are increasingly confronted by requests for transparency regarding their carbon footprint and efficiency. An increased focus on costs, combined with increasing requirements on environmental impact, requires companies to have more insight on their supply chains. Direct emissions and emissions from purchased energy, known respectively as Scope 1 and Scope 2 emissions, have been the focus of data collection and reporting in industrial companies for some time now. The next frontier— indirect emissions, known as Scope 3 emissions—is now coming on to the radar as companies are drafting strategies to accomplish net zero targets. Thus, whereas decarbonization as a theme was recognized, no concrete demand for decarbonization services (including Scope 3) exists. To develop and enhance its service offering, ZeroLab has engaged in dialogues with customers to identify shorter and longer term needs. This resulted in pilots in which TK and customers worked together in developing products and services. To ensure commitment on both ends, pilot customers pay a fee to TK to cover part of the expenses. Next a 'fail fast' strategy is used, thereby quickly stopping initiatives that pose insufficient value for customers. Utilizing the broad competencies, experience and networks of TK, ZeroLab joined forces with Klaveness Digital to successfully introduce 'Emissions', an interactive emissions monitoring solution, enabling users to follow the greenhouse gasses (GHG) footprint of shipments in total, per commodity, per trade lane, and over time and drill down to understand how a specific initiative is performing, forecast emissions based on planned shipments and obtain insights for sustainability reporting and performance management.

In the early days of ZeroLab, the level of sophistication of many ideas and concepts proved too high, and direction had to be altered. Many pivots were made before traction was shown for services that provided basic insight into emissions. This has resulted in a more layered approach for ZeroLab. It develops services on three layers. The first layer is aimed at the visualization of current performance and focuses on the ability to present data. For example, (potential) customers can conduct a ZeroLab Health Check—a quick carbon risk assessment of a seaborne supply chain to enable a realistic and cost-efficient strategy for shipping emissions, including a benchmark with the industry average. The second layer is the ability to add intelligence to that data, that is, the ability to interpret the data, resulting in a better understanding of cause–effect relationships. The third layer focuses on actions which can be taken to influence, in this case, the actual emissions (i.e. through the 'Emissions' digital service application).

In developing and enhancing services, the customer is always centric. ZeroLab is collaborating with internal and external stakeholders. The early phases required extensive experimentation and testing with customers. To provide for the required flexibility, these relationships were not overly formalized and heavily relied on the interpersonal skills to keep parties aligned. Important collaborating partners are other divisions within TK to harness their competencies and expertise. The shipping divisions which have extensive knowledge on ship operations and management. Klaveness Digital, which has ample knowledge on harvesting data, presents data but also business models. Since decarbonization is an important topic in the wider shipping industry, Klaveness ZeroLab is also actively involved in fora discussing decarbonization. As a signatory of the Sea Cargo Charter—a framework for assessing and disclosing the climate alignment of ship chartering activities around the globe—ZeroLab proactively promotes transparency about emissions. Through its membership in the Global Maritime Forum, ZeroLab proactively participates in various committees striving to push decarbonization in shipping. The proposition of 'carbon pricing' could be beneficial for TK, as this would further increase demand in the services being developed. External stakeholders and potential clients are being informed and inspired through publications and webcasts showing the importance of decarbonization and the potential of the services which can be provided by TK.

As industry dynamics change, services and business models change as does the way firms interact with their clients. TK has been moving from a pure shipping company to a more service-oriented company. This has resulted in new business models and new revenue streams. It also leads to an increasing complexity for both customers and the standing organization. Questions arise: who is the customer facing entity? How are revenue streams being aligned? How are priorities being set regarding specific customers and how the organization incentives its divisions? In managing these potential tensions, ZeroLab has taken the route of active personal engagement instead of a formal contractual route. The Senior Vice President responsible for ZeroLab directly reports to the CEO, ensuring leadership support. ZeroLab is providing added value, mainly through the shipping divisions of TK, reducing the potential for internal tensions. Success is primarily measured based on revenue and the ability to strengthen the customer relationships. As ZeroLab makes its services more widely available to the market, it will lead to further adoption of tools and services which will improve shipping efficiency and lower carbon emissions. Klaveness is a family-owned customer centric shipping company; it has a long-term perspective and ensures a commitment to directly and indirectly reduce carbon emissions, thereby improving the nature of shipping. ZeroLab plays a key role in that vision.

Questions

1   Torvald Klaveness is responding to technological and societal developments. Explain why partnering, in addition to internal development, constitutes a tool in effectuating its strategic ambitions.
2   Explain how Torvald Klaveness' alliance approach supports the company's innovative and societal goals. What role do customers fulfil in the alliance portfolio?
3   How does Torvald Klaveness' internal organization support its external (alliance) organization?

Note

1   Interview with Klaveness senior executive; Andriessa (2022); Kalouptsidi (2021); Wikipedia (2022)

27

STRATEGIC ALLIANCE MANAGEMENT

Science and art

A thorough understanding of strategic alliance management is a prerequisite for the twenty-first century, when successful alliances are, and will continue to become increasingly, critical strategic tools in firms' competitive arsenals. They appear in many forms and offer a wide range of benefits—economies of scale, reduced competition, innovation, sustainability and profits, to name just a few. Paradoxically, even as firms increase their focus on and use of alliances, failure rates seem to keep climbing. To disentangle the difference between alliance success and failure, we have connected existing theoretical and practical insights to present a much needed, coherent, academically grounded development framework of strategic alliance management that comprises eight separate but related development stages: alliance strategy formulation, partner selection, alliance negotiation, alliance design, alliance launch, alliance management, alliance evaluation and alliance termination. We also have elaborated on rationales for decision-making steps for each stage. Failure might also be attributed to an unawareness of the alliance practices associated with establishing alliances with unique objectives (for example, learning alliances), diverging partner characteristics (for example, international alliances) and distinct alliance constellations (for example, business ecosystems). Consequently, we have supplemented the generic insights with specific decision-making rationales and steps. Because alliance failure is more likely when firms fail to embed alliance experience in their organizational processes, we have also detailed how firms can use alliance professionals, manage alliance teams, and build and deploy their alliance capabilities. Finally, we discussed three unique alliance challenges: building an alliance mindset, navigating the alliance system and embracing the emergence of new alliance constellations.

As a whole, this book suggests that alliances can be purposively and almost scientifically designed and managed to achieve success. By applying the alliance development framework, managers will be able to organize their alliance decision making systematically. Yet alliances are dynamic organizational arrangements, and decision makers still confront a wide range of contingencies that often affect alliance processes and outcomes adversely. The insights in this book deal with a substantial number of contingencies, but no list can be exhaustive. Successful strategic alliance management also necessitates practices that extend beyond an instrumental approach. The practices of an artist describe an alliance professional who creatively and intuitively resolves adversities and creates opportunities. To elaborate on our view that strategic

DOI: 10.4324/9781003222187-27

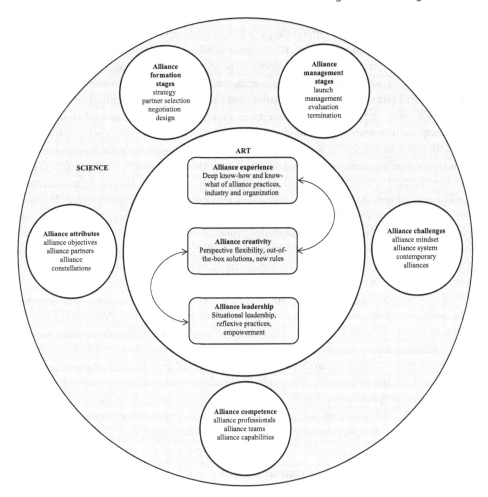

FIGURE 27.1 Strategic alliance management: science and art

alliance management constitutes both a science and an art (see Figure 27.1), we conclude this book by detailing the science of alliance management, followed by a discussion of its art. We end by outlining several future themes that we expect to become salient to the field of strategic alliance management.

The science of strategic alliance management

A scientific approach to strategic alliance management entails the development of a coherent set of theories that inform objective and systematic decision making. The raison d'être of theory is to reduce the complexity of the empirical world by developing and testing theoretical explanations and predictions (Bacharach 1989). A rigorous theory can be generalized beyond the specific context in which it originated. The alliance development framework presented in this book thus draws on wide-ranging theoretical perspectives used by various academics to explain alliance phenomena. That is, the framework and derived decision-making guidelines are well grounded academically.

Yet there are some limitations to the framework. Some theories aim to explain the same alliance phenomena, but their different approaches and assumptions make the related research findings difficult or even impossible to compare (Bell *et al.* 2006; Lumineau and Oliveira 2018). For example, transaction cost economics predicts the conditions, such as asset specificity, frequency or uncertainty, in which certain governance forms are most efficient (Williamson 1981). Thus the theory is normative and prescriptive. The institutional approach is incompatible with such normative assumptions (Teng 2005) because its underlying notion that alliances are inherently behavioural responses to external pressures means there is no need for an efficient governance form. Studies from these two distinct theoretical perspectives are therefore essentially incomparable. In addition, many theories provide only partial explanations. For example, the resource-based view states that an alliance should be terminated if the missing resources or capabilities have been captured or are no longer needed. However, little guidance exists regarding the possibility of changing resource needs in relation to a particular alliance. Although a co-evolutionary view on alliances provides some insights into the relationships between learning and adaptation within an alliance system, the explanations are often confined to specific elements (e.g. environmental dynamics, alliance design or alliance management). No single, unique theoretical perspective can provide a coherent set of explanations for deriving systematic guidelines for successful strategic alliance management.

To overcome these limitations, we have drawn on multiple (though certainly not all) theoretical perspectives to arrive at a coherent set of guidelines for alliance decision making. Because alliances depict socially and economically complex organizational entities operating in a continuously changing environment, consisting of members whose mindsets and interests are likely to shape the relationship, the implications of our academically grounded framework can only go so far. Whereas the science of strategic alliance management values stability, consistency, linearity and simplicity, the art of strategic alliance management draws on principles such as continuous change, inconsistency, non-linearity and complexity.

The art of strategic alliance management

The foundation for our claim that strategic alliance management constitutes an art that is informed by science is our recognition of alliances as inherently complex organizational arrangements. To reduce this complexity, we have disentangled alliance development systematically into separate and manageable parts (see also the strategic alliance management checklist in the Appendix); however, we also note that alliance managers confront opposing, and occasionally mutually exclusive, forces that if left unattended will destroy the alliance. Furthermore, to maintain internal and external alignment, alliances are in a constant flux of learning and adaptation. Also new unknown alliance constellations have emerged, offering new opportunities but also additional coordination complexities. Blueprints, checklists and frameworks are not designed to help alliance managers with these challenges. Strategic alliance management demands, in addition to academic knowledge, the experience, creativity and leadership of alliance managers.

Alliance experience is critical for alliance managers to perform their tasks effectively. Typically, successful alliance managers have deep understanding about the industry, the organization and alliance practices. For example, in finalizing the book, we conducted multiple interviews with alliance professionals. Though their industry and functional expertise varied, consistently they indicate that their effectiveness originates in their deep knowledge of their own organizations. Understanding the functioning of the formal and informal organization and their ability to source internal knowledge, resources and staff enables them to success-fully forge and manage alliance arrangements. Perhaps more often than not, alliance manag-ers need to circumvent the organizational hierarchy to safeguard alliance performance. As alliances bring about multiple disciplines (e.g. legal, R&D, distribution, production, etc.), savvy alliance managers also develop strong interpersonal networks, within their organiza-tions but also crossing organizational boundaries. These networks function as repositories of information, enabling alliance professionals to overcome blind spots in their decision making. Building experience comes with practice; using it to enhance strategic alliance management entails an art.

Successful alliances come with creative solutions which are typically not described in text books. As alliances evolve, managers must address seemingly contradictory, or even mutually exclusive, forces. To resolve these tensions, alliance managers should attempt to reconcile the opposing forces creatively; there is no logical way to put the opposites together in an inter-nally consistent pattern. Possessing a tension-based mindset, alliance managers understand the practice of reconciliation—an intrinsic skill to develop out-of-the-box solutions. Across alliance professionals we interviewed, consensus exists that tools, frameworks and checklist provide guidance and insights, but decision-support systems do not make choices or provide creative solutions. Alliance negotiations are concluded as negotiators develop non-standard incentive schemes to ensure equitable distribution of value among alliance partners. Alliance designs are formalized as professionals creatively reconcile alliance organization, governance form, alliance contract and management control mechanisms. Alliance management drives the alliance forward as alliance managers creatively resolve adversities, challenges and conflicts. The alliance artist embraces perspective flexibility—the skill to direct alliance partners to focus both on safeguarding alliance progress and on developing and capturing new, potentially incompatible, opportunities.

Strategic alliance management necessitates leadership: leadership of oneself, leadership within the organization and leadership across organizational boundaries. A real alliance artist adopts the practice of reflexive action to successfully navigate dynamic, disruptive and unpre-dictable (alliance) environments. They continuously reflect on their behaviours and practices (i.e. self-awareness) as to understand who they are and how they are perceived by others. Several consulted alliance professionals indicate that one misspoken word or sentence can cause an (international) alliance negotiation to break down, or lead to the termination of a successful alliance arrangement. Enhanced self-awareness enables alliance managers to walk the tightrope: advancing individual interests while safeguarding their counterparts' interests. Confronted with various intra- and inter-organizational situations (e.g. harmonious, conflicts, adversities), alliance artists also possess an ability to match their leadership style with unique decision-making situations. For example, an ability to shift between shared and transforma-tional leadership ensures the smooth functioning of alliance teams. Leaders empower alliance team members to make decisions, while simultaneously promoting collective sense-making processes about the team goals and the team's role in the alliance arrangement. The ultimate alliance leadership goal is to forge alliances that are ready to not only benefit in the present but also be prepared for an unexpected future or, more ambitiously, to create the very future that makes current capabilities obsolete.

To conclude, although strategic alliances can improve a firm's competitive advantage, they are also inherently fragile, unstable and difficult to manage. Whereas the 'science' element of strategic alliance management advances informed and systematic decision making, alliance managers need to trust their competences to resolve challenges and adversities. Moreover, confronted with new forms of alliances, the alliance artist understands that contemporary strategic alliance management embodies a shift from competition to cooperation, from firm-centred to multi-centred, from closedness to openness, and from control to orchestration (Tjemkes 2022). This shift may render some traditional instrumental approaches obsolete, necessitating a change in thinking, but in any case, it reemphasizes the salience of the art of strategic alliance management. Not understanding or neglecting the art of strategic alliance management may upset the status quo, leading to premature alliance dissolution. An in-depth understanding of both science and art will help alliance managers better predict, prevent and even deal with specific challenges in their own alliance situations. By combining the alliance development framework in this book with their own managerial experience, creativity and leadership, alliance managers can formulate and implement the right decisions for each unique alliance situation they confront.

The future of strategic alliance management

In this book we provide a coherent and comprehensive understanding of strategic alliance management. During the writing process though, novel ideas kept emerging, both in academia and in practice. Unfortunately, we have not been able to incorporate all these brand-new insights in our book, although on the positive side, this trend suggests a bright future for strategic alliance management, as reflected by numerous review articles presenting directions for future research, including university–industry collaborations (Ankrah and Al-Tabbaa 2015), governance and performance of international alliances (Christoffersen 2013; Contractor and Reuer 2014; Li *et al.* 2015), supply chain management (Grimm *et al.* 2015), societal alliances (Niesten and Jolink 2020), alliance dynamics (Majchrzak *et al.* 2014), alliance termination (Nemeth and Nippa 2013; Rajan *et al.* 2020), alliance capabilities (Kohtamäki *et al.* 2018; Niesten and Jolink 2015; Wang and Rajagopalan 2015), business ecosystems (Cobben *et al.* 2022; Gomes *et al.* 2018), digital transformation (He *et al.* 2020), coopetition (Corbo *et al.* 2022), alliance teams (van der Kamp *et al.* 2022), the dark-side of alliances (Oliveira and Lumineau 2019) and alliance performance issues (Christoffersen *et al.* 2014; Niesten and Stefan 2019; Ryan-Charleton *et al.* 2022). Here, we detail four especially promising areas of interest.

First, mainstream alliance research (still) focuses primarily on alliance governance, with the argument that governance constitutes the primary antecedent of superior alliance performance. However, in line with our alliance development framework, we suggest that some development stages (or elements within stages) may require future attention.

- **Negotiations behaviour.** Building on prior alliance negotiations research (see Chapter 4), future studies could explore a variety of topics: how can alliance managers achieve favourable processes and outcomes during alliance (re)negotiations? What causes firms to initiate renegotiations? What effect do distinct negotiations behaviours have on alliance development? How does opportunistic behaviour manifest itself during alliance negotiations? How do individual (re)negotiation behaviours affect alliance progress?
- **Alliance launch.** Though critical to alliance success, little prior academic work exists detailing on the drivers and mechanisms required to execute an alliance (see Chapter 6). Research may set out to address a variety of questions: when and how should a launch manager become involved? What would make an effective kick-off meeting? How to organize a hand-off? How to deal with the immediate tension between contract application and trust-building? What are critical decisions during the first 100 days?

- **Alliance performance.** Though the majority of alliance research tends to focus on alliance performance, research tends to neglect the multifaceted nature of alliance performance (see Chapters 8–9). Questions that warrant answers include the following: to what extent do antecedents of performance differ from under-performance? What type of intervention (e.g. behaviour, process, structure) is likely to revitalize an alliance? When should an alliance be terminated, such that dissolution does not occur before objective realization or continue after objective realization? How does the interplay between value creation and appropriation affect alliance functioning? How do different alliance performance motives interrelate regarding activities, resources and investments necessitated?

- **Disruptions and shocks.** Prior alliance literature primarily focused on stability and performance of alliance arrangements, with some exceptions seeking to understand how internal disruption can be mitigated and resolved through changes in formal and relational governance (e.g. Keller *et al.* 2021). However, in addition to internal disruptions, external shocks, such as pandemics, natural disasters and (financial) crises, are likely to influence the formation and management of alliance arrangements (see Chapter 25). Questions guiding future research include the following: how do different forms of disruption influence alliance functioning and performance? What preemptive and ex-post mechanisms can be installed to mitigate the impact of disruptions? How do external shocks impact alliance formation decisions? What alliance portfolio configurations buffer against external shocks? How do alliance objectives (e.g. supplier and learning) and partners' attributes (e.g. asymmetry in size and organizational structure) influence the partner firms' ability to cope with disruptions and shocks?

Second, as we have argued throughout this book, alliance processes and managers' behaviours constitute equally important predictors of alliance success. Research on alliance processes and behaviour is advancing (see Chapter 7 for example), but several topics remain open as potentially fruitful research avenues:

- **Alliance teams.** Following in the steps of some recent studies (see Chapter 22), research should explore the relationships among alliance team composition, team processes and team outcomes, such as leadership, decision making, learning and conflicts, while accounting for different types of teams (e.g. negotiation team versus joint venture board) and unique alliance objectives (e.g. supplier versus learning alliance). In addition, alliance arrangements constitute a system of teams (i.e. multi-team system) from both partners and the alliance. Research should explore the dynamics across this set of teams, as well as among individual team members, and explore topics such as goal hierarchies, team interdependencies, inter-team linkages, boundary spanning and the role of informal networks.

- **Alliance professionals.** At the core, alliance professionals make or break an alliance arrangement (see Chapter 21). A better understanding is required about the roles alliance professionals fulfil and which competences and personality traits enable them to work effectively. Or, how alliance professionals construct and deal with tensions (see Chapter 24). Research may explore these topics while focusing on specific topics, such as contract design and application, trust-building and opportunism, handling of emotion and conflicts, and knowledge creation and sharing. In addition, future research may explore how alliance managers use language (e.g. style, fluency and metaphors) to facilitate alliance decision making and processes. Furthermore, how do alliance professionals construct tensions (e.g. as opposed to trade-offs and frictions)? How do they deal with tensions, and under what conditions does tension resolution result in (un)favourable outcomes?

- **Alliances and ICT.** The information and communication technology (ICT) revolution has already affected how digital transformation drives the emergence of new alliance-based business models and how new alliance constellations (see Chapter 26) function, yet how this transformation affects alliance functioning remains an underexplored theme. So how might virtual working provide opportunities for employees in geographically dispersed locations to communicate, share and collaborate so as to achieve private and common goals? How should partners optimize workflows in alliances? How can ICT tools enable social activities in alliances, including finding and getting in contact with people, sharing information and working together? How can firms build, participate and generate value through digital collaboration in various alliance constellations, including portfolios, networks and ecosystems?

Third, with few notable exceptions, most alliance research has adopted a static approach (i.e. cross-sectional, single level of analysis). To advance understanding about strategic alliance management, we need a dynamic perspective to disentangle presumed causal relationships, resolve inconclusive results and unravel multi-level explanations. The following topics may provide inputs for research endeavours:

- **Alliances as dynamic entities.** Though studies provide insights in the development of alliance arrangements, suggesting that successful alliances exhibit patterns of proactive change caused by a recognition to reconcile partner differences and characterized by complex learning and feedback loops (see Chapters 3 and 7), future research may explore a variety of topics to provide a better understanding of the dynamics of alliance evolution. Research questions may focus on the following: what feedback and learning mechanisms drive governance adaptations, and what underlying mechanisms enable these adaptations? How do pre-formation dynamics inhibit or facilitate post-formation development? To what extent, and how, do formal and informal governance mechanisms in concert drive alliance development? And how and under what conditions may alliance instability generate positive alliance outcomes? These and other questions (e.g. learning and contracting dynamics) may also be explored at the portfolio and network levels of analysis.
- **Alliances as multi-level entities.** Studies should explore the dynamics between different levels of analysis (Faems *et al.* 2008; Lumineau and Oliveira 2018; Salvato *et al.* 2017), including internal organizational dynamics, alliance functioning and outcomes, and external contingencies (Brattström *et al.* 2020; Le Roy and Fernandez 2015; Lipparini *et al.* 2014), while focusing on varied, alliance-related phenomena: how do communication, trust and contracting within and between different levels of partner organizations enable or hinder collaborative activities across partners? How do coalition dynamics at different levels within partner organizations, as well as within the alliance, affect one another? What are the differences and tensions in alliance management between alliances initiated at operational or strategic levels? In addition, future research may explore the interrelatedness between individual, team, alliance and network levels of analysis and focus on questions such as the following: how do individual behaviours affect team functioning and alliance progress, and vice versa? Under what conditions are which coordination mechanisms effective to align interests across team- and alliance-levels of analysis? To

what extent do different alliance network structures enable or inhibit alliance formation, management and performance, and vice versa?

- **Alliance capabilities.** Research tends to converge on the salience of alliance capabilities (see Chapter 23) but not on the answers to several remaining issues. In what conditions do internally (e.g. alliance) and externally (e.g. consultants) sourced functions become substitutes or complements? How do alliance capabilities develop over time? How can firms optimize the deployment of alliance capabilities? Regarding contemporary alliance arrangements, what new alliance capabilities (e.g. multi-lateral, openness, cross-sector) would be effective?

Fourth, alliances have become increasingly popular, so new alliance types and constellations keep emerging (Chapter 26). It is important to understand the make-up, motives and management of these new forms; the quality of alliance governance is likely conditioned by the type of alliance chosen:

- **Business ecosystems.** In traditional and emerging industries, such as the financial, IT and services sectors, (platform-based) ecosystems seem to have replaced traditional partnerships as the most dominant form of collaboration. Business ecosystems, conceived as a constellation of multiple alliances, bring about new governance challenges which warrant future research (see Chapter 20). What would constitute an efficient design and effective ecosystem management approach? How are value creation and value appropriation interrelated in business ecosystems? How can ecosystem members fulfil different ecosystem roles while participating in multiple ecosystems? What business and incentive models are effective (e.g. equitable distribution of value) to promote collaboration within business ecosystems? Which coordination mechanisms enable ecosystem leaders to align multiple partners' interests? How to withdraw from a business ecosystem? To what extent vary explanations across ecosystem types?
- **Multi-sided platforms.** While scholars have explored the competitive dynamics of platform ecosystems (see Chapters 20 and 26), less attention has been given to the de novo creation and expansion of multi-sided platform ecosystems, an alliance constellation whereby a digital platform enables direct interactions between two or more distinct sides (e.g. customer and supplier) and each side is affiliated with the platform (e.g. customers can be suppliers and vice versa). Multi-sided platforms are often seen as key disruptors, and they come with new governance challenges. How to align technological, organizational and alliance governance? How to orchestrate value creation and value appropriation? How to safeguard innovation and stimulate growth at the platform and platform member levels of analysis?
- **Service alliance.** Consistent with the development of servitization (Baines *et al.* 2009), firms increasingly forge alliances to attain service provision benefits. Unlike production, services reach outcomes through co-production with customers, so alliances (or ecosystems) based on services tend to be highly interactive, short-term focused and project based (see Chapter 20). In which conditions does such a service alliance support a business strategy? How do organizational identity and customer identity interrelate, and what is their impact on alliance performance? How is it possible to manage the alliance–customer interaction within a service-based ecosystem? How can digitalization enhance service delivery and quality in service alliances?

- **Public–private–plural alliances.** Public–private alliance arrangements are becoming increasingly popular, as well as alliances with and between actors operating in the plural sector. The plural sector refers to any association that is neither public nor private— owned neither by the state nor by private investors (Mintzberg 2015)—and pertains to, for example, non-governmental organizations, cooperatives and foundations. Alliances between public, private and plural actors are forged to deal with social challenges such as (cyber)security, sustainability, corporate social responsibility, housing and climate and environmental changes (see Chapter 26). Although we detailed cross-sector alliance arrangements (see Chapter 15), future research may explore several questions, including the following: how may public and plural organizations use bilateral and multi-lateral alliances to attain their objectives? How and under what conditions can public–private– plural alliances be used to resolve societal issues? How can such alliances be effectively governed, and how can partner misfits (e.g. different values and institutional logics) be resolved?

Academics should explore these research themes and develop and validate rigorous theories (see Box 27.1), which then can inform alliance decision making. Studies also need to build on prior research to develop a conceptually sound and empirically validated body of knowledge (Castañer and Oliveira 2020). The accumulation of such knowledge will allow for verification, falsification and replication, which can help build a theoretically consistent, integrated and logical structure of ideas. These theoretical advances may benefit managers by enhancing their ability to deal with their strategic alliances—which means in turn that research output must be practically applicable, incorporate explanations and guidelines for managers, provide counter-intuitive insights and apply to practitioners at an appropriate time. With this book, we hope to have made one such relevant contribution.

BOX 27.1 SUGGESTIONS FOR EMPIRICAL ALLIANCE RESEARCH

Research studies seeking to interpret and define the complex and dynamic influences associated with strategic alliance management have proliferated in recent years. Many of these studies have been characterized by the adoption of a positivistic perspective in an attempt to quantify identified behaviours in this field. For example, alliance studies used survey, secondary sources and experiment-based (to a lesser extent) methods and techniques to generate quantitative data—data used to test hypotheses. The remainder of the alliance studies have generally pursued a largely exploratory, often case study– based approach, which provides more detail and depth to the existing body of knowledge. Though since its inception the alliance field has become more rigorous and systematic in its use of methodology, as evident in the increasing use of more formalized research processes and sophisticated techniques, there is still room for further improvement. A large part of the alliance literature uses cross-sectional design. Although the results generated valuable and pragmatic knowledge about strategic alliance management to avoid issues with reversed causality (and other endogeneity problems) and simultaneously reduce other measurement biases (e.g. common method bias), data collection preferably should occur at multiple points in time. Alliance research projects also often use subjective and perceptual data; however, collecting both subjective and objective data would enhance the validity and reliability of research findings. In addition, the majority of these studies use one-sided respondents to collect data about alliance phenomena. However, perceptions and experiences may differ between partner representatives (e.g. trust, dependence and information asymmetry), hence the reliability and validity of future results would strongly benefit from two-sided data collection. With regard to operational definitions, to advance the field and enable comparison of empirical findings, more consistency in measures is warranted. Consider for example alliance performance. Despite efforts to develop coherent and multi-dimensional conceptual and operational definitions, across alliance studies, different measurements are employed. Emerging topics may warrant new methods and techniques. Understanding the role of language in alliance negotiations may require more interpretative and possibly action-based research approaches. In addition, multi-level studies demand large data sets and new, sophisticated techniques, whereas understanding alliance dynamics demands longitudinal case-based approaches. Finally, the primary focus in the alliance field appears to be on innovative and original studies. However, more attention should be given to replication, specifically replication of prior findings while accounting for the idiosyncrasies associated with alliance development stages, alliance contextual factors and alliance competences.

Sources: Gomes *et al.* (2016); He *et al.* (2020).

APPENDIX

In this appendix we present a strategic alliance management checklist. The objective of this checklist is to guide alliance professionals in their decision making. Building on the alliance development framework steps presented in this book, we provide for each step the main decision, core activities and example questions.

TABLE A.1 Managerial checklist

Focus	Main decision and core activities	Questions (examples)
Alliance development framework		
Alliance strategy formulation	• Is alliance the most suitable governance mode for realizing your organization goals? • Formulate business strategy. • Develop a governance mode selection framework. • Retrieve internal and external information. • Assess alternative governance mode. • Formulate alliance strategy.	• To what extent is it clear what (strategic) objectives are pursued by the organization? • Is it clear what resources and activities are required to attain these objectives and to what extent the organization lacks these resources and/or activities? • Are all motives clear and assessed, in support of a decision to opt for a strategic alliance (over internal growth, merger and market transaction)? • Has a risk assessment been conducted to explicate the implications of a strategic alliance, both internally and externally? • Is the organization able to forge and manage a strategic alliance? • Are sufficient resources allocated (time, staff, assets and support) to successfully establish a strategic alliance? • Has a business case been developed?

TABLE A.1 (*Continued*)

Focus	Main decision and core activities	Questions (examples)
Alliance partner selection	• Which partner or group of partners is most suitable for realizing the alliance objectives of your organization? • Develop a partner profile. • Make a long and short list of potential partners. • Develop partner fit framework. • Conduct partner fit analysis. • Conduct risk assessment.	• Are all possible partners considered, familiar and unfamiliar? • Are all partner selection criteria clear and assessed, in support of a decision to opt for a specific alliance partner? • Does each partner contribute equitably and uniquely to the alliance, and combined do the contributions provide sufficient value-creation potential? • Is it clear where areas for partner fit and misfit exist and what measures are required for a smooth alliance launch? • Has a risk assessment been conducted to explicate the positive and negative consequences of collaborating with the preferred partner?
Alliance negotiation	• How to create the alliance conditions supporting the execution of alliance in order to realize win–win processes and outcomes for all partners? • Prepare the negotiation: e.g. assemble alliance negotiation team and set the agenda and strategy. • Negotiate: refers to sharing information, assess compatibility and chemistry, balancing interests and considering trade offs. • Post-negotiation: refers to establish relevant documentation and decide to proceed.	• If applicable, has a non-disclosure agreement been signed? • Does the negotiation outcome reflect conditions that enable the partners to attain individual and collective objectives? • Does the negotiation outcome reflect conditions that stimulate the partners to actively collaborate and participate, both short- and long-term? • To what extent does the negotiation process promote a post-formation process exhibiting trust building, mutual learning and adaptability? • Are all agreements formalized in a letter of intent and/or alliance contract?
Alliance design	• Which alliance structure supports your organization and your partners the best for realizing the alliance goals? • Negotiate and document. • Design organization and governance form. • Formulate contractual provisions. • Develop management control. • Assess efficacy alliance design.	• Are the alliance ambition, individual objectives and joint objectives explicated and formalized in an alliance contract? • Has the alliance organization been set with regard to hierarchical structure and operational activities? • Are key staff identified, and has it been formalized with functions and roles they fulfil? • Does the legal arrangement fit with the objective, the organization of activities and the potential risks?

(*Continued*)

TABLE A.1 (*Continued*)

Focus	*Main decision and core activities*	*Questions (examples)*
		• Are all agreements formalized in contractual clauses (e.g. termination, exclusivity), and are appropriate management control mechanisms in place?
		• If applicable, has a code of conduct been explicated and communicated?
		• Is it clear to all partners how conflicts are resolved (if they emerge), how unforeseen circumstances are dealt with (i.e. contingency clauses), how progress is monitored, who has decision-making authority and how stakeholders are informed?
Alliance launch	• How to execute the alliance as to effectuate a smooth transition from alliance negotiation and design to alliance management? • Prepare alliance launch. • Develop alliance launch strategy. • Execute alliance launch strategy. • Transition to alliance management team. • Evaluate and document learnings.	• To what extent is the (joint) alliance launch team assembled? Are members involved in negotiations, and is the team ready to execute the alliance? • Has executive support from both partners been obtained? • Are functional and operational plans prepared, launch activities determined and milestones set? • Has a communication plan to inform internal and external stakeholders been developed? • Has a kick-off meeting been organized? • Has the transition from launch team to management team been organized? • Has the alliance launch been evaluated and documented, as input for future alliances?
Alliance management	• How to manage the day-to-day activities needed to realize alliance goals and how to develop the alliance? • Manage day-to-day activities. • Monitor the alliance. • Decide on corrective measure(s). • Intervene and communicate.	• To what extent does alliance management promote a climate of trust, safety and transparency? • Are learning initiatives supported and monitored? • Are conflicts quickly resolved before they escalate? • Are internal and external developments monitored and assessed on their impact on the alliances? • Are interventions, adaptations and relationship repair initiatives executed before the relationship derails?

Focus	Main decision and core activities	Questions (examples)
Alliance evaluation	• How to evaluate the performance of the alliance? • Design a performance metric system. • Implement the performance metric system. • Interpret metric outcomes. • Assess performance metric system.	• Are the common and individual alliance objectives explicated? • Have you determined, for each objective, (1) input, (2) process and (3) outcome metrics? • Are procedures (who and when) about data collection, data analysis and reporting clear? • Has it been determined at which time intervals alliance evaluation is conducted? • Are adaptations and interventions substantiated and in line with the alliance strategy? • Is the performance metric system regularly updated, and is learning applied to other alliances?
Alliance termination	• Decide when and how to terminate the alliance. • Assess and initiate. • Initiate dyadic communication. • Disengage. • Manage aftermath.	• Are alliance termination clauses explicated in the alliance contract? • Has the decision to withdraw from the alliance been scrutinized, and is it clear what the repercussions are for the organization? • Is it clear how and when the alliance will be dismantled? • Has a communication plan been developed to inform internal and external stakeholders? • Are sufficient precautions being taken to recoup resources and prevent reputational damage? • Are the best and worst alliance practices documented?
Alliance attributes		
Alliance objectives Alliance partners Alliance constellations	• Is it clear how and what alliance context may create unique decision-making situations and affect the choices associated with steps 1–8?	• To what extent and how do alliance objectives (e.g. learning, supplier, co-branding) affect alliance development decisions? • To what extent and how do alliance partners (e.g. international, asymmetrical, cross-sector and coopetition) affect alliance development decisions? • To what extent and how do alliance constellations (e.g. multi-partner, portfolio, network and business ecosystem) affect alliance development decisions?

(*Continued*)

TABLE A.1 (Continued)

Focus	Main decision and core activities	Questions (examples)
Alliance competence		
Alliance professionals Alliance teams Alliance capabilities	• How to build, organize and deploy strategic alliance management practices?	• To what extent and how does a firm employ competent alliance professionals, offer educational alliance programmes and assign the best people to its alliance relationships? • To what extent and how does a firm understand and manage alliance teams, as a stand-alone team or as part of a multi-team system? • To what extent and how does a firm capture, codify, communicate and coach alliance worst and best practices (e.g. alliance function, tool development and training)?
Alliance challenge		
Alliance mindset Alliance system Contemporary alliances	• How to create an alliance mindset enabling professionals to deal with the complexities of alliance systems and emerging forms of alliance constellations?	• To what extent are alliance professional equipped to identify and resolve tensions inherently tied to alliance management? • To what extent does a firm understand the complexity and co-evolutionary (adaptive) nature of alliance systems? • To what extent is a firm aware of emerging alliance practices and thus able to forge and manage technological and societal alliance arrangements?

REFERENCES

Aarikka-Stenroos, L. and Ritala, P. (2017) 'Network management in the era of ecosystems: Systematic review and management framework'. *Industrial Marketing Management*, 67: 23–36.

Accenture (2016) 'Financial technology has been on the rise for five years'. Available online at http://fintechinnovationlabnyc.com/media/830595/FinTech-New-York-Partnerships-Platforms-Open-Innovation.pdf (accessed 14 December 2016).

Accenture (2022) 'Supply chain disruption: Repurposed supply chains of the future must have resilience and responsibility at their heart'. Available online at www.accenture.com/us-en/insights/consulting/coronavirus-supply-chain-disruption (accessed 25 June 2020).

Achrol, R. S. (1997) 'Changes in the theory of interorganizational relations in marketing: Toward a network paradigm'. *Journal of the Academy of Marketing Science*, 25: 56–71.

Adner, R. (2012) 'Amazon vs Apple: Competing ecosystem strategies'. Available online at http://hbr.org/2012/03/amazon-vs-apple-competing-ecos/ (accessed 26 July 2016).

Adner, R. (2017) 'Ecosystem as structure: An actionable construct for strategy'. *Journal of Management*, 43(1): 39–58.

Adner, R. and Kapoor, R. (2010) 'Value creation in innovation ecosystems: How the structure of technological interdependence affects firm performance in new technology generations'. *Strategic Management Journal*, 31(3): 306–333.

Adobor, H. (2004) 'High performance management of shared-managed joint venture teams: Contextual and socio-dynamic factors'. *Team Performance Management*, 10: 65–76.

Agarwal, R., Croson, R. and Mahoney, J. T. (2010) 'The role of incentives and communication in strategic alliances: An experimental investigation'. *Strategic Management Journal*, 31: 413–437.

Agostini, L. and Nosella, A. (2019) 'Inter-organizational relationships involving SMEs: A bibliographic investigation into the state of the art'. *Long Range Planning*, 52(1): 1–31.

Agudelo, M. A. L., Jóhannsdóttir, L. and Davídsdóttir, B. (2019) 'A literature review of the history and evolution of corporate social responsibility'. *International Journal of Corporate Social Responsibility*, 4(1): 1–23.

Ahuja, G. (2000) 'Collaboration networks, structural holes, and innovation: A longitudinal study'. *Administrative Science Quarterly*, 45: 425–455.

Albanese, R. and Van Fleet, D. D. (1985) 'The free-riding tendency in organizations'. *Scandinavian Journal of Management Studies*, 2: 121–135.

Albers, S., Wohlgezogen, F. and Zajac, E. J. (2016) 'Strategic alliance structures: An organization design perspective'. *Journal of Management*, 42: 582–614.

Aldrich, H. E. and Pfeffer, J. (1976) 'Environments of organization'. *Annual Review of Sociology*, 2: 79–105.

Algeanews (2011) 'Solazyme and Bunge sign JDA partnership for production of renewable triglyceride oils'. Available online at http://algaenews.com/?p=384 (accessed 2 August 2011).

Ali, T. and Larimo, J. (2016) 'Managing opportunism in international joint ventures: The role of structural and social mechanisms'. *Scandinavian Journal of Management, 32*: 86–96.

Alliance for Open Media (2015) 'Alliance for Open Media established to deliver next-generation Open Media formats'. Available online at http://aomedia.org/press-releases/alliance-to-deliver-next-generation-open-media-formats/ (accessed 27 July 2016).

Alvarez, S. A. and Barney, J. B. (2001) 'How entrepreneurial firms can benefit from alliances with large partners'. *Academy of Management Executive, 15*: 139.

Amazon (2022a) 'Amazon robotics supports Georgia tech startup incubator'. Available online at www.amazon.science/academic-engagements/amazon-robotics-supports-atdc-georgia-tech-startup-incubator (accessed 5 November 2022).

Amazon (2022b) 'How Amazon is bringing the excitement of Disney's ultimate fan expo to everyone'. Available online at www.aboutamazon.com/news/retail/how-amazon-is-bringing-the-excitement-of-disneys-ultimate-fan-expo-to-everyone (accessed 8 November 2022).

Anand, B. N. and Khanna, T. (2000) 'Do firms learn to create value? The case of alliances'. *Strategic Management Journal, 21*: 295–315.

Anderson, E. (1990) 'Two firms, one frontier: On assessing joint venture performance'. *Sloan Management Review, 31*: 19–30.

Anderson, S. W., Christ, M., Dekker, H. C. and Sedatole, K. L. (2015) 'Do extant management control frameworks fit the alliance setting? A descriptive analysis'. *Industrial Marketing Management, 46*: 36–53.

Andriessa, R. (2022) 'Maritime transport: The backbone of international trade activities'. Available online at https://cwts.ugm.ac.id/en/2022/04/18/maritime-transport-the-backbone-of-international-trade-activities/ (accessed 6 November 2022).

Ang, S. H., Benischke, M. H. and Doh, J. P. (2015) 'The interactions of institutions on foreign market entry mode'. *Strategic Management Journal, 36*: 1536–1553.

Ankrah, S. and Al-Tabbaa, O. (2015) 'Universities-industry collaboration: A systematic review'. *Scandinavian Journal of Management, 31*: 387–408.

Apple (2022a) 'Apple calls on global supply chain to decarbonize by 2030'. Available online at www.apple.com/newsroom/2022/10/apple-calls-on-global-supply-chain-to-decarbonize-by-2030/ (accessed 8 November 2022).

Apple (2022b) 'Apple music and Mercedes-Benz bring premium immersive Spatial Audio to drivers worldwide'. Available online at www.apple.com/newsroom/2022/10/apple-music-and-mercedes-benz-bring-immersive-spatial-audio-to-drivers-worldwide/ (accessed 8 November 2022).

Ariño, A. (2003) 'Measures of collaborative venture performance: An analysis of construct validity'. *Journal of International Business Studies, 34*: 66–79.

Ariño, A. and de la Torre, J. (1998) 'Learning from failure: Towards an evolutionary model of collaborative ventures'. *Organization Science, 9*: 306–325.

Ariño, A., de la Torre, J. and Ring, P. S. (2001) 'Relational quality: Managing trust in corporate alliances'. *California Management Review, 44*: 109–131.

Ariño, A. and Reuer, J. J. (2004) 'Designing and renegotiating strategic alliance contracts'. *Academy of Management Executive, 18*: 37–48.

Ariño, A., Reuer, J. J., Mayer, K. J. and Jané, J. (2014) 'Contracts, negotiation, and learning: An examination of termination provisions'. *Journal of Management Studies, 51*: 379–405.

Arora, A. and Ceccagnoli, M. (2006) 'Patent protection, complementary assets, and firms' incentives for technology licensing'. *Management Science, 52*: 293–308.

Arranz, N., Arroyabe, M. and Fdez Arroyabe, J. C. (2016) 'Alliance-building process as inhibiting factor for SME international alliances'. *British Journal of Management, 27*: 497–515.

Arya, B. and Salk, J. E. (2006) 'Cross-sector alliance learning and effectiveness of voluntary codes of corporate social responsibility'. *Business Ethics Quarterly, 16*: 211–234.

ASAP (2016) 'Alliance management professional development guide'. Available online at www.strategic-alliances.org/?page=cert_overview (accessed 20 July 2016).

ASAP (2022) 'Code of conduct for alliance professionals'. Available online at www.strategic-alliances.org/code-of-conduct-for-alliance-professionals (accessed 25 June 2022).

AT&T (2021) 'AT&T brings 5G connectivity to the GE research campus'. Available online at https://about.att.com/story/2021/ge-research.html (accessed 17 October 2022).

Aulakh, P. S., Kotabe, M. and Sahay, A. (1996) 'Trust and performance in cross-border marketing partnerships: A behavioral approach'. *Journal of International Business Studies*, 27: 1005–1032.

Austin, J. E. (2000) *The collaboration challenge: How nonprofits and business succeed through strategic alliances*. San Francisco, CA: Jossey-Bass.

Bacharach, S. B. (1989) 'Organizational theories—some criteria for evaluation'. *Academy of Management Review*, 14: 496–515.

Baines, T. S., Lightfoot, H. W., Benedettini, J. M. and Kay, J. M. (2009) 'The servitization of manufacturing: A review of literature and reflection on future challenges'. *Journal of Manufacturing Technology Management*, 20: 547–567.

Bakker, R. M. (2016) 'Stepping in and stepping out: Strategic alliance partner reconfiguration and the unplanned termination of complex projects'. *Strategic Management Journal*, 37: 1919–1941.

Bakker, R. M. and Knoben, J. (2014) 'Built to last or meant to end: Intertemporal choice in strategic alliance portfolios'. *Organization Science*, 26: 256–276.

Bamel, N., Pereira, V., Bamel, U. and Cappiello, G. (2021) 'Knowledge management within a strategic alliances context: Past, present and future'. *Journal of Knowledge Management*, 25(7): 1782–1810.

Bamford, J. D., Bhargave, S. and Danie, P. (2022) *Partnership makers shakers: Ankura's 2022 scoreboard of corporate partnering activity*. Washington, DC: Ankura Consulting Group.

Bamford, J. D. and Ernst, D. (2003) 'Growth of alliance capabilities'. In Bamford, J. D., Gomes-Casseres, B. and Robinson, M. S. (eds.), *Mastering alliance strategy: A comprehensive guide to design, management, and organization*. San Francisco, CA: Jossey-Bass, pp. 321–333.

Bamford, J. D., Ernst, D. and Fubini, D. G. (2004) 'Launching a world-class joint venture'. *Harvard Business Review*, 82: 90–100.

Bamford, J. D., Gomes-Casseres, B. and Robinson, M. S. (2003) *Mastering alliance strategy: A comprehensive guide to design, management, and organization*. San Francisco, CA: Jossey-Bass.

Bardsley, J. (2013) 'Oxfam and Marks and Spencer's schwopping partnership'. Available online at http://sofii.org/case-study/oxfam-and-marks-and-spencers-schwopping-partnership (accessed 2 December 2016).

Barkema, H. G., Bell, J. H. J. and Pennings, J. M. (1996) 'Foreign entry, cultural barriers, and learning'. *Strategic Management Journal*, 17: 151–166.

Barney, J. B. (1991) 'Firm resources and sustained competitive advantage'. *Journal of Management*, 17: 99–120.

Barney, J. B. and Hansen, M. H. (1994) 'Trustworthiness as a source of competitive advantage'. *Strategic Management Journal*, 15: 175–190.

Barringer, B. R. and Harrison, J. S. (2000) 'Walking a tightrope: Creating value through interorganizational relationships'. *Journal of Management*, 26: 367–403.

Barroso-Méndez, M. J., Galera-Casqueta, C., Seitanidib, M. M. and Valero-Amaroa, V. (2016) 'Cross-sector social partnership success: A process perspective on the role of relational factors'. *European Management Journal*, 34: 674–685.

Basken, P. (2022) 'MIT ends Skoltech partnership over Ukraine war'. Available online at www.timeshighereducation.com/news/mit-ends-skoltech-partnership-over-ukraine-war (accessed 23 September 2022).

Baum, J. A. C., Calabrese, T. and Silverman, B. S. (2000) 'Don't go it alone: Alliance network composition and startups' performance in Canadian biotechnology'. *Strategic Management Journal*, 21: 267–294.

Beamish, P. W. (1993) 'Characteristics of joint ventures in the people's Republic of China'. *Journal of International Marketing*, 1: 29–48.

Beamish, P. W. and Lupton, N. C. (2016) 'Cooperative strategies in international business and management: Reflections on the past 50 years and future directions'. *Journal of World Business*, 51: 163–175.

Beckman, C. M., Schoonhoven, C. B., Rottner, R. M. and Kim, S.-J. (2014) 'Relational pluralism in De Novo organizations: Board of directors as bridges or barriers to diverse alliance portfolios?' *Academy of Management Journal*, 57(2): 460–483.

Bell, J., den Ouden, B. and Ziggers, G.W. (2006) 'Dynamics of cooperation: At the brink of irrelevance'. *Journal of Management Studies, 43*: 1607–1619.

Bell, J. and Lemmens, C. E. A.V. (2007) 'Alliantievaardigheden als kerncompetentie: een verdiepende case study'. *Tijdschrift voor Management en Organisatie, 61*: 129–138.

Bell, J., Singh, H. and Kale, P. (2010) 'Making strategic alliances work: How Royal Philips tries to build alliance capability'. In Tjemkes, B., van den Hout, T. and Schrijver, I. (eds.), *Strategie in verhouding: Netwerken, stakeholders, samenwerken*. Den Haag: Lemma, pp. 165–174.

Beltagui, A., Rosli, A. and Candi, M. (2020) 'Exaptation in a digital innovation ecosystem: The disruptive impacts of 3D printing'. *Research Policy, 49*: 103833.

Bengtsson, M. and Kock, S. (2000) 'Coopetition in business networks—to cooperate and compete simultaneously'. *Industrial Marketing Management, 29*: 411–426.

Bengtsson, M. and Raza-Ullah, T. (2016) 'A systematic review of research on coopetition: Toward a multilevel understanding'. *Industrial Marketing Management, 57*: 23–39.

Bennis, W. and Nanus, B. (1985) *Leaders: The strategies for taking charge*. New York: Harper & Row.

Berard, C. and Perez, M. (2014) 'Alliance dynamics through real options: The case of an alliance between competing pharmaceutical companies'. *European Management Journal, 32*(2): 337–349.

Berthon, P., Pitt, L. F., Ewing, M.T. and Bakkeland, G. (2003) 'Norms and power in marketing relationships: Alternative theories and empirical evidence'. *Journal of Business Research, 56*: 699–709.

BICO (2022) 'BICO has reached a beneficial and sustainable solution with Organovo'. Available online at https://news.cision.com/bico-group/r/bico-has-reached-a-beneficial-and-sustainable-solution-with-organovo,c3512360 (accessed 5 November 2022).

Bjørkeng, K., Clegg, S. and Pitsis, T. (2009) 'Becoming (a) practice'. *Management Learning, 40*(2): 145–159.

Blankenburg Holm, D., Eriksson, K. and Johanson, J. (1999) 'Creating value through mutual commitment to business network relationships'. *Strategic Management Journal, 20*: 467–486.

Blass, E. (2016) 'Microsoft, Nokia and the burning platform: A final look at the failed Windows phone alliance'. Available online at http://venturebeat.com/2016/02/05/microsoft-nokia-and-the-burning-platform-a-final-look-at-the-failed-windows-phone-alliance/ (accessed 2 December 2016).

Blau, P. M. (1964) *Exchange and power in social life*. New York: Wiley.

Blodgett, L. L. (1991a) 'Partner contributions as predictors of equity share in international joint ventures'. *Journal of International Business Studies, 22*: 63–78.

Blodgett, L. L. (1991b) 'Toward a resource-based theory of bargaining power in international joint ventures'. *Journal of Global Marketing, 5*: 35–54.

Blodgett, L. L. (1992) 'Factors in the instability of international joint ventures—an event history analysis'. *Strategic Management Journal, 13*: 475–481.

Bloomberg (2017) 'AIG, IBM, standard chartered deliver first multinational insurance policy powered by blockchain'. Available online at www.bloomberg.com/press-releases/2017-06-15/aig-ibm-standard-chartered-deliver-first-multinational-insurance-policy-powered-by-blockchain (accessed 25 September 2020).

Boersma, M. F., Buckley, P. J. and Ghauri, P. N. (2003) 'Trust in international joint venture relationships'. *Journal of Business Research, 56*: 1031–1042.

Bonaccorsi, A. and Piccaluga, A. (2000) 'A theoretical framework for the evaluation of university—industry relationships'. *R&D Management, 24*: 229–247.

Bouncken, R. B. and Fredrich, V. (2016) 'Business model innovation in alliances: Successful configurations'. *Journal of Business Research, 69*: 3584–3590.

Boyer O'Leary, M., Mortensen, M. and Williams Woolley, A. M. (2012) 'Multiple team membership: A theoretical model of its effects on productivity and learning for individuals and teams'. *Academy of Management Review, 36*: 461–478.

Bradford, K. D., Stringfellow, A. and Weitz, B. A. (2004) 'Managing conflict to improve the effectiveness of retail networks'. *Journal of Retailing, 80*: 181–195.

Brattström, A. and Faems, D. (2020) 'Inter-organizational relationships as political battlefields: How fragmentation within organizations shapes relational dynamics between organizations'. *Academy of Management Journal, 63*(5): 1591–1620.

Brouthers, K. D. and Bamossy, G. J. (2006) 'Post-formation processes in eastern and western European joint ventures'. *Journal of Management Studies, 43*: 203–229.

Brown, B. and Anthony, S. (2011) 'How P&G tripled its innovation success rate'. *Harvard Business Review:* 66–72.

Brown, T. J. and Dacin, P. A. (1997) 'The company and the product: Corporate associations and consumer product responses'. *Journal of Marketing, 61*: 68–84.

Browning, L. D., Beyer, J. M. and Shetler, J. C. (1995) 'Building cooperation in a competitive industry: SEMATECH and the semiconductor industry'. *Academy of Management Journal, 38*: 113–151.

Bruner, R. F., Eaker, M. R., Freeman, R. E., Spekman, R. E., Olmsted Teisberg, E. and Venkataraman, S. (2003) *The portable MBA*. Hoboken, NJ: John Wiley and Sons.

Büchel, B. (2000) 'Framework of joint venture development: Theory-building through qualitative research'. *Journal of Management Studies, 37*: 636–661.

Büchel, B. (2002) 'Joint venture development: Driving forces towards equilibrium'. *Journal of World Business, 37*: 199–207.

Büchel, B. and Thuy, L. X. (2001) 'Measures of joint venture performance from multiple perspectives: An evaluation by local and foreign managers in Vietnam'. *Asia Pacific Journal of Management, 18*: 101–111.

Burt, R. S. (1982) *Toward a structural theory of action: Network models of social structure, perception, and action.* New York: Academic Press.

Business Times (2022) 'DBS launch 5 partnerships enhance MSEs digital supply chain capabilities'. Available online at www.businesstimes.com.sg/sme/dbs-to-launch-5-partnerships-to-enhance-digital-financing-capabilities-for-smes-across-asia (accessed 5 November 2022).

Businessweek Online (2002) 'Why P&G's smile is so bright: With the fast-growing SpinBrush, the company bent its own rules—and won'. Available online at http://karlulrich.pbworks.com/f/P&G-spinbrush.pdf (accessed 2 August 2011).

Business Wire (2011a) 'Solazyme and Dow form an alliance for the development of micro algae-derived oils for use in bio-based dielectric insulating fluids'. Available online at www.businesswire.com/news/home/20110309005503/en/Solazyme-Dow-Form-Alliance-Development-Micro-Algae-Derived (accessed 2 August 2011).

Business Wire (2011b) 'GE energy financial services expands gas-fired lending portfolio with $73 million for LS power merchant plant'. Available online at www.businesswire.com/news/home/20110613006238/en/GE-Energy-Financial-Services-Expands-Gas-Fired-Lending (accessed 2 August 2011).

Caniëls, M. C. J. and Gelderman, C. J. (2010) 'The safeguarding effect of governance mechanisms in inter-firm exchange: The decisive role of mutual opportunism'. *British Journal of Management, 21*: 239–254.

Canter, A. and Twombly, J. (2016) 'Project vs alliance management'. Available online at www.iienet2.org/Details.aspx?id=21778 (accessed 10 July 2016).

Capaldo, A. (2007) 'Network structure and innovation: The leveraging of a dual network as a distinctive relational capability'. *Strategic Management Journal, 28*: 585–608.

Capaldo, A. (2014) 'Network governance: A cross-level study of social mechanisms, knowledge benefits, and strategic outcomes in joint-design alliances'. *Industrial Marketing Management, 43*: 685–703.

Capgemini (2007) 'Smart energy alliance: Planning next generation distribution with the distribution road-map'. Available online at www.capgemini.com/insights-and-resources/by-publication/distribution_roadmap/ (accessed 2 August 2011).

Castañer, X. and Oliveira, N. (2020) 'Collaboration, coordination, and cooperation among organizations: Establishing the distinctive meanings of these terms through a systematic literature review'. *Journal of Management, 46*: 965–1001.

Castiglioni, M. and Galán González, J. L. (2020) 'Alliance portfolio classification. Which portfolio do you have?'. *Baltic Journal of Management, 15*(5): 757–774.

Castro, I. and Roldan, J. L. (2015) 'Alliance portfolio management: Dimensions and performance'. *European Management Review, 12*: 63–81.

Castro, I., Roldán, J. and Acedo, F. J. (2015) 'The dimensions of alliance portfolio configuration: A mediation model'. *Journal of Management & Organization, 21*: 176–202.

Chai, K. H. (2003) 'Bridging islands of knowledge: A framework of knowledge sharing mechanisms'. *International Journal of Technology Management, 25*: 703–727.

Chang, W. L. (2009) 'Using multi-criteria decision aid to rank and select co-branding partners: From a brand personality perspective'. *Kybernetes, 38*: 954–969.

Chang, W. L. and Chang, K. C. (2008) 'A taxonomy model for a strategic co-branding position'. In Hawamdeh, S., Stauss, K. and Barachini, F. (eds.), *Knowledge management: Competencies and professionalism* (Series on Innovation and Knowledge Management Vol. 7). Singapore: World Scientific Publishing, pp. 355–366.

Chen, C. J. (2004) 'The effects of knowledge attribute, alliance characteristics, and absorptive capacity on knowledge transfer performance'. *R&D Management, 34*: 311–321.

Chen, D., Park, S. H. and Newburry, W. (2009) 'Parent contribution and organizational control in international joint ventures'. *Strategic Management Journal, 30*: 1133–1156.

Chesbrough, H. W. (2003) *Open innovation: The new imperative for creating and profiting from technology.* Boston, MA: Harvard Business School Press.

Chi, T. (1994) 'Trading in strategic resources—necessary conditions, transaction cost problems, and choice of exchange structure'. *Strategic Management Journal, 15*: 271–290.

Chiambaretto, P. (2015) 'Resource dependence and power-balancing operations in alliances: The role of market redefinition strategies'. *Management, 18*: 205–233.

Chiambaretto, P. and Fernandez, A. S. (2016) 'The evolution of coopetitive and collaborative alliances in an alliance portfolio: The Air France case'. *Industrial Marketing Management, 57*: 75–85.

Child, J. (2002) 'A configurational analysis of international joint ventures'. *Organization Studies, 23*: 781–815.

Child, J. and Faulkner, D. (1998) *Strategies of cooperation: Managing alliances, networks, and joint ventures.* Oxford: Oxford University Press.

Child, J. and Yan, Y. N. (1999) 'Investment and control in international joint ventures: The case of China'. *Journal of World Business, 34*: 3–15.

Choi, J. and Contractor, F. J. (2016) 'Choosing an appropriate alliance governance mode: The role of institutional, cultural and geographical distance in international research & development (R&D) collaborations'. *Journal of International Business Studies, 47*: 210–232.

Choi, J. and Yeniyurt, S. (2015) 'Contingency distance factors and international research and development (R&D), marketing, and manufacturing alliance formations'. *International Business Review, 24*: 1061–1071.

Christensen, C. M., McDonald, R., Altman, E. J. and Palmer, J. E. (2018) 'Disruptive innovation: An intellectual history and directions for future research'. *Journal of Management Studies, 55*: 1043–1078.

Christoffersen, J. (2013) 'A review of antecedents of international strategic alliance performance: Synthesized evidence and new directions for core constructs'. *International Journal of Management Reviews, 15*: 66–85.

Christoffersen, J., Plenborg, T. and Robson, M. J. (2014) 'Measures of strategic alliance performance, classified and assessed'. *International Business Review, 23*: 479–489.

Cisco (2019) 'CHILL leads the way to Industry 4.0'. Available online at https://newsroom.cisco.com/c/r/newsroom/en/us/a/y2019/m09/chill-leads-the-way-to-industry-4-0.html (accessed 8 November 2022).

Cisco (2020) 'Cisco merges CHILL accelerator into global innovation center program'. Available online at www.bizjournals.com/sanjose/news/2020/03/23/cisco-merges-chill-accelerator-into-global.html (accessed 8 November 2022).

Climate (2022) 'Climate change: Atmospheric carbon dioxide'. Available online at www.climate.gov/news-features/understanding-climate/climate-change-atmospheric-carbon-dioxide#:~:text=August%20 14%2C%202020-,Highlights,2020%3A%20412.5%20parts%20per%20million (accessed 7 November 2022).

Clubofrome (2022) 'The limits to growth'. Available online at www.clubofrome.org/publication/the-limits-to-growth/ (accessed 7 November 2022).

CNNMoney (2004) 'Pixar dumps Disney'. Available online at http://money.cnn.com/2004/01/29/news/companies/pixar_disney/ (accessed 2 August 2011).

Cobben, D. Y. P., Ooms, W. M., Roijakkers, A. H. W. M. and Radziwon, A. (2022) 'Ecosystem types: A systematic review on boundaries and goals'. *Journal of Business Research, 142*: 138–164.

Coca-Cola (2019) 'Coca-Cola European partners invests in delivery start-ups'. Available online at www.foodbev.com/news/coca-cola-european-partners-invests-in-delivery-start-ups (accessed 5 November 2022).

Coff, R. W. (1999) 'When competitive advantage doesn't lead to performance: The resource-based view and stakeholder bargaining power'. *Organization Science, 10*: 119–133.

Cohen, W. M. and Levinthal, D. (1990) 'Absorptive capacity: A new perspective on learning and innovation'. *Administrative Science Quarterly, 35*: 128–152.

Coleman, J. S. (1990) *Foundations of social theory*. Cambridge, MA: Harvard University Press.

Connelly, B. L., Trevis Certo, S., Ireland, R. D. and Reutzel, C. R. (2011) 'Signaling theory: A review and assessment'. *Journal of Management, 37*: 39–67.

Contractor, F. J. (2001) 'Intangible assets and principles for their valuation'. In Contractor, F. J. (ed.), *Valuation of intangible assets in global operations*. London: Quorum Books, pp. 3–24.

Contractor, F. J. (2005) 'Alliance structure and process: Will the two research streams ever meet in alliance research?'. *European Management Review, 2*: 123–129.

Contractor, F. J. and Ra, W. (2000) 'Negotiating alliance contracts—strategy and behavioral effects of alternative compensation arrangements'. *International Business Review, 9*: 271–299.

Contractor, F. J. and Reuer, J. (2014) 'Structuring and governing alliances: New directions for research'. *Global Strategy Journal, 4*: 241–256.

Contractor, F. J. and Woodley, J. A. (2015) 'How the alliance pie is split: Value appropriation by each partner in cross-border technology transfer alliances'. *Journal of World Business, 50*: 535–547.

Cooper, R. (2012) 'James Bond just sold out: Daniel Craig swaps Vodka Martini for a bottle of Heineken to star in a controversial new 007 ad'. Available online at www.dailymail.co.uk/news/article-2206593/James-Bond-swaps-Vodka-Martini-pint-Heineken-controversial-product-placement-deal-new-film.html (accessed 2 December 2016).

Corbion (2017) 'Innovative microalgae specialist TerraVia acquired by Corbion'. Available online at www.globenewswire.com/news-release/2017/09/29/1134696/0/en/Innovative-microalgae-specialist-TerraVia-acquired-by-Corbion.html (accessed 8 November 2022).

Corbo, L., Kraus, S., Vlacic, B., Dabic, M., Caputo, A. and Pellegrini, M. (2022) 'Coopetition and innovation: A review and research agenda'. *Technovation, 102624*.

Cravens, K., Piercy, N. and Cravens, D. (2000) 'Assessing the performance of strategic alliances: Matching metrics to strategies'. *European Management Journal, 18*: 529–541.

Crunchbase (2022) 'Crunchbase, Hubspot, financials'. Available online at www.crunchbase.com/organization/hubspot/company_financials (accessed 17 October 2022).

Cryptoslate (2022) 'DBS bank enters the metaverse with Sandbox-partnership'. Available online at https://cryptoslate.com/singapores-dbs-bank-enters-the-metaverse-with-sandbox-partnership (accessed 5 November 2022).

CSIS News (2011) 'CARE and Cargill: An innovative NGO—private sector partnership to fight global poverty'. Available online at http://csis.org/event/care-and-cargill-innovative-ngo-private-sector-partnership-fight-global-poverty (accessed 2 August 2011).

Cui, A. S. (2013) 'Portfolio dynamics and alliance termination: The contingent role of resource dissimilarity'. *Journal of Marketing, 77*: 15–32.

Cullen, J. B., Johnson, J. L. and Sakano, T. (1995) 'Japanese and local partner commitment to IJVs: Psychological consequences of outcomes and investments in the IJV relationship'. *Journal of International Business Studies, 26*: 91–115.

Cummings, J. L. and Teng, B.-S. (2003) 'Transferring R&D knowledge: The key factors affecting knowledge transfer success'. *Journal of Engineering and Technology Management, 20*: 39–68.

Dacin, M. T., Hitt, M. A. and Levitas, E. (1997) 'Selecting partners for successful international alliances: Examination of US and Korean firms'. *Journal of World Business, 32*: 3–16.

Dalenogare, L., Benitez, G., Ayala, N. and Frank, A. (2018) 'The expected contribution of industry 4.0 technologies for industrial performance'. *International Journal of Production Economics, 204*: 383–394.

Dan, S. M. and Zondag, M. M. (2016) 'Drivers of alliance terminations: An empirical examination of the bio-pharmaceutical industry'. *Industrial Marketing Management, 54*: 107–115.

Das, T. K. and Kumar, R. (2010) 'Inter-partner negotiations in the alliance development'. In Das, T. K. (ed.), *Researching strategic alliances: Emerging perspectives*. Charlotte, NC: Information Age Publishing, pp. 207–258.

Das, T. K. and Rahman, N. (2001) 'Partner misbehaviour in strategic alliances: Guidelines for effective deterrence'. *Journal of General Management, 27*: 43–70.

Das, T. K. and Teng, B.-S. (2000a) 'Instabilities of strategic alliances: An internal tensions perspective'. *Organization Science, 11*: 77–101.

Das, T. K. and Teng, B.-S. (2000b) 'A resource-based theory of strategic alliances'. *Journal of Management, 26*: 31–61.

Das, T. K. and Teng, B.-S. (2001) 'Trust, control, and risk in strategic alliances: An integrated framework'. *Organization Studies, 22*: 251–283.

Das, T. K. and Teng, B.-S. (2002) 'The dynamics of alliance conditions in the alliance development process'. *Journal of Management Studies, 39*: 725–746.

Das, T. K. and Teng, B.-S. (2003) 'Partner analysis and alliance performance'. *Scandinavian Journal of Management, 19*: 279–308.

Dasi-Rodriguez, S. and Pardo-del-Val, M. (2015) 'Seeking partners in international alliances: The influence of cultural factors'. *Journal of Business Research, 68*: 1522–1526.

D'Aunno, T. A. and Zuckerman, H. S. (1987) 'A life cycle model of organizational federations: The case of hospitals'. *Academy of Management Review, 12*: 534–545.

David, R. J. and Han, S. K. (2004) 'A systematic assessment of the empirical support for transaction cost economics'. *Strategic Management Journal, 25*: 39–58.

Davis, J. P. (2016) 'The group dynamics of interorganizational relationships: Collaborating with multiple partners in innovation ecosystems'. *Administrative Science Quarterly, 61*(4): 621–661.

DBS (2022a) 'DBS our promise to you'. Available online at www.dbs.com/about-us/who-we-are/our-promise-to-you (accessed 5 November 2022).

DBS (2022b) 'DBS our heritage'. Available online at www.dbs.com/about-us/who-we-are/our-heritage (accessed 5 November 2022).

Dedehayir, O., Makinen, S. J. and Ortt, R. (2016) 'Roles during innovation ecosystem genesis: A literature review'. *Technological Forecasting and Social Change 136*: 18–29.

Deeds, D. L. and Hill, C. W. L. (1998) 'An examination of opportunistic action within research alliances: Evidence from the biotechnology industry'. *Journal of Business Venturing, 14*: 141–163.

Deeds, D. L. and Hill, W. L. (1996) 'Strategic alliances and the rate of new product development: An empirical study of entrepreneurial biotechnology firms'. *Journal of Business Venturing, 11*: 41–55.

de Man, A. P. (2005) 'Alliance capability: A comparison of the strength of European and American companies'. *European Management Journal, 23*: 315–323.

de Man, A. P. (2013) *Alliances: An executive guide to designing successful strategic partnerships*. Hoboken, NJ: John Wiley and Sons.

de Man, A. P. and Luvison, D. (2014) 'Sense-making's role in creating alliance supportive organizational cultures'. *Management Decision, 52*: 259–277.

de Rond, M. and Bouchikhi, H. (2004) 'On the dialectics of strategic alliances'. *Organization Science, 15*: 56–69.

de Wit, B. and Meyer, R. (2004) *Strategy process, content, context: An international perspective* (3rd edition). London: Thomson Learning.

de Wulf, K. and Odekerken-Schroder, G. (2001) 'A critical review of theories underlying relationship marketing in the context of explaining consumer relationships'. *Journal for the Theory of Social Behaviour, 31*: 73–101.

Dekker, H. C. (2004) 'Control of inter-organizational relationships: Evidence on appropriation concerns and coordination requirements'. *Accounting Organizations and Society, 29*: 27–49.

Dentoni, D., Pinkse, J. and Lubberink, R. (2021) 'Linking sustainable business models to socio-ecological resilience through cross-sector partnerships: A complex adaptive systems view'. *Business & Society, 60*(5): 1216–1252.

Deutsch, C. H. (2007) 'New York Times, the venturesome giant'. *New York Times*. Available online at www.nytimes.com/2007/10/05/business/worldbusiness/05venture.html (accessed 2 August 2011).

DiMaggio, P. J. and Powell, W. W. (1983) 'The iron cage revisited—institutional isomorphism and collective rationality in organizational fields'. *American Sociological Review, 48*: 147–160.

Ding, D. Z. (1997) 'Control, conflict, and performance: A study of US—Chinese joint ventures'. *Journal of International Marketing, 5*: 31–45.

Ditek Cluster (2017) 'Artificial intelligence technology cluster'. Available online at https://endr.eu/organisation/18/artificial-intelligence-technology-cluster (accessed 30 October 2022).

Dittrich, K., Duysters, G. and de Man, A. P. (2007) 'Strategic repositioning by means of alliance networks: The case of IBM'. *Research Policy, 36*: 1496–1511.

Dorn, S., Schweiger, B. and Albers, S. (2016) 'Levels, phases and themes of coopetition: A systematic literature review and research agenda'. *European Management Journal, 34*: 484–500.

Douma, M. U., Bilderbeek, J., Idenburg, P. J. and Looise, J. K. (2000) 'Strategic alliances—managing the dynamics of fit'. *Long Range Planning, 33*: 579–598.

Doz, Y. L. (1996) 'The evolution of cooperation in strategic alliances: Initial conditions or learning processes?' *Strategic Management Journal, 17*: 55–83.

Doz, Y. L. and Hamel, G. (1998) *Alliance advantage: The art of creating value through partnering*. Boston, MA: Harvard Business School Press.

Drach-Zahavy, A. (2011) 'Interorganizational teams as boundary spanners: The role of team diversity, boundedness, and extrateam links'. *European Journal of Work & Organizational Psychology, 20*: 89–118.

Drupal (2016) 'About'. Available online at www.drupal.org/about (accessed 20 July 2016).

Drupal (2022) 'On its 20th birthday, Drupal poised to capture the next generation of the digital experience market'. Available online at www.prweb.com/releases/on_its_20th_birthday_drupal_poised_to_capture_the_next_generation_of_the_digital_experience_market/prweb17664393.htm (accessed 11 November 2022).

DSM (2016) 'Partnerships: Pharma & bulk chemicals'. Available online at www.dsm.com/corporate/about/business-entities/partnerships.html (accessed 2 December 2016).

DSM (2020) 'DSM and Padang & Co. announce strategic partnership with FoodInnovate to advance food innovation in Singapore'. Available online at www.dsm.com/food-beverage/en_US/insights/insights/innovation/2020-10-19-dsm-and-padang-co-announce-strategic-partnership-with-foodinnovate-to-advance-food-innovation-in-singapore (accessed 18 October 2022).

DSM (2022) 'DSM and the World Food Programme partner to improve nutrition around the world'. Available online at www.dsm.com/corporate/news/news-archive/2022/dsm-and-wfp-partner-to-improve-nutrition-around-the-world.html (accessed 17 October 2022).

Duysters, G. and de Man, A. P. (2003) 'Transitory alliances: An instrument for surviving turbulent industries?'. *R&D Management, 33*: 49–58.

Duysters, G., de Man, A. P., Luvison, D. and Krijnen, A. (2012) *The state of alliance management: Past, present, future*. Eindhoven: Association of Strategic Alliance Professionals.

Duysters, G., Kok, G. and Vaandrager, M. (1999) 'Crafting successful strategic technology partnerships'. *R&D Management, 29*: 343–351.

Dwyer, F. R., Schurr, P. H. and Oh, S. (1987) 'Developing buyer—seller relationships'. *Journal of Marketing, 51*: 11–27.

Dyer, J. H. (1996) 'Specialized supplier networks as a source of competitive advantage: Evidence from the auto industry'. *Strategic Management Journal, 17*: 271–291.

Dyer, J. H. (1997) 'Effective interfirm collaboration: How firms minimize transaction costs and maximize transaction value'. *Strategic Management Journal, 18*: 535–556.

Dyer, J. H., Kale, P. and Singh, H. (2001) 'How to make strategic alliances work: Developing a dedicated alliance function is key to building the expertise needed for competitive advantage'. *Sloan Management Journal, 42*: 37–43.

Dyer, J. H. and Nobeoka, K. (2000) 'Creating and managing a high-performance knowledge-sharing network: The Toyota case'. *Strategic Management Journal, 21*: 345–367.

Dyer, J. H. and Singh, H. (1998) 'The relational view: Cooperative strategy and sources of interorganizational competitive advantage'. *Academy of Management Review, 23*: 660–679.

Dyer, J., Singh, H. and Kale, P. (2008) 'Splitting the pie: Rent distribution in alliances and networks'. *Managerial and Decision Economics, 29*: 137–148.

Eaves, D., Weiss, J. and Visioni, L. J. (2003) 'The relationship relaunch: How to fix a broken alliance'. *Ivey Business Journal, 67*: 1–6.

Ebers, M. and Semrau, T. (2015) 'What drives the allocation of specific investments between buyer and supplier?'. *Journal of Business Research, 68*: 415–424.

Ekici, A. (2013) 'Temporal dynamics of trust in ongoing inter-organizational relationships'. *Industrial Marketing Management, 42*: 932–949.

Endplastic (2019) 'Innovative microalgae specialist TerraVia acquired by Corbion'. Available online at https://endplasticwaste.org/en/about (accessed 8 November 2022).

Energyboom (2011) 'Solazyme and Dow chemicals form algae partnership'. Available online at www.energyboom.com/biofuels/solazyme-and-dow-chemical-form-algae-partnership (accessed 2 August 2011).

Energy Global (2015) 'ExxonMobil and Sinopec announce joint technology development agreement'. Available online at www.energyglobal.com/downstream/gas-processing/30032015/exxonmobil-and-sinopec-announce-joint-technology-development-agreement-544/ (accessed 24 October 2016).

Engbers, P. A. (2021) 'Heineken bewijst met James Bond dat wachten loont'. Available online at www.adformatie.nl/campagnes/heineken-bewijst-met-james-bond-dat-wachten-loont#:~:text=Heineken%20lanceert%20een%20nieuwe%20campagne,campagne%20is%20ontwikkeld%20door%20Publicis (accessed 23 September 2022).

Erevelles, S., Stevenson, T. H., Srinivasan, S. and Fukawa, N. (2008) 'An analysis of B2B ingredient co-branding relationships'. *Industrial Marketing Management, 37*: 940–952.

Etzkowitz, H. and Leydesdorff, L. (1995) 'The triple helix—university-industry-government relations: A laboratory for knowledge-based economic development'. *EASST Review, 14*: 14–19.

Etzkowitz, H. and Leydesdorff, L. (1997) *Universities in the global economy: A triple helix of university—industry—government relations.* London: Cassell Academic.

Evangelista, F. and Hau, L. N. (2009) 'Organizational context and knowledge acquisition in IJVs: An empirical study'. *Journal of World Business, 44*: 63–73.

Faems, D., Janssens, M., Madhok, A. and Van Looy, B. (2008) 'Toward an integrative perspective on alliance governance: Connecting contract design, trust dynamics, and contract application'. *Academy of Management Journal, 51*: 1053–1078.

Farrell, D. (1983) 'Exit, voice, loyalty, and neglect as responses to job dissatisfaction—a multidimensional-scaling study'. *Academy of Management Journal, 26*: 596–607.

Faulkner, D. (1995) *International strategic alliances: Co-operating to compete.* Maidenhead: McGraw-Hill.

Federal Trade Commission (2006) 'Analysis of agreement containing consent orders to aid public comment: In the matter of the Procter & Gamble company and the Gillette company, file no. 051–0115'. Available online at www.ftc.gov/os/caselist/0510115/050930ana0510115.pdf (accessed 2 August 2011).

Fink, R. C., Edelman, L. F., Hatten, K. J. and James, W. L. (2006) 'Transaction cost economics, resource dependence theory, and customer—supplier relationships'. *Industrial and Corporate Change, 15*: 497–529.

Finkelstein, S. (1997) 'Interindustry merger patterns and resource dependence: A replication and extension of Pfeffer (1972)'. *Strategic Management Journal, 18*: 787–810.

Fintech Finance (2016) 'Mizuho financial group partners with cognizant to develop a blockchain solution'. Available online at www.fintech.finance/01-news/mizuho-financial-group-partners-with-cognizant-to-develop-a-blockchain-solution-for-secure-record-keeping-and-improved-customer-experience/ (accessed 14 December 2016).

Flexiblepower Alliance Network (2016) 'Flexiblepower Alliance Network'. Available online at http://flexible-energy.eu/ (accessed 26 September 2016).

Fonda, D. (2006) 'Who gains from a Pixar—Disney merger?' Available online at www.time.com/time/business/article/0,8599,1150674,00.html (accessed 2 August 2011).

Franco, M. and Haase, H. (2015) 'Interfirm alliances: A taxonomy for SMEs'. *Long Range Planning, 48*(3): 168–181.

Franko, L. G. (1971) *Joint venture survival in multinational corporations.* New York: Praeger.

Freeman, R. E. (1984) *Strategic management: A stakeholder approach*. Boston, MA: Pitman.

Fried, I. (2011) 'Nokia's Microsoft partnership: Does the new strategy add up?'. Available online at http://allthingsd.com/20110211/live-from-nokias-investor-meeting-does-the-new-strategy-add-up/ (accessed 2 August 2011).

Fryxell, G. E., Dooley, R. S. and Vryza, M. (2002) 'After the ink dries: The interaction of trust and control in US-based international joint ventures'. *Journal of Management Studies, 39*: 865–886.

Fu, W. H., Wang, Q. and Zhao, X. D. (2017) 'The influence of platform service innovation on value co-creation activities and the network effect'. *Journal of Service Management, 28*(2): 348–388.

Furr, N., O'Keeffe, K. and Dyer, J. H. (2016) 'Managing multiparty innovation'. *Harvard Business Review, 94*(11): 76–83.

Furrer, O., Tjemkes, B. V., Adolfs, K. and Ulgen Aydinlik, A. (2012) 'Responding to adverse situations within exchange relationships: The cross-cultural validity of a circumplex model'. *Journal of Cross-Cultural Psychology, 43*(6): 943–966.

Ganesan, S. (1993) 'Negotiation strategies and the nature of channel relationships'. *Journal of Marketing Research, 30*: 183–203.

García-Canal, E., Duarte, C. L., Criado, J. R. and Llaneza, A. V. (2002) 'Accelerating international expansion through global alliances: A typology of cooperative strategies'. *Journal of World Business, 37*: 91107.

García-Canal, E., Valdes-Llaneza, A. and Ariño, A. (2003) 'Effectiveness of dyadic and multi-party joint ventures'. *Organization Studies, 24*: 743–770.

Garmin (2021) 'Partnerbase'. Available online at www.partnerbase.com/garmin/ispot-tv (accessed 5 November 2022).

Garud, R. (1994) 'Cooperative and competitive behaviors during the process of creative destruction'. *Research Policy, 23*: 385–394.

Gelfand, M. J., Major, V. S., Raver, J. L., Nishii, L. H. and O'Brien, K. (2006) 'Negotiating relationally: The dynamics of the relational self in negotiations'. *Academy of Management Review, 31*: 427–451.

Genewsroom (2017a) 'GE to replace Tva's coal units with cleaner, high-efficiency h-class gas turbines'. Available online at www.genewsroom.com/press-releases/ge-replace-tva%E2%80%99s-coal-units-cleaner-high-efficiency-h-class-gas-turbines-279403 (accessed 26 February 2017).

Genewsroom (2017b) 'GE oil & gas secures long-term services contract to support Yara International's fertilizer complex in the Netherlands'. Available online at www.genewsroom.com/Press-Releases/GE-Oil—Gas-Secures-Long-Term-Services-Contract-to-Support-Yara-Internationals-Fertilizer-Complex-in-the-Netherlands-213247 (accessed 26 February 2017).

Geringer, J. M. and Hebert, L. (1989) 'Control and performance of international joint ventures'. *Journal of International Business Studies, 20*(2): 235–254.

German Robotic Association (2020) 'German Robotics Association launched'. Available online at www.computer-automation.de/robotics-automation/german-robotics-association-launched (accessed 27 October 2022).

Geurts, A., Broekhuizen, T., Dolfsma, W. and Cepa, K. (2022) 'Tensions in multilateral coopetition: Findings from the disrupted music industry'. *Industrial Marketing Management, 105*: 532–547.

Geylani, T., Inman, J. J. and Ter Hofstede, F. (2008) 'Image reinforcement or impairment: The effects of co-branding on attribute uncertainty'. *Marketing Science, 27*: 730–744.

Geyskens, I. and Steenkamp, J. (2000) 'Economic and social satisfaction: Measurement and relevance to marketing channel relationships'. *Journal of Retailing, 76*: 11–32.

Ghosh, A., Ranganathan, R. and Rosenkopf, L. (2016) 'The impact of context and model choice on the determinants of strategic alliance formation: Evidence from a staged replication study'. *Strategic Management Journal, 37*: 2221–2224.

Ghoshal, S. and Moran, P. (1996) 'Bad for practice: A critique of the transaction cost theory'. *Academy of Management Review, 21*: 13–47.

Giller, C. and Matear, S. (2001) 'The termination of inter-firm relationships'. *Journal of Business and Industrial Marketing, 16*: 94–112.

Gilsing, V., Cloodt, M. and Rooijakkers, N. (2016) 'From birth through transition to maturation: The evolution of technology-based alliance networks'. *Journal of Product Innovation Management, 33*: 181–200.

Gimeno, J. (2004) 'Competition within and between networks: The contingent effect of competitive embeddedness on alliance formation'. *Academy of Management Journal, 15*: 584–602.

Glaister, K. W. and Buckley, P. J. (1996) 'Strategic motives for international alliance formation'. *Journal of Management Studies, 33*: 301–332.

Glaister, K. W., Husan, R. and Buckley, P. J. (2003) 'Decision-making autonomy in UK international equity joint ventures'. *British Journal of Management, 14*: 305–322.

Global Energy Alliance (2022) 'Global Energy Alliance for people and planet'. Available online at www.energyalliance.org (accessed 30 October 2022).

Globenewswire (2022a) 'Renault, Nissan & Mitsubishi Motors announce common roadmap alliance 2030: Best of 3 worlds for a new future'. Available online at www.globenewswire.com/news-release/2022/01/27/2373999/0/en/Renault-Nissan-Mitsubishi-Motors-announce-common-roadmap-Alliance-2030-Best-of-3-worlds-for-a-new-future.html (accessed 17 October 2022).

Globenewswire (2022b) 'Terrascope partners with DBS Bank, ERM and Orkiva to facilitate decarbonization of enterprises'. Available online at www.globenewswire.com/news-release/2022/11/03/2547302/0/en/Terrascope-partners-with-DBS-Bank-ERM-and-Workiva-to-facilitate-decarbonisation-of-enterprises.html (accessed 5 November 2022).

Gnyawali, D. R. and Park, B.-J. (2011) 'Coopetition between giants: Collaboration with competitors for technological innovation'. *Research Policy, 40*: 650–663.

Goerzen, A. and Beamish, P. W. (2005) 'The effect of alliance network diversity on multinational enterprise performance'. *Strategic Management Journal, 26*: 333–354.

Golonka, M. (2015) 'Proactive cooperation with strangers: Enhancing complexity of the ICT firms' alliance portfolio and their innovativeness'. *European Management Journal, 33*: 168–178.

Gomes, E., Barnes, B. R. and Mahmood, T. (2016) 'A 22 year review of strategic alliance research in the leading management journals'. *International Business Review, 25*: 15–27.

Gomes, L., Facin, A., Salerno, M. and Ikenami, R. (2018) 'Unpacking the innovation ecosystem construct: Evolution, gaps and trends'. *Technological Forecasting and Social Change, 136*: 30–48.

Gomes-Casseres, B. (1994) 'Group versus group: How alliance networks compete'. *Harvard Business Review, 72*: 62–74.

Google (2022) 'Google'. Available online at https://en.wikipedia.org/wiki/Google (accessed 30 October 2022).

GoPro (2016) 'Two of the world's strongest brands team up to cross-promote and innovate'. Available online at http://gopro.com/news/gopro-and-red-bull-form-exclusive-global-partnership (accessed 22 December 2016).

Granovetter, M. S. (1973) 'The strength of weak ties'. *American Journal of Sociology, 78*: 1360–1380.

Granovetter, M. S. (1985) 'Economic action and social structure: A theory of embeddedness'. *American Journal of Sociology, 91*: 481–510.

Greenberg, J. (1987) 'A taxonomy of organizational justice theories'. *Academy of Management Review, 12*: 9–22.

GreenPeace (2021) 'Greenpeace chief: Alliance to end plastic waste is misfiring, as exposé reveals flagship project failure'. Available online at www.packaginginsights.com/news/greenpeace-chief-alliance-to-end-plastic-waste-is-misfiring-as-expose-reveals-flagship-project-failure.html (accessed 8 November 2022).

Greve, H. R., Mitsuhashi, H. and Baum, J. A. (2013) 'Greener pastures: Outside options and strategic alliance withdrawal'. *Organization Science, 24*: 79–98.

Grimm, C., Knemeyer, M., Polyviou, M. and Ren, X. (2015) 'Supply chain management research in management journals: A review of recent literature (2004–2013)'. *International Journal of Physical Distribution & Logistics Management, 45*: 404–458.

Grooms, L. (2008) 'Grainnet exclusive: Mercedes and algae?' *Biofuels Journal*. Available online at www.biofuelsjournal.com/articles/Mercedes___Algae__Solazyme_Road_Testing_Algae_based_Biodiesel_In_Mercedes-54315.html (accessed 2 August 2011).

Gu, J., Chen, Z., Huang, Q., Liu, H. and Huang, S. (2018) 'A multilevel analysis of the relationship between shared leadership and creativity in inter-organizational teams'. *Journal of Creative Behavior, 52*(2): 109–126.

Gu, Q. and Lu, X. H. (2014) 'Unraveling the mechanisms of reputation and alliance formation: A study of venture capital syndication in China'. *Strategic Management Journal*, *35*: 739–750.

Guidice, R. M., Vasudevan, A. and Duysters, G. (2003) 'From "me against you" to "us against them": Alliance formation based on inter-alliance rivalry'. *Strategic Management Journal*, *19*: 135–152.

Gulati, R. (1995a) 'Does familiarity breed trust—the implications of repeated ties for contractual choice in alliances'. *Academy of Management Journal*, *38*: 85–112.

Gulati, R. (1995b) 'Social structure and alliance formation patterns: A longitudinal analysis'. *Administrative Science Quarterly*, *40*: 619–652.

Gulati, R. (1998) 'Alliances and networks'. *Strategic Management Journal*, *19*: 293–317.

Gulati, R. and Gargiulo, M. (1999) 'Where do interorganizational networks come from?'. *American Journal of Sociology*, *104*: 1439–1493.

Gulati, R., Khanna, T. and Nohria, N. (1994) 'Unilateral commitments and the importance of process in alliances'. *Sloan Management Review*, *35*: 61–69.

Gulati, R. and Kletter, D. (2005) 'Shrinking core, expanding periphery: The relational architecture of high-performing organizations'. *California Management Review*, *47(3)*: 77–104.

Gulati, R. and Nickerson, J. A. (2008) 'Interorganizational trust, governance choice, and exchange performance'. *Organization Science*, *19*: 688–708.

Gulati, R. and Singh, H. (1998) 'The architecture of cooperation: Managing coordination costs and appropriation concerns in strategic alliances'. *Administrative Science Quarterly*, *43*: 781–814.

Gulati, R. and Sytch, M. (2007) 'Dependence asymmetry and joint dependence in interorganizational relationships: Effects of embeddedness on a manufacturer's performance in procurement relationships'. *Administrative Science Quarterly*, *52*: 32–69.

Gulati, R., Sytch, M. and Mehrotra, P. (2008) 'Breaking up is never easy: Planning for exit in a strategic alliance'. *California Review Management*, *50*: 147–163.

Gurcaylilar-Yenidogan, T. and Windsperger, J. (2014) 'Inter-organizational performance in the automotive supply networks: The role of environmental uncertainty, specific investments and formal contracts'. *Procedia-Social and Behavioral Sciences*, *150*: 813–822.

Hagedoorn, J. and Hesen, G. (2007) 'Contract law and the governance of inter-firm technology partnerships—an analysis of different modes of partnering and their contractual implications'. *Journal of Management Studies*, *44*: 342–366.

Hagedoorn, J. and Sadowski, B. (1999) 'The transition from strategic technology alliances to mergers and acquisitions: An exploratory study'. *Journal of Management Studies*, *36*: 87–107.

Haider, S. and Mariotti, F. (2016) 'The orchestration of alliance portfolios: The role of alliance portfolio capability'. *Scandinavian Journal of Management*, *32(3)*: 127–141.

Halinen, A. and Tahtinen, J. (2002) 'A process theory of relationship ending'. *International Journal of Service Industry Management*, *13*: 163–180.

Hambrick, D. C., Li, J., Xin, K. and Tsui, A. S. (2001) 'Compositional gaps and downward spirals in international joint venture management groups'. *Strategic Management Journal*, *22*: 1033–1063.

Hamel, G. (1991) 'Competition for competence and inter-partner learning within international strategic alliances'. *Strategic Management Journal*, *12*: 83–103.

Hamel, G., Doz, Y. and Prahalad, C. (1989) 'Collaborate with your competitors and win'. *Harvard Business Review*. 133–139.

Hannan, M. T. and Freeman, J. (1977) 'Population ecology of organizations'. *American Journal of Sociology*, *82*: 929–964.

Harbison, J. and Pekar, P. (1998) *Smart alliances: A practical guide to repeatable success*. San Francisco, CA: Jossey-Bass.

Harrigan, K. R. (1988) 'Strategic alliances and partner asymmetries'. In Contractor, F. J. and Lorange, P. (eds.), *Cooperative strategies in international business*. Lexington: Lexington Books.

Harrington, S. J. (1991) 'What corporate America is teaching about ethics'. *Academy of Management Executive*, *5*: 21–30.

He, Q., Meadows, M., Angwin, D., Gomes, E. and Child, J. (2020) 'Strategic alliance research in the era of digital transformation: Perspectives on future research'. *British Journal of Management*, *31*: 589–617.

Heide, J. B. and John, G. (1992) 'Do norms matter in marketing relationships?'. *Journal of Marketing, 56*: 32–44.

Heide, J. B. and Miner, A. S. (1992) 'The shadow of the future—effects of anticipated interaction and frequency of contact on buyer—seller cooperation'. *Academy of Management Journal, 35*: 265–291.

Heide, J. B., Wathne, K. H. and Rokkan, A. I. (2007) 'Interfirm monitoring, social contracts, and relationship outcomes'. *Journal of Marketing Research, 44*: 425–433.

Heidl, R. A., Steensma, H. K. and Phelps, C. (2014) 'Divisive faultlines and the unplanned dissolutions of multipartner alliances'. *Organization Science, 25*: 1351–1371.

Heimeriks, K. H., Bingham, C. B. and Laamanen, T. (2015) 'Unveiling the temporally contingent role of codification in alliance success'. *Strategic Management Journal, 36*: 462–473.

Heimeriks, K. H. and Duysters, G. (2007) 'Alliance capability as a mediator between experience and alliance performance: An empirical investigation into the alliance capability development process'. *Journal of Management Studies, 44*: 25–49.

Heimeriks, K. H., Klijn, E. and Reuer, J. J. (2009) 'Building capabilities for alliance portfolios'. *Long Range Planning, 42*: 96–114.

Hennart, J. F. (1988) 'A transaction costs theory of equity joint ventures'. *Strategic Management Journal, 9*: 361–374.

Hennart, J. F. (2006) 'Alliance research: Less is more'. *Journal of Management Studies, 43*: 1621–1628.

Hennart, J. F., Kim, D. J. and Zeng, M. (1998) 'The impact of joint venture status on the longevity of Japanese stakes in US manufacturing affiliates'. *Organization Science, 9*: 382–395.

Hennart, J. F. and Zeng, M. (2005) 'Structural determinants of joint venture performance'. *European Management Review, 2*: 105.

HFN Daily News (2010) 'Philips Sonicare partners with Susan G. Komen for the cure'. Available online at www.hfnmag.com/housewares/philips-sonicare-partners-susan-g-komen-cure (accessed 2 August 2011).

Hill, R. C. and Hellriegel, D. (1994) 'Critical contingencies in joint venture management—some lessons from managers'. *Organization Science, 5*: 594–607.

Hirschman, A. O. (1970) *Exit, voice and loyalty: Responses to decline in firms, organizations and states*. Cambridge, MA: Harvard University Press.

Hite, J. M. and Hesterly, W. S. (2001) 'The evolution of firm networks: From emergence to early growth of the firm'. *Strategic Management Journal, 22*: 275–286.

Hitt, M. A., Dacin, M. T., Levitas, E., Arregle, J. L. and Borza, A. (2000) 'Partner selection in emerging and developed market contexts: Resource-based and organizational learning perspectives'. *Academy of Management Journal, 43*: 449–467.

Ho, C.-H., Böhm, S. and Monciardini, D. (2022) 'The collaborative and contested interplay between business and civil society in circular economy transitions'. *Business Strategy and the Environment*, 2714–2727.

Hoang, H. and Rothaermel, F. T. (2005) 'The effect of general and partner-specific alliance experience on joint R&D project performance'. *Academy of Management Journal, 48*: 332–345.

Hoehn-Weiss, M. N. and Karim, S. (2014) 'Unpacking functional alliance portfolios: How signals of viability affect young firms' outcomes'. *Strategic Management Journal, 35*: 1364–1385.

Hoffmann, W. H. (2005) 'How to manage a portfolio of alliances'. *Long Range Planning, 38*: 121–143.

Hoffmann, W. H. (2007) 'Strategies for managing a portfolio of alliances'. *Strategic Management Journal, 28*: 827–856.

Hoffmann, W. H. and Schlosser, R. (2001) 'Success factors of strategic alliances in small and medium-sized enterprises: An empirical survey'. *Long Range Planning, 34*: 357–381.

Hofstede, G. (1991) *Cultures and organizations: Software of the mind*. London: McGraw Hill.

Hofstede, G. and Bond, M. H. (1988) 'The Confucius connection: From cultural roots to economic growth'. *Organizational Dynamics, 16*: 5–21.

Hogg, M. A., van Knippenberg, D. and Rast, D. E. III (2012) 'Intergroup leadership in organizations: Leading across group and organizational boundaries'. *Academy of Management Review, 37*(2): 232–255.

Horrel, P. (2016) 'Mitsubishi has joined Renault-Nissan. Here's what you need to know'. Available online at www.topgear.com/car-news/mitsubishi-has-joined-renault-nissan-heres-what-you-need-know (accessed 1 December 2016).

House, R. J. (2004) *Culture, leadership, and organizations: The GLOBE study of 62 societies.* Thousand Oaks, CA: Sage Publications.

Howard, M., Steensma, H. K., Lyles, M. and Dhanaraj, H. (2016) 'Learning to collaborate through collaboration: How allying with expert firms influences collaborative innovation within novice firms'. *Strategic Management Journal*, 37: 2092–2103.

HSD (2016) 'About HSD'. Available online at www.thehaguesecuritydelta.com/about (accessed 26 July 2016).

HSD (2022) 'TNO and IMEC launch photonics collaboration: Pivotal role for Holst Centre in Eindhoven'. Available online at https://holstcentre.com/insights/news/tno-and-imec-launch-photonics-collaboration/ (accessed 14 November 2022).

Hubspot (2022a) 'Sequoia, Google ventures, and Salesforce.com invest $32 million in HubSpot'. Available online at www.hubspot.com/blog/bid/10491/Sequoia-Google-Ventures-and-Salesforce-com-Invest-32-Million-in-HubSpot (accessed 17 October 2022).

Hubspot (2022b) 'HubSpot announces strategic partnership with Google Cloud, further fueling the growth of the HubSpot CRM'. Available online at www.hubspot.com/company-news/hubspot-announces-strategic-partnership-with-google-cloud (accessed 17 October 2022).

Hutt, M. D., Stafford, E. R., Walker, B. A. and Reingen, P. H. (2000) 'Case study: Defining the social network of a strategic alliance'. *Sloan Management Review*, 41(2), 51–62.

Hwang, P. and Burgers, W. P. (1997) 'The many faces of multi-firm alliances: Lessons for managers'. *California Management Review*, 39: 101–117.

Iansiti, M. and Levien, R. (2004) *The Keystone Advantage: What the new dynamics of business ecosystems mean for strategy, innovation, and sustainability.* Boston, MA: Harvard Business School Press.

IBM (2007) 'Lenovo and IBM expand global alliance'. Available online at www.-03.ibm.com/press/us/en/pressrelease/21589.wss (accessed 2 August 2011).

IBM (2011a) 'Our history of progress, 1890s to 2001'. Available online at www.-03.ibm.com/ibm/history/interactive/ibm_ohe_pdf_13.pdf (accessed 28 September 2011).

IBM (2011b) 'Louis V. Gerstner, Jr. CEO 1993–2002'. Available online at www.-03.ibm.com/press/us/en/biography/10153.wss (accessed 28 September 2011).

IBM (2016) 'It's a brave new world out there'. Available online at www.-356.ibm.com/partnerworld/wps/servlet/ContentHandler/partnerworld-public (accessed 2 December 2016).

IBM (2022a) 'IBM and Vodafone join forces in exploration of quantum computing technology and quantum-safe cryptography'. Available online at https://newsroom.ibm.com/2022–11–09-IBM-and-Vodafone-Join-Forces-in-Exploration-of-Quantum-Computing-Technology-and-Quantum-Safe-Cryptography (accessed 14 November 2022).

IBM (2022b) 'Bosch partnering with IBM on strategic quantum computing materials science engagement'. Available online at https://newsroom.ibm.com/2022-11-09-Bosch-Partnering-with-IBM-on-Strategic-Quantum-Computing-Materials-Science-Engagement (accessed 14 November 2022).

IBM (2022c) 'Sierra Space and IBM collaborate on the next generation of space technology and software platforms'. Available online at https://newsroom.ibm.com/2022-10-26-Sierra-Space-and-IBM-Collaborate-on-the-Next-Generation-of-Space-Technology-and-Software-Platforms (accessed 14 November 2016).

IBM (2022d) 'IBM transforms business operations with the RISE with SAP Solution in expanded partnership with SAP'. Available online at https://newsroom.ibm.com/2022-05-11-IBM-Transforms-Business-Operations-with-the-RISE-with-SAP-Solution-in-Expanded-Partnership-with-SAP (accessed 14 November 2022).

IBS Center for Management Research (ICMR) (2006) 'Disney's acquisition of Pixar, case # BSTR203'. Available online at www.icmrindia.org/casestudies/catalogue/Business%20strategy/Business%20Strategy%20Disney's%20Acquisition%20of%20Pixar.htm (accessed 2 August 2011).

Inditex.com (2016) 'Inditex and Coruña University set up an international researcher recruitment programme'. Available online at www.inditex.com/en/media/news_article?articleId=218413 (accessed 25 October 2016).

Inkpen, A. C. (2000) 'Learning through joint ventures: A framework of knowledge acquisition'. *Journal of Management Studies*, 37: 1019–1043.

Inkpen, A. C. and Beamish, P. W. (1997) 'Knowledge, bargaining power, and the instability of international joint ventures'. *Academy of Management Review, 22*: 177–202.

Ireland, R. D., Hitt, M. A. and Vaidyanath, D. (2002) 'Alliance management as a source of competitive advantage'. *Journal of Management, 28*: 413–446.

Ireland, R. D. and Webb, J. W. (2007) 'A multi-theoretic perspective on trust and power in strategic supply chains'. *Journal of Operations Management, 25*: 482–497.

Isabella, L. A. and Spekman, R. E. (2001) 'Alliance leadership: Template for the future'. In Mobley, W. H. and McCall, M. W. Jr. (eds.), *Advances in global leadership* (Vol. 2). Bongley: Emerald Group Publishing, pp. 217–244.

Isckia, T. and Lescop, D. (2009) 'Open innovation within business ecosystems: Lessons from Amazon. com'. *Communications & Strategies, 74*: 37–55.

iSpotTV (2022) 'iSpotTV'. Available online at www.ispot.tv/about (accessed 5 November 2022).

Jacobides, M. G. and Winter, S. G. (2005) 'The co-evolution of capabilities and transaction costs: Explaining the institutional structure of production'. *Strategic Management Journal, 26*: 395–413.

Janowicz-Panjaitan, M. and Noorderhaven, N. G. (2008) 'Formal and informal interorganizational learning within strategic alliances'. *Research Policy, 37*: 1337–1355.

Jap, S. D. (1999) 'Pie-expansion efforts: Collaboration processes in buyer—supplier relationships'. *Journal of Marketing Research, 36*: 461–475.

Jap, S. D. (2001) '"Pie sharing" in complex collaboration contexts'. *Journal of Marketing Research, 38*: 86–99.

Jap, S. D. and Ganesan, S. (2000) 'Control mechanisms and the relationship life cycle: Implications for safeguarding specific investments and developing commitment'. *Journal of Marketing Research, 37*: 227–245.

Jarvensivu, T. and Moller, K. (2009) 'Metatheory of network management: A contingency perspective'. *Industrial Marketing Management, 38*: 654–661.

Jarzabkowski, P., Bednarek, R., Chalkias, K. and Cacciatori, E. (2021) 'Enabling rapid financial response to disasters: Knotting and reknotting multiple paradoxes in interorganizational systems'. *Academy of Management Journal, 65*(5): 1477–1506.

Jemison, D. B. (1984) 'The importance of boundary spanning roles in strategic decision making'. *Journal of Management Studies, 21*: 131–152.

Jiang, R. J., Tao, Q. T. and Santoro, M. D. (2010) 'Alliance portfolio diversity and firm performance'. *Strategic Management Journal, 31*: 1136–1144.

Jiang, X., Li, M., Gao, S., Bao, Y. and Jiang, F. (2013) 'Managing knowledge leakage in strategic alliances: The effects of trust and formal contracts'. *Industrial Marketing Management, 42*: 983–991.

Johnson, J. P., Korsgaard, M. A. and Sapienza, H. J. (2002) 'Perceived fairness, decision control, and commitment in international joint venture management teams'. *Strategic Management Journal, 23*: 1141–1160.

Joshi, A. M. and Lahiri, N. (2015) 'Language friction and partner selection in cross-border R&D alliance formation'. *Journal of International Business Studies, 46*: 123–152.

Joshi, A. W. and Arnold, S. J. (1997) 'The impact of buyer dependence on buyer opportunism in buyer—supplier relationships: The moderating role of relational norms'. *Psychology and Marketing, 14*: 823–845.

Joskow, P. L. (1985) 'Vertical integration and long term contracts: The case of coal burning electric generation plants'. *Journal of Law, Economics and Organization, 1*: 33–80.

Kale, P., Dyer, J. H. and Singh, H. (2001) 'Value creation and success in strategic alliances: Alliancing skills and the role of alliance structure and systems'. *European Management Journal, 19*: 463–471.

Kale, P., Dyer, J. H. and Singh, H. (2002) 'Alliance capability, stock market response, and long-term alliance success: The role of the alliance function'. *Strategic Management Journal, 23*: 747–767.

Kale, P. and Singh, H. (2007) 'Building firm capabilities through learning: The role of the alliance learning process in alliance capability and firm-level alliance success'. *Strategic Management Journal, 28*: 981–1000.

Kale, P. and Singh, H. (2009) 'Managing strategic alliances: What do we know now, and where do we go from here?'. *Academy of Management Perspectives, 23*: 45–62.

Kale, P., Singh, H. and Perlmutter, H. (2000) 'Learning and protection of proprietary assets in strategic alliances: Building relational capital'. *Strategic Management Journal, 21*: 217–237.

Kalouptsidi, M. (2021) 'The role of shipping in world trade'. Available online at https://econofact.org/the-role-of-shipping-in-world-trade (accessed 6 November 2022).

Kang, N. H. and Sakai, K. (2001) 'New patterns of industrial globalization: Cross-border mergers and acquisitions and strategic alliances'. *Report of the Industry Division of the OECD*: 1–174.

Kanter, R. M. (1994) 'Collaborative advantage—the art of alliances'. *Harvard Business Review, 72*(4): 96–108.

Kaplan, R. S., Norton, D. P. and Rugelsjoen, B. (2010) 'Managing alliances with the balanced score card'. *Harvard Business Review, 88*(1): 114–120.

Kapoor, R. and Lee, J. M. (2013) 'Coordinating and competing in ecosystems: How organizational forms shape new technology investments'. *Strategic Management Journal, 34*: 274–296.

Katila, R., Rosenberger, J. D. and Eisenhardt, K. M. (2008) 'Swimming with sharks: Technology ventures, defense mechanisms and corporate relationships'. *Administrative Science Quarterly, 53*: 295–332.

Kaufmann, J. and O'Neill, H. M. (2007) 'Do culturally distant partners choose different types of joint ventures?'. *Journal of Worm Business, 42*: 435–448.

Kauppila, O. P. (2015) 'Alliance management capability and firm performance: Using resource-based theory to look inside the process black box'. *Long Range Planning, 48*: 151–167.

Keller, A., Lumineau, F., Mellewigt, T. and Ariño, A. (2021) 'Alliance governance mechanisms in the face of disruption'. *Organization Science, 32*(6): 1542–1570.

Kellogg (2022) 'Kellogg and Nickelodeon's green apple flavored'. Available online at www.intribe.co/blog/2022-brand-collaborations (accessed 18 October 2022).

Kelly, E. (2015) 'Introduction: Business ecosystems coming of age'. In Canning, M. and Kelly, E. (eds.), *Business ecosystems coming of age*. Stamford, CT: Deloitte University Press, pp. 3–12. Available online at https://www2.deloitte.com/content/dam/insights/us/articles/platform-strategy-new-level-business-trends/DUP_1048-Business-ecosystems-come-of-age_MASTER_FINAL.pdf (accessed 22 February 2023).

Kelly, M. J., Schaan, J. and Joncas, H. (2002) 'Managing alliance relationships: Key challenges in the early stages of collaboration'. *R&D Management, 32*: 11–22.

Kersten, G. E. (2001) 'Modeling distributive and integrative negotiations: Review and revised characterization'. *Group Decision and Negotiation, 10*: 493–514.

Khademi, B. (2020) 'Ecosystem value creation and capture: A systematic review of literature and potential research opportunities'. *Technology Innovation Management Review, 10*(1): 16–34.

Khan, Z., Shenkar, O. and Lew, Y. K. (2015) 'Knowledge transfer from international joint ventures to local suppliers in a developing economy'. *Journal of International Business Studies, 46*: 656–675.

Khanagha, S. (2021) 'Leading digital strategy'. In Tjemkes, B. V. and Mihalache, O. (eds.), *Transformative strategies: Strategic thinking in the age of globalization, disruption, collaboration and responsibility*. Abingdon: Taylor & Francis Ltd, pp. 82–103.

Khanna, T. (1998) 'The scope of alliances'. *Organization Science, 9*: 340–355.

Khanna, T., Gulati, R. and Nohria, N. (1998) 'The dynamics of learning alliances: Competition, cooperation, and relative scope'. *Strategic Management Journal, 19*: 193–210.

Kiefer, B. (2022) 'Heineken drops its Heinekicks, a sneaker that lets wearers walk on beer'. Available online at www.adweek.com/brand-marketing/heineken-drops-its-heinekicks-a-sneaker-that-lets-wearers-walk-on-beer/ (accessed 18 October 2022).

Killing, J. P. (1983) *Strategies for joint venture success*. New York: Praeger.

Kim, J. (2014) 'Formal and informal governance in biotechnology alliances: Board oversight, contractual control, and repeated deals'. *Industrial and Corporate Change, 23*: 903–929.

King, L. (2015) 'L'Oreal seeks quantum leap with 3D printed skin'. Available online at www.forbes.com/sites/leoking/2015/05/20/loreal-3d-printed-skin-organovo/#11f1d918168e (accessed 6 August 2016).

Kipnis, D. and Schmidt, S. (1985) 'The language of persuasion'. *Psychology Today, 19*: 40–46.

Kittel, J. (2013) 'Strategic alliance manager role (identity): A unique, holistic and empowering perspective'. *SPiBR.org LLC*. Available online at www.spibr.org/strategic_alliance_manager_role.pdf (accessed 10 July 2016).

Klein, B., Crawford, R. G. and Alchian, A. A. (1978) 'Vertical integration, appropriable rents, and the competitive contracting process'. *Journal of Law and Economics, 21*: 297–326.

Knight, L. (2002) 'Network learning: Exploring learning by interorganizational networks'. *Human Relations, 55*: 427–454.

Knight, L. and Harland, C. (2005) 'Managing supply networks: Organizational roles in network management'. *European Management Journal, 23*: 281–292.

Kogut, B. (1988) 'Joint ventures—theoretical and empirical—perspectives'. *Strategic Management Journal, 9*: 319–332.

Kogut, B. (1989) 'The stability of joint ventures: Reciprocity and competitive rivalry'. *Journal of Industrial Economics, 38*: 183–198.

Kogut, B. (1991) 'Joint ventures and the option to expand and acquire'. *Management Science, 37*: 19–33.

Köhler, J., Sönnichsen, S. D. and Beske-Jansen, P. (2022) 'Towards a collaboration framework for circular economy: The role of dynamic capabilities and open innovation'. *Business Strategy and the Environment, 31*(6): 2700–2713.

Kohtamäki, M., Rabetino, R. and Möller, K. (2018) 'Alliance capabilities: A review and future research directions'. *Industrial Marketing Management, 68*: 188–201.

Kok, G. and Wildeman, L. (1997) 'Succesvolle allianties'. *Nijenrode Management Review, 4*: 78–84.

Koka, B. R. and Prescott, J. E. (2008) 'Designing alliance networks: The influence of network position, environmental change, and strategy on firm performance'. *Strategic Management Journal, 29*: 639–661.

Kotabe, M., Martin, X. and Domoto, H. (2003) 'Gaining from vertical partnerships: Knowledge transfer, relationship duration, and supplier performance improvement in the U.S. and Japanese automotive industries'. *Strategic Management Journal, 24*: 293–316.

Kotler, P. (1991) *Marketing management: Analysis, planning, and control*. Englewood Cliffs, NJ: Prentice-Hall.

Koza, M. P. and Lewin, A. Y. (1998) 'The co-evolution of strategic alliances'. *Organization Science, 9*: 255–264.

Koza, M. P. and Lewin, A. Y. (1999) 'The coevolution of network alliances: A longitudinal analysis of an international professional service network'. *Organization Science, 10*: 638–653.

Koza, M. P. and Lewin, A. Y. (2000) 'Managing partnerships and strategic alliances: Raising the odds of success'. *European Management Journal, 16*: 146–151.

Kramer, M. W., Day, E. A., Nguyen, C. and Cooper, O. D. (2019) 'Leadership in an interorganizational collaboration: A qualitative study of a statewide interagency taskforce'. *Human Relations, 72*(2): 397–419.

Krishnan, R., Geyskens, I. and Steenkamp, J.-B. E. M. (2016) 'The effectiveness of contractual and trust-based governance in strategic alliances under behavioral and environmental uncertainty'. *Strategic Management Journal, 37*: 2521–2542.

Kumar, M. V. S. (2010) 'Differential gains between partners in joint ventures: Role of resource appropriation and private benefits'. *Organization Science, 21*: 232–248.

Kumar, N., Scheer, L. K. and Steenkamp, J. (1995) 'The effects of perceived interdependence on dealer attitudes'. *Journal of Marketing Research, 32*: 348–356.

Kumar, R. (2016) 'Alliance process: A micro behavioral view'. *International Journal of Business and Management, 11*: 20–30.

Kumar, R. and Nti, K. O. (1998) 'Differential learning and interaction in alliance dynamics: A process and outcome discrepancy model'. *Organization Science, 9*: 356–367.

Kwak, Y. H., Chih, Y. Y. and Ibbs, C. W. (2009) 'Towards a comprehensive understanding of public—private partnerships for infrastructure development'. *California Management Review, 51*: 51–78.

Lahiri, N. and Narayanan, S. (2013) 'Vertical integration, innovation, and alliance portfolio size: Implication for firm performance'. *Strategic Management Journal, 34*: 1042–1064.

Lambe, C. J., Spekman, R. E. and Hunt, S. D. (2002) 'Alliance competence, resources, and alliance success: Conceptualization, measurement, and initial test'. *Journal of the Academy of Marketing Science, 30*: 141–158.

Lampel, J. and Shamsie, J. (2003) 'Capabilities in motion: New organizational forms and the reshaping of the Hollywood movie industry'. *Journal of Management Studies, 40*: 2189–2210.

Lane, P. J. and Lubatkin, M. (1998) 'Relative absorptive capacity and interorganizational learning'. *Strategic Management Journal, 19*: 461–477.

Lane, P. J., Salk, J. E. and Lyles, M. A. (2001) 'Absorptive capacity, learning, and performance in international joint ventures'. *Strategic Management Journal, 22*: 1139–1161.

Lardinois, F. (2015) 'Amazon, Netflix, Google, Microsoft, Mozilla and others partner to create next-gen video format'. Available online at http://techcrunch.com/2015/09/01/amazon-netflix-google-microsoft-mozilla-and-others-partner-to-create-next-gen-video-format/ (accessed 27 July 2016).

Lavie, D. (2006) 'The competitive advantage of interconnected firms: An extension of the resource-based view'. *Academy of Management Review, 31*: 638–658.

Lavie, D. (2007) 'Alliance portfolios and firm performance: A study of value creation and appropriation in the US software industry'. *Strategic Management Journal, 28*: 1187–1212.

Lavie, D., Haunschild, P. R. and Khanna, P. (2012) 'Organizational differences, relational mechanisms, and alliance performance'. *Strategic Management Journal, 33*: 1453–1479.

Lavie, D., Lechner, C. and Singh, H. (2007) 'The performance implications of timing of entry and involvement in multipartner alliances'. *Academy of Management Journal, 50*: 578–604.

Lavie, D. and Rosenkopf, L. (2006) 'Balancing exploration and exploitation in alliance formation'. *Academy of Management Journal, 49*: 797–818.

Lavie, D. and Singh, H. (2012) 'The evolution of alliance portfolios: The case of Unisys'. *Industrial Corporate Change, 21*: 763–809.

Lax, D. A. and Sebenius, J. K. (1986) *The manager as negotiator: Bargaining for cooperation and competitive gain.* New York: Free Press.

Lee, H. U. and Park, J. H. (2008) 'The influence of top management team international exposure on international alliance formation'. *Journal of Management Studies, 45*: 961–981.

Lee, J., Hoetker, G. and Qualls, W. (2015) 'Alliance experience and governance flexibility'. *Organization Science, 26*: 1536–1551.

Lee, S.-C., Chang, S.-N., Liu, C.-Y. and Yang, J. (2007) 'The effect of knowledge protection, knowledge ambiguity, and relational capital on alliance performance'. *Knowledge and Process Management, 14*: 58–69.

Lee, Y. and Cavusgil, S. T. (2006) 'Enhancing alliance performance: The effects of contractual-based versus relational-based governance'. *Journal of Business Research, 59*: 896–905.

Lei, D. (2003) 'Competition, cooperation and learning: The new dynamics of strategy and organisation design for the innovation net'. *International Journal of Technology Management, 26*: 694–716.

Leipämaa-Leskinen, H., Närvänen, E. and Makkonen, H. (2022) 'The rise of collaborative engagement platforms'. *European Journal of Marketing, 56*(13): 26–49.

Leischnig, A., Geigenmueller, A. and Lohmann, S. (2014) 'On the role of alliance management capability, organizational compatibility, and interaction quality in interorganizational technology transfer'. *Journal of Business Research, 67*: 1049–1057.

Le Roy, F. and Fernandez, A. S. (2015) 'Managing coopetitive tensions at the working-group level: The rise of the coopetitive project team'. *British Journal of Management, 26*(4): 671–688.

Lewicki, R. J., Weiss, S. E. and Lewin, D. (1992) 'Models of conflict, negotiation and 3rd party intervention—a review and synthesis'. *Journal of Organizational Behavior, 13*: 209–252.

Lewis, R. (2004) 'Renault/Nissan: A successful partnership'. Available online at www.carkeys.co.uk/features/renaultnissan-successful-partnership (accessed 2 August 2011).

Li, J. T. and Hambrick, D. C. (2005) 'Factional groups: A new vantage on demographic faultlines, conflict, and disintegration in work teams'. *Academy of Management Journal, 48*: 794–813.

Li, J. T., Tian, L. and Wan, G. (2015) 'Contextual distance and the international strategic alliance performance: A conceptual framework and a partial meta-analytic test'. *Management and Organization Review, 11*: 289–313.

Li, J. T., Xin, K. and Pillutla, M. (2002) 'Multi-cultural leadership teams and organizational identification in international joint ventures'. *International Journal of Human Resource Management, 13*: 320–337.

Li, J. T., Xin, K. R., Tsui, A. and Hambrick, D. C. (1999) 'Building effective international joint venture leadership teams in China'. *Journal of World Business*, *34*(1): 52–68.

Li, L., Qian, G. and Qian, Z. (2013) 'Do partners in international strategic alliances share resources, costs, and risks?'. *Journal of Business Research*, *66*: 489–498.

Lin, H. (2012) 'Strategic alliances for environmental improvements'. *Business & Society*, *51*(2), 335–348.

Lin, X. H. and Germain, R. (1998) 'Sustaining satisfactory joint venture relationships: The role of conflict resolution strategy'. *Journal of International Business Studies*, *29*: 179–196.

Lin, Z., Yang, H. B. and Arya, B. (2009) 'Alliance partners and firm performance: Resource complementarity and status association'. *Strategic Management Journal*, *30*: 921–940.

LinkedIn (2022a) 'Alliance partner manager—phoenix market'. Available online at www.linkedin.com/jobs/view/3328546623 (accessed 30 October 2022).

LinkedIn (2022b) 'Alliance manager-Deloitte'. Available online at www.linkedin.com/jobs/view/3280944673 (accessed 30 October 2022).

LinkedIn (2022c) 'Alliance manager-Cisco'. Available online at www.linkedin.com/jobs/view/3309656436 (accessed 30 October 2022).

Lipparini, A., Lorenzoni, G. and Ferriani, S. (2014) 'From core to periphery and back: A study on the deliberate shaping of knowledge flows in interfirm dyads and networks'. *Strategic Management Journal*, *35*: 578–595.

Litwak, E. and Hylton, L. F. (1962) 'Interorganizational analysis—a hypothesis on coordinating agencies'. *Administrative Science Quarterly*, *6*: 395–420.

Liu, L. A., Adair, W. L. and Bello, D. C. (2015) 'Fit, misfit, and beyond fit: Relational metaphors and semantic fit in international joint ventures'. *Journal of International Business Studies*, *47*: 830–849.

Liu, Y. and Ravichandran, T. (2015) 'Alliance experience, IT-enabled knowledge integration, and ex ante value gains'. *Organization Science*, *26*: 511–530.

London, T., Rondinelli, D. A. and O'Neill, H. (2006) 'Strange bedfellows: Alliances between corporations and nonprofits'. In Shenkar, O. and Reuer, J. J. (eds.), *Handbook of strategic alliances*. Thousand Oaks, CA: Sage Publications, pp. 353–366.

López-Duartea, C., González-Loureirob, M., Vidal-Suáreza, M. M. and González-Díaza, B. (2016) 'International strategic alliances and national culture: Mapping the field and developing a research agenda'. *Journal of World Business*, *51*: 511–524.

López-Navarro, M. Á. and Camisón-Zornoza, C. (2003) 'The effect of group composition and autonomy on the performance of joint ventures (JVs): An analysis based on Spanish export JVs'. *International Business Review*, *12*: 17–39.

Lorenzoni, G. and Baden-Fuller, C. (1995) 'Creating a strategic centre to manage a web of partners'. *California Management Review*, *37*: 1–18.

Loza, J. (2004) 'Business—community partnerships: The case for community organization capacity building'. *Journal of Business Ethics*, *53*: 297–311.

Lubatkin, M., Florin, J. and Lane, P. (2001) 'Learning together and apart: A model of reciprocal interfirm learning'. *Human Relations*, *54*: 1353–1382.

Lui, S. S. and Ngo, H. Y. (2004) 'The role of trust and contractual safeguards on cooperation in nonequity alliances'. *Journal of Management*, *30*: 471–485.

Lumineau, F., Eckerd, S. and Handley, S. (2015) 'Inter-organizational conflicts: Research overview, challenges, and opportunities'. *Journal of Strategic Contracting and Negotiation*, *1*: 42–64.

Lumineau, F. and Oliveira, N. (2018) 'A pluralistic perspective to overcome major blind spots in research on interorganizational relationships'. *Academy of Management Annals*, *12*: 440–465.

Lumineau, F., Wang, W. and Schilke, O. (2020) 'Blockchain governance—a new way of organizing collaborations?'. *Organization Science*, *32*(2): 500–521.

Lunnan, R. and Haugland, S. A. (2008) 'Predicting and measuring alliance performance: A multidimensional analysis'. *Strategic Management Journal*, *29*: 545–556.

Luo, Y. D. (2002) 'Contract, cooperation, and performance in international joint ventures'. *Strategic Management Journal*, *23*: 903–919.

Luo, Y. D. (2005) 'How important are shared perceptions of procedural justice in cooperative alliances?'. *Academy of Management Journal*, *48*: 695–709.

Luo, Y. D., Liu, Y., Yang, Q., Maksomov, V. and Hou, J. (2015) 'Improving performance and reducing cost in buyer-supplier relationships: The role of justice in curtailing opportunism'. *Journal of Business Research*, 68: 607–615.

Luo, Y. D. and Park, S. H. (2004) 'Multiparty cooperation and performance in international equity joint ventures'. *Journal of International Business Studies*, 35: 142–160.

Luvison, D. and Marks, M. A. (2013) 'Team coordination in strategic alliances: Identifying conditions that reduce team willingness to cooperate'. *International Journal of Strategic Business Alliances*, 3: 1–22.

Lyles, M. A. and Salk, J. E. (1996) 'Knowledge acquisition from foreign parents in international joint ventures: An empirical examination in the Hungarian context'. *Journal of International Business Studies*, 27: 877–904.

Lynn, M. L. (2005) 'Organizational buffering: Managing boundaries and cores'. *Organization Studies*, 26: 37–61.

Lyons, T. F., Krachenberg, A. R. and Henke, J. W. (1990) 'Mixed motive marriages—what's next for buyer—supplier relations?' *Sloan Management Review*, 31: 29–36.

Macdonald, S. and Chrisp, T. (2005) 'Acknowledging the purpose of partnership'. *Journal of Business Ethics*, 59: 307–317.

Macmillan, I., Purowitz, M. and Prakash, S. (2022) 'Charting new horizons: M&A and the path to thrive'. Available online at https://www2.deloitte.com/content/dam/Deloitte/global/Documents/About-Deloitte/gx-charting-new-horizons-ma-strategies.pdf (accessed 7 November 2022).

MacNeil, I. R. (1978) 'Contracts—adjustment of long-term economic relations under classical, neoclassical, and relational contract law'. *Northwestern University Law Review*, 72: 854–905.

Madhok, A. (1995) 'Opportunism and trust in joint venture relationships: An exploratory study and a model'. *Scandinavian Journal of Management*, 11: 57–74.

Madhok, A., Keyhani, M. and Bossink, B. (2015) 'Understanding alliance evolution and termination: Adjustment costs and the economics of resource value'. *Strategic Organization*, 13(2): 91–116.

Madhok, A. and Tallman, S. B. (1998) 'Resources, transactions and rents: Managing value through inter-firm collaborative relationships'. *Organization Science*, 9: 326–339.

Majchrzak, A., Jarvenpaa, S. L. and Bagherzadeh, M. (2014) 'A review of interorganizational collaboration dynamics'. *Journal of Management*, 41: 1338–1360.

Makhija, M. V. and Ganesh, U. (1997) 'The relationship between control and partner learning in learning-related joint ventures'. *Organization Science*, 8: 508–527.

Makino, S., Chan, C. M., Isobe, T. and Beamish, P. W. (2007) 'Intended and unintended termination of international joint ventures'. *Strategic Management Journal*, 28: 1113–1132.

Malhotra, D. and Murnighan, J. K. (2002) 'The effects of contracts on interpersonal trust'. *Administrative Science Quarterly*, 47: 534–559.

March, J. G. (1991) 'Exploration and exploitation in organizational learning'. *Organization Science*, 2: 71–78.

Marks, M. A. and Luvison, D. (2012) 'Product launch and strategic alliance MTSs'. In Zaccaro, S. J., Marks, M. and DeChurch, L. A. (eds.), *Multiteam systems: An organization form for dynamic and complex environments*. New York: Routledge, pp. 33–52.

Martino, M. (2010) 'Galapagos, Roche enter $588.7m COPD alliance'. Available online at www.fiercebiotech.com/story/galapagos-roche-enter-588-7m-copd-alliance/2010-01-11?utm_medium=rss&utm_source=rss&cmp-id=OTC-RSS-FB0 (accessed 2 August 2011).

Masten, S. E., Meehan, J. W. and Snyder, E. A. (1991) 'The cost of organization'. *Journal of Law, Economics and Organization*, 7: 1–25.

M&S (2022) 'M&S rewards customers for donating used clothing to Shwopping scheme'. Available online at www.retailgazette.co.uk/blog/2022/01/ms-rewards-customers-for-donating-used-clothing-to-shwopping-scheme/ (accessed 8 November 2022).

Mayer, K. J. and Argyres, N. S. (2004) 'Learning to contract: Evidence from the personal computer industry'. *Organization Science*, 15: 394–410.

McCann, J. (2013) '007 effect lifts Heineken sales: Amount sold up to 5.2% after Bond swaps vodka martini for beer'. Available online at www.dailymail.co.uk/news/article-2278331/007-effect-lifts-Heineken-sales-Amount-sold-5-2-Bond-swaps-vodka-martini-beer.html (accessed 2 December 2016).

McGuire, M. (2002) 'Managing networks: Propositions on what managers do and why they do'. *Public Administration Review, 62*: 599–609.

Meena, A., Dhir, S. and Sushil, S. (2022) 'A review of coopetition and future research agenda'. *Journal of Business & Industrial Marketing, 38*: 118–136.

Meier, M. (2011) 'Knowledge management in strategic alliances: A review of empirical evidence'. *International Journal of Management Reviews, 13*: 1–23.

Mellewigt, T. and Das, T. K. (2010) 'Alliance structure choice in the telecommunications industry: Between resource type and resource heterogeneity'. *International Journal of Strategic Change Management, 2*: 128–144.

Mercedes-Benz Group Media (2022) 'Mercedes-Benz partners with Luminar to enhance pioneering work in next-generation automated driving systems'. Available online at https://group-media. mercedes-benz.com/marsMediaSite/en/instance/ko/Mercedes-Benz-partners-with-Luminar-to-enhance-pioneering-work-in-next-generation-automated-driving-systems.xhtml?oid=52432970 (accessed 17 October 2022).

Meschi, P.-X. (1997) 'Longevity and cultural differences of international joint ventures: Toward time-based cultural management'. *Human Relations, 50*: 211–228.

Meschi, P.-X. (2005) 'Environmental uncertainty and survival of international joint ventures: The case of political and economical risk in emerging countries'. *European Management Review, 2*: 143–152.

Meta (2022a) 'MetaL company office'. Available online at https://about.meta.com/company-info/ (accessed 9 November 2022).

Meta (2022b) 'Meta connect 2022: Meta Quest Pro, More social VR and a look into the future'. Available online at https://about.fb.com/news/2022/10/meta-quest-pro-social-vr-connect-2022/ (accessed 9 November 2022).

Meyer-Krahmer, F. and Smoch, U. (1998) 'Scientific based technologies university—industry interaction in four fields'. *Research Policy, 27*: 835–851.

Microsoft (2022a) 'Microsoft details metaverse partnership with Facebook'. Available online at https:// businessplus.ie/news/microsoft-meta-metaverse (accessed 18 October 2022).

Microsoft (2022b) 'Microsoft partner code of conduct'. Available online at www.microsoft.com/en-us/ legal/compliance/anticorruption/trustworthy-representatives (accessed 9 November 2022).

Microsoft (2022c) 'Microsoft and Meta partner to deliver immersive experiences for the future of work and play'. Available online at https://blogs.microsoft.com/blog/2022/10/11/microsoft-and-meta-partner-to-deliver-immersive-experiences-for-the-future-of-work-and-play/ (accessed 9 November 2022).

Microsoft (2022d) 'General'. Available online at www.microsoft.com/investor/reports/ar13/financial-review/business-description/index.html (accessed 9 November 2022).

Microsoft News Center (2001) 'Microsoft and Nokia form global alliance to design, develop and market mobile productivity solutions'. Available online at www.microsoft.com/presspass/press/2009/ aug09/08–12pixipr.mspx (accessed 2 August 2011).

Mintzberg (2015) 'Time for the plural sector'. Available online at http://ssir.org/articles/entry/time_ for_the_plural_sector (accessed 8 June 2017).

Mittelman, M. (2016) 'JPMorgan to Adopt Fintech startups with in-house incubator'. Available online at www.bloomberg.com/news/articles/2016–06–30/jpmorgan-to-adopt-fintech-startups-with-in-house-incubator (accessed 16 January 2017).

Moghaddam, K., Bosse, D. A. and Provance, M. (2016) 'Strategic alliances of entrepreneurial firms: Value enhancing then value destroying'. *Strategic Entrepreneurship Journal, 10*: 153–168.

Mohr, V., Garnsey, E. and Theyel, G. (2014) 'The role of alliances in the early development of high-growth firms'. *Industrial and Corporate Change, 23*: 233–259.

Moon, H. and Sprott, D. E. (2016) 'Ingredient branding for a luxury brand: The role of brand and product fit'. *Journal of Business Research, 69*: 5768–5774.

Moore, J. F. (1993) 'Predators and prey: A new ecology of competition'. *Harvard Business Review, 71*: 75–86.

Moore, J. F. (1996) *The death of competition: Leadership and strategy in the age of business ecosystems.* New York: HarperBusiness.

Moore, J. F. (1998) 'The rise of a new corporate form'. *The Washington Quarterly, 21*(1): 167–181.

Moore, J. F. (2006) 'Business ecosystems and the view from the firm'. *The Antitrust Bulletin, 51*(1): 31–75.

Morgan, R. M. and Hunt, S. D. (1994) 'The commitment-trust theory of relationship marketing'. *Journal of Marketing, 58*: 20–38.

Mowery, D. C., Oxley, J. E. and Silverman, B. S. (1996) 'Strategic alliances and interfirm knowledge transfer'. *Strategic Management Journal, 17*: 77–91.

Mowery, D. C., Oxley, J. E. and Silverman, B. S. (1998) 'Technological overlap and interfirm cooperation: Implications for the resource-based view of the firm'. *Research Policy, 27*: 507–523.

Muthusamy, S. K. and White, M. A. (2005) 'Learning and knowledge transfer in strategic alliances: A social exchange view'. *Organization Studies, 26*: 415–441.

Nabec, L., Pras, B. and Laurent, G. (2016) 'Temporary brand-retailer alliance model: The routes to purchase intentions for selective brands and mass retailers'. *Journal of Marketing Management, 32*: 595–627.

Nair, A., Narasimhan, R. and Bendoly, E. (2011) 'Coopetitive buyer—supplier relationship: An investigation of bargaining power, relational context, and investment strategies'. *Decision Sciences, 42*: 93–127.

Nakamura, M., Shaver, J. M. and Yeung, B. (1996) 'An empirical investigation of joint venture dynamics: Evidence from US—Japan joint ventures'. *International Journal of Industrial Organization, 14*: 521–541.

NBS (2022) 'Partnering with NGOs: The 4 keys to success'. Available online at https://nbs.net/partnering-with-ngos-the-4-keys-to-success/ (accessed 8 November 2022).

NEA (2022) 'DBSD foundation and national environment agency to engage Singapore's youth in nationwide challenge to reduce food waste'. Available online at www.nea.gov.sg/media/news/news/index/dbs-foundation-and-national-environment-agency-to-engage-singapore-s-youth-in-nationwide-challenge-to-reduce-food-waste (accessed 5 November 2022).

Nemeth, A. and Nippa, M. (2013) 'Rigor and relevance of IJV exit research'. *Management International Review, 53*: 449–475.

Niederkofler, M. (1991) 'The evolution of strategic alliances—opportunities for managerial influence'. *Journal of Business Venturing, 6*: 237–257.

Niesten, E. and Jolink, A. (2015) 'The impact of alliance management capabilities on alliance attributes and performance: A literature review'. *International Journal of Management Reviews, 17*: 69–100.

Niesten, E. and Jolink, A. (2020) 'Motivations for environmental alliances: Generating and internalizing environmental and knowledge value'. *International Journal of Management Reviews, 22*: 356–377.

Niesten, E. and Stefan, I. (2019) 'Embracing the paradox of interorganizational value co-creation and value capture: A literature review towards paradox resolution'. *International Journal of Management Reviews, 21*: 231–255.

Nippa, M. and Reuer, J. J. (2019) 'On the future of international joint venture research'. *Journal of International Business Studies, 50*: 555–597.

Noble, G. and Jones, R. (2006) 'The role of boundary-spanning managers in the establishment of public—private partnerships'. *Public Administration, 84*: 91–117.

Noel, J. (2022) 'EY announces alliance with Logility to help provide insights-driven supply chain management'. Available online at www.ey.com/en_gl/news/2022/06/ey-announces-alliance-with-logility-to-help-provide-insights-driven-supply-chain-management (accessed 17 October 2022).

Nokia (2011) 'Nokia and Microsoft sign definitive agreement ahead of schedule'. Available online at http://press.nokia.com/2011/04/21/nokia-and-microsoft-sign-definitive-agreement-ahead-of-schedule/ (accessed 2 August 2011).

Nonaka, I. (1994) 'A dynamic theory of organizational knowledge creation'. *Organization Science, 5*: 14–37.

Nooteboom, B. (2004) 'Governance and competence: How can they be combined?' *Cambridge Journal of Economics, 28*: 505–525.

Norman, P. M. (2002) 'Protecting knowledge in strategic alliances: Resource and relational characteristics'. *Journal of High Technology Management Research, 13*: 177–202.

Noseleit, F. and de Faria, P. (2013) 'Complementarities of internal R&D and alliances with different partner types'. *Journal of Business Research, 66*: 2000–2006.

Olekalns, M., Smith, P. L. and Walsh, T. (1996) 'The process of negotiating: Strategy and timing as predictors of outcomes'. *Organizational Behavior and Human Decision Processes, 68*: 68–77.

Oliveira, N. and Lumineau, F. (2019) 'The dark side of interorganizational relationships: An integrative review and research agenda'. *Journal of Management, 45*(1): 231–261.

Oneworld Trust (2009) '2008 global accountability report'. Available online at http://oneworld trust. org/publications/doc_view/270–2008-cargill-accountability-profile?tmpl=component&format= raw (accessed 2 August 2011).

Oral Health America (2008) 'Philips Sonicare partners with OHA to conduct public opinion survey of oral health in America'. Available online at www.orthodontic productsonline.com/news/2008–05– 16_01.asp (accessed 2 August 2011).

Organovo (2015) 'L'Oreal USA announces research partnership with Organovo to Develop 3-D bio-printed skin tissue'. Available online at http://ir.organovo.com/phoenix.zhtml?c=254194&p=irol-newsArticle&ID=2129344 (accessed 6 August 2016).

Organovo (2022) 'Organovo and BICO (CELLINK) Reach Licensing Agreement on bioprinting patents'. Available online at https://ir.organovo.com/news-releases/news-release-details/organovo-and-bico-cellink-reach-licensing-agreement-bioprinting (accessed 5 November 2022).

Osborn, R. N. and Baughn, C. C. (1990) 'Forms of interorganizational governance for multinational alliances'. *Academy of Management Journal, 33*: 503–519.

Oxfam (2016a) 'Working together: Oxfam's partnership principles'. Available online at www.oxfam. org/sites/www.oxfam.org/files/file_attachments/story/oxfam-partnership-principles_1_0.pdf (accessed 2 December 2016).

Oxfam (2016b) 'M&S and Oxfam shwopping'. Available online at www.oxfam.org.uk/donate/donate-goods/mands-and-oxfam-shwopping (accessed 2 December 2016).

Oxfam (2021) 'Marks and Spencer and OXFAM shwopping'. Available online at www.oxfam.org.uk/ donate/donate-to-our-shops/marks-and-spencer-and-oxfam-shwopping/ (accessed 8 November 2022).

Oxley, J. E. (1997) 'Appropriability hazards and governance in strategic alliances: A transaction cost approach'. *Journal of Law Economics and Organization, 13*: 387–409.

Oxley, J. E. (1999) 'Institutional environment and the mechanisms of governance: The impact of intellectual property protection on the structure of inter-firm alliances'. *Journal of Economic Behavior and Organization, 38*: 283–309.

Oxley, J. E. and Sampson, R. C. (2004) 'The scope and governance of international R&D alliances'. *Strategic Management Journal, 25*: 723–749.

Oxley, J. E. and Wada, T. (2009) 'Alliance structure and the scope of knowledge transfer: Evidence from US—Japan agreements'. *Management Science, 55*: 635–649.

Ozmel, U. and Guler, I. (2015) 'Small fish, big fish: The performance effects of the relative standing in partners' affiliate portfolios'. *Strategic Management Journal, 36*: 2039–2057.

Packaginginsights (2021) 'Alliance to end plastic waste fires back at Greenpeace over criticism of flagship project failure'. Available online at www.packaginginsights.com/news/alliance-to-end-plastic-waste-fires-back-at-greenpeace-over-criticism-of-flagship-project-failure.html (accessed 8 November 2022).

Palmatier, R. W., Dant, R. R. and Grewal, D. (2007) 'A comparative longitudinal analysis of theoretical perspectives of interorganizational relationship performance'. *Journal of Marketing, 71*: 172–194.

Pangarkar, N. (2009) 'Do firms learn from alliance terminations? An empirical examination'. *Journal of Management Studies, 46*: 982–1004.

Pangarkar, N. and Klein, S. (1998) 'Bandwagon pressures and inter-firm alliances in the global pharmaceutical industry'. *Journal of International Marketing, 6*: 54–73.

Panteli, N. and Sockalingam, S. (2005) 'Trust and conflict within virtual inter-organizational alliances: A framework for facilitating knowledge sharing'. *Decision Support Systems, 39*: 599–617.

Panwar, R. and Niesten, E. (2022) 'Jump-starting, diffusing, and sustaining the circular economy'. *Business Strategy and the Environment, 31*(6): 2637–2640.

Panwar, R., Pinkse, J. and De Marchi, V. (2022) 'The future of global supply chains in a post-COVID-19 world'. *California Management Review, 64*: 2, 5–23.

Parise, S. and Casher, A. (2003) 'Alliance portfolios: Designing and managing your network of business-partner relationships'. *Academy of Management Executive, 17*: 25–39.

Park, C. W., Jun, S. Y. and Shocker, A. D. (1996) 'Composite branding alliances: An investigation of extension and feedback effects'. *Journal of Marketing Research, 33*: 453–466.

Park, G., Kim, M. J. and Kang, J. (2015) 'Competitive embeddedness: The impact of competitive relations among a firm's current alliance partners on its new alliance formations'. *International Business Review, 24*: 196–208.

Park, S. H. and Russo, M. V. (1996) 'When competition eclipses cooperation: An event history analysis of joint venture failure'. *Management Science, 42*: 875–890.

Park, S. H. and Ungson, G. R. (1997) 'The effect of national culture, organizational complementarity, and economic motivation on joint venture dissolution'. *Academy of Management Journal, 40*: 279–307.

Parkhe, A. (1991) 'Interfirm diversity, organizational learning, and longevity in global strategic alliances'. *Journal of International Business Studies, 22*: 579–601.

Parkhe, A. (1993) 'Strategic alliance structuring: A game theoretic and transaction cost examination of interfirm cooperation'. *Academy of Management Journal, 36*: 794–829.

Patzelt, H. and Shepherd, D. A. (2008) 'The decision to persist with underperforming alliances: The role of trust and control'. *Journal of Management Studies, 45*: 1217–1243.

PC World (2009) 'Microsoft, Nokia target 'Crackberry' crowd with Mobile Office'. Available online at www.pcworld.com/businesscenter/article/170091/microsoft_nokia_target_crackberry_crowd_with_mobile_office.html (accessed 2 August 2011).

Pearce, R. J. (2001) 'Looking inside the joint venture to help understand the link between inter-parent cooperation and performance'. *Journal of Management Studies, 38*: 557–582.

Pekar, P. and Allio, R. (1994) 'Making alliances work—guidelines for success'. *Long Range Planning, 27*: 54–65.

Peng, M. W. and Shenkar, O. (2002) 'Joint venture dissolution as corporate divorce'. *Academy of Management Executive, 16*: 92–105.

Perkmann, M., Neely, A. and Walsh, K. (2011) 'How should firms evaluate success in university—industry alliances? A performance measurement system'. *R&D Management, 41*: 202–216.

Pfeffer, J. and Nowak, P. (1976) 'Joint ventures and interorganizational interdependence'. *Administrative Science Quarterly, 21*: 398–418.

Pfeffer, J. and Salancik, G. R. (1978) *The external control of organizations: A resource dependence perspective.* New York: Harper and Row.

Pfizer (2020) 'Pfizer and BioNTech announce vaccine candidate against COVID-19 achieved success in first interim analysis from phase 3 study'. Available online at www.pfizer.com/news/press-release/press-release-detail/pfizer-and-biontech-announce-vaccine-candidate-against (accessed 17 October 2022).

PG (2022) 'Oral-B partners to make oral care more inclusive'. Available online at https://us.pg.com/blogs/oralb-partners-iadh-to-make-oral-care-more-inclusive/ (accessed 5 November 2022).

Philips (2004) 'Philips en Procter & Gamble kondigen alliantie aan voor de introductie van de Intelliclean van Philips' Sonicare® en Crest®'. Available online at www.newscenter.philips.com/nl_nl/standard/about/news/press/article-14525.wpd (accessed 2 August 2011).

Ping, R. A. (1993) 'The effects of satisfaction and structural constraints on retailer exiting, voice, loyalty, opportunism, and neglect'. *Journal of Retailing, 69*: 320–352.

Pisano, G. P. (1989) 'Using equity participation to support exchange—evidence from the biotechnology industry'. *Journal of Law Economics and Organization, 5*: 109–126.

Pixar Planet Forum (2008) 'The truth about the Disney/Pixar partnership . . . many answers'. Available online at www.pixarplanet.com/forums/viewtopic.php?f=6&t=2945&start=0 (accessed 2 August 2011).

Pondera (2022) 'Elements for energy'. Available online at https://ponderaconsult.com/en/ (accessed 6 November 2022).

Poniatowski, M., Lüttenberg, H., Beverungen, D. and Kundish, D. (2022) 'Three layers of abstraction: A conceptual framework for theorizing digital multi-sided platforms'. *Information Systems and e-Business Management, 20*: 257–283.

Poole, M. S. and van de Ven, A. H. (1989). 'Using paradox to build management and organization theories'. *Academy of Management Review, 14*(4): 562–578.

Poppo, L. and Zenger, T. (2002) 'Do formal contracts and relational governance function as substitutes or complements?' *Strategic Management Journal, 23*: 707–725.

Poppo, L. and Zhou, K. Z. (2014) 'Managing contracts for fairness in buyer-supplier exchanges'. *Strategic Management Journal, 35*: 1508–1527.

Porter, M. E. (1987) 'From competitive strategy to cooperative strategy'. *Harvard Business Review, 65*: 43–59.

PovertyAlliance (2022) 'Poverty alliance'. Available online at www.povertyalliance.org (accessed 30 October 2022).

Powell, W. W. (1990) 'Neither market nor hierarchy—network forms of organization'. *Research in Organizational Behavior, 12*: 295–336.

Powell, W. W., Koput, K. W. and SmithDoerr, L. (1996) 'Interorganizational collaboration and the locus of innovation: Networks of learning in biotechnology'. *Administrative Science Quarterly, 41*: 116–145.

PRNewswire (2015) 'AT&T and GE strengthen alliance, fuel innovation with smart energy solutions: Technology leaders work together to bring new opportunities to energy sector'. Available online at www.prnewswire.com/news-releases/att-and-ge-strengthen-alliance-fuel-innovation-with-smart-energy-solutions-300030432.html (accessed 3 January 2017).

PRNewswire (2016) 'Lendico and PostFinance launch joint venture in Switzerland'. Available online at www.prnewswire.com/news-releases/lendico-and-postfinance-launch-joint-venture-in-switzerland-586285301.html (accessed 25 October 2016).

Proctor & Gamble (2017) 'What is connect + develop'. Available online at www.pgconnectdevelop.com/what-is-connect-develop/ (accessed 17 February 2017).

Pruitt, D. G. (1983) 'Strategic choice in negotiation'. *American Behavioral Scientist, 27*: 167–194.

Pruitt, D. G. and Lewis, S. A. (1975) 'Development of integrative solutions in bilateral negotiation'. *Journal of Personality and Social Psychology, 31*: 621–633.

PR Web (2008) 'Worldwide market for personal care appliances to reach 460 million units by 2010, according to a new report by Global Industry Analysts, Inc'. Available online at www.prweb.com/releases/appliances_personal_care/hair_care_oral_care/prweb765894.htm (accessed 2 August 2011).

PWC (2016) 'Redefining business success in a changing world: CEO survey'. PWC 19th Annual Global CEO Survey. Available online at https://www.pwc.com/kz/en/publications/ceo-assets/pwc-19th-annual-global-ceo-survey.pdf.

Rahman, N. and Korn, H. J. (2014) 'Alliance longevity: Examining relational and operational antecedents'. *Long Range Planning, 47*: 245–261.

Rai, R. K. (2016) 'A co-opetition-based approach to value creation in interfirm alliances: Construction of a measure and examination of its psychometric properties'. *Journal of Management, 42*: 1663–1699.

Rajan, R., Dhir, S. and Sushil (2020) 'Alliance termination research: A bibliometric review and research agenda'. *Journal of Strategy and Management, 13*(3): 351–375.

Rao, A. and Schmidt, S. M. (1998) 'A behavioral perspective on negotiating international alliances'. *Journal of International Business Studies, 29*: 665–693.

Renault (2010) 'The Renault—Nissan alliance'. Available online at www.renault.com/en/groupe/l-alliance-renault-nissan/pages/l-alliance-renault-nissan.aspx (accessed 2 August 2011).

Renault–Nissan–Mitsubishi Alliance (2022) 'Renault—Nissan—Mitsubishi Alliance'. Available online at https://en.wikipedia.org/wiki/Renault—Nissan—Mitsubishi_Alliance (accessed 17 October 2022).

Reuer, J. J. and Ariño, A. (2007) 'Strategic alliance contracts: Dimensions and determinants of contractual complexity'. *Strategic Management Journal, 28*: 313–330.

Reuer, J. J., Klijn, E. and Lioukas, C. S. (2014) 'Board involvement in international joint venture'. *Strategic Management Journal, 35*: 1626–1644.

Reuer, J. J. and Ragozzino, R. (2005) 'Agency hazards and alliance portfolios'. *Strategic Management Journal, 27*: 27–43.

Reuer, J. J. and Tong, T. W. (2005) 'Real options in international joint ventures'. *Journal of Management, 31*: 403–423.

Reuer, J. J. and Zollo, M. (2005) 'Termination outcomes of research alliances'. *Research Policy, 34*: 101–115.

Revilla, E., Sarkis, J. and Acosta, J. (2005) 'Towards a knowledge management and learning taxonomy for research joint ventures'. *Technovation, 25*: 1307–1316.

Reynolds, M. and Yuthas, K. (2008) 'Moral discourse and corporate social responsibility reporting'. *Journal of Business Ethics, 78*: 47–64.

Ring, P. S. (2000) 'The three T's of alliance creation: Task, team, and time'. *European Management Journal, 18*: 152–163.

Ring, P. S. and Van de Ven, A. H. (1994) 'Developmental processes of cooperative interorganizational relationships'. *Academy of Management Review, 19*: 90–118.

Ritchie, H. and Roser, M. (2022) 'Energy mix'. Available online at https://ourworldindata.org/energy-mixaccessed (accessed 9 June 2022).

Robson, M. J., Leonidou, L. C. and Katsikeas, C. S. (2002) 'Factors influencing international joint venture performance: Theoretical perspectives, assessment, and future directions'. *Management International Review, 42*: 385–418.

Rochemont, M. H. (2010) *Opening up for innovation: The antecedents of multi-partner alliance performance.* Eindhoven: Technical University Eindhoven.

Rockmann, K. W., Pratt, M. G. and Northcraft, G. B. (2007) 'Divided loyalties—determinants of identification in interorganizational teams'. *Small Group Research, 38*: 727–751.

Rondinelli, D. A. and London, T. (2003) 'How corporations and environmental groups cooperate: Assessing cross-sector alliances and collaborations'. *Academy of Management Executive, 17*: 61–76.

Rusbult, C. E., Zembrodt, I. M. and Gunn, L. K. (1982) 'Exit, voice, loyalty, and neglect—responses to dissatisfaction in romantic involvements'. *Journal of Personality and Social Psychology, 43*: 1230–1242.

Russo, M. V. (1992) 'Power plays—regulation, diversification, and backward integration in the electric utility industry'. *Strategic Management Journal, 13*: 13–27.

RWE (2021) '50 billion euros, 50 gigawatts of capacity by 2030: RWE launches investment and growth offensive'. Available online at www.rwe.com/en/press/rwe-ag/2021-11-15-rwe-launches-investment-and-growth-offensive (accessed 7 November 2022).

RWE (2022) 'RWE history, from 1898 until today: Over 120 years of successful history'. Available online at www.rwe.com/en/the-group/history (accessed 7 November 2022).

Ryall, M. D. and Sampson, R. (2009) 'Formal contracts in the presence of relational enforcement mechanisms: Evidence from technology development projects'. *Management Science, 55*: 906–925.

Ryan-Charleton, T. and Gnyawali, D. R. (2022) 'Value creation tension in coopetition: Virtuous cycles and viscous cycles'. *Strategic Management Review.* Available online at extension://bfdogplmn-didlpjfhoijckpakkdjkkil/pdf/viewer.html?file=https%3A%2F%2Fstrategicmanagementreview.net%2Fassets%2Farticles%2FRyan-Charleton%2520and%2520Gnyawali.pdf.

Ryan-Charleton, T., Gnyawali, D. R. and Oliveira, N. (2022) 'Strategic alliance outcome: Consolidation and new directions'. *Academy of Management Annals, 16*: 719–758.

Sadovnikova, A. and Pujari, A. (2017) 'The effect of green partnerships on firm value'. *Journal of the Academy Marketing Science, 45*(2): 251–267.

Salk, J. E. (2005) 'Often called for but rarely chosen: Alliance research that directly studies process'. *European Management Review, 2*: 117–122.

Salk, J. E. and Brannen, M. Y. (2000) 'National culture, networks, and individual influence in a multinational management team'. *Academy of Management Journal, 43*: 191–202.

Salk, J. E. and Shenkar, O. (2001) 'Social identities in an international joint venture: An exploratory case study'. *Organization Science, 12*: 161–178.

Salvato, C., Reuer, J. J. and Battigalli, P. (2017) 'Cooperation across disciplines: A multilevel perspective on cooperative behavior in governing interfirm relations. *Academy of Management Annals, 11*: 960–1004.

Sampson, R. C. (2004a) 'The cost of misaligned governance in R&D alliances'. *Journal of Law Economics and Organization, 20*: 484–526.

Sampson, R. C. (2004b) 'Organizational choice in R&D alliances: Knowledge-based and transaction cost perspectives'. *Managerial and Decision Economics, 25*: 421–436.

Sampson, R. C. (2005) 'Experience effects and collaborative returns in R&D alliances'. *Strategic Management Journal, 26*: 1009–1031.

Samuelsen, B. M., Olsen, L. E. and Keller, K. L. (2015) 'The multiple roles of fit between brand alliance partners in alliance attitude formation'. *Marketing Letters, 26*: 619–629.

Sanzo-Pérez, M. J. and Álvarez-González, L. (2022) 'Partnerships between Spanish social enterprises and nonprofits: A rich hybridity-based setting for social innovation'. *Technovation, 110*: 102376.

SAP (2022) 'What is SAP?'. Available online at www.sap.com/about/company/what-is-sap.html#:~:text=What%20does%20SAP%20do%3F,midsize%20companies%2C%20and%20large%20corporations (accessed 24 September 2022).

Sarkar, M. B., Aulakh, P. S. and Madhok, A. (2009) 'Process capabilities and value generation in alliance portfolios'. *Organization Science, 20*: 583–600.

Sarkar, M. B., Echambadi, R., Cavusgil, S. T. and Aulakh, P. S. (2001) 'The influence of complementarity, compatibility, and relationship capital on alliance performance'. *Journal of the Academy of Marketing Science, 29*: 358–373.

Saxton, T. (1997) 'The effects of partner and relationship characteristics on alliance outcomes'. *Academy of Management Journal, 40*: 443–461.

SBMC (2022a) 'Smart Biomaterials Consortium (SBMC) members announce first collaboration to prevent thousands of amputations worldwide'. Available online at www.globenewswire.com/news-release/2022/07/08/2476448/0/en/Smart-Biomaterials-Consortium-SBMC-members-announce-first-collaboration-to-prevent-thousands-of-amputations-worldwide.html (accessed 8 November 2022).

SBMC (2022b) 'Corbion helps reduce emissions from agriculture through support for Cargill soil health program'. Available online at www.globenewswire.com/news-release/2022/10/20/2537951/0/en/Corbion-helps-reduce-emissions-from-agriculture-through-support-for-Cargill-soil-health-program.html (accessed 8 November 2022).

SBR (2022) 'DBS launch 5 partnerships enhance SMES digital supply chain capabilities'. Available online at https://sbr.com.sg/news/dbs-launch-5-partnerships-enhance-smes-digital-supply-chain-capabilities (accessed 5 November 2022).

Schaan, J. L. (1983) 'Parent control and joint venture success: The case of Mexico'. Unpublished doctoral dissertation. University of Western Ontario.

Scheer, L. K., Kumar, N. and Steenkamp, J. (2003) 'Reactions to perceived inequity in US and Dutch interorganizational relationships'. *Academy of Management Journal, 46*: 303–316.

Schifrin, M. (2001) 'Is your company magnetic?' *Forbes*, May 21, p. 16.

Schilke, O. and Cook, K. S. (2015) 'Sources of alliance partner trustworthiness: Integrating calculative and relational perspectives'. *Strategic Management Journal, 36*: 276–297.

Schilke, O. and Goerzen, A. (2010) 'Alliance management capability: An investigation of the construct and its measurement'. *Journal of Management, 36*: 1192–1219.

Schneider, S. C. and Barsoux, J.-L. (1997) *Managing across cultures*. London: Prentice-Hall.

Schoenmakers, W. and Duysters, G. (2006) 'Learning in strategic technology alliances'. *Technology Analysis and Strategic Management, 18*: 245–264.

Schreiner, M., Kale, P. and Corsten, D. (2009) 'What really is alliance management capability and how does it impact alliance outcomes and success?' *Strategic Management Journal, 30*: 1395–1419.

Scott, J. (2000) *Social network analysis: A handbook*. London: Sage Publications.

Scott, W. R. (2003) *Organizations: Rational, natural and open systems*. Upper Saddle River, NJ: Prentice Hall.

Segil, L. (1998) *Measuring the value of partnering: How to use metrics, to plan, develop, and implement successful alliances*. New York: Amacom.

Shan, W. J., Walker, G. and Kogut, B. (1994) 'Interfirm cooperation and startup innovation in the biotechnology industry'. *Strategic Management Journal, 15*: 387–394.

Shenkar, O. and Zeira, Y. (1992) 'Role-conflict and role ambiguity of chief executive officers in international joint ventures'. *Journal of International Business Studies, 23*: 55–75.

Shih, W. C. (2020) 'Global supply chains in a post-pandemic world: Companies need to make their networks more resilient. Here's how'. *Harvard Business Review, 98*(5): 82–89.

Shortell, S. M. and Zajac, E. J. (1988) 'Internal corporate joint ventures—development processes and performance outcomes'. *Strategic Management Journal, 9*: 527–542.

Simonin, B. L. (1997) 'The importance of collaborative know-how: An empirical test of the learning organization'. *Academy Management Journal, 40*: 1150–1174.

Simonin, B. L. (1999) 'Ambiguity and the process of knowledge transfer in strategic alliances'. *Strategic Management Journal, 20*: 595–623.

Simonin, B. L. and Ruth, J. A. (1998) 'Is a company known by the company it keeps? Assessing the spillover effects of brand alliances on consumer brand attitudes'. *Journal of Marketing Research, 35*: 30–42.

Simoons, P. (2016) 'Are alliance managers a different kind of people?' Available online at www.peter-simoons.com/2012/07/are-alliance-managers-a-different-kind-of-people/ (accessed 20 July 2016).

Singh, H., Bell, J. and Kale, P. (2008) *Philips: Building alliance capabilities.* Philadelphia, PA: Wharton.

SkyTeam (2021) 'SkyTeam expands SkyCare&Protect Pledge with new digital, health and safety measures'. Available online at www.skyteam.com/en/about/press-releases/press-releases-2021/skyteam-expands (accessed 8 November 2022).

SkyTeam (2022) 'Delta and Aeromexico launch touchless check-in, powered by SkyTeam technology'. Available online at www.skyteam.com/en/about/press-releases/press-releases-2022/delta-and-aeromexico-launch-touchless-check-in-powered-by-skyteam-technology (accessed 8 November 2022).

Smith, P., Haslam, S. A. and Nielsen, J. F. (2018) 'In search of identity leadership: An ethnographic study of emergent influence in an interorganizational R&D team'. *Organization Studies, 39*(10): 1425–1447.

SolarDuck (2022) 'Our purpose'. Available online at https://solarduck.tech/#purpose (accessed 7 November 2022).

SotaTek (2022) 'Strategic partnership announcement: SotaTek x Dvision network'. Available online at www.sotatek.com/strategic-partnership-announcement-sotatek-dvision-network/ (accessed 17 October 2022).

Spekman, R. E., Forbes, T. M. III, Isabella, L. A. and MacAvoy, T. C. (1998) 'Alliance management: A view from the past and a look to the future'. *Journal of Management Studies, 35*(5): 747–772.

Stadtler, L. and Van Wassenhove, L. N. (2016) 'Coopetition as a paradox: Integrative approaches in a multi-company, cross-sector partnership'. *Organization Studies, 37*: 655–685.

Stafford, E. R. (1994) 'Using co-operative strategies to make alliances work'. *Long Range Planning, 27*: 64–74.

Stafford, E. R., Polonsky, M. J. and Hartman, C. L. (2000) 'Environmental NGO—business collaboration and strategic bridging: A case analysis of the Greenpeace—Foron alliance'. *Business Strategy and the Environment, 9*: 122–135.

Starbuck Coffee Company (2021) 'Starbucks pickup and Amazon go collaborate to launch new store concept in New York City'. Available online at https://stories.starbucks.com/press/2021/starbucks-pickup-and-amazon-go-collaborate-to-launch-new-store-concept-in-new-york-city/ (accessed 8 November 2022).

Starbuck Coffee Company (2022a) 'Starbucks affirms commitment to a planet positive future through innovation and learnings from store partners'. Available online at https://stories.starbucks.com/press/2022/starbucks-affirms-commitment-to-a-planet-positive-future-through-innovation-and-learnings-from-store-partners (accessed 8 November 2022).

Starbuck Coffee Company (2022b) 'Delta Air Lines and Starbucks launch loyalty partnership'. Available online at https://stories.starbucks.com/press/2022/delta-air-lines-and-starbucks-launch-loyalty-partnership (accessed 8 November 2022).

Starbuck Coffee Company (2022c) 'Company profile'. Available online at https://stories.starbucks.com/uploads/2022/05/AboutUs-Company-Profile-5.5.22.pdf (accessed 8 November 2022).

StartPath (2016) 'StartPath global'. Available online at www.startpath.com/global/ (accessed 14 December 2016).

Statista (2017) 'Size of the global oral care market from 2013 to 2021'. Available online at www.statista.com/statistics/326389/global-oral-care-market-size/ (accessed 19 December 2016).

Steensma, H. K., Marino, L. and Weaver, K. M. (2000) 'The influence of national culture on the formation of technology alliances by entrepreneurial firms'. *Academy of Management Journal, 43*: 951–973.

Sterling, B. (2013) 'A crowdsourcing alliance between Quirky and General Electric'. Available online at www.wired.com/2013/04/a-crowdsourcing-alliance-between-quirky-and-general-electric/ (accessed 1 September 2022).

Stock, R. M. (2006) 'Interorganizational teams as boundary spanners between supplier and customer companies'. *Journal of the Academy of Marketing Science, 34*: 588–599.

Stock, R. M. (2014) 'How should customers be integrated for effective interorganizational NPD teams? An input-process-output perspective'. *Journal of Product Innovation Management, 31*: 535–551.

Street, T. and Cameron, A. F. (2007) 'External relationships and the small business: A review of small business alliance and network research'. *Journal of Small Business Management, 45*: 239–266.

Stuart, T. E. (2000) 'Interorganizational alliances and the performance of firms: A study of growth and innovation rates in a high-technology industry'. *Strategic Management Journal, 21*: 791–811.

Stubbs, W., Dahlmann, F. and Raven, R. (2022) 'The purpose ecosystem and the United Nations sustainable development goals: Interactions among private sector actors and stakeholders'. *Journal of Business Ethics, 180*: 1097–1112.

Sukoco, B. M. (2015) 'Interrelatedness, interdependencies, and domain learning in alliance portfolios'. *International Journal of Business, 20*: 160–177.

Swait, J., Erdem, T., Louviere, J. and Dubelaar, C. (1993) 'The equalization price: A measure of consumer-perceived brand equity'. *International Journal of Research in Marketing, 10*: 23–45.

Szulanski, G. (1996) 'Exploring internal stickiness: Impediments to the transfer of best practice within the firm'. *Strategic Management Journal, 17*: 27–43.

Tan, K. C. (2001) 'A framework of supply chain management literature'. *European Journal of Purchasing and Supply Management, 7*: 39–48.

Taras, V., Rowney, J. and Steel, P. (2009) 'Half a century of measuring culture: Review of approaches, challenges, and limitations based on the analysis of 121 instruments for quantifying culture'. *Journal of International Management, 15*: 357–373.

Teece, D. (1992) 'Competition, cooperation, and innovation: Organizational arrangements for regimes of rapid technological progress'. *Journal of Economic Behavior & Organization, 18*: 1–25.

Teece, D. J., Pisano, G. and Shuen, A. (1997) 'Dynamic capabilities and strategic management'. *Strategic Management Journal, 18*: 509–533.

Teng, B. (2005) 'The emergence and popularization of strategic alliances: Institutional and entrepreneurial views'. *International Entrepreneurship and Management Journal, 1*: 61–82.

Tesla (2013) 'Panasonic and Tesla reach agreement to expand supply of automotive-grade battery cells'. Available online at www.tesla.com/blog/panasonic-and-tesla-reach-agreement-expand-supply-automotivegrade-battery-cells (accessed 24 October 2016).

Tesla (2016) 'Tesla and Panasonic to collaborate on photovoltaic cell and module production in Buffalo, New York'. Available online at www.tesla.com/blog/tesla-and-panasonic-collaborate (accessed 24 October 2016).

The Rhythm of Business (2016) 'Sample pages alliance management guidebook: Managing BioPharma strategic alliances'. Available online at http://static1.1.sqspcdn.com/static/f/1139545/23746222/1456624855150/AMguideSample.pdf?token=MPwT7y1pJX04edu FTTT9468h%2BZs%3D (accessed 20 July 2016).

The TechScoop (2011) 'IBM processors power Wii U'. Available online at www.thetechscoop.net/2011/06/11/ibm-processors-power-wii-u/ (accessed 2 August 2011).

Thibaut, J. W. and Kelley, H. H. (1959) *The social psychology of groups*. New York: Wiley.

Thompson, L. (1990) 'Negotiation behavior and outcomes—empirical-evidence and theoretical issues'. *Psychological Bulletin, 108*: 515–532.

Tjemkes, B. (2008) *Growing and sharing the pie: A study of performance in strategic alliances*. Nijmegen: Radboud University Nijmegen.

Tjemkes, B. and Furrer, O. (2010) 'The antecedents of response strategies in strategic alliances'. *Management Decision, 48*: 1103–1133.

Tjemkes, B. and Furrer, O. (2011) 'Behavioral responses to adverse situations in strategic alliances'. In Das, T. K. (ed.), *Behavioral perspectives on strategic alliances*. Charlotte, NC: Information Age Publishing Researching Strategic Alliances, pp. 227–249.

Tjemkes, B. V. (2021) 'Collaborative transformation'. In Tjemkes, B. V. and Mihalache, O. (eds.), *Transformative strategizing: Strategizing the unknown in the age of globalization, disruption, collaboration, and responsibility*. Abingdon: Taylor & Francis Ltd, pp. 107–136.

Tjemkes, B. V. (2022) *I feel the earth move: Reigniting strategic management with purpose*. Amsterdam: Vrije Universiteit Amsterdam.

Tjemkes, B. V. and Mihalache, O. (eds.). (2021) *Transformative strategizing: Strategizing the unknown in the age of globalization, disruption, collaboration, and responsibility* (edited book). Abingdon: Routledge.

Today in Windows (2001) 'What does the Nokia—Microsoft partnership mean?'. Available online at www.todayinwindows.com/2011/04/what-does-the-nokia-microsoft-partnership-mean/ (accessed 2 August 2011).

Tokio Marine (2022) 'Singapore: Tokio Marine and Bolttech form strategic alliance'. Available online at www.asiainsurancereview.com/News/View-NewsLetterArticle/id/82627/Type/eDaily/Singapore-Tokio-Marine-and-bolttech-form-strategic-alliance (accessed 18 October 2022).

Toyota (2021) 'Kawasaki Heavy Industries, Subaru, Toyota, Mazda, and Yamaha take on challenge to expand options for producing, transporting, and using fuel toward achieving carbon neutrality'. Available online at https://global.toyota/en/newsroom/corporate (accessed 17 October 2022).

Trompenaars, F. (1993) *Riding the waves of culture: Understanding cultural diversity in business*. London: The Economist Books.

Turiera, T. and Cros, S. (2013) *Co-businesses: 50 examples of business collaboration*. Valencia: Co-Society.

Ul-Haq, R. U.-H. (2005) *Alliances and co-evolution: Insights from the banking sector*. Basingstoke: Palgrave Macmillan.

UNFCCC (2022) 'The Paris Agreement: What is the Paris Agreement?'. Available online at https://unfccc.int/process-and-meetings/the-paris-agreement/the-paris-agreement (accessed 7 November 2022).

Vandaie, R. and Zaheer, A. (2014) 'Surviving bear hugs: Firm capability, large partner alliances, and growth'. *Strategic Management Journal, 35*: 566–577.

van der Kamp, M., Tjemkes, B. V., Duplat, V. and Jehn, K. (2022) 'On alliance teams: Conceptualization, review, and future research agenda'. *Human Relations.* https://doi.org/10.1177/00187267221104985.

van der Meer-Kooistra, J. and Kamminga, P. E. (2015) 'Joint venture dynamics: The effects of decisions made within a parent company and the role of joint venture management control'. *Management Accounting Research, 26*: 23–39.

van Dyck, W. (2012) 'Building and leveraging your ecosystem to spark innovation-based growth'. Available online at http://iveybusinessjournal.com/publication/building-and-leveraging-your-ecosystem-to-spark-innovation-based-growth/ (accessed 20 July 2016).

Vangen, S. and Huxham, C. (2003) 'Enacting leadership for collaborative advantage: Dilemmas of ideology and pragmatism in the activities of partnership managers'. *British Journal of Management, 14*: S61–S76.

van Wijk, R. and Nadolska, A. (2020) 'Making more of alliance portfolios: The role of alliance portfolio coordination'. *European Management Journal, 38*(3): 388–399.

Venkatraman, N., Koh, J. and Loh, L. (1994) 'The adoption of corporate governance mechanisms: A test of competing diffusion models'. *Management Science, 40*: 496–507.

Villalonga, B. and McGahan, A. M. (2005) 'The choice among acquisitions, alliances, and divestitures'. *Strategic Management Journal, 26*: 1183–1208.

Vink, J., Koskela-Huotari, K., Tronvoll, B., Edvardsson, B. and Wetter-Edman, K. (2021) 'Service ecosystem design: Propositions, process model, and future research agenda'. *Journal of Service Research, 24*(2): 168–186.

Visioni, L. J., Palmer, N., Hughes, J., Weiss, J. and Kliman, S. (2010) 'Right from the start: The seven virtues of a successful alliance launch'. *International Journal of Strategic Business Alliances, 1*: 401–423.

Vlaar, P. W. L. (2006) *Making sense of formalization in interorganizational relationships: Beyond coordination and control*. Rotterdam: Erasmus Universiteit Rotterdam.

Vlaar, P. W. L., Van den Bosch, F. A. J. and Volberda, H. W. (2007) 'Towards a dialectic perspective on formalization in interorganizational relationships: How alliance managers capitalize on the duality inherent in contracts, rules and procedures'. *Organization Studies, 28*: 437–466.

Volberda, H.W. and Lewin, A.Y. (2003) 'Guest editors' introduction—co-evolutionary dynamics within and between firms: From evolution to co-evolution'. *Journal of Management Studies, 40*: 2111–2136.

Votolato, N. L. and Unnava, H. R. (2006) 'Spillover of negative information on brand alliances'. *Journal of Consumer Psychology, 16*: 196–202.

Walmart (2016) 'Collaboration'. Available online at http://corporate.walmart.com/sourcing/collaboration (accessed 2 December 2016).

Walmart (2021) 'Walmart partners with Netflix on new product lines'. Available online at www.pymnts.com/news/retail/2021/walmart-partners-with-netflix-on-new-product-lines (accessed 17 October 2022).

Walter, G. A. and Barney, J. B. (1990) 'Research notes and communications management objectives in mergers and acquisitions'. *Strategic Management Journal, 11*: 79–86.

Wang, Y. G., Wange, Y., Wanga, N., Jiang, L., Yang, Z. and Cuie, V. (2016) 'Managing relationships with power advantage buyers: The role of supplier initiated bonding tactics in long-term buyer-supplier collaborations'. *Journal of Business Research, 69*: 5587–5596.

Wang, Y. K. (2015) 'The impact of prestigious top management team on international alliance formation: Evidence from Taiwanese electronics firms'. *Journal of Management & Organization, 21*: 835–852.

Wang, Y. Z. and Rajagopalan, N. (2015) 'Alliance capabilities: Review and research agenda'. *Journal of Management, 41*: 236–260.

Washburn, J. H., Till, B. A., Priluck, R. and Boughton, P. D. (2000) 'The effect of co-branding on search, experience, and credence attribute performance ratings before and after product trial'. American Marketing Association Summer Marketing Educators' Conference, Chicago IL, Volume 11, 117.

Wassmer, U. (2008) 'Alliance portfolios: A review and research agenda'. *Journal of Management, 36*: 141–171.

Wassmer, U. (2010) 'How to manage alliance better than one at a time'. *MIT Sloan Management Review, 51*: 77–84.

Wassmer, U. and Dussauge, P. (2012) 'Network resource stocks and flows: How do alliance portfolios affect the value of new alliance formations?'. *Strategic Management Journal, 33*: 871–883.

Wassmer, U., Paquin, R. and Sharma, S. (2014) 'The engagement of firms in environmental collaborations: Existing contributions and future directions'. *Business & Society, 53*(6): 754–786.

Wathne, K. H. and Heide, J. B. (2000) 'Opportunism in interfirm relationships: Forms, outcomes, and solutions'. *Journal of Marketing, 64*: 36–51.

Weber, L. and Mayer, K. J. (2011) 'Designing effective contracts: Exploring the influence of framing and expectations'. *Academy of Management Review, 36*(1): 53–75.

Weick, K. (1979) *The social psychology of organizing*. New York: McGraw-Hill, Inc.

Weis, S. E. (2011) 'Negotiating the Renault—Nissan alliance: Insights from Renault's experience'. In Benoliel, M. (ed.), *Negotiation excellence*. Singapore: World Scientific Publishers Company, pp. 315–340.

Weitz, B. E. and Jap, S. D. (1995) 'Relationship marketing and distribution channels'. *Journal of the Academy of Marketing Science, 23*: 305–320.

Westman, C. and Thorgren, S. (2016) 'Partner conflicts in international joint ventures: A minority owner perspective'. *Journal of International Management, 22*: 168–185.

Wickert, C. (2021) 'Strategizing corporate social responsibility'. In Tjemkes, B. V. and Mihalache, O. (eds.), *Transformative strategizing: Strategizing the unknown in the age of globalization, disruption, collaboration, and responsibility*. Abingdon: Taylor & Francis Ltd, pp. 137–158.

Wikipedia (2022) 'Environmental effects of shipping'. Available online at https://en.wikipedia.org/wiki/Environmental_effects_of_shipping#:~:text=Maritime%20transport%20accounts%20for%20 3.5,ranking%20between%20Japan%20and%20Germany (accessed 6 November 2022).

Williams, T. (2005) 'Cooperation by design: Structure and cooperation in interorganizational networks'. *Journal of Business Research, 58*: 223–231.

Williamson, O. E. (1975) *Markets and hierarchies: Analysis and antitrust implications*. New York: Free Press.

Williamson, O. E. (1981) 'The economics of organization—the transaction cost approach'. *American Journal of Sociology, 87*: 548–577.

Williamson, O. E. (1985) *The economic institutions of capitalism*. New York: Free Press.

Williamson, O. E. (1991) 'Comparative economic organization—analysis of discrete structural alternatives'. *Administrative Science Quarterly, 36*: 269–296.

Williamson, P. J. and De Meyer, A. (2012) 'Ecosystem advantage: How to successfully harness the power of partners'. *California Management Review, 55*(1): 24–46.

Wilson, J. and Hynes, N. (2009) 'Co-evolution of firms and strategic alliances: Theory and empirical evidence'. *Technological Forecasting and Social Change, 76*: 620–628.

Wit de, B. and Meyer, R. (2004) *Strategy process, content, context: An international perspective.* London: Thomson Learning.

Wittmann, C. M. (2007) 'Strategic alliances: What can we learn when they fail?' *Journal of Business-to-Business Marketing, 14*: 1–19.

White, G. O., Joplin, J. R. W. and Salama, M. F. (2007) 'Contracts and conflict resolution strategies in foreign ventures: A transaction cost perspective'. *International Journal of Conflict Management, 18*: 376–390.

Wojciszke, B., Brycz, H. and Borkenau, P. (1993) 'Effects of information-content and evaluative extremity on positivity and negativity biases'. *Journal of Personality and Social Psychology, 64*: 327–335.

Wolfe, R. J. and McGinn, K. L. (2005) 'Perceived relative power and its influence on negotiations'. *Group Decision and Negotiation, 14*: 3–20.

Wood, G. (2002) 'A partnership model of corporate ethics'. *Journal of Business Ethics, 40*: 61–73.

WWF (2020) 'Bolton Food: Together to support more sustainable fishing and our oceans'. Available online at https://wwf.panda.org/act/partner_with_wwf/corporate_partnerships/who_we_work_with/bolton_food/ (accessed 18 October 2022).

Xu, L. D., Xu, E. L. and Ling, L. (2018) 'Industry 4.0: State of the art and future trends'. *International Journal of Production Research, 56*(8): 2941–2962.

Yan, A. M. and Gray, B. (1994) 'Bargaining power, management control, and performance in United States—China joint ventures: A comparative case study'. *Academy of Management Journal, 37*: 1478–1510.

Yan, A. M. and Gray, B. (2001) 'Antecedents and effects of parent control in international joint ventures'. *Journal of Management Studies, 38*: 393–416.

Yan, A. M. and Luo, Y. (2001) *International joint ventures: Theory and practice.* New York: Routledge.

Yan, A. M. and Zeng, M. (1999) 'International joint venture instability: A critique of previous research, a reconceptualization, and directions for future research'. *Journal of International Business Studies, 30*: 397–414.

Yang, H. B., Zheng, Y. and Zaheer, A. (2015) 'Asymmetric learning capabilities and stock market returns'. *Academy of Management Journal, 58*: 356–374.

Yang, H. B., Zheng, Y. and Zhao, X. (2014) 'Exploration or exploitation? Small firms' alliance strategies with large firms'. *Strategic Management Journal, 35*: 146–157.

Yang, M.-H., Liao, C.-H. and Liu, S.-C. (2007) 'Applying internet-based information systems to facilitate business alliance activities'. *Internet-based Information Systems, 107*: 125–140.

Yeheskel, O., Zeira, O., Shenkar, Y. and Newburry, W. (2001) 'Parent company dissimilarity and equity international joint venture effectiveness'. *Journal of International Management, 7*: 81–104.

Yin, J. and Jamali, D. (2021) 'Collide or collaborate: The interplay of competing logics and institutional work in cross-sector social partnerships'. *Journal of Business Ethics, 169*: 673–694.

Yin, X. L. and Shanley, M. (2008) 'Industry determinants of the "merger versus alliance" decision'. *Academy of Management Review, 33*: 473–491.

Yli-Renko, H. and Autio, E. (1998) 'The network embeddedness of new, technology-based firms: Developing a systemic evolution model'. *Small Business Economics, 11*: 253–267.

Yli-Renko, H., Autio, E. and Sapienza, H. J. (2001) 'Social capital, knowledge acquisition, and knowledge exploitation in young technology-based firms'. *Strategic Management Journal, 22*: 587–613.

Yoon, W. J., Lee, D. Y. and Song, J. (2015) 'Alliance network size, partner diversity, and knowledge creation in small biotech firms'. *Journal of Management & Organization, 21*: 614–626.

Zaccaro, S. J., Marks, M. A. and DeChurch, L. A. (2012) *Multiteam systems: An organization form for dynamic and complex environments.* New York: Routledge.

Zagt, A. (2015) 'Bond moet weer aan het bier, én de wodka'. Available online at www.ad.nl/show/bond-moet-weer-aan-het-bier-en-de-wodka~acf5fa35/ (accessed 2 December 2016).

Zahoor, N., Khan, Z. and Shenkar, O. (2023) 'International vertical alliances within the international business field: A systematic literature review and future research agenda. *Journal of World Business*, *58*(1): 101385.

Zahra, S. A. and George, G. (2002) 'Absorptive capacity: A review, reconceptualization, and extension'. *Academy of Management Review*, *27*: 185–203.

Zahra, S. and Nambisan, S. (2012) 'Entrepreneurship and strategic thinking in business ecosystems'. *Business Horizons*, *55*: 219–229.

Zajac, E. J. and Olsen, C. P. (1993) 'From transaction cost to transactional value analysis—implications for the study of interorganizational strategies'. *Journal of Management Studies*, *30*: 131–145.

Zeng, J., Zaheer, K. and De Silva, M. (2019) 'The emergence of multi-sided platform MNEs: Internalization theory and networks'. *International Business Review*, *28*(6): 101598.

Zeng, M. and Chen, X. P. (2003) 'Achieving cooperation in multiparty alliances: A social dilemma approach to partnership management'. *Academy of Management Review*, *28*: 587–605.

Zeng, M. and Hennart, J. F. (2002) 'From learning races to cooperative specialization: Towards a new framework for alliance management'. In Contractor, F. J. and Lorange, P. (eds.), *Cooperative strategies and alliances*. Amsterdam: Pergamon International Business and Management Series, pp. 189–210.

Zhang, Y. and Li, H. (2001) 'The control design and performance in international joint ventures: A dynamic evolution perspective'. *International Business Review*, *10*: 95–113.

Zhang, Y., Chang, X., Liu, Y., Wang, Y. and Li, H. (2021) 'Urban expansion simulation under constraint of multiple ecosystem services (MESs) based on cellular automata (CA)-Markov model: Scenario analysis and policy implications'. *Land Use Policy*, *108:* 105667.

Zheng, Y. and Yang, H. (2015) 'Does familiarity foster innovation? The impact of alliance partner repeatedness on breakthrough innovations'. *Journal of Management Studies*, *52*: 213–230.

Ziggers, G. W. and Tjemkes, B. V. (2010) 'Dynamics in inter-firm collaboration: The impact of alliance capabilities on performance'. *International Journal of Food System Dynamics*, *1*: 151–166.

Zineldin, M. (2004) 'Coopetition: The organisation of the future'. *Marketing Intelligence & Planning*, *22*: 780–790.

Zinn, W. and Parasuraman, A. (1997) 'Scope and intensity of logistics-based strategic alliances—a conceptual classification and managerial implications'. *Industrial Marketing Management*, *26*: 137–147.

Zollo, M., Reuer, J. J. and Singh, H. (2002) 'Interorganizational routines and performance in strategic alliances'. *Organization Science*, *13*: 701–713.

Zoogah, D. B., Vora, D., Richard, O. and Peng, M. W. (2011) 'Strategic alliance team diversity, coordination, and effectiveness'. *International Journal of Human Resource Management*, *22*: 510–529.

INDEX

Note: Page numbers in *italic* indicate a figure and page numbers in **bold** indicate a table on the corresponding page.

absorptive capacity 159–161, 165–166
acceptance tactics 212–219
accommodated exit 133–134
accountability conflict 225
aggressive voice 98–99
alliance capabilities 352–355, **355**, 359–362, **359**; alliance office 265, 361–364; alliance tools 355–357, **357**, 361–363; competence levels 326, 358–360, **359**; Philips 363–364
alliance champion role 324, 327
alliance co-evolution: alliance system 376–388; co-evolutionary view 376–379; drivers of 379–386; Nexia 380
alliance competence 10–11
alliance contracts 52–53, 64–67, 69–75, 92–95, 129–132, 184–185, 213–221, 247–249; contractual clauses **65**, 168–169, 200–201; learning alliances 156–172
alliance coordination routines 353–354
alliance coordinator role 324–327
alliance design 57–77; alliance contracts 52–53, 64–67, 69–75, 92–95, 129–132, 167–169, 184–185, 213–221, 247–249; alliance mirror design 70, *70*; contractual clauses **65**, 168–169, 200–201; control dimensions 68–69; control modes 67–68, 71; joint ventures 59–60, 200–201; L'Oreal-Organovo 75–77; management control 67–69, 101–103; non-equity and equity-based governance forms 58–62, **61**; structural configuration 69–71
alliance development stages 6–11, *8*
alliance evaluation 109–123, *118*; performance metric system 104–105, 109–112, 116–121;

economic approach 113–114; learning approach 115; operational approach 114; performance metric approaches 112–117; relational approach 115–116; strategic approach 114
Alliance for Open Media **237**
alliance function 254–255, 258–261, 405–406
alliance launch 78–91, **80**, **82**, *86*; alliance relaunch 88–89; Capgemini–Eneco 89–91; conflict management 93, 96–97, 103, 230; inter-partner learning 100–101, 104–106; organizational justice 96; relational governance theory 93–95; response strategies 98–100; TNO–Hoogendoorn 107–108; types of trust 94–95
alliance management 92–108; approaches 92–101; decision-making steps 103–106; and design 101–103; TNO–Hoogendoorn 107–108
alliance manager role 327–330
alliance mindset 365–375; meaning of 365–367; Microsoft 374–375; tensions 367–373
alliance negotiation 43–56; negotiation behavior 43–48; negotiation dynamics 46–48; negotiation stage 49–53; negotiation strategies 43–48, **45**; negotiation tactics 45–46, **45**; negotiation team 50–53; post-negotiation 49, 52, 411; pre-negotiation 49, 51, 72; Renault–Nissan 54–56
alliance networks 284–299; IBM 297–299; network configurations *289*; network dynamics 292; network management **287**, 290–293; network position 286–290, 293–295
alliance offices 265, 361–364

alliance paradox: cooperative vs competitive **369**; corporate vs societal **369**; deliberate vs emergent **369**; structure vs process **369**

alliance partner selection 30–42; partner fit analysis 36, 38, 218, 231; partner fit framework 36–37, 104–106; risk assessment 38–39; SolarDuck 39–42

alliance portfolios 267–283; General Electric 281–283; governance 269–277; portfolio design 269–275; Toyota's suppliers' portfolio 270

alliance proactiveness 353–354, 361

alliance professionals 320–335; alliance manager 327–330; competences 327–330; eVision 333–335; Ivan Vogels 333–335

alliance relaunch 88–89

alliance strategy formulation 13–29; Google–HubSpot 28–29; governance mode rationales 15–25, **14**; institutional theory 15–16, 22–23; organizational learning perspective 21–22, 63; resource-based view 15–19; resource dependence perspective 15, 19, 24, 63; social network theory 21; transaction cost economics 15–16

alliance system 376–388, *383*; co-evolutionary view 376–379; drivers of alliance co-evolution 379–386; oral care appliances 386–388

alliance team member role 324–326, 337, 343, 346, 350, 403

alliance teams 336–351; Dutch Optics Centre 349–351; multi-team system 344–349, *345*

alliance termination 124–137; disengage 125–126, 131, 133; Nokia–Microsoft 135–137

alliance training 332, 355–356, 360–361

alliance transformation routines 354

'ally' governance mode 7, 13–15, **14**

Amazon 317–318

Apple 317–318

ASAP certification 329

asymmetrical alliances 208–221; acceptance tactics 212–219; defensive tactics 211–219; Disney–Pixar 219–221; offensive tactics 211–219

behavioural control 67–68, 111, 385

BMW 176

bounded rationality 17, 94, 370, 384

brand and product fit 177–179, **177**

brand associations 176–181, 185

brand attitudes 177–181

brand awareness 173, 179, 183, 239, 321

brand equity 173, 177–186

brand loyalty 179, 185

business ecosystems 300–318; Apple vs Amazon 317–318; attributes 303–309; challenge 300–303; decision-making steps 312–316; managing 309–312

'buy' governance mode 7, 13–15, **14**

Capgemini–Eneco alliance 89–91

CARE–Cargill alliance **223**

Cargill **223**

Cisco Hyperinnovation Living Labs (CHILL) **301**

closure *see* network density

coach role 355

co-branding alliances 173–188; brand and product fit 177–178; brand equity 179–180; contractual provisions 73–74; Heineken–James Bond 186–188

Cognizant **157**

collaborative commitment 226–232

collective identity 142–147, 150–151

Compaq 298

compatibility 30–32, 35–39

competences (Levels 1–3) 358–361

competition law 246–247

complementary resource alignment 31

conflict management 93, 96–97

considerate voice 98–99

contemporary alliances 389–399; societal responsibility 392–394; technological innovation 389–392; theoretical implications 394–396; Torvald Klaveness 397–399

contractual completeness 64

contractual governance 102, 218, 255, 257–258

control dimensions 68–69

control modes 67–68

coopetition alliances 236–252; competition law 246–247; Reckitt Benckiser 250–252

co-partnering *see* co-branding alliances

Coruna University **223**

creative voice 98–99

cross-sector alliances 222–234; culture of collaborative commitment 226, 227–228; Marks & Spencer–Oxfam 232–234

crowdsourcing 308

cultural competence 196–197

cultural fit 34–35, 165–166

Damen Shipyards 40, 204–206

DBS Singapore 121–123

decision-making steps: alliance capabilities 360–362; alliance design 71–75; alliance evaluation 117–120; alliance launch 85–89; alliance management 103–106; alliance negotiation 48–53; alliance networks 293–297; alliance partner selection 35–39; alliance portfolios 277–281; alliance professionals 330–332; alliance strategy formulation 25–28; alliance teams 346–349; alliance termination 131–134; asymmetrical alliances 215–219; business ecosystems 312–316; co-branding alliances 181–185; coopetition alliance 244–250; cross-sector alliances 228–232; international alliances

198–203; learning alliances 164–170; supplier alliances 146–151
defensive tactics 213–214, 217–219
director of alliances 326
Disney–Pixar alliance 219–221
distributive negotiation 44–46, 52–53
DOC (Dutch Optics Centre) 349–351
Drupal **301, 304**
DSM **3, 190**
dual branding 173, 182
Dutch Optics Centre (DOC) 349–351

ecosystems *see* business ecosystems
egocentric alliance network 287
Eneco 89–91
entrepreneurial ecosystem 306–307
eVision 333–335
EVO Electric 144
Evoque 144
executive sponsor role 135, 324, 327
exit 59–61, 98–99, 129–134, 259–263
expert role 355
exploration strategy 270, 273–274, 280, 289
ExxonMobil 151

financial experts 356
Ford–Mazda alliance 55
FORTRAN 297
free riding 58, 255–264, 310–311
Fujitsu 298

General Electric (GE) 281–283
General Motors 195, **285**
Gillette 176, 387
GKN 144
GLT PLUS 151–155
goal hierarchy **341,** 344–345, 347–348
Google–HubSpot alliance 28–29
GoPro–Red Bull alliance **174**
governance dimension 271–272

Hague Security Delta (HSD) **301**
hard tactics 45–47, 53, 194
Heineken 186–188
Hewlett Packard (HP) 298, 354, 356
hold-up problems 58
Holst Centre 170–172
Hoogendoorn 107–108
human fit **32,** 35–36, 38, 49, 106

IBM 297–299
Inditex–Coruna University alliance **223**
individualism–collectivism 191–192, 368
innovation ecosystem 306
institutional conflicts 224
institutional theory (IT) 15–16, 22–23, **24,** 63, **128,** 370, 395
integrative negotiation 44, 52–53, 165–167

Intel 135, 180, 398, 306, 308
intellectual property rights (IPR) 48, 64–66, 74–76, 133, 375
IntelliClean 387
intended termination 134
inter-firm learning 23–24, 31–33, 157–160, 166–169
international alliances 189–206; cultural competence 196–197; culture as a barrier 193–194; culture as a challenge 194; culture as opportunity 194–196; Damen Shipyards 40, 204–206; Hofstede's five cultural dimensions **192;** national cultural dimensions 191–193
international joint venture (IJV) 60, 200–201, 342–343
inter-partner learning 100–101, 104–106
Ivan Vogels 333–335

joint advertising 176, 182
joint promotion 175–178, 181–183, 187
joint venture 2–4, 58–61, 64–65, 200–202, 337–343
JP Morgan Chase & Co.: In-Residence **209**

knowledge ambiguity 162–163
knowledge characteristics 159, **159,** 162–163
knowledge management 275, 354–355
knowledge manager (alliance function) 164, 355
knowledge practices 159, 163
knowledge protection 156–159, 162–166, 169–170

learning alliances 156–172; absorptive capacity 160; alliance contracts 64–67; alliance design 57–77; alliance evaluation 109–123; alliance launch 78–91; alliance management 92–108; alliance negotiation 43–56; alliance partner selection 30–42; alliance strategy formulation 13–29; alliance termination 124–137; governance form 161; Holst Centre 170–172; knowledge characteristics 159, 162–163; knowledge practices 159, 163; open innovation 158, 170–172, 387–390; relational capital 93–95
legal experts 126, 131–132, 355–356
Lendico–PostFinance alliance **190**
litigated exit 133–134
L'Oreal–Organovo alliance 75–77

'make' governance mode 7, 13–15, **14**
management control 67–69
management development programmes 361
Marks & Spencer–Oxfam alliance 232–234
MasterCard:StartPath™ **209**
mediated exit 133
MeeGo 135, 137
Microsoft 135–137, 374–375
mirror structure design 70

Mizuho Financial Group–Cognizant alliance **157**
multi-partner alliances 253–266; orchestrator role 255, **256**, 258–259; relational governance 255–258, 263; resource complementarity 255–256; SkyTeam 264–266
multi-team system 344–349, *345*
multi-sided platforms **391**

NAM–GLT PLUS 151–155
national culture: cultural competence 196–197; Hofstede's five cultural dimensions **192**
Nederlandse Aardolie Maatschappij (NAM) 151–152
negotiation behaviour 43–48
negotiation dynamics 46–48
negotiation stage 49–53
negotiation strategies 43–48, **45**
negotiation tactics 45–46
network centrality 288
network criteria 26
network density 288
network dynamics 292
network facilitator (alliance function) 355
network management **287**, 290–293
network position 284–290, 293–297; configurations 286–295
Nexia 380
NGO–business partnerships 222, 224–225
Nike 176, 179, 285, 363
Nintendo 314
Nissan 54–56
Nokia–Microsoft alliance 135–137
non-equity and equity-based governance 58–63, **61**
NUMMI 195

offensive tactics 142, 212–218
open innovation 157–158, 170–172, 389–390
operational fit 34, **36**–38
opportunism 62–66, 93–99, 142–144
opportunistic behaviour 57–58, 64–68, 142–145, 149–151, 200–201
Oral-B 387–388
oral care appliances 386–388
orchestra model 306
orchestrator role **256**, 258–265
organizational fit **32**, 33–34, 37, 106, 166
organizational justice 96
organizational learning perspective (OLP) 15, 21–22, **24**, 63
Organovo 75–77
output control 111, 380
Oxfam 232–234, **367**

partner fit 30–35, **32**
partner profile 36–37, 353

partner selection 30–42, *36*, 197, 216, 229–230, 245–246, 259–261, 278–279, 294, 314
patience 98, 197, 331
performance metrics 117: approaches **113**; economic approach 113–114; learning approach 115; operational approach 114; relational approach 115–116; strategic approach 114
performance metric system 109, 111–112, 116–121, 131–132, 249–250
Pfizer–BioNtech **237**
Philips 363–364
Pixar 219–221
platform ecosystem 307
portfolio management 171, 267–271
PostFinance **190**
post-negotiation stage 49, 52, **411**
power distance 191–195, 205
power neutrality 226, 229, 231–232
pre-negotiation stage 49, 51, 72
private benefits 110, 240
Proctor & Gamble (P&G) 304, 386
public–private partnerships 222–225
public–private–plural alliances 408

rational tactics **45**, 46
Reckitt Benckiser 250–252
Red Bull **174**
relational capital 93–95, 140–143, 167–170
relational governance 93–95, 102–106, 144–151, **256**, 258
relational governance theory (RGT) 93–95
Renault–Nissan alliance 54–56
resource-based motives 26, 31
resource-based view (RBV) 18–23, 394–396
resource complementarity 30–32, 35–39, 165–166, 245–246, 255–256
resource dependence perspective (RDP) 19–20, **24**, 63
response strategies **93**, 98–100
Royal Dutch Shell *see* Shell
Royal Philips *see* Philips

SEMATECH **254**, 258, **304**
senior alliance manager role 324, 326–327, **338**, 347
Sensiplant 107–108
service alliances 407
service-based ecosystems 407
Shell 151, 175
shirking 58
SkyTeam 264–266
social control 67–68, 111, 194, 371
social exchange theory 99, **128**, 142
social network theory (SNT) 21, 23, **24**, 63
soft tactics 46–49, 183, 230
SolarDuck 39–42

Solazyme 268
Spectre-Heineken alliance 187
strategic alliance management 1–12; alliance
    competence 10; alliance development
    stages 6–8, *8, 11*; alliance segmentation 9;
    cooperative vs competitive alliance paradox
    368–370; science and art 400–409
strategic fit **32**, 33, 37, 106, 112, 246
strategic management theory (SMT) 20–21, **24**, 33
supplier alliances 139–155; NAM–GLT Plus
    151–155

Tata Group **285**
Tension 368–373, **369**

Tesla–Panasonic alliance **141**
TNO–Hoogendoorn 107–108
Torvald Klaveness 397–399
Toshiba **285**
Toyota 54, 195, **237**, 270, 275–276
transaction cost economics (TCE) 16–18, **24**, 62
trust 52–54, 63–66, 84–85, 94–97, 102, 162,
    190–191, 198, 205–206, 214

under-performing alliances 38, 386
unintended termination 125–126, 134, 215, 219
university–industry partnerships 223, 404

Walmart **3**

Taylor & Francis eBooks

www.taylorfrancis.com

A single destination for eBooks from Taylor & Francis
with increased functionality and an improved user
experience to meet the needs of our customers.

90,000+ eBooks of award-winning academic content in
Humanities, Social Science, Science, Technology, Engineering,
and Medical written by a global network of editors and authors.

TAYLOR & FRANCIS EBOOKS OFFERS:

A streamlined
experience for
our library
customers

A single point
of discovery
for all of our
eBook content

Improved
search and
discovery of
content at both
book and
chapter level

REQUEST A FREE TRIAL
support@taylorfrancis.com

 Routledge
Taylor & Francis Group

 CRC Press
Taylor & Francis Group

Printed in the United States
by Baker & Taylor Publisher Services